A Singer's Guide to
THE
AMERICAN ART SONG
1870–1980

VICTORIA ETNIER VILLAMIL

FOREWORD BY THOMAS HAMPSON

The Scarecrow Press, Inc.
Metuchen, N.J., & London 1993

British Library Cataloguing-in-Publication data available

Library of Congress Cataloging-in-Publication data

Villamil, Victoria Etnier
    A singer's guide to the american art song, 1870–1980 / by Victoria
Etnier Villamil ; foreword by Thomas Hampson.
        p.   cm.
    Includes bibliographical references (p.   ), discography (p.   ), and indexes.
    ISBN 0-8108-2774-3 (acid-free paper)
        1. Songs, English—United States—Bibliography. 2. Songs, English—
United States—History and criticism. I. Title.
ML128.S3V5   1993
016.78242168'0973—dc20   93-34664

To the American song composer,
and to the memory of my mother.

TABLE OF CONTENTS

ACKNOWLEDGMENTS

I am deeply grateful to the composers and relatives of composers who so generously took the time to answer my inquiries. I thank the many libraries who supplied my needs either through the mail or in person, especially the efficient staff of the Free Library of Philadelphia, who tirelessly met my requests and who allowed me unrestricted access to their impressive collection of sheet music. Over the years I was fortunate to have excellent pianists with whom I performed or read through the American art song repertoire; in particular, Doris Coleman (over whose kitchen table I first expressed my dream of writing this book), Patricia Walmsley, Joel Sachs, and Ruben Del Pilar. Special thanks to Michael Höhne, whose good sense and skill in preparing this book for publication gave me peace of mind; to my husband, who repeatedly and good naturedly, at the precise moment I felt I had to have it, stopped what he was doing to give me the benefit of his wisdom; and to my daughter, Marisol Villamil Greenberg, who patiently, cheerfully, and expertly edited my attempts at writing. And finally, I am indebted to the singularly gifted artist, baritone Thomas Hampson, for taking time from his busy schedule to contribute such a thoughtful, moving, and provocative Foreword.

Philadelphia, 1993

FOREWORD

To introduce a new guide/compendium of American song is a grateful, rewarding, and somewhat daunting task. When confronted with the vast and myriad influences—inspirations borne out in any type of collection of American song (much less a book dedicated to the description and awareness of this vastness)—I am again overwhelmed with enthusiasm, wonder, and respect for our heritage of poetic/musical expression.

The condition of American song today is rather paradoxical in that, while in the short history of this nation there has never lacked a voracious attempt by our composers and poets to produce "song," there has always been a certain lag or gap—never more apparent than in today's concert scene—between its creation and its realization or re-creation. In fact, we have been so singularly dedicated to responding to the many pleas for "the song of self" or to finding "the voice of a nation" from various religious, philosophical, poetic and folkloric prophets that the staggeringly prolific output is matched only by its perplexing diversity.

The study of American song invites one into the study of the American psyche as do few other disciplines. American composers and poets have, for one thing, consistently spent almost as much time articulating the contemplation of their existence as American artists as they have spent with their own unique productivity as American artists. This continued self-examining is indicative of a far greater collective experience we call the American experiment: i.e., the challenge of existence of the one among many; the tolerance of the specific in the context of the greater good; the obsessive love/hate dialogue with form, whether political, social, religious, or musical; the confusing preoccupation with "art" versus "popular" as concepts; and certainly, above all, the persistent longing to define "it" as "American."

What then becomes fascinating through the history of American song is that the repertoire almost becomes the diary of the development of the American consciousness. While this seems a lofty pronouncement, the point is to invite somehow a different perspective to the well-known American adjectives of "eclecticism" and "plurality."

American song is by definition eclectic. And its ensuing plight has always been one of suffered, even belabored negative comparison with the very "eclectic" roots of musical ideas, styles, and forms from which it has drawn its inspiration. Eclecticism is not superficiality! Poly-cultural influences do not belie or make less "American" a piece of music. "Truly

American" cannot mean the severance from the many cultural circumstances and influences that gave, and still give, us "things American"!

It seems to me that song in almost any context is a fascinating, transcendent suspension of life's successive moments or pulses to the expanded reflection of a greater present. The specific use of that moment is then defined by its sentiment. Art becomes the transformer, the active ingredient of expression and is not belittled to usage as a qualitative adjective. In American song that active ingredient is as multifarious as the peoples from whence it came.

Walt Whitman said, *I say no land or circumstances ever existed so needing a race of singers and poems differing from all others.* Whitman is not pleading for a "type" or "style" of song, but for an active expression. *Oneself I sing,* says Whitman again with willful confidence, unapologetic naïveté, and mystical curiosity. These are the passionate ingredients of American song. A compendium or guidebook such as Ms. Villamil's *A Singer's Guide to the American Art Song: 1870-1980* fills a major gap in the current vocal research literature. Even more so, it exemplifies the kind of resourceful, self-study research tools so needed in a society determined to replace the broadminded humanities foundation of education with the inevitably short-sighted emphasis on technical proficiency. In the world of singing we must never allow "the voice" to be trained away or separated from the spirit or soul from which it comes. Thoughts in language, transmitted through and with music—not the curious technical phenomenon of vocal acoustics or coincidental properties of articulation and diction in various linguistic symbols—realize the landscape of the soul, the human condition, in singing. Song is like the lamppost or roadsign in the landscape.

Everyone of us who is involved at any level with the singing of songs shares the responsibility to shatter what Ms. Villamil rightly calls *the destructive notion that American song is the property of specialists.* My own commitment to the American song repertoire stems curiously enough from my first acquaintance with it—in other words, from a "hands on" approach.

An adventure of continual associations, recognitions, and expressions that are, both musically and poetically, peculiarly American in their attitude, yet dramatically human in their substance, awaits the student of this guidebook. But as with any guidebook, the journey it describes remains theoretical, obsolete, or—even worse—not your own, unless you travel the adventure yourself.

Thomas Hampson
Zürich, September 1993

INTRODUCTION

A Singer's Guide to the American Art Song took root in my mind in the early 1970s when, while browsing through the shelves of the Free Library of Philadelphia, I came upon an album called *Seventeen Songs of Sidney Homer*. Intrigued that the collection had been compiled by Samuel Barber, who introduced himself as Homer's nephew, and attracted by the look of the songs, I took it home. There, wide-eyed with delight, my pianist and I read through all 17 songs. But who was Sidney Homer? And what other hidden treasures were out there?

It turned out library shelves were rife with forgotten American composers of forgotten American songs. It would take a long time to sort them all out. Over the years I tried to do just that and gradually imagined a book that would not only assist singers like myself in making sense of the material, but also keep lesser known composers of our art song heritage (who, like Homer, were approaching obscurity) clearly identified for posterity.

There are many, experienced and knowledgeable in the field, who might have been perfect for the job, but time passed and no such book appeared. Armed with little more than my considerable experience in, and lifelong love affair with, singing, song, and American song (in that order), I therefore determined to fill the void myself. The other essential qualifications, writing and researching, I set out to acquire and, in doing so, greatly enjoyed the process.

A Singer's Guide brings under one cover all relevant and useful information pertaining to the American art song repertoire, and also documents the men and women who produced it. Though I believe that teachers, scholars, accompanists, and coaches will find the book useful, it is not an analytical work. It is, rather, precisely what its title purports—a practical handbook written by a singer, for singers.

THE SELECTION PROCESS

Composers and songs were initially selected on the basis of the guidelines described below, and ultimately at my own discretion. As it was not possible to look at *every* published song by *every* American composer, there are bound to be omissions. However, in my endeavor to review all relevant and significant material, I have culled library stacks and store shelves; read books, catalogues, periodicals, and old programs; and, in short, sought out every informational source on the subject of American song known to me.

Composers

(*A Singer's Guide* includes 21 women composers, but for reasons of expediency, I refer to composers by the masculine pronoun).

1. Each composer must be American, either born in America or naturalized at some time. In the latter case, he must also be generally regarded as American; e.g. though he became a citizen in 1947, Schoenberg would not be included.

2. The greater part of the composer's song catalogue must have been published after 1870 or before 1980. Though both dates are essentially arbitrary, the year 1870 approximates the appearance of Dudley Buck's first published song. ("With Buck," William Treat Upton wrote, "the floodgates of American song were opened and the deluge was upon us.") As it is not possible to stay totally up to date nor to evaluate the significance of the most recent song composers, the year 1980 simply serves as a convenient cut-off date. It does not, however, apply to the songs published after 1980 by already established composers, such as Ned Rorem and Lee Hoiby. Rather, it applies to the catalogues of young composers, such as John Musto and Christopher Berg, *none* of whose songs, according to *Classical Vocal Music in Print* (1985 Supplement), appeared before 1980.

3. The songs of the composer must either have some history of performance, regardless of my personal assessment; warrant performance, in my estimation; or have a visibility (or availability) that calls attention to them in such a way they must be considered. Size of output played only a small part in my considerations. The composer of a mammoth catalogue certainly could not be ignored, but neither could the composer of a single song or cycle if it was a major contribution to the repertoire.

Songs

1. Each song must be for solo voice.
2. Each song must be either unaccompanied or with piano accompaniment. Songs with other instruments are not listed. Piano reductions of orchestral or other scores are rarely included.
3. Each song must, at some point, have been published.
4. Each song must be deemed *art song* or have a close relationship with it; e.g. concert ballads are included; except in rare instances, popular songs, folk songs, and songs intended for religious services are not. Each song must be set to a text; vocalises are not included.
5. Each song must have either quality, interest, significance, or a combination of all three. This must be either my opinion or that of a significant enough number of other singers. Exceptions are made for the songs that are included to complete a certain composers catalogue. At all times, however, I make it clear if I cannot personally recommend the song. Wherever possible, I considered the composer's entire output. However, when dealing with a large, long out-of-print, hard-to-find catalogue of a more obscure composer, I studied such well known early critics in the field as Upton and Hughes, perused the listings in reference books such as *The New Grove Dictionary of American Music,* and read countless reviews and articles in old periodicals to be certain that, at the very least, the most important songs had been considered.
6. A Supplement of Songs (Appendix A) is comprised of noteworthy songs by composers who, because their output is not of significant interest, do not appear in the main body of the book.

GUIDE TO THE GUIDE

A Singer's Guide to the American Art Song is arranged alphabetically by composer. However, depending on the quality, quantity, and significance of his contribution, the focus and depth of coverage each composer receives varies greatly. For instance, a composer who is included on the basis of one outstanding work is identified by only a few sentences, but the particular song or cycle in question receives full coverage. On the other hand, only a brief summary is accorded the life and contribution of a composer: whose former popularity or historical significance is indisputable, but whose work has virtually no place in today's repertoire; who bears some name recognition but whose output, though large, is generally disappointing; whose songs are worth exploring though they are hardly known and difficult to find. Most composers, however, receive the full coverage described in detail below.

Biographies

In addition to providing the usual data regarding parentage, education, awards, positions, and so forth, I attempt to give some human dimension to each composer with emphasis on information that may be of special interest to singers. In most cases, my principal sources have been the biographical reference works noted in each composer's bibliography. For lesser known composers, periodicals were especially helpful. In a few cases, when information was scarce or confusing, I personally approached those composers who were still alive.

Song discussion

These brief essays focus on the aspects of a composer's song output that a singer may find interesting or helpful. They may include the influences that shaped his style; characteristics of that style; poets he tended to set; size and significance of output; any special knowledge the composer may have of singing; and any technical, musical, or interpretative difficulties the singer, and sometimes the pianist, can expect to find.

Publication and recording information

Basic publication information regarding a composer's songs is provided at the end of the song discussions. If the composer has an album devoted to his songs alone, an abbreviation for that title is provided (e.g. *Paul Bowles: Selected Songs* becomes *PBSS*). From that point on, all references to that title in that composer's entry employ the abbreviation.

Specific data about the principal song recordings of each composer is also provided at the end of the song discussion. Thereafter, only the performer's last name is given to indicate that recording. Isolated recordings, however, only appear with their respective song entry, at which time full data is provided. All recordings are LP unless otherwise noted. If an LP has been reissued on CD, data for the CD and not the LP is given. Every effort has been made to keep recording and publication information complete and up to date. A discography of American song in collection is also provided as an appendix. Though most recordings are naturally out of print, many can be found in recording libraries or stores that specialize in such material. Furthermore, though the list is far from complete, by noting some of the singers who recorded these songs, one gets additional insight as to their history.

Song lists

The annotated listing of the composer's songs may be partial or complete. A partial listing will be comprised of representative examples and/or my personal recommendations, and will always include the better known works. If feasible and appropriate, a complete listing (or that which is believed to be complete) is accorded important outputs of consistently high quality. As there is ongoing interest in virtually all the songs of Ned Rorem and Charles Ives, I provide complete listings of their songs despite the huge numbers involved.

An addenda of songs, which I call "Also of interest," may appear at the end of a composer's song listing, and is described later.

I have personally reviewed the sheet music for every song listed. In addition, I have either listened to one or more recordings of that song, read through it at least once with a pianist, performed it myself, or any combination of the above.

Song annotations

The annotations described below are in two parts: publication data and descriptive information. Cycles and sets are annotated in the same manner as individual songs. If it seems permissible to extract songs from such a work, I usually provide modified annotations for each individually. But when the songs involved are too numerous, or the set/cycle is clearly intended to be kept intact, it is annotated as a single work.

Publication data:

1. *Title*. Titles are written exactly as the composer has given them. Subtitles are included when significant; translations of titles in a foreign language are provided if there seems to be a need. If opus numbers have been used, they follow the title.
2. *Poet*. Where the composer has only provided a last name, I have filled in first names when I am certain of the information. Otherwise they are given as noted on the sheet music. (Though some composers do not capitalize E. E. Cummings, others do; I have taken the liberty of uniformly capitalizing the name, except when it appears as part of a song title.)
3. *Publishers and Copyright*. Publishers names are shortened; e.g. Peters for C. F. Peters (see Appendix C for full names and other data on all publishers). Wherever possible, the original publisher and original copyright date are given. When a song has been transferred to a totally separate publisher I usually provide both. I do

not, however, concern myself with changes the publisher itself
may have undergone since the song was first printed. Again, the
reader will want to refer to the publisher's appendix for the most
recent information on that complicated issue.

4. *Anthologies.* If the song is also included in a collection of that composer's songs or in a multi-composer anthology the entry will read
"also incl." followed by the abbreviation for that collection. If the
word "also" is eliminated, the song *only* appears in that collection.
Abbreviations for single composer collections are given at the end
of the song discussion. Abbreviations for multi-composer anthologies are provided both at the end of this introduction and, with full
publication data and contents in Appendix B.

5. *Date of composition.* When known, date of composition is usually
provided.

6. *Dedications.* Only dedications of particular interest, such as a
known singer, another composer, or a family member, are noted.

7. *Commissions and first performances.* This information is provided
only if a well known performer was involved or if the occasion
was historic.

Descriptive information:

1. *Type of voice.* Type of voice is either specified by the composer
(spec.); designated by the publisher (pub.); or recommended by
the author (rec.). This may vary as I see fit or be a combination of
these options. I avoid specificity in my personal recommendations,
mainly because voices are too individual for anyone to *really*
know the correct designation for that particular voice and I would
not want to needlessly deter a prospective singer from a particular
song. Similarly, the tiresome issue of whether a particular song is
appropriate for a man or a woman is also kept open wherever possible. Gender is noted only when the composer specifies it or when
everything about a song cries out for either a man or a woman.
When the gender implied in a song *may* affect a singer's decision
to program that particular song, I state that the text *suggests* one
gender over the other. Otherwise, I leave the issue alone.

2. *Range of voice.* Lowest and highest notes are given. Compass of
range are notated as follows: working up from middle C, the first
octave would be c1–b1; second octave c2–b2; third octave c3–b3.
The octave starting with c below middle c would be c–b; the
octave below that, C–B. Optional notes are given in brackets next

to the notes they alter, but *only* when the range of the *entire* song
is affected. When the song is published in more than one key, in
the interests of space, only one range is provided. I feel confident
that with that much information the singer can make a satisfactory estimate as to what the other ranges would be.

3. *Timing.* Timings are taken either from recordings (sometimes the
average between two well regarded recordings); from specified
timings stated on the sheet music itself; or from my own timing of
the song. With so many variables of interpretation to take into
account, timings are approximate. Consequently, seconds have
been rounded off to the nearest quarter minute.

4. *Tempo.* The tempo noted is virtually always that given by the composer at the beginning of a piece. As composers always capitalize
the first letter of these markings, I do the same. Therefore, if the
capital is omitted the indication is my own, which means that none
was provided by the composer. Tempo changes made as the song
progresses are noted when significant.

5. *General description.* This includes any or all of the following:
mood; type; form; vocal style; accompanimental feeling; technical, interpretive, or musical concerns (difficulty is described from
the point of view of the advanced or professional singer); historical interest; subject matter; use; and total impression.

6. *Recordings.* Except for isolated recordings, only the singer's name
is provided. For full recording data the reader should refer back to
the end of the song discussion. (See recording and publication
information.)

Also of interest

This addenda of titles serves as a melting pot for songs which, either
because they are not as highly recommended as the other songs, or
because they do not fit the guidelines of the book, are not included in the
main list, but may be of interest to a performer wishing to explore the
composer further. Annotations are greatly shortened (for instance: poet's
first names are eliminated; vocal type and publishing information is only
provided when it is unusual or of special interest).

Bibliography

The bibliography provided at the end of each composer's entry always
opens with the abbreviated titles of the best standard references that offer
substantive information on the composer. Full titles and publication data

for these works are provided both in the list of abbreviations that follows this introduction and in the bibliography at the end of the book. The remainder of the bibliography is comprised of the titles I found to be the most useful, interesting, and relevant to that particular composer and his songs.

FINDING THE SONGS

Anyone in the business of singing classical song knows how difficult it is to find any but the most standard repertoire. American art song being no exception, I make a few suggestions for tracking down those hard-to-find items. I had originally envisioned providing a full listing of the libraries that can claim the best collections, but soon realized that the research involved was beyond the scope of this book. However, if your local store does not have what you are looking for and cannot order it because it is no longer in print, your best hope is usually libraries. From my own experience the Library of Congress, the New York Public Library for the Performing Arts at Lincoln Center, and the Free Library of Philadelphia are all excellent sources.

If you do not have access to these or other big libraries, or if your local library cannot produce what you want, the interlibrary loan, which virtually all libraries have access to, is an amazingly efficient service. If you are not in a hurry, it can produce almost anything. The American Music Center, 30 West 26th Street, New York, NY 10010 also offers library services for its collection. Finally, I recommend Classical Vocal Reprints, P.O. Box 20263, New York, NY 10023 (telephone: (212) 517-8114; fax: (212) 570-9125). Run by Glendower Jones, it is an excellent source for all kinds of solo vocal music, including a great many of the titles I recommend in this guide.

Other than the above suggestions, one must both cull old collections and watch for reprints and new publications.

ABBREVIATIONS

All abbreviations used in the guide, except those for publishers and for single-composer albums, are given below. Abbreviations for publishers are given in Appendix C. Abbreviations for individual composer collections are given in the paragraph preceding the listing of his or her songs. See the bibliography and various appendixes at the end of the book for full data on books and anthologies.

AAA	*American Artsong Anthology* (Galaxy c1982)
AAS	*American Art Songs* (Associated c1982)
AASBAC	*Anthology of Art Songs by Black American Composers* (Marks c1977)
AASGS	*Anthology of American Song* (G. Schirmer c1911)
AASTC	*American Art Songs of the Turn of the Century* (Dover c1991)
ACA	American Composers Alliance
AmerGroves	The New Grove Dictionary of American Music
Ammer	*Unsung* (Christine Ammer)
arr.	arranged
ASA	*Art Song Argosy* (G. Schirmer c1937)
ass.	assigned
A12S	*Album of Twelve Songs by American Composers* (G. Schirmer c1958)
b.	born
Baker	*Baker's Biographical Dictionary of Music*
c (e.g. c1980)	copyright date
CAAS	*Contemporary American Art Songs* (Ditson c1977)
CAS	*Contemporary American Songs* (Summy-Birchard c1960)
CASS	*Contemporary American Sacred Song* (G. Schirmer c1985)

CAS28	*Contemporary Art Songs: 28 Songs by British and American Composers* (G. Schirmer c1958)
CBY	*Current Biography Yearbook*
CC	*Cos Cob Song Volume* (Cos Cob c1935)
comm.	commissioned
comp.	composed
CSE	*Contemporary Songs in English* (Fischer c1956)
CVR	Classical Vocal Reprints
d.	died
ded.	dedicated
der.	derived
ed.	edited
Ewen	*American Composers* (David Ewen)
Ewen (ACT)	*American Composers Today* (David Ewen)
Ewen (1900)	*Composers Since 1900* (David Ewen)
50AS	*Fifty Art Songs from the modern repertoire* (G. Schirmer c1939)
50SS	*Fifty Shakspere* [sic] *Songs* (Ditson c1906)
Flanagan	"American Songs: A Thin Crop" (William Flanagan)
Friedberg (I, II, III)	*American Art Song and American Poetry; Vols. I–III* (Ruth Friedberg)
Goss	*Modern Music Makers* (Madeleine Goss)
Greene	*Greene's Biographical Encyclopedia of Composers*
Gruen	*The Party's Over Now* (John Gruen)
Hall	*The Art Song* (James Husst Hall)
Howard (OAM)	*Our American Music* (John Tasker Howard)
Howard (OCC)	*Our Contemporary Composers* (John Tasker Howard)
Hughes	*American Composers* (Rupert Hughes)
incl.	included
Ivey	*Song: Anatomy, Imagery, and Styles* (Donald Ivey)
LF1	*Lyric Fancies: Volume 1* (Schmidt c1919)
LF2	*Lyric Fancies: Volume 2* (Schmidt c1919)
Manning	*New Vocal Repertory* (Jane Manning)
med.	medium
Mellers	*Music in a New Found Land* (Wilfrid Mellers)

NAAS	*A New Anthology of American Song* (G. Schirmer c1942)
Nathan	"United States of America" (Hans Nathan)
NVS	*New Vistas in Song* (Marks c1964)
opt.	optional
orig.	original, originally
perf.	performed
pub.	published
RAAS	*Romantic American Art Songs* (G. Schirmer c1990)
rec.	recommended
Recital Pub. Reprint	Recital Publications Reprint Edition
rev.	revised
SE	*Songs in English* (Fischer c1970)
SIA	*Songs of an Innocent Age* (G. Schirmer c1984)
SSSR	*Singable Songs for Studio and Recital* (Ditson c1936)
S30A	*Songs by 30 Americans* (Ditson c1904)
S22A	*Songs by 22 Americans* (G. Schirmer c1960)
Southern	*The Music of Black Americans* (Eileen Southern)
spec.	specified
Tawa	*The Coming of Age of American Art Music* (Nicholas Tawa)
Thompson	*The International Cyclopedia of Music and Musicians* (Oscar Thompson)
Thorpe	"Interpretative Studies in American Songs" (Harry Colin Thorpe)
trans.	translated
20CAS	*20th Century Art Song* (G. Schirmer c1967)
Upton	*Art-Song in America* (William Treat Upton)
Upton (Sup)	*A Supplement to Art-Song in America* (William Treat Upton)
VN	*Vote for Names* (Peer Southern)
vol.	volume
WW (1-5)	*Wa-Wan Press Reprint Edition: Vols. I–V* (ed. Vera Brodsky Lawrence)

A Singer's Guide to
THE
AMERICAN ART SONG
1870–1980

SAMUEL ADLER
b. March 4, 1928, Mannheim, Germany

Samuel Adler is best known for his instrumental and liturgical music. Nonetheless, his prolific catalogue includes many songs of which his earlier settings are especially effective.

Adler was born into a Jewish family filled with music and religion.[1] His father was a cantor and a composer of Jewish liturgical music; his mother had studied voice and piano. As a child, Adler studied violin but set his sights on becoming a composer. In 1939 the family immigrated to the United States (Adler became an American citizen in 1945) and settled in Worcester, Massachusetts. While still in high school Adler studied theory with Herbert Fromm, then continued his musical studies at Boston University (1946–1948), and at Harvard University (1948–1950), where he worked with Walter Piston, Irving Fine, Randall Thompson, and Paul Hindemith. During summer vacations he studied composition with Aaron Copland and conducting with Serge Koussevitsky at the Berkshire Music Center. In the early 1950s Adler served in the U.S. Army in Germany and was honored for organizing the Seventh Army Symphony. In 1953 he went to Texas where he was musical director of Temple Emanu-El in Dallas and a professor at North Texas State University. In 1966 he joined the faculty of the Eastman School of Music, becoming chairman of the department in 1970. Married to Carol Ellen Stalker, an author and poet, the couple have raised two daughters.

THE SONGS
Written in a conventional modern idiom, Adler's early songs convincingly depict mood and scene, and abound in lyricism and vitality. The fluid, gracious vocal writing makes only moderate demands on performers. Later songs, however, labor in their effort to communicate more serious and dramatic subject matter. Vocal lines become increasingly rigid, disjunct, and long. Intervals, especially some unwieldy approaches to high notes, are awkward, and much thought must be given to phrasing if one is to find a place to breathe. Although most of Adler's songs have some tonal centering, in later years they become decidedly more atonal and dissonant. Rhythms are generally straightforward. In 1991 Southern published *Samuel Adler: Collected Songs for Voice and Piano (SACS)*. This album of 22 songs includes some early sets (formerly pub-

lished by Hinshaw), as well as a considerable amount of later unpublished material. The following recommendations favor early settings.

Four Poems of James Stephens, Oxford c1963; pub. separately.
Pub. high voice (c#1–b♭2), rec. voices with stamina and weight
especially in upper range; 6:30; titles are: *The Wind; Chill of the Eve;
The Piper; And It Was Stormy Weather;* best as a set; generally fast
tempos with only one slow song; high tessitura with a few vocally
demanding passages; small rhythmical difficulties; big ending; colorful; and effective.

Three Songs, various poets; Hinshaw c1979; also incl. *SACS;* comp.
1953/54.
Spec. medium voices (a–g2); 4:15; these songs (on youth, old age,
and time itself) make an excellent cycle, but any one could also be
used individually.
But I Was Young and Foolish, William Butler Yeats; (b–f#2), text
suggests men; 1:00; Quite fast, and very crisp throughout; light
and lyrical.
Old Age, Judah Stampfer; (a–e2); 1:45; Slowly, but do not drag; lyrical; subdued.
Time You Old Gypsy Man, Ralph Hodgson; (b♭ –g2); 1:30; Excitedly
rushing; small rhythmical difficulties; dramatic; striking; recorded by Jan DeGaetani on Electra-Nonesuch CD (79248-2-ZK).

Three Songs about Love, various poets; Hinshaw c1978; also incl.
SACS; comp. 1953/54.
Spec. high voice (b–a2); 4:30; makes a good set but can be used
individually; in a lyrical declamation; light and attractive.
Go Lovely Rose, Edmund Waller; (b–g#2); 2:15; Moderately fast; the
least appealing of the set.
A Ditto,[2] Sir Philip Sidney; (e1–a2); 1:45; Gently flowing.
Song (from the Vicar of Wakefield), Oliver Goldsmith; (d1–g#2);
0:30; Fast; light.

Two Songs For Three Years, various poets; Boosey c1974; to my
beloved daughter Deborah on her third birthday.
Spec. medium voices (a–f2); 5:00; Adler makes a note that
although these may both be sung by a baritone, the first is best for
mezzo-soprano.
My Daughter the Cypress, Ruth Whitman; (c#1–f2); 2:00; Gently
rocking; a lullaby.

Song To Be Sung By the Father of Infant Female Children, Ogden Nash; (a–e2); 3:00; With verve; a fast moving comic narrative; builds as the doting father plots against his daughter's future suitors.

Two Songs from the Portugese, Gil Vincente (H. W. Longfellow); Hinshaw c1978; also incl. *SACS;* comp. 1953/54.

Rec. medium voices (bb–f#2); 2:30; titles are: *Simple Song; Ballad;* best kept together; folk texts, but the tunes are by Adler; rhythmically fun; light, lyrical, and happy.

Unholy Sonnets (Five Love Songs), John Donne; incl. *SACS.*

Spec. tenors (c#1–cb3); 12:15; best as a cycle but could be used individually; from Donne's early poems (not sonnets) on experiences with women and love; the title is Adler's and is probably meant to contrast with Donne's more famous late *Holy Sonnets;* verbally elaborate; highly disjunct with many high notes; generally passionate, intense, declamatory, and very demanding for the voice; the most effective of Adler's later songs.

The good-morrow, (d#1–b2); 2:45; Fast and excited.

The Broken Heart, (c#1–a2); 2:45; Fast and wild.

Woman's Constancy, (eb 1–cb3, falsetto); 3:15; With a great deal of pathos.

The Indifferent, (db1–a2); 2:00; With abandon.

The Triple Foole, (db1–bb2); 2:30; Gently moving; subdued ending.

BIBLIOGRAPHY

AmerGroves, Baker, Ewen, Greene.
"American Composer Sketches: Samuel Adler," *Music Educators Journal* 53 (March 1967): 41–45.

---

[1] The famous philosopher and theologian Martin Buber was a family friend.
[2] This is Adler's title for the famous sonnet which begins "My true love has my heart and I have his."

GEORGE ANTHEIL
b. July 8, 1900, Trenton, NJ; d. Feb. 12, 1959, New York, NY

After studying with Ernest Bloch, George Antheil found notoriety in Europe with his avant-garde compositions. He returned to New York in 1933 and eventually moved to Hollywood, where he composed film scores. In addition to *Five Songs,* written when he was still a student,

Antheil composed *Songs of Experience,* a set of nine beautiful songs in the neo-romantic style of his later years. Currently in manuscript at the Library of Congress, they were recorded by Uta Graf, with the composer at the piano, on SPA (1). *Night Piece,* a setting of James Joyce, was recorded by Myron Myers on Musical Heritage (MHS 912016M).

Five Songs: 1919-1920, Adelaide Crapsey; Cos Cob c1934; reissued Boosey c1961.

Spec. soprano (c1–a#2); 5:30; titles are: *November Night; Triad; Susanna and the Elders; Fate Defied; The Warning;* must be performed as a set; straight, dispassionate declamation over various atmospheric chord patterns; two songs call for an unrelenting high tessitura; rhythmic complexity in the last song; concentrated, poignant, and totally without tune, these striking, diminutive songs perfectly capture Crapsey's terse, chilling imagery.

BIBLIOGRAPHY
AmerGroves, Baker, Ewen, Goss, Greene, Thompson, Upton (Sup).
Antheil, George. *Bad Boy of Music.* Garden City, New York: Doubleday, Doran and Co., 1945. Antheil was a first-rate raconteur and his life is endlessly fascinating.
Whitesitt, Linda. *The Life and Music of George Antheil, 1900–1959.* Ann Arbor, Michigan: UMI Research Press, 1983.

DOMINICK ARGENTO
b. Oct. 27, 1927, York, PA

Dominick Argento is one of our most vocally sympathetic composers and, with his songs, operas, and choral works all regularly performed, one of the most successful. Yet, by living apart from musical centers and holding to an eclectic, albeit very personal, compositional style, he is not widely known outside of the vocal world and its audiences.

Argento was the eldest of three children, whose parents, immigrants from Sicily, ran a restaurant and hotel. There was no music at home but as a child, fascinated by biographies of composers, he taught himself theory and harmony. When his father gave him a piano for his 16th birthday, Argento began to study formally. In 1947, after two years of military service, he enrolled in the Peabody Conservatory of Music, where his composition teachers were Nicolas Nabakov, Hugo Weisgall,[1] and later, Henry Cowell. Luigi Dallapiccola in Italy (on a 1951 Fulbright fellowship), and Howard Hanson, Bernard Rogers, and Alan Hovhaness at the Eastman School of Music, round out his large, diverse, and distinguished array of teachers.

Argento's early one-act opera *The Boor* premiered in 1957 and paved the way for a dozen more. In 1958 he accepted what he believed would be only a temporary teaching position at the University of Minnesota, but soon realized the advantages of developing a musical identity away from the mainstream and the pressures that attend it. Moreover, Minneapolis was a city coming to life culturally, and Argento found himself with enviable commissions from the Minneapolis Symphony, the Minnesota Opera,[2] and Tyrone Guthrie's newly formed repertory theater. A Pulitzer Prize in 1975 for the song cycle *From the Diary of Virginia Woolf* secured his reputation. Currently on a light schedule at the University, Argento lives in Minneapolis most of the year but summers in Florence, Italy, where he composes eight hours a day. Since 1954 he has been married to soprano Carolyn Bailey, a fellow Peabody student who first performed his *Spring Songs.*

THE SONGS
One has only to read Argento's thoughtful, eloquent addresses to two NATS conventions, given ten years apart, to appreciate that a profound feeling for the singing voice is at the root of his compositional drive. It is moving to hear him describe the voice as the "original instrument, the one for which and with which music was invented."[3] And it is reassuring that he should so thoroughly understand the vulnerability of the singer, the excitement and danger under which performance is undertaken, and the impossibility of separating a singer's persona from his instrument. He has suggested that self-discovery is the theme for much of his work.[4] Hence, of his five cycles for voice and piano, diaries and letters are the textual source for three—an idea with little precedent.

Happily eclectic, whether calling for a major triad or a twelve-tone row, Argento's compositional style is essentially traditional. Given his Italian background, his love for literature, and the inspiration that comes with being married to a soprano, it is also essentially lyrical, with a strong literary and theatrical thrust. At first acquaintance these songs seem difficult. A profusion of subtle detail, changing tempos and meters, intricate rhythmic patterns, and expression markings all take time to work out, especially in conjunction with the piano. But this intelligent and conscientiously crafted music works so well performers will quickly realize that these difficulties, by virtue of the naturalness of the expression, are easily surmountable. Much of the vocal writing, especially in the cycles, is a blending of conversational and cantabile styles. The lightness of declamation, graceful contours, and moderate ranges all ensure the singer's comfort and ease. Argento gives enormous credit to his wife's ongoing counsel. (Carolyn Bailey had a high, flexible voice and introduced many of his earlier works.) The widely diverse textures of the gracious, evocative piano writing are always perfectly balanced with the vocal line. Argento's songs are unabashedly emotional and warm but always tempered by exquisite refinement and taste. They will not only show a singer's voice to advantage but allow him to reach deep into his emotional and artistic make-up.

Singers might also consider *Letters from Composers* for tenor and guitar, and *To Be Sung Upon the Water* for piano and clarinet. *From the Diary of Virginia Woolf* has been recorded by Virginia Dupuy on Gasparo CD (GSCD-273) and Linn Maxwell on Centaur CD (CRC 2092); *Six Elizabethan Songs* by Barbara Martin (with instruments) on CRI (C 380); *The Andrée Expedition* by William Parker on Centaur CD (CRC 2092). The following is believed to be a complete listing of Argento's published songs.

The Andrée Expedition, Boosey c1987, comp. 1983.

Spec. baritone (B♭–g1); 40:00; titles are: *Prologue; The Balloon Rises; Pride and Ambition; Dinner Aloft; The Unforseen Problem; The Flight Aborted; Mishap with a Sledge; The King's Jubilee; Illness and Drugs; Hallucinations; Anna's Birthday; Epilogue; Final Word;* in two parts: *In the Air,* comprised of six songs, and *On the Ice,* seven songs; extracts from letters and diaries of three Swedes, whose frozen bodies were found 33 years after their 1897 attempt to reach the North Pole in a hot air balloon; published in a clear manuscript; a blend of declamation and cantabile but with a preponderance of the former; tessitura is on the high side; musically difficult, especially ensemble. The optimistic opening, drama of the aborted flight, gradual recognition of the true situation, and painful, poetic final words are powerful stuff—almost too much for music—but a compelling experience if delivered by a performer with finely honed theatrical instincts; recorded by Parker.

Casa Guidi, Elizabeth Barrett Browning; Boosey c1984; comp. 1983; for Federica von Stade.

Spec. mezzo-soprano (a♭–a2[a♭2]); 20:00; titles are: *Casa Guidi; The Italian Cook and the English Maid; Robert Browning; The Death*

of Mr. Barrett; Domesticity; a cycle of five songs taken from letters
Elizabeth Barrett Browning wrote from Florence, Italy, to her sister,
Henrietta, in England. These nicely varied songs follow the text
wherever it takes us. The result is a score of many moods saturated
with subtle rhythmic and tempo fluctuations. Although the cycle
opens and closes lyrically, it builds to a passionate climax in the emotional *Robert Browning.* Originally composed for orchestra, Argento
immediately reduced it for piano. However, not only does the piano
version require the services of an exceptionally dexterous pianist to
solve such problems as the repeated notes in the second song, but
many of the effects, such as the lone high notes in *The Death of Mr.
Barrett,* seem empty without instrumental color. Beautifully crafted
for the voice, the greatest challenge is the ensemble; a thoroughly
romantic cycle in the same manner as the Virginia Woolf cycle, but
without its drama and tension.

From the Diary of Virginia Woolf, Boosey c1975; comp. 1974; for
Janet Baker.
    Spec. medium voice (b–g#2); 30:00; titles are: *The Diary; Anxiety;
Fancy; Hardy's Funeral; Rome; War; Parents; Final Entry;* a cycle,
excerpted from the famous diaries of this great English novelist and
essayist; the entries range from 1919 to 1941 just before her suicide.
A wide variety of ideas are used here to express the many facets of
Woolf's complex persona. Though she first contemplates the shape
her diary will assume in a supple twelve-tone row, elsewhere the
musical vocabulary is from the mainstream of contemporary writing.
Of moderate musical difficulty; flexible, sensitive vocal lines are
beautifully crafted in a relaxed middle tessitura; a first-rate, probing
work of beauty and imagination; one of the best in the literature;
recorded by Dupuy and Maxwell.

Six Elizabethan Songs, various poets; Boosey c1970; comp. 1957; for
Nicholas DiVirgilio; second version arr. for baroque ensemble in
1962.
    Spec. high voice (d#1–a2); 15:00; can be used as a set or individ-
ually; in the Elizabethan spirit these tuneful, colorful songs also evoke
Benjamin Britten; wonderful variety of mood; the voice in a generally high tessitura needs control and flexibility; pianist requires considerable dexterity; the instrumental version is preferable; recorded
by Martin.

Spring, Thomas Nash; (e♭1–f2); 1:30; Allegretto piacevole; light over a sprightly piano.

Sleep, Samuel Daniel; (d#1–f2); 2:45; Lentamente; sustained; more animated central section.

Winter, William Shakespeare; (e1–a2); 1:30; Allegro vivace con slancio; some sustained high notes; very colorful.

Dirge, William Shakespeare; (e1–e2); 3:15; Largo e semplice; a poignant, liquid vocal line over a slight accompaniment; *piano* throughout.

Diaphenia, Henry Constable; (f#1–g2); 1:45; Allegro brillante; lyrical, parlando, and sustained passages; spirited.

Hymn, Ben Jonson; (d#1–g#2); 3:00; Andante maestoso; some declamation; mostly sustained; generally quiet; noble.

Songs About Spring, E. E. Cummings; Boosey c1980; comp. 1951; for Carolyn Bailey; also arr. for small orchestra.

Rec. light, high voices (c#1–c3 [b♭2]); 9:30; written while still a student, Argento only reluctantly permitted publication of these songs many years later; nevertheless, they are justifiably popular; can be used individually but make a good upbeat set; light and lyrical with a reasonably good variety of tempo and mood, despite single poet and single theme.

who knows if the moon's a balloon; (e1–a2); 1:45; Allegretto piacevole; light; coloratura passages.

Spring is like a perhaps hand; (d#1–g2); 3:00; Larghetto semplice; sustained.

In Just-spring; (d1–c3 [a♭2]); 1:00; Leggiero e giojoso; brilliant, then fades.

in Spring comes; (c#1–f#2); 1:30; Adagietto, innocentemente; a lovely lyric recitative in canon with a single piano line.

when faces called flowers float out of the ground; (d1–b♭2); 2:15; tempo di valse; exuberant.

BIBLIOGRAPHY

AmerGroves, Baker, CBY (1977), Ewen, Greene.

Altman, Peter. "The Voyage of Dominick Argento," *Opera News,* April 17, 1976.

Argento, Dominick. "The Composer and the Singer," *The NATS Bulletin* 33 (May 1977). A reprint of the address Argento gave to the NATS convention in Philadelphia in 1976.

————. "The Matter of Text," *The NATS Journal* 44 (March/April 1988). A reprint of the address Argento gave to the NATS convention in San Antonio in 1987.

Davis, Peter G. "Miss Havisham Goes to the Opera," *New York Times*, March 18, 1979.

Steele, Mike. "Dominick Argento: Musician of the Month," *High Fidelity/Musical America* (September 1975).

---

[1] Argento would later work in Hugo Weisgall's Hilltop Opera of Baltimore.
[2] Co-founded by Argento as the Center Opera.
[3] Address to 1976 NATS convention, reprinted in *NATS Bulletin* (May 1977), p. 19.
[4] Ibid, 20.

FREDERIC AYRES[1]
b. March 17, 1876, Binghamton, NY; d. Nov. 23, 1926, Colorado Springs, CO

After studying engineering at Cornell University, Ayres worked briefly in that field. Then from 1897 till 1901 he studied composition with Edgar Stillman Kelley and, for one summer, with Arthur Foote. In 1901, however, he became ill with tuberculosis and was obliged to move to New Mexico and, the following year, to Colorado Springs. There he lived out his life, teaching privately and composing.

THE SONGS
Ayres's approximately 50 songs, over half of which were published, span his compositional career from 1906 to 1926. Several have real substance, wonderful mood, and even a kind of restrained theatrical quality. However, a great many others suffer from being seriously overwritten. Too often Ayres seems to be composing in a vacuum, unable to curb a restless searching, and unaware that excesses of chromaticism and shifting harmonics wear thin. His vocal writing is idiomatic, often melodic, and rarely demanding. But given Ayres's penchant for sharps, flats, elaborate textures, and intricate patterns, which often require very wide stretches for the hand, the pianist will find his work cut out for him. William Treat Upton held Ayres in great esteem, and Arthur Farwell admired his early work enough to publish a piano piece and five songs in the Wa-Wan Press. Paul Sperry has recorded two on Albany CD

(TROY034-2). Though uneven and hard to find, a few of Ayres's unusual songs must be recommended.

Christmas Eve at Sea, John Masefield; G. Schirmer c1925.
   Spec. medium voices (c#1–f#2); 3:15; Andante tranquillo, ma con moto; the atmospheric opening builds, then closes on a hushed, refrain-like "Nowell"; much happens in this evocative song with its dramatic undercurrents.

My Love in Her Attire, Anonymous; G. Schirmer c1924.
   Spec. medium and higher voices (d1–g2), text suggests men; 1:00; Andante con moto; lyrical; piano and vocal lines interweaving; though on the surface simple, straightforward, and tuneful, this is an exquisitely constructed song of great sophistication.

Sea Dirge, Op. 4, No. 2, William Shakespeare; Wa-Wan c1907, incl. *WW (4).*
   Rec. medium and lower voices (b♭–c2); 2:45; Lento misterioso; lyric declamation over slowly rocking chords; hushed and eerie; an excellent setting of "Full fathom five thy father lies."

Three Songs, various poets; G. Schirmer c1921.
   Spec. high voices (d1–a2), rec. bigger voices; 8:30; a good set, but could be sung individually; melodic, cantabile vocal writing over rich, occasionally very difficult accompaniments; serious, romantic, and strong.
   The Song of the Panthan Girl, Rudyard Kipling; (d1–g♭2), text suggests women; 3:45; Lento; strophic; nostalgic.
   Strong as Death, Henry Cuyler Bunner; (e♭1–a2), text suggests men; 3:00; Adagio; the uncharacteristically straightforward opening builds to a powerful climax before the hushed, mysterious close.
   Triumph, William Vaughn Moody; (d1–a♭2); 1:45; Allegro moderato; big singing; dramatic and uplifting.

Also of interest:

Sappho, a paraphrase of the Sixty-eighth Fragment, Adagio, ma cantando; *Sunset Wings,* Dante Gabriel Rossetti, for high voices, elaborate; *Take, O Take Those Lips Away,* Shakespeare, incl. *WW (3),* and *AASTC,* recorded by Sperry; *The Twa Corbies,* Anonymous, a traditional narrative; *Where the Bee Sucks,* Shakespeare, incl. *WW (4)* and *AASTC,* recorded by Sperry.

BIBLIOGRAPHY
AmerGroves, Baker, Howard (OAM and OCC), Thompson, Upton.
Upton, William Treat. "Frederic Ayres," *Musical Quarterly* 18 (January 1932): 39–59. A major article with emphasis on the songs; also a complete listing of his works.

---

[1] Ayres was sometimes referred to by his real name, Frederic Ayres Johnson.

MILTON BABBITT
b. May 10, 1916, Philadelphia, PA

Milton Babbitt grew up in Jackson, Mississippi, where he received his early music training. He later studied with Marion Bauer in New York and with Roger Sessions at Princeton University. A leader of the serial and electronic movements, Babbitt has been on the faculties of Princeton, Columbia University, and the Juilliard School.

Disjunct vocal lines, formidable rhythms, and a generally theoretical approach have not endeared Babbitt to the average singer. Nevertheless, his attention to the sonic properties of words and his expressive, if unorthodox, feeling for the text, distinguish his vocal music.[1] *The Widow's Lament in Springtime* is an outstanding example of song in the twelve-tone idiom.

The Widow's Lament in Springtime, William Carlos Williams; Boelke-Bomart c1959.

Spec. soprano, but range suggests lower voices (f#–f#2); 2:30; slow quarter given for tempo; serial; though the vocal and piano lines are disjunct and complex, their limpid lyricism are woven into a cohesive whole; quiet dynamics; low notes need only be brushed gently; plaintive and disquieting; a song of singular beauty and mood; recorded by Jan DeGaetani on Elektra/Nonesuch CD (79248-2-ZK).

Also of interest:

Du, Stramm, spec. soprano, a short twelve-tone cycle in German; *Sounds and Words,* incl. *New Vistas in Songs,* rec. high agile voices, serial, very difficult; *Three Theatrical Songs,* Babbitt, comp. 1946; straightforward, tonal show songs reflecting Babbitt's early interest in jazz.

BIBLIOGRAPHY
AmerGroves, Baker, Ewen, Greene, Manning (on *Three Theatrical Songs*), Nathan (on *Du*), Thompson.

---

[1] In addition to his few songs, *Vision and Prayer* and *Philomel*, long monologues for soprano and tape, and *A Solo Requiem*, a cycle for soprano and two pianos, are notable works in their genre. They have all been recorded by Bethany Beardslee, the leading exponent of Babbitt's vocal music.

ERNST BACON
b. May 26, 1898, Chicago, IL; d. March 16, 1990, Orinda, CA

Answering only to his wholly original and inventive mind, Ernst Bacon has written some of America's most unusual, forthright, and affecting music. At the heart of this bountiful and intriguing catalogue are more than 200 songs.

His father was a prominent physician; his mother, an amateur pianist and singer, who taught him piano. While continuing music studies with teachers that included Glenn Dillard Gunn and Alexander Raab, at his father's insistence, Bacon pursued an academic course of education at Northwestern University and the University of Chicago. Then, in 1924 he went to Vienna where, in addition to his piano studies, he took composition with Karl Weigl and Franz Schmidt. On his return, he studied conducting with Eugene Goosens in Rochester, New York. Subsequently, he studied composition with Ernest Bloch in California and, in 1935, received a masters degree from the University of California at Berkeley. From 1934 to 1937 he was supervisor of the Federal Music Project in San Francisco. During this period he also founded the famous Bach Festival in Carmel, California.

Bacon's own distinguished teaching career took him throughout the United States with long periods spent at Converse College in Spartanburg, South Carolina (1937–1948), where he also directed the New Spartanburg Festival, and at Syracuse University in New York (1948–1963). In addition, he won Pulitzer and Guggenheim Fellowships, concertized as a pianist, conducted, wrote criticism, articles, and books,[1] and composed an extraordinary output of music, much of it—like the wonderful *Ford's Theater*—based on American themes. Married four times, Bacon fathered six children. After his retirement from Syracuse, he returned to California and lived in the hills overlooking the San Francisco Bay area. Late in life he began to lose some vision, but assisted by his last wife (a young musician and teacher, whom he had married in 1972), he continued composing into his nineties.

THE SONGS

Angry chords or tender lyricism, rugged declamation or melting cantilena, dissonance or consonance, the voice of the people or the music of the spheres—all, embraced with equal naturalness, make up Bacon's unique expression. Though his earliest songs, settings to German poetry, lack distinction, they demonstrate the ingredients of the superlative song composer he would become.[2] But in the songs that began to appear in 1942 and continued over the next decade, culminating in 1952 with *Quiet Airs,* he found his highly individualistic voice. These are vintage Bacon. Later volumes *(Fifty Songs* and *Tributaries)* reveal yet further probing.

Bacon's selection of text is vast, but he is best known for his settings of American poets. His Emily Dickinson settings have perhaps brought him his greatest renown, and he may well be her best interpreter. Comfortable with the Amherst spinster's quirks and sensibilities, amazingly, his virile, forthright, expansive voice never overwhelms her delicate, cryptic, economic verse. What's more, these songs reveal him as a captivating melodist. Conversely, in his settings of Walt Whitman, Bacon perfectly matches the amplitude, mystery, vision, and challenging exuberance of the grand poet, who in his free-wheeling celebration of America, the common man, life, and the unknown, was surely Bacon's soul mate. Carl Sandburg was another favorite, and from Sandburg's use of the vernacular, it is only a small step to Bacon's gutsy folk realizations.

Limpid melody, steely declamation, whimsical melismas, and romantic outpouring are but some of the styles and timbres that make up Bacon's rich vocal palette. Clear, firm, flexible voices are generally best, but singers must also be masters of both poise and temperament; capable of imparting both power and tenderness. While he often writes in a straightforward, conventional manner, some songs, especially later ones, may have a harmonic vocabulary so densely dissonant that finding or holding pitch becomes difficult. Rhythms can also be knotty, refusing to settle into any single prescribed pattern, so that one has to stay alert to their constant fluctuations. In these songs, the piano rarely doubles the voice but often works contrapuntally or in cross meters to it. And, although the richly expressive, individualistic accompaniments may well be as intriguing as the voice, they can also be virtuosic and very intricate.

Only a few Bacon songs were published separately. Most appear in a confusing variety of collections, and many appear in more than one, occasionally with changes. Of these, especially recommended is *Quiet Airs* (Mercury Music c1952). The classic *Five Poems by Emily Dickinson* (G. Schirmer c1944) is now reprinted in *RAAS*. The other Dickinson settings appear in sundry collections. *Six Songs* and *Four Songs* (Music Press c1949) are settings of diverse poets. *Ernst Bacon: Fifty Songs,* attractively published in manuscript form by Dragon's Teeth Press c1974, duplicates some of the above but also offers new material. A similar volume, *Tributaries* (Musical Offering c1978) has even more revisions and new songs. Several of the publishers are no longer in existence, but authorized copies for many of these and other Bacon songs can now be obtained from Classical Vocal Reprints. Helen Boatwright has recorded 22 Dickinson settings with Bacon at the piano on Cambridge CRS (1707). Though long out of print, this is a classic, and well worth tracking down. In addition, Carolyn Heafner sings seven songs on CRI (SD 462), Eleanor Steber sings four on Desto (6411/6412), and John Hanks two on Duke, Vol. 1, (DWR 6417). Some recommendations from Bacon's prodigious catalogue follow.

The Banks of the Yellow Sea, Emily Dickinson;[3] incl. *Six Songs* and *Tributaries.*
   Pub. low and medium (low, b♭–d♭2, in *Six Songs,* and medium, c1–e♭2 in *Tributaries)* 2:00; With a slow and nostalgic swing; a mournful cantilena; melismatic passages; mysterious; recorded by Heafner.

Eden, Emily Dickinson; incl. *Quiet Airs* and *Fifty Songs.*[4]
   Rec. lyric high voices (b♯–g♯2 in *Quiet Airs,* and a half tone higher in *Fifty Songs);* 2:30; Languidly; an intensive, steady, seductive melodic line insinuates its way over eerie, rocking chords; requires great control; a song of haunting beauty; recorded by Boatwright and Heafner.

Eternity, Emily Dickinson; incl. *Fifty Songs* and *Tributaries.*
   Rec. robust higher voices (f1–a♭2); 1:00; Andante maestoso; the fervent, taut vocal line builds relentlessly over angry, surging chords; powerful, exciting, challenging; recorded by Boatwright.

Five Poems of Emily Dickinson, G. Schirmer c1944; also incl. *RAAS.*
   Rec. higher, lyric voices; issued as a group but often sung separately or mixed with other Dickinson settings.

It's all I have to bring,[5] (c1–f2); 1:00; Andante; a lovely, flowing, affecting melody; heartfelt and ingenuous; perhaps Bacon's best known song; recorded by Steber, Boatwright, and Hanks.

So bashful, (c#1–g2); 1:15; Allegretto grazioso; recorded by Steber and Boatwright.

Poor little heart, (c1–f2); 2:00; Rather slowly; spare, fragile; exquisite; recorded by Heafner.

To make a prairie, also incl. *Tributaries* under title *If Bees Are Few;* (d#1–g2[a2]); 0:45; Quasi allegretto; recorded by Steber and Boatwright.

And this of all my hopes, (e♭1–f2); 1:15; Rather slowly; lilting; recorded by Steber and Hanks.

Fond Affection, Anonymous; incl. *Quiet Airs.*
    Rec. medium and higher lyric voices (c#1–f2); 2:15; With quiet tenderness; folklike over a fluid accompaniment, later intensified by cross rhythms; a final vocalized refrain.

Gentle Greeting, Emily Brontë; incl. *Quiet Airs.*
    Rec. lyric voices (c#1–g2); 2:00; Larghetto; a quiet melody over pulsing eighths; develops some surprising dissonances; sad and touching.

The Grass, Emily Dickinson; Associated c1944.
    Spec. medium voices (c1–a2), rec. higher voices; 2:15; Allegretto moderato; the simple opening becomes increasingly involved; a warm central section; lyrical; contemplative; recorded by Boatwright.

The Heart, Emily Dickinson; incl. *Quiet Airs;* to Ethel Luening.[6]
    Rec. lyric voices (e♭1–e♭2); 1:30; Slowly; lyrical over widely spaced chords; fragile, serious, and sober; recorded by Heafner.

Is There Such a Thing as Day, Emily Dickinson; Associated c1944.
    Spec. medium voices (d#1–f#2); 1:00; Andantino; a lovely, parlando melody over flowing eighths; delicate and fresh; recorded by Boatwright.

The Lamb, William Blake; incl. *Quiet Airs;* to the memory of Janet Fairbank.
    Rec. medium and higher lyric voices (c#1–f#2); 2:30; Andante con moto; a fluid accompaniment carries the warm melody; grows in intensity and feeling; some rhythmic intricacies; affecting and strong.

O Friend, Emily Dickinson; Associated c1946.
   Spec. medium voice (c#1–g2), rec. higher voices; 1:45; Sustained and with fervor; expansive; intense; affecting; recorded by Boatwright.

The Red Rose, Robert Burns; Boosey and Hawkes c1949; also incl. *Tributaries* (rev.).
   Rec. medium and lower voices (a–f2, orig. version); 1:30; Andantino; simple melody; traditional; a lovely, gentle song.

Song of Snow-White Heads, Cho Wen-chün (tr. Arthur Waley); incl. *Quiet Airs;* to Henry and Sydney Cowell.
   Rec. medium lyric voices (c1–f2), best for women; 2:00; Quasi allegretto; low tessitura; intricate piano texture; difficult for both performers to bring out all the countering lines; a Chinese wife to her Lord on the break up of their marriage; unusual.

A Spider, Emily Dickinson; incl. *Fifty Songs.*
   Rec. high lyric voices (e1–ab2); 1:00; Un poco vivace; short sustained phrases over light, scurrying filigree figurations; recorded by Boatwright.

Stars, A. E. Housman; incl. *Quiet Airs* and *CAAS;* to John Edmunds.
   Rec. higher lyric voices (c1–f2); 2:00; Placido; long, sustained lines cushioned by a spare, gently undulating accompaniment; broad and mysterious.

A Threadless Way, Emily Dickinson; incl. *Fifty Songs*
   Rec. higher lyric voices (eb1–f2); 1:15; Andante; sustained over spare chords; fragile; poignant; recorded by Boatwright.

Twilight, Sara Teasdale; incl. *Quiet Airs;* to Douglas Moore.
   Rec. medium voices (c#1–e2); 1:00; Grave; sustained over slow chords; broad and solemn.

Velvet People, Emily Dickinson; Fischer c1948.
   Rec. medium and lower voices (c1–e2); Rather fast; a delightful accompaniment of quirky running figures; the voice, enjoying some quirky moments of its own, must cut through the confusion; tricky, but fun and different.

Also of interest:

Alabaster Wool, Dickinson, incl.*Tributaries,* Allegretto, recorded by Boatwright; *As Well as Jesus?* Dickinson, incl. *Fifty Songs,* Andante, recorded by Boatwright under the title *As I Love Thee; The Bat,* Dickinson, incl. *Fifty Songs* and *Tributaries,* Allegro; *The Imperial Heart,* Dickinson, incl. *Fifty Songs,* Andante, recorded by Boatwright; *In the Silent West,* Dickinson, incl. *Fifty Songs,* dramatic, recorded (with many changes) by Boatwright under the title *On This Wondrous Sea; Lingering Last Drops,* Whitman, incl. *Tributaries,* Becalmed; *The Little Stone,* Dickinson, incl. *Quiet Airs,* Allegretto; recorded by Heafner; *No Dew Upon the Grass,* Dickinson, incl. *Six Songs,* Grave; *Omaha,* Sandburg, incl. *Six Songs,* Moderato; *The Simple Days,* Dickinson, incl. *Tributaries,* Semplice, recorded by Boatwright and Heafner; *She Went,* Dickinson, incl. *Fifty Songs,* Un poco lento; recorded by Boatwright; *Summer's Lapse,* Dickinson, incl. *Fifty Songs* and *Tributaries,* Larghetto, recorded by Boatwright; *Sunset,* Dickinson, incl. *Fifty Songs* and *Tributaries,* Sostenuto, recorded by Boatwright under the title *A Nameless Bird; The Swamp,* Dickinson, incl. *Fifty Songs,* Allegretto, recorded by Boatwright under the title *The Snake; Weeping and Sighing,* Dickinson, incl. *Fifty Songs,* Animato, recorded by Boatwright; *World Take Good Notice,* Whitman, incl. *Six Songs* and *Tributaries,* Marziale.

BIBLIOGRAPHY

AmerGroves, Baker, Ewen, Friedberg (I), Greene, Thompson.
Bacon, Ernst. *Words on Music.* Syracuse University Press, 1960.
————. "On Words and Tones," preface to *Fifty Songs,* Dragon's Teeth Press, 1974.
Edmunds, John. "The Songs of Ernst Bacon," *Sewanee Review* (October 1941): 499–501.
Fleming, William. "Ernst Bacon," *Musical America,* April 15, 1949.
Horgan, Paul. "Ernst Bacon: A Contemporary Tribute," foreword to *Fifty Songs,* Dragon's Teeth Press, 1974.
Kerr, R. M. "Seeking the Native American Note Is Task of Composers," *Musical Courier,* April 1, 1951.

---

[1] These include *Words on Music* (1960) and *Notes on the Piano* (1961).
[2] Found in the collection *Ten Songs,* which is available from Classical Vocal Reprints.

[3] Because scholars later believed it to be Dickinson's preference, the last line is changed from "with fairy sails" in *Six Songs* to "like orioles" in *Tributaries*.
[4] Bacon made some changes to the ending, but the early version, as found in *Quiet Airs*, is preferred.
[5] Also found in *Tributaries*, a half tone higher, under the title *This and My Heart*.
[6] Ethel Luening, the first wife of composer Otto Luening, was a fine soprano.

ROBERT BAKSA
b. Feb. 7, 1938, New York, NY

As a "frustrated singer,"[1] who has done his share of singing in choruses, Robert Baksa admits to an undeniable affinity for singers, singing, and song. Two short operas *(Aria da Capo* and *Red Carnation)* and numerous choral works have been especially successful. His songs, though seldom heard, are tasteful, well made, and very appealing.

Of Hungarian descent, when Baksa was seven, the family moved from New York City to Tucson, Arizona. Having studied piano since the age of six, he began to compose in his teens. Baksa has a degree in composition from the University of Arizona and has studied at the Berkshire Music Center, but considers himself to be self-taught.[2] Since 1962 he has lived in New York City where, in addition to working as a music copyist, he has quietly amassed a catalogue of over 500 compositions. Though he has written in a great variety of idioms, since the early 1970s chamber music has been a major focus, and some of these works have been recorded.

THE SONGS
Most of his published songs were composed in the 1960s, but reveal little interest in any of the experimental trends of the era. Instead, Baksa has drawn his inspiration from the clarity and proportions of classicism and, with a rare gift for creating atmosphere with little ado, has composed unaffected songs that are models of restraint, moderation, and lightness of texture.

Tonally oriented, Baksa's linear, contrapuntal style is, nevertheless, seasoned with considerable chromaticism producing a certain amount of free-falling dissonance. At the severest of such times singers may find some difficulty with pitches. Otherwise, rhythms are conventional, tessitura moderate, ranges modest, phrases short, and vocal demands altogether minimal. His effective piano writing is, in fact, often more emphatic than that of the voice. Not designed to show off either voice, technique, or temperament, Baksa's songs are best served if allowed to speak for themselves. Composers Library Edition is the composer's own press. Though the songs were originally distributed by Alexander Broude, they were assigned to Theodore Presser in the early 1980s. A new volume of selected songs is in preparation. Otherwise, the following is a complete listing.

A Cynic's Cycle, Op. 41, (Four Songs to poetry from "The Devil's Dictionary"), Ambrose Bierce; Composers Library Editions c1978; comp. 1968; to John Stewart.

Rec. medium and high voices (c1–a2), two texts suggest men; 8:30; titles are: *Allah's good laws; To Men; The Graverobber; The Troutlet;* low-key humor and nuggets of wisdom from a mild cynic on a variety of subjects; an attractive, lightweight cycle.

Housman Songs, Composers Library Edition c1967/1981; comp. 1964; rev. 1978.

Spec. baritone (c1–f#2), but other voices, including women, could sing some of these songs; 10:00; though designated a cycle, smaller groupings could be made.
When I was one-and-twenty, (c1–c2); 2:15; Moderately; short lyrical phrases.
On your midnight pallet lying, (c1–f2); 2:30; Moderately slow; somber.
When the lad for longing sighs, (c#1–f#2); 1:15; Brightly, not too fast; crisp moving chords.
If it chance your eye offend you, (c1–eb2); 1:30; Moderate march; rhythmic; incisive; builds to a *ff*.
Oh, when I was in love with you, (c1–eb2); 1:15; Freely, not too slow; with the voice in 2/4 and the piano in 6/8, the play between the two ideas has effective and really lovely results.
Think no more, lad! (b–f2); 1:15; Fast; brisk repeated chords; ends *ff*.

More Songs to Emily Dickinson, Op. 40; Composers Library Editions c1978; comp. 1967; for Carolyn Reyer.[3]

Rec. medium lyric voices (bb–g2); a sequel to *Seven Songs of Emily Dickinson*; any groupings could be made from the two sets; good songs with nice variety of mood.
Two butterflies went out at noon, (f1–f2); 2:45; Lively; with changing tempos; waltz-like.

The morns are meeker than they were, (e1–a2); 1:45; Moderate; measures 23–28 should be twice as fast as notated; warm vocalism over gently flowing accompaniment; a good song.
There's a certain slant of light, (b♭–e♭2); 3:30; Slow; sustained; subdued.
Poor little Heart! (d1–g2); 2:00; Moderate; touching and tuneful.
No matter— now— Sweet, (d#1–f2); 1:15; Fast; curious setting; curious poem.
When night is almost done, (c1–f#2); 2:15; Tranquil; expansive; sustained.
Who robbed the woods, (f1–g2); 1:15; Quite fast; sustained over a scurrying accompaniment.

Seven Songs to Poems of Emily Dickinson, Op. 38; Composers Library Editions c1977; comp. 1963–1966.
    Rec. medium lyric voices (a#–g2); the first of two sets, from which any groupings could be made.
Much madness is divinest sense, (c#1–f#2); 1:00; Moderato; gentle.
What inn is this, (c#1–e2); 1:45; Agitated; dramatic and mysterious.
I took my power in my hand, (f1–f2); 2:00; Moderato; broad; dignified.
I died for beauty, (a#–f#2); 2:15; Moderately slow; subdued, atmospheric.
A shady friend for torrid days, (f#1–g2); 1:15; Bouncy; quite fast.
The soul selects his own society, (d1–g♭2); 3:00; Rubato; quite slow.
I'm nobody, (d1–f2); 2:30; Moderate; half note, not quarter note, equals 60.

BIBLIOGRAPHY
AmerGroves, Friedberg (III).
Roffman, Frederick S. and Scribner, Louise. Liner notes. *Robert Baksa: Octet for Woodwind Instruments: Nonet: Chamber Concerto No. 2,* Musical Heritage Society(MHS 512446X).

---

[1] Ruth C. Friedberg, *American Art Song and American Poetry: Vol. III,* p. 268.
[2] Ibid, 266.
[3] Both sets of Emily Dickinson songs were premiered by mezzo-soprano Carolyn Reyer as part of her New York recitals: Op. 38 in 1967, Op. 40 in 1968. The latter was commissioned by her.

SEYMOUR BARAB
b. Jan. 9, 1921, Chicago, IL

Barab is not well known, but his catalogue, primarily comprised of song and opera, is admired for its tasteful humor and unaffected charm.

Seymour Barab studied keyboard as a boy and was a professional church organist by the time he was 13. His career as a pianist, however, was abandoned when, in high school, he discovered the cello. He studied the instrument with important teachers (including Gregor Piatigorsky), played in major orchestras and chamber groups, and concertized as a recitalist. After he settled in New York, he helped found Pro Musica, with whom he played viola da gamba, and the Composer's Quartet. Unsuccessful efforts in interesting other composers to write for his instrument prompted Barab, in his early 30s, to compose himself. A recording of his early songs, *Child's Garden of Verses,* brought him recognition. Though self-taught as a composer, Barab has been a teacher of composition at the New England Conservatory, Black Mountain College, and Rutgers University.

THE SONGS
Although Barab is a performing string player, as a composer he prefers the immediacy of the voice to the abstraction of instruments. His hefty catalogue is primarily vocal, and includes 12 operas (ten of which are in one act) and approximately 200 songs, many of which have been published. Almost anyone with a little training can sing Barab's sensible, accessible songs and practically anyone will enjoy them. Most are tasteful, intelligent, and though they employ only the most elementary musical language, remarkably resourceful. Tuneful—though not memorably so—vocal lines are natural, gracious, and often in a relaxed conversational style. Piano parts are comprised of a nice variety of crisp, descriptive accompanimental figures. Singers may also want to consider several of Barab's works for voice with instruments, such as *Bits and Pieces, Airs and Fancies, Moments Macabres* (for which a piano score is available), and *Alice, A Cabaret* (spoken songs with cello). Russell Oberlin has recorded *A Child's Garden of Verses* in its orchestrated version on Counterpoint (CPT 539). The following is believed to be a complete listing of Barab's published songs for voice and piano.

A Child's Garden of Verses, Robert Louis Stevenson; Boosey c1985; available with orchestral accompaniment.

Spec. medium voices (c#1–f2); 30:00; in two volumes of 12 songs each; best with instruments; early sets on the fancies, pleasures, and concerns of a child's world; excellent variety, but too many at one time become tedious; small groupings are recommended; tuneful and fresh; recorded by Oberlin.

An Explanation, Walter Learned; Boosey c1964.
Spec. medium voices (d1–eb2), text suggests men; 1:00; Con moto; conversational; tuneful; charming; a nice encore.

Four Songs, various poets; Boosey c1955.
These four songs are so diverse and of such uneven quality, each must be considered on its own merits.
Go, Lovely Rose, Edmund Waller; rec. medium voices (d1–f#2); 1:30; Andante; a comely melody in a parlando style; a lovely song.
She's somewhere in the sunlight strong, Richard Le Gallienne; rec. higher lyric voices (e1–g2); 1:15; Allegretto; the 5/4 meter with off accents is a little treacherous; melismatic passages; requires flexibility; a questionable setting.
Minstrel's Song, Thomas Chatterton; rec. medium and higher voices (b1–g2), text suggests women; 3:00; Moderato; changing tessituras; a rocking motif throughout; cantabile; mournful.
I Can't Be Talkin' of Love, Esther Mathews; rec. medium voices (c#1–d#2); 1:15; Allegretto; folklike; a catchy, light song; could be an encore.

A Maid Me Loved, Patrick Hanney; Boosey c1964.
Spec. medium voices (c1–e2), man's text; 2:00; Allegro commodo; parlando with some ornamental turns and sustained tones; an attractive, interesting song.

Parodies (As some traditional jump-rope rhymes might have been set to music by the Masters); Boosey c1986.
Spec. high soprano (b–b2), several would be feasible for medium voices; 15:00; six spoofs on composers' styles, ranging from Handel to DeFalla; can be performed as a group or individually; expertly done and humorous.

The Rivals, James Stephens; Presser c1971.
Spec. high voice (d1–bb2); 5:45; lyrical songs of moderate difficulty; could be used individually; agreeable but routine.
The Daisies, (f1–g2); 1:30; Allegro moderato; light.

The Rose in the Wind, (d1–g2); 1:30; Slow; a lullaby and more; best of the set.

The Hawk, (e♭1–a♭2); 1:00; Allegretto; becomes progressively slower; light.

The Rivals, (e1–b♭2); 1:45; Allegro moderato; a sprightly vocal line with melismatic passages over a stacatto accompaniment.

Songs of Perfect Propriety, Dorothy Parker; Boosey c1959/1984; also available with instrumentation.

Spec. medium voices; 40:00; most texts suggest women; in two volumes of 12 songs each; smaller groupings should be made; some recommended titles are: *Social Note; A Very Short Song; Comment; Sympton Recital; Chant for Dark Hours;* uneven, but in the best, without sacrificing his innate charm, Barab has perfectly matched the dry, caustic humor of Parker's verse; accessible, sophisticated, clever, witty; good fun; warmly recommended.

BIBLIOGRAPHY
Nathan, Thompson.
Heglund, Gerald. "Barab Opera Wins Praise," *Music Journal* (May 1975).

SAMUEL BARBER
b. March 9, 1910, West Chester, PA; d. Jan. 23, 1981, New York, NY

Content to uphold the romantic label but ever true to his personal voice, Samuel Barber maintained a rare standard of excellence throughout his distinguished career. Though a singer himself, he left fewer than 40 published songs,[1] but every one in this magnificent body of work is noteworthy.

Barber's father was a physician. His mother came from a large musical family; one of her sisters, in fact, married composer Sidney Homer, and became world renowned as the contralto Louise Homer.[2] Exceptionally gifted, Barber was intent on becoming a musician and, as a boy, studied piano and attempted some composition. In 1926 he entered the newly opened Curtis Institute of Music as a triple major, studying voice with renowned baritone, Emilio de Gogorza, piano with Isabelle Vengerova, and composition with Rosario Scalero.

A steady stream of awards, grants, and commissions supported Barber throughout his life and financed many trips to Europe. On one of them, accompanied by his lifelong friend from Curtis days, Gian Carlo Menotti, he met Arturo Toscannini who, in 1938, programmed Barber's *Adagio for Strings* and *First Essay* with the newly formed NBC Symphony Orchestra. Though his compositions were already attracting attention, this tribute from the great maestro, known to eschew contemporary music, virtually hurtled the young composer to the forefront of American composition.

After serving in World War II, Barber returned to Capricorn, the rambling mansion outside Mt. Kisco, New York, which he and Menotti had purchased earlier.[3] In 1958 his first full opera *Vanessa,* to a libretto by Menotti, was premiered at the Metropolitan Opera and won the Pulitzer Prize. In 1962 his Piano Concerto earned him yet another Pulitzer. His next opera, *Antony and Cleopatra,* was commissioned for the 1966 opening of the new Metropolitan Opera House, but its production, a tasteless extravaganza, overwhelmed the music giving Barber his only significant failure. Withdrawing to the Italian Alps he lived in seclusion for several years. In 1974 he moved into a New York apartment where he lived alone, rarely composing. Ill with cancer, he was unable to attend the numerous 70th birthday celebrations in his honor.

THE SONGS

Though commonly categorized as a "neo-Romantic," Barber did not wear his heart on his sleeve. His is a guarded emotion, guided by inherent good taste and twentieth-century sensibility. His style develops in complexity over the years but never loses its innate lyricism, and late songs recapture much of the early simplicity. His cosmopolitan tastes are apparent from his choice of texts. British, Irish, and French poets, as well as translations of other foreign poets, far outnumber American settings.

A fine lyric-baritone himself, Barber was comfortable writing in a lyric, dramatic, or declamatory style. Several songs (premiered by first-rate artists such as Eleanor Steber and Leontyne Price) call for expansive, full-throated, even operatic vocalism. His piano writing is also anything but timid. Often highly contrapuntal, it can demand the technical facility of a virtuoso. Rhythms, with their irregular and constantly changing meters, especially in some of the faster moving songs, can be perilous. Melodies, despite an abundance of chromaticism and shifting harmonies, are inherently—though often ambiguously—tonal.

It is no trouble to obtain these songs. G. Schirmer, as sole publisher, has issued virtually everything Barber approved for publication both separately and in the album *Samuel Barber: Collected Songs.* As this volume was reprinted several times while Barber was still composing, earlier editions will not include later works. And, though available for low and high voice, not every song is published in two keys. Comprehensive recordings have been made by Glenda Maurice on Globe CD (GLO 5017) and Roberta Alexander on Etcetera CD (KTC 1055). Leontyne Price, with Barber at the piano, has recorded *Hermit Songs,* a reissue on Odyssey (32 16 0230); Eleanor Steber, *Hermit Songs* on Columbia (ML 5843); Dietrich Fischer-Dieskau, Opus 45 on Musical Heritage Society (MHS 824794K); Pierre Bernac, *Mélodies passagères* on New World (NW 229); Christopher Trakas, *Despite and Still* on Music Masters CD (MMD6 0170 M). Sharon Mabry, *Three Songs* on Owl CD (35); Dale Moore, eight songs on Cambridge (CRS 2715); Joan Patenaude, nine songs on Musical Heritage Society (MHS 3770), and John Hanks, four songs on Duke, Vol. 1 (DWR 6417). Happily, New World reissued what had been a collector's item—Barber's own singing of *Dover Beach* (NW 229). Other miscellaneous recordings are noted with their respective song entries.

A complete listing of Barber's published songs follows.[4] Designated cycles are kept intact, but all other songs are listed by the usual alphabetical procedure regardless of opus number. It should be kept in mind, however, that opus numbers can be a valuable tool in choosing the best groupings. (The tradition of whimsically juxtaposing Barber songs will probably continue; he seems to have given no indication that he disapproved the practice.) Unless otherwise noted, it can be assumed each song has been published in a high and low key. As all songs are available in *Collected Songs* published by Schirmer, there is no further mention of that essential album.

Bessie Bobtail, Op. 2, No. 3, James Stephens; G. Schirmer c1936; comp. 1934.

Pub. medium only (c1–f2), rec. dramatic voices; 3:15; Andante, un poco mosso; halting motifs evoke the homeless woman's unsteady walk; intensifies to a central *ff* largamente; a powerful and profoundly moving narrative; recorded by Alexander and Hanks.

The Daisies, Op. 2, No. 1,[5] James Stephens; G. Schirmer c1936; also incl. *NAAS;* comp. 1927; to Daisy.[6]

Pub. medium voices (d1–f2);[7] 1:00; Allegretto con grazia; flowing; lyrical; folklike simplicity; Barber's first song; recorded by Alexander and Moore.

Despite and Still, Op. 41, various poets; G. Schirmer c1969; comp. 1968; ded. to Leontyne Price.

Pub. high and medium keys (high, c1–b♭2[a2]); 10:30; though designated a cycle, these songs are occasionally used individually; only moderately difficult; an underlying theme of aloneness;[8] recorded by Alexander and Trakas.

A Last Song,[9] Robert Graves; (d1–g#2); 2:00; Moderato; lyrical over a pulsing accompaniment; melancholy.

My Lizard (Wish for a Young Love), Theodore Roethke; (d1–b♭2[g2]); 1:00; Fast and light; graceful and fluid over a scurrying accompaniment, builds to an impassioned climax, then trails off.

In the Wilderness, Robert Graves; (c1–g2); 3:00; Flowing; an affecting melody frames an intense, strange, central section.

Solitary Hotel, James Joyce: *Ulysses;* (c1–f2); 2:45; Like a rather fast tango in 2; a suspenseful little scena, narrated in parlando style over a nostalgic accompaniment; also recorded by Patenaude.

Despite and Still, Robert Graves; (e1–a2); 1:45; Fast and darkly impassioned; a heartrending song requiring grand, expansive phrasing.

A Green Lowland of Pianos, see *Three Songs,* Op. 45.

Hermit Songs, Op.29, Anonymous texts of Irish monks and scholars from the 8th to 13th centuries; various translations; G. Schirmer c1955; comp. 1952; comm. by the Elizabeth Sprague Coolidge Foundation; first perf. by Leontyne Price with the composer at the piano, Oct. 30, 1953 at the Library of Congress in Washington D.C.

Pub. high and low (high, c1–b♭2; low, g#–f#2); 17:00; though these songs are best kept intact, many, such as the captivating *Monk and his Cat* or the intensely moving *Crucifixion,* can be sung individually; on the general theme of seclusion; much is asked of the singer from simplest lyricism to impassioned outpourings; generally declamatory; no time signatures; steady eighths; from these small poems Barber has produced a big cycle of great variety and interest—one of his most acclaimed works; recorded by Alexander and Price.

At Saint Patrick's Purgatory; (high, c#1–f#2); 1:30; Allegretto, in steady rhythm.

Church Bell at Night; (high, d#1–c#2); 0:45; Molto adagio.

St. Ita's Vision; (high, c1–a♭2); 3:45; Recit., then Andante con moto.

The Heavenly Banquet; (high, d1–a♭2); 1:15; Lively, with good humor.

The Crucifixion; (d1–f2); 2:00; Moderato; also recorded by Nancy Tatum on London (OS 26053).

Sea-Snatch; (high, c1–b♭2); 0:30; Allegro con fuoco, surging.

Promiscuity; (high, g#1–c2); 0:45; Sostenuto, then Allegro moderato.

The Monk and His Cat; (high, d1–e2); 2:30; Moderato, flowing; also recorded by Nancy Tatum on London (OS 26053).

The Praises of God; (high, e1–g2); 1:00; Poco allegro.

The Desire for Hermitage; (high, e1–g2); 3:30; Calmo e sostenuto.

I Hear an Army, Op. 10, James Joyce, from *Three Poems from Chamber Music;* G. Schirmer c1939; comp. 1936.

Pub. high and low (high, d1–a♭2), rec. dramatic voices; 2:30; Allegro con fuoco; requires a solid middle and high voice; alternately lyrical and dramatic with an impassioned ending; difficult but stunning; recorded by Alexander, Fischer-Dieskau, Maurice, Hanks, Moore, Myron Myers on Musical Heritage (MHS 912016M), and Patenaude.

Mélodies passagères, Op. 27, Rainer Maria Rilke; G. Schirmer c1952; comp. 1950/51; ded. to Francis Poulenc and Pierre Bernac.[10]

Pub. high and low (high, d1–b♭2); 8:30; titles are: *Puisque tout passe; Un cygne; Tombeau dans un parc; Le clocher chante; Départ;* not as difficult vocally as much of Barber's work; generally subdued and lyrical; images of things passing, departing. Probably because of the French it is hard to recognize Barber in these songs, but Barber was fluent in French and living in France at the time of their composition;[11] they certainly have appeal and all the care, craft, and sensitivity of any Barber song. *Le clocher chante,* the only one that doesn't require sustained singing, is particularly interesting, and *Départ* is very moving; recorded by Bernac.

Monks and Raisins, Op. 18, no.2, José Garcia Villa; G. Schirmer c1944; comp. 1943.

Rec. medium voice, one key only (d1–f2); 1:15; Allegro; the fast moving parlando 7/8 is tricky, but this clever "exercise in counterpoint and rhythm"[12] is well worth some patience; humorous and fun; recorded by Alexander and Moore.

Nocturne, Op.13, No.4, Frederic Prokosch; G. Schirmer c1941; comp. 1940.

Pub. high and low, (high, d#1–a♭2); 3:45; Andante, un poco mosso; difficult; long, sustained phrases over sextuplets; an unusual and profound love song; recorded by Alexander, Maurice, Moore, Patenaude, Fischer-Dieskau, and Hanks.

Now Have I Eaten Up the Rose, see *Three Songs,* Op. 45

A Nun Takes the Veil (Heaven-Haven), Op.13, No. 1, Gerard Manley Hopkins; G. Schirmer c1941; comp. 1937.

Pub. high and low (high, g1–g2), title (more than text) suggests women; 1:45; Broad and sustained, in exact rhythm; lyrical declamation over rolled chords; the longing for peace as found in nature; eloquent and expressive; recorded by Alexander, Maurice, and Patenaude.

Nuvoletta, Op.25, James Joyce *(Finnegan's Wake);* G. Schirmer c1952; comp. 1947.

Rec. high sopranos, one key only (b#–b#2); 5:00; Allegretto; basically a rapid waltz but with a variety of rhythms, tempos, and other surprises (including a cadenza); a delightful showpiece of operatic proportions; very difficult; a crazy text but it is the spirit that counts; recorded by Alexander and, with great abandon, by Eleanor Steber on Desto (411/412).

O, Boundless, Boundless Evening, see *Three Songs,* Op. 45.

The Queen's Face on the Summery Coin, Op. 18, No. 1, Robert Horan;[13] G. Schirmer c1944; comp. 1942.

Rec. medium voice, one key only (c1–e2); 2:45; Andante con moto; lyrical; a somewhat dramatic central section; an enigmatic poem of shifting moods; recorded by Alexander.

Rain Has Fallen, Op. 10, James Joyce from *Three Songs from Chamber Music;* G. Schirmer c1939; comp. 1935.

Pub. high and low (high, f1–g2); 2:30; Moderato; over quiet sextuplets, the subdued, longing vocal line builds to an appassionato before tapering; difficult; recorded by Alexander, Moore, Myron Myers on Musical Heritage (MHS 912016M), and Patenaude.

The Secrets of the Old, Op. 13, No. 2, William Butler Yeats; G. Schirmer c1941; comp. 1938.

Pub. high and low (high, e♭1–g2), text suggests women; 1:15; Allegro giocoso; parlando over vamp-like accompaniment; tricky shifting meters; a gossipy, charming, touching song about three old women pleased with the secrets of their youths; recorded by Alexander, Maurice, and Patenaude.

Sleep Now, Op. 10, James Joyce from *Three Songs from Chamber Music;* comp. 1935.

Pub. high and low (high, e♭1–g2); 2:45; Andante tranquillo; the lyrical opening and closing frame an impassioned central section; difficult; recorded by Alexander, Maurice, Moore, Myron Myers on Musical Heritage (MHS 912016M), and Patenaude.

Sure on This Shining Night, Op. 13, No. 3, James Agee; G. Schirmer c1941; also incl. *S22A;* comp. 1938.

Pub. high and low (high, d1–g2); 2:30; Andante; a seamless, shimmering, yearning cantilena (in canon with the piano right hand) hovers over pulsing chords; an impassioned central climax; a beautiful song, probably Barber's most famous; recorded by Alexander, Lucine Amara on Cambridge (CRM 704), Elly Ameling on Phillips CD (422 333-2), Bethany Beardslee on New World (NW 243), Hanks, Maurice, Moore, and Patenaude.

Three Songs, Op. 45, translations of German and Polish writers; G. Schirmer c1974; comp. 1972; commissioned by the Chamber Music Society and premiered by Dietrich Fischer-Dieskau.

Pub. high and low (high, d1–g2); 8:45; These, Barber's last songs, are clearly intended to be sung as a group, but any one could stand on its own; more conservative than the songs of Barber's middle period; generally calm and lyrical; recorded by Maurice and Fischer-Dieskau.

Now Have I Fed and Eaten Up the Rose, James Joyce (trans. from the German of Gottfried Keller); (high, f#1–f#2); 2:15; Moderato; a prayer issued from the grave; delicate; subdued.

A Green Lowland of Pianos, Czeslaw Milosz (trans. from the Polish of Jerzy Harasymowicz); (high, [e♭1]d1–f#2); 2:30; Allegretto con grazia; some tricky rhythms; melodious and lilting; the nonsensical text is charmingly understated.

O Boundless, Boundless Evening, Christopher Middleton (trans. from the German of George Heym); (high, e1–g2); 4:00; Tranquillo, un poco mosso; a lovely, serene cantabile.

Three Songs to Poems from "Chamber Music" by James Joyce, Op. 10;
G. Schirmer c1939; see separate entries for *Rain Has Fallen, Sleep
Now,* and *I Hear an Army;* the connection to *Chamber Music* is all
that unites these songs and they are rarely performed as a group, but
they do shape well as one.

With Rue My Heart Is Laden, Op. 2, No. 2; A. E. Housman; G.
Schirmer c1936; comp. 1928.
    Pub. high and low (high, e1–f2); 1:15; Andante cantabile; a
melancholy cantabile over broken-chord patterns; shifting meters;
recorded by Alexander, Moore, and Patenaude.

BIBLIOGRAPHY

AmerGroves, Baker, Ewen, Friedberg (III), Greene, Hall, Ivey, Mellers
    (on *Hermit Songs*), Nathan, Thompson.
Ardoin, John. "Samuel Barber of Capricorn," *Musical America,* March,
    1960.
Broder, Nathan. *Samuel Barber.* New York: G. Schirmer, 1954.
Gruen, John. "And Where Has Samuel Barber been...?" *New York Times,*
    October 3, 1971, Sec. 2.
Heyman, Barbara B. *Samuel Barber: The Composer and His Music.*
    New York: Oxford University Press, 1992.
Horan, Robert. "American Composers, X1X: Samuel Barber." *Modern
    Music* 20 (March/April 1943): 161–69.
Ramey, Phillip. Liner notes, "A Talk with Samuel Barber." *The Songs
    of Samuel Barber and Ned Rorem,* New World Records (NW 229).
Salzman, Eric. "Samuel Barber." *Hi Fi/Stereo Review,* October, 1966.
Quillian, James W. "The Songs of Samuel Barber," *Repertoire* 1
    (October 1951): 17–22.

---

[1] According to Barbara Heyman *(Samuel Barber),* there are 68 unpublished
    songs; most are at the Library of Congress.
[2] Both the Homers were enormously influential in Barber's career. Sidney
    Homer, who Heyman considers to be "one of the heroes of his (Barber's)
    story," *(Samuel Barber,* 512) was his mentor and earliest supporter. Louise
    Homer performed several of her nephew's early songs.
[3] This was done with the financial help of Mary Curtis Bok (1876-1970), a
    philanthropist, the founder of Curtis Institute, and a loyal supporter of Barber.
[4] The beautiful *Dover Beach* (for medium voice) and *Knoxville: Summer of
    1915* (for soprano), scored for string quartet and orchestral accompaniment
    respectively, are beyond the scope of this book. Though there are piano

scores of each—and *Knoxville* is often performed in this manner—too much is lost in the piano reductions.

5 In a 1985 nationwide survey of 214 voice teachers conducted by the National Association of Teachers of Singing, this song was selected number one as an American art song suitable for beginning students. *Sure on This Shining Night* was the second choice.

6 Daisy was Barber's mother.

7 A low version can be found in the low edition of *NAAS*.

8 Heyman points out that these songs were written at a difficult period in Barber's life and there is much biographical significance in the bleak themes that are probed. *(Samuel Barber,* 465).

9 Barber has substituted the word "song" for Graves's original "poem."

10 Bernac and Poulenc also premiered the cycle at Town Hall in 1952, although Barber had performed three of the songs in Washington D.C. in 1950 with soprano Eileen Farrell.

11 The Ramey interview (NW 229) tells us that even Poulenc approved their prosody.

12 Dale Moore, liner notes *Favorite American Concert Songs by Samuel Barber and others* (CRS 2715).

13 This is the same Robert Horan who writes about Barber in *Modern Music* (see bibliography).

ALICE BARNETT
b. May 26, 1886, Lewistown, IL; d. Aug. 28, 1975, San Diego, CA

Alice Barnett was one of the most imaginative of the many women who, in the early 1900s, composed songs virtually to the exclusion of every other genre.[1]

After studying music with her father, a piano and organ teacher, Barnett went to Chicago to be raised by her maternal grandfather, a man of some means. Pretty and precocious, in 1905 she graduated with high honors from the Chicago Musical College, where her music teachers included Felix Borowski (composition) and Rudolf Ganz (piano). In 1909, chaperoned by an older singer, Barnett left to study in Berlin. Her composition teacher there, Hugo Kaun, considered her gifted and was distressed when she gave up her studies in order to marry a young vocal student. The newlyweds lived in San Diego, where Barnett continued to compose, but after four years and two children, the marriage failed. To earn a living Barnett taught high school music, but retired in 1926 to marry a prominent local physician. Turning their home into a popular center for musicians, she stopped composing around 1930, but remained active in the city's musical affairs for a long time after.

THE SONGS

Barnett's songs are colorful, original, vigorous, and tasteful; a few are exceptionally beautiful. Never sentimental, she was quite willing to take whatever risks were needed to express herself. Unexpected progressions and what were then considered to be ultra-modern harmonies are especially common.

If Barnett was not always knowledgeable in technical matters, her vocal writing nevertheless has intensity and melodic sweep—often with an easy interchange of cantabile and declamatory styles. The piano writing, equally vital, can be dense with black notes and unconventional figurations. Although her output is flawed and uneven, William Treat Upton astutely singled Barnett out for special praise.[2] Of her approximately 50 songs, a few representative and recommended works are listed.

In a Gondola, Robert Browning; G. Schirmer c1920; pub. separately.

Spec. high voice (d1–a♭2); rec. lyric or dramatic voices; 12:00; titles are: *Serenade; Boat-Song; The moth's kiss; What are we two?; He Muses—Drifting; Dip your arm o'er the boatside; Tomorrow, if a harp-string, say; It was ordained to be so, sweet.* Judith Elaine Carman suggests this cycle could be sung jointly by a soprano and a tenor since Browning indicates that certain of the verses are spoken by the man, others by the woman.[3] (Browning, in fact, does not give titles at all, only "He speaks" and "She speaks.") If this procedure were followed, the tenor would sing the majority of the songs (1, 2, 4, 5, and 8). While this is a possibility, it should not dissuade either a soprano or a tenor from singing the whole work. Though strongly cyclic both in narrative and music, Barnett indicates that groupings could be made. Browning's poetry is rather obscure, but Barnett has her own obscure language and is quite able to follow all the unexpected twists and turns of the highly charged story. Vigorous and imaginative, this is Barnett's most important work; recommended to all full-throated, adventurous singers in search of something romantic, dramatic, and out-of-the-ordinary.

Music, When Soft Voices Die, Percy Bysshe Shelley; G. Schirmer c1926.

Rec. medium voices (c1–e2); 1:45; Andante; opulent chords nurture the broad, mournful vocal line as it builds to a *ff* before the quiet close; a beautiful song.

Nightingale Lane, William Sharp;[4] G. Schirmer c1918.

Rec. higher, full voices (b#1–g#2); 0:45; Vivace; urgent, with sweep, spontaneity, and many notes for the pianist; written as a student in Berlin and retrieved from the wastebasket when her teacher threw it out; later, it so impressed Efrem Zimbalist that he showed it to Schirmer; her first published song; rather unusual.

Panels from a Chinese Screen, F. M;[5] Fischer c1924; pub. separately.

Rec. lyric medium voices (c1–f2); 5:15; could be used individually; a less adventurous set, but very attractive.

The Singing Girl of Shan, (c1–e2) 1:15; Allegretto con moto; some melismas; light and colorful.

On a Moonlit River, (c#1–e2); 2:30; Tranquillo; generally chordal with a warm, sustained melody.

In the Time of Saffron Moons, (c1–f2); 1:30; Andante grazioso; melodious and colorful.

BIBLIOGRAPHY
AmerGroves, Ammer, Baker, Howard (OAM), Upton.

Ridgely, Roberta. "Alice Price Stevenson: A Woman's Life and Music," *San Diego Magazine* (June 1978). An in-depth article with good photographs. The name given in the title would be that by which Barnett was known in community affairs. Price was her first husband's name; Stevenson was her second husband's name.

---

[1] Barnett also composed some violin pieces and a trio.

[2] William Treat Upton, *Art Song in America,* 214–22; repeated in "Some Recent Representative American Song-Composers," *Musical Quarterly* 2 (1925): 398–400.

[3] Judith Elaine Carman, "The Song Cycle in the United States: 1900–1970, Part 1," *NATS Bulletin* (October 1976), 23.

[4] William Sharp is the real name of Fiona MacLeod, the pen name by which he is best known.

[5] F. M. is Fritz Mertz.

HOMER BARTLETT
b. Dec. 28, 1845, Olive, NY; d. April 3, 1920, Hoboken, NJ

Homer Bartlett is best known for his sacred music, but his large catalogue of secular song, sophisticated for its time, helped move the genre out of the parlor and on to the concert stage. As a child Bartlett had such difficulty articulating words that he sang before he spoke. After learning the violin he went to New York City, where he studied music with O. F. Jacobson and Max Braun. At age 14, and for the next 31 years, he was organist at the Madison Avenue Baptist Church. With good reason William Treat Upton regretted Bartlett's tendency to the saccharine and the superfluous which gave rise to a very uneven output. However, songs such as the lovely, expansive *The Two Lovers,* and the comely, lyrical *Come to me, dearest* are fine examples of the period.

BIBLIOGRAPHY
AmerGroves, Baker, Howard (OAM), Hughes, Thompson, Upton.

LESLIE BASSETT
b. Jan. 22, 1923, Hanford, CA

Bassett's music is primarily instrumental, but some of his songs have found appeal with singers looking for vocal music in a modern idiom.

His father was a rancher, and when Bassett was seven, the family moved to Fresno, California. As a child he took piano lessons with his mother, but when he was 14, he became an enthusiastic trombone student. During high school he performed in and composed for various concert and band groups. After first serving in World War II and then graduating from Fresno State College, he studied with Ross Lee Finney at the University of Michigan. Other of his prestigious teachers include Arthur Honneger, Nadia Boulanger, Robert Gerhard, and for electronic music, Mario Davidovsky. In 1952 Bassett joined the faculty of the University of Michigan, and has been a professor there ever since. He has received numerous awards and grants, including the 1966 Pulitzer Prize for his *Variations for Orchestra.* In 1949 he married pianist Anita Denniston and they had three children.

THE SONGS
Bassett took a long time to find a convincing expression in his songs. The earliest set available, *Four Songs,* is in a spare, conventionally atonal idiom, badly handicapped by unidiomatic vocal writing. The next, *To*

Music, is often so overcomposed that the music virtually overwhelms the text. In later sets, however, Bassett seems to find his personal voice and shows a far better understanding of the idiom. All of Bassett's songs are atonal; rhythms can be complicated. Though not as difficult as many modern settings, secure, mature musicianship is essential. The following is believed to be a complete listing of his published songs.

Five Love Songs, various poets; Merion c1977.
    Spec. soprano (c#1–a2); 13:00; titles are: *Love, Like a Mountain Wind* (Anonymous, Greece); *The Tides of Love* (Walter Savage Landor); *To My Dear and Loving Husband* (Anne Bradstreet); *Teach Me Your Mood, O Patient Stars* (Ralph Waldo Emerson); *Madrigal* (Henry Harrington); though each is very different from the others, love is a unifying theme and these songs are clearly best kept as a set; performance directions given; many passages without bar lines; a given number of seconds indicate time lapse; the piano plays a major role, and abounds in special effects; vocal lines are relatively straightforward, mostly declamatory; a whisper and a whistle are the singer's only extra effects; evocative; effective.

The Jade Garden (Four Miniatures of Ancient Japanese and Chinese Poetry); Presser c1977.
    Spec. soprano (c#1–g#2); 9:00; titles are: *Maple Leaves; Pine Tree; Night; Nightingale;* performance directions are given; mostly without bar lines, time lapse is indicated by a given number of seconds; despite a certain sameness, these Haiku-like settings are atmospheric and inventive.

To Music, various poets; Galaxy c1966; pub. separately.
    Spec. high voice (b–a2); 10:00; though rightly considered a cycle, even with a recurring musical theme, any one of these songs could stand on its own; for the most part, however, they are overwritten.
    Slow, Slow Fresh Fount, Ben Jonson; (b–f#2); 3:45; Slow; somber; more contained and forthright than the other two.
    To Music, Robert Herrick; (f#1–f2); 2:45; Moderately slow; elaborate piano writing.
    Great Art Thou, William Billings; (c#1–a2); 3:30; Rather fast and with strong pulse; extravagant piano score; some florid singing; big ending.

Also of interest:
Four Songs, various poets, ACA, for high voices.

BIBLIOGRAPHY
AmerGroves, Baker, Ewen, Greene.
Scanlan, Roger. "Spotlight on Contemporary American Composers:
Leslie Bassett," *NATS Bulletin* 32 (December 1975).

MARION BAUER

b. Aug. 15, 1887, Walla Walla, WA; d. Aug. 9, 1955, South Hadley, MA

Though best remembered as a tireless promoter of American music, Marion Bauer was also a respected composer. She was born into a musical family of French origin. Her composition teachers included Henry Holden Huss in New York, Nadia Boulanger in Paris, and Paul Ertel in Berlin. A noted writer on music, Bauer was a correspondent for the Chicago magazine *Musical Leader* (a position she held till her death), a regular contributor to music journals, and an author (often in collaboration with Ethel Peyser) of several books, including the very successful *How Music Grew* and *Twentieth Century Music*. Bauer also lectured throughout the country, co-founded the American Music Guild, served on the board of the League of Composers, and taught at New York University and the Juilliard School. Her own compositions were mostly in smaller forms. Her impressionistic songs were admired by William Treat Upton, who compared her *Four Poems,* Op. 16, to the songs of her good friend Charles Griffes. Though not easy to find, a few, such as *The Harp, The Red Man's Requiem,* and a little gem, *Epitaph of a Butterfly,* warrant the search.

BIBLIOGRAPHY
AmerGroves, Ammer, Baker, Ewen, Goss, Howard, Thompson, Upton.

AMY (MRS. H. H. A.) BEACH[1]

b. Sept. 5, 1867, Henniker, NH; d. Dec. 27, 1944, New York, NY

Though Amy Beach was America's first important woman composer, following her death she fell into oblivion. In recent years, however, her music, including a large catalogue of songs, has enjoyed a positive reevaluation and a spate of new recordings and reprints.

Descended from New England colonists, she was born Amy Marcy Cheney, the only child of a paper manufacturer. In 1871 the family moved to Chelsea (now part of Boston), and soon the musically precocious Beach began piano lessons with her mother, an amateur pianist and singer. After further studies, Beach made her professional debut at the age of 16. But her concert career all but ended when, in 1885, she married Dr. Henry Harris Aubrey Beach, a prominent Boston physician and amateur musician. For the next 25 years, with her husband's encouragement, Mrs. H. H. A. Beach (as she properly called herself) fulfilled her musical calling through composition.

Though she was mostly self-taught in compositional technique, Beach's first work, the song *Ariette,* was published only a year after her marriage. Other small pieces followed until, in 1892, her Mass in E-flat was performed by the Handel and Haydn Society in Boston. The result of almost three years of work, it was probably the first composition in a large form to be written by a woman, and she soon followed up on its success with symphonies and concertos. After her husband died in 1910, Beach, who had hardly ever been away from Boston, spent four years in Europe. There she resumed her career as a concert pianist and also became the first American woman to earn international recognition as a composer. On her return, she settled in New York, but always spent the summer in New England, often at the MacDowell Colony. She remained active in music until her death.

THE SONGS

Amy Beach's singular position in the story of American music is best explained by her accomplishments in large forms—an area, at that time, considered to be both inappropriate for and beyond the capabilities of women. But her approximately 120 songs were also successful and, indisputably solid and masterful, even today have much that recommends them. Texts are drawn from many sources, both classical and contemporary, and include both her own and her husband's poems. Several songs, set in their original French or German, adroitly assume the stylistic characteristics of those two countries. Others—best exemplified by the Robert Burns settings—are straightfoward, simple, even folklike. But many, bursting with emotional fervor, are huge in dimension and require full-bodied voices to negotiate the expansive melodic lines that have been set over accompaniments teeming with elaborate figurations.

Originally all were published individually—some in one key, others in several—and a few were available with obbligato parts (usually violin). In 1985 Recital Publications Reprint Editions *(RPRE)* issued 28 songs in four volumes. In 1992 Da Capo Press issued *Amy Beach:*

Twenty-Three Songs (AB23S).[2] Many songs in the Da Capo volume duplicate those of Recital Publications, but are easier to read since, unlike the Recital Publications edition, they have not been reduced in size. Classical Vocal Reprints also includes many Beach titles in its catalogue. There is a fine recording devoted to Beach songs (with some violin pieces) by mezzo-soprano D'Anna Fortunato, who performs both soprano and mezzo settings with equal ease, on Northeastern CD (NR 9004). Three songs are recorded by Paul Sperry on Albany CD (TROY034-2), three by Yolanda Marcoulescou-Stern on Gasparo CD (GSCD-287), and Barbara Heafner sings the *Three Browning Songs* on CRI (SD 462). A few recommendations follow.

Ariette, Op. 1, No. 4, Percy Bysshe Shelley; Schmidt c1886; also incl. *RPRE* (Vol. 1) and *AB23S;* comp. 1886.
 Rec. lighter high voices (c#1–f#2); 2:00; Allegretto ma non troppo; a fetching tune over guitar-like strumming; recorded by Fortunato and Sperry.

Dark Is the Night, Op. 11, No. 1, William Ernest Henley; Schmidt c1889; also incl *RPRE* (Vol. 1); comp. 1890.
 Rec. big high voices (e1–b2); 1:30; Allegro con fuoco; a tumultuous setting, only briefly subdued; moody, exciting, dramatic; very effective; recorded by Fortunato.

Ecstasy, Op. 19, No. 2, Amy Beach; Schmidt c1892; also incl. *RPRE* (Vol. 2) and *AB23S;* comp. 1892.
 Pub. high and low (high, c1–g2); 2:00; Andantino con molto espressione; lyrical and—despite the title—restrained; sentimental, but once very popular; recorded (with violin obbligato) by Fortunato.

Empress of Night, Op. 2, No. 3, H.H.A.B.;[3] Schmidt c1891; also incl. *RPRE* (Vol. 1); comp. 1891.
 Rec. full medium-high voices (f#1–g2); 1:45; Allegretto ma non troppo; tender lyricism over delicate figurations; a lovely song, rarely heard; recorded by Marcoulescou-Stern.

The Lotus Isles, Op. 76, No. 2, Alfred Lord Tennyson; G. Schirmer c1914; also incl. *RAAS;* to Madame Elena Gerhardt.
 Rec. medium voices (d♭1–g♭2); 3:30; Lento, molto tranquillo; sustained over gently undulating eighths; a mesmerizing evocation of a pastoral scene.

Take, O Take Those Lips Away, Op. 37, No. 2, William Shakespeare; Schmidt c1897; also incl. *RPRE* (Vol. 4) and *SIA*.

Rec. high lyric voices (e1–a2); 1:45; Andantino con espressione; a mournful cantabile intensifies to a central climax; an exquisite melisma rounds out this touching song; recorded by Sperry.

Three Browning Poems, Op. 44; Schmidt c1900; also incl. *AB23S* and *AASTC*.

Often performed individually; romantic, operatic-scale songs that were immensely popular in their time; recorded by Heafner.

The Year's at the Spring, pub. med. and high (high, a♭1–a♭2); 1:00; Allegro di Molto; short melodic phrases build over pulsing chords; joyous; always popular; also recorded by Johanna Gadski on New World (NW 247), and Marcoulescou-Stern.

Ah, Love, But a Day, pub. low, medium, and high (high, e♭1–a2), 3:15; Lento con molto espressione; operatic; sustained; builds to a fervid climax; ends quietly; a bit inflated but still effective; also recorded by Fortunato.

I Send My Heart Up to Thee! pub. med. and high (high, d♭1[e♭1]–b♭2[a♭2]), *AB23S* offers this song in the medium key; 3:00; Andante con affetto; more subdued and lyrical; a central climax.

Also of interest:

Dearie, Burns, incl. *DC,* for low voices, Largo con molto espressione, Scottish dialect, recorded by Fortunato; *Fairy Lullaby,* Shakespeare, incl. *RPRE* (Vol.3), Allegro ma non troppo, light with florid passages; *Far Awa'!* Burns, incl. *RPRE* (Vol. 3) and *DC,* Andantino, Scottish dialect; *Just for This!* Fabbri, incl. *RPRE* (Vol. 2), Allegretto a capriccio, recorded by Fortunato; *O Mistress Mine,* Shakespeare, incl. *RPRE* (Vol. 4), *DC,* and *SIA,* recorded by Fortunato and Sperry; *Oh were my love yon lilac fair,* Burns, incl. *RPRE* (Vol. 3), Allegretto semplice, Scottish dialect; *Springtime,* Heywood, incl. *RAAS,* Limpido; *The Thrush,* Sill, incl. *RPRE* (Vol. 1); *Ye Banks and Braes of Bonnie Doon,* Burns, also incl. *RPRE* (Vol. 2), recorded by Fortunato; *The Western Wind,* Henley, incl. *RPRE* (Vol. 1); *Wind o' the Westland,* Burnet, Andantino espressivo, incl. *RAAS*.

BIBLIOGRAPHY

AmerGroves, Ammer, Baker, Ewen, Greene, Hall, Howard (OAM, OCC), Hughes, Tawa, Thompson, Upton.

Kinscella, Hazel Gertrude. "Play No Piece in Public When First Learned, Says Mrs. Beach," *Musical America,* Sept. 7, 1918. This article gives considerable insight into Beach's beliefs and methods.

Ledbetter, Steven. Liner notes, *Amy Beach: Songs and Violin Pieces.* Northeastern Records (NR 202).

Tuthill, Burnet C. "Mrs. H.H.A. Beach," *Musical Quarterly* 26 (July 1940): 297–310.

---

[1] In keeping with modern practice, she is now referred to as Amy Beach. During her lifetime, however, Beach was known as Mrs. H. H. A. Beach, which is how she signed her compositions.

[2] Neither of these editions specifies a particular voice. Though higher voices are favored, especially in the Recital Publications Reprint Editions, there is a variety of range in both editions.

[3] H.H.A.B. is Amy Beach's husband, Henry Harris Aubrey Beach.

JACK BEESON
b. July 15, 1921, Muncie, IN

Jack Beeson, nurturing his lifelong passion for vocal music, is best known for a handful of operas. His songs, however, have theatrical qualities of their own, and are too rarely heard.

Born partially paralyzed, with a broken left arm and a metabolic disorder, Beeson defied all predictions of an early demise. Growing up in the Midwest, he was inspired by the live Saturday afternoon broadcasts from the Metropolitan Opera, and he saved his money to buy piano scores so that he could accompany the operas. In high school he studied music and attempted his own opera composition. On an honorary fellowship to the Eastman School of Music, he studied composition with Bernard Rogers, Burrill Phillips, and Howard Hanson; then worked for one year with Bela Bartok in New York City. A recipient of the Prix de Rome and a Fulbright Fellowship, Beeson lived from 1948 to 1950 in Rome, where he composed his first opera. Though it won an honorable mention in a La Scala competition, it was never produced. But subsequent operas—some resembling musical theater—have fared much better. *Hello Out There, Lizzie Borden, My Heart's in the Highlands* (written for television), and *Captain Jinks of the Horse Marines,* are a few that are performed (especially on college campuses) and recorded.

After advanced study and a teaching fellowship at Columbia University, in 1945 Beeson joined its faculty. He has since held a long series of positions at the University and been fully involved in its highly regarded opera program. In 1967 he was selected as the MacDowell Professor of Music and, two years later, received the Columbia Great Teacher's Award. Beeson married Nora Sigerist in 1947. The couple had a son, who died in an automobile accident, and a daughter.

THE SONGS

Beeson's strong, energetic songs are striking for their off-beat texts; probably no other composer's catalogue lists such a curious array of titles. Potent interpretations of untraditional themes, which range from the obscure to the mundane; if the performer is not attracted to the poem, there is little sense proceeding. However, if not put off by the unorthodox subject matter, there are real rewards for those with a theatrical flair. Vocal writing is generally declamatory and angular, and several, virile in both subject matter and style, specify the baritone voice. Though there are no key signatures, there is usually a central note and a feeling that tonality is not too far distant. Harmonies are dense; dissonances can be biting. With a few notable exceptions, the vigorous rhythms are straightforward. In the hands of a solid musician who can deliver the texts with imagination and incisive enunciation, these songs can provide an effective change of pace on recital programs.

Though Beeson's songs are generally published individually, many are also available in two albums: *Nine Songs and Arias for Soprano (NSAS)* and *Nine Songs and Arias for Baritone (NSAB)*, both published by Boosey and Hawkes c1991. Singers interested in chamber music will want to consider two works for voice and string quartet—*A Creole Mystery* and *The Day's No Rounder Than Its Angels Are,* both of which are available in piano reduction. Three songs are recorded by Carolyn Heafner on CRI (SD 462). A virtually complete listing of Beeson's published songs follows.[1]

Against Idleness and Mischief and in Praise of Labor (A practice session for voice and piano), Issak Watts; Boosey c1973; also incl. *NSAS;* to Madeleine Marshall.[2]

   Spec. high voice (d1–c3), rec. lyric coloratura; 2:45; Purposefully and strictly in time; bright, energetic, occasionally florid, singing; a big, busy piano part, replete with arpeggios, scales, and other practice figures; a little crazy and great fun.

Big Crash Out West, Peter Viereck; Mills c1963; Galaxy c1989; also incl. *NSAB;* comp. 1951.

Spec. baritone, in bass clef (c#–e1); 2:00; Vigorously; robust declamation and sizable chords evoke the vast western landscape, where speed is "the bridge for spanning loneliness" and the auto crash is inevitable; a final quiet reflection.

Calvinistic Evening, John Betjeman; Boosey c1962; also incl. *NSAB;* comp. 1952.

Spec. baritone (or bass-baritone), in bass clef (c–f1); 3:00; Heavily; declamatory over chords, which bring out the melody of psalm 50; the pessimism and repression of the Calvinistic doctrine is drawn with cynicism and some quiet drama; recorded by Donald Gramm (Desto 411/412).

Cat, John Keats; incl. *NSAS;* comp. 1979.

Spec. sopranos (or mezzos) (b–g2); 3:00; Stealthily; very slow; declamation over rapid, intricate piano figurations; rhythmically very complex, especially in ensemble; an affectionate ode to an old alley cat, but of questionable effectiveness.

Cowboy Song, Charles Causley; Galaxy c1989; also incl. *NSAB;* comp. 1979.

Spec. baritone, in bass clef (B–f1); 4:00; Rolling along; while the piano depicts the cowboy swagger, the voice describes, in flowing melody, the pros and cons of a cowboy's life; a quiet, cryptic ending.

Death by Owl-Eyes, Richard Hughes; Boosey c1973; also incl. *NSAS.*

Rec. high voices (d1–g2); 2:30; Straightforwardly; after the simple, consonant opening we are hurtled into the contemporary musical idiom; generally declamatory with a long trill; active piano; abstract and different; recorded by Heafner.

Eldorado, Edgar Allen Poe; Galaxy c1982; also incl. *AASA;* comp. 1951; rev. 1967/77.

Rec. high, somewhat dramatic voices (c#1–a2); 1:15; Swinging; fast with a meno mosso central section; shifting meters and cross rhythms; this narrative of the knight who becomes old in his search for Eldorado's gold builds to a climactic end; recorded by Heafner.

Fire, Fire Quench Desire, George Peele; incl. *NSAS;* comp. 1959.

Spec. soprano (or mezzo) (b–ab2); 2:30; Lentissimo; rhythmically complex; difficult to sustain the slow tempo; vivid declamation and spare piano figures portray the images of burning in this sensuous poem from David and Bethsabe.

Five Songs, Francis Quarles; Peer c1954.

Rec. medium or high lyric voices (c1–a♭2); 8:00; titles are: *On a Spiritual Fever; A Good Night; On the World; Epigram; On Death;* should be kept as a set; rhythms and ensemble very difficult; serious, philosophical songs on man's spiritual state; alternately lyrical and declamatory, ending in a subdued reflection.

Indiana Homecoming, adapted from Abraham Lincoln;[3] Boosey c1973; also incl. *NSAB.*

Spec. baritone, in bass clef (B–e1); 2:00; Slowly; quiet; warm, lyrical declamation; a sympathetic, effective evocation of childhood.

Senex, John Betjeman; Boosey c1979; also incl. *NSAB.*

Spec. baritone, in bass clef (c–f♭1); 2:15; Quick and repressed; syllabic, tuneful declamation over chords; incisive rhythms, pungent dissonances and caustic words from a man battling lust with humor and bitterness.

To a Sinister Potato, Peter Viereck; Boosey c1973; also incl. *NSAB.*

Spec. baritone, in bass clef (B-f1); 3:30; Purposefully; disjunct declamation over a colorful piano score; requires perfect diction and a straight face; a somber but humorous ode to the neglected potato.

The You Should Have Done It Blues, Peter Viereck; Boosey c1973; also incl. *NSAS.*

Rec. medium and high voices (b–g2), text suggests women; 2:30; Slow and bluesy; musing, then agitated; ends nostalgically; the monologue of a rejected lover; effective as a character song; recorded by Heafner.

BIBLIOGRAPHY
AmerGroves, Baker, Ewen, Friedberg (III), Greene, Thompson.
Eaton, Quintance. "Beeson on Camera," *Opera News,* March 21, 1970.

---

[1] Theresa Treadway has recorded a Beeson cycle, *From a Watchtower,* on Orion (ORS 84467). As the recording jacket acknowledges Boosey and Hawkes, the author checked with the publishers, but they show no record of these songs.

[2] Madeleine Marshall, well known for her teaching of English diction and her book *The Singer's Manual of English Diction,* is a natural choice for this dedication. The extra note provided for the "t" (page 4) is surely for her benefit.

[3] According to Friedberg, this is adapted from a poem Lincoln included in a letter, dated April 18, 1846, to his step-brother John D. Johnston. In 1816 the

Lincoln family moved from Kentucky to Indiana, where Lincoln's mother died two years later. In 1844, while practicing law in Illinois, he made the visit to Indiana which inspired the poem.

JEAN BERGER
b. Sept. 27, 1909, Hamm, Germany

Jean Berger, the son of Orthodox Jews, was born in Germany but grew up in the Alsace Lorraine. He studied music at the universities of Heidelberg and Vienna, and composition with Louis Aubert in Paris. In 1935 Berger became a French citizen but, with the outbreak of World War II, left for Rio de Janeiro, where he taught at the Conservatorio Brasileiro de Musica and coached for the opera company. In 1941 he went to the United States, becoming an American citizen in 1943. He spent his first years in New York, where he was an arranger for CBS and NBC and a vocal coach. Since then he has taught at Middlebury College, the University of Illinois at Urbana, and the University of Colorado.

THE SONGS
Better known for his choral music, Berger's numerous songs are uneven and somewhat pedestrian. An extremely eclectic composer, he is successful in evoking ethnic color and facile at adapting himself to any style the text suggests. Given his international background, it is not surprising that, in addition to settings in English (especially early English), he often uses texts in foreign languages (French, Portugese, Spanish, Italian, and German). At their worst, Berger's songs are contrived, awkward, and repetitive. At their best, they are colorful and singable. Despite some rhythmic intricacies, technical and musical difficulties in these very tonal songs are minimal. Probably for that reason they are best known in teaching circles. Many sets and cycles are available, primarily from John Sheppard Music Press. Some preferences follow.

Four Songs, Langston Hughes; Broude Bros. c1951.
　　Rec. medium voices (b–f2); 6:45; titles are: *In Time of Silver Rain; Heart; Carolina Cabin; Lonely People;* tuneful vocal writing over simple, mostly chordal accompaniments; no difficulties whatsoever; a very attractive, rather melancholic, folklike set.

Of Love, various 16th- and 17th-century poets; Sheppard c1970.
　　Spec. high voice (c#1–bb2), texts suggest men; 8:30; titles are: *He or she that hopes to gain* (Anonymous); *Fair Julia* (Philipott); *A lit-*

tle ground well tilled (Anonymous); *When I admire the rose* (Thomas Lodge); *My love in her attire* (Anonymous); a cycle with good variety and a nice early English flavor; *When I admire the rose* is a lovely, straightforward cantabile; the other songs have more of the quirky rhythmic effects that are typical of Berger; generally lively, with nice feeling.

Three Songs, James Thomson; Sheppard c1985.

Spec. medium high voice (b♭–g2); 5:30; titles are: *Gifts; The Vine; Song;* though repetitive, these songs have lilt and personality, especially the last two; nice set for students.

Also of interest:

Five Shelley Poems, for low voices, the last is lively and humorous; ***Quatre Chants D'Amour,*** early French poems, colorful.

BIBLIOGRAPHY
AmerGroves, Baker, Greene.

WILLIAM BERGSMA
b. April 1, 1921, Oakland, CA

William Bergsma's prolific catalogue includes two operas and several major choral works. Though his songs are few in number, they abound in personality and lyricism.

His mother, a former opera singer, gave Bergsma his first piano lessons. When he was six, the family moved south to Redwood City, where he grew up and learned to play the violin. During high school he both composed for and conducted the school orchestra. After studying at Stanford University, he entered the Eastman School of Music as a composition student of Howard Hanson and Bernard Rogers. Graduating with a master's degree, Bergsma taught for a year at Drake University in Des Moines. Then, from 1946 to 1963, he was a teacher and administrator at the Juilliard School, leaving to become director of the School of Music at the University of Washington in Seattle. He married Nancy Nickerson in 1946, and they had two children.

THE SONGS
With scrupulous attention to text and detail, and an abundant supply of melodic, rhythmic, and harmonic invention, Bergsma has given us a handful of songs that are expressive, individualistic, and distinguished.

Relatively early works, they operate within a tonal, conventional framework and are essentially lyrical. Musically and interpretatively, however, they are difficult. Other than *Cantilena from "In Space"* (a long excerpt from a large multimedia work in a piano reduction), it is believed all published songs are listed.

Bethsabe Bathing, George Peele; Galaxy c1962; comp. 1961.

Spec. mezzo-soprano (b–f2); 3:00; somewhat dramatic declamation over secco rhythmic figures; some vocalization on "ah"; piano harmonics; a spare, yet sensuous, setting concerning the beauteous Bethsabe (better known as Bathsheba, the forbidden love of biblical David); unusual; strong.

Lullee, Lullay, Janet Lewis; Fischer c1950; incl. *CSE.*

Pub. high and low (high, e1–g2); 2:45; Andante; warm, lyrical, flowing; medieval in character; recorded by Eleanor Steber on Desto (D 411/412).

Six Songs, E. E. Cummings; Fischer c1947.

Rec. high, but not too light, voices (d#1–bb2); 12:30; though any one of these stunning settings can stand on its own, they are especially effective as a group if the singer can handle the various vocal timbres.

When God lets my body be; (e1–a2); 2:15; ringing, dramatic declamation; interior lyric sections.

Doll's boy's asleep; (e1–bb2); 2:00; a quasi lullaby to a curious poem; a central high melismatic passage.

Hist whist; (d#1–f2); 1:30; a brilliant, magical scherzo; tricky rhythms; fun vocal effects.

Thy fingers make early flowers of all things; (e1–a2); 2:45; linear, contrapuntal; lyrical and fragile.

It may not always be so; (e1–g#2); 4:00; slow; long, sustained phrases; a big, somewhat dramatic, love song.

Jimmie's got a goil; (g1–a2); 1:00; Presto; lively, earthy; in dialect; syncopated; tricky; fun.

BIBLIOGRAPHY

AmerGroves, Baker, Ewen, Goss, Greene.
Skulsky, Abraham. "The Music of William Bergsma," *Juilliard Review* 3 (Spring 1956): 12–20.

LEONARD BERNSTEIN

b. Aug. 25, 1918, Lawrence, MA; d. Oct. 14, 1990, New York, NY

In a corpus which embraced everything from symphony to Broadway musical, Leonard Bernstein—composer, conductor, pianist, teacher, author, quintessential music-maker—left only a small place for the art song.

The eldest of three children of Jewish Russian immigrants, as a child Bernstein revealed dazzling musical gifts. After attending the prestigious Boston Latin School, he entered Harvard University, where his principal teachers were composers Edward Burlingame Hill and Walter Piston. Graduating with honors in 1939, he then studied piano, conducting, and composition at the Curtis Institute. Summers were spent as a conducting protégé of Serge Koussevitsky at Tanglewood's Berkshire Music Center. In 1943 Bernstein made history when, substituting on short notice for an ailing Bruno Walter, he conducted the New York Philharmonic. In the whirlwind career that followed, he lavished his multifarious talents and passionate personality upon the world. Despite a controversial private life, he was married to an aspiring actress from Chile,[1] with whom he had three children. Only days after retiring from conducting he died from a heart attack in his Manhattan apartment.

THE SONGS

In an honest response to his times Bernstein convincingly straddled the fence between classical and popular music. For the purposes of this book, however, songs that are expressly theatrical or popular are excluded. Most of those that remain are in a fun-loving vein and can only tenuously be called classical. Some, unfortunately, border on cute, others on sentimentality—problems that are exacerbated when Bernstein wrote his own texts.[2] Otherwise, Bernstein's infectious songs are so skillfully crafted, rhythmically inventive, and melodically pleasing that they would be a lively addition to any recital.

Since Jennie Tourel was the original recipient of many Bernstein songs, one would expect them to have been written in lower keys. Instead, the tessitura tends to be high and, unless Tourel transposed them down (which is unlikely), they are testament to the great mezzo's upper range. Singers will need flexibility and quick, crisp enunciation to get around a great deal of fast-moving patter. And, though on the surface these songs are not musically difficult, the tiniest deviation from or laziness towards the exacting rhythms can—in an instant—kill the tension and, ultimately, the sparkle. Singers might also want to consider *So Pretty* (a cross-over song, first performed by Barbra Streisand), *Arias and Barcarolles* (for two singers and piano four hands), and vocal solos in piano reduction from his theater and orchestral works. Roberta Alexander has recorded virtually all the art songs on Etcetera CD (1037). All have been published individually and most are included in *Leonard Bernstein: An Album of Songs (LBAS)*, Amberson c1974. The following is believed to be a complete listing of Bernstein's published art songs.

Afterthought, Leonard Bernstein; G. Schirmer c1945; comp. 1945.[3]

   Rec. medium and high voices (a-g#2); Lento; plaintive; sustained; worth finding.

I Hate Music,[4] A Cycle of Five Kid Songs, Leonard Bernstein; Witmark c1943; for Edys.[5]

   Spec. soprano (c1–a2); 6:30; titles are: *My mother says that babies come in bottles; Jupiter has seven moons; I hate music!* (often extrapolated as an encore); *A big Indian and a little Indian; I just found out today;*[6] the childlike character of the texts suggests that lighter, lyric voices are best, but Bernstein gives directions that "coyness is to be assiduously avoided"; witty and clever; light relief on a program (Jane Manning finds them appropriate for a party as well); some rhythms (especially changing meters) and large intervals are treacherous; recorded by Alexander.

La Bonne Cuisine (Four Recipes), from "La Bonne Cuisine Française" by Émile Dumont, English version by Bernstein; G. Schirmer c1949; also incl. *LBAS;* for Jennie Tourel.

   Rec. flexible voices with a good top (b–b2), only the first song calls for many high notes; 4:15; titles are: *Plum Pudding;*[7] *Queues de Boeuf* (Ox-tails); *Tavouk Gueunksis; Civet à Toute Vitesse* (Rabbit at top speed); considerably more sophisticated than *I Hate Music;* musically tricky; some passages in a high tessitura; ends low; gossamer lightness, lyric fullness, articulation, flexibility, wit, theatricality, and personality, are all required to bring off this delightful, funny set of French recipes from a Victorian cookbook; recorded, first in French and then in English, by Alexander.

Silhouette (Galilee), Leonard Bernstein; G. Schirmer c1951; also incl. *LBAS* and *S22A;* for Jennie Tourel on her birthday in Israel.

   Rec. medium or high voices (b♭–g#2); 2:00; Allegretto, molto ritmico; light staccato effect; strophic, with refrains comprised of melismas and Arabic vocalisms; the last stanza drops radically from the otherwise high tessitura; a pretty song; recorded by Alexander.

Two Love Songs, Rainer Maria Rilke, trans. Jesse Lemont; G. Schirmer c1960; also incl. *LBAS* and *CAS28;* comp. 1949; for Jennie.[8]

   Rec. medium or high lyric voices (c1–g2); 3:30; set to the English translation of these two moving poems; sustained, cantabile; the most serious of Bernstein's art songs; recorded by Alexander.

Extinguish My Eyes, (c1–g2); 1:30; Fast; translucent and flowing; ends with humming.

When My Soul Touches Yours, (c1–gb2); 2:00; Moderately slow and sustained; declamation and heavy chords give way to lyricism.

BIBLIOGRAPHY

AmerGroves, Baker, CBY (1944, 1960), Ewen, Goss, Greene, Manning (on *I Hate Music*), Thompson.

Peyser, Joan. *Bernstein: A Biography.* New York: William Morrow, 1987. Though the fullest biography currently available, it does not include a discography, bibliography, or catalogue of his works.

---

[1] The beautiful Felicia Montealegre Bernstein died from cancer in 1978.

[2] Bernstein was fortunate that most of his songs made their entrance into the world in the tasteful, artistic hands of his close friend, the great mezzo Jennie Tourel.

[3] Though well reviewed when mezzo Nell Tangman gave the first performance of this song as part of her New York recital on October 24, 1949, according to *AmerGroves* it was withdrawn in 1948.

[4] This little cycle was first introduced by Jennie Tourel as encores in a Lennox, Massachusetts recital. With Bernstein accompanying, it was first heard in New York as part of her debut recital on November 13, 1943, the night before his historic conducting performance as substitute for Bruno Walter.

[5] Edys Merrill was a young woman who shared an apartment with Bernstein when he first came to New York. She described working all day in a war factory and going crazy at night with the constant music in the apartment. "I would walk around the apartment with my hands over my ears screaming, 'I hate music—la de da de da,' and Bernstein wrote a cycle of songs based on what I screamed and dedicated it to me." (Peyser, 77, 78)

[6] As Bernstein does not provide titles for these songs, first lines are provided in their place.

[7] *Plum Pudding* is also incl. *S22A* in a lower key.

[8] Presumably this is Jennie Tourel and not Bernstein's mother who was also a Jennie.

GORDON BINKERD
b. May 22, 1916, Lynch, NE

Gordon Binkerd is probably best known for his symphonies and choral works, but he has also produced an impressive catalogue of unusual and compelling songs.

Though he was born in Nebraska, Binkerd's family moved around, eventually settling in Gregory, South Dakota.[1] Binkerd entered South Dakota Wesleyan as a piano major, but his studies there with Russell Danburg and Gail Kubik inspired him to try a career in composition. After graduation, he taught in Kansas and Indiana. Then, in 1940, he went to the Eastman School of Music, where he studied with Bernard Rogers, and graduated with a master's degree. In 1942 he married Patricia Walker and, that same year, enlisted in the Navy. After service in the Pacific, he earned a doctoral degree in musicology at Harvard University (1952), where he also studied composition with Irving Fine and Walter Piston. In 1949 Binkerd joined the faculty of the University of Illinois at Urbana and began to compose on a regular basis. Retiring in 1971 to devote himself to composing, he lives with his wife on a farm outside Urbana.

THE SONGS
Binkerd has written an uncommonly personal and poetic body of song, which for its scope, candor, and boldness, is also decidedly American. Why, then, do do these potent and important songs "lie asleep in the warehouse?"[2] Probably because Binkerd, by his own admission, has never pressed singers to take them up, while those who do often find them to be formidably difficult and unusually long. Moreover, with his Midwestern residency placing him outside the musical mainstream, Binkerd is easily overlooked.

There is a marked difference between Binkerd's early and late songs and, despite the lyricism that seems intrinsic to his style, singers may find themselves drawn more to one period than the other. Once described as coming from the "radical center,"[3] Binkerd's early musical vocabulary can be extremely complex. Though tonal centers are usually apparent, he freely employs twelve-tone elements. The simply stated ideas which so often open his songs (a characteristic common to both periods), in the earlier songs assume complex, ranging, and dissonant contrapuntal textures, over which elaborate vocal lines are contoured. Listener and performer may feel they have embarked on an exciting but uncertain voyage of uncharted waters. Without sacrificing any of his individual voice, however, since the 1970s Binkerd has gradually softened and simplified his language. Recent songs are tonal, even to the point of using key signatures. Vocal lines, though just as vivid and fresh, are more grounded and melodic; accompaniments more supportive.

As a young man, Binkerd did some singing himself and even studied voice for a year, but it is his lifelong love of poetry that provided much of the impetus behind his vocal writing. A discerning poetic sensibility and a willingness to set some unconventional texts are certainly factors in his success with the idiom. A consummate craftsman, whether writing declamation or cantilena, he is assured in his handling of the voice. Even his most disjunct vocal lines flow. With a few notable exceptions, however, these songs (early or late) are only for mature singers. Wide range, control, support, and exceptional stamina are required for what can be unusually broad and extensive vocal writing. In fact, several songs are on an operatic scale and could stand alone—aria-like—on a program.[4] Binkerd is himself a pianist and, as with his writing for the voice, he expresses himself on the instrument with a similar grandeur of design. Expansive and technically demanding, accompaniments, with their evocative sonorities and many solo passages, are often so interesting they might stand on their own.[5]

Boosey and Hawkes is the only publisher. (Inexplicably, none have been commercially recorded.) Virtually all published songs for voice and piano are listed, though singers should also consider his three chamber works with voice, of which *Portrait Interieur* and *Three Songs for Mezzo Soprano* have also been arranged for piano. Note that some songs were incorporated into cycles either after being issued separately or the other way around. Most are in one key only.

Ae Fond Kiss, Robert Burns; Boosey c1980.

Pub. medium voices (db–f2), but a higher version can be found in the cycle *Heart Songs* (see entry below); 3:45; With a lilt; in Scottish dialect, to a traditional tune; the accompaniment becomes more involved with each stanza but closes quietly.

Alleluia for St. Francis, From the Roman-Seraphic Missal; Boosey c1970.

Spec. medium voice ([c1]bb1–f2); 3:15; Moderato-lilting; tonal; melismatic; mostly to the word "alleluia"; unaccompanied passages sit low; quiet dynamics; fluid and linear; mysterious and beautiful.

And I Am Too Old To Know, Pauline Hanson; Boosey c1971; comp. 1958.

 Rec. high, ample voices (c#1–b♭2 [a♭2]); 6:00; slow; lungs of steel and a gorgeous sound required for the long, intensive lines which build to a *ff* climax; textures thicken dramatically, and then abruptly thin out; a powerful song on love and death.

A Bygone Occasion, see *Shut Out That Moon.*

The Fair Morning, Jones Very; Boosey c1971; also incl. *Four Songs for High Soprano;* comp. 1968.

 Rec. stratospheric high voices (b–f♭3); 8:00; Allegro moderato; many tempo and dynamic changes; generally spirited; elaborate piano part; an exultant ode to morning; formidably difficult, but striking.

Four Songs for High Soprano, various poets; Boosey c1976.

 Spec. high voices (d♭1–f♭3); 20:30; high tessitura and great flexibility required; piano score is spare but intricate; generally atonal; very difficult; any of these songs can be used individually.

 Lightly Like Music Running, Jean Garrigue; (g#1–c♭2) 4:00; flows in a moderate tempo; very high tessitura; romantic piano interlude; a spoken passage; lovely song.

 Her Silver Will, (high, d♭1–a2); the only one of this set with a key signature; see separate entry (in a medium key).

 Mermaid Remembered, Babette Deutsch; (d#1–d3); 5:45; bright and moving; meno allegro central section; somewhat fantastical; major piano score; very difficult.

 The Fair Morning, see separate entry.

Heart Songs, Robert Burns; Boosey c1980.

 Spec. tenor (d1–a2); 20:00; titles are: *Bonnie Bell; Long, Long the Night; Wilt Thou Be My Dearie; Ae Fond Kiss; Blythe Hae I Been;* on traditional Scotch airs, the last two are in Scottish dialect; can be used individually or in a smaller group; tonal; strophic; the voice sings the original tunes over accompaniments that occasionally undergo amazing transformations, particularly *Ae Fond Kiss* and *Blythe Hae I Been;* the latter song is especially recommended.

Her Definition, Thomas Hardy; Boosey c1968; comp. 1966; to my wife.

 Rec. baritone, in bass clef (G–e♭1); 4:15; Moderato; the hushed opening breaks out into ascending, fitful lines as the poet searches for the words to describe his love; difficult and unusual.

Her Silver Will (Looking Back at Sposalizio),[6] Emily Dickinson;
Boosey c1976; comp. 1974; also incl. (in a higher version) in *Four
Songs for High Soprano* .
  Spec. medium voice (b♭–f#2); 2:45; Andante sognante; tonal; a
kind of lyrical recitando, delivered as in a trance; a lovely, contem-
plative song.

If Thou Wilt Ease Mine Heart, Thomas L. Beddoes; Boosey c1971;
comp. 1970.
  Rec. baritones, in bass clef (A–f1); 6:00; a contained, hypnotic
recitando in dialogue with a spare and wide-ranging piano score; a
più mosso central section; on sleep and death as balm for the pains of
love; translucent; mysterious; a beautiful song.

Is It You I Dream About? Kate Flores; Boosey c1980.
  Spec. medium voice (c#1–f#2); 4:00; Moderato; tonal; with its
simple, forthright melody this lovely song has the feeling of a popular ballad, even with a piano interlude; not difficult; tender, haunting.

A Nursery Ode, Ambroise Philips; Boosey c1971; comp. 1970.
  Rec. lyric baritones, in bass clef (F–f#1); 4:45; as the poet watch-
es the little girl in the nursery, he speculates as to how she will grow
up; insinuating, disjunct, but lyrical over a colorful piano score; complex rhythms; difficult; witty; coy; effective.

O Darling Room, Alfred Lord Tennyson; Boosey c1977.
  Spec. medium voice (d♭1–g♭2), also rec. lyric voices; 4:00;
Moderato; tonal; lyrical; the lovely melody is gracefully recast as the
song evolves; tender and warm.

One Foot in Eden, Edwin Muir; Boosey c1977; comp. 1974.
  Spec. medium voice; (c1–e♭2); 8:00; Broad; steady and majestic;
tonal; two more active central sections; primarily chordal; evokes a
Thanksgiving hymn; if a clear, ample voice can communicate Muir's
profoundly moving ideas and images with sensitivity and simplicity,
and, despite the song's grandeur, not lose sight of its affecting lyricism, this should be a memorable moment on any program.

Peace, Henry Vaughan; Boosey c1968; comp. 1966.
  Pub. high (high, c♭1–a♭2) and low (g♭–e♭2); 2:45; Moderato;
Emphatic and sonorous; changing moods and tonalities; many dotted
rhythms; some hymnlike effects; difficult; strong.

Shut Out That Moon, Thomas Hardy; Boosey c1968; comp. 1965.
    Spec. high voice (b–a2), texts suggest women; 15:00; any one of these songs could stand on its own, but it is a strong cycle and best kept as such; Binkerd has effectively captured an aging woman's bitter regret and bleak rumination in spare textures and vocal writing that is at times limpid, at other times intense and anxious; quite difficult; many beautiful elements, but the general impression is one of great sadness.
    She, to Him, (b–a♭2); 4:30; Slow; lyric; sustained; high passages.
    Shut Out That Moon, (c♭1–a2); 4:00; Fast, light and rhythmic; staccato and sustained passages; changing meters.
    A Bygone Occasion, (c1–g♭2); 3:00; a slow half-note, mostly in canon; sustained; lyrical; quiet; a very lovely song; published separately for low voice, but Binkerd also uses the identical music in his setting of *What Sweeter Music* (see entry below).
    The Riddle, (d1–g#2); 3:15; Tempo rubato; long, sustained phrases; haunting.

Somewhere I Have Never Travelled, E. E. Cummings; Boosey c1969; comp. 1950.
    Rec. high voices (b♭–a♭2); 7:00; Andante con moto; lyrical, disjunct declamation over an elaborate piano score; closely following the text, it builds in tempo, dynamic, and textural complexity to a central climax; difficult; an unusual love song.

Song of Praise and Prayer (Children's Hymn), William Cowper; Boosey c1972; comp. 1971.
    Rec. medium and high voices (e♭1–f2); 2:15; Flowing; in 5/8; a syllabic melody; strophic; straightforward.

What Sweeter Music, Robert Herrick; Boosey c1968.
    Pub. high (c1–g♭2) and low (a–e♭2); the text is on the birth of Christ; see *A Bygone Occasion* from *Shut Out That Moon* for the original setting of this song.

The Wishing Caps, Rudyard Kipling; Boosey c1971; comp. 1970.
    Rec. baritones, in bass clef (B–f1); 6:00; Allegro moderato; later, Più allegro and Presto sections; tricky; a delightful, sprightly romp on an operatic scale.

BIBLIOGRAPHY
AmerGroves, Baker, Thompson.

Hagen, Dorothy Veinus. "Gordon Binkerd," *ACA Bulletin* 10 (September 1962): 1–4.

Scanlan, Roger. "Spotlight on Contemporary American Composers," *NATS Bulletin* 31 (May/June 1975).

Shakelford, Rudy. "The Music of Gordon Binkerd," *Tempo,* No. 114 (1975): 2–13.

---

[1] Most biographical information on Binkerd gives the impression that he grew up among American Indians on reservations. But in a letter to the author, dated July 15, 1991, he explains that the town where he was born was later designated The Ponca Indian Reservation, while Gregory, the location of his subsequent home, was simply the pay office for Sioux Indians from the Rosebud Reservation.

[2] Letter from the composer dated January 18, 1990.

[3] David Cohen. "Music From the Radical Center," *Perspectives of New Music* 3 (1964), p. 131.

[4] Binkerd, however, has never written an opera.

[5] Binkerd has, in fact, made several piano transcriptions of his songs.

[6] In a letter to the author dated June 23, 1991, the composer explains that the subtitle is a reference to the four measures he has "borrowed" from Liszt's *Années de Pelerinage.*

ROBERT FAIRFAX BIRCH
b. Nov. 19, 1917, Chevy Chase, MD

Growing up in a music-loving home, Birch studied piano and sang in church. When serious illness held him back from pursuing his musical interests, he became a promoter of various performers in Washington D.C. and, after the war, New York City. In lieu of a formal music education, he has described his training in voice and composition as an assimilation of knowledge from the artists with whom he spent time. Settling in New York, where he has lived since 1950, for 20 years Birch worked at the Joseph Patelson Music Store. At the same time he composed songs, which Patelson's published and distributed. A lyric baritone, he often performed his own songs on radio and recital programs.

THE SONGS
Today Birch is best known for his settings of Haiku poets; the attractive little albums are still readily available. However, though no longer in print, a large catalogue of his other songs was also published. The endorsements on their covers by well-known singers, such as Bidú

Sayão, Martha Lipton, Eileen Farrell, and Gladys Swarthout, are evidence of their early success. Written in a conventional style and set to a wide variety of excellent poetry, Birch's poorer songs suffer from sentimentality and awkward construction. The best, however, are simple, straightforward, and—benefiting from the composer's own experience with singing—lyrical, expressive, and melodious. Theodore Presser is now the sole representative for Birch's song catalogue. A few recommendations follow.

Epitaph for a Poet, Robert Nathan; Presser c1957.
Pub. medium voices (d1–f#2); 2:00; Rather slow; a warm melody; delicate, tender.

Haiku, various Haiku poets; eight volumes; Joseph Patelson and Theodore Presser (copyrights range from 1963 to 1985).
Rec. lyric medium voices; titles of the volumes in order of publication are *Haiku; All Snow; Bugs; Another Flower; Among the Bamboos; Rippling Sounds; Now for Cherry Bloom; Way of Haiku.* Each volume averages between 50 and 100 songs, each of which is well under a minute (some are just a few seconds). Never requiring a page turn, they have been carefully arranged for pacing and variety. Although the volumes tend to be on a theme, the songs can be mixed to make any grouping the performer likes. Without departing from a conventional western musical idiom, Birch matches the various moods in succinct, attractive sketches.

It is a Beauteous Evening, William Wordsworth; Presser c1952; to Grete Stueckgold.
Pub. medium low voices (d♭1–f2); 1:45; Quietly - Rubato; a melting, sustained melody over moving chords; simple; atmospheric.

The Moralist, Omar Khayyam; Presser c1953.
Rec. all voices (d#1–e2); 1:00; Heavy, then lighter; dialogue between a mullah and a harlot; cute and a little different.

The Owl and the Pussy Cat, Edward Lear; Presser c1953.
Rec. all voices (d♭1–g♭2); 2:15; Staccato (lightly with humor); dotted rhythms; an easy, flowing tune; a charming narrative.

Repose, Erasmus Darwin; Presser c1952.
Rec. higher lyric voices (d♭1–g♭2); 1:30; Slowly and quietly; a lovely, sustained melody over undulating sixteenths; reflective.

The River, Patrick MacDonogh; Presser c1953; to Gladys Swarthout.
Rec. lower lyric voices (a–f#2); 2:00; Flowing - moderato; sustained over murmuring sixteenths; quiet and warm.

Sonnet, Robert Nathan; Presser c1956.
Spec. high voices (e♭1–g2); Slow; recitative followed by a warm cantabile.

Also of interest:

The Green River, Douglas, Moderato; ***If There Were Dreams,*** Beddoes, Andante; ***The Philosophist,*** Raleigh, With satire; ***Snowfall,*** Carducci, Quietly and Slowly; ***Upon a Child That Died,*** Herrick, Andante cantabile; ***Weep You No More,*** Anonymous, Slowly.

BIBLIOGRAPHY
There is virtually no mention of Birch in standard references. Biographical information for this entry came from a publicity release found at the American Music Center, reviews from *Musical America* (July, 1955; May, 1960), information (including reviews, with no dates given, from the *New York Times*) provided on the covers of certain of the songs, and the author's interview with the composer at his home on January 24, 1991.

MARC BLITZSTEIN
b. March 2, 1905, Philadelphia, PA; d. Jan. 22, 1964, Fort-de-France, Martinique

Marc Blitzstein, celebrated in the annals of socially conscious music theater, also composed in a purely classical idiom. His art songs are vivid and skillful, but rarely heard.

Blitzstein was of Russian Jewish descent. His father, who had come to the United States in 1889, was a banker. Exceptionally bright and musically precocious, Blitzstein played the piano by the age of three, performed publicly by five, and at 14 was a soloist with the Philadelphia Orchestra. Though he remained a formidable pianist, he was intent on a career in composition. After two years at the University of Pennsylvania he entered the Curtis Institute and studied with Rosario Scalero. In 1926 he went to Europe, where he did the unthinkable and studied for brief periods with the great adversaries: Nadia Boulanger in Paris and Arnold Schoenberg in Berlin. Returning to America, Blitzstein found himself with a growing reputation as a controversial modernist. Like many artists of the era, he flirted with leftist political views. Though he was an acknowledged homosexual, in 1932 he married author Eva Goldbeck,[1] continuing a relationship based on their mutual beliefs in the principles of communism. Eva died only three years later, but Blitzstein's music continued to address social concerns, culminating with *The Cradle Will Rock*.[2]

During World War II Blitzstein was stationed in England with the U.S. 8th Army Air Force. In 1949 he returned to Broadway with *Regina,* an opera with spoken dialogue, but it was his 1954 English version of Brecht/Weill's *Threepenny Opera* that brought him popular recognition. Blitzstein also wrote articles and criticism for various music journals, and was a founder of the Arrow Music Press. He was completing an opera, *Sacco and Vanzetti* (commissioned for the Metropolitan Opera), when while vacationing in Martinique, he was robbed and beaten by three sailors he had met in a bar, and died from the injuries.

THE SONGS

Blitzstein, who liked to sing himself, experimented with a wide variety of vocal styles from quasi-Broadway to quasi-operatic. There is, however, no question but that the vernacular songs from his theatrical compositions are at the heart of his vocal music. But he also wrote art song in a surprisingly conventional style.[3] Spare and beautifully proportioned, his serious settings have feeling and mood; light ones have wit and charm. Often polytonal, dissonances are pungent. Initially, the singer will find it difficult to hold his or her pitch against the piano (and the pianist dismayed by the endless accidentals), but the unusual color soon defines itself, and he or she will find the clean writing tuneful and wonderfully complimentary to the voice. Many Blitzstein songs, including *It's 5* (an earlier set of Cummings poetry), remain unpublished. Karen Holvik and William Sharp have recorded an album on Koch CD (3-7050-2), which is primarily comprised of Blitzstein's theater songs, but includes Sharp singing four art songs. More of Blitzstein's cabaret style songs can also be heard on Premier CD (PRCD 1005). All art songs known to have been published are listed.

From Marion's Book, [4] E. E. Cummings; Chappell c1962; comp. 1960; to Alice Estey (sic).

   Rec. medium and low lyric voices (a#–f2); 12:30; not difficult vocally; no key signatures; generally polytonal; spare in texture; linear; more erudite than most of Blitzstein's vocal music but, at the same time, lyrical, colorful, and warm. Blitzstein is light with Cummings's verbal magic and, with a deft, sensitive touch, imaginatively conveys the modern poet's many romantic moods; rarely heard; a smaller group could be programmed; highly recommended.

o by the by, (a#–e2); 1:30; Allegro; a charming song about flying kites; recorded by Sharp.

when life is quite through with, (d#1–b1); 1:30; Andantino; subdued, tender.

what if a much of a which of a wind, (c1–e2); 1:45;Vivace; a whirlwind.

silent unday by silently not night, (b♭–e2); 3:15; Calmo; an excited central section; a big song, strange, spiritual.

until and i heard, (b♭–f2); 1:15; Allegro; waltzlike; light and ebullient; recorded by Sharp.

yes is a pleasant country, (b–e♭2); 1:00; Allegretto; straightforward; warm.

open your heart, (c1–f2 [g♭2]); 2:15; Molto moderato; builds but ends quietly; emotional; recorded by Sharp.

Jimmie's got a goil,[5] E. E. Cummings; Cos Cob Press c1935; incl. *CC.* Rec. medium and high voices (c1–f#2); 0:45; Vivo; in dialect; spicy rhythms and dissonances; fun and funny; good ender; recorded by Sharp.

Six Elizabethan Songs,[6] various poets; Chappell c1959; comp. 1958; for Leonard Bernstein.[7]
  Spec. soprano or tenor (e♭1–a♭2); 8:30; high tessitura; lyrical and straightforward with a suggestion of Elizabethan style; key signatures; some dissonance but less difficult than *From Marion's Book;* one could program any of these songs individually, but they also make a delightful, colorful set.

Sweet Is the Rose, Amoretti; (f1–g2);1:30; Andante; lilting.

Shepherd's Song, William Shakespeare; (f1–f2); 1:30; Andante... Allegro; mostly unaccompanied.

Song of the Glove, Ben Jonson; (f1–g2); 1:30; Moderato; sustained high tessitura.

Court Song, Anonymous; (e♭1–g2); 1:00; Allegro commodo; strophic with a fa la la refrain; charming.

Lullaby, William Shakespeare; (f1–a♭2); 1:45; Andantino.

Vendor's Song, William Shakespeare; (f1–a♭2); 1:15; Allegro vivo; centers on high G; rhythmic and brilliant; wonderful ender.

BIBLIOGRAPHY
AmerGroves, Baker, CBY (1940), Ewen, Goss, Greene, Ivey (on
Jimmie's got a goil), Thompson.
Gordon, Eric A. *Mark the Music: The Life and Work of Marc Blitzstein.*
New York: St. Martin's Press, 1989. Highly recommended.

---

[1] Goldbeck was the daughter of the popular light opera soprano, Lina
Abarbanell, who remained close to Blitzstein after her daughter's death.

[2] The 1936 opening-night of this opera (or theater piece with music), which
had been awarded to him as a Federal Theater project, became the stuff of
legends when Blitzstein and his actors defied the WPA's last minute attempt
to cancel the show for being "subversive." Abandoning the WPA theater, in
a matter of hours a new theater was found to which the audience followed the
company. There, Blitzstein played the piano on a bare stage (the WPA had
taken scenery and costumes), while the actors, forbidden by the union to
appear on a different stage, performed from their seats among the audience.

[3] Though four of the early, unpublished Whitman settings are designated to be
sung in a "coon shout," no further unorthodox requests in his art songs are
ever again asked of his singers.

[4] Marion was Cummings's wife.

[5] This is the last of his otherwise unpublished set, *It's 5.*

[6] Composed as incidental music for *A Midsummer's Night Dream* and *The
Winter's Tale* at the American Shakespeare Festival Theater.

[7] Blitzstein had been an early mentor to Bernstein. They became devoted
friends.

HOWARD BOATWRIGHT
b. March 16, 1918, Newport News, VA

Though probably best known as a composer of choral music, Howard
Boatwright has made notable contributions in many areas of music. He
began as a concert violinist, making his New York recital debut in 1942.
In 1943—the same year he married soprano Helen Boatwright (née
Strassburger), with whom he would often perform—he was appointed to
the faculty at the University of Texas (Austin). From 1945 to 1948 he
studied theory and composition with Paul Hindemith at Yale University,
then remained there to teach and conduct the Yale University Orchestra.
He also served as Director of Music at St. Thomas Church in New
Haven, where he built a major reputation for his concerts and recordings
of early music. From 1964 until his retirement in 1983 he taught at
Syracuse University, and for many years was dean of the School of

Music. Boatwright is also recognized for his writings on subjects as diverse as music theory, classical Indian music, and Charles Ives.[1]

THE SONGS

With Helen Boatwright's clear-voiced soprano[2] as a steady source of inspiration, not surprisingly Howard Boatwright has written a great deal for solo voice. Though his refined, intelligent, atonal songs require advanced musicianship, the natural declamation and pliant, expressive vocal lines make them gratifying to sing. Boatwright has also made some folk song arrangements, which were published by Oxford University Press. His art songs are available in a crisp, totally legible manuscript from Walnut Grove Press.

Five Early Songs, various poets; Walnut Grove c1993; comp. 1946–1954.

> Spec. sopranos (d1–a2); 11:00; titles are: *Requiescat* (Oscar Wilde); *On Hearing the Birds Sing* (Irish); *o by the by* (E. E. Cummings); *At the Round Earth's Imagined Corners* (John Donne); *Revelation* (B. T. Coler); despite the various poets, subject matter, and dates of composition, Boatwright has nicely shaped these songs to work as a group; generally lyrical, with some long sustained passages, over clear piano textures; vivid and imaginative.

Six Prayers of Kierkegaard, Walnut Grove c1985; comp. 1978.

> Spec. soprano (d1–a♭2); 10:00; first lines are: Grant that our prayer; And when at times; It is from thy Hand; When the thought of thee; Thou hast commanded us to forgive; Be near to us with thy power; a continuous cycle; atonal, with passages that are, in essence, serial; lyrical declamation with some sustained and dramatic singing; slow to moderate tempos; some intricate, and often independent piano writing; intense and profoundly spiritual.

Also of interest:

Five Songs, Victoria Hill, a difficult, but picturesque set for lyric soprano; *From Joy to Fire,* Ursula Vaughan Williams, for mezzo soprano; *Three French Songs,* various poets; *Three Love Songs,* Emily Dickinson, for sopranos.

BIBLIOGRAPHY
AmerGroves, Baker, Ewen.

Boatwright, Howard. Program Notes. "Seventy-Fifth Anniversary Concert," March 17, 1993 (Everson Museum of Art, Syracuse, New York).

---

[1] In particular, he is the author of *Introduction to the Theory of Music* (1956), and the editor of Charles Ives's *Essays before a Sonata and Other Writings* (1962).

[2] Helen Boatwright, a prominent concert singer and voice teacher, is especially well known for her performances of American art song. See Ernst Bacon and Charles Ives for more on her pioneering recordings of their songs.

CARRIE JACOBS BOND

b. Aug. 11, 1862, Janesville,WI; d. Dec. 28, 1946, Glendale, CA

Born into a musical family, as a child Carrie Jacobs improvised songs and studied piano. Divorced from her first husband, then widowed by her second husband (Dr. Frank Bond), Carrie Jacobs Bond, living in Chicago and needing to make a living, composed and published songs. She illustrated the pretty covers herself, and with only the help of a young son from her first marriage,[1] under the imprint of Carrie Jacobs Bond & Son, she printed them in her own home (the Bond Shop). Then, as advertisement, she sang and played them at functions and sent them to famous singers. Baritone David Bispham was especially instrumental in launching Bond's career. The first, other than herself, to include *A Perfect Day* in recital,[2] in 1905 he courageously devoted most of a recital to the, as yet, unknown composer. Bond went on to compose almost 200 small pieces, primarily songs. She also sang at the White House and Buckingham Palace, published her autobiography and a book of poetry, and moved the Bond Shop to Hollywood, where she built her dream house in the nearby mountains.

Bond's songs are undeniably sentimental, but their ingenuousness easily explains their extraordinary former popularity. Melodies are comely and appealing, while the texts, usually written by Bond herself, express cherished truisms. Though most are what were once called "heart" songs, there are also a surprising number of witty songs. A few of the most popular are still in print, but most, including some collections, are library items. Published in several keys, often available with obbligato, best known are: *I Love You Truly,* recorded by Jan DeGaetani on Elektra/Nonesuch CD (79248-2-ZK), Rosa Ponselle on BIM CD (701-2), and Elisabeth Suderburg (OLY-104); *A Perfect Day,* recorded by Ponselle on Nimbus CD (7805) and Suderburg (OLY-104); and *Just a Wearyin' for You.*

BIBLIOGRAPHY
AmerGroves, Ammer, Baker, Greene, Thompson.
Bond, Carrie Jacobs. *The Roads of Melody: My Story.* New York: D. Appleton and Company, 1927. "The Story of Carrie Jacobs-Bond," *Music Journal* (September 1955).
"Writes the Verses, Composes the Music, Publishes Songs and Then Sings Them," *Musical America,* October 26, 1907.

---

[1] Frederick Jacobs Smith committed suicide in 1928, a tragedy that abruptly curtailed Bond's creativity.

[2] The sheet music of *A Perfect Day* eventually sold over eight million copies and appeared in 60 different arrangements.

GENE BONE
b. April 14, 1915, Newman, CA; d. Sept. 26, 1992, New York, NY

HOWARD FENTON
b. date unknown, New York, NY

Known as Bone and Fenton, this intriguing pair may be the only composers in classical music to write as a team. Both had training in vocal and instrumental music. Fenton supplemented his income by acting and singing while Bone, the more classically trained of the two,[1] primarily accompanied and coached. Though little is written about how they worked, this would suggest that Fenton may have written the vocal lines and Bone the accompaniments. They first met in 1941 when Bone was hired as an accompanist for a revue that Fenton had written and in which he was also performing. It was not until a chance meeting in 1943, however, that their collaboration got underway. Though each also pursued other avenues in show business, as late as 1977 a Bone and Fenton show was produced.[2]

THE SONGS
In addition to a Broadway show and a popular Christmas cantata, Bone and Fenton composed a multitude of songs—classical, sacred, and popular—which were performed by such well known singers as Leonard Warren, Eugene Conley, Gladys Swarthout, and Eileen Farrell. These art

songs readily show the pair were not only talented but very sensitive to poetry (often writing their own texts as well). They also had imagination and— not surprisingly, considering their background in show business— a keen dramatic sense. What is surprising is their fine taste in the face of what must have been real pressure to be commercial. Though a *Music Journal* article they wrote in 1960 reveals nothing about their composing process, it does tell us a great deal about the pleasure they had in doing it. This spirit comes through in their songs and accounts for much of their appeal. A few recommendations follow.

The April Hill, Janet Lewis; Fischer c1947.
    Pub. high and medium voices (med., c1–f#2); 2:15; Slow; many tempo and dynamic changes; lyric, sustained; an unusual and moving song about death.

Deborah, Alice Kilmer; Fischer c1947; also incl. *CSE* .
    Pub. medium and low voices (med., c#1–f#2); 1:30; Lively, with a lilt; mostly in waltz time; a delightful song about the changes a little girl undergoes from the age of two to three.

Everything That I Can Spy, James Stephens; Morris c1946.
    Pub. high and medium (high, e1–g♭2); 1:30; Allegro ma non troppo; many tempo changes; melodious; spirited; broadening in the central sections; big ending; unusual.

Green Fields, Gene Bone and Howard Fenton; Morris c1945.
    Pub. high and low (high, e1–a2); 1:45; With tranquil motion; sustained over a full-bodied accompaniment; warm and nostalgic; a lovely song.

Wind in the Tree-tops, Gene Bone and Howard Fenton; Boosey c1943.
    Pub. high and low (high, e♭1–g♭2); 2:30; Moderately with expression; a pretty, rocking melody; big ending; this lovely song, when introduced by Eileen Farrell on the radio, brought Bone and Fenton their first recognition.

Also of interest:

Blue Water, Mally, Sweeping; *Captain Kidd,* Stephen Vincent Benét, a colorful narrative for men; *Distances,* Bone and Fenton, Slowly; *Finnegan's Wake,* Old Irish Folk Poem, Allegro, jaunty dialogue in Irish brogue; *Tryst,* Cullen, Con moto, lyrical.

BIBLIOGRAPHY

"Bone and Fenton – Team of Versatile Writers," *Musical Courier*, February 15, 1952.

Bone, Gene and Howard Fenton, "The Wedding of Words and Music," *Music Journal* (April/May, 1960).

---

[1] Bone studied at the San Francisco Conservatory and the Juilliard School.

[2] Their show called "Fixed" was given at Theater of the Riverside Church in Manhattan on Dec. 20, 1977.

PAUL BOWLES
b. Dec. 30, 1910, Jamaica, NY

His stature as a writer has eclipsed his considerable contribution as a composer, but the music of Paul Bowles is still recalled with affection. Many of his songs—deft and "delicious"[1]—are finding their way into the established repertoire.

As the precocious son of an abusive father (a dentist), Bowles entered into a solitary world of fantasy. He first dreamed of being a poet, but was also interested in art and, as a boy, studied piano and wrote music. Uncertain as to which artistic bent to follow, after two attempts at college, he showed some compositions to Henry Cowell, who, finding them stylistically French, sent him on to Aaron Copland. When Copland offered to give him lessons, Bowles happily followed his new mentor to Paris, Berlin, and Morocco. It was but the beginning of such a peripatetic lifestyle he would later title his autobiography *Without Stopping*.

From 1933 until 1947 Bowles worked out of New York City, where he built a solid reputation for theater, ballet, and film music. Between commissions, he traveled extensively in Latin America, especially Mexico, and wrote articles and short stories. In 1947 he made his way back to Morocco, where his transformation from composer to author culminated with the 1949 publication of his most important novel, *The Sheltering Sky*.[2] From this point on, but for a few incidental commissions, he virtually ceased to compose.

Bowles's 1937 marriage to novelist Jane Auer (Bowles) somehow survived long separations, endless travel, extra-marital affairs, homosexuality, drugs, serious illness, and an altogether exotic lifestyle. Since her death in 1973 he has only written short stories but continues to live in a flat in Tangiers. Although his books and expatriate status first made him something of a cult figure, more recently there has been widespread interest in all facets of his life and work.

THE SONGS

The easygoing, infectious music of Bowles's younger days seems at opposite ends to the dark, existential prose of his later years. His musical style—personal and artless—blends the lightness, precision, and sophistication of the French influence with American folk and popular elements. His songs are delicate, graceful, fresh, clever, and evocative. Though many were written for theatrical productions, texts generally came either from the poets of his own literary circles, including his wife, or from his own works.

With an unerring ability to match words with music, Bowles's beguiling, irresistible melodies flow with the ease of a popular song. Lyric voices are generally best to accommodate what Virgil Thomson has described as their "weightlessness."[3] Meanwhile, jazz and rag rhythms, the basis of many of the clever accompaniments, will keep pianists alert. Though a fairly large number of songs remain either lost or unpublished, at one time a substantial number were published individually and a few others appear in anthologies.[4] Best, however, is the 1984 *Paul Bowles: Selected Songs (PBSS)*, edited by Peter Garland, from Soundings Press. This collection includes both published and previously unpublished works. There are various recordings: John Hanks sings two of the *Blue Mountain Ballads* on Duke, Vol. 1 (DWR 6417); Donald Gramm, the *Blue Mountain Ballads* on Desto (411/412) and two songs on New World (243); Yolanda Marcoulescou-Stern, four Spanish settings on Orion (OC 685) and three songs on Gasparo CD (GSCD 287); Paul Sperry, five songs on Albany CD (TROY043); and William Sharp, *The Blue Mountain Ballads* and seven songs on New World CD (NW 369-2). Some recommendations follow.

April Fool Baby, Gertrude Stein; incl. *PBSS;* comp. 1935.
> Rec. medium or high voices (d♭1–f2), text suggests men; 1:15; a lively ragtime, followed by a tender meno mosso; big piano interlude; recorded by Sharp and Sperry.

Baby, Baby, Paul Bowles; Mercury Music c1946; also incl. *PBSS* (slightly revised under the title *Sleeping Song).*
> Rec. lyric higher voices (f1–f2); 2:00; high tessitura; a lullaby; warm and winsome; recorded Sharp and Sperry.

Blue Mountain Ballads, Tennessee Williams;[5] G. Schirmer c1946; also
pub. individually.

Rec. medium voices (b–f#2); 7:00; best as a set, but can be used
individually; not difficult vocally; many subtle changes of dynamic,
tempo, and meter; some dialect; folklike; probably Bowles's best
known songs; recorded by Sharp and Gramm.

Heavenly Grass, also incl. *CAS28;* (b–e2); 2:30; With flowing simplicity; musing, melting, exquisite; also recorded by Hanks.

Lonesome Man, also incl. *PBSS;* (d♭1–e♭2); 1:15; Very rhythmically; raglike.

Cabin, also incl. *20CAS;* (c#1–c#2); 1:45; Like a ballad; melancholy;
also recorded by Hanks.

Sugar in the Cane, also incl. *PBSS;* (d1–f#2); 1:30; In absolutely
strict tempo; spirited; jazz rhythms; comical.

Farther from the Heart *(Song of an Old Woman),* Jane Bowles; G.
Schirmer c1946; also incl. *PBSS;* comp. 1942.

Rec. medium and lower lyric voices (c#1–e2); 2:30; Andante;
quiet and plaintive; recorded by Gramm (NW).

Letter to Freddy, Gertrude Stein; New Music c1935; G. Schirmer c1946;
also incl. *PBSS.*

Rec. medium voices (e♭1–e♭2); 1:30; Lento...Allegro; dreamy,
then a bright waltz; a serious incident prompted this real letter;[6]
recorded by Sharp and Sperry.

My Sister's Hand in Mine, Jane Bowles; incl. *PBSS.*

Rec. medium and higher lyric voices (d1–g2); 1:15; as the cold
truth of the dream becomes apparent, the spirited opening becomes
subdued; recorded by Sharp.

Once a Lady Was Here, Paul Bowles; G. Schirmer c1946; also incl.
PBSS and *S22A.*

Rec. medium and lower voices (c1–e♭2); 1:30; sustained over
vamping accompaniment; nostalgic; recorded by Gramm,
Marcoulescou-Stern, and Sperry.

Secret Words, Paul Bowles; incl. *PBSS;* comp. 1943.

Rec. medium and higher lyric voices (d1–g2); 2:30; languorous;
melodious, romantic; recorded Sharp.

Sleeping Song, see *Baby, Baby.*

Song of an Old Woman, see *Farther from the Heart.*

Three, Tennessee Williams; Hargail c1947; also incl. *PBSS.*
Rec. medium lyric voices (e1-d2); 1:30; slow and sustained; hushed, haunting; recorded by Sharp and Sperry.

Also of interest:
Ainsi parfois nos seuils, St. John Perse, incl. *CC,* considerable motion, unusual; *Cuatro Canciones de Garcia Lorca,* incl. *PBSS,* varying tempos and moods in a Spanish style, recorded by Marcoulescou-Stern; *In the Woods,* Paul Bowles, Adagio, molto semplice, some high tessitura; *The Heart Grows Old,* David, incl. *PBSS,* active but reflective; *A Little Closer Please,* Saroyan, also incl. *PBSS;* jazzlike, recorded by Sharp; *On a Quiet Conscience,* Charles the First, also incl. *PBSS;* with quiet motion; *The Piper,* O'Sullivan, incl. *PBSS;* spirited, fun.

BIBLIOGRAPHY
AmerGroves, Baker, CBY (1990), Ewen, Friedberg (III), Greene, Thompson.
Bowles, Paul. *Without Stopping.* New York: Putnam, 1972. A fun read, but Bowles reveals little about himself and tends to ramble.
Dagel, Gena. "A Nomad in New York: Paul Bowles 1933-48," *American Music* 7 (Fall 1989): 278–314.
Glanville-Hicks, Peggy. "Paul Bowles: American Composer," *Music and Letters* 26 (1945): 88–95.
Rorem, Ned. "Come Back Paul Bowles," *The New Republic,* April 22, 1972. Reprinted as "Paul Bowles," *Pure Contraption.* New York: Holt, Rinehart and Winston, 1974.
Sawyer-Lauçanno, Christopher. *An Invisible Spectator: A Biography of Paul Bowles.* New York: Weidenfeld and Nicolson, 1989. Highly recommended, though the focus is on Bowles's career as a writer.

---

[1] Virgil Thomson, *American Music Since 1910,* p.127.
[2] This partially autobiographical novel was made into a motion picture by Bernardo Bertolucci in 1991. Bowles appears in a cameo role.
[3] Virgil Thomson, Preface to *Paul Bowles: Selected Songs,* 2.
[4] Though Bowles also had his own short-lived press (Editions de la Vipère), it printed only one hundred copies of a few songs.
[5] Tennessee Williams was a close friend. Bowles wrote incidental music for the original productions of Williams's plays *Glass Menagerie, Summer and Smoke,* and *Sweet Bird of Youth,* and he set other poems as late as the 1960s.

⁶ Freddy (his middle name) was Stein's preferred name for Bowles, as she felt
it more aptly reflected his youthful personality. In this incident, Bowles was
mistakenly diagnosed as having syphilis and his friend Harry Dunham was
frantic he may have contracted it. See Sawyer-Lauçanno, 126.

GENA BRANSCOMBE
b. Nov. 4, 1881, Picton, Ontario, Canada; d. July 26, 1977, New York, NY

Gena Branscombe is best known as a composer and conductor of choral
music, but her large catalogue also includes a sizable number of noteworthy art songs.

   Though born in Canada, Branscombe's ancestry, dating back to
1640, was American. She studied with Felix Borowski at the Chicago
Musical College, where she was twice awarded the gold medal for composition. While remaining at the college to teach piano, she studied
songwriting with Alexander von Fielitz. Later studies included a year
with Englebert Humperdinck in Berlin. In 1910 Branscombe became an
American citizen and, in the same year, married a New York lawyer. As
the mother of four daughters, she understood her responsibilities to the
family, but was also mindful of her own career and concerned about
problems facing women musicians. She gradually earned a considerable
reputation as a conductor of women's orchestras and, in 1934, founded
her own women's chorus with whom she toured extensively. Active in
the music world for many decades, she composed well into her nineties.

THE SONGS
Branscombe's art songs mostly date from the early 1900s, before she
became seriously involved with choral music. While most women composers of the period were turning out sentimental ballads, Branscombe
was writing strong songs of appreciable individuality, sophistication, and
assurance. Her forthright, yet comely, vocal lines are a pleasure to sing,
and pianists will enjoy the descriptive and richly textured accompaniments. Though Recital Publications has reprinted two small cycles *(Love
in a Life* and *A Lute of Jade)*, unfortunately, they are not representative
of her best work. Some recommendations follow.

Old Woman Rain, Louise Driscoll; incl. *CAS.*
   Pub. high and low (low, c1–e2); 2:00; Andantino; a warm, lyrical
narrative about the approach of rain; a little different.

Serenade, Robert Browning; incl. *WW(3).*

Rec. medium voices (c1–f#2); 0:45; Fervently; lyrical over a fluid accompaniment.

Sleep, Then, Ah Sleep! Richard Le Gallienne; Schmidt c1906; also incl. *WW(3)*.

Pub. high and low (high, d1-a2); 2:00; Adagio lamentabile; a plaintive melody over slow chords with dramatic surges; effective.

Also of interest:

Across the Blue Aegean Sea, Moody, for high voices, Andante tranquillo; ***Boots and Saddle,*** Robert Browning, best for men, Con spirito ma moderato, dated but fun; *I Bring You Heartsease,* Branscombe; Allegretto cantabile, a straightforward, somewhat sentimental waltz; ***Love in a Life,*** Elizabeth Barrett Browning, Recital Pub. Reprint; six songs for medium voice; an uneven set, but songs such as *How do I love thee* and *The face of all the world is changed* might be used individually; *A Lute of Jade,* trans. from the Chinese, Recital Pub. Reprint, four songs in high and low editions, a nice lyric group.

BIBLIOGRAPHY
AmerGroves, Ammer, Baker, Ewen, Goss, Thompson.
Crothers, Stella Reid. "Women Composers of America - 28," *Musical America,* Dec. 11, 1909.

DUDLEY BUCK
b. March 10, 1839, Hartford, CT; d. Oct. 6, 1909, West Orange, NJ

In the late 1800s, Dudley Buck was a commanding figure in American music. Renowned for his sacred compositions, his songs are relatively insignificant. He is, nevertheless, credited with having opened "the floodgates of American [art] song."[1]

Though his parents, who were both from distinguished New England families, did not approve music as a vocation, by the time Buck reached his teens, his obvious gifts could not be ignored. After two years in Trinity College, he was sent to Europe (Paris and the Leipzig Conservatory) to receive a proper music education. Returning to America in 1862, he built a distinguished career as an organist and teacher. When his cantata, commissioned for the opening of the 1876 Centennial exhibition, received acclaim, he became equally well known as a composer. Married in 1865, Buck eventually settled in Brooklyn,

New York. One of his three children, Dudley Buck Jr., became a singer and, later, a very popular voice teacher.

THE SONGS

Most of Buck's composition was vocal—sacred and secular. From today's vantage point his songs appear old-fashioned and badly flawed, but his efforts to express emotion and drama in his melodies clearly sets him apart from the innocuous tune-machines of his predecessors. In addition, as Upton points out, Buck's "fluency" and "facility" in the medium was evidence that song-writing in America had become "an ordinary rather than an extraordinary procedure."[2] A few of the best and most representative songs are listed.

Bedouin Love Song, Op. 87, No. 2, Bayard Taylor; G. Schirmer c1881.
    Spec. baritone (a–e2); 3:30; Allegro molto energico; many changing tempos and vocal styles as this swashbuckling tale of love unfolds; rhythmic; mostly dramatic.

The Capture of Bacchus, Op. 87, No. 3, Charles Swain; incl. *SIA.*
    Rec. higher voices (d#1–g#2 [a2]), men best; 3:00; Allegretto giocoso; a rollicking narrative in light opera style; encore material; recorded by Sperry on Albany CD (TROY034-2).

Spring Song ("It was a lover and his lass"), Op. 76, No. 2, William Shakespeare; G. Schirmer c1904.
    Spec. alto or baritone (d1–e2), rec. lyric medium voices; 2:00; In happy mood, lively; a nicely constructed, charming setting.

Sunset, Op. 76, No. 4, Sidney Lanier,[3] G. Schirmer c1877.
    Spec. altos or baritones (ab–f2); 3:30; Molto moderato; broad vocal melody over rippling figurations; low tessitura; last pages designated Con Molto Appasionato; a little stiff and long but some good moments.

Where are the Swallows fled? Op. 36, No. 1, Adelaide Proctor; G. Schirmer 1868.
    Spec. mezzo-soprano (c1–f2); 2:45; Con moto; lyrical; two stanzas to the same melody, but the prosody of the second is bad and could be eliminated (the above timing is for one stanza); otherwise, a lovely song; Buck's first song and the oldest one in this book.

BIBLIOGRAPHY
AmerGroves, Baker, Greene, Howard, Hughes, Thompson, Upton.

"Dudley Buck Dead at Age Seventy," *Musical America,* Oct. 16, 1909.

[1] William Treat Upton, *Art Song in America,* 78.
[2] Ibid, 80. Upton also includes Homer Bartlett in these remarks.
[3] This popular American poet and musician also collaborated with Buck on *The Centennial Meditation of Columbus,* the cantata which opened the Philadelphia Centennial exhibition in 1876.

HARRY THACKER BURLEIGH[1]
b. Dec. 2, 1866, Erie, Pa; d. Sept. 12, 1949, Stamford, CT

Harry T. Burleigh was America's first prominent black composer. He is best known for his arrangements of spirituals, but his catalogue of original songs is large and distinguished.

As a boy, Burleigh learned the melodies of plantation life from his maternal grandfather, a former slave. Though Burleigh's parents were free-born, the family was poor and he held numerous menial jobs to help out. He also sang in a fine baritone voice at local churches. In 1892 he won a scholarship to the National Conservatory of Music in New York, which was then under the direction of Anton Dvořák.[2] In 1894, from a field of 60 white applicants, he was hired as baritone soloist at the wealthy, all-white St. George's Episcopal Church in New York. A popular figure, he remained there for 52 years. He also became an acclaimed recitalist (occasionally accompanying himself), toured Europe and America, and even gave command performances for royalty. Meanwhile, he found the time to arrange old spirituals and to compose his own music. In 1911 the famous publishing house of Ricordi, where Burleigh had been made an editor, began to issue his spirituals; their unforeseen and incalculable success would pave the way for his original songs.

Burleigh's private life was not very happy. His marriage in 1898 to Louise Alston, an actress and a poet, whose verses he occasionally set, ended early in a lifelong separation. Their one child, Alston, spent much of his life away from his father. In his declining years Burleigh suffered increasing senility. He was released by Ricordi and, in 1946, he retired from St. George's. Leaving his home in the Bronx, he entered a private nursing home in Connecticut, where he died. A loved and respected artist, he had done a great deal to lower the barriers of racial prejudice.

THE SONGS

Burleigh's balanced, tasteful, richly harmonized arrangements were the first to bring the Negro spiritual to the concert stage. Embraced by singers (both black and white), their popularity continues to this day.[3] But Burleigh's own songs (almost 150, sacred and secular) were also championed by some of the finest artists of the era.[4] Grandeur of design, quality poetry, sensitivity to text, and deep feeling distinguish his best work, and even his quainter songs have a sincerity that disallows sentimentality. If performed tastefully, many would do well on a contemporary recital. Dramatic voices are rewarded with some especially unusual songs, but lyrics will find some uncommonly lovely ones. Four are recorded by Cynthia Haymon on Argo CD (436 117 2ZH). A representative sampling, all originally published in two or more keys, follows.

Ethiopia Saluting the Colors, Walt Whitman; Ricordi c1915; dedicated to and sung by Mr. Herbert Witherspoon.

   Rec. dramatic voices, mezzos and baritones probably best (high, c#1–f2); 4:30; Tempo di marcia; the narrator and an old black woman (Ethiopia) recall slavery's history as the Union armies pass; an unusual and impressive dramatic song.

The Grey Wolf, Arthur Symons; Ricordi c1915.

   Rec. big voices (high, b♭–g2); 4:00; Moderato; a dramatic scena with cantabile sections; the narrator pleads with a grey wolf to leave his door as he has no food to give him; a strange poem but very effective in this setting.

Jean, Frank L. Stanton; Maxwell c1913, ass. Theodore Presser, 1914.

   Rec. lyric voices (medium, d♭1–f2), text suggests men; 1:30 Fervently with good rhythm; a lovely melody with a waltz-like lilt; a love song for one departed; sentimental but simple and true; Burleigh's first hit.

Saracen Songs, Fred G. Bowles; Ricordi c1914; available from Classical Vocal Reprints (high voice only).

   Pub. high and low (high, d♭1–a2); 9:30; seven fairly brief songs with an Eastern theme involving four characters;[5] ends on a dramatic farewell; lyrical, succinct, and tasteful; good diversity; a fine period cycle.

The Soldier, Rupert Brooke;[6] Ricordi c1916.

Rec. heavier voices (medium, d♭1–g♭2); 4:30; Moderato; warm, broad, and lyric with some martial effects and interesting thematic material, including an evocation of *Rule Britannia*.

Also of interest:

By the Pool at the Third Rosses, Symons, a lovely cantabile for lyric voices; *Five Songs of Laurence Hope,*[7] a big, expansive, lush set on Eastern (Indian) themes, from which *Kashmiri Song* is especially recommended; *Among the Fuschias* and *Till I Wake* are recorded by Haymon; *Her Eyes Twin Pools,* Johnson, lyric and liquid; *Little Mother of Mine,* Brown, a sentimental ballad and (as sung by John McCormack) a favorite with audiences; *O, Perfect Love,* Blomfield, popular as a wedding song.

BIBLIOGRAPHY

AmerGroves, Baker CBY (1941), Greene, Thompson.

Simpson, Anne Key. *Hard Trials: the life and music of Harry T. Burleigh*. Metuchen, N.J.: Scarecrow Press, 1990. Includes a discography, bibliography, and full catalogue of Burleigh's music.

---

[1] *Henry* Thacker Burleigh, Burleigh's father's name and Burleigh's given name, occasionally appears in print. *Harry,* however, was generally adopted, and is Anne Key Simpson's choice for her recent, authoritative biography.

[2] Dvořák, the famous Czech composer, who urged American composers to look to native sources for inspiration, was inspired by Burleigh's singing of spirituals. Some of these Dvořák incorporated into his *New World Symphony*.

[3] Originally issued under separate cover, they are now available in a collection *The Spirituals of Harry T. Burleigh* (Belwin Mills c1984).

[4] Christine Miller, Oscar Seagle, George Hamlin, Mary Jordon, Roland Hayes, and John McCormack, were especially loyal.

[5] In his prefatory note, W.G. Henderson suggests the cycle could be performed by two singers.

[6] This famous sonnet, beginning "If I should die," written by England's beloved poet soldier who fell shortly thereafter, was recently published and had captured the public's imagination.

[7] Laurence Hope was a pseudonym for Adela Florence Cory. Some critics felt this set was Burleigh's best work, but this author cannot agree. The writing seems inflated in relation to his other work and it was not surprising to discover the songs had been orchestrated soon after their publication. They would be better served with instrumentation.

CHARLES WAKEFIELD CADMAN
b. Dec. 24, 1881, Johnstown, PA; d. Dec. 30, 1946, Los Angeles, CA

Pretty though they may be, Cadman's songs are generally too naïve for today's concert stages. Nevertheless, as a popularizer of American Indian melodies and as one of the best selling composers of his era, his place in the story of American song is assured.

When Cadman was a boy, his family moved to the Pittsburgh area, where he was a messenger in the same steel mill his father worked. But Cadman burned with artistic aspiration. After studying all aspects of music (including voice), he held numerous jobs in the field, including that of music critic for the Pittsburgh *Dispatch*. He also composed and, to seemingly no avail, hustled his music.[1] However, when he and a local poet, Mrs. Nelle Richmond Eberhart, began to collaborate on songs based on Indian themes, they met with astounding success.[2] And when John McCormack finally programmed an earlier song, *At Dawning,* Cadman's career was secured.

Pursuing his interest in American Indians, Cadman visited reservations, recorded Indian melodies, and toured the country giving 'Music-Talks,' assisted by Indian princess (and mezzo-soprano) Tsianina Redfeather. All would culminate in his opera *Shanewis,* based on Princess Redfeather's life, which was presented by the Metropolitan Opera in 1918. Eventually, plagued by poor health, he had a house built in the warm climate of Los Angeles, where he helped found the Hollywood Bowl Concerts. In addition to a vast array of instrumental, choral, and chamber pieces, songs of all types continued to pour from his pen, each one duly noted by the national press. But with the approach of World War II and a growing interest in modern trends, his conventional, sentimental style gradually lost its appeal. Though Cadman never married, he did enjoy a serious romance with the beautiful English soprano, Maggie Teyte.[3]

THE SONGS
Of his several hundred songs, those devoted to American Indian themes comprise a relatively small part of Cadman's output. But, written with great enthusiasm while he was still very young, they do represent some of his freshest and most spontaneous efforts. Using the poems of Nelle Richmond Eberhart practically to the exclusion of all others, his catalogue includes sentimental settings of the South Seas, Ancient Greece, and the Orient. Occasionally he attempted more fully developed songs,

but generally he is remembered for his melodious ballads. Several cycles are available from Recital Publications Reprints, and Classical Vocal Reprints has many titles in its catalogue. Otherwise, except for the occasional song that turns up in an anthology, these are library items. (The Cadman *Album of Songs,* Ditson c1911, offers little of interest.) William Parker has recorded *Four American Indian Songs* on New World (213). Despite Cadman's former popularity, only a few songs from his huge output can be recommended. Practically all were published in several keys.

At Dawning, Nelle Richmond Eberhart; Ditson c1906.
    Pub. in four keys (high, e♭1–g2); 2:30; cantabile; this song's former 'hit' status is best explained by its straightforward, nostalgic melody;[4] recorded with long, lingering rallentandos by Mary Garden on New World (247), and by Thomas Hampson on EMI CD (7-540512).

Black Butterflies, Nelle Richmond Eberhart; Galaxy c1937; to Constance Eberhart.[5]
    Rec. high or medium lyric voices (b♭–g2); 2:15; Allegro non troppo; black butterflies, in Irish lore, signify "the blues;" rhythmic, sprightly, endearing; one of his best late works.

Four American Indian Songs, Nelle Richmond Eberhart; White-Smith c1909; pub. both separately and as a set.[6]
    Pub. high and low (low, d1–e2), some weight needed for the last song; 9:00; can be sung individually; straightforward and quite beautiful; recorded in entirety by Parker.
    From the Land of the Sky-blue Water, also incl. *AASTC;* (low d♭1–d♭2); 1:45; Con moto; a lilting, nostalgic melody; also recorded by Paul Sperry on Albany CD (TROY034-2).
    The White Dawn Is Stealing, (low, d1–d2); 2:00; With simplicity and lightness of tone.
    Far Off I Hear a Lover's Flute, (low, d1–d2); 2:45; Smoothly and softly; builds to a dramatic middle section.
    The Moon Drops Low, (low d1–e2); 2:30; Majestically, with great dignity; dramatic; also recorded by Jan DeGaetani on Elektra/Nonesuch CD (79248-2-ZK).

I Hear a Thrush at Eve (Serenade); Nelle Richmond Eberhart; Morris c1913.

Pub. high, medium, and low (high e_b1-a_b2); 1:45; Graziosa con anima; waltzlike; a charming ballad; requested by McCormick after the great success of *At Dawning.*

Idylls of the South Sea, Nelle Richmond Eberhart; Recital Pub. Reprint (high voice only); probably comp. 1912.

Pub. high and low (high, d#1–g#2); 9:00; titles are: *Where the Long White Waterfall; The Great Wind Shakes the Breadfruit; The Rainbow Waters Whisper; Withered is the Green Palm;* best kept as a cycle; a good example of Cadman's flair for exotic imagery.

O Moon Upon the Water, Nelle Richmond Eberhart; White-Smith c1915.

Pub. high, medium, and low (med., c1–f2), text suggests men; 1:30; Amabile con moto; a tasteful sentimental ballad.

Also of interest:

Sayonara: A Japanese Romance, Eberhart, Recital Pub. Reprint, a cycle for one or two voices; *Music of the American Indian,* a Bicentennial edition, includes drawings by George Catlin, a tribute to Cadman, reminiscences by Mrs. Eberhart, and nine songs, the first four of which comprise Cadman's second American Indian cycle, *From Wigwam and Tepee.*

BIBLIOGRAPHY

AmerGroves, Baker, Ewen, Greene, Howard, Thompson, Upton.
"Opportunities for the American Composer: A Conference with Charles Wakefield Cadman," *Etude* (November 1943).
"Charles Wakefield Cadman: An American Composer," *The Musician* (November 1915).

---

[1] Cadman published his first composition, the *Carnegie Library March,* himself, then sold it door to door.

[2] *The Moon Drops Low* (from *Four American Indian Songs*) immediately won a prize in a contest sponsored by the Carnegie Art Institute, and *From the Land of the Sky-Blue Water* (from the same cycle) was programmed by opera stars Lillian Nordica and Frances Alda.

[3] Garry O'Conner, *The Pursuit of Perfection: A Life of Maggie Teyte,* New York: Atheneum, 1979, 125–127. Teyte was one of the rare foreign singers who regularly performed American songs.

[4] The melody was so well known, it was parodied by Charles Ives in his song, *On the Counter.*

[5] Mrs. Eberhart's daughter, who sang.
[6] The original edition includes at the beginning of each song the Omaha or Iroquois tribal melody on which it is based.

JOHN CAGE
b. Sept. 5, 1912, Los Angeles, CA; d. Aug. 12, 1992, New York, NY

John Cage, who stands at the epicenter of the twentieth century's musical avant-garde, also wrote a choice handful of unconventional songs in a relatively conventional idiom.

The son of an inventor, Cage studied composition with Adolph Weiss, Arnold Schoenberg, and Henry Cowell. While employed as an accompanist in a dance studio, he inserted rubber bands, screws, and other objects among the strings to create percussive sounds, and developed what came to be known as the "prepared piano." In the early 1940s he moved to New York, where he collaborated with dancer/choreographer Merce Cunningham on a variety of radically innovative works. Since then he has worked in aleatory, multimedia, electronic, and other experimental idioms, including the one that brought him the greatest notoriety—silence.

THE SONGS
In most of his large vocal catalogue, Cage seeks to extend the possibilities for the voice, and, in so doing, takes it beyond the traditional perception of song. Often unaccompanied or employing electronics, his scores instruct the singer on how to produce certain sounds, phonetics, or fragments of text. One of the most popular of these is the colorful, aleatory *Aria*. But Cage also wrote several wholly lyrical songs that fit the traditional definition of art song. Though a few call for special effects, none are especially radical or difficult, and all are fresh and winsome. Joan La Barbara has recorded an album devoted to Cage's vocal works on New Albion CD (NA035CD), but with the exception of her precise, mesmerizing rendition of *Wonderful Widow*, it offers no art song. Meriel Dickinson has recorded *5 Songs for Contralto* on Unicorn (UN1-72017). The following are the best known of Cage's published songs for voice and piano.

5 Songs for Contralto, E. E. Cummings; Henmar c1960; comp. 1938.
     Spec. contralto (g♭–f♯2), rec. lyric lower voices; 9:00;[1] titles are: *little four paws; little Christmas tree; in Just-; hist whist; Tumbling*

hair; despite the low tessitura, the lightness of the vocal writing makes this set possible for many voices; atonal; frequently changing meters cause some rhythmic complexities; spare textures; no dynamic markings but *piano* is clearly intended; the last song is sustained and slow; the first four are lyrical and fluent; a wonderful set, which perfectly complements Cummings's magical imagery; recorded by Dickinson.

The Wonderful Widow of Eighteen Springs, James Joyce; Peters c1961.
    Rec. all voices (key is optional; tessitura should be comfortable); 2:30; instructions given by the composer; moderate tempo; employing just three pitches the vibratoless vocal line (as in folksinging) is intoned over intricate rhythmic patterns tapped with fingers and knuckles on various areas of a closed piano; some difficult ensemble; generally hushed, but becomes quite agitated as it builds to the central climax; a long, slow vocal glissando at the end; despite its seemingly unaffected and simple expression, this song is highly sophisticated, abounding in nuance, invention, and inner intensity; a spellbinding moment on any program.

Also of interest:
A Flower, no words, sustained vibratoless vocalizing over closed piano, some nonmusical sounds; *Nowth upon nacht,* a difficult Joyce text intoned (like a town crier) on a high pitch, at full dynamic strength, over the vibrations of a banged piano lid; written later than, but intended to be paired with, *The Wonderful Widow of Eighteen Springs.*

BIBLIOGRAPHY
AmerGroves, Baker, CBY (1961), Ewen, Greene, Manning (on *A Flower* and *Wonderful Widow*), Thompson.

---

[1] This timing is taken from Dickinson's recording which closely follows metronome markings; the score itself indicates 12:00.

LOUIS CALABRO
b. Nov. 1, 1926, New York, NY

A student of Vincent Persichetti at the Juilliard School, in 1955 Calabro joined the faculty at Bennington College in Vermont. His compositions are primarily instrumental, but include numerous works for chorus. His one published solo song cycle demonstrates a solid command of the vocal idiom and is highly recommended.

Macabre Reflections, Howard Nemerov; Elkan-Vogel c1969; *Each a Rose* and *It Is Forbidden* are also incl. *CAAS;* comp. 1956; for my wife Leontina.

Spec. mezzo-soprano (g♭–g2); 16:00; titles are: *The Ground Swayed; The Officer; Each a Rose; No More Than Dust; It Is Forbidden; The Sunlight Pierced;* in a generally low tessitura; incisive and expressive declamation with glissandos and whispering; illustrative piano ideas; interesting color and sonorities; atonal with an effective interplay of consonance and dissonance; wonderful invention within a conventional framework; reflections (witty, ironic, deadly serious) on disease and death; dramatic and somewhat theatrical; without being especially difficult, this is a solidly crafted, imaginative, strong contemporary work.

BIBLIOGRAPHY
Baker.

LOUIS CAMPBELL-TIPTON
b. Nov. 21, 1877, Chicago, IL; d. May 1, 1921, Paris, France

He left two operas and some orchestral works, but Campbell-Tipton's reputation was built on smaller forms, including a good number of luxuriant and rather unusual songs.

Campbell-Tipton abandoned an interest in law to study music. His education began in Chicago and Boston, then continued in Leipzig, Germany, where he worked with Carl Reinecke. After teaching at the Chicago Musical College (1901-1904), he and has wife settled in France where he taught and composed until his early death after a brief illness.

THE SONGS
Critics and performers of the time were respectful, even enthusiastic about the youthful Campbell-Tipton. Today many of his songs seem dated, but *Memory* certainly has a timeless beauty, and a few other songs have imagination and excitement. More often than not, however, they are encumbered by a surfeit of long vocal lines, sustained high notes, sweeping arpeggios, changing tonalities and dynamics, and opulent harmonies dripping with chromaticism. Heard in quantity, the songs wear thin, but one or two could be a real bonus in an American group.

Campbell-Tipton was especially drawn to the sensuous texts of the English symbolist poet, Arthur Symons (who was also beguiled by France), and to the mystical, exuberant celebrations of Walt Whitman. Most, probably because of Campbell-Tipton's firm belief in translation as well as his association with France, offer French translations. Dramatic voices, especially tenors,[1] show themselves and the songs to best advantage. Following are a few of the most notable.

Elegy, Walt Whitman; Boston c1918.
Pub. high and low (high, c#1–f#2[b2]), rec. bigger voices; 2:30; Moderato; subdued opening builds to an appassionato; ends quietly and contemplatively.

Four Sea Lyrics, Arthur Symons; Recital Pub. Reprint; also incl. *WW(5);* comp. 1907; written for and dedicated to George Hamlin.
Pub. high voice (d1–a2), best for tenors; 9:15; French translations provided; sea imagery and some common thematic material make these strong as a group, but they can be used individually; exceedingly demanding vocally.
After Sunset, also inc. *AASTC;* (d#1–a2); 2:15; Andante espressivo; tranquil, lyrical.
Darkness, (d1–a2); 2:30; Allegro Moderato – Andante misterioso; much hefty singing.
The Crying of Water, also incl. *NAAS;* also pub. for low voice (high, f#1–g#2); 2:00; Moderato ma con passione; long, sustained phrases and high notes; most popular of the set.
Requies, (e1–a2); 2:30; Andante; big singing but ends quietly.

Memory (A Miniature), Arthur Symons; G. Schirmer c1907.
Rec. all medium voices (d#1–d#2); 1:45; Andante espressivo; sustained over flowing arpeggios; hushed dynamics throughout; uses only a fragment of the poem; simpler in materials and on a much smaller scale than other Campbell-Tipton songs; a jewel.

The Opium-Smoker (Tone Poem), Arthur Symons; G. Schirmer c1907.
Rec. bigger medium voices (c1–f#2); 3:15; Allegro molto; aided by a variety of ecstatic piano figures (characterizing the effects of smoking opium), the singer expounds in lurching phrases; then, a quasi recitative as he deals with the terrible reality of his poor life; ends impassioned *fff*; despite some weaknesses, evocative and unusual.

Rhapsodie, Walt Whitman; G. Schirmer c1913.
> Pub. high and low voices (high, d1–a2), rec. dramatic voices; 2:00; Very fast, with joyous abandon; explosive phrases surge out of the charged accompaniment; some sustained high notes; big dynamics; requires undaunting brilliance from both performers to be effective.

The Spirit Flower, B. Martin Stanton; G. Schirmer c1908.
> Pub. in many keys (high, d♭1–a2); 2:00; Moderato; sustained; syrupy, but one of the most performed songs of its time.

BIBLIOGRAPHY
AmerGroves, Baker, Howard, Hughes, Thompson, Upton.
"Instruction at Home Advocated by American Composer Abroad," *Musical America,* March 21, 1914. This lengthy interview elicits Cambell-Tipton's interesting ideas on such matters as vocal study, Americans abroad, translation, and diction.

---

[1] Several were composed for tenor George Hamlin, who performed them with great success.

JOHN ALDEN CARPENTER
b. Feb. 28, 1876, Park Ridge, IL; d. April 26, 1951, Chicago, IL

By throwing off the yoke of German influence John Alden Carpenter became one of the first to lighten the fabric of American music. His catalogue, which primarily favors French impressionism, but also incorporates popular American materials, includes a sizable number of superb songs.

Born into a wealthy, aristocratic family, Carpenter was named for his famous ancestor, the pilgrim John Alden. Though he was expected to follow his father into the family transportation supply business, his mother, a serious amateur singer,[1] began to teach him music at the age of five. After further studies in piano and theory, Carpenter entered Harvard University, where he studied music with John Knowles Paine and, in 1897, graduated with highest honors. Returning to Chicago, he became a junior partner, and later a vice-president, in George B. Carpenter & Co. Though he never neglected the business, he did manage to study briefly with Edward Elgar in Rome and, from 1908 to 1912, with the theorist Bernard Ziehn in Chicago.

Carpenter's early works, especially the song cycle *Gitanjali* and the witty orchestral suite *Adventures in a Perambulator,* were well received. Embarking on a major career in music he went on to garner numerous awards and honors, and on his 60th birthday finally retired from business to devote himself to composition. Carpenter was married in 1900 to Rue Winterbotham,[2] with whom he had a daughter. When Rue died after 31 years of marriage, he married Ellen Waller Borden.

THE SONGS

Carpenter composed a vigorous, highly diverse catalogue of over 50 songs, of which a good percentage rank with the best. Clearly his first love, the idiom perfectly suited his innate cultivation and refinement. He had excellent taste in poetry and such a natural, fluid way with text that in his best settings— especially the exquisite songs on nature themes— each poem manifests its singularity as if music and words had been written as one.

Though most are published in only one voice range, determining which voice category is suitable for a particular song is not always easy. Many are designated for medium voice, but are often too high or low for a true medium voice. Generally speaking, lower voices work best. The beautiful, evocative accompaniments can be demanding. According to contralto Mina Hager, who sang Carpenter's songs and worked with him personally, he was an exciting and unusual pianist.[3] Masters Music Publications has reprinted *Water-Colors* and *Eight Songs for Medium Voice (8S),* and Classical Vocal Reprints has many Carpenter songs in its catalogue. Alexandra Hunt has recorded *Gitanjali* on Orion (ORS 77272). Other miscellaneous recordings are noted below. The following is a selection of both recommended and well known songs.

Berceuse de Guerre (A War Lullaby), Emile Cammaerts; G. Schirmer c1918.
> Rec. medium or low women's voices (c1–g2); 5:00; in French; a monologue, almost operatic in scope, about World War I; while a storm rages the mother, filled with foreboding, visualizes her husband in the trenches; the lullaby she attempts is broken by agitated parlando musings which eventually swell into powerful outpourings of dread; original and affecting; one of Carpenter's best.

The Day Is No More, Rabindranath Tagore[4] ("Gitanjali" No. 74);[5] G. Schirmer c1915; comp. 1914.

Rec. medium and low voices (g#–d#2); 3:30; Larghetto; the lovely, melancholy vocal line could almost be sung by a high voice but
for four measures that plummet below the staff; subdued dynamics;
highly atmospheric.

Don't Ceäre, William Barnes; G. Schirmer c1912; also incl. *8S.*
Rec. medium voices (c1–d2), text suggests man; 2:00; in
Dorsetshire dialect; Animato Giocoso; while the voice tells the story,
the piano makes merry and steals the show.

Four Negro Songs, Langston Hughes; G. Schirmer c1927; pub. separately.
Rec. lower voices (a–f2); 7:00; titles are: *Shake your brown feet
honey; The Cryin' Blues; Jazz-Boys; That Soothin Song;* can be used
individually; in dialect; a pioneering work in the use of jazz and blues
in serious song; *Jazz Boys* is recorded by Donald Gramm on Desto
(411/412).

Four Poems by Paul Verlaine, G. Schirmer c1912; pub. separately.
Voice type varies with each song (b–f#2); in French, with English
translations; all but *Chanson D'Automne* are recorded by Yolanda
Marcoulescou on Orion (OC 685).
Il pleure dans mon coeur (The tears fall in my heart).
Rec. medium voices (d1–d2); 2:00; Modéré; steady eighths; hushed,
evocative.
Chanson d'Automne (Song of Autumn).
Pub. low voices (b–c#2); 2:00; Lent et grave; generally sustained over
chords; hushed and atmospheric.
Le Ciel (The Sky).
Rec. lyric medium or high voices (c#1–f#2); 3:15; Lent; a central
anguished climax; bleak; spare; haunting; recorded by
Marcoulescou under the title *Le Prison.*[6]
Dansons la Gigue! (Let's Dance the jig).
Rec. lower voices (b–e2), text suggests men; 2:15; Mouvementé,
light.

Gitanjali (Song-Offerings), Rabindranath Tagore; G. Schirmer c1914;
comp. 1913.
Rec. medium or high voices (b–g2); 19:00; each "an entity within
itself—a philosophical expression...,"[7] these songs need not be kept
as a cycle; romantic, rich in harmonic color; ample in vocal line; dif-

ficult; though *Gitanjali* is his most famous vocal work, it seems more
dated than much other Carpenter; recorded by Hunt.

When I bring to you colour'd toys, also incl. in *CAS28* and *AASTC;*
(c#1–f#2); 2:15; Animato; a beguiling, flowing melody; Carpenter's most popular song; also recorded by Rose Bampton on New
World (247), John Hanks on Duke Vol. 1 (DWR 6417), and
Conchita Supervia on Pearl CD (9969).

On the day when death will knock at thy door, (c1–f2); 3:15; Grave
maestoso, declamatory and lyrical; some big singing.

The Sleep that flits on Baby's Eyes, also incl. *50AS,* (b–f#2); 2:30;
Lento; più mosso sections; subdued, quiet; also recorded by
Yolanda Marcoulescou on Gasparo CD (287).

I am like a Remnant of a Cloud of Autumn, (b♭–f2); big voices
required; 3:45; Grave; declamatory; often very grand.

On the Seashore of Endless Worlds, (c1–f#2); 5:00; Andantino, con
moto grazioso; gentler but building to some big climaxes; difficult
to sustain; also recorded by Yolanda Marcoulescou on Gasparo
CD (287).

Light, My Light, (e1–g2); big voices only; 3:00; Carpenter indicates
Presto giocoso, but do not be fooled. "Perhaps archangelic voices
might cope with its long-drawn trumpet-like phrases, but no earth-
ly voice should attempt these soaring flights!"[8] Also recorded by
Rose Bampton on New World (247).

Go, Lovely Rose, Edmund Waller; G. Schirmer c1912; also incl. *8S.*
Rec. lyric voices (d♭1–e♭2), text suggests man; 2:15; Larghetto
grazioso, metronome marking seems slow; a charming parlando
melody over delicate, fluid triplets; chordal middle section; an especially graceful rendition of this oft set poem.

The Green River, Lord Alfred Douglas; G. Schirmer c1912; also incl.
8S.
Rec. medium voices (b–e2); 4:00; Slowly; the hushed spare recitative-like opening takes on color and motion, then tapers to close *ppp;*
subtle and poetic; an exquisite, magical song.

Little Fly, William Blake; G. Schirmer c1912; also incl. *8S.*
Rec. medium voices (c1–d♭2); 1:00; Allegretto grazioso; a consideration of a man's life in relation to that of a fly; a curious little
song, but it works.

Looking-Glass River, Robert Louis Stevenson; G. Schirmer c1912. comp. 1909; also incl. *8S, NAAS,* and *AASTC.*

Rec. medium and lower voices (b–d2); 2:15; Largo; the languid vocal line describes the smooth sliding river over lazily flowing eighths; a wonderful, atmospheric song; superbly recorded by Donald Gramm on Desto (411/412).

Morning Fair (Sonnet XX), James Agee; G. Schirmer c1936; also incl. *RAAS;* comp. 1935.

Rec. higher voices (c#1–g#2); 4:45; Moderato; this beautiful invocation to the dawn calls for both full throated singing and controlled lyricism; difficult; somewhat romantic; rich in nuance and ideas.

The Player Queen, William Butler Yeats (from an unfinished play); G. Schirmer c1915.

Rec. medium or high voices (d♭1–f#2); 4:00; Lento (but seems moderato); lilting and ballad-like; five stanzas; the third builds to a stunning climax; eerie ending; mystical, haunting, and different; recorded by Elizabeth Suderburg on OLY (104).

Les Silhouettes, Oscar Wilde; G. Schirmer c1913; also incl. *AASTC.*

Spec. medium voices (c1–g2), rec. higher voices; 2:15; Largo mistico; in English; constantly changing moods and images; difficult musically and vocally; a beautiful and unusual seascape.

Watercolors (Four Chinese Tone Poems), Chinese poems (5th to 10th centuries); G. Schirmer c1916; reprint by Master Music c1992; various dedications.

Rec. medium, light voices (b♭–f2); 7:00; titles are: *On a Screen; The Odalisque; Highwaymen; To a Young Gentleman;* though not really a cycle, definitely a set with each complementing the others; lyrical declamation, occasionally tuneful, over gossamer accompaniments; light Oriental flavor; highly impressionistic, deft miniatures.[9]

When the Misty Shadows Glide (En Sourdine), Paul Verlaine (trans. by Carpenter); Ditson c1912.

Rec. medium and high voices but pub. in two keys which seem incorrectly specified as low and medium (medium, c1–f2; low, a–d2); 3:45; Slowly and in pensive mood; can be sung in English or French; very sustained over chords; a lovely song.

Also of interest:

Bid Me to Live, Herrick, also incl. *8S,* Lento, in the lieder tradition; **Serenade** (from *Two Night Songs*), Sassoon, also incl. in *S22A* and *RAS,* Moderato, a big song, recorded by Marcoulescou on Gasparo CD (287); **Young Man, Chieften!** (An Indian Prayer), Austin, Lento maestoso, unusual.

BIBLIOGRAPHY

AmerGroves, Baker, CBY (1947), Ewen, Goss, Greene, Hall, Howard, Nathan, Thompson; Thorpe (on *Serenade*), Upton, Upton (Sup).

Borowski, Felix. "John Alden Carpenter," *Musical Quarterly* 16 (October 1930): 449–468.

Downes, Olin. "J. A. Carpenter, American Craftsman," *Musical Quarterly* 16 (October 1930): 443–448.

Hager, Mina. "Speak for Yourself, John Alden Carpenter," *Music Journal* 28 (March 1970).

Howard, John Tasker. "John Alden Carpenter," *Modern Music* 9 (1931–1932): 8–16.

---

[1] The mother of four sons, Elizabeth Carpenter had studied abroad with renowned voice teachers: William Shakespeare in London and Mathilde Marchesi in Paris.

[2] A kindred artistic spirit, Rue wrote and illustrated *Improving Songs for Anxious Children* and *When Little Boys Sing,* two of Carpenter's earliest works.

[3] Mina Hager, "Speak for Yourself, John Alden Carpenter," *Music Journal,* 67.

[4] Rabindranath Tagore (1861-1941), perhaps the most important poet and philosopher of modern India, won the Nobel Prize in literature for *Gitanjali: Song Offering* in 1913. He was also a musician and composer .

[5] This song is totally separate from the cycle *Gitanjali.* There are over 100 poems in the Tagore collection.

[6] *Le prison* is one of several titles for this song, which was also set by Debussy, Faure, and Hahn.

[7] Edwin McArthur, liner notes for *Songs by Carpenter, Griffes and MacDowell* (ORS 77272).

[8] William Treat Upton, *Art-Song in America,* 211.

[9] According to David Mason Greene *(Greene's Biographical Encyclopedia of Composers, 958),* a recording was once made by Mina Hager with Carpenter at the piano.

ELLIOT CARTER
b. Dec. 11, 1908, New York, NY

The intensely complex, intellectual idiom with which Elliot Carter's name is generally associated is nowhere to be found in his five warmly lyrical art songs.

He was expected to join his father in the import business, but Carter's passion for music was too strong. After graduate studies with, among others, Walter Piston and Gustav Holst at Harvard University, he spent three years in Paris with Nadia Boulanger. Carter's own teaching includes positions at Columbia University, the Peabody Conservatory, the Juilliard School, Cornell University, and the American University in Rome. In 1960 and, again, in 1971 he was awarded the Pulitzer Prize, each time for a string quartet.

THE SONGS
Carter's few art songs all date from the early 1940s. Their language reflects his traditional schooling, but their energy and invention is pure Carter, and the American texts perfectly suit his forthright, individualistic style. Meriel Dickinson has recorded all Carter's songs (except *Warble for Lilac Time*) on Unicorn (UN1-72017). Other recordings of the Frost settings are noted below.[1] All published songs for voice and piano are listed.

Three Poems of Robert Frost, Associated c1947; comp. 1942; *Dust of Snow* and *The Rose Family,* both of which are also incl. *AAS,* were originally pub. separately.
>   Rec. medium voices (b–f#2); 4:15; best as a set although *Line Gang*, lacking the charm of the other two, is often excluded; all very different, but with their shared vigor and appealing freshness, they all have an American ring; not difficult in any way; recorded in entirety by Dickinson; *Dust of Snow* and *Rose Family* by DeGaetani on Elektra/Nonesuch CD (79248-2-ZK).

Dust of Snow, (d1–e2); 1:00; Allegro; slower final section; the contrast of long, sustained, lush vocal lines over an active, dry, jazzy accompaniment creates an unusual effect.

The Rose Family, (eb1–f2); 1:30; Allegretto, con moto; some fun made about Gertrude Stein's famous definition of a rose; light and lyrical.

The Line Gang, (b–f#2); 1:45; Vigorously (fast quarters); declamatory; chordal.

Voyage, Hart Crane; Associated c1973; comp. 1945; to Hope and John
Kirkpatrick.

Spec. medium voices (c#1–g2); 5:15; Andante espressivo; a faster
more dramatic central section and a hushed, slower final section;
long, sustained phrases; a love song with complex symbolism; intimate; intense; recorded by Dickinson.

Warble for Lilac Time, Walt Whitman; Peer c1956; comp. 1943.

Rec. big high voices ([c1]bb–a2); 7:00; Vivace; lyrical over waves
of rolling triplets; a stark, chordal, slow central section; opulent voices, capable of both long legato lines and quick, pliant, parlando passages, are required to ride the full-bodied accompaniment; tedious if
attention is not paid to the many gradations of tempo and dynamics;
a stirring paean to spring, nature, and remembrance.

BIBLIOGRAPHY
AmerGroves, Baker, CBY (1960), Greene, Manning (on Frost settings),
Nathan, Thompson.

---

[1] Various singers also recorded vocal works composed by Carter from 1975 to
1981 on Bridge CD (9014). Though all are with instruments, the recording
includes a 1980 arrangement of the Frost settings with orchestra.

GEORGE W. CHADWICK
b. Nov. 13, 1854, Lowell, MA; d. April 4, 1931, Boston, MA

As an educator, administrator, conductor, organist, and leading composer of the Second New England School,[1] George Chadwick was a
commanding figure on the late nineteenth- and early twentieth-century
American music scene. Today his symphonies have found new favor,
but many of his large catalogue of songs, though once very popular, are
either flawed or dated.

His mother died just days after his birth, leaving Chadwick to be
cared for by his grandparents. When his father remarried, the family
reunited and, in 1860, moved to Lawrence, Massachusetts, where the
elder Chadwick founded a successful insurance company. Chadwick
first learned piano from an older brother. Later, he commuted to Boston,
where he was a special student at the New England Conservatory. In
1877, after briefly heading the music department at Olivet College in
Michigan, he joined the exodus of young Americans to the music capi-

tals of Europe. There, he studied with Karl Heinrich Reinecke and Salomon Jadassohn in Leipzig, and Josef Rheinberger in Munich.

In 1882, two years after opening a studio in Boston, Chadwick joined the faculty of the New England Conservatory of Music. In 1897 he became its director (a position he held until his retirement in the year of his death) and built it into a musical institution able to compete with those in Europe. In addition, he wrote textbooks on music, directed major festivals at Springfield and Worcester, and taught many of the young composers who would achieve recognition at the turn-of-the-century.[2] His own compositions, usually written while summering on Martha's Vineyard, were performed repeatedly, often under his own baton. Chadwick was married in 1885 and had two sons.

THE SONGS

Generally speaking, Chadwick's many songs[3] are more sophisticated and artistic than the quaint dallyings associated with the period. The wide assortment ranges from those inspired by the nineteenth century lieder tradition to comic songs, ballads, and quasi folk settings. There is much to like about many of them, not the least of which are the beautiful melodies and inventive accompaniments. Moreover, despite his advocacy of the German and French schools, his infectious rhythms (he was crazy about syncopations) and sense of humor have a genuine American flavor. However, many songs suffer from inferior, old-fashioned poetry and, not withstanding his considerable experience with opera and choral music, clumsy vocal writing. In some of the bigger ones especially, extreme fluctuations of tessitura, unwieldy intervals, and quirky prosody are all too frequent. Fully trained voices, occasionally of operatic proportions, are often required. The important Arlo Bates cycles *(A Flower Cycle* and *Told in the Gate)* are available in a fine reprint edition from Da Capo. Classical Vocal Reprints includes several songs in its catalogue, and some appear in anthologies; others in various Chadwick albums of the period, in particular, *Song Album: 15 Songs for Soprano or Tenor by George Chadwick (SA15)*. Three songs are recorded by Paul Sperry on Albany CD (TROY034-2). The following is a representative sampling.

Allah, H. W. Longfellow; Schmidt c1887; also incl *SA15*.
    Pub. high and low (high, c#1–g#2); 1:30; Serioso; in a moderate tempo; a warm melody; straightforward and dignified; an appreciation of Allah's goodness.

A Ballad of Trees and the Master, Sidney Lanier; Ditson c1927; comp.
1899.

    Pub. high, medium, and low (med., a–f2); 2:45; Moderato alla
Marcia; sustained, in a generally low tessitura; militant and chordal;
central lyrical section; an impressive climax followed by a subdued
ending; winner of the *Musical Record* competition in 1899, one of the
most famous sacred songs of the period and a favorite on concert
stages as well.[4]

Bedouin Love Song, Bayard Taylor; Schmidt c1890.

    Pub. high and low (high, b–a2), best for men; 1:45; Animato assai;
robust singing over a big accompaniment; dynamic changes and an
effective central *Maestoso assai* have the interest in this vigorous
period-piece.

La Danza, Op. 14, No. 1, Arlo Bates; Schmidt c1885; also incl. *AASTC*
and *SA15.*

    Pub. high and low (high, f1–g2 [b♭2]), considered a man's song
because of text but traditionally sung by anyone with a strong voice
and plenty of stamina; 2:00; Allegretto grazioso; high tessitura; like
a Spanish dance; an exuberant song with a catchy tune; recorded by
Sperry.

A Flower Cycle, Arlo Bates; Schmidt c1892; reprint Da Capo c1980.

    Spec. different voices; lyrics generally best; 13 songs with flower
titles, of which *The Trilliums; The WaterLily; The Cyclamen; The
Cardinal Flower;* and *The Jacqueminot Rose* are preferred; a cycle in
name only; songs could be sung individually or in groups; most are
strophic and, as the titles would indicate, pretty in a quaint way; far
less interesting than Chadwick's other collaboration with Bates—
Lyrics from "Told in the Gate."

Lyrics from "Told in the Gate," Arlo Bates; Schmidt c1897; reprinted
Da Capo c1980.

    Orig. pub. high and low, but the Da Capo reprint is only for low
voice;[5] though some of the texts indicate gender, the songs are too
old-fashioned to warrant any concern about that issue; Chadwick
probably envisioned the cycle for two, or even three singers alternating; too long to program in entirety, but a good selection could be
made; some are prime Chadwick; based on Persian themes at the time
of Omar Khayyam.

Sweetheart, thy lips are touched with flame, (c1–f2[g2]); 2:15;
   Molto appassionato; sweeping vocal lines; big song.

Sings the nightingale to the rose, (b–e2); 2:30; Andante con moto;
   quaint.

The rose leans over the pool, (b–e2); 2:00; Scherzando; charming
   syncopations; graceful; a good song.

Love's like a summer rose, (b–e2); 2:00; Andantino; traditional.

As in waves without number, (a–f2); 2:30; Molto moderato e
   sostenuto; an ample voice is needed to sustain the rich melodic
   line as it builds to a *ff* ending; flawed but with beautiful moments.

Dear love, when in thine arms, (bb–f2); 2:30; Larghetto, Molto
   espressivo; hymnlike.

Was I not thine, (bb–eb2); 1:30; Andante maestoso; the straightforward opening becomes increasingly opulent.

In mead where roses bloom, (a–e2); Moderato e mesto; 1:30; a dialogue with a rose.

Sister fairest, why art thou sighing, (c1–f2); 1:45; Andante and
   Allegro agitato; dialogue.

Oh, let night speak of me, (c1–f2); 1:30; Molto moderato; warm;
   lyrical; a lovely song; recorded by John Hanks on Duke, Vol. 1
   (DWR 6417).

I said to the wind of the south, (g–e2); 2:15; Allegretto con moto;
   brightly moving and slower, sustained sections alternate.

Were I a prince Egyptian, (bb–f2); 1:45; Andante moderato; this
   poem was not part of the original Bates narrative.

Nocturne, Thomas Bailey Aldrich; Schmidt c1886; also incl. *SA15*.
   Rec. high voices, tenors best (c1–a2); 1:30; Con moto; an arching
   melody in a high tessitura; briefly impassioned; happy and winsome.

When stars are in the quiet skies, Bulwer Lytton, Schmidt c1910.
   Pub. high and low (high, c1–gb2), text suggests men; 4:15; Molto
   tranquillo; sustained, warmly lyric; contemplative; expansive.

Also of interest:

Before the Dawn, Andante con tenerezza; **Euthanasia,** Macy, from *Six
Songs,* incl. *SIA,* Lusinghiero, recorded by Sperry; **In My Belovèd's
Eyes,** Chauvenet, incl. *AASGS,* Adagio espressivo; **The Maiden and the
Butterfly,** incl. *LF1,* Capriccioso e semplice; **Song from the Persian,**
Aldrich, incl. *SA15,* Andante con sentimento, high tessitura.

BIBLIOGRAPHY

AmerGroves, Baker, Ewen, Greene, Hall, Hughes, Stevens, Tawa, Thompson, Upton.

Engel, Carl. "George W. Chadwick." *Musical Quarterly* 10 (July 1924): 438–57.

Ledbetter, Steven. Introduction to *George Chadwick: Songs to Poems by Arlo Bates*. New York: Da Capo Press, 1980.

Yellin, Victor Fell. "Chadwick, American Musical Realist." *Musical Quarterly* 61 (January 1975): 77–97.

————. *Chadwick: Yankee Composer*. Washington and London: Smithsonian Institution Press, 1990.

---

[1] The Second New England School refers to the many classicist composers who were centered in the Boston area in the late nineteenth century. Chief among them were John Knowles Paine, Daniel Gregory Mason, Parker, Foote, Beach, and Chadwick. The First New England School refers to the composers of the late eighteenth century singing schools.

[2] Parker, who became a lifelong friend, was one of his first students. Hadley, Homer, Daniel Gregory Mason, Edward Burlingame Hill, Shepherd, and Farwell are but a few who followed.

[3] *The New Grove Dictionary of American Music* lists 137 songs.

[4] In an article "Von Warlich discovers 'The Best American Song'" *Musical America,* Nov. 23, 1912, the Russian baritone effusively recommends this song, commending Chadwick on his restraint.

[5] All ranges given are for the low version used in the Da Capo reprint edition.

THEODORE CHANLER
b. April 29, 1902; Newport, RI; d. July 27, 1961, Boston, MA

He wrote little else, but Theodore Chanler's handful of songs are prized as masterpieces of the genre—"probably the best we have," Virgil Thomson wrote.[1]

Though born in Rhode Island, Chanler grew up in western New York. His parents were wealthy and cultivated. His mother, whose career aspirations as a pianist had been thwarted by her Victorian parents, would later author various books. A Roman Catholic, she brought up their eight children, of whom Theodore was the youngest, liberally, but in the Church. Chanler studied music in a desultory fashion until 1920 when, just as he was about to enter Harvard University, he met Ernest Bloch. Inspired by the composer, Chanler followed him to Cleveland where Bloch was director of the Institute of Music. After three years studying with Bloch, to appease his parents Chanler attended Oxford University for two years. During this time, however, and until 1928, he also studied intermittently with Nadia Boulanger in Paris. Then, for several years, he hardly composed. Remaining in Paris, he married Maria de Acosta Sargent in 1931 and, two years later, returned to the United States. Finally, crediting the Catholic Church, marriage, and music for helping him out of his "coma,"[2] in 1935 he began to compose again. Chanler's *Eight Epitaphs* was performed at the Library of Congress in 1937 and, in 1940, his *Four Rhymes from Peacock Pie* won the League of Composers Town Hall Award. He continued to compose, primarily setting the poetry of his friend Father Leonard Feeney,[3] until the late 1940s. After that, other than a chamber opera, *The Pot of Fat,* he wrote little.

Chanler was also a regular contributor to the journal, *Modern Music,* and, for a brief time, a critic for the *Boston Herald.* From 1945 to 1947 he was on the faculty of the Peabody Conservatory. Then, making his home in Cambridge, Massachusetts, he taught at the Longy School of Music until his early retirement due to illness.

THE SONGS

Even the slightest of Chanler's approximately 30 published songs are noteworthy. Gossamer lightness masks their tidy precision and scrupulous craftsmanship. Melodies flow like musical speech with prosody so artless as to seem unremarkable. Only the rather sentimental and precious rhymes of Leonard Feeney diminish their excellence.

Though, with their clear-eyed candor and infectious rhythms, Chanler's songs seem wholly American, his training and proclivity were French (Fauré was his model), and one is struck, above all, by their intimacy and refined lyricism. They are totally out of place in a large hall, for communication between performer and listener must be direct, personal, and immediate. With rare exception vocal lines are in the middle range, but a lush voice will not be comfortable if the singer cannot temper his or her instrument. Higher voices, in fact, often work well because their middle ranges are not so ample. The clean look of the elegant, often independent, piano writing is deceptive because much of it requires technical dexterity. Musical difficulties, except for occasional shifting meters, are modest. But musicality, precision, and care for detail are essential to retain the lucidity of Chanler's concentrated expression. *Eight Epitaphs* are recorded by Glenda Maurice on Etcetera CD (KTC

1099), Sanford Sylvan on Elektra Nonesuch CD (9 79259-2), and Phyllis
Curtin on Columbia (AMS 6198);[4] *Four Rhymes from 'Peacock Pie'* is
recorded by William Parker on New World (300); other miscellany by
Paul Sperry on Albany CD (TROY043-2), and Donald Gramm and
Bethany Beardslee on New World (243). Virtually all Chanler's pub-
lished songs are listed.

The Children, Leonard Feeney; G. Schirmer c1946; comp. 1945.
    Spec. medium voices (c1–g2); 15:00; good variety; despite the
rather insipid poems, which mostly give the child's point of view,
these songs are fresh and charming; a bit too long and insubstantial to
perform as a whole, but smaller groups could provide a welcome
change on a serious program.
The Children, (d1–f2); 1:00; Allegro; tuneful with a swinging pulse;
    recorded by Gramm.
Once Upon a Time, (c1–f2); 1:45; Moderato; parlando; recorded by
    Gramm.
Wind, (c1–g2); 1:30; Animato; spirited.
Sleep, (c#1–f2); 2:30; Andante; short sustained phrases over softly
    flowing sixteenths.
The Rose, (c1–f#2); 2:30; Lento; sustained; recorded by Gramm, and
    by John McCollum on Desto (411/412).
Grandma, (c1–f2); 1:30; Allegro; waltz-like.
Spick and Span, (d1–f2); 0:30; Lento moderato; staccatos.
Moo Is a Cow, (d♭1–f2); 2:45; Allegretto; bright and moving; an
    optional lower obbligato vocal part, which would require another
    singer, is included; recorded by Gramm, who uses electronic
    devices to sing as a duet with himself.
One of Us, (c1–f2); 1:45; Molto lento; sustained over chords; serious,
    quiet.

The Doves, Leonard Feeney; Hargail c1946; comp. 1935.
    Rec. higher voices (c1–f2); 2:00; Allegretto molto moderato; tes-
situra sits a little high; sustained over a light, vamping, staccato piano;
a lovely, wistful song; recorded by Sperry.

Eight Epitaphs, Walter de la Mare; Arrow c1939; ass. to Boosey c1956;
    comp. 1937; to Israel Citkowitz.
    Rec. medium voices (b–f2);[5] 11:45. This exquisite cycle set to de
la Mare's imaginary gravestone inscriptions is widely considered to
be both Chanler's masterpiece and a masterpiece of the repertoire. De

la Mare and Chanler bring the odd, lovable characters so vividly back to life that, at the end of a good performance, the silence in the hall is palpable. The songs are varied and colorful, but the spare melodies and chaste harmonies are daring in their restraint. They are not as easy as they appear, requiring control, sensitive musicianship, and careful attention to detail. Though it is often done, it is better not to extract any of these songs; its perfectly balanced cyclic form, from the introspective lyricism of the opening through the very active character sketches of the middle, and finally the gradual pulling back until time seems suspended, is a major component of its greatness; recorded by Curtin, Sylvan, and Maurice.

Alice Rodd, Non troppo lento; a mournful triplet figure in the piano intertwines with the poignant declamation.

Susannah Fry, Lento; a tender, lyrical recitative in dialogue with the piano.

Three Sisters, Molto vivace; a straightforward description of the busy life of the spinsters, depicted in the piano with all manner of rapid scale patterns.

Thomas Logge, Allegro assai, alla burla; a scherzo riddled with meter changes; a wild, disjointed piano part; also recorded by Gramm.

A Midget, Molto moderato; the staccato, ostinato-like bass depicts the walk of the little man, lovingly described in the lightly declaimed melody. Since Chanler reworked this song after it was first published, two versions exist.

"No Voice to Scold," Tranquillo; lyrical.

Ann Poverty, Un poco più Andante.

"Be Very Quiet Now," Largo; spare chords; perfect quietude.

The Flight, Leonard Feeney; Associated c1948; comp. 1944.

Rec. medium voices (c1–g2); 3:45; Allegro moderato; lyric declamation over fluid sixteenths; the story, with some dialogue, of the angel's warning for Joseph to escape Herod's decree; the continually shifting meters, though difficult for the singer, add to the feeling of urgency and suspense; strange, yet quite effective.

Four Rhymes from Peacock Pie, Walter de la Mare; Associated c1948; comp. 1940.

Rec. medium voices (b–f#2); 5:00; tessitura on the higher side; not difficult; these delightful songs are best as a set but can be used individually; recorded by Parker.

The Ship of Rio, (b–f#2); 1:15; Allegro vivace; a jaunty ballad over
rippling sixteenths.

Old Shellover, (e♭1–f♭2); 1:15; Andante con moto; lyrical and quiet.

Cake and Sack, (e♭1–f2); 1:00; Allegretto; light and delicate.

Tillie, (d1–f#2); 1:30; Waltz; light and graceful.

I Rise When You Enter, Leonard Feeney; G. Schirmer c1945; comp.
1942.

Spec. medium voice (d1–g2), text suggests men; 1:30; Allegro
assai; parlando; offbeat rhythms; a sparkler with a bit of 'pop'; good
fun; recorded by John McCollum on Desto (411/412) and Sperry.

The Lamb, William Blake; Associated c1946; also incl. *CASS;* comp.
1941.

Spec. medium voices (c1–d2); 1:45; Andante; a tender, parlando
melody; simple; pretty.

Memory, William Blake; Associated c1946; comp. 1919.

Rec. medium voices (c1–f#2); 1:45; Andantino; a dreamy, lyric
melody over undulating triplets; an attractive but less memorable
song; recorded by Sperry.

O Mistress Mine, William Shakespeare; Boosey c1962; comp. 1936; to
Eva Gauthier.

Rec. medium voices (c1–g♭2), text suggests men; 1:15; Vivace;
sustained over a rippling accompaniment; recorded by Sperry.

The Patient Sleeps, William Ernest Henley; G. Schirmer c1949.

Rec. low voices (g–c#2); 1:45; Allegro; low tessitura; fast moving
parlando; a crazy, excited, fun song about going under anesthesia.

The Policeman in the Park, Leonard Feeney; G. Schirmer c1948.

Rec. low voices (a♭–d♭), text suggests men; 2:15; Andante; low
tessitura; tuneful, smooth, and flowing; syncopated; told from the
policeman's point of view; somewhat like a sophisticated show tune;
nice song.

These My Ophelia, Archibald MacLeish; incl. *CC;* comp. 1925.

Rec. medium high lyric voices (e♭1–g♭2); 2:45; long, sustained
lines over moving chords; shifting meters and offbeats; mysterious,
haunting; recorded by Sperry and Beardslee.

Three Husbands, Epitaph No. 9,[6] Walter de la Mare; Boosey c1962;
comp. 1940.

Rec. medium voices (c1–f#2); 1:00; Allegro vivace; rhythmic; jaunty and saucy.

BIBLIOGRAPHY

AmerGroves, Baker, Ewen, Ewen (ACT), Flanagan, Greene, Mellers (on *Eight Epitaphs*), Nathan, Thompson.

Chanler, Theodore. "Poetry and Music," *Modern Music* 18 (May/June, 1941): 232–234.

———. "Poetry, Music and Time," *Modern Music* 21 (Nov/Dec, 1943): 3–5.

Collins, Thomas. "Theodore Ward Chanler: American Song Composer," *NATS Bulletin,* 30 (December 1973).

Tangman, Robert. "The Songs of Theodore Chanler," *Modern Music* 22 (May/June 1945): 227–233.

---

[1] Virgil Thomson, *American Music Since 1910*, p. 88.

[2] As quoted in David Ewen's *American Composers Today*, 54.

[3] The Jesuit priest Father Leonard Feeney was Chanler's friend, but in the late 1940s Chanler stayed with the Church when it broke with Feeney.

[4] This recording is actually titled *Nine Epitaphs* because it includes *Three Husbands*, the only one of a later set, *Three Epitaphs*, to be published.

[5] The author has never seen the lower version implied by the ranges given for this cycle in *Art Song in the United States: An Annotated Bibliography*.

[6] This is one of *Three Epitaphs* which Chanler wrote after the original eight. The other two remain unpublished. The manuscripts are held by the American Music Center.

ERNEST CHARLES[1]
b. Nov. 21, 1895, Minneapolis, MN; d. April 16, 1984, Beverly Hills, CA

Composition came easily to Ernest Charles, and he was also an able pianist. Singing, however, was his passion, and he studied voice with Charles Modini Wood,[2] developing his light tenor enough to enjoy a small career in revues and recital. But it was as a composer that he won recognition. After the popular baritone John Charles Thomas included *Clouds* in a New York recital, G. Schirmer offered Charles a contract. As a result he provided the publishers with a steady stream of concert ballads, which he dashed off with his customary ease. During the 1940s he lived with his wife, a mezzo-soprano, in New York City, where he produced the radio program *Great Moments in Music*. In 1953 they settled in Beverly Hills.

THE SONGS

Rendered with tantalizing rubato and the lustrous sound of some of the era's major artists, Charles's 45 songs were favorites on the concert stage and especially the radio. Though in a somewhat popular vein, they are definitely for trained voices. In fact, their sweeping lines, often rising to an emotive, sustained high note, do best with an operatic approach. The poorest songs, facile and unimaginative settings of syrupy, simplistic poems, indulge in a confusing glut of ideas, lavish harmonies, and predictable devices. Rather than ravishing the ear, they exhaust it. (Charles has confided that he was not proud of many of his songs, especially those he failed to edit when Schirmer pressed him too hard.)[3] The best, however, either have an ingenuous charm, or boast melodies so sumptuous and expressive of their charged poetic messages that even the crustiest listener will be stirred if the song is delivered by a warm, sincere voice. Though several of the most popular are still available individually, *Songs of Ernest Charles (SEC)*, a representative selection of 19 songs, available in high and low editions, was published by G. Schirmer in 1990. Various recordings are noted with the song entries. Some recommendations follow.

Clouds, author unknown; G. Schirmer c1932; also incl *SEC*.
    Rec. all but light voices (high, f1–ab2); 2:00; Tranquillo; sustained with an agitated central section.

The House on a Hill, Ernest Charles; G. Schirmer c1933; also incl. *SEC*.
    Rec. lyric voices (high, d1–g2); 1:15; Leisurely but fluent; broadens to a final *fff*; straightforward, warm, and happy.

Let My Song Fill Your Heart (Viennese Waltz), Ernest Charles; G. Schirmer c1936; also incl. *SEC*.
    Rec. bigger voices (high, eb1–ab2); 3:15; Alla Valzer; expansive; this exuberant quasi Viennese operetta aria was made famous on the radio by Eileen Farrell; recorded by Maryanne Telese on Premier (002).

My Lady Walks in Loveliness, Mona Modini Wood; G. Schirmer c1932; also incl. *SEC;* to John Charles Thomas.
    Rec. lyric voices (high, e1–g2); text suggests men; 2:45; Andante; tender and relatively subdued; recorded by Dale Moore on Cambridge (CRS 2715).

Night, Sydney King Russell; G. Schirmer c1944; also incl *SEC;* to my wife.

Rec. full lyric voices (high, f1–a♭2); 1:45; Poco lento; sustained over a fluid accompaniment; intensifies to long high notes and *fff* dynamics.

The Sussex Sailor, Alfred Noyes; G. Schirmer c1933; also incl. *SEC;* to John Charles Thomas.
Rec. any full voice (d1–g2); 3:15; Con brio; an English style ballad; varying tempos and moods, from lusty to lyrical; narration and dialogue; effective change of pace.

When I Have Sung My Songs, Ernest Charles; G. Schirmer c1934; also incl. *SEC*.
Pub. high and low (high, d1–g2), rec. bigger voices; 2:15; Calmly; sustained but moving; this famous melody to the words "When I have sung my songs to you, I'll sing no more" makes the classic encore; it also pulls out all the stops and shows the voice to great effect; recorded by Kirsten Flagstad on New World (247), Rosa Ponselle on RCA CD (7810-2-RG) and on BIM CD (701-2), and Thomas Hampson on EMI CD (7-54051 2).

The White Swan, Mona Bonelli; G. Schirmer c1941; also incl. *SEC*.
Rec. full lyric voices (high, e1–a2); 2:00; Dreamily; long, sustained lines over rippling piano figurations with a central *ff* section.

Also of interest:

And So, Goodbye, Charles, also incl. in *NAAS* and *SEC,* Restless; ***The Message,*** Teasdale, also incl. *SEC,* Moderato; ***Spendthrift,*** Naidu, also incl. *SEC,* Moderate; ***Sweet Song of Long Ago,*** Charles, Valzer lento.

BIBLIOGRAPHY
Baker.
Miller, Philip L. Liner notes, *When I Have Sung My Songs: The American Art Song, 1900-1940.* (New World 247).
Wolz, Larry. "The Songs of Ernest Charles," *NATS Bulletin* 39 (Mar/Apr 1983). This article includes a complete listing of the songs.

---

[1] As his parents had the surname of Grosskopf, one assumes Charles changed his name when his career began to develop; Charles may have been his middle name.

[2] Father-in-law of the famous operatic baritone, Richard Bonelli.

[3] Letter from Charles to Larry Wolz, quoted in his NATS article (Mar/Apr 1983).

ISRAEL CITKOWITZ

b. Feb. 6, 1909, Skierniewice, Poland;[1] d. May 4, 1974, London, England

Israel Citkowitz's brief career as a composer produced a handful of choice, poetic songs.

Brought to America when he was three, he first studied in New York with Aaron Copland, who became a special friend and supporter, and with Roger Sessions. In 1927 Citkowitz went to Paris and studied for four years with Nadia Boulanger. With Copland's help, his small compositions were presented in concerts by the League of Composers, the Yaddo Festival, and the Copland-Sessions concerts. By the end of the 1930s, however, he had stopped composing. Instead, he taught composition and counterpoint at the Dalcroze School in New York City, gave piano lessons to nonprofessionals, and wrote articles for *Modern Music*, *Musical Mercury,* and *Poetry* magazines. A complicated man who, according to Ned Rorem, went in and out of marriages and money,[2] in 1969 Citkowitz went to London where he lived out his life.

THE SONGS

Citkowitz's small output elicits some regret for promise unfulfilled.[3] His reputation lies entirely with his Joyce *Chamber Music* settings, which some regard as classics of the repertoire. In these finely wrought songs Citkowitz emerges as a lyric musician with an uncommon sensitivity for Joyce's poetry. A fine recording by Bethany Beardslee on New World (243) is a reminder that these songs are too seldom heard.

Five Songs from "Chamber Music," James Joyce; Boosey c1930.

Rec. high lyric voices (d1–a2), some texts suggests men; 8:30; titles are: *Strings in the Earth and Air; When the Shy Star Goes Out in Heaven; O It Was Out by Donneycarney; Bid Adieu; My Love Is in a Light Attire;* should be kept as a set; because of the fluid declamation and high tessitura, the right voice is critical (only the low, declamatory opening of *When the Shy Star* provides relief); few dynamic markings given, but *piano* is clearly intended; no key signatures; shifting meters of steady eighths; the spare, bell-like, accompaniment, primarily in the treble clef, gives an illusion of the music of the spheres; a vivid, evocative set of gossamer lightness; recorded by Beardslee.

Gentle Lady, James Joyce; incl. *CC*.
      Rec. medium lyric voices (f1–d2); 1:45; Rubato...Giusto; a soli-
tary, independent treble line in the piano intertwines with the singer's
folklike melody; plaintive, subdued; beguiling.

BIBLIOGRAPHY
AmerGroves, Baker, Greene, Upton (Sup).
Ewen, David. "New Blood in American Music," *Musical Courier,*
      September 16, 1933.
Rorem, Ned. Liner notes. "The American Art Song from 1930-1960: A
      Personal Survey," New World 243. Reprinted as "The American Art
      Song," in *Setting the Tone.* New York: Coward McCann, 1983.
Upton, William Treat. "Aspects of the Modern Art Song." *The Musical
      Quarterly* 24 (January 1938).

---

[1] A few reference works give Citkowitz's birthplace as Russia, but
   Skierniewice is in Poland.
[2] Ned Rorem, liner notes New World (243).
[3] Other than his songs, only a handful of choral and small instrumental pieces
   exist. Unpublished works for solo voice are settings to William Blake (with
   string quartet) and to Frost (with piano).

HENRY CLOUGH-LEIGHTER
b. May 13, 1874, Washington D.C.; d. Sept. 15, 1956, Wollaston, MA

In the early 1900s Henry Clough-Leighter was a highly regarded composer of choral music and songs. His father was Scotch and German, and
his mother, his first music teacher, was French and English. After studying in Washington D.C., he moved to New England and, in 1901, settled
in Boston. In addition to his composition, he taught, held positions as
church organist, and from 1901 to 1908, was an editor at the Oliver
Ditson Company. He then became director of the Boston Music
Company, leaving that position in 1921 to become editor-in-chief of E.
C. Schirmer, a position he held till his death. He was married to Grace
Marshall, who composed under the pseudonym G. Marscal-Loepke.

THE SONGS
Clough-Leighter's 100-plus songs seem to have been written by several
different composers. Some are straightforward and ingenuous; others
elaborate and lush; some are totally conventional, even trite, while still

others were regarded by critics of the time as "ultra-modern." One can find good examples of all the styles. A few recommendations follow.

Her Songs - My Tears, Op. 60, No.1, Christina G. Rossetti; Ricordi c1914.
  Rec. high voices (e♭1–g♭2); 3:15; Andante quasi allegretto, e placido; sectional, in various tempos; sustained singing; fussy piano writing; somewhat confusing, but nice feeling.

It Was a Lover and His Lass, William Shakespeare; Ditson c1906; also incl. *50SS* and *AASTC.*
  Pub. high and low (high, d1–a2), rec. lyric voices; 1:30; Poco allegro animoso; bouncy, fresh, and appealing; recorded by Paul Sperry on Albany CD (TROY034-2).

Love's Magnificat, Op. 57, No. 1, Arthur Symons; Boston c1914.
  Rec. high big voices (e1–a2); 5:30; Poco andante: molto sentito; many mood and harmonic changes; much rubato; the decadent symbolist poem, which opens "Praise God, Who wrought for you and me, Your subtle body, made for love," may bother some; otherwise, a large, sensual, and unusual song.

My Lover, He Comes on the Skee (Norwegian Love-Song), Hjalmar Hjorth Boyesen; G. Schirmer c1901; also incl. *A12S.*
  Rec. medium voices (d1–f2), text suggests women; 1:30; Allegro ben marcato; the lilting, quasi-traditional tune is clothed in a variety of elaborate, lively accompanimental figures.

Requiescat, Op. 57, No. 6, Oscar Wilde; Boston c1914.
  Rec. medium to higher voices (e♭1–g♭2), text suggests men; 3:15; Lento: pensieroso e mesto; straightforward, lyrical, and affecting; a good song, one of Clough-Leighter's best.

Also of interest:

I Drink the Fragrance of the Rose, Towne, also incl. *S30A,* Allegretto grazioso; ***A Love Garden,*** Towne, Recital Pub. Reprint, cycle of six songs for high voice; ***O Perfect Love,*** a wedding song.

BIBLIOGRAPHY
AmerGroves, Baker, Hughes, Thompson.
"Clough-Leighter's 'Magnum Opus' to Receive Early Performance," *Musical America,* February 17, 1917.

AARON COPLAND
b. Nov. 14, 1900, Brooklyn, NY; d. Dec. 2, 1990, North Tarrytown, NY

Aaron Copland, whose extensive catalogue spans the greater part of the twentieth century, is probably America's most admired and recognized composer. Though accessible works such as *Appalachian Spring* and *Fanfare for the Common Man* have made him a household name, his long career also included many periods of erudite compositional exploration. His songs are few in quantity but outstanding in quality.

The youngest of five children, whose Russian-Jewish parents owned a dry goods store, as a child Copland studied piano and, by age 13, had decided to become a musician. After studying privately with Rubin Goldmark, in 1920 he went to Paris. There his studies with the, as yet, unknown Nadia Boulanger opened the floodgates to the countless Americans who, for decades to come, would seek the services of this enormously influential composition teacher. Returning to New York in 1924, Copland lectured, taught, performed as a conductor and pianist, and composed. He also tirelessly promoted American music. The League of Composers, Copland-Sessions concerts, Yaddo Festival, American Composer's Alliance, and Cos Cob Press are but a few projects that owe their existence, at least in part, to his efforts. Copland finished his last composition in 1971 and made his last public appearance in 1980. From then on he lived quietly in Peekskill, New York, at his hilltop home overlooking the Hudson River.

THE SONGS
Copland's few songs come in two batches separated by 22 years. The first is the sundry fruits of his student days (prior to 1928). The second is primarily his settings of Emily Dickinson (1950), but also includes the *Old American Songs* (written as a form relaxation while composing the complex Dickinson set), and his last song, *Dirge in the Woods*. Though earlier songs are more lyrical, both periods are pure Copland—linear, spare, and luminous.

Never very comfortable with the vocal idiom, Copland once wrote that he hated "an emotion-drenched voice."[1] Later he elaborated on the remark by explaining that he liked "a certain purity in the presentation of the vocal line" and didn't want to be "personally involved in the performer's private emotions."[2] While this might be kept in mind when performing his songs, the operative word is "drenched," for Copland's songs by no means lack melody or expressivity. All the same, the powerfully sculpted vocal lines are somewhat instrumental. Often long and sustained, they can hang cruelly in high tessituras or, as in the case of the Dickinson songs, be markedly disjunct. Meanwhile, pitch and rhythm, especially in ensemble with the highly independent and intricate piano accompaniments, can be challenging. Nevertheless, at all times, the extraordinary intelligence and sensibility of the writing provides a gratifying and absorbing experience for performer and listener.

All published songs are currently in print. The most recent addition is *Four Early Songs,* Boosey and Hawkes c1989. *Song Album: Aaron Copland (SAAC),* Boosey and Hawkes c1980, contains various selections for high voices. Singers may also want to consider *Old American Songs,* two very popular sets of folk song arrangements; *Vocalise,* an early piece for voice and piano without words; *As It Fell Upon a Day,* for soprano, flute, and clarinet. The most comprehensive recording of Copland's art songs (complete except for *Dirge in the Woods*) is by Roberta Alexander on Etcetera CD (KTC 1100). In addition, *Twelve Poems of Emily Dickinson* are recorded by: soprano Adele Addison, with Copland at the piano, on CBS (32 11 0017); mezzo-soprano Martha Lipton, also with Copland and with some transpositions, on Columbia (ML 5106); and baritone Sanford Sylvan on Elektra/Nonesuch CD (9 79259 2).[3] Other isolated recordings are noted below. All published songs are listed.

Alone, Arabic text by John Duncan, trans. by E. Powys Mathers; incl. *Four Early Songs,* comp. 1922; also exists in a version for voice, viola and piano.

   Rec. high lyric voices (d1–f#2); 2:00; Lento; sustained over a fluid piano score; mysterious, haunting; recorded by Alexander.

Dirge in the Woods, George Meredith; Boosey c1957; comp. 1954; in honor of Nadia Boulanger's fiftieth year of teaching.

   Rec. high voices ([eb1]d1–bb2); 3:00; Not too slow; sustained over broken chords; a dramatic central climax; many meter changes and cross rhythms; mysterious and intense; recorded by John McCollum (Desto 411/412).

My Heart Is in the East, Aaron Schaffer,[4] comp. 1918; incl. *Four Early Songs.*

   Rec. high voices (e1–g2); 2:15; Mournfully; sustained; romantic; recorded by Alexander.

Night, Aaron Schaffer; comp. 1918; incl. *Four Early Songs.*

Rec. high voices (c1–g2); 4:00; Adagio molto; sustained; a more active central section; lyrical, musing; recorded by Alexander.

Old Poem,[5] Chinese, trans. by Arthur Waley (also with a French trans.); Senart c1923; comp. 1920; also incl. *SAAC.*

Rec. high lyric voices (e1–g2), text suggests women; 2:00; Very slowly; warm and sustained over hushed, translucent chords, a more restless central section; fragmented, musing, and moody; recorded by Alexander.

Pastorale, trans. from the Kafiristan by E. Powys Mathers; Boosey c1979; comp. 1921; also incl. *SAAC.*

Spec. high voice (d1–a2); rec. lyric sopranos; 2:30; Not too slowly, serenely; a stunning, arching, sustained vocal line opens and closes this beautiful love song; interior parlando passages; vocally difficult but very effective; recorded by Alexander, and Arleen Auger on Delos CD (3029).

Poet's Song, E. E. Cummings; Boosey c1967; comp. 1927; also incl. *CCA* (under the title, *Song*) and *SAAC.*

Rec. high lyric voices (e1–a2); 1:45; Lento molto; sustained with many long tones over a spare piano motif; vocally difficult but unusual and quite beautiful; recorded by Alexander, Bethany Beardslee on New World (243), and Meriel Dickinson on Unicorn (72017).

A Summer Vacation, Aaron Schaffer; comp.1918; incl. *Four Early Songs.*

Rec. high voice (g1–g2); 2:15; Moderato; a luxuriant piano score supports this expansive, lovely romantic song; recorded by Alexander.

Twelve Poems of Emily Dickinson, Boosey c1951; comp. 1949/50; several have also been issued separately; each song dedicated to a different composer friend.

Conceived for medium-high voice[6] (a–b♭2), best for women; 28:00; Copland said the songs can be sung separately or in groupings but that he preferred it as a cycle seeing it as "cumulative."[7] However, as Alice Howland (who sang the first performance) points out: in addition to its length, singers will find that not all songs suit their voices—factors that have kept the cycle from being heard in full.[8] Traditional keys with some chromaticism and considerable dissonance; many instructions as to dynamics, timbre, and small tempo adjustments. The voice, stretched in both directions with hefty singing on either end, must also contend with widely spaced, angular intervals, broadly sculpted lines, changing vocal styles, and subtle mood changes; one of the most distinguished works in the American song repertoire; recorded by Addison, Alexander, Lipton, and Sylvan.

Nature, the gentlest mother, (bb–g2); 3:45; Quite slow; delicate; lyrical declamation.

There came a wind like a bugle, (b–g2); 1:30; Quite fast; loud and excited; also recorded by Jan DeGaetani on Elektra/Nonesuch CD (79248-2-ZK).

Why do they shut me out of heaven? (b–ab2); 1:45; Moderately; declamatory, humorous; also recorded by Nancy Tatum on London (OS 26053), and by Federica von Stade on CBS (37231).

The world feels dusty, (a#–f#2); 1:45; Very slowly; sustained, somber; also recorded by Tatum and DeGaetani.

Heart, we will forget him, (bb–g2); 2:15; Very slowly (dragging), lyrical also recorded by Arleen Auger on Delos CD (3029).

Dear March, come in! (a–f#); 2:15; With exuberance; declamatory.

Sleep is supposed to be, (bb–bb2 [ab2]); 2:45; Sustained; dramatic.

When they come back, (c1–f#2); 1:45; Moderately, builds.

I felt a funeral in my brain, (c#1–g2); 2:15; Rather fast.

I've heard an organ talk sometimes, (bb–f2); 1:45; Gently flowing; big end.

Going to Heaven! (a–f2); 2:45; Fast; an excited but light parlando; subdued ending.

The Chariot, (b–f#2); 3:00; With quiet grace; dramatic central section.

BIBLIOGRAPHY

AmerGroves, Baker, Ewen, Flanagan, Friedberg (I), Goss, Greene, Nathan, Thompson.

Copland, Aaron, *Copland on Music.* 1945. Paperback reprint. New York: W.W. Norton & Company, Inc., 1963.

Copland, Aaron and Vivian Perlis. *Copland: 1900 through 1942.* New York: St. Martin's/ Marek, 1984.

———. *Copland Since 1943.* New York: St. Martin's Press, 1989. In this volume Copland and singers Alice Howland, Phyllis Curtin, and William Warfield discuss his vocal music in depth.

"The Reluctant Composer: A Dialogue with Aaron Copland," *Opera News,* Jan. 26, 1963.

Young, Douglas. "Copland's Dickinson Songs," *Tempo* 103 (1972): 33–37.

---

[1] *Copland on Music,* 137.

[2] "The Reluctant Composer," *Opera News,* 16. Repeated almost verbatim in *Copland Since 1943,* p. 212.

[3] Marni Nixon has made a recording of eight of the Dickinson poems in their later orchestral version on Reference CD (RR-22).

[4] Aaron Schaffer, a French professor, who died in 1957, was the good friend from Copland's youth who first encouraged him to go to Paris. The songs, a gift from Schaffer to the University of Texas, turned up among uncatalogued manuscripts in 1986.

[5] Also called *Vieux Poème.*

[6] *Copland Since 1943,* p.159.

[7] Ibid.

[8] Ibid, 160.

JOHN CORIGLIANO
b. Feb. 16, 1938, New York, NY

Though few composers of his generation have been as effective in communicating with their audiences as John Corigliano, his published songs are regrettably few and tell us little of his considerable gifts.

His mother was a pianist; his father a noted concertmaster of the New York Philharmonic, who opposed his son's interest in composition, viewing it as a hapless career. Nevertheless, Corigliano took courses with Otto Luening at Columbia University, and later studied with Vittorio Giannini and Paul Creston. For several years, he earned a living by working for classical music radio stations. Then, in 1964, his Sonata for violin and piano (composed for his father, who at first refused to play it) won first prize at the Spoleto Festival Competition. Since that time Corigliano's career has developed smoothly, culminating in acclaim for his first symphony (inspired by the AIDS quilt) and his opera, *The Ghosts of Versailles*, commissioned by the Metropolitan Opera. He continues to live in New York City, where he has taught at the Manhattan School of Music and is currently on the faculty of the Juilliard School.

THE SONGS

Corigliano's song output is, as yet, too small to confirm the growing suspicion that the profound lyric and communicative gifts which have earned him recognition in recent years make him a natural for the idiom. At present, all that is available from a catalogue that abounds in large forms are two small cycles. Composed in a conventional contemporary idiom early in his career, they are dynamic and intelligent, but little more than routine. One waits for him to turn his hand to art song again. Henry Herford has recorded *The Cloisters* on New World (327).

The Cloisters, William Hoffman;[1] G. Schirmer c1967; comp. 1965.
    Rec. medium voices (a–g2); 10:00; titles are: *Fort Tryon Park: September; Song to the Witch of the Cloisters* (also incl. *CAS28); Christmas at the Cloisters* (also incl. *CAS28); The Unicorn.* The jubilant *Christmas at the Cloisters* is occasionally performed individually; otherwise the cycle is best kept intact; opening with an autumnal setting and closing with spring, it depicts various seasons at this famous museum of medieval art, located in upper Manhattan's Fort Tryon Park overlooking the Hudson River; a medieval ambiance is evoked despite the generally romantic (sometimes jazzlike) idiom; stamina and weight in the voice are required for the primarily declamatory, occasionally lyrical, writing; no key or time signatures; of modest musical difficulty; an attractive set; recorded by Herford.

Petit Fours (A Song Cyclette), various poets; G. Schirmer c1981; comp. 1959.
    Rec. high lyric voices (bb–a2); 3:00; titles are: *Upon Julia's Clothes* (Robert Herrick); *The Turtle* (Ogden Nash); *Une Allée du Luxembourg* (Aloysius Bertrand), in French; *The Ancient Mariner, Verse 1* (Samuel Taylor Coleridge); there appears to be no unifying theme whatsoever for these highly eclectic, clever songs; though none is big enough to stand on its own, as a mini-set they make a colorful, amusing, effective splash.

BIBLIOGRAPHY
AmerGroves, Baker, CBY (1989), Ewen, Friedberg (III), Greene.
Holland, Bernard. "Highbrow Music to Hum," *New York Times Magazine,* Jan. 31, 1982.
Nott, Michael C. "The Long Road to Versailles," *Opera News,* Jan. 4, 1992.

---

[1] Hoffman is also the librettist for Corigliano's opera, *The Ghosts of Versailles.*

RAMIRO CORTÉS

b. Nov. 25, 1933,[1] Dallas TX; d. July 2, 1984, Salt Lake City, UT

Perhaps the first Mexican-American to achieve recognition as a composer of music in the classical idiom, Cortés's small handful of compelling songs are too rarely heard.

His Mexican-born father, who played the guitar, sang, and wrote poetry, abandoned the family when Cortés was a child. Cortés showed exceptional musical talent and, at the age of 8, began piano lessons. In Denver, Colorado, where the family moved after his mother remarried, he continued piano lessons, composed, and—supported by an anonymous benefactor who envisioned, for Cortés, a major career as a tenor—studied voice. In the summer of 1952, as winner of the Charles Ives Scholarship, Cortés studied with Henry Cowell. Further studies followed with Richard Donovan at Yale University; Ingford Dahl and Halsey Stevens at the University of California; Vittorio Giannini at the Juilliard School (where Cortés earned his master's degree); Roger Sessions at Princeton University; and, on a Fulbright Fellowship, Goffredo Petrassi in Rome. Cortés also performed as a pianist, and was a conductor of contemporary music. He taught at the University of California (Los Angeles) and the University of Southern California, then, in 1972, joined the faculty of the University of Utah, where he remained until his death. Married, divorced, then remarried to Nancee Charles, a ballet dancer, their stormy relationship mirrored Cortés's own troubled personality.

THE SONGS

Only four of Cortés's striking, intelligent, unusual songs have ever been published. Though somewhat difficult, both musically and vocally, they are profoundly expressive and gratifying to sing. The piano writing is expansive, colorful, and at times virtuosic. These are exciting songs, which should be performed. It can only be hoped that an enterprising singer will seek out the approximately 50 that remain unpublished.[2]

The Falcon, Anonymous; Peters c1958.

     Spec. soprano (c#1–bb2); 4:45; Lento; contemplativo; atonal; a disjunct, yet passionate, vocal line; difficult intervals; chords of chilling harmonies; complex rhythms; an evocation of the Dies Irae theme; rises to a *ff* climax but recedes to a tragic and subdued conclusion; a dramatic, intense setting of this famous mystical poem.

Three Spanish Songs, Federico Garcia Lorca; Peer c1961; pub. separately.

   Rec. full medium voices (b♭–a2); 6:30; titles are: *La Guitarra* (The
Guitar); *Las Seis Cuerdas* (The Six Strings); *Adivinanza de la
Guitarra* (The Riddle of the Guitar); despite being published separately these songs are best sung as a set; in Spanish (the English translation provided is not recommended); not in any key but tonally
centered; many embellishments; Flamenco rhythms; although the
expressive vocal lines have an intrinsic darkness, the singer is
required to perform in cantabile, declamatory, and florid styles; many
guitar effects in the exciting piano score; the first and last songs are
imposing, dramatic, and agitated; the central song is subdued with
long, legato lines; perfectly matching the spirit of García Lorca, these
elegant, incisive, vivid songs explore the mysterious emotive powers
of the guitar.

BIBLIOGRAPHY
AmerGroves, Baker.
Hathaway, Nancee Cortés. "Ramiro Cortés." Nancee Cortés Hathaway,
   1992. A privately printed biographical summary by the composer's
   widow.

---

[1] *The New Grove Dictionary of American Music* gives Cortés's birth year as
   1938, which according to his widow is incorrect.

[2] Cortés's widow has informed the author that her late husband's songs are
   located at the Special Collections Department, University of Utah Libraries,
   Salt Lake City, UT 84112.

HENRY COWELL
b. March 11, 1897, Menlo Park, CA; d. Dec. 10, 1965, Shady, NY

Henry Cowell is primarily known for his experimental music, but his
immense output shows that he was receptive to all kinds of influences.
With few exceptions his appealing handful of published songs are in a
conventional idiom.

   His Irish father deserted the family when he was a boy, leaving
Cowell's mother, a writer, to informally educate her son. Though he was
a precocious student of the violin, Cowell had to give up the instrument
due to a nervous disease. For a few years mother and son tried living in

Des Moines and then New York but, unable to support themselves, returned to Menlo Park. Saving enough to buy an old piano, Cowell experimented at the keyboard and attracted attention with his striking compositions incorporating tone clusters and other unorthodox effects. In 1914 he began formal study at the University of California (Berkeley), and privately with Charles Seeger.

In the 1920s and 1930s Cowell gave controversial performances of his radical compositions throughout the United States, Europe, and the Soviet Union. In 1927 he founded *New Music,* a quarterly publication of modern composition. But in 1936 his career was cruelly halted when he was imprisoned in San Quentin on a morals charge. Released on parole in 1940, two years later he was pardoned by the governor of California at the request of the prosecuting attorney, who now believed him to be innocent. Cowell resumed his busy career although his years of experimentation seemed to be over. Highly regarded as a lecturer and teacher, he held positions at, among others places, the New School for Social Research, the Peabody Institute, and Columbia University. In 1941 he married Sidney Robertson, an ethnomusicologist. Later, they collaborated on *Charles Ives and His Music* (1955), the first book devoted to Ives, whose music Cowell had been one of the first to promote.

THE SONGS

The New Grove Dictionary of American Music provides a lengthy listing of Cowell songs. Only a few, however, were published and, of those, most were written with Cowell's experimental years behind him. Nevertheless, they retain his special feeling for color and atmosphere. Melodic and fluid, most call for warm, lyric singing over conventional accompaniments. Only three early examples employ any of the groundbreaking effects for which he is best known. Sopranos may also be interested in the lovely *Vocalise* with flute and piano, or *Toccanta* with flute, cello, and piano. Virtually all published songs are listed.

Daybreak, William Blake; Peer c1950; comp. 1946.
> Rec. higher lyric voices (d1–g2); 1:15; Andante; linear and fluid; a lovely, unaffected song of reawakening.

The Donkey, G. K. Chesterton; Music Press c1947; comp. 1946; for Roland Hayes.[1]
> Spec. medium voice (d1–a2[g2]), rec. high voices; 2:15; Andante; contrasting sections; the donkey laments the derision he has endured

through history, but exalts that he bears Jesus Christ; a moving, dramatic song; recorded by John McCollum on Desto (411/412).

Firelight and Lamp, Gene Baro; Peters c1964; comp. 1962; for Theodore Uppman.
Rec. higher lyric voices (c1–g2); 2:15; Andante; atmospheric with central dramatic passages evoking the winter winds raging outside and the passion of the relationship experienced inside; an effective mood piece.

How Old Is Song, Harry Cowell;[2] Williams c1943; comp. 1929.
Rec. high voices (b–g2); 2:15; no tempo indication; an expansive, rather stately vocal line over plucked and swept open strings on the piano.

The Little Black Boy, William Blake; Peters c1964; comp. 1952/54.
Rec. higher voices (d1–a2 [f2]), text suggests men; 2:15; Vivo; tricky shifting meters; colorful and fervent.

The Pasture, Robert Frost; Marks c1964; comp. 1944;[3] also incl. *NVS.*
Rec. high lyric voices (e1–a2); 1:15; Andante; a bright, supple, syllabic vocal line in a high tessitura over a twinkling accompaniment; fresh and innocent.

Spring Comes Singing, Dora Hagemeyer; Associated c1958; comp. 1954; also incl. *AAS;* commissioned by and dedicated to the Juilliard School of Music.
Rec. high lyric voices (d1–a2); 2:30; Allegro; despite its seemingly innocuous opening and relentless motion, this song surprises at every turn with a variety of moods, tempos, and dynamics, all building to the final buoyant ending.

St. Agnes Morning, Maxwell Anderson; Music Press c1947; comp. 1914.
Rec. medium voices (c1–g2); 2:45; Andante con moto; sustained over a pulsing accompaniment; some dramatic areas; intense.

Two Songs, Catherine Riegger;[4] New Music; comp. 1933.
Spec. low voice (g–e2); 4:30; titles are: *Sunset; Rest;* as it describes potent and poetic images, the voice is alternately mystical (with occasional eerie glissandos), majestic, and fierce; some massive clusters, played with the flat of the hand and the forearm; startling,

striking songs; recorded by Raymond Murcell on Musical Heritage (7370Y).

BIBLIOGRAPHY

AmerGroves, Baker, Ewen, Goss, Greene, Ivey (on *The Pasture*), Thompson.

Brant, Henry. "Henry Cowell: Musician and Citizen," *Etude* (February/March/April 1957).

Peyser, Joan. "Henry Cowell: An Influential 'American Original'," *New York Times*, December 6, 1981.

---

[1] Roland Hayes, the famous black tenor, was the first American musician to visit the USSR. Cowell was the second.

[2] Harry Cowell, Henry's father, was an aspiring poet. Several other unpublished songs, with similarly evocative titles, are also set to his poetry.

[3] Composed for his wife on their anniversary.

[4] Catherine Riegger was the eldest daughter of composer Wallingford Riegger.

RUTH CRAWFORD (SEEGER)[1]

b. July 3, 1901, East Liverpool, OH; d. Nov. 18, 1953, Chevy Chase, MD

Though Ruth Crawford is probably best known as a compiler of folk-songs, she was also one of the most forward-looking and original composers of her time.

Her father was a Methodist minister; her mother an accomplished pianist and Crawford's first teacher. When Crawford was ten, the family moved to Jacksonville, Florida, where, two years later, her father died. Crawford helped the family by teaching piano in the local schools. During this time she also studied at the American Conservatory in Chicago and, in 1929, graduated summa cum laude with a master's degree. In 1930 she went to New York, where she studied with the noted teacher and composer, Charles Seeger. That same year she became the first woman to receive a Guggenheim fellowship and she used it to travel through Europe. On her return in 1931, she married Seeger. In 1935 the family moved to Silver Spring, Maryland, where, while raising four children,[2] she worked as a music teacher. In 1937 she and Seeger began to collect American folk music. Crawford not only used the songs for teaching, but also edited and arranged eight volumes of them. Except for one piece in 1941 and one other shortly before her untimely death from cancer, she did no composing of her own after 1932.

THE SONGS

Crawford composed her songs early in her career. They are intense, cere-
bral, and deadly serious. Her obvious empathy with her poetic subject,
however, elicits a profound expressiveness which softens the cool exte-
riors. Atonal and rhythmically complex, Crawford's songs are musically difficult but vocally idiomatic. Three of the Sandburg settings have
been recorded by Jan DeGaetani on Elektra/Nonesuch CD (79248-2-
ZK).

Chinaman, Laundryman, H. T. Tsiang; Merion c1973/76; comp. 1932.
    Rec. higher voices (d1–g2); 3:00; Moderato; the voice in a 2/2
meter is alternately sung and spoken on an indefinite pitch (like
"sprechstimme") with many slides over a linear piano part in 3/4; if
one can conquer this treacherous rhythmic exercise, the impact of this
protest song over immigrant conditions is disturbing and striking; less
effective, however, than the more commanding *Sacco and Vanzetti,*
with which it can be paired.[3]

Five Songs, Carl Sandburg; Peters c1990; comp. 1929.
    Spec. contralto (a–f#2), *Home Thoughts* is also suitable for medi-
um voices; 10:00; titles are: *Home Thoughts; Loam; Joy; White
Moon; Sunsets;* though not conceived as a cycle, these songs can be
used as one; brief, disjunct, declamatory vocal lines over spare,
sketchy accompaniments; in a twelve-tone idiom; with the exception
of the biting, fast moving *Joy,* tempos are generally slow and the
overall mood is subdued, introspective, and evocative; *Home
Thoughts, White Moon,* and *Joy* are recorded by DeGaetani.

Sacco and Vanzetti, H. T. Tsiang; Merion c1973/76; comp. 1932.
    Rec. solid middle voices (b–g2); 4:30; Tempo giusto; declaimed,
in same vocal style as *Chinaman, Laundryman,* over chords; difficult
to sustain the intensity; important dynamic changes; Crawford has
carefully set the words to be clearly understood; the anguish many
people still felt one year after the execution of two Italian-Americans,
who may have been innocent of the murder with which they were
charged, is powerfully imparted in this second of the protest songs.

BIBLIOGRAPHY

AmerGroves, Ammer, Baker, Ewen, Greene, Thompson.
Gaume, Matilda. *Ruth Crawford Seeger: Memoirs, Memories, Music.*
    Metuchen, New Jersey: Scarecrow Press, 1986.

[1] Though often referred to as Ruth Crawford Seeger, her songs are published under the name, Ruth Crawford.

[2] The famous folksinger Pete Seeger was the son of Charles Seeger by his first wife. However, two of Ruth and Charles Seeger's four children also had careers as folksingers; they are Mike Seeger and Peggy Seeger.

[3] *Two Ricercari* was the original cover title for *Chinaman, Laundryman* and *Sacco and Vanzetti*. These two political protest songs were set to texts found in the Communist newspaper *The Daily Worker*.

PAUL CRESTON
b. Oct. 10, 1906, New York, NY; d. Aug. 24, 1985, San Diego, CA

Creston's abundant catalogue includes some luxuriant songs. Born Giuseppi Guttoveggio, Paul Creston was the son of Italian immigrants. Despite the family's poverty, as a child he managed to learn piano and organ. Subsequently, he held a variety of jobs (including organist for silent movies), married a dancer, changed his name, had children, and finally, in 1932, decided on a career in composition. Though recognition for his conventional but vigorous and distinctive compositions came quickly, he also taught, held administrative positions, and wrote theoretical books. In 1976 he moved to San Diego.

THE SONGS
To glance at Creston's lush, colorful songs is to meet with a sea of black ink. Though discernible patterns soon emerge from the tiny notes riddled with accidentals, good-sized voices, also endowed with stamina and ringing top notes, are needed to cut through the lavish textures. The impression of excess and the stamina required make it difficult to program more than one or two of these exuberant songs at a time, but if used sparingly, several can be strongly recommended. Five have been recorded by Yolanda Marcoulescou-Stern on Gasparo CD (GSCD 287). A virtually complete listing of the published songs follows.

The Bird of the Wilderness, Rabindranath Tagore; G. Schirmer c1950; also incl. *S22A.*
    Pub. high and low (high, f#1–a2); 2:00; Andante; full-bodied singing over a fluid accompaniment; a brief chordal section; romantic; recorded by Marcoulescou-Stern.

Fountain Song, John G. Neihardt; Leeds c1952.

Rec. bigger high voices (e1–b2[g#]); 1:30; With spirit; lyrical; virtuosic arpeggios of shifting harmonies evoke the fountain; the final high B can just as well be replaced by the optional lower note; colorful; effective; recorded by Marcoulescou-Stern.

Lullaby, John G. Neihardt; Leeds c1952.
Rec. high lyric voices (f1–f2); 1:45; Slow; a pretty melody over a gently flowing accompaniment; recorded by Marcoulescou-Stern.

Psalm XXIII, Op. 37; G. Schirmer c1945; also incl. *20CAS.*
Rec. full medium voices (d1–f2); 3:45; With tranquility; becomes rather charged; recorded by Marcoulescou-Stern.

Serenade, Edward C. Pinkney; Leeds c1952.
Rec. secure high voices (f1–ab2), text suggests men; 1:45; Rather fast; evokes a Latin serenade, but the complex rhythmic scheme and many notes creates considerable ensemble difficulties; demanding but quite effective; recorded by Marcoulescou-Stern.

A Song of Joys, Op. 63, Walt Whitman; Colombo c1963.
Rec. full high voices, possibly medium (eb1–gb2); 2:15; Moderately fast; long cantabile lines over a sweeping accompaniment; some sustained high tones; exuberant.

Three Songs, Op. 46; see *Serenade, Lullaby* and *Fountain Song;* published separately, but a well balanced set, which could be sung by a man or woman despite the varying connotations of the texts; can also be programmed individually.

BIBLIOGRAPHY
AmerGroves, Baker, Ewen, Goss, Greene, Thompson.
Bloomingdale, Wayne; "Creston's Songs: The Art of Communication," *The American Music Teacher* (January 1979).

BAINBRIDGE CRIST
b. Feb. 13, 1883, Lawrenceburg, IN; d. Feb. 7, 1969, Barnstable, MA

For a time after World War I, Bainbridge Crist was a well-known figure on the music scene. Today he is yet another obscure composer of that era. This is unfortunate because a number of Crist's fresh, imaginative songs exemplify the period at its colorful best.

He was the only son of caring, artistic parents. His father, a businessman, was also an accomplished poet, painter, inventor, and flutist. His mother, whose maiden name was Bainbridge, was a pianist and writer. Crist began studying piano with his mother at age five, and flute with Theodore Hahn soon after. He dreamed of becoming a composer but, after the family moved to Washington, D.C., recognizing the difficulties of such a career, he stoically studied law at the University of Washington.

Crist, however, was haunted by his muse and in 1912, after six years of successful practice in Boston, he abandoned the legal profession and left for Europe to begin full music studies. In Berlin, he studied composition with Carl Landi and Paul Juon, and voice with Franz Emerich. In London, he continued vocal studies with the eminent teacher, William Shakespeare. With the outbreak of World War I he returned to the United States, where he established himself as a voice teacher in Boston and later Washington D.C. Meanwhile, his compositions were published and performed. Married, with one son, Crist eventually settled on Cape Cod, where he taught, sang, wrote about music (including a treatise, *The Art of Setting Words to Music),* and continued to compose songs. After the early 1940s, however, little more is heard from or about him.

THE SONGS

Though his huge output of song is uneven,[1] when Crist unleashed his fanciful imagination, he was a master of mood and evocation. Settings of favorite poets, Walter de la Mare and Conrad Aiken, or poetry on exotic themes, primarily the Orient, show him at his best. He also had a talent for children's subjects and for making tasteful arrangements of traditional and folk melodies. Otherwise, his songs, though invariably well crafted, are either routine or, often because of a poor choice of poetry, sentimental.

It is doubtful Crist ever had aspirations to be a singer himself. More likely he studied voice for the security the voice teacher's profession would provide[2] and for the knowledge it would give him for his composition. While carefully balancing declamation with beautiful melody, he could write the kinds of delectable vocal lines that really show a singer's instrument to good advantage. The pianist is similarly well served by the vivid, often exotic, and always interesting accompaniments. Skilled in orchestration and a wonderful colorist, several of the songs were also arranged for orchestra. A few recommendations follow. Most songs are published in one key only; those in more than one are so noted.

By a Silent Shore, Conrad Aiken (Verses from Senlin); G. Schirmer
c1934; from *Four Songs.*
    Rec. lyric voices with good middle (c#1–g#2); 3:00; Largo e lan-
guidamente; a warm, sensuous melody over chords; hushed; poetic.

Chinese Mother Goose Rhymes, trans. from the Chinese by Prof. I. F.
Headland; Fischer c1917; for my son.
    Rec. medium or high lyric voices (c1–g2); 4:00; these seven trans-
lations of authentic Chinese Mother Goose rhymes are somewhat different from the Western version; "delightfully droll" and of an "odd
humor";[3] sophisticated, incisive, and very clever.

Coloured Stars, trans. from the Chinese (19th century) by E. Powys
Mathew; Fischer c1921; from the cycle, *Coloured Stars.*
    Spec. high or medium voices (d♭1–g♭2[b♭2]); 1:45; Allegretto;
optional high note is not recommended; lustrous, energetic vocalism
over a kaleidoscopic array of piano figurations and shifting harmonies—"a veritable riot of color."[4]

The Dark King's Daughter, Conrad Aiken; Church c1920.
    Rec. high voices (d1–b2), tenors best; 1:45; Allegretto; a lovely,
surging cantabile building to a climactic high B over colorful, rippling broken chords; then slows and fades; magical.

Drolleries from an Oriental Doll's House, trans. from the Chinese and
Japanese; Fischer c1920; for my son.
    Rec. medium lyric voices (c1–g2); 6:00; music based upon
Japanese and Chinese themes; six charming and imaginative songs;
similar to, but more developed than *Chinese Mother Goose Rhymes.*

Enchantment, Conrad Aiken; Church c1920.
    Rec. high full voices (c#1–g2); 1:30; Andante; the tentative, lyric
opening builds to a powerful climax; charged and romantic.

Evening, Conrad Aiken (Verses from Senlin); G. Schirmer c1934; from
Four Songs.
    Rec. high lyric voices (c1–a2); 1:30; Andante; a nostalgic melody
over quiet chords; final sustained *pp* high A.

If There Were Dreams to Sell, Thomas Lowell Beddoes; Boston c1915.
    Rec. medium voices (e♭1–e♭2); 3:00; Moderato; a wistful melody
over an exquisite fluid accompaniment of evocative harmonies.

Into a Ship, Dreaming, Walter de la Mare; Fischer c1918; ded. to Reinald Werrenrath.

    Pub. high, medium, and low (high, e♭1–g#2); 1:45; Moderato, non troppo allegro; haunting lyricism over a fluid accompaniment; considered one of Crist's best; recorded by John Hanks on Duke, Vol. 1 (DWR 6417).

Knock on the Door, Conrad Aiken (Verses from Senlin); G. Schirmer c1934; also incl. *NAAS;* from *Four Songs.*

    Pub. high and low (high, e♭1–a♭2); 0:45; Presto; segmented; declamatory; dramatic; a peculiar but interesting song.

Languor, Li-Tai-Pe, trans. E. Powys Mathers; Fischer c1923.

    Rec. medium voices (e♭1–f2); Lento, e molto tranquillo; over gong-like chords, a hushed voice slowly rouses itself to render an evocative account of the Chinese king as he languishes before Syche's voluptuous dancing; sensuous and special.

Mistletoe, Walter de la Mare; Boston c1916.

    Rec. high lyric voices (g1–g2); 2:00; Lento; a beguiling melody over a colorful accompaniment; enchanting.

The Mocking Fairy, Walter de la Mare; Galaxy c1949.

    Spec. medium voices (c#1–e2); 2:00; Allegro; alternating faster and slower tempos; declamatory; late Crist; different, but with all the fantasy and imagination of the early songs.

O Come Hither! George Darley; Fischer c1918.

    Rec. coloratura sopranos (d1–b2[d3]); 2:30; Allegro, con grazia; florid; a good showpiece of its type.

The Old Soldier, Walter de la Mare; Fischer c1919.

    Pub. high, medium, and low (med., c1–f2); 2:00; Allegretto; a strophic narrative; one lyrical verse, the others marchlike, each with a little refrain; charming, touching.

Queer Yarns, Walter de la Mare; Fischer c1925.

    Spec. medium voices (c1–g2); 4:00; titles are: *Alas, Alack; Tired Jim; Five Eyes; Jim Jay;* bizarre little narratives; some tricky rhythms; pictorial piano writing.

Also of interest:

April Rain, Aiken, Allegretto, cascading piano figures; *Leila,* from the Chinese, operatic; *The Ship of Rio,* de la Mare, Allegro, a humorous narrative; *The Way That Lovers Use,* Brooke, Moderato, lyrical.

BIBLIOGRAPHY

AmerGroves, Baker, Hall, Thompson, Thorpe (on *Into a Ship, Dreaming),* Upton, Upton (Sup).

Crist, Bainbridge. *The Art of Setting Words to Music.* New York: Carl Fischer, 1944.

Howard, John Tasker. *Studies of Contemporary American Composers: Bainbridge Crist.* New York: Carl Fischer, 1929.

Upton, William Treat. "Bainbridge Crist—A Study in Contemporary Song." *The Musical Observer* (August 1924).

---

[1] He also composed many orchestral and choral pieces as well as ballets. They were usually based on literary themes.

[2] Very serious in his role as a voice teacher, Crist took students abroad to prepare them for operatic roles. He also wrote an article called "The 'Missing Link' in Voice Production," (*Emerson Quarterly,* Nov. 2, 1930) in which he compared the teachings of Lamperti, Garcia, and Lehmann.

3 William Treat Upton, *Art Song in America,* 241 and 242, respectively.

4 Ibid, 247.

RICHARD CUMMING
b. June 9, 1928, Shanghai, China

Born in China to American parents, Cumming was raised in Manila, where his father was in the import-export business. In 1941 the family returned to America and settled in California. Cumming studied at the San Francisco Conservatory and spent summers at the Music Academy of the West, the Griller Quartet Summer School, and later the Aspen School of Music. His teachers included Lili Krause and Rudolf Firkusny for piano, and Roger Sessions, Ernest Bloch, and Arnold Schoenberg for composition. Cumming concertized as a pianist in the early 1950s and, for many years, was accompanist to such well known singers as Phyllis Curtin, Jennie Tourel, and Donald Gramm. He has also accompanied and written musical scores for productions of the Trinity Repertory Company in Providence, Rhode Island, where he has been composer-in-residence.

THE SONGS

Cumming's conventional, romantic style is pleasing for its easy lyricism and smooth, attractive melodies. He writes for the voice with exceptional naturalness and facility. His accompaniments support and describe. Not difficult for either performer or listener, there is little that is especially original, but much to admire and enjoy, as well as a nice diversity of mood and subject matter. While those with rhythmic verve make an immediate effect, the quieter, more thoughtful songs have an ingenuous warmth. Donald Gramm and Carole Bogard have made a fine recording of Cumming's songs (including several not yet published) on Cambridge (CRS 2778); John Hanks has also recorded three on Duke, Vol. 2 (DWR 7306). Virtually all published songs are listed.

Go, Lovely Rose, Edmund Waller; Boosey c1956; comp. 1949.
　　　Spec. medium lyric voices (c1–g2), text suggests men; 3:00; Allegro moderato; the earliest and weakest of Cumming's songs; recorded (transposed up) by Hanks.

The Little Black Boy, William Blake; Boosey c1966; comp. 1963; to Helen Vanni.
　　　Rec. high voices (c1–c3[a2]); 4:15; Ritmico e poco allegro; syncopations and other jazz-like effects; a big setting of a difficult poem; only partially successful; recorded by Bogard and Hanks.

Memory, Hither Come, William Blake; Boosey c1966; comp. 1956.
　　　Rec. medium and lower lyric voices (b♭–e2); 1:15; Allegro moderato; a straightforward melody over an undulating accompaniment; delicate; recorded by Bogard and Hanks.

Other Loves, Philip Minor; Galaxy c1982; comp. 1974; incl. *AAA;* for Helen Vanni.
　　　Spec. high voice (b♭–a♭2); 6:30; titles are: *Summer Song; Night Song; Love Song;* no key signatures but tonally centered; nicely balanced with a sprightly ending; recorded by Bogard.

We Happy Few, various poets; Boosey c1969; comp. 1963; various dedications; comm. by Donald Gramm.
　　　Rec. medium and lower voices (g–e2, with glissando from a low d♭ to shouted f#2), men best; 24:00. War is the theme of this cycle, but since it is not given a particularly weighty treatment, one could easily make smaller groups. Despite the smattering of low notes, the

tessitura is generally middle range. All in all, an appealing work with moments of real beauty and feeling; recorded by Gramm.

The Feast of Crispian, William Shakespeare; (g–e2); 3:00; Maestoso; a quasi recitative.

To Whom Can I Speak Today? Anonymous Egyptian (ca. 3000 B.C.); (a–c2); 2:15; Adagio; hushed; with mystery; an unusual song.

Fife Tune, John Manifold; (a–e♭2); 1:30; Andante amabile; parlando; charming.

Here Dead Lie We, A. E. Housman; (c♭1–b1); 1:15; Adagio.

A Ballad of the Good Lord Nelson, Lawrence Durrell; (a–d2); 3:15; Allegro Moderato; a spirited narrative in Gilbert and Sullivan style patter.

Going to the Warres (to Lucasta), Richard Lovelace; (a–d2); 1:15; Allegro commodo; tender.

A Sight in Camp, Walt Whitman; (a♭–e2); 3:30; Lento e misterioso; three moving portraits of fallen soldiers.

The End of the World, Archibald MacLeish; (a–e♭2); 1:45; Moderate waltz-time; bright and full, then hushed and halting over eerie chords.

Grave Hour, Rainer Maria Rilke; (b–e2); 2:30; Adagio; restrained.

The Song of Moses, from Exodus; (g–e2); 3:30; Rather fast - with joyous exaltation; jazzy; somewhat obvious.

BIBLIOGRAPHY
Friedberg (III).
Rorem, Ned. Liner notes. "The Songs of Richard Cumming." *Richard Cumming: Cycles and Songs.* Cambridge (CRS 2778).

PEARL CURRAN
b. June 25, 1875, Denver, CO; d. April 16, 1941, Larchmont, NY

Born Pearl Gildersleeve, Curran studied at the University of Denver, but did not begin composing until her mid-thirties. She then produced approximately 40 lyric songs, including some sacred pieces. Unquestionably the greatest detriment to her work was her insistence on setting her own simplistic, old-fashioned texts. Otherwise, her songs are imaginative, melodious, and well crafted. Despite their naiveté, they can also be surprisingly elaborate and expansive. *Life* (introduced by Caruso), *Rain,* and *Nocturne* are good examples of songs that enjoyed some popularity. Virtually all, usually in more than one key, were published by Schirmer and are easily found in libraries.

BIBLIOGRAPHY
Howard (OAM), Thompson.

REGINALD DE KOVEN
b. April 3, 1859, Middletown, CT; d. Jan. 16, 1920, Chicago, IL

In 1872 De Koven's father, a minister, moved his family to England, where De Koven was educated. After graduating from Oxford University in 1879, he studied music in Germany; singing with Luigi Vannuccini in Florence; and composition with the great operetta composer Carl von Suppé in Vienna, and with Léo Delibes in Paris. In 1892 he returned to Chicago, where he married into affluence. He was a music critic in Chicago and New York, and also helped found the Washington Philharmonic Orchestra, which he conducted from 1902 to 1905. De Koven's large catalogue is primarily vocal, with two operas, one of which was premiered by the Metropolitan Opera, and numerous operettas, including his one success, *Robin Hood*. In addition, he wrote approximately 400 songs. Tuneful, lightweight, and facile, they are mostly sentimental ballads. Today he is best remembered for the wedding song *O Promise Me*.

BIBLIOGRAPHY
AmerGroves, Baker, Greene, Thompson.
De Koven, Mrs. Reginald. *A Musician and His Wife*. New York: Harper and Brothers, 1926.

NORMAN DELLO JOIO[1]
b. Jan. 24, 1913, New York, NY

Best known for his compositions in large forms, Norman Dello Joio's superb songs are too easily passed over.

His father, an Italian immigrant, was a musician who coached for the Metropolitan Opera; his mother was also of Italian descent. The elder Dello Joio taught his only child theory and keyboard, then turned him over to renowned organist Pietro Yon for further study. Expected to continue in the line of organists from which his father had descended, Dello

Joio, at the age of 12, took the first of several important church positions. In these formative years, however, he also played in dance bands, formed a touring jazz group, played baseball (even considered an offer to try the sport professionally), and endured his parents divorce and his mother's attempted suicide.

Dello Joio began to seriously study composition in 1939, when he began lessons with Bernard Wagenaar at the Juilliard School of Music. Later he studied at the Berkshire Music Center and at Yale University with Paul Hindemith. He went on to build a prolific and diversified catalogue which earned him many awards, including the 1957 Pulitzer Prize.[2] An energetic man, Dello Joio also held many administrative positions. From 1945 to 1950, he headed the music department at Sarah Lawrence College. In the late 1950s, while chairing a project for the Ford Foundation, he joined the faculty at the Mannes School of Music, leaving to become dean of the Fine Arts School at Boston University (1972-1978). In 1942 he married an amateur ballerina, Grace Baumgold, and they raised three children. Divorced in 1973, Dello Joio married professional actress, Barbara Boulton, the following year. Since leaving Boston, they have lived in East Hampton, New York.

THE SONGS
Written with wonderful vocal and theatrical instincts, Dello Joio's songs attest to his Italian heritage. Some are like mini operatic scenes with delicate dramas played out on the microscopic stage of song. Others are small arias, intensified by the containment of the song form. Most, however, are simply warm, expressive, lyrical utterances of love, death and leave taking. (Giuseppi Verdi was, after all, an idol.) But, inspired as well by his liturgical ancestry, especially that of the Gregorian chant, Dello Joio's songs are essentially spare and true. A superior craftsman, with much beautiful detailing, he varies, develops, and shapes his material into songs of the utmost refinement. He has that rare ability to create a song which, on first hearing appears straightforward but, in time, reveals unexpected delicacies. The harmonic palette is broad and colorful; dissonances have purpose; rhythms are inventive and expressive.

Dello Joio's sensitivity for prosody, combined with a deft ability to turn the vocal phrase, make his songs a pleasure for the singer. Cantilena and declamation seamlessly intertwine as they attend the textual nuances. Only *Un Sonetto di Petrarca* and *Three Songs of Adieu* push above moderate ranges. They are, in fact, the only works of real difficulty. Elsewhere, despite the dissonances and the piano's seeming independence, the common sense behind the writing precludes any real difficulties. *Eyebright* and *Meeting at Night* are recorded by John Hanks on Duke, Vol. 1 (DWR 6417), and *The Listeners* by William Parker on New World (300). Most of Dello Joio's published songs are listed. Unless otherwise noted they are published in one key only.

All Things Leave Me, Arthur Symons; Fischer c1950.
> Spec. medium voice (f1–f2); 1:45; Allegro grazioso; vocal and piano lines gracefully intertwine in this lovely, vivid waltz.

The Assassination (Two fates discuss a human problem), adapted by the composer from the poem by Robert Hillyer; Fischer c1949.
> Spec. low voice (bb–d2); 4:00; Andante; difficult interpretively; a spare and subdued dialogue in many sections and tempos; much dramatic characterization in the piano; of what was probably the first performance, one critic wrote: "It is a scena, based on a metaphysical conceit, the destruction of hope; yet Miss Howland's superb performance made it as exciting as Italian *verismo.*"[3]

The Dying Nightingale, Stark Young;[4] one of *Six Love Songs;* Fischer c1954.
> Spec. high voice (db1–gb2); 4:30; Molto Adagio; bird song motifs and other delicate detail; lyrically declaimed; briefly impassioned; intense, somber, haunting; a beautiful song.

Eyebright, J. Addington Symonds; one of *Six Love Songs;* Fischer c1954.
> Spec. medium voice (eb1–f2), text suggests man; 2:30; Andante, con tenerezza; flowing, warm, and expressive; recorded by Hanks.

How Do I Love Thee? words adapted by the composer from Elizabeth Barrett Browning; one of *Six Love Songs;* Fischer c1954; also incl. *SE.*
> Spec. high voice (d1–g2); 2:30; Andante, molto espressivo; like a lyric recitative; a wide range of dynamics and expression.

Lament,[5] Chidiock Tichborne; Fischer c1959.
> Spec. for medium voice (c1–f2), rec. dramatic weight; 4:30; Adagio; intense declamation over spare, dissonant piano textures; a powerful song of operatic proportions.

The Listeners, Walter de la Mare; Fischer c1960.
> Spec. medium voices (b–f2), rec. dramatic weight; 5:00; Allegro non troppo e misterioso; the striking piano writing underscores the

narration of the dramatic, unsettling scene; requires a first-rate story teller; powerful and different; recorded by Parker.

Meeting at Night, Robert Browning; one of *Six Love Songs;* Fischer c1954.

Spec. high voice (f1–g2); 1:45; Allegro molto deciso; like the beating of two hearts, the ostinato bass conveys the anticipation of the meeting; a perpetual ebb and flow of dynamics; the most dramatic of the *Six Love Songs;* exciting; recorded by Hanks.

Mill Doors, Carl Sandburg; Fischer c1948; also incl. *CSE.*

Rec. all but light voices[6] (high e1–f#2); 3:00; Very slow; a heavy vocal line over a droning ostinato bass; bleak dissonances; evokes the bleeding of the working man by industrial society; cheerless but strong.

Note Left on a Doorstep, Lily Peter; Marks c1969; to Lily Peter.

Spec. medium voice (e♭1–f2); 2:30; Lento espressivo; recitative-like but over a full accompaniment; serene in the assertion that death can take the body but not the soul.

Six Love Songs, see separate entries for: *Eyebright; Why So Pale and Wan, Fond Lover?; Meeting at Night; The Dying Nightingale; All Things Leave Me; How Do I Love Thee?* Published separately, there is little reason to keep these songs together. Three are specified for high voice, three for medium. Because, however, all are in an average range well suited to lyric voices, and because all are about various aspects of love, they do work as a group if one chooses. *The Dying Nightingale* was written in 1950, the others in 1948.

Un Sonetto di Petrarca (a Sonnet by Petrarch) Francesco Petrarca, Marks c1964; also incl. *NVS.*

Rec. high full voices (f#1–b♭2), text suggests men; 2:30; Andante appassionato; in Italian; English translation provided; the sweeping, cascading phrases for voice and piano barely relax, driving exultantly to the grand finale; requires a singer with a gorgeous sound and plenty of stamina, who can handle the high tessitura; Petrach's passionate homage to his beloved Laura is the most opulent of Dello Joio's settings.

There Is a Lady Sweet and Kind, Anonymous Elizabethan; Fischer c1948; also incl. *CSE.*

Spec. medium voices (high, d1–g2),[7] text suggests men; 2:00; Amabile; graceful, elegant and charming.

Three Songs of Adieu, Marks c1962.

Rec. high lyric voices (f1-b♭2); 6:00; titles are: *After Love* (Arthur Symons); *Fade, Vision Bright* (Anonymous); *Farewell* (John Addington Symonds); a short, deeply felt cycle on the theme of pain in parting; the high tessitura, angular vocal line, and potent dissonances make these the most difficult of Dello Joio songs.

Why So Pale and Wan, Fond Lover? John Suckling; one of *Six Love Songs;* Fischer c1954; also incl. *SE.*

Spec. medium voice (d1–e2); 1:45; Andante movendo; over a lively piano part, the poet, with a taunting melody, questions the lover's efforts to win his woman.

Also of interest:

Ballad of Thomas Jefferson, Lerman, folklike, best for men; **Bright Star,** Andante Semplice, a Christmas song; **The Holy Infant's Lullaby,** Andantino, a Christmas song; **New Born,** Marshall, Andante con tenerezza; **Songs of Remembrance,** Wheelock, four songs for baritone in the bass clef, a major work originally for orchestra, but a good piano reduction is available.

BIBLIOGRAPHY

AmerGroves, Baker, Ewen, Friedberg (III), Goss, Greene, Nathan, Thompson.

Bumgardner, Thomas A. *Norman Dello Joio.* Boston: G.K. Hall & Co., 1986.

Downes, Edward. "The Music of Norman Dello Joio." *Musical Quarterly* 48 (April 1962): 149–72.

Sabin, Robert. "Norman Dello Joio." *Musical America,* December 1, 1950.

---

[1] The original family name was Ioio.

[2] The Pulitzer was given for *Meditations on Ecclesiastes,* for string orchestra.

[3] This review of a recital by Alice Howland is found in *Musical America,* Nov. 15, 1948.

[4] Stark Young was a friend of Dello Joio's. A full discussion of this song can be found in Friedberg (III).

[5] Written on the eve of his execution, this poem is usually referred to as *Tichborne's Elegy*. It was also set by David Diamond under the title *Life and Death*.

[6] Originally conceived for baritone (according to Bumgardner), but specified for medium voice, and available high and low in *CSE*.

[7] Published separately for medium voice; also available high and low in *CSE*.

DAVID DEL TREDICI
b. March 16, 1937, Cloverdale, CA

Though Del Tredici began as a pianist, he also studied composition with Andrew Imbrie, Arnold Elson, and Seymour Shifrin. Encouraged by Darius Milhaud to make composition a career, Del Tredici spent two years at Princeton University on a Woodrow Wilson fellowship. He has taught at Harvard University, Boston University, and City College of New York.

The Joyce settings were written in what Del Tredici has called "a scrim of wrong notes, a haze of atonality" to placate the fiercely modern composers of the Princeton school.[1] Since then, no more of his songs have been published. Nevertheless, by virtue of his compositions based on "Alice in Wonderland" for soprano and orchestra, Del Tredici will forever be linked to the vocal idiom.[2] *Four Songs*, a compelling, expressive set in a modern idiom, is highly recommended. *Two Songs*, also to Joyce, composed at the same time, but published later, is less cohesive, and consequently less effective.

Four Songs, James Joyce; Boosey c1974; comp. 1958–1960.
Rec. medium and high, full voices (a–a2), a solid low register is needed; 13:00; titles are: *Dove Song; She Weeps Over Rahoon; A Flower Given to My Daughter; Monotone;* not originally intended as a cycle, but best when treated as such; Del Tredici's earliest work; musically very challenging; cross rhythms and frequent meter changes; many tiny tempo and dynamic fluctuations notated; though the vocal writing is disjunct, it is also idiomatic and conducive to warm, lyrical singing; a few effects, such as slides and glissandos, are called for; multi-textured; a complex, often pictorial, piano part; much rehearsal required; intellectual, yet profoundly felt songs in a modern idiom.

BIBLIOGRAPHY
AmerGroves, Baker, Ewen, Greene, Manning (on *Four Songs*), Thompson. Suttoni, Charles. "David Del Tredici: Musician of the Month," *Musical America*, September, 1980.

---

[1] Interview with Charles Suttoni, *Musical America*, 4.
[2] One of these, *In Memory of a Summer Day*, won the 1980 Pulitzer Prize.

DAVID DIAMOND
b. July 9, 1915, Rochester, NY

With neo-romanticism again in favor, David Diamond's orchestral works have been reheard with new enthusiasm. Meanwhile, his impressive catalogue of art song continues to be inexplicably overlooked.

The son of Austrian-Polish Jewish immigrants, Diamond's father was a cabinetmaker; his mother a dressmaker for the Yiddish theater. By age seven Diamond had not only taught himself to play violin but also composed odd little tunes using notation of his own invention. When he was ten, the family found themselves in such financial straits they went to live with relatives in Cleveland. There, a Swiss musician, André de Ribaupierre, was impressed enough to give Diamond some formal training, and to provide him with the funds to study at the Cleveland Institute of Music. In 1929 the family returned to Rochester. Still in high school, Diamond took additional classes at the Eastman School of Music, where his principal teacher was Bernard Rogers. But after one year as an undergraduate, he rebelled against the conservative training and left for New York City, where—while taking menial jobs to support himself—he studied with Roger Sessions.

In 1935 Diamond receievd a commission to work in Paris, enabling him to make the first of several influential trips to that city. There he studied with Nadia Boulanger and met many prominent artists. But with war imminent, he returned to America, where his compositions were beginning to be heard. In the early 1950s, a series of Fulbright fellowships made it possible for him to work in Italy. Since his return to the United States in 1965, Diamond has continued to compose prolifically. He has also taught at a number of institutions including SUNY (Buffalo), the Manhattan School of Music, and the Juilliard School of Music from which he retired in 1986. Eventually he resettled in

Rochester. Diamond has a command of seven languages. He is also a serious painter and has written an—as yet unpublished—autobiography.

THE SONGS

Diamond's nearly 100 published songs have met with mysterious and shocking neglect. Perhaps their sheer number, variety of styles, and lack of consistency have dismayed singers from giving them the attention required to sort out the best. Diamond is quick to put any text to music, and does so with such facility and lack of self censorship, it is not surprising that many fail. Nevertheless, at his best, his highly personal style and unerring sense for prosody have resulted in some unusually compelling and poignant songs.

Despite a certain sameness, the early songs, mostly from the 1940s, are especially recommended. The writing is lyrical but spare and intense. Moody and philosophical, often about death, the tendency is to slower tempos; harmonies, though primarily tonal, are spartan, sometimes astringent. A few of the songs take on operatic dimensions but, in general, the vocal writing is contained and presents few difficulties. The songs of Diamond's later years, however, are altogether different and can be treacherous. With a wider variety of personality and text (though still tending to the melancholy), they neither have the restraint nor the lyricism of the earlier works. Generally atonal, very chromatic, harmonically and rhythmically intricate, vocal writing is declamatory and disjunct, accompaniments formidably difficult and elaborate. It is in this period that one finds the unwieldy, somewhat bombastic—with the notable exception of *Love and Time*—cycles.

Having emphasized the somber side of Diamond, it would be negligent not to mention that he has also written some successful humorous songs, which may be helpful in shaping an appealing group for a recital. Most of Diamond's songs are available individually. There is no album of his songs, but some appear in anthologies. Sopranos will want to consider the lively, long *Mad Maid's Song* with flute and harpsichord (or piano). The very beautiful *David Mourns for Absalom* and *Brigid's Song* are recorded by Mildred Miller on Desto (411/412). Personal recommendations from Diamond's large, uneven, but compelling corpus of songs follow. This author finds even the best of the cycles of questionable merit, but in deference to their magnitude, they are all cited under "Also of interest." Keep in mind that virtually all earlier songs are, at least, somewhat tonal, but that later songs (after about 1960) are atonal.

Anniversary in a Country Cemetery, Katherine Anne Porter; Arrow
c1942; comp. 1940.
   Rec. medium and high voices (c1–g2); 2:45; Lento e mesto; dirge-
like, but builds to a poignant *ff*.

As Life What is So Sweet, Anonymous (circa 1624); Arrow c1941;
comp. 1940.
   Rec. medium and high voices (d♭1–g2); 1:30; Andante; lyrical and
warm.

Billy in the Darbies,[1] Herman Melville; Elkan Vogel c1946; comp.
1944.
   Rec. medium voices (c1–g2), text suggests men; 3:00; Allegretto;
this moving soliloquy of an innocent man facing execution in the
morning has been to music many times. Diamond sets the whole
ballad, following all the ramblings of Billy's dazed mind; hypnotic
undulations in the accompaniment evoke both the ocean and the
drowsiness overtaking Billy.

Brigid's Song, James Joyce; Mercury c1947; comp. 1946; also incl.
CAAS.
   Rec. medium voices (c1–g2); 1:00; Andante; simple, lyrical;
recorded by Miller.

Chatterton, John Keats; Southern c1950; comp. 1946.
   Rec. high, heavier voices (b–b2); 3:00; Adagio non troppo; expansive; an impassioned central section; rises to a climactic high B; dignified and strong.

David Mourns for Absalom, from the Second Book of Samuel (18:33);
Mercury c1947; comp. 1946.
   Rec. dramatic voices (c1–a2); 2:45; Andantino; an expansive
vocal line over chords; an eloquent, impassioned lament, almost operatic in scope; one of Diamond's best; recorded by Miller.

Don't Cry, Marilyn Monroe (as published in *McCall's* magazine, August,
1972); G. Schirmer c1983; comp. 1981.
   Spec. high voice; (d1–b2), rec. lyric or coloratura; 1:00; Allegretto; sustained with melismatic passages; a despairing cradle song
which ends "Help, I feel life coming closer when all I want is to die;"
a curiosity because of the poet, but could be very effective.

Epitaph (On the Grave of a Young Cavalry Officer Killed in the Valley of Virginia),[2] Herman Melville; Associated c1946; also incl. *AAS;* comp. 1945.

Rec. higher voices (c1–g2); 1:15; Poco Adagio; short phrases; sensitive, delicate, gentle.

The Epitaph, Logan Pearsall Smith (from "More Trivia"); Elkan-Vogel c1947; comp. 1946; to Leonard Bernstein.[3]

Rec. medium or low voices (bb–f2); 1:00; Allegretto; over light staccatos the poet, in conversational style, contemplates his own funeral; different and refreshing.

For an Old Man, T. S. Eliot; Southern c1951; also incl. *VN;* comp. 1943.

Rec. big medium voices (d1–f2); 1:00; Allegro barbaro; an old man vents his feelings about age.

Four Ladies, Ezra Pound; Southern c1966; comp. 1935; rev. 1962.

Rec. medium and low voices (a–eb2), text suggests men; 3:00; the titles of this mini-cycle are: *Agathas; Young Lady; Lesbia Illa; Passing;* engaging miniatures of ladies past their prime.

Homage to Paul Klee, Babette Deutsch; Elkan-Vogel c1973; comp. 1960.

Rec. lyric, high voices (bb–a#2); 2:00; Allegretto; disjunct; fragmented; intricate; much staccato; difficult musically; charming, different, and fun—like a Paul Klee drawing.

I am Rose, Gertrude Stein; Elkan-Vogel c1973; comp. 1973.

Rec. medium voices (d1–e2); 1:00; Andante, molto semplice; winsome and lyrical; more subdued than Rorem's setting of the same poem.

I Shall Imagine Life, E. E. Cummings; Southern c1968; comp. 1962.

Rec. medium voices (b–f#2); 1:00; Andante; contemplative and lyric; expansive even in its brevity.

If You Can't, E. E. Cummings; Leeds c1950; comp. 1949.

Rec. medium voices (d1–g#2); 1:00; Allegro; a catchy encore-type novelty; colloquial, on the problems of being a bum; fun but not characteristic of Diamond or Cummings.

Let Nothing Disturb Thee, St. Teresa of Avila (English version by Henry Wadsworth Longfellow); Associated c1946; comp. 1945; ded. to Mr. and Mrs. Igor Stravinsky.

   Spec. medium voices (c1–f2); 1:30; Adagio tranquillo; lyrical; a soothing prayer.

Life and Death, Chidiock Tichborne; Southern c1971; comp. 1971.

   Rec. medium voices (a–g2); 4:00; Andante; a disjunct, haunting melody in different sequences; pitches are difficult; compelling.

The Lover as Mirror, Edward Stringham; Elkan Vogel c1946; comp. 1944; to Jennie Tourel.

   Rec. medium voices (c1–g2); 1:45; Andante; independent piano and vocal lines; reflective; interesting.

The Millennium, Isak Dinesen (from "Out of Africa"); Southern c1969; comp. 1960.

   Rec. medium or low voices (a–f#2); Adagio; narrative; recitando; describes the preparations for the return of Christ and his desire to, once more, walk the road to Calvary; strange, but persuasive.

Music, When Soft Voices Die, Percy Bysshe Shelley; Associated c1944; also incl. *AAS;* comp. 1943.

   Rec. medium or low voices (c1–e2); 0:45; Moderato; warmly lyrical over flowing eighths.

My Papa's Waltz, Theodore Roethke; Southern c1968; comp. 1964.

   Rec. medium voices (b–e2); 1:00; Tempo di Valzer triste, un po' macabro; to the dizzying rhythms of a drunken waltz, the child just manages to hold on to his father.

My Spirit Will Not Haunt the Mound, Thomas Hardy; Southern c1952; comp. 1946.

   Rec. medium and low voices (c1–e2); 1:45; Adagio; lyrical; warm and unaffected.

On Death, John Clare; Associated c1944; also incl. *AAS;* comp. 1943.

   Rec. medium or high voices (c1–g2); 2:45; Adagio e mesto; opens unaccompanied voice; sustained, expansive; stirring and bleak.

A Portrait (the Marchioness of Brinvilliers), Herman Melville; Elkan-Vogel c1947; comp. 1946.

Rec. medium voices (c1–g2); 1:00; Allegretto grazioso; a comely vocal line and filigree piano describe the many shadings the artist has woven into the portrait.

The Shepherd Boy Sings in the Valley of Humiliation, John Bunyan; Southern c1949; comp. 1946.

Rec. high voices (d♭1–b2); 1:00; Allegretto grazioso; an ebullient, supple melody; straightforward and vigorous.

Sister Jane, Jean de la Fontaine; Elkan-Vogel c1946; comp. 1943.

Rec. high voices (d1–g2); 0:45; Allegretto scherzando; a lively patter; a witty seventeenth-century poem about "Sister Jane, who had produced a child."

This World Is Not My Home, Anonymous; Elkan-Vogel c1947; comp. 1946; dedicated to James and Mia Agee.[4]

Rec. medium voices (d1–f2); 0:45; Andante sostenuto; folklike; simple and affecting; would make a nice encore.

The Twisted Trinity, Carson McCullers; Elkan-Vogel c1946; comp. 1943.

Rec. medium or high voices (c1–g2); 1:45; Lento; subdued, builds to an expansive central section; twisted lines interweave; a final cryptic chord; strange, stark, ironic.

Also of interest:

L'ame de Debussy, letters of Debussy; a cycle for medium voice; **Do I Love You?** (Theme and Variations), Larson, for high voices; **The Fall,** cycle of nine songs to the sonnets of James Agee, for medium and high voices; **Hebrew Melodies,** Byron, cycle of four songs for higher voices, best for men, dramatic, demanding; **Love and Time,** Loucheim, a cycle of four songs; **We Two,** a cycle of nine Shakespeare sonnets.

BIBLIOGRAPHY

AmerGroves, Baker, CBY (1966), Ewen, Flanagan, Friedberg (III), Goss, Greene, Nathan, Thompson.

Crociata, Francis. "Our 'Youngest' Symphonic Composer Turns 60," *The New York Times,* July 6, 1975.

Diamond, David. "From the Notebook of David Diamond," *Music Journal* 22 (April 1964).

Freed, Richard D. "Music is Diamond's Best Friend," *The New York Times*, August 22, 1965.

Kimberling, Victoria. *David Diamond: A Bio-bibliography.* Metuchen, NJ: The Scarecrow Press, 1987.

Peyser, Joan. "A Composer Who Defies Categorization," *The New York Times,* July 7, 1985.

---

[1] Darbies are handcuffs or shackles. This well known ballad serves as an epilogue to Melville's *Billy Budd.*

[2] Diamond's subtitle for this song is Melville's original title.

3 Diamond's temper, egomania, and morbidity were legendary. However, he enjoyed the fact that his close friends, Aaron Copland and Leonard Bernstein, wanted to start a fund for him to see a psychiatrist. Here he seems to be poking fun at them about it.

4 According to Victoria Kimberling in *David Diamond: A Bio-bibliography,* the poem was not only dedicated to but also written by Agee, the young writer who had such trouble reconciling with the ways of the world. Mia was his third wife. Diamond must have known them in his Greenwich Village days.

TOM DOBSON
b. Aug. 17, 1890, Portland, OR; d. Nov. 5, 1918, New York, NY

Tom Dobson was a performer, a composer, and for a few brief seasons, a minor celebrity. As a boy soprano he joined choirs in San Francisco and Washington D.C., not to return home until he was 13. After musical studies in Berkeley, California, in 1911 he proceeded to New York City, where he studied voice, piano, and composition. In 1914 Dobson gave the first of his unusual one-man recitals at the quaint Punch and Judy Theater. Immensely successful, his performances, in which he accompanied himself, often in his own compositions, became a seasonal event until his tragic early death following a brief illness.

Dobson's singing and playing were not, in themselves, especially remarkable. It was, rather, his artistry, delivery, personal charm, and unusual programming, that enabled him to command the stage alone and establish a rare intimacy with his audiences. This same gift for communication is reflected in his own vivid and imaginative compositions. Big settings of John Masefield's *Cargoes* and *An Old Song Resung* are the best known of his songs. However, if one can track down a copy, the charming little cycle, *The Rocky Road to Dublin,* to poems of James Stephens, is a winner.

BIBLIOGRAPHY
Wiggin, Kate Douglas. "Biographical Sketch...In Memoriam." Boston:
  Oliver Ditson, 1919. These brief essays serve as introduction to
  Dobson's cycle *The Rocky Road to Dublin*.
"A Unique Singer of Unique Songs," *Musical America,* June 17, 1916.

CELIUS DOUGHERTY
b. May 27, 1902, Glenwood, MN; d. Dec. 22, 1986, Effort, PA

Younger performers may never have heard of Celius Dougherty, but in
the 1940s and 1950s, his songs were fixtures in American teaching studios and on standard recital programs.

Dougherty graduated from the University of Minnesota, where he
studied composition and piano with Donald Ferguson, and performed his
own piano concerto with the University orchestra. In 1924, as winner of
a competition sponsored by the St. Paul Schubert Club, he went to New
York City to study composition with Rubin Goldmark, and piano with
Josef Lhevinne on scholarship at the Juilliard School of Music. He soon
became a favorite accompanist to well known singers, such as Maggie
Teyte, Eva Gauthier, Povla Frijsh, Jennie Tourel, Marian Anderson, and
Alexander Kipnis, all of whom often included Dougherty's songs on
their programs. In 1939 Dougherty began a 16-year association with
Vincenz Ruzicika. As a duo piano team, the adventurous pair performed
the American premieres of works by Stravinsky, Schoenberg,
Hindemith, and Milhaud. Dougherty retired to a small town in Pennsylvania, where he died from cancer.

THE SONGS
Other than one opera, *Many Moons* (based on a James Thurber story),
and a smattering of choral, piano, and chamber pieces, Dougherty composed songs. Often written for the singers he accompanied, they date
from the 1920s to the 1960s, but the hey day of their popularity was the
1950s. Their simple— generally optimistic, often humorous—sentiments, perfectly suited that complacent era, and Doughtery rendered
them with taste and skill.

Occasionally, when dealing with serious themes, Dougherty develops an unattractive heavy hand, which muddies textures and weights
vocal lines. Otherwise, he knew singers well and the writing is idiomatic. Few of the songs present difficulties though several call for an operatic sound. Not surprisingly, this accompanist/composer crafted the

piano parts with particular care and, at times, they contain the most interesting material. There are some old recordings of Dougherty as an accompanist but virtually none of his songs. A sampling of the most popular as well as some personal recommendations follow.

Heaven-Haven, Gerard Manley Hopkins; Fischer c1956; also incl. *SE.*
     Rec. medium voices (eb1–f2); 2:30; Very quietly and very sustained; chordal; warm, subdued, and eloquent.

The K'e, From the Chinese, 718 B.C.; G. Schirmer c1954; also incl. *20CAS.*
     Rec. medium women's voices (d1–f2); 3:00; Slowly; sustained; animated central section; a woman recalls her love for the foreign lad whose rejection has made her old; simply and touchingly told.

Love in the Dictionary, From Funk and Wagnalls Students' Standard Dictionary; G. Schirmer c1949; also incl. *S22A;* for Blanche Thebom.
     Rec. any voice (high, c1–g2); 2:15; Leisurely at first...then, in spirited waltz rhythm; many subtle changes to convey the various kinds of love defined by this dictionary, ending with "love" as a term used in tennis; this clever, fun, tasteful song is still often used as an encore; according to the cover, it was recorded by Blanche Thebom on RCA Victor; also by Cynthia Haymon on Argo CD (436-117-2ZH).

Loveliest of Trees, A. E. Housman; Boosey c1948.
     Rec. medium to high lyric voices (eb1–gb2); 3:15; With rapture, but quietly; sustained over a finely wrought, flowing accompaniment; serene and very lovely.

A Minor Bird, Robert Frost; G. Schirmer c1958; also incl *20CAS.*
     Rec. medium voices (f1–eb2); 2:00; Melancholy; a lyric recitative responds to the piano's plaintive bird motif; later, full chords accompany the poet's growing insight.

Music, Amy Lowell; Row c1953; for Winifred Cecil.
     Rec. medium voices (c1–f2), text suggest women; 3:15; Quietly, not dragging; nightly, the poet muses over the beauty of her neighbor's flute playing (nicely evoked by the piano) but, in the day, avoids looking at the fat bald musician; well done; different.

Primavera, Amy Lowell; G. Schirmer c1948; also incl. *S22A;* for Margaret Speaks.

Rec. high lyric voices (high, c1–bb2), best for sopranos; With joyous enthusiasm; in operatic style, a quasi recitative followed by a joyous arioso; one of Dougherty's most popular songs.

Songs by e. e. cummings, G. Schirmer c1966; pub. separately.
Rec. higher lyric voices (c1–bb2); 5:30; these four songs, often sung individually, also make a nice group. The arbitrary order given on the covers (and below) might best be changed.
thy fingers make early flowers of all things, also incl. *20CAS;* (eb1–g2); 2:15; Andantino; lyrical and quiet; briefly impassioned.
until and i heard, (f1–bb2); 1:30; Allegretto; opens quietly, intensifying throughout; some big singing and sustained high notes.
o by the by, (c1–g2); 1:00; Leggero; bright; rhythmic; charming.
little fourpaws, (db1–eb2); 0:45; Moderato; metronome marking seems fast; a delicate parlando over flowing sixteenths.

Also of interest:

Green Meadows, Anonymous, Andante; ***Hushed Be the Camps Today,*** Whitman, With simple fervor; ***Listen the Wind,*** Wolfe, best for baritone, active; ***Madonna of the Evening Flowers,*** Lowell, Broadly; ***Pianissimo,*** Collins, best for women, With steady pulsing rhythm; ***Portrait of a Lady,*** Lowell, Andantino; ***The Song of the Jasmine,*** Dolcissimo, sustained; ***Sound the Flute!*** Blake, also incl. *CAS28,* Quickly and lightly; ***The Taxi,*** Lowell, also incl. *SE,* Monotonously. Also ***Five American Folk Songs*** and ***Five Sea Shanties.***

BIBLIOGRAPHY
AmerGroves, Baker, Greene.
Obituary, *The New York Times,* Dec. 23, 1986.

JOHN DUKE
b. July 30, 1899, Cumberland, MD; d. Oct. 26, 1984, Northampton, MA

John Duke is not widely known outside the singing world, but within those confines, he is regarded as one of America's foremost composers of art song. Although his songs enjoyed their greatest popularity in the mid twentieth century, recent recordings and new publications have spurred renewed interest and reaffirmed their appeal.

Duke's father, who engaged in various business pursuits, loved literature and at one time owned a bookstore; his mother sang and taught her son to read music. Duke, the eldest of six children, began piano lessons when he was 11. At age 16, he won a scholarship to the Peabody Conservatory in Baltimore where, for three years, he studied piano with Harold Randolph and composition with Gustav Strube. After service in the Student Army Training Corps during World War I, Duke settled in New York City. While working at the Ampico recording laboratories, he continued his musical studies and, in 1920, gave his debut recital as a concert pianist. In 1923 his first songs were published by G. Schirmer, and that same year, he accepted the teaching position at Smith College he would hold until his retirement 44 years later. In 1929, on a one year's sabbatical, he studied piano with Arthur Schnabel in Berlin, and composition with Nadia Boulanger in Paris.

For much of Duke's career, composition was an activity he did on the side. His duties at Smith were as a pianist and teacher of piano, and he also concertized. Beginning in 1954, summers included visits to the Seagle Colony in Schroon Lake, New York, a camp devoted to vocal studies, where he gave master classes and lectures. His long marriage to Dorothy Macon of Virginia was an exceptionally happy one.[1] With their two children—a daughter, Karen[2] (who also sang and composed) and son, Jay —they lived a quiet life in their comfortable home in Northampton, Massachusetts. In 1960 Duke was named to the Henry Dike Sleeper Chair of Music. In 1967 the amiable, soft-spoken professor emeritus retired, but he continued to compose till the week before his death.

THE SONGS

Duke produced his most vital and original work during his early years of composition. Though he has said that he was little affected by modern developments and simply wrote as he pleased,[3] in these early songs he clearly seems inspired by the exciting musical trends of the 1920s and 1930s. Subsequently, in the 1940s, 1950s, and early 1960s his work is notably less adventuresome. It is, however, his most fertile and consistent period and the one that established his reputation. The songs of his middle years are not only his best known and loved, but also his most accessible and conventional. Here and there one senses the original passion and vitality, but the daring is gone. Though he continued to be prolific in his late years, inspiration and ideas were increasingly at a premium. One also suspects a lack of self-criticism and a growing failure to edit; unchecked, these songs ramble and lose definition.

Duke wrote little instrumental music.[4] It is song that tantalized him—"the strange and marvelous chemistry of words and music."[5]

Preoccupied with their proper integration, he dismissed the concept that the aim is to enhance the poem with music. He believed, rather, that words become elements of music themselves. To the singer, he warns: "It is the ability to feel how the text of a song is assimilated by the music which distinguishes the singer of real interpretative insight from the vocal virtuoso."[6]

Having great affection for the voice, Duke gave it ample opportunity to shine in a natural, unpressed manner and lovingly fashioned supple, often sustained vocal lines. Declamation and recitative bring out some of his finest invention, but he employed it sparingly in later songs. An accomplished pianist himself, Duke's accompaniments are fluid, expert, and often virtuosic—at times, just short of overwhelming the vocal line. The songs of the middle and late years are generally of moderate musical difficulty, but some of the earlier ones, especially those that have discarded time and key signatures, even bar lines, can be challenging.

Duke's songs have suffered needlessly (even on recordings) as a result of unimaginative programming. There is far more variety, interest, and outright fun in his catalogue than one would suppose given the sameness of the selections performers have historically made. Early songs, especially the witty and wild ones, are almost never heard. Recently there has been a plethora of new publications and now the great majority of his approximately 265 songs are easily available. Southern has issued vast numbers, including three volumes of previously unpublished ones. Titled *Songs of John Duke,* each volume is comprised of those songs that are geared to a specific voice range. Volume One *(SJD1)* is specified for high voice; Volume Two *(SJD2)* for medium voice; Volume Three *(SJD3)* is not specified but inclines towards medium and lower voices. In addition, Schirmer has issued an especially wonderful volume, *Songs of John Duke (SJD),* containing some new material, but mostly valuable reprints of early songs. It is available for low and high voices, though not all songs are transposed. In addition, Recital Publications has issued *Eight Songs on Translations from the Greek and Latin Poets.*

There are several recordings. Most have Duke himself, expert but a bit loose (probably due to age), at the piano. Carole Bogard (with Duke) features the Cummings settings and songs from the 1960s and 1970s on Cambridge (CRS 2776); Donald Boothman (with Duke) offers a nice variety on Golden Age (1004), and the two pair up again on AFKA CD (SK-505) with a less interesting selection. A few of the earlier songs are recorded by John Hanks on Duke, Vols. 1 and 2 (DWR 6417 and 7306, respectively). Yolanda Marcoulescou-Stern sings four songs on Gasparo CD (287). Best of all is Donald Gramm's rendition of the E. A. Robinson poems on New World (243). Most Duke songs were written and published in one key alone. However, because *SJD* and certain other anthologies published high and low volumes, singers may be able to find preferable transpositions in these collections. In an effort to point out the diversity in Duke's songs, recommendations emphasize the more unusual in addition to those that, despite their conventionality, are well known or otherwise successful.

Acquainted with the Night, Robert Frost; Southern c1964; also incl. *VN;* comp. 1950.
   Rec. medium voices (b–f2); 3:15; At the rate of a slow, casual walk; the night wanderer contemplates the deserted city streets in a light declamation over delicate, descriptive figurations; uneasy; evocative.

Be Still as You Are Beautiful, Patrick MacDonogh; Fischer c1968; also incl. *SE;* comp. 1961.
   Rec. medium voices (c1–f2), text suggests men; 2:30; Quiet and flowing; cantabile over a fluid accompaniment; a poignant love song; recorded by Boothman (Golden Age) and Marcoulescou-Stern.

Bells in the Rain, Elinor Wylie; Fischer c1948; comp. 1945.
   Pub. high voice (e1–g2); 2:30; Quietly, with bell-like evenness; delicate and sustained over high sixteenths; a fine example of Duke's appealing lyricism; recorded by Marcoulescou-Stern.

The Bird, Elinor Wylie; G. Schirmer c1947/1949; issued with *Little Elegy* under the title *Two Songs;* also incl. *SJD;* comp. 1946; to Bidú Sayão.
   Rec. high lyric voices (f1–a2); 2:00; Simply and very quietly; the bird song motif is heard in the introduction, interlude, and postlude; the sustained vocal line, though requiring the greatest clarity and delicacy, develops a surprising intensity in its plea for the bird to sing again; one of Duke's best known songs; recorded by Bidú Sayão on Columbia (ML 4154).

Bredon Hill, A. E. Housman; incl. *SJD3;* comp. 1981.

Rec. medium and low lyric voices (a#–e2), text suggests men; 3:15; Moderato; a warm lyric line over bell-like chords; recorded by Boothman (Afka).

Dirge, Adelaide Crapsey; incl. *SJD2;* comp. 1935.
Rec. medium and high voices (c#1–g2); 2:00; Slow and sustained; long lines intertwine with the piano; wide range of dynamics; spare and linear; grave and intense.

The End of the World, Archibald MacLeish; Valley Music c1953; comp. 1935.
Rec. medium voices with some weight (c1–f2); 2:45; Allegro giusto; a jaunty parlando, like a nonsense song, until with the words "Quite unexpectedly the top blew off," it does just that; then, mysterious and sustained; highly theatrical; an amazing song; recorded by Boothman (Golden Age).

Evening, Frederic Prokosch; Fischer c1954; also incl. *SE;* comp. 1948.
Pub. medium voice (a–g2); 2:15; With a quiet steady swing; the pure, hushed opening builds dramatically; strange imagery; different and effective.

February Twilight, Sara Teasdale; G. Schirmer c1926; also incl. *SJD* and *RAAS;* comp. 1924.
Rec. lyric voices (f#1–f#2); 1:45; Very sustained; spare, fragile chords and a thread of melody; evocative and beautiful.

Fragment, Adelaide Crapsey; also incl. *SJD;* comp.1935.
Rec. lyric voices (c#1–e2); 1:00; With a quiet swing; succinct; spare; strange and evocative.

The Grunchin Witch, Jessica Jackson; G. Schirmer c1926; also incl. *SJD;* comp. 1924.
Rec. medium voices (b–g2); 1:15; With a great rush; some tempo changes; wild chords; highly rhythmic; a colorful, crazy, fun song.

hist...whist, E. E. Cummings; Southern c1957; comp. 1952.
Rec. high lyric voices ([a]b–g2); 1:15; Very lively; all about witches and goblins, with a whisper and a squeal thrown in for good measure; good fun; very effective; recorded by Bogard.

just-spring, E. E. Cummings; Fischer c1954; also incl. *SE;* comp. 1949.
Rec. high lyric voices (d1–bb2); 1:30; Joyous; running sixteenths and a childhood chant motif in the piano; fun vocalism for the right

voice; ends quietly, but altogether a happy, colorful song; recorded by Bogard, Hanks (Vol. 2), and Marcoulescou-Stern.

The Last Word of a Bluebird (as told to a child), Robert Frost; G. Schirmer c1959; comp. 1955; also incl. *SJD*.

Rec. medium and lower voices (a–f2); 1:00; Strict tempo; the bluebird's message, that he has to move on but will be back in the spring, is delivered in short conversational phrases over a lively accompaniment; sprightly, fun.

Little Elegy, Elinor Wylie; G. Schirmer c1949; issued with *The Bird* under the title *Two Songs;* also incl. *SJD* and *RAAS;* comp. 1946.

Rec. high lyric voices (f1–a2); 1:00; Plaintively; spare; delicate.

Loveliest of Trees, A. E. Housman; G. Schirmer c1934; also incl. *22SA, SJD,* and *RAAS;* comp. 1928; to Lawrence Tibbett.

Pub. high and low (high, d#1–f2), rec. lyric voices; 2:00; Allegretto grazioso; a lovely cantilena over delicate, lilting piano figures; a more animated central section; one of Duke's most melodious and popular songs; recorded by Hanks (Vol. 1) and Boothman (Golden Age).

Luke Havergal,[7] Edward Arlington Robinson; Fischer c1948; also incl. *CSE;* comp. 1945.

Spec. medium voice (b–f2); 4:30; Sadly, tenderly; flowing; a haunting melodic line over a lush piano score; melodic and smooth even in dramatic sections; a chilling central section; powerful emotions in this mystical poem of unexplained longing; one of Duke's best; recorded by Gramm, by Thomas Hampson on EMI CD (7 54051 2), and by Dale Moore on Cambridge (CRS 2715).

Miniver Cheevy (A Satire in the form of variations),[8] Edward Arlington Robinson; Fischer c1948; comp. 1945.

Spec. low voice (g–f2); 5:00; the theme, set forth in the piano introduction, is followed by nine telling variations (Melancholy; Sprightly; Dreamy; Dolorous; Grandiose; Indignant; Puzzled; Tipsey; and an Epilogue) on the town drunkard—Miniver Cheevy; expert characterization; good fun; perfectly recorded by Gramm.

Morning in Paris, Robert Hillyer; Fischer c1956; comp. 1953.

Spec. high voice (eb1–a2); 1:15; Quiet and graceful; lilting, charming, nostalgic.

My Soul Is an Enchanted Boat, Percy B. Shelley; Valley c1953; comp.
1934.
    Rec. medium and high lyric voices (d♭1–g2); 1:45; a high ostina-
to octave figure fills the air through which the voice quietly makes its
way, its delicate line at times afloat in the rarified atmosphere; an
unusual, magical song.

Old Ben Golliday, Mark Van Doren; incl. *SJD3;* comp. 1971.
    Rec. low and middle voices (c1–e2); 2:30; Moderato; a tuneful,
ballad-like narrative, becoming increasingly poignant, with colorful
touches and good descriptive changes.

Rapunzel, Adelaide Crapsey; Mercury c1947; comp. 1935
    Rec. high voices (e1–a2); 2:15; Lento, quasi recitativo; many
tempo and dynamic changes; fragmented, declamatory building to a
big ending; suspenseful, strange, and dramatic.

Richard Cory, Edward Arlington Robinson; Fischer c1948; comp. 1945.
    Spec. low voice (a–e2); 2:30; Quietly and decorously but with an
elegant swing; the Richard Cory "strut" is depicted in the cool 6/8
accompaniment, over which, in 2/4, the story of a man who appeared
to have everything but "Went home and put a bullet through his
head," is told; excellent song; eloquently recorded by Gramm.

Silver, Walter de la Mare; G. Schirmer c1961; incl. *20CAS.*
    Rec. lyric lower voices (a–d?); 2:30; Slowly, with hushed intensi
ty; sustained over a spare, delicate accompaniment; poetic; atmospheric; a lovely song.

Six Poems by Emily Dickinson; Southern c1978; comp. 1968.
    Spec. soprano (b♯–a2); 10:00; titles are: *Good morning, Midnight;
Heart! We will forget him; Let down the bars, Oh Death; An awful
tempest mashed the air; Nobody knows this little Rose; Bee! I'm
expecting you!* This is the first and more distinguished of Duke's two
Dickinson sets; a cohesive group, though individual songs could be
excerpted; Duke sets the terse poetry in a romantic, expansive idiom;
recorded by Bogard.

Spring Thunder, Mark Van Doren; incl. *SE;* comp.1960.
    Pub. high and medium (e♭1–g2); 1:30; Moderato; some recitative;
alternately lyrical and dramatic; a moving depiction of the anticipation, approach, arrival, and significance of a spring storm.

Three Gothic Ballads, John Heath-Stubbs; Southern c1959; comp. 1952.
Rec. baritones (a–f2); 10:45; titles are: *The Old King; The Mad Knight's Song; The Coward's Lament;* originally published separately; now issued under one cover and definitely a cycle; mostly declamatory narratives in rather operatic style; musically complex; intense, somber, and thoughtful; a dramatic and different mini-cycle.

Two Songs, Elinor Wylie; see separate entries for *Little Elegy* and *The Bird.*

White in the Moon the Long Road Lies, A. E. Housman; Valley c1948; comp. 1934.
Rec. medium voices (c1–eb2); 3:15; the poet reflects over a hypnotic piano line, signifying the long road that leads him away from his lover; no key or time signatures; one of Duke's most original and beautiful songs, shattering in its evocation of dispassion and weariness; recorded by Hanks (Vol. 1).

Wild Swans, Edna St. Vincent Millay; Mercury c1947; reissued Southern c1985 with editing by Ruth C. Friedberg; comp. 1935.
Rec. high voices (db1–a2); 1:30; With great abandon; steady eighths in shifting meters; the voice, independent of the ranging piano, intensifies but ends *ppp;* wonderfully strange and evocative.

Also of interest:

Counting the Beats, Graves, also incl. *SJD2,* grim and intense; ***Elaine,*** Millay; incl. *SJD,* Andante; ***For a Dead Kitten,*** Hay, Funeral March Tempo; ***From the Sea***, Teasdale, incl. *SJD1,* five songs for soprano, pretty and conventional, recorded by Bogard; ***I can't be talkin' of love,*** Matthews, incl. *SJD,* With a quiet and steady swing, folksy; ***I carry your heart,*** Cummings, incl. *SJD,* recorded by Bogard and Hanks (Vol. 2); ***I Ride the Great Black Horses,*** Nathan, incl. *SJD,* dramatic, rhythmic, recorded by Boothman (Golden Age); ***I watched the Lady Caroline,*** de la Mare; incl. *SJD* and *20CAS,* With flowing rhythm and flexible tempo; ***the mountains are dancing,*** Cummings, for high lyric voices, joyous, recorded by Bogard and Hanks (Vol. 2); ***O, It Was out by Donneycarney,*** Joyce, incl. *SJD2,* delicate, folklike; ***Peggy Mitchell,*** Stephens, incl. *CAS28* and *SJD,* Tenderly, flowing; ***Penguin Geometry,*** Wheelock, incl. *SJD3,* Allegro moderato, long and humorous; ***A Piper,*** O'Sullivan, incl. *S22A* and *SJD,* In brisk March tempo; ***The Puritan's Ballad,*** Wylie, incl. *SJD1,* rec. dramatic sopranos, long, different;

Shelling Peas, Jessica Jackson, incl. *SJD*, Allegro, funny; *Stillness,* Karen Duke, incl. *SJD3*, Very quiet and sustained; *Stopping by Woods on a Snowy Evening,* Frost; incl. *SJD1*, Tempo giusto e molto dolce, recorded by Bogard; *To the Thawing Wind,* Frost; rec. big voices, With great excitement; *XXTH Century,* Hillyer; fast, different, recorded by Boothman (Golden Age); *Viennese Waltz,* Wylie, Dreamily, in moderate waltz tempo, recorded by Hanks (Vol. 1); *The White Dress,* Wolfe, incl. *SJD*, rec. low voices, sustained, recorded Boothman (Golden Age).

BIBLIOGRAPHY

AmerGroves, Baker, Friedberg (II), Thompson.

Beaver, Martha de B. "To Believe in Song, 'Man's Sweetest Joy,' Is at the Heart of His Career in Music," *Daily Hampshire Gazette,* March 27, 1973.

Duke, John. "Some Reflections on the Art Song in English," *The American Music Teacher* (Feb/March 1976).

————. "The Nature and Significance of Song," *NATS Bulletin* 40 (Jan/Feb 1984).

Friedberg, Ruth C. "The Songs of John Duke," *NATS Bulletin* 19 (May 1963).

————. "The Recent Songs of John Duke," *NATS Bulletin* 36 (Sept/Oct 1979).

Hayes, Gregory. "Finding his music in the world's great poetry," *Hampshire Gazette,* Jan. 26, 1983.

---

[1] Devoted to the literary arts, Dorothy wrote librettos for two of her husband's little operas, and the poem for the song *Reality*.

[2] Duke wrote the words and music for a song he called *To Karen, Singing* (Elkan-Vogel c1946). Karen herself wrote the poem *Stillness*, which Duke set in 1949.

[3] *Hampshire Gazette,* Jan. 26, 1983, p. 30.

[4] Some orchestral and chamber works were composed in the 1930s and 1940s. A few chamber operas and choral works were written as late as the 1960s.

[5] John Duke, "Words as Musical Elements," *The Bulletin (NATS)* (September 1954) p. 6.

[6] Ibid.

[7] *Luke Havergal, Miniver Cheevy,* and *Richard Cory* are all psychological portraits of people from fictional Tillbury Town, believed to actually be Robinson's home town of Gardiner, Maine.

[8] See note 7. The subtitle is provided by Duke, not Robinson.

VERNON DUKE
b. Oct. 10, 1903, Parfianovka, Russia; d. Jan. 16, 1969, Santa Monica, CA

Vernon Duke, born Vladimir Dukelsky, studied under Reinhold Glière at the Kiev Conservatory. In 1919 Duke fled the Russian revolution and spent the next two years in Turkey. He then made his way to the United States, where in 1936 he became a naturalized citizen. To support his career as a classical composer he began writing popular music. At the suggestion of George Gershwin, he adopted the pen name of Vernon Duke and, until 1955, reserved Dukelsky for his serious composition. He eventually settled in Hollywood, where he wrote for films.

Although Duke received considerable recognition as a classical composer, he was immensely successful in popular music with *April in Paris* and *Autumn in New York* among his best known works. His art songs, all published under the name Duke, include: *The Musical Zoo,* an amusing set of 20 short songs to Ogden Nash; *Six Songs from "Shropshire Lad,"* A. E. Housman, for medium voice; *Four Songs,* William Blake, for medium voice; and *An Italian Voyage,* a translation of Russian texts by M. Kuzmin, for high voice. Though they employ key signatures, the last three sets are very dissonant and give a strong impression of atonality. Unpredictable and inconsistent, they have effective moments, but cannot be recommended without reservation. Singer Kay McCracken, a former student of Lotte Lehmann, who Duke married when he was 54, recorded some of his songs on Glendale (GLS-6016).

BIBLIOGRAPHY
AmerGroves, Baker, CBY (1941), Ewen, Greene, Thompson.

JOHN EDMUNDS[1]
b. June 10, 1913, San Francisco, CA; d. Dec. 9, 1986, Berkeley, CA

"Where has John Edmunds gone? He is not so much underrated as unknown, yet at least half his four hundred songs (like many a song composer, he tends to be only a song composer) are programmable ... Edmunds rates a plaque for his lifelong proselytizing on behalf of Song in English."[2]

Edmunds inherited a passion for poetry from his Welsh and English mother, while singing could be found in the ancestry of his Scottish father.[3] As a child Edmunds studied piano. Later, at the University of California in Berkeley, he majored in English literature but also began to compose. Encouraged after hearing a performance of his songs, he entered the Curtis Institute of Music in Philadelphia, where he studied composition with Rosario Scalero. At Harvard University he studied with Walter Piston, receiving a master's degree in 1941. Other noted teachers were Roy Harris, Otto Luening, and—specialists in early English music—Arnold Goldsbrough and Thurston Dart.

In 1946 Edmunds returned to San Francisco where, with the help of his wife, Beatrice (a pianist), he founded the Campion Society, an organization devoted to the promotion of song in English.[4] He also taught for brief periods at Syracuse University and the University of California (Berkeley). Then, from 1957 to 1961, he headed the Americana collection at the New York Public Library and concurrently served as president of the American Music Center. In the 1960s and early 1970s, with the help of numerous grants and fellowships, he worked abroad. In Italy he prepared realizations of Vivaldi and Marcello;[5] in England, he completed his 12 volumes of arrangements and transcriptions of early English song.[6] After Beatrice died, Edmunds married again and, in 1977, settled in the Berkeley hills overlooking San Francisco Bay. There he continued to work on his many projects until his death from cancer.

THE SONGS
Whether realizations of Purcell, arrangements of the great seventeenth century English masters, settings of American and British folk songs, or the art song itself, Edmunds devoted himself almost exclusively to song in English.[7] For a time, especially in the late 1950s, his enormous catalogue[8] received considerable attention, but when he left the country, publications and performances dropped off.

Edmunds's eloquent, highly individual expression seems to be derived from his rare sensibility for poetry. A clear and vigorous illumination of the text, balanced with personal warmth and intimacy, distinguishes his style. Rhythms are flexible; prosody, with unexpected turns and accented syllables falling on off-beats, is idiosyncratic; his broad, colorful harmonic vocabulary accentuates all manner of textual nuances and shadings. Primarily setting the poetry of his British heritage, especially that of the Middle English period, like Benjamin Britten, he was strongly influenced by Henry Purcell and the early English masters.

Edmunds could write ravishing, supple melodies, highly complementary to the intrinsic lyricism of the voice, though in his fidelity to the text, he sometimes strayed into awkward tessituras or forgot the singer's need to breathe. He was a firm believer that expression is already inherent in the music and that nothing more than a clear and honest reading is required of the performer. Consequently, his failure to supply expression markings is totally calculated; retards and accelerandos are rare; dynamic range is modest; and piano writing, though intricate and vivid, primarily accompanimental.

In addition to a few songs that were published separately, Edmunds prepared several collections of his songs, and either oversaw their publication or printed them himself. The best are *Hesperides* (Dragon's Teeth Press c1975) and *The Faucon* (The Musical Offering c1978), containing 50 and 21 songs respectively. Though the original publishers are no longer in existence, these albums and other Edmunds songs can now be obtained from Classical Vocal Reprints. Folk song arrangements and the well-known Purcell realizations are still generally available. Dorothy Renzi and John Langstaff recorded 11 songs on Desto (DST-6430), but especially recommended is Donald Gramm's recording of *The Drummer* and *The Faucon* on Desto (411/412). Some recommendations follow.

Come Away Death, William Shakespeare; incl. *Hesperides;* comp. 1936; in memoriam - Povla Frijsh.[9]

Rec. middle and high lyric voices (e♭1–gb2); 1:30; Allegretto sospirando; a limpid, importuning melody, wafted on a stream of murmuring broken chords.

The Drummer, Thomas Hardy; Mills c1952.[10]

Rec. low voices (g#–d2); 2:00; Largo; over dry, drumlike effects in the piano, the singer recalls the poignant death of young Drummer Hodge; intense; powerful; recorded by Gramm.

The Faucon, Anonymous, Middle English; Mercury c1947; also incl. (in a rev. version) in the *The Faucon;*[11] comp. 1938; for Randall Thompson.

Pub. high voice (d1–g2), rev. version (c1–f2[g♭2]); 2:15; Freely; each stanza, introduced by a descending melisma on "Ah!" and with a "Lullee, lullay" refrain, assumes a different melodic contour as the drama enfolds; a chilling, mystical ballad; uneasy; haunting; perhaps Edmunds's best; recorded by Gramm.[12]

Helen, Edgar Allen Poe; incl. *Hesperides;* comp. 1935.

Rec. low and medium voices (d♭1–e2), text suggests men; 2:00; Andante con moto; cantabile over euphonious chords; an ode to the beauteous Helen; mellifluous, romantic.

The Isle of Portland, A. E. Housman; Boosey c1950; also incl. *The Faucon* (rev. under the title *The Star Filled Seas);* to Janet Fairbank.

Rec. lyric medium voices (e1–e2); 1:45; Largo sostenuto; sustained; flowing; chordal (the more active accompaniment of the revised edition is recommended); a lovely melody of disarming simplicity; recorded by Langstaff.

The Lonely, AE (George William Russell); Fischer c1948; incl. *CSE;* to Janet Fairbank.

Pub. high and low voices (high, e♭1–f2), rec. lyric voices; 1:15; Gently; a lovely undulating melody, almost like a lullaby, over broken chords; tender.

Milkmaids, Anonymous, 17th century; Mercury c1947; comp. 1946.

Rec. lyric voices (d♭1–f2); 0:45; Briskly; staccato; light and witty; recorded by Langstaff.

O Death, Rock Me Asleep, Anonymous, 16th century (Anne Boleyn?); Southern c1955; also incl. in *The Faucon* (rev. under the title *The Lament of Anne Boleyn).*

Rec. medium voices (d#1–e2); 2:45; Lento; sustained over steady chords; poignant and somber; recorded by Renzi.

On the Truth, Coventry Patmore; incl. *Hesperides;* comp. 1946; in memoriam - Edgard Varèse.

Rec. medium and low voices (c1–f2); 2:30; Very slow; a ground bass, in steady eighths, joined by the voice builds to a final *ff* of stunning amplitude; powerful and different; recorded by Langstaff (under the title *On the Nature of Truth).*

To Music, Robert Herrick; incl. *Hesperides;* comp. 1935.

Rec. lyric medium and high voices (d1–g♭2); 1:15; Andantino; the caressing melody gives balm to the senses; a lovely song (not to be confused with Edmunds's Shelley setting of the same title in the same volume).

Weep You No More Sad Fountains, Anonymous; incl. *Hesperides;* comp. 1938.

Rec. high lyric voices (e♭1–g2); Evenly, with motion; a heartbreaking melody over pulsing chords; difficult for the quiet dynamics and sustained lines in a high tessitura; beautiful and affecting.

Why Canst thou Not, Samuel Daniel; incl. *Hesperides;* comp. 1939; for Dorothy Renzi.

Rec. medium voices (d1–f2); 2:00; Andantino; a lovely, beseeching line over chordal accompaniment; recorded by Renzi.

Also of interest:

Have These For Yours, Housman, delicate, sustained; **Instinctively, Unwittingly,** Lewis, incl. *Hesperides,* lyrical and delicate; **O Love, How Strangely Sweet,** Marston, incl. *Hesperides,* Largo, sustained; **Seal Up Her Eyes,** Cartwright, incl. *Hesperides,* for lower voices, lyrical with florid passages, different; **Take, O Take Those Lips Away,** Shakespeare, incl. *Hesperides,* lyrical and flowing; **Whenas in Silks My Julia Goes,** Herrick, incl. *Hesperides,* lyrical; **When Daises Pied,** Shakespeare, incl. *Hesperides,* light and sprightly.

BIBLIOGRAPHY
AmerGroves, Baker, Greene, Thompson.

Additional information for this entry is taken from Edmunds's personal letters to the author (1980–1986) and telephone interviews with his widow and his sister.

---

[1] Occasionally Edmunds referred to himself as John St. Edmunds. According to his widow, he felt there were too many people named John Edmunds.

[2] Ned Rorem, "The American Art Song from 1930 to 1960," liner notes to *But Yesterday Is Not Today* (NW 243).

[3] His grandfather, Edmund Edmunds, was a tenor, renowned throughout the British Isles. Among other accomplishments he appeared with Paganini and, in 1831, was Count Almaviva in the first production of Rossini's *Barber of Seville* in Scotland. Several of his children also sang.

[4] Leonard Ralston, a colleague, was also one of the original founders. Part of the Campion Society's work was the Campion Library, a collection limited to music for solo voice that is housed in the San Francisco Public Library. The Society, however, is best remembered for the major song festival it sponsored for several years.

[5] Published by Carl Fischer in 1957 and 1967 respectively.

[6] *The Major Epoch of English Song: The 17th Century from Dowland to Purcell.* Edmunds worked on it from 1940 to 1976, but it remains unpublished.

[7] Even in later years, when he began to experiment in larger forms, Edmunds turned to ballet and choral works—always something that would fulfill his passion for literature and the word.

8 *The New York Times* (April 18, 1937) reported that Edmunds won the Bearns prize on the basis of nearly 40 songs he had submitted out of the 200 he had already composed.

9 Since soprano Povla Frijsh did not die until 1960, the dedication was probably added later. Edmunds was an inveterate reviser.

10 This song is available in a higher key in another Edmunds collection called *Boreas*. The album is available from Classical Vocal Reprints.

11 In notes supplied for this collection, Edmunds explains some of the symbolism of this mystical poem.

12 This appears to be the revised edition but a half-tone lower and with some other changes. If there is yet another edition, it has not come to the author's attention.

CLARA EDWARDS
b. April 18, 1887, Mankato, MN; d. Jan. 17, 1974, New York, NY

Clara Edwards was a singer, an accompanist, and a composer of over 100 songs[1]—often to her own words. While studying singing in Vienna, she married a physician, who died shortly after their daughter was born. Edwards made a few European concert tours but, in 1914, returned to America. A single mother in New York City, she composed her songs out of financial necessity. Quickly taken up by publishers, programmed by such stars as Lily Pons and John Charles Thomas, and performed on the popular radio show, the Telephone Hour, they became immensely successful.

Distinguished for their tasteful and truly lovely melodies, Edwards's songs are some of the best of the ballad style concert song. The early *With the Wind and the Rain in Her Hair* was considered 'popular' and even played at the top of the Hit Parade in 1940. *By the Bend in the River* (to words of Bernhard Haig, a pen name of the composer) and *Into the Night* are deservedly still in print. *The Fisher's Widow* was another favorite. *By the Bend in the River* is recorded by Maryanne Telese on Premier (002).

BIBLIOGRAPHY
AmerGroves, Baker.
Brant, Leroy V. and Clara Edwards. "The Heart of the Song: From a Conference with Clara Edwards," *Etude,* January, 1948.

---

1 This is the figure given in the *Etude* interview. Baker and AmerGroves, probably referring to her published songs, gives the number as being over 50.

HERBERT ELWELL
b. May 10, 1898, Minneapolis, MN; d. April 17, 1974, Cleveland, OH

Best known as a teacher and critic, Herbert Elwell's output is small but includes a number of distinctive songs. After three years at the University of Minnesota, Elwell studied with Ernest Bloch in New York, then with Nadia Boulanger in Paris. In 1923 he received a Prix de Rome and on a subsequent fellowship spent the next three years at the American Academy in Rome. Marrying an Italian, Maria Cecchini, the couple returned to America. From 1928 to 1945, Elwell taught at the Cleveland Institute of Music, and from 1932 to 1964 he was a critic for the *Cleveland Plain Dealer*. He also taught summer classes at the Eastman School of Music and the Oberlin Conservatory.

THE SONGS
Much of Elwell's output is vocal. In addition to choral music and chamber music with voice, he wrote a number of solo songs, about half of which have been published.Though quite romantic, their refinement, lucidity, and harmonic palette reveal a strong French influence. Set to poems that are rich in vivid imagery, they abound in lovely ideas, but are somewhat handicapped by a lack of cohesion. Singers will find Elwell's writing lyrical and vocally gratifying. Maxine Makas has recorded six songs on CRI (SD 270). Some recommendations follow.

Agamede's Song, Arthur Upton; Valley c1948.
    Rec. medium and higher voices (f1–f2); 2:15; Moderato, tranquillo e moderato; lyrical declamation over octave patterns; becomes quite dramatic; spare; somber and melancholy; a strong song; pairs well with *Suffolk Owl.*

In the Mountains, Chang Yu; Broadcast c1946.
    Rec. medium voices (d♭1–f2); 3:15; Moderato; lyrical and sustained over light, fluid piano figures; atmospheric; dreamy; a lovely song.

Suffolk Owl, Thomas Vautor; Valley c1948.
    Rec. higher voices (d1–g2); 2:15; Lento; lyrical with melismatic passages; evokes the owl's call; spare; melancholy; philosophical; about death, it pairs well with *Agamede's Song.*

Three Poems of Robert Liddell Lowe, Fema c1969.

Rec. high voices (c1–a2); 8:00; titles are: *All Foxes; This Glittering Grief; Phoenix Afire;* excellent diversity of mood and tempo among these generally philosophical texts; some melismatic passages; the brilliant final song ends on a difficult long high A; an effective, somewhat unusual, set; *This Glittering Grief* is recorded by Makas.

Also of interest:

Music I Heard With You, Aiken, Moderato, lush and warm; *Renouncement,* Meynell, Comodo, lyrical declamation; *The Road Not Taken,* Frost, Allegretto.

BIBLIOGRAPHY
AmerGroves, Baker, Ewen, Greene, Thompson.

CARL ENGEL
b. July 21, 1883, Paris, France; d. May 6, 1944, New York, NY

Though born in France, his parents were German, and Engel was educated at the universities of Strasbourg and Munich. In 1905 he went to the United States, where he became a citizen and, for decades, was a central figure in the country's musical life. Among his many influential positions, he was editor of the Boston Music Company (1909–1921), president of G. Schirmer (1929–1932 and 1934–1944), editor of the *Musical Quarterly* (1929–1944), head of the Music Division of the Library of Congress (1922–1934), and consultant to the Library (1934–1944). His large body of writing on music, especially on the composers who were his contemporaries, is highly regarded. Of his own impressionistic compositions, his songs probably enjoyed the greatest success. *Chansons Intimes* (now a Recital Publications Reprint Edition) and several settings of the poet Amy Lowell are still viable. Two early Robert Lowell settings (G. Schirmer c1911), the charming, bright *The Trout,* and especially its companion piece, the lovely, undulating *Sea Shell* (also incl. *50AS),* were very popular in their day.

BIBLIOGRAPHY
AmerGroves, Baker, Howard (OCC and OAM), Thompson, Upton.

BLAIR FAIRCHILD
b. June 23, 1877, Belmont, MA; d. April 23, 1933, Paris, France

The expatriate Blair Fairchild, whose healthy catalogue includes some opulent songs, was one of the first American composers to introduce exotic material into his music.

His aristocratic parents disapproved of his interest in music, but while at Harvard University preparing for a career in business, Fairchild also took composition with Walter Spalding and John Knowles Paine. On holiday in Italy, he studied piano and immersed himself in the country's folk music. Then, after a brief attempt at business, he compromised with his parents by entering the diplomatic service. Assigned to Teheran, he was again captivated by ethnic music and began to notate the Persian melodies. Finally freed from parental pressures by an inheritance, in 1905 Fairchild left for Paris to pursue a career in music. There, he studied with Charles Widor, established his own teaching career, and eventually won recognition for his compositions.[1] With his American wife he adopted a young Polish violinist, Samuel Dushkin, who later had a significant career on both sides of the Atlantic. Though Fairchild often visited America himself, Paris remained his home.

THE SONGS
Most of Fairchild's songs were influenced by his stays in Italy or Iran (then Persia) and by his feeling for France. His four volumes of *Canti Popolari Italiani* and six settings of *Stornelli Toscani* (folklike melodies of his own invention but in the Italian style) were very popular. His art songs, a mix of Eastern effects and French impressionism, were well received by the critics. William Treat Upton, in particular, admired their rich scoring and shifting harmonic colors. Modern ears, however, may find the beautiful melodic and harmonic writing commendable, but the use of exotic (mostly Near Eastern) materials excessive and distorted. Most Fairchild songs are library items, but Recital Publications has issued a reprint volume of miscellany for medium voice, *Blair Fairchild: Ten Songs (BFTS)*. A few recommendations, emphasizing those available from this album, follow.

Les Amours de Hafiz, Op. 38, Hafiz; Augener c1914; comp. 1914.
   Rec. medium voices (b–f#2), texts suggest men; 12:00; in French; seven songs from which a smaller group could easily be made up; notable are *Le Soir parfumé, Dans la nuit profonde, Oh regarde-moi,* and *Extase;* in the style of Fauré with a good sprinkling of Duparc;

one of Fairchild's best cycles and, owing to its reasonable length in comparison to many of his cycles, one of the most practical.

Lake Isle of Innisfree, Op. 22, No. 1, William Butler Yeats; also incl. *BFTS.*
    Rec. medium voices (c1–f2); 1:45; Andantino con moto; a lovely, nostalgic melody over a delicately flowing accompaniment.

Lament of Mahomet Akram, Op. 22, No. 2, Laurence Hope; also incl. *BFTS.*
    Rec. medium voices (d1–f2); men best; 2:30; Andante; sustained over a luxuriant flowing accompaniment; exotic Eastern figurations between the stanzas; a poignant song of lost love.

Music, When Soft Voices Die, Op. 9, No. 2, Percy B. Shelley; also incl. *BFTS.*
    Rec. medium voices (b–e2); 2:15; Slowly; a creamy, sustained vocal line over undulating chords.

Also of interest:
Quatrains d'Al-Ghazali, Lahor, a cycle of eight songs, pub. high and low, in French, especially admired by Upton but tediously opulent and long.

BIBLIOGRAPHY
AmerGroves, Baker, Howard, Thompson, Upton.
Bromfield, Louis. "The Henry James of American Music," *The Sackbut* (April 1923): 281–285.

---

[1] In 1921 his ballet-pantomine, *Dame Libelulle,* became the first work by an American to be performed at the Paris Opèra.

ARTHUR FARWELL
b. April 23, 1872, St. Paul, MN; d. Jan. 20, 1952, New York, NY

Arthur Farwell is probably best known as an indefatigable crusader for an American music free from European influences. Unfortunately, his early arrangements of American Indian melodies have somewhat over-shadowed his original compositions, which include some outstanding settings of Emily Dickinson.

Although Farwell studied violin as a child, he prepared for a career in electrical engineering at the Massachusetts Institute of Technology, but inspired by the music he heard at Boston Symphony Orchestra concerts, he decided instead to become a composer. After graduation he studied with Homer Norris in Boston, then with Engelbert Humperdinck and Hans Pfitzner in Berlin. Returning to the United States, Farwell lectured at Cornell University and began writing compositions that incorporated American Indian themes. Unable to find a publisher for his music and distressed to meet other composers in similar straits, in 1901 he founded his own non-profit publishing enterprise in Newton Center, Massachusetts—the Wa-Wan Press.[1]

To support himself and Wa-Wan, Farwell lectured across America and, in 1905, also founded the American Music Society, whose 20 centers nationwide arranged concerts of American composers. From 1909 until 1918 he lived in New York City, where he joined the staff of *Musical America* and, as its chief critic, espoused the cause of American music. During these years he was also Supervisor of Municipal Concerts, Director of the Settlement Music School of New York, and an organizer of the New York Community Chorus. In addition to composing and teaching, for the next two decades, first in California and later in Michigan, Farwell sought ways to involve people directly with music.[2] Retiring in 1939, he once again tried publishing, this time hand lithographing and promoting only his own music. His last years were spent in New York. Married twice (in 1917 to Gertrude Everts Brice, niece of a U.S. Senator from Ohio, with whom he had six children; and, in 1939, to Betty Richardson with whom he had a daughter), after Farwell's death some of his children worked to make his music available.

THE SONGS

Farwell's 39 settings of Emily Dickinson's poetry, mostly written late in life, were his largest and most significant contribution to song. Had he written nothing else, these wholly original settings would stand as a major achievement. Earlier settings to a variety of poets (some of which were published by Wa-Wan) are not on the same level. Mild-mannered, routine, even quaint, only a handful anticipate his later work.[3]

In a superb fusion of poetry and music, Farwell set Dickinson's pithy verse in cogent, fragmentary phrases that seem to stand out as in relief against a kaleidoscopic array of vivid piano accompaniments. Singers need little more than poetic sensibility and a solid, clear middle range to communicate the largely declamatory idiom. More serious demands are found in the illustrative piano writing, which, even within the confines of Farwell's succinct expression, can be intricate, elaborate, and virtuosic. However, the massing of small black notes in an endless array of piano figurations make these songs appear more difficult than they actually are. Rhythms (with a penchant for dotted figures) are conventional and commonsensical, and the singer will find pitches regularly doubled in the piano. The tenor Paul Sperry has done much to see these wonderful songs into print. With an introduction by Sperry, 34 were published by Boosey and Hawkes in 1983. In addition, he has recorded 11 on Albany CD (TROY043-2). William Parker sings the Indian settings on New World (213). Some recommendations follow.

Drake's Drum, Henry Newbolt; Wa-Wan c1907; incl. *WW(4)*.
    Spec. baritone (b♭–f2); 3:00; With spirit, not too fast; many small tempo changes; boldly rhythmic; wide dynamic range; drum and other effects in the piano; the voice, in a sort of brogue, narrates about Sir Francis Drake; spirited and effective.

Love's Secret, William Blake; Wa-Wan c1903; incl. *WW(4)*.
    Rec. medium voices (c1–f2), text suggests men; 1:15; Moderato; a simple lyric melody develops; a little narrative of rejected love.

Thirty-Four Songs on Poems of Emily Dickinson (two volumes); Boosey c1983; introduced by Paul Sperry.
    Volume 1 contains songs from 1936 through 1941; volume 2, from 1944 through 1949. Only one song was published previously.[4] No single opus necessarily forms a group; rather, one can cull a varied grouping from any or all, as Sperry did on his recording. Different songs call for different ranges, but most are suited to medium voices. A clean delivery, clear enunciation, and careful attention to detail, rhythms, and markings (especially the numerous tempo fluctuations) are essential. All 34 songs are of interest, but due to the sheer number, only this author's highest recommendations are listed. Performers are sure to find other favorites and should study the volumes carefully.

Ample Make This Bed, Op. 108, No. 7; incl. Vol. 2.
    Rec. medium and high voices (e1–f2); 1:15; Very Slowly; controlled, solemn; recorded by Sperry.

And I'm a Rose! Op. 108, No. 4; incl. Vol. 2.

Rec. higher lyric voices (d1–g#2); 0:30; Moderately; crisp melodic snippets in dotted rhythms; elaborate piano figurations; an exquisite miniature.

Dropped into the Ether Acre, Op. 108, No. 10; incl. Vol. 2.

Rec. medium and high voices (cb–g♭2); 1:30; Very Slowly; descriptive fragments and a final funeral march; fascinating, and different.

The Grass So Little Has To Do, Op. 112, No. 2; incl. Vol. 2.

Rec. higher voices (d1–g2); 1:00; Moderately fast; in dotted rhythms the voice cheerfully describes the pastoral scene over a running 12/8; recorded by Sperry.

I Had No Time to Hate, (no opus given), incl. Vol. 2; comp. 1949.

Rec. medium and low voices (b–d2); 0:45; Very Slowly; clear, controlled, straightforward.

The Level Bee, Op. 105, No. 10; incl. Vol. 1; comp. 1940.

Rec. medium and higher voices (c1–g2); 1:00; With motion; whirring sixteenths depict the busy bee's activities; recorded by Sperry.

Presentiment, Op. 105, No. 12; incl. Vol. 1.

Rec. medium and lower voices (b–d2); 1:30; Very slowly; ominous chords; then, a murmuring unaccompanied voice and a slow releasing of the tension; an insightful song of only ten measures; recorded by Sperry.

Safe in Their Alabaster Chambers, Op. 105, No. 2; incl. Vol. 1.

Rec. medium voices (e♭1–e2); 2:00; Slowly; sustained over an ostinato rhythmic figure evoking eternity's rest; an active middle section depicting living nature; haunting; recorded by Sperry.

The Sea Said "Come" to the Brook, Op. 108, No. 5; incl. Vol. 2; comp. 1944.

Rec. medium voices (b#–g2); 1:00; Slowly; over various water figurations brook and sea converse.

Summer's Armies, Op. 105, No. 9; incl. Vol. 1.

Rec. medium and higher voices (c#1–g♭2); 2:30; opens "Slowly and smoothly," but with each new awakening of nature, a brighter tempo and character is introduced; ends big; a wonderful song; recorded by Sperry.

These Saw Vision, Op. 105, No. 4; incl. Vol. 1.

Rec. medium and lower voices (c1–e2); 1:45; Slowly; halting fragments in dotted rhythms over spare chords; an exquisite, tender farewell.

Tie the Strings to My Life, Op. 107, No. 2; incl. Vol. 2.

Rec. medium and high voices (d1–g2); 1:00; With agitation; breathless and racing with the anticipation of the ride to Judgement; ends *sffff*; could close a program; recorded by Sperry.

Two Songs for medium voice on poems of William Blake, printed and published by Arthur Farwell c1931.[5]

Lamb (f1–f2); 1:15; Simply; two verses; delicate.

A Cradle Song (b–f2); 2:45; Quietly, rocking; builds briefly.

Also of interest:

Three Indian Songs, for medium voice, arrangements of melodies transcribed from the songs of the Omaha tribe, recorded by Parker.

BIBLIOGRAPHY

AmerGroves, Baker, Ewen, Greene, Howard (OAM), Thompson, Upton.

Culbertson, Evelyn Davis. *He Heard America Singing: Arthur Farwell, Composer and Crusading Music Educator.* Metuchen, N.J.: Scarecrow Press, 1992.

Farwell, Brice. *A Guide to the Music of Arthur Farwell and to the Microfilm Collection of his Work.* Briarcliff Manor, New York: 1972.

---

[1] Named for an Omaha Native ceremony, the Wa-Wan Press published, in periodical form, the music of 37 progressively minded composers (ten of whom were women), who had found themselves rejected by commercial publishers. In addition, the beautifully designed volumes included articles— the majority written by Farwell— championing the cause of American music. By 1911 Wa-Wan was on the decline, so in 1912 it was sold to G. Schirmer, who let it fall by the way side. In 1970 all the periodicals were reprinted in five volumes by the Arno Press, New York, edited by Vera Brodsky Lawrence, with an introduction by the historian Gilbert Chase.

[2] This included arranging and composing gigantic community choruses and other works with audience participation.

[3] In addition to conventional art song, Farwell's songs based on Indian themes, arrangements of Negro spirituals, Cowboy songs, and Spanish-Californian folk songs are also from this early period.

[4] *These Saw Vision* was published by Galaxy c1944. Five additional Dickinson settings were published by G. Schirmer in the 1920s.

[5] Attempting to find a way to avoid the restrictions imposed by publishers, these were the first two compositions Farwell printed on his own lithographic press.

IRVING FINE
b. Dec. 3, 1914, Boston, MA; d. Aug. 23, 1962, Boston, MA

Fine's small but highly regarded catalogue includes some excellent songs.

Born and raised in Boston, Fine studied under Edward Hill Burlingame and Walter Piston at Harvard University, graduating with a master's degree in 1938. He also worked at various times with Nadia Boulanger. From 1939 to 1950 he taught at Harvard, then became composer-in-residence at Brandeis University. Married to Verna Rudnick in 1941, the couple had three daughters. He had just conducted his only symphony at the Tanglewood Festival when he died of a heart attack.

THE SONGS
Fine's catalogue, which has loosely been described as neo-classic, is primarily made up of chamber and choral music. His two works for solo voice and piano, both written in the 1950s, are first-rate, but their totally contrasting subject matters elicit very different approaches (as described in their entries below). Although *Childhood Fables* is considerably more conventional than Fine's usual style, which is better exemplified by the cycle *Mutability,* both works share in his vitality, imagination, elegance, and clarity. Vocal writing is intelligent and sensitive, but *Mutability* is very demanding. In both works the piano is an equal and active partner, at times requiring technical prowess. *Childhood Fables* was recorded in its entirety by Susan Daveny Wyner on CRI CD (574), and in part by Mildred Miller on Desto (411/412) and William Parker on New World (300); *Mutability* was recorded by Eunice Alberts on CRI CD (630).

Childhood Fables for Grownups, Gertrude Norman; Boosey c1955/58/59; orig. pub. as two sets, they are now under a single cover; each song is dedicated to a different composer.

    Rec. medium or lower voices (a–f2); 14:00; animal fables; excellent variety; tonal; straightforward but with vigorous, clever rhythms; any grouping of these colorful songs would be possible, including some combination of the two sets; to do all six, however, might be excessive; though not difficult vocally or musically, these songs require flexibility, quick enunciation, and a first-rate storyteller; fun, humorous, and intelligent; recorded by Wyner.
Set One:
Polaroli, (a–e2); 1:45; Moderato; recorded by Miller.

Tigeroo, (b♭–f2); 1:15; Allegro Moderato; recorded by Parker.
Lenny the Leopard, (c1–e♭2); 3:00; Andante; recorded by Parker.
The Frog and the Snake, (d1–e♭2); 1:15; Allegro vivace; recorded by Miller.
Set Two:
Two Worms, (d1–f2); 3:45; Andante, with a final Allegretto; recorded by Parker.
The Duck and the Yak, (b♭–f2); 3:00; Allegro; recorded by Parker.

Mutability, Irene Orgel;[1] Belwin-Mills c1959; comp. 1952.[2]
   Spec. mezzo-soprano (g–g♭2); 14:00; titles are: *I Have Heard the Hoofbeats of Happiness; My Father; The Weed; Peregrine; Jubilation; Now God Be Thanked for Mutability;* this cycle covers a wide spectrum of color, mood, and performance styles; though generally romantic and employing key signatures, certain songs are strongly dissonant and atonal; despite the low range, nimble, clear voices are required to deal with the many words, disjunct lines, and diverse vocal styles, ranging from declamatory and dramatic to lyrical and florid; a major piano score—active, independent, and inventive; though the piano often doubles the singer's pitches, this is a difficult work for both performers; the philosophical poems concern life's changes; a virtuosic, intense, and important cycle; recorded by Alberts.

BIBLIOGRAPHY
AmerGroves, Baker, Ewen, Greene, Manning (on *Mutability)*, Thompson.

---

[1] Irene Orgel was an English poet. She was at the MacDowell Colony with Fine the same summer he composed the cycle.
[2] Conceived for Eunice Alberts, who recorded it.

ROSS LEE FINNEY
b. Dec. 23, 1906, Wells, MN

So much of Ross Lee Finney's long career has been spent in academic settings that he has not received the exposure befitting his stature. Nonetheless, his eclectic but strongly defined catalogue, including a distinguished output of solo song, is highly regarded.
   Born in Minnesota, Finney grew up in Valley City, North Dakota, but in 1918 the family settled in Minneapolis. His father was a writer,

sociologist, and a university professor. His mother had a degree in piano and, with her three sons,[1] formed a quartet in which Finney, the youngest, played the cello. He also played the piano and, accompanying himself on the guitar, later performed (even toured) as a folksinger. After one year at the University of Minnesota, where he studied with Donald Ferguson, Finney was invited to be a student and part time teacher at Carleton College. There he met his future wife, a violinist in the school string quartet, who as Gretchen L. Finney, would later write about music. After graduating in 1927, Finney studied in Paris with Nadia Boulanger. Other teachers include Edward Burlingame Hill, Alban Berg, Francesco Malpiero, and Roger Sessions. Except for time spent serving in World War II (he was wounded and awarded a Purple Heart) Finney, from 1929 to 1947, taught at Smith College. While there, he founded the Smith College Music Archives and Valley Music Press. From 1949 to 1973 he was professor of music and composer-in-residence at the University of Michigan.

THE SONGS

Finney's catalogue is primarily comprised of instrumental and choral music. But his clean, economical, resolute style combined with his poetic sensibility and restrained lyricism has resulted in five eloquent, sophisticated, and beautifully crafted song cycles. Because of its length, *Chamber Music* presents a programming problem; otherwise, Finney's songs have no unusual musical or technical difficulties and should engage discerning audiences. It is astonishing that they are so seldom performed.

Finney never specifies a particular voice category, but tessitura and many of the texts suggest that lyric voices—tenors especially—are well served. No display singing here; vocal lines are neither melting nor lush and, in their interaction with the accompaniment, are often treated instrumentally. Evenness of tone for the long sustained lines and clarity of delivery are essential to balance the lucid, independent piano writing. Ensemble is, in fact, the greatest challenge. The dearth of Finney song recordings is inexplicable. It is believed that the following is a complete listing of his published songs.

Chamber Music, James Joyce; Peters c1985; comp. 1952.
   Spec. high voices (a–a2), best for lyric tenors (low notes are usually given higher options); 60:00; this cycle of 36 songs is probably the only one to use the complete volume of poems which Joyce titled *Chamber Music*. It is clear from both the emotional development and

from certain recurring similarities in the songs, that Finney, as did Joyce, regarded his work as a single "arc of expression."[2] It is about love, beginning with adolescence and courtship, tasting physical love, and ending in disillusionment, loneliness, and despair. Though, ideally, the cycle should be heard in its entirety, it contains some exceptional single songs, which might be programmed individually or in smaller groupings. The music, like the poems, has something of an Elizabethan feeling. Though the songs are not especially difficult, the singer requires great poetic sensitivity and a clear delivery, being careful not to press the lightness of the poetry. *Chamber Music* is a major contribution to our song literature.

Poems by Archibald MacLeish, American c1955; comp. 1934; to Archibald and Ada MacLeish.[3]
  Rec. high lyric voices (d1–a2[g2]); 12:00; titles are: *They seemed to be waiting; Go secretly; The flowers of the sea; Salute; These, my Ophelia;* a variety of tempos but generally on the slow side, and with quiet dynamics; only moderately difficult; a beautiful, sensitive, finely wrought cycle, matching the mood and mystery of the poetry.

Poor Richard,[4] Benjamin Franklin; G. Schirmer c1950; various dedications.
  Rec. high voices (d1–a2), best for tenors;[5] 9:30; titles are: *Epitaph; Here Skugg Lies; Wedlock, As Old Men Note; Drinking Song; When Mars and Venus; Epitaph on a Talkative Old Maid; In Praise of Wives;* Franklin's lightweight, clever lyrics are a delight and Finney has set them in an appropriately understated eighteenth-century style; a deftly balanced cycle of good variety; not difficult and a little different. John Hanks has recorded *Wedlock* and *Drinking Song* on Duke, Vol. 1 (DWR 6417).

Three Love Songs to Words by John Donne, Valley c1957.
  Rec. high lyric voices (d1–a2), best for tenors; 8:00; titles are: *A Valediction: Of Weeping; A Valediction: Forbidden Mourning; Love's Growth;* little contrast here; all three songs move in slow, steady, similarly restrained eighths; linear, polyphonic; an impressive work for the erudite performer and listener.

Three 17th Century Lyrics, Valley c1949; comp. 1936–38.
  Rec. higher lyric voices (b–f#2); 5:00; tonal, linear; these songs are short and with similar tempos, but each develops in a singular

fashion; Finney's most warmly lyrical songs; a beautiful, small, reflective set.

On the Life of Man, Henry Vaughan; Andante (with a spherical motion); builds to an unexpectedly dramatic ending.

Look How the Floor of Heaven, William Shakespeare; Andante (with a gentle rolling motion); many cross rhythms; generally quiet and restrained.

On May Morning, John Milton; Larghetto (with movement); ends up and full.

BIBLIOGRAPHY

AmerGroves, Baker, Ewen, Friedberg (II), Greene, Thompson.

Borroff, Edith. *Three American Composers.* Lanham, Maryland: University Press of America, Inc., 1986.

Finney, Ross Lee. *Ross Lee Finney: Profile of a Lifetime.* New York: C. F. Peters, 1993.

---

[1] One of these sons, Theodore, has written on music; particularly noteworthy is his *History of Music* (1935).

[2] Ross Lee Finney, from the Preface to *Chamber Music.*

[3] Ada MacLeish, Archibald's wife, was a soprano often heard on the new music scene of the 1930s and 1940s.

[4] Not all come from the famous *Poor Richard's Almanac.*

[5] According to *Art-Song in the United States (NATS),* a low voice version was issued by Independent Music, but the author has never seen it.

NICOLAS FLAGELLO
b. March 15, 1928, New York, NY

The eldest son of Italian parents, Flagello studied piano and violin as a boy. At the Manhattan School of Music he accompanied the vocal classes of Friedrich Schorr (teacher of his younger brother, Ezio, who would become a leading operatic basso), earned his bachelor's and master's degrees, and taught conducting and composition (1950-1977). Though Flagello studied for a while with Ildebrando Pizzetti in Rome, Vittorio Giannini was his principal teacher. Flagello has also performed as a pianist (primarily as an accompanist to singers), and has had a considerable career in conducting.

THE SONGS
Given his Italian heritage, Flagello's appealing songs are—not surpris-

ingly—grand, theatrical, and eloquently fashioned for the voice. They are also bold and imaginative, and while remaining within a conventional idiom, totally modern. Regrettably, all his published cycles for solo voice (*Contemplazoni di Michelangelo, L'Infinito, The Land,* and *Songs from William Blake's "An Island in the Moon"*) appear to have originally been conceived for voice with orchestra or smaller instrumentation. Although all are available in piano reduction, only the William Blake settings are convincing in this form, and even here the piano part is formidable. The Michelangelo and Blake settings have been recorded, with orchestra, by Nancy Tatum on Serenus (12005); *The Land,* with orchestra, by Ezio Flagello on Musical Heritage Society (1559); three of the Blake settings by John Reardon, with piano, on Serenus (12019).

Songs from William Blake's "An Island in the Moon" General c1965; pub. separately.

Spec. high voice (b–bb2), several are best for men; these curious poems have wonderful diversity ranging from the comic to the tragic; a smaller group could be made; some demanding piano writing; occasional operatic-like singing; an effective and distinctive set.

As I Walked Forth, (f#1–f#2), man's text; 2:15; Andantino; long piano introduction; lilting and lyrical; recorded by Reardon.

This Frog He Would A-Wooing Ride, (d1–g2); 1:45; Allegretto; a highly sophisticated nursery-type song.

O Father, O Father, (c#1–a2); 2:15; Allegro Giusto; emotional and agitated with a central lento misterioso recitative; powerful, dramatic, moving.

Good English Hospitality, (d1–a2) 2:25; Allegro Giocoso; a robust parlando with vamp-like accompaniment; final long high A; recorded by Reardon.

Leave, O Leave Me To My Sorrows, (b–g2); 3:00; Andante Lento; lyrical; subdued; recorded by Reardon.

Dr. Clash and Signor Falalasole, (d1–bb2); 3:30; Allegro Energico; many tempo changes; a comical sketch on musicians; big ending.

BIBLIOGRAPHY
AmerGroves, Baker, Ewen, Greene.

WILLIAM FLANAGAN

b. Aug. 14, 1923, Detroit, MI; d. Aug. 31, 1969, New York, NY

At his untimely death, William Flanagan left a small but choice cata-logue containing some of the most individual and compelling songs in the American literature.

Flanagan first became interested in music through the background scores he heard at the movies. Then, while ushering for the Detroit Symphony, he was so inspired by the classical music he heard that, at the age of 20, he abandoned his studies in journalism to attempt a career as a composer. Though virtually untrained, he was nevertheless accepted at the Eastman School of Music, where for three years he studied under Bernard Rogers and Burrill Phillips. Later he worked with David Diamond in New York City, and with Aaron Copland, Arthur Berger, and Arthur Honegger at the Berkshire Music Center in Tanglewood. In addition to his composition, in the late 1950s and 1960s Flanagan wrote criticism for the *Herald Tribune, Stereo Review,* and *Musical America.* He also presented a series of concerts (Music for the Voice) with his friend Ned Rorem, and collaborated on projects with the playwright Edward Albee.[1] In 1967 Flanagan won the National Institute of Arts and Letters Award and was also a Pulitzer Prize nominee. Though his career appeared to be moving forward, he was found dead in his Manhattan apartment, a probable suicide.

THE SONGS

Flanagan's inspired musical-poetic sensibility, as expressed through his painfully sensitive soul, resulted in songs of beauty and profound pathos. And his style, though executed within a conventional, even romantic idiom (especially in line and sonority) was wholly his own. Flanagan has said he probably turned to songwriting because he lacked the training to write extended instrumental works.[2] Nevertheless, his unmistakable affinity for the vocal idiom was evident from the beginning, and his out-put was almost entirely vocal.[3] It was also very small, for each work was born only after great anxiety.[4]

Flanagan's songs were composed at two separate stages of his life, and though the intensity of his personal expression is common to both, there is a notable difference between the two. Early efforts produced somber, sad, introspective miniatures that remained well within the accepted confines of the genre, while the songs of his relative maturity take on a lighter cast, and even—at least in one notable example—abundant (albeit sarcastic) humor. Big, expansive, strongly defined, warm, and unafraid, although musically more complex, by opening out to the listener, these later songs are actually more accessible.

Impressed with Copland's Emily Dickinson settings and that composer's "concept of a hyperlyrical vocal line treating wide skips and conscious octave displacements as easily as if they were thirds or fifths,"[5] Flanagan incorporated this idea into his own music. His personal brand of lyricism and expressivity, however, somehow transforms these unorthodox intervals into vocal lines that sing with all the affecting mellifluousness of a Schubert song and poignancy of a Puccini aria. Initially it takes work to absorb the unusual contours, but with time the singer will find that, despite the sudden leaps and unexpected turns, the pliant lines unfold with a grace that is exceedingly complimentary to the voice. Accompaniments are lightly textured, expressive, and give the impression of independence, whereas in actuality, they closely interact with the voice. Musical difficulties are moderate, primarily incurred by frequent changes of key and meter and the aforementioned unorthodox intervals. Carol Bogard and Herbert Beattie made an excellent recording, devoted exclusively to Flanagan's vocal music, on Desto (6468) and Mildred Miller sings two other songs on Desto (411/412).[6] Virtually all Flanagan's published songs are listed below.[7]

The Dugout, Siegfried Sassoon; Peer c1953; comp. 1946.
> Rec. high voices (d#1–g2); 1:30; Andante con moto; lyrical; profoundly and quietly agonizing.

Go and Catch a Falling Star, John Donne; Peer c1954; comp. 1949.
> Rec. high voices (e1–bb2), text suggests men; 1:15; Moderato; wordiness in a high tessitura presents some difficulties; a strange, abbreviated setting of this cynical ode on woman's inconstancy.

Heaven Haven, Gerard Manley Hopkins; Peer c1952; comp. 1947.
> Rec. higher voices (f1–f#2), text suggests women; 1:30; Andante con moto; lyrical declamation; mysterious and quietly beautiful.

Horror Movie, Howard Moss; Peters c1965; comp. 1962; for Veronica Tyler.
> Rec. medium and higher voices (c1–g2); 4:00; Largo misterioso (piano prelude), then Fast and light; a mix of parlando and sustained passages over an expansive, animated piano score; some grand singing; shifting meters and cross rhythms; big ending; very colorful; great fun; truly funny; recorded by Bogard.

If You Can, Howard Moss; Peters c1963; incl. *Two Songs;* comp. 1961.
Rec. high voices (d♭1–a2); 3:15; Largo Andante; four dramatic
stanzas with a lyrical refrain, which each time adds a new line of text;
vivid imagery; fervent vocal writing over an intricate piano fabric of
widely spaced sonorities; a reflective postlude; operatic in scope; one
of Flanagan's best; a stunning, haunting song; recorded by Bogard.

Plants Cannot Travel, Howard Moss; Peters c1963; incl. *Two Songs;*
comp. 1959.
Rec. high lyric voices (e1–a2); 1:00; Allegretto; essentially a
waltz; light and lilting with darker shadings; recorded by Bogard.

See How They Love Me, Howard Moss; Peters c1965.
Rec. high lyric voices (d1–a2); 2:30; the tempo approximates an
andante; an arioso, alternately sustained and lightly declaimed; rich
in nuance; an exquisitely beautiful, deeply affecting song; recorded
by Bogard.

Send Home My Long Strayed Eyes, John Donne; Peer c1955.
Rec. higher lyric voices (e1–g2); 2:15; Andante; sustained declamation over a spare piano part; poignant, introspective, emotionally
restrained; recorded by Miller, transposed down.

Song for Winter Child, Edward Albee; Peer c1964; comp. 1950; for
Edward.
Rec. high lyric voices (d1–a2); 1:30; Very slow; delicate, some-
what disjunct parlando; tender; quiet; curiously effective.

Two Songs, see *Plants Cannot Travel* and *If You Can.* The two songs
need not be programmed together despite their similar themes.

Upside-Down Man, Howard Moss; Peer c1964; comp. 1962; also incl.
VN.
Rec. high voices (c1–g2); 4:00; opens and closes smoothly with a
"cold" tone but builds to an impassioned climax; some shattering
chords; legato, disjunct declamation over a linear piano counterpart;
doubling of difficult pitches; shifting meters and "quasi-serial
devices";[8] the world as seen from an upside-down vantage point;
dramatic; different; effective; recorded by Bogard.

Valentine to Sherwood Anderson, Gertrude Stein; Peer c1951; comp.
1947; for Florence Kopleff.

Rec. medium voices (b–e2); 2:30; Moderato; light declamation over clear, delicate piano writing; charming; tender; recorded by Miller.

BIBLIOGRAPHY

AmerGroves, Baker, Friedberg (III), Greene, Gruen, Thompson.

Albee, Edward and Ned Rorem. "William Flanagan...and his Music," *Bulletin of the American Composer's Alliance*, 9 (1961). In two parts; Albee considers the man, Rorem the music. The Rorem part is reprinted in *Music and People*. New York: George Braziller, 1968.

Flanagan, William. Liner notes. *Songs and Cycles by William Flanagan*. Desto (DC 6468).

Reilly, Peter. "William Flanagan," *Stereo Review* (November 1968).

Rorem, Ned. "Bill Flanagan: 1923–1969," *Critical Affairs*, 119–122. New York: George Braziller, 1970.

Thomson, Virgil. "William Flanagan," *A Virgil Thomson Reader*, 446–447. Boston: Houghton Mifflin Company, 1981. A reprint of the tribute read by Thomson at the Flanagan Memorial Concert, Whitney Museum, New York, April 14, 1970.

Trimble, Lester. "William Flanagan (1923-1969): An Appreciation," *Stereo Review* (November 1969).

---

[1] Flanagan describes his long and complicated personal relationship with Albee in some detail in John Gruen's *The Party's Over Now.*

[2] Liner notes, *Songs and Cycles by William Flanagan,* Desto DC6468.

[3] He also wrote several chamber works with voice, and a short opera.

[4] Ned Rorem, "William Flanagan," *The New Grove Dictionary of American Music.*

[5] Flanagan, liner notes.

[6] Four songs are on an old release by Sara Carter (New Editions 2), which the author has not located.

[7] Peer International has been credited with publishing the cycle *Time's Long Ago* which was recorded by Bogard in 1951, but the company reports that it was never printed. A few other songs were once held by the American Composers Alliance but no longer appear in their catalogue.

[8] Flanagan, liner notes.

ARTHUR FOOTE
b. March 5, 1853, Salem, MA; d. April 8, 1937, Boston, MA

America's "last Victorian,"[1] interest in Arthur Foote today lies with his instrumental music. His many songs, immensely popular in their day, are fetching but old-fashioned.

His father was editor of the local Salem newspaper. His mother died when he was four and Foote was raised, for the most part, by his older sister. Though there was no music in the family, he took some piano lessons as a child and studied harmony at the New England Conservatory. While preparing at Harvard University for a business career, he studied music on the side with John Knowles Paine and conducted the Glee Club. Then, after graduation, he studied organ with Benjamin Lang, who encouraged him to pursue a musical career. Reentering Harvard as a graduate student, in 1875 Foote received the first master of arts degree to be given by an American university. He soon became a major force on the Boston concert scene and one of America's most performed and honored composers. Though he stopped composing around 1918, he continued to teach and also published several theoretical books on music. After his death, his daughter arranged for publication of his autobiography.[2]

THE SONGS

Though Foote was one of the few late nineteenth-century American composers to be educated entirely in this country, his style, ultimately, was formed by the deeply entrenched German traditions of the New England Conservatory. The most sophisticated of his more than 100 songs, at their best, resemble Mendelssohn, but too often they are pedantic and prosaic. On the other hand, his charming, straightforward period songs survive as fine examples of a quaint genre, and still have genuine appeal. There are many recordings of Foote's instrumental music but very few of his songs. Chief among these would be Paul Sperry's *Oh Swallow, Swallow* and *It Was a Lover and His Lass* on Albany CD (TROY034-2). Though virtually all are library items, Classical Vocal Reprints include several songs in its catalogue. An *Album of Selected Songs by Arthur Foote* Arthur P. Schmidt c1907 *(ASSAF)* offers a nice selection. A sampling of the author's personal favorites as well as the best known follows.

Constancy, Op. 55, No. 1, Anonymous; Schmidt c1904.
  Pub. high and medium (high, d1–g2); 1:30; Rather fast, with free diction; tuneful, fluent, and full; warm and happy; an excellent closer.

A Ditty, Sir Philip Sidney; Schmidt c1882; also incl. *ASSAF.*

Pub. high and low (high, c#1–f#2), women best; 1:00; Allegretto grazioso; a sprightly, unusually disjunct melody to the words "My true love hath my heart."

I'm Wearin' Awa', Op. 13, No. 2; Lady Nairn; Schmidt c1899.

Pub. high and low (high, d♭1–f2); 1:00; Expressively; a poignant melody in a traditional vein; subdued with a slow lilt; a touching Scotch poem; one of his most popular songs.

Irish Folk Song, Gilbert Parker; Schmidt c1894.

Pub. high and low (high, d1–g2); 2:15; Moderato espressivo; delicate, nostalgic verses with a more sprightly refrain on "ah"; also very popular.

Lilac Time, from the poem "The Barrel Organ" by Alfred Noyes; Schmidt c1917.

Pub. high and low (high, e1–a2); 1:45; Moderately fast: gracefully; lyrical, light, tuneful; a nice period piece; fresh and ingenuous.

The Night Has a Thousand Eyes, Francis W. Bourdillon; Schmidt c1882.

Pub. high and low (high, e♭1–f2); 0:45; Andante espressivo; straightforward; affecting.

BIBLIOGRAPHY
AmerGroves, Baker, Ewen, Greene, Hall, Howard, Hughes, Tawa, Thompson, Upton.
Foote, Arthur. *Arthur Foote: An Autobiography.* New York: Da Capo Press, 1979. A reprint of the 1946 privately printed edition.

---

[1] Frederic Jacobi, "Homage to Arthur Foote," in *Modern Music* (May-June 1937) as found in *Arthur Foote: An Autobiography,* 133.

[2] See bibliography.

VITTORIO GIANNINI
b. Oct. 19, 1903, Philadelphia, PA; d. Nov. 28, 1966, New York, NY

Vittorio Giannini composed in a variety of forms, but steeped in the lyric traditions of his Italian ancestry, he made his mark with his romantic operas and songs.

Giannini was born into a musical family. His grandfather was a poet and song composer from Tuscany, who had emigrated to America as a political refugee. His father, Ferruccio, had had a career as a tenor[1] before running an art shop and theater in Atlantic City. His mother, Giannini's first music teacher, was a violinist. His brother played the cello. One sister, Dusolina Giannini became an internationally celebrated soprano. The other, Euphemia Giannini Gregory, also a soprano, is best remembered for her distinguished career as a singing teacher at the Curtis Institute.

When he was ten Giannini went to Italy with his mother on a violin scholarship from the Verdi Conservatory in Milan. On his return four years later he studied privately until, in 1925, he began studies in composition with Rubin Goldmark at the Juilliard School. His conservative but pleasing compositions won awards and commissions, including one from NBC-TV for the opera *The Taming of the Shrew,* probably his best known work. He was also a popular teacher at a variety of institutions, including Juilliard (1939–1956) and the Curtis Institute (1956–1964). Twice married and divorced, he never had children.

THE SONGS

Of Giannini's 36 published art songs, 19 are set to the verses of his friend, Karl West Flaster.[2] Though only *Tell Me, Oh Blue, Blue Sky* has had lasting success, these highly romantic, occasionally sentimental, songs were once programmed by such favorite singers as Grace Moore, Giovanni Martinelli, Jan Peerce, and Eileen Farrell. Melodious and expressive, they show the voice in a lyric, at times, operatic style. But there are drawbacks: careless prosody too often diminishes the attractiveness of the vocal line; piano writing can be cumbersome; 'purple passages' abound; and there is a predictability and sameness which discourages the programming of more than a few at one time.

Singers should be sure to also look up Giannini's irresistible transcriptions of Italian folk songs. But don't be misled by the word "folk," for these are big numbers. A more exciting song than *Zompa Llari Llira* or more infectious encore than *Ohie Menechè* would be hard to find. The latter is recorded by Dusolina Giannini on Preiser CD (90124). Jeffrey Price has recorded all the Flaster settings (including five that are unpublished) on a CD (aca CM 20011-11) aptly titled *Hopelessly Romantic: Songs of Vittorio Giannini. Tell Me, Oh Blue, Blue Sky* is also recorded by baritones Thomas Hampson on EMI CDC (7 54051 2) and Leonard Warren on RCA CD (7807-2-RG). Giannini's songs are so similar in mood that it is difficult to recommend one over another. The following are this author's preferences, but singers may want to consider others.

Far Above the Purple Hills, Karl Flaster; Ricordi c1939.
Rec. high lyric voices (c#1–a2); 2:45; Moderato; sustained over hushed, undulating piano figures; some recitative-like passages; a more dramatic, declamatory central section; a lovely song; recorded by Price.

It Is a Spring Night, Karl Flaster; Ricordi c1942.
Rec. high voices (e♭1–a2); 3:30; Andante sostenuto; delicate, lyric, subdued; broadens into a romantic central section; recorded by Price.

Longing, Karl Flaster; Elkan-Vogel c1950.
Rec. high and medium lyric voices (b#–g♭2); 2:15; Adagio; a filigree of piano figures carries the delicate, cantabile vocal line; quietly effective; a personal favorite of this author; recorded by Price.

Tell Me, Oh Blue, Blue Sky, Karl Flaster; Ricordi c1927; to Marcella Sembrich.
Rec. high lyric voices (c#1–g#2); 2:45; Adagio; very lyrical and sustained over a fluid accompaniment; builds briefly to an appassionato before the final beautiful refrain; recorded by Price, and (transposed down) by Hampson and Warren.

There Were Two Swans, Karl Flaster; Elkan-Vogel c1944.
Pub. high and medium (high, c1–g#2); 2:30; Moderato; subdued, restrained; spare; impressionistic; recorded by Price.

Three Poems of the Sea, Karl Flaster; Ricordi c1935; comp. 1935.
Rec. for tenors (c#1–b2); 5:15; though published separately, best kept as a romantic mini-cycle; recorded by Price.
Sea Dream, (e1–a♭2); 1:30; Andante sonnolento; subdued love song.
Waiting, (c#1–g#2); 2:00; Andante; gently flowing; lyrical; tuneful.
Song of the Albatross, (e#1–b2); 1:45; Allegro; "the wild sea's foam" is evoked in a flood of charged romantic piano figures, over which the voice valiantly exerts itself in a treacherously high tessitura; can be dramatic and effective, but only with a singer who sounds comfortable.

Also of interest:
I Shall Think of You, Flaster, Adagio; recorded by Price; ***If I Had Known,*** Flaster, Moderato, recorded by Price; ***I Only Know,*** Flaster,

Cantabile, recorded by Price; *Sing To My Heart A Song,* Flaster, Allegro moderato, recorded by Price.

BIBLIOGRAPHY
AmerGroves, Baker, Ewen, Greene, Thompson, Upton (Sup).

Parris, Robert. "Vittorio Giannini and the Romantic Tradition," *Juilliard Review* 4 (Spring 1957): 33–46.

Price, Jeffrey. Liner notes. *Hopelessly Romantic: Songs of Vittorio Giannini* (aca CM 20011-11).

Simpson, Anne and Karl Wonderly Flaster. "A Working Relationship: The Giannini-Flaster Collaboration," *American Music* 6 (Winter 1988): 375–408.

---

[1] Ferruccio Giannini (1868–1948) toured with the Mapleson Opera Company. In 1896 he became one of the first singers to make an operatic recording.

[2] Flaster was a reporter, florist, and poet. He and Giannini met as young men while waiting for a trolley car. The collaboration lasted 40 years and included four operas.

MIRIAM GIDEON
b. Oct. 23, 1906, Greeley, CO

Although much of Gideon's large catalogue for solo voice employs additional instrumentation, it also includes some fine songs with piano.

Born to cultured but non-musical parents, Gideon was nonetheless fascinated by music as a child. She began studying piano in Chicago, where the family moved in 1915, and continued lessons the following year in New York. In 1921, in the care of her uncle, a professional musician, she went to Boston, where she completed her studies and also developed an interest in composition. In 1926 she settled in New York and studied with various teachers, including Lazare Saminsky and, most importantly, Roger Sessions. Gideon has been on the faculties of Brooklyn College, City College of New York, The Jewish Theological Seminary, and the Manhattan School of Music. The recipient of countless awards and honors, she was only the second woman composer to be elected to the American Academy and Institute of Arts and Letters. She is married to Frederic Ewen, a writer and professor at Brooklyn College.

THE SONGS
Gideon balances a musicianly and thoughtful intelligence with a warm, poetic, feminine expression. Although her idiom is atonal and rather dis-

sonant, she writes lyrically for the voice. Her textures are spare and clear, often contrapuntal. Many works that have not been commercially published are available from the American Composers Alliance in their Composers Facsimile Edition. A Gideon Retrospective was recorded on New World CD (80393-2) and includes Constantine Cassolas and William Sharp singing various songs for voice and piano. The following are especially recommended.

Epitaphs from Robert Burns, ACA; comp. 1952.

Pub. high, medium, low; (low, g#–f#2); 4:00; titles are: *Epitaph for a Wag in Mauchline; Epitaph on Wee Johnie; Epitaph on the Author; Monody on a Lady Famed for Her Caprice;* mostly declamatory; atonal; spare piano textures; a humorous, pithy, potent, little cycle; recorded by Sharp.

Gone in Good Sooth You Are, (from "Fatal Interview") Edna St. Vincent Millay; ACA c1961; also incl. *AAA.* comp. 1952.[1]

Rec. sopranos (d#1–a♭2); 2:00; Distant; flowing, lyrical; atmospheric and mysterious.

The Seasons of Time, based on Tanka Poetry of Ancient Japan; General c1971; also set with instrumentation.

Rec. high lyric voices (e1–a2); 8:30; ten seasonal images of various lengths; a radiant opening and a delicate *ppp* close; the expansive and exuberant no. 5 (beginning "Each season more lovely") is the pinnacle of the cycle; though somewhat disjunct, the vocal writing is warmly expressive; of only moderate difficulty; atonal; delicate, filigreed, impressionistic textures; an elegant contemporary work; recorded by Evelyn Mandac with flute, cello, and piano on Desto (7117), and Paul Sperry on Serenus (12078).

Also of interest:

Mixco, Asturias, Spanish and English, ACA, a big song, recorded by Cassolas; ***Poet to Poet,*** various poets, ACA, three songs, recorded by Cassolas; ***To Music,*** Herrick; ACA, Dolce ma un poco agitato, recorded by Cassolas.

BIBLIOGRAPHY
AmerGroves, Ammer, Baker, Ewen, Greene, Nathan, Thompson.

---

[1] Other titles from this small set *(Night is my sister* and *Moon that against the lintel of the west)* are available from ACA, but the author feels they are not on the same level as *Gone in Good Sooth You Are.*

HENRY F. GILBERT
b. Sept. 26, 1868, Somerville, MA; d. May 19, 1928, Cambridge, MA

A leader of the nationalist movement, Gilbert both incorporated ethnic materials into his work and composed some of the most original American music of his era. His songs, however, though sacrificing none of the vitality associated with his style, are disappointing.

Born to musical parents (his mother was a professional singer; his father a church composer, organist, and singer), Gilbert studied at the New England Conservatory, and also with Edward MacDowell. He began as a violinist but soon abandoned music altogether and, instead, held jobs that ranged from real estate to silkworm farming. While cutting pies at the Chicago World's Fair, he met a friend of Rimsky-Korsakov, who inspired him with stories about the Russian nationalist school. But it was not until 1900, when he went to France and heard Charpentier's *Louise,* that Gilbert finally committed himself to composition. His music was admired abroad but received little attention in the United States. Married with two daughters, he lived most of his life grappling with the frail health which had plagued him since birth, and struggling to make a living from music.

With their ponderous piano parts, bursting with tremolos and massive chords, Gilbert's songs seem better suited to orchestral accompaniment. Tending to the dramatic and theatrical, vocal lines are robust but lack suppleness. Most are best for men. Many can be found in various volumes of the reprint edition of the Wa-Wan Press, originally published by Arthur Farwell, whom Gilbert had met in 1902 and who was an enthusiastic admirer. Probably Gilbert's most admired songs were the four *Celtic Studies (WW3),* which are best for tenors. Also, the lusty *Pirate Song (WW1)* and *Fish Wharf Rhapsody (WW5),* once made popular by baritone David Bispham, are fun and different. Paul Sperry sings three songs on Albany CD (TROYO34-2).

BIBLIOGRAPHY
AmerGroves, Baker, Ewen, Greene, Howard, Hughes, Thompson.
Carter, Elliot. "American Figure, with Landscape," *Modern Music* 20 (May/June 1943): 219–225.
Narodny, Ivan. "A Troubador of the New Age: Gilbert's Rich Bequest to American Posterity," *Musical America,* June 16, 1928.

HALLET GILBERTÉ

b. March 14, 1872, Winthrop, ME; d. Jan. 5, 1946, New York, NY

Hallet Gilberté (changed from Gilbert) was a student of Ethelbert Nevin and one of the most performed, prolific, and popular American song composers in the period that led to the end of World War I. He was also a tenor who sometimes filled as many as 100 engagements in a season. Expert at handling publishers, attracting press coverage, and getting his songs heard, on annual nationwide tours Gilberté not only sang himself but arranged to accompany local singers in performances of his own songs. Though he and his wife, who occasionally wrote the verse for her husband's songs, lived in New York, the couple reserved summers for "Melody Manse," the dream home they built in Lincolnville, Maine.

It is not an injustice that Gilberté has been totally forgotten, for his songs are altogether too sentimental and superficial to be taken seriously by contemporary audiences. Nevertheless, as prototypes of his era's commercial approach to 'serious' song writing, they make fun encore material, and would be of interest to the performer with an eye to historical programming. While most are lush, grand, and romantic in the extreme, they can also be charming and innocent. Always melodious, skillfully crafted, and vocally idiomatic, they make excellent showpieces for full-throated singers. In their heyday, the most popular titles from Gilberté's huge catalogue were the sumptuous *Ah, Love, But a Day* for high voice, and *The Devil's Love's Song,* a potboiler for baritone.

BIBLIOGRAPHY
Baker, Thompson.
Kramer, A. Walter. "Vacation Procedure Reversed by Gilberté," *Musical America,* June 23, 1917.

PEGGY GLANVILLE-HICKS

b. Dec. 29, 1912, Melbourne, Australia; d. June 25, 1990, Sydney, Australia

Peggy Glanville-Hicks had associations with so many nationalities some may dispute her inclusion here. However, she became an American citizen in 1948 and is usually classified as American. More importantly, her songs, primarily written during her time in the United States, are too exceptional to risk exclusion.

After growing up in Australia, in 1931 Glanville-Hicks went to London. She studied at the Royal College of Music, where Ralph Vaughan Williams was her composition teacher. Later she studied with Nadia Boulanger in Paris and with Egon Wellesz in Vienna. Married in 1938 to the English composer Stanley Richard Bate (divorced after eight years) the couple came to the United States in 1942. Settling in New York City, she immersed herself in the city's music scene. Then, from 1959 to 1976 she took up residence in Athens, Greece, only returning to New York in 1969 to be operated on for a brain tumor. In 1976 she returned to Australia, where she helped found the East-West Music Centre in Sydney.

THE SONGS

Glanville-Hicks wrote three excellent small song cycles in a contemporary, highly individual idiom with impressionistic overtones. They are cleanly crafted works—incisive and succinct. The vocal writing is gratifying and natural. Rhythms can be treacherous, but pitches, often doubled by the piano, present few problems, even in the more atonal songs. Accompaniments are especially colorful and evocative. The challenge for both performers is to communicate the fleeting, shifting moods of these poetic miniatures with the same nimbleness and precision with which they have been set. In addition to the three cycles given below, Hayes's bio-bibliography on Glanville-Hicks notes five early songs and *Ballade,* a song to the poetry of her good friend, Paul Bowles.[1]

Five Songs, A. E. Housman; Weintraub c1952; comp. 1944; to Paul.
    Rec. high voices (b–a2); 5:30; titles are: *Mimic Heaven; He Would Not Stay; Stars; Unlucky Love; Homespun Collars;* best kept as a set; technically and musically the more difficult of the three cycles for both performers; a strong feeling of tonality; wonderful diversity, including a rhythmically incisive opening, various evocative and emotional interior settings, and a spirited, folklike ending; colorful and imaginative; highly recommended.

Profiles from China, Eunice Tietjens; Weintraub c1951.
    Rec. high voices (e1–a2); 5:30; titles are: *Poetics; A Lament of Scarlet Cloud; The Dream; Crepuscule; The Son of Heaven;* definitely should be treated as a cycle; the five brief sketches range from a humorous opening to a somewhat dramatic close; of moderate difficulty; one of the better cycles on Oriental themes.

13 Ways of Looking at a Blackbird, Wallace Stevens; Weintraub c1951; comp. 1947.

   Rec. medium and lower voices (a–g#2); 9:00; opens incisively and closes quietly over an ethereal fragment of trills and glissando piano figures; in between all manner of effects, including spoken passages; some florid phrases; an easily managed contemporary cycle.

BIBLIOGRAPHY
AmerGroves, Baker, Ewen, Greene, Thompson.
Antheil, George. "Peggy Glanville-Hicks," *ACA Bulletin* 4 (1954).
Hayes, Deborah. *Peggy Glanville-Hicks: A Bio-Bibliography.* New York and Westport, Connecticut: Greenwood Press, 1990.

---

[1] See the Paul Bowles bibliography for an article on Bowles by Glanville-Hicks. Some biographical writings on Bowles note her friendship—sometimes described as an infatuation—with the composer.

ERNEST GOLD
b. July 13, 1921, Vienna, Austria

After studying music in Austria, Gold came to the United States in 1938. (He became a citizen in 1946.) In 1945 he settled in Hollywood, where he studied with George Antheil and had considerable success as a film composer, winning an Academy Award in 1960 for *Exodus.* He was married for a time to soprano Marni Nixon, for whom he wrote *Songs of Love and Parting.*

Songs of Love and Parting, various poets; G. Schirmer c1963; pub. separately.

   Spec. high voice (a–b2), some texts suggest a certain gender, but in the interest of the universality of the feelings explored, Gold has said he "deliberately ignored whether a given poem was addressed to a man or a woman";[1] 18:00; best kept as a set but smaller groupings could be made; dramatic and lyrical; employs a wide vocal range; no key signatures; generally tonal with straightforward rhythms; a big romantic set; effective; though originally composed for piano accompaniment, these songs were later orchestrated on a commission; recorded in its entirety, with orchestra, by Marni Nixon on Crystal CD (501); with guitar by Helen Dilworth on Cambria (1062); and four songs, with piano, by Nancy Tatum on London (OS 26053).

Gifts, James Thomson; (d1–a2); 2:15; Allegretto; rhythmic.

Shall I Compare Thee, William Shakespeare; (c#1–b2); 4:00; Leisurely; introspective.

A Red, Red Rose, Robert Burns; (b–a2); 2:30; Allegretto con grazia; lilting and lyrical.

Peace, Emily Dickinson; also incl. *20CAS;* (f1–ab2); 1:15; Allegro agitato; intense.

Parting, Emily Dickinson; (a–ab2); 2:15; Tempo rubato; slowly declaimed over sustained arpeggiated chords.

Time Does Not Bring Relief, Edna St. Vincent Millay; (a–g2); 4:15; Appassionato; dramatic declamation; hushed inner sections.

Music, When Soft Voices Die, Percy Bysshe Shelley; also incl. *20CAS;* (eb1–f#2); 1:30; Tempo rubato; sustained; flowing.

BIBLIOGRAPHY
AmerGroves, Baker, Greene.

---

[1] Liner notes, Crystal (S 501).

CHARLES TOMLINSON GRIFFES
b. Sept 17, 1884, Elmira, NY; d. April 8, 1920, New York, NY

One of the most poetic and personal voices in American music, his catalogue, though modest in size, is major in significance, and includes some of this country's finest songs.

Charles Griffes was the third of five children, whose middle-class parents cared deeply about literature and the arts. When he was 11, he began studying piano with his older sister, who, after four years, sent him to her own teacher, Mary Selena Broughton. Recognizing Griffes's potential, the enlightened Broughton taught him for another four years and then recommended, and even financed, further study in Germany for her talented pupil.[1] Arriving in Berlin in 1903, while studying piano and composition for two years at the Stern Conservatory, Griffes devoured the city's rich culture. He then remained for further study, including some lessons with Englebert Humperdinck, outside the Conservatory. In 1907 Griffes reluctantly returned to America and took a position as piano teacher, organist, and choir director at the Hackley School for Boys in Tarreytown, New York. Despite the tedium and drain on his energies, he would hold this job for the rest of his life. Meanwhile, as he hustled his growing portfolio of music in nearby New York City, he slowly acquired a small, but enthusiastic following of performers, composers, and critics, and in 1909 even convinced a skeptical G. Schirmer to give him a contract. In the last years of his short life recognition for his work grew widespread, culminating in 1919 with the Boston Symphony Orchestra's premiere of his tone poem *The Pleasure Dome of Kubla Khan*. But only days later, Griffes fell seriously ill. After months of suffering, he was taken to New York City for a last desperate operation, but died soon after.[2]

Keenly responsive to nature and color, Griffes was an amateur visual artist, who painted watercolors, made etchings in copper, and was a serious photographer. He also loved theater, movies, dance, the circus, parades, everything about the Orient, and literature of all kinds. Sensitive and shy, he treasured his friendships, struggled with homosexuality and, though deeply spiritual, was attracted by mystical concepts and opposed to any dependence on God.[3]

THE SONGS

Against the unparalleled backdrop of the romantic lieder tradition, Griffes, a student in Berlin, set the greater part of his 25 lyrical, melodious, harmonically colorful, partially imitative songs to German texts.[4] Then, upon his return to America, he began to compose what would amount to 34 settings in English (including some translations of Japanese, Chinese, and Rumanian texts). The first of these reflected his new interest in French impressionism and the Orient, but as he became increasingly experimental in his search for a personal voice, he turned to more modern and exotic poetry. These late compositions, which were described by critics of the day as "ultra-modern," exude the full potency of his expression.

Griffes was fortunate in the kinds of intelligent singers he was able to attract, particularly the beautiful Vera Janacopoulos and the inimitable Eva Gauthier, both of whom had the vivid imagination needed to communicate such evocative, descriptive music.[5] His knowledge of vocal craft came first from his experience in Germany with singers and the lieder tradition. Later, he learned about singing technique both from his friend, Laura Moore Elliot, a former singer and distinguished voice consultant, and from the well known teacher, William Earl Brown.[6]

Vocally, musically, and interpretively, Griffes's songs require considerable maturity. Many, especially those from later periods, are miniature tone poems, often on mystical themes. With his "unerring sense of the appropriate fusion of text and music,"[7] the long, intensive vocal lines build to powerful climaxes, calling for considerable stamina in addition to restraint and control. The elaborate, richly textured accompaniments also require advanced performers. (An excellent pianist himself, Griffes often accompanied his own works.) Ensemble is especially challenging, for vocal lines are rarely doubled, while rhythmic schemes, fraught with cross rhythms and changing meters, can be intricate.

G. Schirmer was Griffes's sole publisher until 1951, but since 1967, C. F. Peters has been bringing out previously unpublished songs. In 1989 Schirmer issued two volumes of reprints compiled according to vocal range. Edited by Paul Sperry, these are: *The Songs of Charles Griffes: Volume One for High Voice (SCG1)* and *The Songs of Charles Griffes: Volume Two for Medium Voice (SCG2)*. Masters Music Publications has also issued some collections, including *Six Songs to German Poems (6SGP)*.

Of the many recordings, two are comprehensive with Faith Esham, Irene Gubrud, Jan Oplach, and Lucy Shelton on a two disc set by Musical Heritage Society (824678M), and Phyllis Bryn-Julson, Sherrill Milnes and Olivia Stapp with orchestra (under Sejii Ozawa) and piano on New World CD (NW 273-2). In addition, Thomas Hampson has recorded most of the German settings on Teldec CD (9031-72168-2); Alexandra Hunt and William Parker have each recorded selections on Orion (ORS 77272) and New World (NW 305) respectively. Additional isolated recordings are noted with the individual entries. Most of the songs were published in only one key and many transpositions are made on these recordings, especially by the lower voiced performers. The Griffes catalogue is of such importance that virtually all published songs are noted— in some form—in the following song list. Though most appear in their original groupings, performers can make other arrangements of the songs. Only *Five Poems of Ancient China and Japan* and, possibly, *Four Impressions* are best kept intact.

Auf geheimem Waldespfade (By a Lonely Forest Pathway), Nikolaus Lenau; from *Five German Songs* (pub. separately); G. Schirmer c1909; also incl. *S22A, 50AS,* and *6SGP*.

   Pub. low, medium, and high voice (high, d1–a♭2); 2:15; Molto tranquillo; often sung in English; sustained over broken chords; recorded in German by Yolanda Marcoulescou on Orion (OC 685), Gubrud, Hampson, Milnes, and John Hanks on Duke, Vol. 1 (DWR 6417); in English by Eleanor Steber on New World (247).

Auf ihrem Grab (Upon Their Grave), Heinrich Heine; G. Schirmer c1941; also incl. *SIA*.

   Rec. high voices (c1–g2); 2:45; Moderato; lyrical over a fluid accompaniment; piano postlude; recorded by Hampson and Shelton.

Les Ballons, Oscar Wilde; Peters c1986; incl. *Seven Songs;* probably comp. 1912; some reconstruction by Donna K. Anderson.

   Rec. high voices (e♭1–a♭2); 2:30; Gently throughout; in English despite French title; a lovely lyrical melody (requiring some high floating tones) over rippling harmonies, like air currents; recorded by Shelton.

By a Lonely Forest Pathway, see *Auf geheimem Waldespfade.*

Cleopatra to the Asp, John B. Tabb; Peters c1986; incl. *Seven Songs;* comp. around 1912; reconstructed by Donna K. Anderson.

   Rec. medium and high women's voices (d♭1–g2); 3:15; Languido; cross rhythms; almost operatic in its theatrical character; mysterious, sensual, effective.

Come, Love, across the Sunlit Land, see *Two Rondels.*

Evening Song, Sidney Lanier; G. Schirmer c1941; also incl. *SCG1.*

   Rec. high voices (d#1–g#2); 2:45; Quietly but not too slowly; over a pulsing accompaniment, each verse begins quietly, then grows to an exuberant *f*; recorded by Oplach (transposed down), Hunt, and Marcoulescou-Stern on Gasparo CD (287).

The First Snowfall, John B. Tabb; G. Schirmer c1941; also incl. *SCG2.*

   Rec. medium voices (d1–f2); 1:45; Slowly and softly; lyrical over a veiled accompaniment; atmospheric and mystical; recorded by Esham and Parker.

Five German Songs, various poets; G. Schirmer c1909; only pub. separately.

   Pub. various ranges; not conceived as a set; titles are: *Auf dem Teich, dem Regungslosen* (Lenau) also incl *6SGP; Auf geheimen Waldespfade* (see separate entry); *Nacht liegt auf den fremden Wegen* (Heine), also incl. *6SGP; Der traümende See* (Mosen), also incl. *6SGP; Wohl lag ich einst in Gram und Schmerz* (see separate entry).

Five Poems of Ancient China and Japan, Op. 10;[8] various translations of Oriental poets; G. Schirmer c1917; reprinted 1945 as *Five Poems* *of the Ancient Far East;* also incl. *SCG2* as *Five Songs from the Chinese;* comp. 1917.

Spec. medium voice (a#–e2); 8:00; titles are: *So-fei Gathering Flowers; Landscape; The Old Temple Among the Mountains; Tears; A Feast of Lanterns;* excellent variety; impressionistic; each composed on a five or six tone scale; vocal lines flow effortlessly; the range is moderate but often dips below the staff; generally quiet dynamics; light textures; technically and musically not difficult; lyrical; evocative; recorded by Gubrud.

Four German Songs, various poets; Peters c1970; trans. & ed. by Donna K. Anderson; probably comp. between 1903 and 1907; not conceived as a set; titles are: *An den Wind* (Lenau), medium voices; *Am Kreuzweg wird begraben* (Heine), medium voices; *Meeres Stille* (see separate entry); *So halt' ich endlich dich umfangen* (see separate entry); all recorded by Hampson.

Four Impressions, Oscar Wilde; Peters c1970; comp. between 1912 and 1915.

Spec. medium (high) voice (d1–b♭2), rec. lyric spinto voices; 10:00; in English, despite the French titles; best kept as a set, but can be used individually; technically and interpretively difficult; appropriately titled "impressions," the rich imagery of Wilde's poetry is perfectly suited to Griffes's evocative colors; the long, sustained vocal lines require singing on a grand scale; rejected by Schirmer and never heard in his lifetime, but one of Griffes's most beautiful and substantive works; recorded in its entirety by Shelton, who sings the 1916 version of *La Mer* that is not included in the Peters edition (Esham sings the 1912 version on the same recording), and by Stapp.

Le Jardin (The Garden); Mesto; a desolate song of an autumn garden; dramatic central section.

Impression du Matin (Early Morning in London); Tranquillo; evocative harmonies; an exquisite song; also recorded by Elizabeth Suderburg (OLY 104) under its English title.

La Mer (The Sea); 1912 version;[9] Molto tempestoso; haunting misterioso in the middle; ends *ppp*.

Le Réveillon (Dawn); misterioso building to a tremendous finale.

La Fuite de la Lune, Oscar Wilde; G. Schirmer c1915; also incl. *SCG2*.

Pub. medium (c#1–f2); 3:30; Tranquillo; English text despite French title; an impressionistic song full of strange images; subdued; unusual; recorded by Oplach.

The Half-Ring Moon, John B. Tabb; G. Schirmer c1941; incl. *SCG2.*
     Rec. full medium voices (d#1–e2); 1:00; With a very quick movement; dramatic over pulsing chords; unbridled and passionate; ends mournfully; recorded by Shelton.

In a Myrtle Shade, Op. 9, No. 1, William Blake; G. Schirmer c1918; also incl. *SCG1* and *RAAS;* comp. 1916.
     Rec. high voices (f#1–a2); 2:00; Tranquillo; expansive and sustained over moving triplets; a beautiful song; recorded by Esham, Hunt, Marcoulescou-Stern on Gasparo CD (287), and by Cynthia Haymon on Argo CD (436 117 2ZH).

The Lament of Ian the Proud, see *Three Poems by Fiona MacLeod.*

Meeres Stille (Calm Sea), Johann Wolfgang von Goethe; Peters c1970; from *Four Songs.*
     Rec. medium or low voices (a#–e2); 2:00; Ruhig; lyrical declamation over slow chords; recorded by Hampson and Milnes.

Nachtlied (Night Song), Emanuel Geibel, Peters c1984.
     Spec. high voice (d♭1-a2 [a♭2]); 3:15; Moderato; cantabile over a flowing accompaniment of luxuriant harmonies; probably the last of the German settings; a hushed, magical, highly romantic night scene; recorded by Hampson.

An Old Song Resung, see *Two Poems by John Masefield.*

Phantoms, Arturo Giovannitti; G. Schirmer c1918; also incl. *SCG2.*
     Spec. medium voice (b♭–f2); 3:30; Moderato; cantabile over mysterious, pulsing chords; builds to moments of anguish; a recitative-like central passage; recorded by Oplach.

Phantoms, Op. 9, No. 3, John B. Tabb; Peters c1986; incl. *Seven Songs;* probably comp. around 1912.
     Rec. medium or high voices (e♭1–f2 [a♭2]); 2:00; Rather slowly and with tender sadness; a mournful lyric melody over rippling arpeggios of phantom snowflakes; recorded by Oplach.

Pierrot, Sara Teasdale; Peters c1986; incl. *Seven Songs;* comp. 1912.
     Rec. higher lyric voices (d1–g#2), text suggests women; 1:15; Allegretto scherzando; waltzing, over a lute-like accompaniment; not characteristic of Griffes; recorded by Shelton.

The Rose of the Night, see *Three poems by Fiona MacLeod.*

Seven Songs, various poets; edited and compiled into an album by Donna T. Anderson; Peters c1986; spec. medium to high voice; a miscellaneous but interesting collection; see separate entries for: *Two Birds Flew into the Sunset Glow; Les Ballons; In the Harem; The Water-Lily; Phantoms* (John B. Tabb); *Pierrot; Cleopatra to the Asp.*

Six Songs, various German texts; edited and compiled by Donna T. Anderson; Peters c1986; comp. between 1903 and 1911.

Spec. medium voices (many seem best for low voices); 11:00; though all are translated by either Griffes or Donna T. Anderson, the original German is definitely preferable; titles are: *Das ist ein Brausen und Heulen* (Heine); *Mit schwarzen Segeln* (Heine); *Das Müden Abendlied* (Geibel); *Das sterbende Kind* (Geibel); *Mein Herz ist wie die dunkle Nacht* (Geibel); *Wo ich bin, mich rings umdunkelt,* (Heine); miscellaneous early settings; not conceived as a set; recorded in its entirety by Hampson, and three by Parker.

So halt' ich endlich dich umfangen *(At Last I Hold You),* E. Geibel; Peters c1970; from *Four Songs.*

Rec. higher voices (b–g#2); 2:00; Nicht zu langsam; romantic over moving chords; builds to an impassioned ending; recorded by Hampson.

Song of the Dagger, translated Rumanian folk poem, Peters c1983.

Rec. dramatic baritones, in bass clef (A♭–f1); 4:30; Presto; with slower sections; rhythmic; grand piano writing; dialogue of the dagger and his master; very colorful; virile and dramatic; recorded by Milnes and Oplach.

Sorrow of Mydah, see *Two Songs by John Masefield.*

Symphony in Yellow, Oscar Wilde; from *Tone Images;* G. Schirmer c1915; also incl. *SCG1, 20CAS,* and *RAAS.*

Rec. high voices (d1–g♭2); 2:45; Languidamente; a restrained but liquid vocal line over atmospheric chords; a middle section of some movement; the color imagery in this curious poem describing London scenes is marvelously portrayed; different and very effective; recorded by Oplach, and by John Hanks on Duke, Vol. 1 (DWR 6417).

This Book of Hours, see *Two Rondels.*

Three Poems, Op. 9; various poets; G. Schirmer c1918; pub. separately; see separate entries for *In a Myrtle Shade, Waikiki, Phantoms* (Giovannitti).

Three Poems by Fiona MacLeod, Op. 11;[10] G. Schirmer c1918; comp. 1918; pub. separately; also incl. (in their entirety) *SCG1*.

Rec. high, bigger voices (c#1–a#2); 10:00; arranged for piano or orchestra;[11] many long sustained lines and high notes; difficult, big, and occasionally romantic singing; often used individually but gorgeous as a set; recorded by Esham (with piano) and by Bryn-Julson (with orchestra).

The Lament of Ian the Proud, also incl. *NAAS* and *S22A;* to Povla Frijsh.

Rec. big voices (d#1–a#2);[12] 3:45; Lento; opens with a haunting leitmotif; develops motion and intensity as the old man's agitation builds to a powerful climax; difficult; a dramatic song of great beauty; also recorded by Elizabeth Suderburg (OLY 104), by Dale Moore on Cambridge (2715), and by John Hanks on Duke, Vol. 1 (DWR 6417).

Thy Dark Eyes to Mine, to Marcia van Dresser; (e♭1–a♭2); 2:30; Andantino; the seductive, sustained vocal line hovers over lush undulating chords; beautiful; romantic; also recorded by Hunt.

The Rose of the Night, (c#1–a2); 3:30; Moderato; sustained, dramatic singing; opens mysteriously and builds over three stanzas to a powerful climax; a big, exotic, passionate song.

Thy Dark Eyes to Mine, see *Three Poems by Fiona MacLeod.*

Time Was When I in Anguish Lay, though well known in its English version, see *Wohl lag ich einst in Gram und Schmerz.*

Tone Images, Op. 3; various poets; G. Schirmer c1915; pub. separately; also published under the title *Three Songs* by Masters Music; see separate entries for *La Fuite de la Lune, Symphony in Yellow,* and *We'll to the woods and gather may.*

Two Birds Flew into a Sunset Glow, Rumanian folk text; Peters c1986; incl. *Seven Songs;* comp. 1914.

Rec. medium voices (c1–f2); 2:45; a simple setting of a folk-like melody develops over the first three stanzas, but the last is stark and mournful; different from other Griffes; recorded by Shelton.

Two Poems by John Masefield for Medium Voice, G. Schirmer c1920; pub. separately; also incl. *SCG2*.

　　An Old Song Resung, pub. high and low (high, e1–f2); best suited to men's voices; 1:45; Giocoso ma non troppo presto; a sea-shanty with much characterization and drama; seemingly robust, rhythmic, and energetic, yet "as sinister as it is powerful";[13] recorded by Oplach and Parker, and by John Hanks on Duke, Vol. 1 (DWR 6417).

　　Sorrow of Mydah, pub. medium (b–f#2), rec. dramatic male voices; 3:00; Molto appassionato, ma non troppo allegro; probably Griffes's most "ultra-modern" song with startling effects including glissandi for the voice and polytonal passages; virtuosic, explosive piano writing; a gripping song of despair and desolation; recorded by Oplach.

Two Rondels, Op. 4; G. Schirmer c1915; also pub. by Masters Music and incl. *SCG1*.

　　Spec. sopranos (c#1–f#2), rec. lyric voices; 3:15; can be sung individually; recorded by Gubrud.

　　This Book of Hours, Walter Crane; rec. medium or high voice (c#1–f#2); 2:00; Molto moderato e semplicemente; a pure melody over spare accompaniment.

　　Come, Love, across the Sunlit Land, Clinton Scollard; rec. medium or high voice (e1-f#2); 1:15; Allegro con spirito; a lilting melody with a sustained central section; bubbling accompaniment; pretty.

Waikiki, Op. 9, No. 2; Rupert Brooke; G. Schirmer c1918; comp. 1916; also incl. *SCG1* and *RAAS*.

　　Spec. high voice (d#1–g#2); 4:00; Andante con moto; strong imagery, especially of Hawaii and its ukalelee; essentially lyrical but becoming passionate in recalling an uncertain love "by some other sea"; unusual and difficult; recorded by Shelton and Hunt, and by Eleanor Steber on Desto (411/412).

We'll to the woods and gather may, William Ernest Henley; from *Tone Images;* G. Schirmer c1915; incl. *SCG2*.

　　Rec. medium voices (e♭1–f2); 1:00; Molto vivace; an ecstatic melody over broken chords; romantic and straightforward; a rare happy song; recorded by Esham, and by Marcoulescou-Stern on Gasparo CD (287).

Wohl lag ich einst in Gram und Schmerz (Time Was, When I in Anguish Lay), Emanuel Geibel; from *Five German Songs;* G. Schirmer c1909; also incl. *SIA* and *6SGP;* to Miss Geraldine Farrar.

Spec. high voices (e1–g#2); 0:45; Allegro appassionato; soaring over triplets; recorded by Sperry on Albany CD (TROY034-2), Esham, and Hampson.

Also of interest:

Elfe, Eichendorff, Allegro vivace, high voices recorded by Shelton; **In the Harem,** Ch'ing-yü, incl. *Seven Songs,* Moderato, recorded by Gubrud; **Könnt ich mit dir dort oben gehen,** Mosen, recorded by Shelton; **The Water-Lily,** Tabb, incl. *Seven Songs,* with a quiet movement, recorded Gubrud; **Zwei Könige sassen auf Orkadal,** Geibel, also incl. *6SGP,* a dramatic ballad, recorded by Hampson and Parker.

BIBLIOGRAPHY

AmerGroves, Baker, Ewen, Friedberg (I), Greene, Hall, Nathan, Thompson, Upton.

Anderson, Donna K. *Charles T. Griffes: An Annotated Bibliography-Discography.* Boulder, Colorado: College Music Society, 1977.

————. *The Works of Charles T. Griffes: A Descriptive Catalogue.* Ann Arbor, Michigan: UMI Research Press, 1983. A comprehensive guide to Griffes, including a biography and a chapter on his songs.

Bauer, Marion. "Charles Griffes as I Remember Him," *Musical Quarterly* 29 (July 1943): 355-380.

Maisel, Edward M. *Charles T. Griffes.* New York: Knopf, 1943; updated 1984.

Upton, William Treat. "The Songs of Charles T. Griffes," *Musical Quarterly* 9 (1923): 314–328.

---

[1] Broughton, a New Zealander (and a cousin to the author Katherine Mansfield), believed in Griffes's talents so strongly that she considered her financial aid an investment to be paid back when he became successful.

[2] Griffes died from empyema (abscesses of the lungs), which was caused by influenza.

[3] Griffes's beliefs are discussed in depth in Maisel, 99–107.

[4] Five of these songs were the first of Griffes's works to be published by Schirmer in 1909. The last date of composition for a German text is 1912.

[5] Gauthier also contributed greatly to his studies of Oriental music and, when she lived in Java, she transcribed native melodies, some of which Griffes

arranged for her. Later she withheld these from publication claiming they had been a personal gift to her.

[6] Brown, once a student of the great Lamperti, is the author of the excellent book on singing *Vocal Wisdom: Maxims of Giovanni Battista Lamperti.*

[7] Donna K. Anderson, Preface to *Seven Songs.*

[8] These songs were first performed by Eva Gauthier with Griffes at the piano to mixed reviews.

[9] Griffes composed two versions of this same poem. It appears that the 1916 version is not published.

[10] Fiona MacLeod was a pseudonym for the Celtic poet William Sharp. Primarily used for his works about the mystical Celtic world, this secret was carefully kept until Sharp's death in 1905. Other poems and prose works were published under his real name.

[11] Griffes played the first piano performance with Vera Janacopulos; two days later the Philadelphia Orchestra performed them with Marcia van Dresser as soloist.

[12] Available for low voice in collection *S22A.*

[13] William Treat Upton, "The Songs of Charles T. Griffes," *Musical Quarterly*, 324.

HENRY K. HADLEY

b. Dec. 20, 1871, Somerville, MA; d. Sept. 6, 1937, New York, NY

Both as a conductor and as a composer, Henry Hadley was an immensely successful figure in his lifetime. Of his nearly 200 songs many can still be recommended for their unaffected, buoyant lyricism.

His ancestors were distinguished pre-revolutionary New Englanders, who settled in Somerville, Massachusetts, in the early nineteenth century. His father, who taught Hadley violin and piano was, as his father before him, director of music for the local schools. His mother was a pianist and contralto soloist, and his younger brother would become a well-known cellist.[1] Hadley studied theory and composition with George Chadwick in Boston and later with Eusebius Mandyczewski in Vienna. From 1895 to 1902, he taught music at St. Paul's Episcopal School for Boys in Garden City, New York, and, during that time, wrote the symphony *(Youth and Life)* which would establish him as a composer. Prolific in all idioms, he not only enjoyed the rare distinction of a premiere at the Metropolitan Opera House,[2] but also composed and conducted possibly the first score to be synchronized with a movie.[3]

Married in 1918 to Inez Barbour, a well-known lyric soprano,[4] the couple made New York their home base. But Hadley was a man of irrepressible energy and spirit, and his second career as a conductor kept him busy around the world.[5] A tireless promoter of American music, the Manhattan Symphony, which he organized in 1929, performed 36 American compositions under his three years of leadership. He also founded the National Association of American Composers and Conductors which, after his death, sponsored the Henry Hadley Memorial Library of works by American composers. In 1938 a Henry Hadley Foundation for the Advancement of American Music was formed.

THE SONGS

Although Hadley's highly accessible, colorful style occasionally met with raised eyebrows from critics, audiences responded to it with enthusiasm. His generally happy songs are a feast of melodic and harmonic delights, and show a refreshing spontaneity. The supple vocal lines, sensitive to poetic concerns, unfold effortlessly and offer ample, but tasteful, opportunity for vocal display. The accompaniments are primarily supportive and, though rarely difficult, can be inventive and evocative. But Hadley was prolific to a fault and permitted flaws of prosody and other technicalities a less facile composer would have corrected. In addition, a good number of his songs are trite or quaint. The following recommendations, however, are deft, engaging, often very beautiful, and would still be an asset if programmed today.

Evening Song, Sidney Lanier; G. Schirmer c1915.
> Rec. warm, full voices (high c1–f2); 2:45; Very slowly and peacefully; a gorgeous, arching melody over an arpeggiated accompaniment; a truly beautiful love song.

I Heard a Maid with Her Guitar, Op. 44, No. 3; Clinton Scollard; Church c1909.
> Rec. lighter lyrical voices (high, d1-g2), text suggests men; 1:30; Allegretto; a bright melody over a sparkling guitar-like accompaniment; charming.

Il pleut des pétales de fleurs (It is raining flower petals), Alfred Samain; G. Schirmer c1909; also incl. *NAAS.*
> Rec. warm lyric voice (low, c1–eb2); 2:30; Lente avec langueur; in French; undulating eighths evoke the desolate dropping of petals; an expansive central section; a poignant, atmospheric song.

If You Would Have It So, Op. 84, No. 3; Rabindranath Tagore; Fischer c1921.

Rec. lighter lyric voices (high, f1–ab2), text suggests men; 1:00; Allegretto scherzando; bright, with many staccatos; busy accompaniment; flirtatious and happy.

The Lute Player of Casa Blanca, Op. 84, No. 1; Laurence Hope; Fischer c1921; for Inez.

Rec. light lyric voices (high, f1–a2), text suggests women; 1:30; Allegretto con gentilezza; lyric and melodious over lute effects; some sustained high notes; ardent and infectious.

Stille, träumende Frühlingsnacht (Dreamy, wonderful summer night), Op. 42, No. 1; Otto Julius Bierbaum; G. Schirmer c1911.

Rec. lyric voices (c1–f2); 2:00; Sanft und träumerisch; in German; undulating; subdued dynamics; delicate, intimate and very lovely.

The Time of Parting, Op. 84, No. 2; Rabindranath Tagore; Fischer c1921; for my wife.[6]

Rec. lyric voices, but not pub. lower than medium (medium, d1–f2); 2:15; Andantino teneramente; a soothing cantilena over flowing broken chord patterns; justly famous for its lovely melody and affecting sentiment.

Also of interest:

Colloque Sentimental, Verlaine, Broadly with dignity, in French;[7] *I Plucked a Quill from Cupid's Wing,* Boucicault, for high voices, Allegretto scherzando; *My True Love,* Sydney [sic], Allegro giocoso; *A Spring Night,* Towne, Allegro appassionato; *Twelve Songs for Medium Voice,* Op. 12, Recital Publications Rep. Edition, especially rec. from this opus are the Heine settings in their English translations *(Dear when I look into thine eyes, A lonely fir-tree,* and *The Butterfly is in Love with the Rose); Under the April Moon,* Carman, lyric and moving; *The Year's at the Spring,* Browning, slow and restrained, an unusual setting.

BIBLIOGRAPHY

AmerGroves, Baker, Ewen, Greene, Hughes, Thompson, Upton.

Boardman, Herbert R. *Henry Hadley: Ambassador of Harmony.* Georgia: Emory Press, 1933.

Gideon, Henry L. "Examining the Achievements of Henry Hadley," *Musical America,* June 22, 1918.

MacArthur, Pauline Arnoux. "Henry Hadley's Place in American Music," *Musical America,* Oct. 29, 1921.

---

[1] Arthur Hadley became a member of the Boston Symphony. Hadley wrote several works for him.

[2] *Cleopatra's Night* premiered in 1920. It was the first opera at the Metropolitan to be conducted by its composer.

[3] *When a Man Loves* (1926).

[4] Inez Barbour grew up in Pittsburgh, where she began her career as a pianist. But also encouraged in her singing, she studied in Europe, making her operatic debut in Vienna as Aida. Even after marriage, she maintained a busy concert and operatic career on both sides of the Atlantic.

[5] In addition to his guest appearances, Hadley was, at various times, conductor of the Seattle and San Francisco symphony orchestras, and associate conductor of the New York Philharmonic.

[6] Written for one of her annual recitals, Inez Barbour herself suggested the poem. It became her favorite Hadley song.

[7] Favorably compared to Debussy's famous setting in *Art Song in America* (Upton, 159).

RICHARD HAGEMAN
b. July 9, 1882, Leeuwarden, Netherlands; d. March 6, 1966, Beverly Hills, CA

Composer, conductor, coach, and accompanist, for many years Richard Hageman was a popular figure with singers and audiences. His large output of songs includes some of the more colorful and attractive of the genre often referred to as "concert song."

Hageman's Dutch father was a violinist, composer, and director of the Amsterdam Conservatory; his Russian mother a court singer in Holland. Under his father's tutelage, Hageman exhibited exceptional musical gifts, and at age ten, was sent to the Brussels Conservatory, where he studied with composers Arthur de Greef (a pupil of Liszt) and François Gevaert. Returning to Amsterdam he became a rehearsal pianist and subsequently a conductor at the Royal Opera House. In 1904 Hageman moved to Paris, where he accompanied in the studio of the great voice teacher, Mathilde Marchesi. But two years later he joined the diseuse Yvette Guilbert on her tour of the United States and, when it ended, decided to remain in New York. Joining the staff of the Metropolitan Opera, Hageman made his official conducting debut in 1913 and for six seasons served as principal conductor for its popular

Sunday evening concerts. Later, he conducted the Chicago Opera (with summers at the Ravinia Festival) and the Los Angeles Grand Opera. He also briefly headed the Opera Department of the Curtis Institute in Philadelphia. Establishing a busy and successful studio wherever he worked, he coached and accompanied such illustrious singers as Claudia Muzio, Frieda Hempel, and Giovanni Martinelli. Eventually he settled in Los Angeles and became a film score composer and conductor for Paramount Studios.[1]

A lady's man, Hageman married three different sopranos. The first marriage (to Rosina Van Dyck from the Metropolitan Opera) ended in a messy court affair in which he claimed she threatened to kill him. The threat, she claimed,was motivated by his amorous involvement with Renée Thornton, who coached with Hageman. Thornton did indeed become the second Mrs. Hageman, but though the couple concertized together, they also divorced, and in 1931, he married his last soprano, Eleanore Rogers.

THE SONGS

As a prominent figure in the vocal world, Hageman had a ready platform for his songs. The vocal recital was enjoying heady days, and it had become standard fare to program an English group. A composer who could write music that provided a winding down from all the seriousness that preceded it—and still call it 'art' music—found himself in the right place at the right time.[2] Taking an accessible poem in English, serious or light, Hageman enhanced it with lovely melodies, rhythmic vitality, and lush, colorful harmonies. He also saw to it that both singer and pianist had ample opportunity to display the riches of their instruments. All this, coming under the guise of serious music making, was immensely satisfactory to audiences.[3]

Most of Hageman's songs are appropriate for any lyric voice. Some, however, with their long lines, sustained high notes, and robust accompaniments sound better with a more opulent sound. Pianists will need dexterity for the endless supply of imaginative figurations that make Hageman's accompaniments a particular delight. Few songs are still in print, but most are easily found in libraries, often published in more than one key. Isolated recordings are noted with their respective entries. Some recommendations follow.

At the Well, Rabindranath Tagore; G. Schirmer c1919; also incl. *50AS*.
         Pub. high and low (high e♭1–c♭3[a♭2]); 2:15; Allegro; but don't go too fast or the subtleties and grace might be lost, and the delightful

piano figurations won't sparkle; some tricky meter changes; a narrative of two sisters who, when they go to fetch water, enjoy being observed by a secret admirer; charming, different; recorded by Marcoulescou-Stern on Gasparo CD (287).

Do Not Go, My Love, Rabindranath Tagore; G. Schirmer c1917; also incl. *S22A* and *RAAS;* to George Hamlin.
    Pub. high (d#1–g2); 3:00; Adagio; sustained and lyrical with a più mosso; mostly quiet dynamics; a poignant love song; recorded by Rose Bampton on New World (247), Thomas Hampson on EMI CD (7 54051 2), John Hanks on Duke, Vol. 1 (DWR 6417), Dale Moore on Cambridge (2715), and Maggie Teyte on Pearl Gemm CD (9326).

Hush, Robert Nathan; Galaxy c1951.
    Pub. high voices only (c1–g2); 2:00; Molto tranquillo; lyrical.

May Night, Rabindranath Tagore; G. Schirmer c1917; to Oscar Seagle.
    Rec. high or medium voices (d1–gb2); 1:45; Allegro molto; excited, over chromatic scales evoking the breezes of a May night.

Me Company Along, James Stephens; Fischer c1925.
    Pub. high and low (high, f1–bb2); 2:30; Allegro non troppo; busy piano figurations propel this happy song; fun and effective.

Miranda, Hilaire Belloc; Galaxy c1940.
    Pub. high, medium and low (high, e1–a2); 2:15; Con spirito; tuneful; infectious Spanish rhythms (some tricky); big ending; colorful and evocative; an excellent setting of a wonderful poem; fun for everyone; recorded by Maryanne Telese on Premiere (002) and Marcoulescou-Stern on Gasparo CD (287).

Music I Heard With You, Conrad Aiken; Galaxy c1938.
    Pub. high and low (high, e1–a2); 3:00; Andante; the lyrical opening develops into some full throated singing over a lush accompaniment; nostalgic; romantic; recorded by Lucine Amara on Cambridge (CRM 704).

Velvet Shoes, Elinor Wylie; Galaxy c1954.
    Rec. high lyric voices (fb1–bb2[g#2]); 3:00; Molto tranquillo; delicate and sustained; intensifies briefly; a nice version of the oft set "Let us walk in the white snow."

Also of interest:
Beggar's Love, Storm, high only, Adagio; ***Charity,*** Dickinson, in three

keys, Andante molto tranquillo; ***Christ went up into the hills,*** Adams, big voices, a bit grandiose but effective; ***Fiddler of Dooney,*** Yeats, high only, Allegro giocoso; ***The Night Has a Thousand Eyes,*** Bourdillon, in two keys, irresistible bathos; ***O Why Do You Walk*** (To a Fat Lady seen from the Train), quiet and unusual; ***The Town,*** Storm, high only, somber.

BIBLIOGRAPHY[4]

AmerGroves, Baker, Greene, Thompson, Upton, Upton (Sup).

"Hageman Advocates Prohibition of Singers," *Musical America,* May 28, 1921. An interview in which Hageman declares that about 500 of the vocal recitals given each season in New York are superfluous.

"Hasty Debut May Bring Repentance, Renée Thornton Warns," *Musical America,* April 12, 1924. This interview with Hageman's second wife gives a good idea of how he worked as a coach.

---

[1] In 1940 he won an Academy Award for his musical score to the film *Stage Coach.* One also catches glimpses of the tall, austere Hageman in the role of the conductor in *The Great Caruso* (1951).

[2] 'Popular' music was still not considered appropriate for the concert stage. Eva Gauthier was considered very daring when she included Gershwin, Kern, and Berlin in a 1923 recital.

[3] The ascendancy of radio, with its wonderful semi-classical musical programs, was another outlet for this type of song.

[4] Some of the information for this entry comes from the countless stories that appeared in the music magazines of the 1910s and 1920s, describing Hageman's social and public life. His unorthodox opinions about the music world resulted in fascinating interviews, one of which is cited here.

LEE HOIBY

b. Feb. 17, 1926, Madison, WI

With his unaffected lyric gift and warm personal voice, Lee Hoiby has excelled in vocal writing. He is best known for his operas, but his contribution to song is also significant.

Beginning lessons at age five, Hoiby first aspired to be a pianist. At the University of Wisconsin he studied the instrument with Gunnar Johansen and, after graduation, continued with Egon Petri at Mills College in California. He also took composition with Darius Milhaud, and by the time he had earned his master's degree in 1952, Hoiby had produced a respectable portfolio of compositions. Then, while preparing

for his first New York piano recital, he was sidetracked by an offer to
work with composer Gian Carlo Menotti at the Curtis Institute. When
Menotti encouraged him to try his hand at opera, Hoiby's gift for the
idiom quickly revealed itself. His first success, *The Scarf*, premiered in
1958 at the Festival of Two Worlds in Spoleto, Italy, and the commissions that followed firmly established him as a composer.[1] Although in
1978 he finally gave his long anticipated New York piano debut, and he
still does some performing, Hoiby has continued to focus on composition. After living in Manhattan for many years, he now makes his home
in Long Eddy, New York, on the Delaware River.

THE SONGS
Rejected in 1953 by the Accademia di Santa Cecilia for being too tonal,
Hoiby, sticking to his convictions in an atonal world, has known artistic
isolation, but finds himself once again in the mainstream. He credits
Mozart, Richard Strauss, Puccini, Barber, and Menotti as major influences and singles out Schubert as the composer who taught him "how to
use the human voice." He has also admired the "arching melodic line"
and "simple harmonic means" of Cat Stevens and Joni Mitchell, popular songwriters who inspired him in the 1970s.[2] Hoiby's forthright songs
have beauty as well as personality and backbone. The truly romantic settings are especially fine, and the lighter songs are genuinely infectious.
Most were copyrighted in the 1980s, but some were composed as far
back as the 1950s. Though these early songs seem self-conscious compared to his later free-wheeling creations, his innately lyrical voice is
readily apparent from the beginning.

Hoiby is passionate about singing and knows singers well. Many,
including Leontyne Price, whose lustrous vocalism has inspired some of
his finest songs, have supported his work. His writing for voice is knowledgeable, but can be demanding, especially when it gets bogged down
in overly long sustained lines or in tessituras too high for clear enunciation of the words. And, while he claims not to be a "high C buff,"[3] he
may well end a song on an operatic high note. In keeping with his own
talents, the piano writing is, at times, even more sumptuous and arresting than that of the voice, and can be quite virtuosic. Other than occasional rhythmical complexities, difficulties for both performers are more
likely to be technical than musical.

Some songs appear in random anthologies or are published separately, but best sources are: *Thirteen Songs for High Voice (13SHV)*, G.
Schirmer c1990, and *Songs for Leontyne: Six Songs for High Voice* [4]

(SL), Southern c1985. In addition, Hoiby has issued the following collections from Aquarius Music, his own company: *Songs and Arias for High Voice (SAHV), Songs and Arias for Middle Voice (SAMV),* and *Baritone Songs and Arias (BSA).* Published in manuscript form, they are completely legible, though there is a confusing overlapping from volume to volume, and some duplicate the Southern and Schirmer publications. *Night Songs* are recorded by Carolyn Heafner, with Hoiby at the piano, on CRI (SD 462); also five songs are recorded by Kristine Ciesinski on Leonardo (LP1 120); two by William Sharp on New World CD (369-2); two by Cynthia Haymon on Argo CD (436 117-2ZH). Following are some recommendations.

Autumn, Rainer Maria Rilke (trans. Harry Duncan); incl. *SL;* comp. 1979; for David Garvey.[5]

Rec. high voices (d1–g2); 4:00; Andante sostenuto; vocally difficult with long, high, sustained passages; big; philosophic; very serious; recorded by Ciesinski.

A *Clear Midnight,* Walt Whitman; incl. *SAMV* and *BSA;* comp. 1988.

Rec. lower voices (b–c♭2); 2:15; Lento; Sustained and succinct; eloquent and affecting.

Evening, Wallace Stevens; incl. *SL;* comp. 1983.

Rec. high full voices (f1–a2); 4:30; Still; translucent, serene piano introduces an introspective voice; then, high sustained phrases suspended over fast moving figurations; demanding high tessitura; formidable piano part; too many high notes and a bit long, but beautiful and passionate.

Four Dickinson Songs, Southern c1988; comp 1986/87.

Spec. high voice (b–g#2); 9:15; may be used individually, though *A Letter* needs something to follow.

***A Letter,*[6]** (b–f#2); 2:45; Moderato; lyrical; prosaic piano figure sets the domestic mood and Emily's desire to communicate with her new friend; a nice opening.

How the Waters Closed, (d1–g2); 1:45; Mesto; slow; intense; strong dynamic changes.

Wild Nights, (c1–g2); 2:15; Allegro; soaring and sustained over rushing piano figurations; a good setting of this famous poem.

There Came a Wind Like a Bugle, (e1–a2); 2:30; Molto allegro; hefty singing over active piano part; the predictable and excessive ending disappoints.

Go, and Catch a Falling Star, John Donne; Boosey c1965.
   Rec. high, agile voices (d♭1–a♭2), text suggests men; 2:00; Vivace;
a disjunct but fetching vocal line over running sixteenths; sustained
central section; the idea is that one is as likely to find a woman who
is true as to catch a falling star; an excellent, spirited song.

An Immorality, Ezra Pound; G. Schirmer c1956; incl. *CAS28* and
13SHV.
   Rec. medium and higher lyric voices (e♭1–g2); 1:00; Poco allegro;
forthright and tuneful; shifting meters; attractive and cheerful.

In the Wand of the Wind, John Fandel; incl. *SL;* comp. 1952.
   Rec. high voices (e♭1–a♭2); 1:00; Allegro molto; spirited; rhythmic; a nice opener.

Jabberwocky, Lewis Carroll; c1986; incl. *SAMV* and *13SHV;* comp.
1986.
   Rec. all voices (medium b♭–g2); 4:45; Molto moderato; this wild
narrative begins and ends easily enough, but gets excited and
involved with the killing of the jabberwock; many nonsensical words;
good characterization for both performers; fun; recorded by Sharp.

Night Songs, Adelaide Crapsey; incl. *SAHV.*
   Rec. higher lyric voices (c#1–a♭2); 10:00; titles are: *Night;
Pierrot; Angélique; The Shroud;* could be used individually; moderate tempo indications; only *Angélique* gets briefly excited; sustained
and highly lyrical; contained, atmospheric, attractive songs; recorded
by Heafner.

O Florida, Op.39; Wallace Stevens; incl. *SAMV* and *BSA;* comp. 1983
   Spec. medium voice (a–g♭2); 22:00; titles are: *Floral Decorations
for Banana; Gubbinal; Continual Conversation with a Silent Man;
Contrary These; O Florida;* complex musically; many cross rhythms;
only an occasional feeling of tonality; starts out propitiously but
meanders in the last songs; nevertheless, much of it captures exceedingly well the strange and sensuous imagery.

The River-Merchant's Wife: A Letter, Rihaku (trans. Ezra Pound);[7]
Southern c1987; incl. *SAHV* and *VN;* comp. 1956; rev. 1981.
   Rec. lyric voices (d1–a2), text suggests women; 6:30; Andante; a
variety of tempos and many shifting meters; lightly declaimed with
some recitative and sustained passages; requires clarity and delicacy;

in this long letter to her husband, the wife reviews their whole relationship; different and effective.

The Serpent, Theodore Roethke; incl *SL;* comp. 1979; for Leontyne Price.

Rec. high lyric voices (c1–b♭2); 4:00; Allegro giocoso; a fast paced narrative, in various colorful sections, about a serpent who gave up serpenting for singing; this he proceeds to do in a mild coloratura style much to the other animals distress; many tricky shifting meters; fun, successful, and entertaining; recorded by Ciesinski, who adds some unnotated but nice effects, such as the exaggerated use of 's' when the serpent talks.

She Tells Her Love While Half-Asleep, Robert Graves; incl. *13SHV;* comp. 1952.

Rec. medium lyric voices (d1–e2); 1:15; Moderato; long sustained lines over a flowing accompaniment; hushed.

What If..., Samuel Taylor Coleridge; incl. *SAMV* and *BSA;* comp. 1986.

Rec. medium lyric voices (b–f2); 3:00; Con moto espressivo; warm and suggestive over a softly moving accompaniment; whimsical; lovely; recorded by Sharp.

Also of interest:

always, it's Spring, Cummings, incl. *13SHV,* Allegro molto; recorded by Haymon; **Christmas 1951,** Fandel, incl. *SAHV,* Andante sostenuto; **Jean qui Rit,** Williams, *SAHV,* Andantino; **Love Love Today,** Mew, incl. *SAHV,* Moderato; **O Star,** Fandel, incl. *SAHV,* Lento; **Where the Music Comes From,** incl. *13SHV,* Moderato, recorded by Haymon; **Why Don't You?** Beers, incl. *SAMV* and *BSA,* Bouncy, crazy, tricky but fun.

BIBLIOGRAPHY

AmerGroves, Baker, CBY(1987), Ewen, Greene, Thompson.

Cavalieri, Walter. "Lee Hoiby: A Summer of Success," *Music Journal* (Nov/Dec 1980).

Ericson, Raymond. "Music Notes: Mr. Hoiby's New Career," *New York Times,* Oct. 19, 1980.

Hoiby, Lee. "Making Tennessee Williams Sing," *New York Times,* June 13, 1971.

Schmidgall, Gary. "A Long Voyage," *Opera News* (June 1986).

---

1 Commissions include: *Natalia Petrovna* (changed to *A Month in the Country*) by the City Center Opera in 1964; *Summer and Smoke* (based on the play by Tennessee Williams) by the St. Paul Opera in 1971; and *The Tempest* by the Des Moines Metro Opera in 1986.

2 Gary Schmidgall, *Opera News,* 13.

3 "Lee Hoiby: A Summer of Success," *Music Journal* (Nov/Dec 1980), 11.

4 Leontyne is, of course, Leontyne Price. This is a collection of the songs Hoiby wrote for her at different times.

5 David Garvey is a pianist who has often accompanied Leontyne Price.

6 This was Dickinson's second letter in what became a celebrated correspondence with Thomas Higginson, an author and critic, who had taken an early interest in her work after she sent him some poems. Here she answers some of his first inquiries. Only a small fragment of the letter is used for the song.

7 Rihaku is an eighth century Chinese poet. This translation is found in Pound's collection *Personae.*

SIDNEY HOMER
b. Dec. 9, 1864, Boston, MA; d. July 10, 1953, Winter Park, FL

"The songs of Sidney Homer ... need no introduction, as they are sufficiently known to every American singer."[1] So wrote Sergius Kagen in 1949, but today Homer's vigorous, expressive, heartfelt songs lie untouched on library shelves.

The third and last child of deaf parents, Homer, though born with perfect hearing, used sign language before he ever spoke. His father worked as a customs agent, but an annuity left by a wealthy uncle secured the family's comfort.[2] When he was 16, Homer chose to study in London where he felt he could explore his literary interests. A music critic there, however, recognized his unusual musical sensibility and urged him in that direction. He studied first in Leipzig, then with George Chadwick in Boston, and finally with Josef Rheinberger in Munich. Back in Boston, in 1888 Homer opened his own studio, to which, the following year, Louise Beatty, a promising young contralto from Philadelphia, came to complete her general music studies. Two years later they married and left for Paris. There, Louise completed her vocal studies and Homer began to compose in earnest. When the couple returned to New York, G. Schirmer began to publish his songs, while Louise Homer—rapidly becoming one of the great singers of the Golden Age of Opera—and her illustrious colleagues gave them widespread exposure.

Despite their successful careers, the happy couple still found time to have six children.[3] When not in New York for Louise's career they lived in "Homeland," the house they built on Lake George, New York. In 1939 they retired to Winter Park, Florida, where Homer died seven years after Louise, having devoted his final years to editing his songs.

THE SONGS

The 100-plus songs of Sidney Homer have remarkable character and vitality. His response to text is, in fact, so strong that if these songs have a failing, it is their lack of full compositional development—as though, without the words, there is nothing more to say. The diversity of his catalogue is a delight for, despite his excellent taste in poetry, Homer also enjoyed setting less highbrow texts. William Blake, Robert Browning, Mother Goose, and "Casey at the Bat" are all approached with equal gusto. There are also a number of songs on political and social concerns of the day, such as *To Russia* and *The Song of the Shirt,* as well as emotional potboilers like *Prospice* and *Babylon the Great.* Though popular in their time, few of this type are viable for today's audiences. Otherwise, in addition to some of the best narrative and dramatic settings of the period, Homer's catalogue abounds with songs that are sincere, original, forthright, and occasionally very beautiful.

Because—through Louise—Homer's world was peopled with the finest operatic stars, many of his songs seem better suited to big voices. Vocal lines can be bold,[4] but are always sympathetic and beautifully crafted. Piano writing, abounding in large, and, often, unusual chords, tends to be homophonic. All Homer's songs were published individually but, excepting the occasional anthology item, are out of print. However, Classical Vocal Reprints includes many in its catalogue. A collection, *Seventeen Songs of Sidney Homer (SSSH),* was lovingly compiled by his nephew, Samuel Barber,[5] and published by G. Schirmer (c1943) in high and low editions. Louise Homer's recording of 12 songs, including six *Mother Goose* settings, is available on Pearl Gemm CD (9950). Some recommendations follow. Though virtually all were published in a high and a low key, the low is usually the original, having been written with his wife's contralto voice in mind.

Dearest, Op. 23, No. 1, William Ernest Henley; G. Schirmer c1910; to my wife; also incl. *SSSH.*

Rec. all voices (high, eb1–ab2); 1:00; Andante sostenuto; builds in intensity, then tapers; a touching love song with a compelling melodic line; recorded by Homer.

The Fiddler of Dooney, Op. 20, William Butler Yeats; G. Schirmer c1909/1941; also incl. *SSSH*.

Rec. big voices (high, d1–g2), text suggests men; 1:00; Allegro molto; a parlando builds to a final *ff*; rhythmically spirited; effective.

General William Booth Enters into Heaven, Op. 38, Vachel Lindsay; G. Schirmer c1926.

Spec. low or medium voice but only published in A♭ Major (c1–e♭2), rec. bigger voices; 4:00; marchlike Allegro giubiloso sections alternate with passages of flowing lyricism. Unlike the famous Ives version, Homer uses the entire Lindsay poem. Booth, the founder of the Salvation Army, is extoled as he makes his triumphant entrance into paradise; the hushed Lento, when Booth and Christ come face to face, makes a striking, unexpected ending; a vigorous, thrilling, moving song.

The House That Jack Built, Op. 36, from Mother Goose; John Church c1920.[6]

Rec. strong, agile voices (high, c1–a♭2); 2:00; Allegro, gaily with increasing animation; ends prestissimo; stamina required; infectious and great fun without being cute; recorded by Homer.

"How's My Boy?" Op. 17, No. 1, Sydney Dobell; G. Schirmer c1906/ 1934; to my wife; also incl. *SSSH*.

Rec. dramatic voices (low, c#1–e2); 3:00; Allegro; many recitative-like passages as the mother questions a sailor as to her son's fate; this unusual, dramatic dialogue was a favorite recital ender for Louise Homer; recorded by Homer.

Infant Sorrow, Op. 26, No. 2; William Blake, G. Schirmer c1913; also incl. *SSSH*.

Rec. big voices (low, g–f2); 1:00; Allegro molto (furiously); intense and driving throughout; ends *fff*; an exciting song describing one's own birth.

The King of the Fairy Men, Op. 34, No. 1, James Stephens; G. Schirmer c1917/ 1943; also incl. *SSSH*.

Rec. all voices (c1–f2); 1:00; Allegro energico; rhythmically incisive; the irony of this curious poem which opens "I know the man without a soul" is neatly drawn; a startling little song.

Mary's Baby, Op. 34, No. 3; Irene Rutherford McLeod; G. Schirmer c1917; also incl. *SSSH*.

Rec. lyric voice (high, e1–f2); 1:45; Andante; moves through slower tempos to end lento; the eloquent, concise phrases disallow sentimentality; mystical, poignant.

My Star, Op. 12, No. 1, Robert Browning; G. Schirmer c1902.
Rec. lyric voices (low, c#1–d#2); 1:00; Allegretto; a breathless, fluid melody over a twinkling accompaniment; fresh and beguiling.

Pirate Story, Op. 16, No. 1, Robert Louis Stevenson; G. Schirmer c1906; to my children.
Rec. all voices (low, c1–d2); 1:30; Allegro (with grace and merriment); an irresistible setting from the *Child's Garden of Verses,* tuneful and catchy.

Sheep and Lambs, Op. 31, Katherine Tynan Hinkson; G. Schirmer c1914/1942; also incl. *SSSH;* to my wife.
Rec. bigger voices (high, c1–f#2); 3:00; Andante; a lovely, sustained melody over fluid accompaniment; builds to a central climax; not a church piece despite the religious theme (Christ as the Lamb of God); a favorite on Louise Homer's programs.

The Sick Rose, Op.26, No. 1, William Blake; G.Schirmer c1913/1941; also incl. *SSSH.*
Rec. big voices (high, c#1–g2); 1:30; Molto lento; very sustained, quiet dynamics with a central climax of stunning intensity; unusual harmonies; an impressive song; recorded by Dale Moore on Cambridge (CRS 2715).

A Woman's Last Word, Op. 12, No. 2; Robert Browning; G. Schirmer c1903.
Rec. women's voices (low, b–c2); 2:45; Andante; tends to lie low; the subservience of the Victorian woman is portrayed in an unusually restrained melodic line; unless one is troubled by the text, this is an effective and different song.

Also of interest:

April, April, Watson, Con moto, lyrical; *A Banjo Song,* Weeden, in dialect, tuneful but dated, one of his most popular songs; recorded by Homer; *Break, break, break,* Tennyson, somewhat dramatic; *The Country of the Camisards,* Stevenson, Moderato; *In the meadow— what in the meadow?* Christina Rossetti, Vivace, delicate; *Lullaby, oh Lullaby!* Christina Rossetti, Molto lento, very sustained; *Michael*

Robartes Bids His Beloved be at Peace, Yeats, best for men, Allegro
molto; ***Requiem,*** Stevenson, Adagio, succinct, warm; recorded by
Homer; ***Sing to Me, Sing,*** Henley, Allegro molto, recorded by Telese on
Premier (002) and Homer; ***The Stormy Evening,*** Stevenson, dramatic
women's voice, Allegro molto; ***Sweet and Low,*** Tennyson, a rocking lullaby; ***"Thy voice is heard 'thro rolling drums,"*** Tennyson, impassioned;
The Unforgotten, Stevenson, a lovely miniature; ***When Death to either
shall come,*** Bridges, warm, lyrical.

BIBLIOGRAPHY

AmerGroves, Baker, Greene, Hall, Howard, Nathan, Thompson, Upton.
Barber, Samuel. Preface to *Seventeen Songs of Sidney Homer*. New
    York: G. Schirmer, c1943.
Gilman, Lawrence. "The Songs of Sidney Homer," *The Musician*
    (January 1906).
Homer, Sidney. *My Wife and I*. New York: Macmillan, 1939. This is an
    enjoyable autobiography. In Homer's characteristically modest man-
    ner, he focuses on Louise Homer's career, but also offers many inter-
    esting insights on song-writing, singing, and singers.
Homer, Anne. *Louise Homer and the Golden Age of Opera*. New York:
    William Morrow & Company, 1974.
Thorpe, Harry Colin. "The Songs of Sidney Homer," *Musical Quarterly*
    17 (1931): 47–73.

---

[1] Sergius Kagen, *Music for the Voice*, 327. This remark was retained in the
revised edition of 1964.

[2] Also an artistic family, the great American painter Winslow Homer was a
cousin of Homer's father.

[3] Two of the children became musicians: Louise, the eldest, was a soprano;
Kay was a pianist who occasionally served as her mother's accompanist. Joy
and Ann were both writers.

[4] Homer applauded the singularity of the voices of his era and deplored any
standardization of singing, which he feared was the coming trend. *My Wife
and I*, 191.

[5] Barber was Homer's nephew, the son of Louise's sister. He happened to be
a fine singer and became, of course, an important composer of songs in his
own right. See Barber, footnote 2, for more on his important relationship with
his uncle.

[6] In an effort to see music made available in bookstores, Homer's 35 *Mother
Goose* settings were originally published by Macmillan.

EDWARD HORSMAN
b. 1873, Brooklyn, NY; d. July 27, 1918, Summit, NJ

Edward Horsman adroitly combined a career in his family's toy business with that of composition. He was also an organist and, for five years, music critic for the *Herald Tribune*. Though for many years Horsman was primarily a composer of choral music, the overwhelming success of his first published song, *The Bird of the Wilderness,* assured him a reputation as a song writer. His untimely death from a heart attack, however, ended the early promise.

THE SONGS
Though Horsman is remembered solely for *The Bird of the Wilderness,* he, in fact, left a handful of beautiful songs. An adamant believer that the accompaniment should be an equal partner to the vocal line (conceivably able to stand on its own), his rich, expressive songs are akin to small tone poems. However, as most are in similarly slower tempos, programming too many at one time would do them a disservice. Appropriate for all but light voices, Horsman's sensitivity for the vocal line is a special pleasure.[1] The six songs listed below appear to be all that were published. All are worthwhile.

The Bird of the Wilderness, Rabindranath Tagore; G. Schirmer c1915; to Miss Alma Gluck; also incl. *NAAS.*
    Pub. low, medium, high (med., bb–g2), rec. bigger voices; 1:45; Moderato; a lush, attractive melody over a sumptuous accompaniment; a big ending; an ecstatic love song; less interesting than some of the others, but very popular in its time.[2]

The Dream, from "The Mastersingers of Japan"; G. Schirmer c1917.
    Pub. high voice only (f1–g2); 3:15; Adagio; long sustained vocal lines over a languidly flowing piano; begins and ends quietly; builds to a central climax; despite the excessive repetitions of the text, an unusual and atmospheric song.

In the Yellow Dusk, from the Chinese of Li-Po (circa A.D. 700); G. Schirmer c1916; to Mr. Oscar Seagle.
    Pub. medium and high voices (high, f#1–ab2); 3:00; Tranquillamente; a woman weaves alone in the quiet dusk and recalls a lost love; the evocative music matches the changing imagery; impressionistic; a fine song.

The Shepherdess, Alice Meynell; G. Schirmer c1916; to my wife.
  Pub. low and high voices (high, d♭1–a♭2), text suggests man; 2:15; Larghetto semplice; more tuneful and less involved than other Horsman; borderline sentimental; lyrical, pretty.

Thus Wisdom Sings, from the Chinese of Chang-Chih-Ho; G. Schirmer c1916.
  Pub. high voice only (e♭1–a2); 1:30; Allegretto; the melodious opening praising the joys of nature becomes somewhat dissonant as the less pleasant company of men is considered; not as well crafted as other Horsman.

You Are the Evening Cloud, Rabindranath Tagore; G. Schirmer c1916.
  Pub. high and low (high, d#1–a2); 3:00; Lento, ma non troppo; the counter melody carried by the top note of the rolled chords is rather awkward; otherwise, lush, melodic, and unabashedly romantic.

BIBLIOGRAPHY
Thorpe (on *In the Yellow Dusk*).
"Horsman Dedicates New Song to Seagle," *Musical America,* Oct. 7, 1916.
"The Man Who Wrote 'Bird of the Wilderness'," *Musical America,* Oct. 30, 1915.

---

[1] Another of his guiding principles was that texts primarily made up of one syllable words are best for musical settings.

[2] In a poll of major artists, taken by *Musical America,* to determine their favorite American song, *The Bird of the Wilderness* (only one year after its publication) won handily, beating out the more established favorites.

ALAN HOVHANESS[1]
b. March 8, 1911, Somerville, MA

Drawing heavily on non-Western influences, Alan Hovhaness has developed an idiom so singularly his own that he remains a novelty on the sidelines of American music. His many evocative and distinctive songs are admired but seldom programmed.

  His father, a chemistry professor at Tufts University, was Armenian; his mother Scottish. But Hovhaness's upbringing in Arlington, Massachusetts, where the family moved when he was five, was altogether American. As a child, he took piano lessons with Adelaide

Proctor, and also devised his own notational system. Briefly attending
Tufts, he soon transferred to the New England Conservatory, where he
studied composition with Frederick Converse and built up a considerable reputation locally for his work. Then, in the early 1940s he began
to immerse himself in the languages, religions, philosophies, and music
of his Eastern European heritage. Boldly destroying his previous compositions, he began again and, in 1945, presented an all-Hovhaness program in New York City. By the early 1950s, his compositions were
being performed by major orchestras. In 1959, with the aid of a Fulbright
Research Scholar grant, he embarked on a world tour, which lasted several years and included visits to India, Japan, Germany, France, Korea,
and a residency at the University of Hawaii. On his return, with his first
wife, pianist Naru Whittington, Hovhaness established a recording company, Poseidon Records, but when they divorced, she was awarded control of the business. In 1972 he settled in Seattle and, in 1977, married
Hinako Fujihara, a coloratura soprano.

THE SONGS

Hovhaness's many songs were mainly composed in the 1940s and 1950s.
Though highly accessible, they are not to everyone's liking. One must
have a taste for such extremely distinctive flavors, and some may charge
the songs favor effect over substance. Employing a small vocal, dynamic, and emotional range, most are chantlike and move in a kind of perpetual motion. Within this framework, however, invention is unending.
And, although the impression is that musical materials were taken from
ethnic sources, they are, in fact, original. The ancient modes, rhythms,
musical devices, and styles of the Near, Middle, and Far East, are merely the foundation through which Hovhaness filters his own modern
Occidental techniques and sensibilities. Texts generally evoke the serenity and contemplation that is the essence of the East, but more often than
not, the poets are Western—very often Hovhaness himself. What
emerges—evocative, exotic, mystical, simple, pure— is altogether different from anything else in the singer's library.

Tessitura is a determining factor when considering who should sing
which songs. Otherwise, their modest ranges make them accessible to
most singers, though the long sustained lines and melismatic passages
readily expose poor support or uneven voice quality. Nimble-fingered
pianists can revel in long solo passages. Musical difficulties are rare.
Melodic lines, often modal, move stepwise and orbit a tonal center. On
occasion, seemingly for timbral effect, tiny microtones are called for.

With meters frequently changing or abandoned altogether, rhythms often have an improvisatory feeling. Programming these songs to their advantage can be problematic for, despite the endless invention, too large a dose can easily wear thin.

There should be no trouble in finding these songs. If not available at local stores, they can be ordered from C. F. Peters. Poseidon Records[2] has issued much of Hovhaness's music, including three albums of songs with piano, all sung by bass, Ara Berberian (with high songs transposed down), and the composer at the piano. These are Vol. 1 (Poseidon 1005) and Vol. 3 (Poseidon 1009). Vol. 2 contains only Armenian language settings.The following is a small sampling of recommendations from a very large catalogue. Anyone drawn to this distinctive style will want to investigate further, and also consider Hovhaness's works for voice with instruments.

Black Pool of Cat, Op. 84, No. 1, Jean Harper; Peters c1969; comp. 1949.

   Rec. medium or high voices (g1–f♭2); 3:30; a long piano introduction; then, a simple melody over a variety of evocative, fast moving figurations; the poet envies the tranquility of the sleeping cat; quiet; recorded by Berberian (Vol. 1).

Innisfallen, Op. 95, No. 4,[3] Jean Harper; Peters c1960; comp. 1949.

   Rec. medium or high lyric voices (d1–e2); 2:00; a chantlike invocation with microtones over a spare piano; mystical; cool.

Love Songs of Hafiz,[4] Op. 33, Alan Hovhaness; Peters c1968; comp. 1935 (second version 1957).

   Spec. medium voice (b–f2); 18:00; titles are: *Hafiz, like Lord Krishna; Hafiz Is a Merry Old Thief; O Flowing of My Tears; Hafiz Wanders, Weeping; Day of Hafiz' Vision; O Love, Hear My Cry; Where Is My Beloved; Love for the Soul;* narratives; folklike; recorded by Berberian (Vol. 1).

The Moon Has a Face, Op. 156, Robert Louis Stevenson; Peters c1968; comp. 1930.

   Rec. lyric voices (e1–e#2); 2:00; Lento misterioso; recitando on a repeated note over soft chords evoking the moonlit scene; finally, a simple melody steals forth; magical.

Out of the Depths, Op. 142, No. 3, from Psalm 130; Peters c1958; comp. 1938, rev. 1958; also for organ.

Rec. big high voices (e1–a2); 2:30; Andante; chordal; builds without letup to a powerful close; a prayer.

Pagan Saint, Op. 74, No. 1, Consuelo Cloos; Peters c1960; comp. 1948.
Rec. medium and high voices (g1–g2); 1:45; Presto for the long piano opening, then, with the entrance of the voice, Allegro; changing meters; jazz-like rhythms; an abrupt ending; a strong song with a certain wild abandon; recorded by Berberian (Vol. 3).

Persephone, Op. 154, Alan Hovhaness; Peters c1968; comp. 1957.
Rec. low or medium low voices (b–d2); 5:00 (this specified time seems impossibly short); Very free; various figurations well up from the bowels of the piano (the depths of Hades); the voice haltingly describes the coming of spring; a tone poem which could stand alone on a program.

Raven River, Consuelo Cloos; Peters c1960.
Rec. low voices (g–a1); 2:45; Allegro; the singer weaves his low line in a tempo independent of the high piano writing; the pianist also strikes a suspended Chinese Gong at stipulated moments; a cumulative effect of thick, stifling sonority intimates death's imminence.

Starlight of Noon, Op. 32,[5] Alan Hovhaness; Peters c1968.
Rec. high lyric voices (g#1–f#2); 1:45; Allegro; long piano introduction; both piano and voice are set in a high range; sparkling effect; short and sweet.

Three Songs, Op. 95, Jean Harper; Peters c1960; comp. 1949.
Rec. medium lyric voices (b–e2); 4:30; titles are: *Describe Me!; Green Stones; Fans of Blue;* these descriptive songs complement each other and, ideally, should stay together; moderate in range, dynamic, and difficulty; includes microtones and melismas; a spare piano in perpetual motion; sensitive and effective, little songs.

Also of interest:

Dawn at Laona, Hovhaness, in several parts, a cantata for low voice; *Lullaby of the Lake,* Cloos, Allegro, recorded by Berberian (Vol. 1); *O Goddess of the Sea,* Hovhaness, Very free with a strange and fierce expression; *O World,* Shelley, for tenor or baritone, free, melismatic, chantlike, powerful.

BIBLIOGRAPHY
AmerGroves, Baker, CBY (1965), Ewen, Greene, Thompson.

Daniel, Oliver. "Alan Hovhaness," *ACA Bulletin* 2 (Oct. 1952).

Kostelanetz, Richard. "Alan Hovhaness Does Things Differently," *New York Times*, Nov. 12, 1978.

Wolverton, Vance D. "The Solo Vocal Music of Alan Hovhaness," *The NATS Journal* 47 (May/June 1991).

---

[1] Alan Hovhaness Chakmakjian was his birth name. At various times, he also took the name Vaness as well as his mother's maiden name of Scott.

[2] Crystal Records is now distributor for Poseidon and, under its own label, has reissued several recordings on CD. None, as yet, are of the songs.

[3] This opus number suggests that Hovhaness added this song to other Jean Harper texts in *Three Songs*, Op. 95. *AmerGroves,* however, lists it as Op 84, No. 2, which connects it more logically to *Black Pool of Cat*. All were composed in 1949.

[4] Hafiz was the pseudonym for a fourteenth century Persian poet.

[5] Though none is given here, there are two numbers to this opus, the other being *O World.*

MARY HOWE
b. April 4, 1882, Richmond, VA; d. Sept. 14, 1964, Washington, D.C.

Mary Howe's catalogue of music includes a large number of songs ranging from the highly unusual to the conventionally pretty. Though many would be a welcome addition to the repertoire, they are seldom heard.

She was born Mary Carlisle and grew up in Washington D.C., where her father was an international lawyer. Her mother was musical and had studied singing. As was customary for affluent families of the time, Howe was educated at home by tutors. She studied piano from an early age and later commuted to Baltimore's Peabody Conservatory to work with Ernest Hutcheson. In 1912 she married Walter Bruce Howe, a Washington lawyer, who supported his wife's musical interests. Within six years Mary Howe had three children and had learned to balance her role at home with her busy performance schedule. In addition to her solo work, for decades she periodically toured the country with her friend Anne Hull as a duo piano team. Later, with her musical children singing and herself at the virginal, "The Four Howes" also toured, performing madrigals, glees, and catches.

Howe did not begin composing seriously until she was almost 40, at which time she returned to Peabody to study composition with Gustave Strube. At the same time, she not only continued to perform but also gave tirelessly of herself to the founding and organizing of many of Washington D.C.'s musical organizations.[1] In 1927 she began spending part of every summer at the MacDowell Colony where she found the quiet she needed for composing. She also took a year to study with Nadia Boulanger in France. Throughout her life Howe remained active in all her musical endeavors. Her 80th birthday was celebrated in grand fashion with performances of her works.

THE SONGS

Howe's compositional style is conventional, but her writing abounds with unusual ideas and can be highly individualistic. Though some songs are brief, euphonic, and straightforward, others are long, aggressively dissonant, and complex. Some of the latter can be very powerful, but others ramble or get bogged down in arbitrary dissonance. Generally speaking, the best of Howe's songs are a combination of the two extremes of her style.

Her selection of texts is also wide-ranging. Howe was clearly drawn to women poets of her own generation, such as Amy Lowell and Elinor Wylie, but she also set French and German poetry (in the original language), the Elizabethans, the Romantics, and many unknown contemporaries (always of high quality) who were probably her friends. With a special gift for effortlessly moving from quasi recitative into full-throated song, her vocal writing is, for the most part, idiomatic and rewarding. The appearance on the printed page, however, is disconcerting, for Howe tended to compose in white notes, using the half note as the standard unit of time. Visually, this detracts from the linear effect and gives an incorrect impression that the vocal line will be ponderous. Though meters shift frequently, rhythms are not difficult. Pitches are only difficult in the most chromatic passages, at which time the pianist will also have a difficult job. Other than some earlier songs, which were issued individually, Howe's published songs are found in Galaxy's 1959 publication of seven volumes devoted to her songs. Three of these are English settings; another is German; yet another is French; an additional one, in English, is specified for baritone; and, finally, there is a volume devoted entirely to Goethe settings. The only recording is Sharon Mabrey singing five of the Goethe—songs that are not very representative of Mary Howe's style or special qualities—on Coronet (LPS 3127). Recommended songs are either individually published or selected from the Galaxy albums of English Songs: Parts 1, 2, and 3 *(ESP1, ESP2,* and *ESP3).*

Avalon (Where men are sent to be healed of their grievous wounds), Nancy Byrd Turner; Galaxy c1959; incl. *ESP3*.
   Rec. medium and high voices (d1–g2); 2:15; Andante comodo; sustained over broken chord patterns; builds briefly; warm; nostalgic.

The Bailey and the Bell, Anonymous 15th century; incl. *ESP1*.
   Rec. high lyric voices (d1–a2); 4:00; Gravely; organ-like chordal passages frame a bell-like, allegretto central section; vocally challenging; mystical; evocative; different.

The Birds, D. C.; incl. *ESP1*.
   Rec. lyric voices (e1–g2); 1:30; Slowly; chords, then a lyrical parlando over a spare piano; graceful, with a carefree, improvisational feeling; different.

In Tauris, Euripides, from "Iphigenia in Tauris"; trans. Gilbert Murray; incl. *ESP2*.
   Rec. voices with a rich middle (d♭1–g2); 9:00; Larghetto serioso; many diverse sections including recitative, sustained passages over chords, and flowing lyricism over various piano effects; a lament for a lost love in grand operatic scale (one can imagine it with orchestra) but not a display piece; interpretatively difficult and dangerously long, but original and—given a first-rate performance—potentially very moving.

Let Us Walk in the White Snow (Velvet Shoes), Elinor Wylie; Fischer c1948; also incl. *CSE*.
   Pub. medium high and medium low (medium high, d1–g2); 4:00; Andantino, molto tranquillo; shifting meters; lyrical; atmospheric; a beautiful, expansive setting of this wonderful poem.

Little Elegy, Elinor Wylie; G. Schirmer c1939.
   Rec. medium lyric voices (e1–e2); 2:00; Andantino; warm, flowing but somber.

Men, Dorothy Reid; incl. *ESP2*.
   Rec. any woman's voice (f1–f2); 1:00; Casually, not too fast; lightly declaimed; concerns the odd things men do, but ends "I like men."

My Lady Comes, Chard Powers Smith; incl. *ESP2*.
   Rec. tenors (d1–g2); 2:15; Tranquillo; lyrical; a lovely, delicate love song.

O Mistress Mine, William Shakespeare; incl. *ESP3*.

Rec. medium voices (d1–e2[f#2]), text suggests men; 1:00; a light allegretto in a sprightly parlando; not at all difficult; nice subtleties; charming.

O Proserpina, William Shakespeare (from The Winter's Tale); incl. *ESP1.*
Rec. high lyric voices (g1–a2); 2:30; opens Slowly; alternately recitando and lyrical; strange and affecting.

Three Hokku,[2] from the Japanese, Amy Lowell; incl. *ESP2;* to Adele Addison.
Rec. lyric voices (g1–g2); 3:00 (about 1:00 each); three haiku inspired sketches of flower images, which must be sung together; lyrical and spare; effective.

When I Died in Berners Street (A Strange Story), Elinor Wylie; G. Schirmer c1947.
Rec. medium and high voices (c1–g2); 3:00; Allegretto; many tempo changes; a series of deaths (some macabre) in various London locations; only the last is gentle; as interesting and original a song as its title suggests.

Also of interest:

Berceuse, Anonymous, pub. separately, Andantino; *Fair Annet's Song,* Wylie, incl. *ESP1,* active, big; *Fragment,* Lee, incl. *ESP1,* Moderato; *Old English Lullaby,* 15th cent., incl. *ESP3,* Andante semplice; *Were I to Die Tonight,* Valeur, incl. *ESP3,* Moderato. Also keep in mind the four remaining albums: *Seven Goethe Songs, Baritone Songs* (in English), *French Songs,* and *German Songs.*

BIBLIOGRAPHY[3]

AmerGroves, Ammer, Baker, Friedberg (II), Goss, Greene, Thompson, Upton (Sup).
Craig, Mary. "Mary Howe, Composer, Honored for Works," *Musical Courier,* Feb. 1, 1953.

---

[1] These included the National Symphony Orchestra, the Friends of Music at the Library of Congress, and the National Federation of Music Clubs.

[2] See Friedberg (II), 23–26, for an especially good analysis of this set.

[3] In 1959 Howe's autobiography, *Jottings,* was privately published.

RICHARD HUNDLEY
b. Sept. 1, 1931, Cincinnati, OH

Though generally overlooked by the non-vocal world, Richard Hundley is, nonetheless, very popular with singers—and with good reason: in a career dedicated to the vocal idiom, he has furnished them with some of the more pleasing, singable songs of recent years.

Hundley was raised in Kentucky, where he went to live with his grandmother after his parents divorced. At age eight he began piano lessons and, answering to an irrepressible urge to sing, invented little songs with which he would entertain his grandmother's friends. In his teens Hundley performed as a pianist and studied at the Cincinnati College Conservatory. In 1952 he went to New York, where he coached and accompanied singers, and studied composition with three masters of the art song—William Flanagan, Virgil Thomson, and Israel Citkowitz. In 1960 Hundley, a light baritone, joined the Metropolitan Opera chorus and seized the opportunity to show his work to prominent artists. By the early 1970s, Annaliese Rothenberger, Anna Moffo, Frederica von Stade, and other Metropolitan stars, as well as American song advocate Paul Sperry, had all added Hundley songs to their repertoires.

THE SONGS
A "maverick"[1] who has kept his distance from the musical establishment, Hundley has unabashedly remained true to his romantic muse. It took time for his songs to find a place, but when they did, they met with a warm reception. Though some people have complained they are too folksy, sweet, and inconsequential (of the encore variety), many more have welcomed them as "balm for weary throats and weary ears."[2] Indeed, there is much to admire and enjoy, not the least of which is Hundley's discerning selection of texts. Whether a gravestone inscription or a poem by his good friend, James Purdy, they are pithy, lyrical, well defined, and perfect for the song form. What's more, the subject matter—both poignant and witty—is accessible and straightforward. Add to that a knack for good tunes, careful craftsmanship, and an endearing humor and charm, and you have the essence of Hundley's success.

Hundley credits his four years with the Metropolitan Opera Chorus, as well as his experience as coach and accompanist (especially in the teaching studio of the diva Zinka Milanov) with providing the bel canto foundation that feeds his profoundly lyrical style.[3] His own slight, yet very intimate, expression, however, is not inflated by the "grand" of grand opera. Never sacrificing lyric beauty, each poem is set for total comprehensibility, while the supple vocal lines (most often in comfortable middle ranges) and light piano textures disallow any weighty or pressed singing. Tonal and with only minor rhythmic complexity (mainly meter changes), these songs present little musical difficulty. Apparently, a good number are not yet published, including the charming *Some Sheep Are Loving* and the haunting *Waterbird* (both recorded by Sperry). Otherwise, the published songs appear individually and/or in one of two albums—*Four Songs* (Boosey c1985) and *Eight Songs* (Boosey c1981).[4] Paul Sperry has recorded many on Albany CD (TROY043) and Serenus (SRS 12078). Additional isolated recordings are included with the song entries. The following is believed to be a virtually complete listing of Hundley's published songs.

The Astronomers, An Epitaph (based on an inscription found in Allegheny, PA.); Boosey c1961; also incl. *Eight Songs;* comp. 1959.
     Rec. higher voices (c#1–f#2); 1:45; Slowly; a hushed reading of names, then a warm cantabile builds; a memorable text and a lovely, evocative song; recorded by Federica von Stade on CBS (37231) and Sperry (Albany).

Ballad on Queen Anne's Death, Anonymous, 1619; General c1964; comp. 1962.
     Rec. medium voices (bb–d2); 1:30; Allegretto; a light syllabic melody; recorded by Sperry (Albany and Serenus), transposed up and with several alterations.

Bartholomew Green, James Purdy; incl. *Eight Songs;* comp. 1978.
     Rec. lighter medium voices (d1–f2); 0:45; Lively and spirited; fun with the lost art of gravestone inscription; recorded by Sperry (Albany).

Birds, U.S.A., James Purdy; incl. in *Eight Songs;* comp. 1972; to Billie Lynn Daniel.
     Rec. medium voices (f1–f2); 0:45; Grandly (chordal opening), then, Lively; rhythmic.

Come Ready and See Me, James Purdy; incl. *Eight Songs* and *Four Songs;* comp. 1971.
     Rec. higher voices (db1–gb2), transposed for lower voices in *Four Songs* (bb–eb2); 2:00; cantabile over a flowing accompaniment; almost like a "pop" love ballad; both the lovely poem and the com-

pelling melody have made this a favorite; recorded by Frederica von Stade (CBS 37231), Sperry (Albany), and Cynthia Haymon on Argo CD (436 117-2).

Epitaph on a Wife, Anonymous; Boosey c1961; also incl. *Four Songs;* comp. 1957.
   Rec. medium men's voices, in bass clef (c–e♭1); 0:45; Spirited and rhythmic; declamatory; humorous; recorded by Sperry (Albany), transposed up, under the title *On a Wife.*

Evening Hours, James Purdy; incl. *Four Songs;* comp. 1975.
   Rec. medium voices (c1–f#2); 2:00; Nostalgic; warmly melodic; intensifies; a lovely, tender song.

For Your Delight (A Romance), Robert Louis Stevenson; General c1962; comp. 1962.
   Rec. light medium voices (c1–f2), text suggests men; 2:45; Gracefully; waltzlike; routine; recorded by John Reardon on Serenus (1019).

I Do, James Purdy; Boosey c1981; incl. *Eight Songs;* comp. 1974; to Paul Sperry.
   Rec. high lyrics (g1–a♭2, with lower options); text suggests men; 0:45; Allegro grazioso; a marriage proposal; lightweight, somewhat jazzy; recorded by Sperry (Albany).

Isaac Greentree, Based upon an epitaph found in Samuel Palmer's collection "Epitaphs and Epigrams: Curious, Quaint, Amusing"; Boosey c1981; incl. *Eight Songs;* comp. 1960; to Paul Sperry.
   Rec. higher lyric voices (c1–g♭2); 1:00; fairly slow; lyrically declaimed over spare chords; intimate, delicate; recorded by Sperry (Albany).

Maiden Snow, Kenneth Patchen; General c1961; to Anna Moffo.
   Rec. higher lyric voices (d1–g2); 1:30; Andante sostenuto; a supple recitando, building in intensity to a final searing phrase before drifting away; wistful piano interludes; the pathos of this simple love poem is conveyed with restraint and tenderness; a beautiful song.

My Master Hath a Garden, Anonymous, Elizabethan; Boosey c1981; incl. *Eight Songs;* comp. 1963.
   Rec. light higher voices (d1–g2); 1:30; Brightly; chordal; light and lilting; a cantabile central section.

Postcard from Spain, Richard Hundley; General c1964; comp. 1963.

    Rec. high voices (f1–a2); 1:00; Gaily; waltzlike with syncopations; a melismatic passage; a good encore song; recorded by John Reardon on Serenus (1019).

Softly the Summer, Richard Hundley; General c1963; comp. 1957.

    Rec. high lyric voices (f1–b♭2), 2:00; Tempo a piacere (gently flowing); this shimmering vocal line uncharacteristically sits in an unrelenting high tessitura;[5] hushed, atmospheric; different; beautiful (if beautifully sung).

Spring, William Shakespeare; General c1963; comp. 1962; to Virgil (Thomson).

    Rec. higher light voices (f1–a2); 1:15; Light, airy, and with sparkle; opening recalls Virgil Thomson's setting of Jasper Fisher's *At the Spring;* a charming setting; recorded by Sperry (Albany and Serenus).

Sweet Suffolk Owl, Anonymous; Boosey c1981; incl. *Eight Songs;* comp. 1979; to Paul Sperry.

    Rec. medium voices (e♭1–f2); 1:30; Deliberately; a rhythmically incisive melody over heavy staccato chords; good song; recorded by Sharp (NW 369) and Sperry (Albany).

When Orpheus Played, William Shakespeare; Boosey c1985; also incl. *Four Songs;* comp. 1979; to Paul Sperry.

    Rec. medium voices (c#1–f#2); 1:30; Rapturous; a nice melody, but tepid.

Wild Plum, Orrick Johns; General c1961.

    Rec. light medium voices (d1–f2); 0:45; Allegretto; a light, detached parlando; fun meter shifting; recorded by Sperry (Serenus).

BIBLIOGRAPHY

Friedberg (III).

Finn, Robert. "Richard Hundley, non-conformist," *The Cleveland Plain Dealer,* June 3, 1983.

Some of the information for this article was taken from a Richard Hundley Master Class, Art Song Minnesota (University of Minnesota School of Music), June 11, 1990.

---

[1] Hundley's word for himself as quoted in Friedberg (III), 248.

2 A review by Thor Eckert in *The Christian Science Monitor* (no date given), quoted in a press release.

3 Richard Hundley Master Class, Art Song Minnesota, June 11, 1990.

4 In prefaces to these two collections, Hundley supplies background to his songs, and thoughts about their interpretation.

5 In his collection *Eight Songs*, Hundley lets it be known that transpositions are acceptable. However, in a masterclass, the author heard him complain about inappropriate transpositions. In particular, he cited *Softly the Summer*, a song Anna Moffo wanted to lower, which he felt would have made it too "pop."

CHARLES IVES
b. Oct. 20, 1874, Danbury, CT; d. May 19, 1954, New York, NY

He produced most of his extraordinary output in relative obscurity, isolated from the music world, but, since his death, the world has come to view Charles Ives as, perhaps, America's most remarkable composer. His song catalogue is a huge, all-important body of work with a mystique that continues to lure new enthusiasts.

Ives's father had been the youngest bandleader in the Union army. A versatile musician, who led his community in its musical affairs, he was also an inveterate experimenter in sound and his son's first and most influential teacher. By his early teens the younger Ives was beginning to compose. Shortly after entering Yale University, however, his father died, and Ives's studies with his new teacher, the conservative composer Horatio Parker, were a constant frustration for him.

Fully cognizant of the difficulties he would encounter were he to try to make a living composing the kind of music he envisioned, after graduating from Yale in 1898, Ives became a clerk at Mutual Life Insurance Company in New York City. There he met and, in 1907, formed a business partnership with a friend, Julian Myrick. As Myrick and Ives grew into one of the most successful and innovative insurance agencies of its time, Ives acquired both a sizable fortune and a respected reputation as a business executive. That he composed music nights and weekends was known only to a select few.

In 1908 Ives married Harmony Twitchell, and the couple raised an adopted daughter, Edith, and made homes in New York City and West Redding, Connecticut. But weakened by a serious heart attack in 1918, during the 1920s Ives virtually stopped composing, and by 1930 medical factors had ended his business career as well. Stalked by poor health, he became increasingly eccentric and reclusive, refusing interviews and photographs, even when, in 1947, he was awarded the Pulitzer Prize for his *Third Symphony*. On the other hand, he remained active on the perimeters of the contemporary music world, and provided generous financial support to colleagues and projects. Ives died of a stroke, while recovering from yet another operation, but with the comfort of knowing that his music was finally being heard.

THE SONGS

The financial prosperity Ives enjoyed from his business career enabled him to make private printings of his *Concord Sonata* and *114 Songs,* which he sent to all possibly interested parties during the early 1920s.[1] A few took notice and pressed important early performances. One of these took place in 1932 at the first Yaddo Festival, when baritone Hubert Linscott, accompanied by Aaron Copland, performed seven Ives songs— a performance that, with others of the 1930s, electrified the younger generation, though recognition by the mainstream would not come till decades later.

Copland has described *114 Songs* as "thrown together helter-skelter, displaying an amazing variety and fecundity of imagination…."[2] The endless invention and diversity of these songs fill admirers with wonder and delight. Their scope, complexity, and depth stagger us. But it is Ives as a gentle humanitarian, outspoken in his love for home and country, that explains their direct and enduring emotional appeal. To really study an Ives song is to enter into an intense relationship—personal, elusive, and unpredictable.

Donald Walker has distinguished three periods of song composition that may help the performer orient himself in Ives's confusing catalogue,[3] where conventional lyricism takes its place beside some of the most innovative, idiosyncratic vocal writing ever heard. In the early years, between 1890 and 1902, Ives confronted a dual, but conflicting, obligation: write what was expected of him and—somehow—answer to his own voice. Most of the conventional songs and all the foreign language settings come from this period, and serve as proof that Ives knew the rules of composition so well he could, in fact, write in any style. But the period also includes songs, such as *Circus Band* and *Children's Hour,* that are lightly seasoned with the beginnings of later experimentation and that bode exciting things for the future. The middle period, from 1903 to 1911, contains considerably more radical than traditional material. It includes the amazing *Requiem, Soliloquy,* and *General William Booth,* but also some works that caused Ives to express shame for what he called his "slumps," by which he meant succumbing to pressure to write accessible songs.[4] From 1912 to 1924, however, there are no more "slumps." Writing with freedom and confidence, finally immune to outside opinion, he produces (especially from 1919 to 1921) his most experimental, difficult, and—very often—greatest songs.

Ives set anything: the classics, Whitman, Emerson, both his own and Harmony's poems, a phrase from something he had heard, a newspaper clipping—whatever stirred him. (Curiously, he did not set the important contemporary American poets.) Though he altered it in any way that suited his purposes, text was everything. He followed its flow, like a stream of consciousness, using any means to express each image or thought as vividly as possible. For the singer, clarity of word is everything. "To lose the words is to lose the song."[5] Ives had once studied singing and felt singers were timid about wide leaps or awkward intervals.[6] Vocal writing, therefore, may be jagged and disjunct (especially in later periods) but is rarely demanding in range or tessitura. As for the colorful written asides Ives sprinkled through his scores, most can be enjoyed and then ignored. In a few, however, he seems to want the singer or pianist to speak (or shout) something at an indicated spot, and although there is no proscribed manner of dealing with these notations, it would seem contrary to Ives's nature to restrain the impulse. The spirit of an Ives performance is best revealed by his nephew's recollection of his own attempt to sing the song *He is There!* for his excited Uncle Charlie: "There was one little passage that called for a real shout, but I shouted very timidly and he nearly hit the roof. 'Can't you shout better than that? That's the trouble with this country—people are afraid to shout!'"[7]

Ives himself was considered to be a formidable, if eccentric, pianist, and his writing for that instrument can be bold and technically challenging, with unwieldy stretches for an average hand. Musically, conventional settings from the first period present no problems, but polyrhythms; cross rhythms; atonality; polytonality; tone clusters; absence of key signatures, bar lines, or meters; and multiple layers of quotations and musical ideas creating overwhelming dissonances and textural density are but a few of the difficulties performers will experience in the more experimental songs.

In addition to the 1975 reprint of *114 Songs (114S),* there are 12 smaller albums available to the performer, most of which were published in the 1950s. These are: *Three Songs,* Associated c1968 *(3S); Four Songs,* Mercury c1950 *(4S); Seven Songs,* Associated c1957, transferred from Arrow c1939*(7S); Nine Songs,* Peer c1956 *(9S); Ten Songs,* Peer c1953 *(10S); Eleven Songs & Two Harmonizations,* Associated c1968 *(11S2H); Twelve Songs,* Peer c1954 *(12S); Thirteen Songs,* Peer c1958 *(13S); Fourteen Songs,* Peer c1955 *(14S); Nineteen Songs,* Merion c1935 *(19S); Thirty-four Songs,* Merion c1933 *(34S); Sacred Songs,* Peer c1958 *(SS).* As these albums not only contain important songs not found in *114 Songs,* but also include tiny revisions and corrections, they—not *114 Songs*— should be the singer's ultimate source for performance.[8] A few songs have been issued individually. *40 Earlier Songs,* which will include some new and some previously published songs, is in preparation.[9] According to *AmerGroves* there are a total of 151 songs.

Unless otherwise noted the following recordings are primarily devoted to Ives songs. (Isolated recordings are given only with the specific song entry.) Roberta Alexander, soprano, has two volumes on Etcetera CD (KTC 1020 and 1068); Mordecai Bauman, baritone, six songs on a reissue by CRI (SRD 390); Helen Boatwright, soprano, on Overtone (7),[10] and also on the historic *Charles Ives: The 100th Anniversary* Columbia (M4 32504); Corrine Curry, soprano, one side on Cambridge (CRS 1904); Jan DeGaetani, mezzo-soprano, on Elektra/Nonesuch CD (713252) and half of the Bridge CD (BCD 9006); Dietrich Fischer-Dieskau, baritone, on Deutsche Grammophon (2530 696); Thomas Hampson, 14 German settings on Teldec CD (9031-72168-2); Henry Herford, baritone, two volumes on Unicorn-Kanchana CD (DKP 9111 and 9112); Michael Ingham, baritone, on AmCam CD (ACR-10306);[11] Charles Ives (himself) sings and plays on *Charles Ives: The 100th Anniversary* Columbia (M4 32504);[12] Evelyn Lear, soprano, and Thomas Stewart, baritone, together on Columbia (M 30229); Marni Nixon, soprano, one side on Nonesuch (H 71209); William Parker, baritone, nine songs on New World (300); Ted Puffer, tenor, two volumes on Folkways (FM 3344 and 3345); Samuel Ramey, baritone, 10 songs on Argo CD (433 027-2); Sheila Schonbrun and Victoria Villamil, sopranos, six songs, on Musical Heritage CD (512292Y). Finally (and most recently), soprano Dora Ohrenstein, mezzo soprano Mary Ann Hart, tenor Paul Sperry, and baritone William Sharp come together on Albany CD (TROY 077) on Volume One of a planned edition of the complete songs of Charles Ives. This recording features early songs, both published and, as yet, unpublished.

As confusions over Ives's song catalogue abound, to best service the performer, pertinent information is provided for every song that, at the time of this writing, has been published regardless of its merit.

Therefore, only those which will be published for the first time in *40 Earlier Songs* are excluded. Names of poets that are given by the author when none is indicated on the score, are taken from the scholarship provided in *Charles Ives: A Bio-Bibliography*. Question marks following dates of composition are as given in the score. Ives rarely specified voice types. Therefore, because most of his songs are appropriate for, and have been traditionally sung by, practically any voice (high or low, man or woman) recommendations regarding voice type are left very flexible. Tonal songs are noted as such; otherwise, the songs are in Ives's free harmonic style. When a performer has recorded more than one volume of Ives song, the volume number is indicated in parentheses. Asterisks (*) indicate the songs that Ives declared "be not sung, at least in public, or given to students except as examples of what not to sing."[13]

Abide With Me, Rev. Henry Francis Lyte; *13S* and *SS;* comp. 1890.
    Higher voices (d1–g2); 3:15; Adagio; strophic; tonal; lyrical; recorded by Boatwright (Overtone), Fischer-Dieskau, and Sperry.

Aeschylus and Sophocles, Walter Savage Landor; *19S;* comp. 1922.
    Voices that can project through the dense textures (a–g2), best with two singers and string quartet; 4:00; Adagio, then Allegro; other tempo changes; a dialogue; very difficult; recorded, with string quartet, by Schonbrun and Villamil.

Afterglow, James Fenimore Cooper; *34S* and *114S;* comp. 1919.
    Lyric voices (d1–d2); 2:00; Slowly and very quietly; sustained over veiled, rolled chords; impressionistic; recorded by DeGaetani (Bridge), Herford (2); Lear, Puffer (2).

Allegro, Harmony T. Ives; *13S* and *114S;* comp. 1900.
    Higher voices (c1–g2); 1:15; Allegro; tonal; strophic; tuneful over rippling piano figurations; subdued Largo ending.

Amphion, see *from "Amphion."*

Ann Street, Maurice Morris; *34S* and *114S;* comp. 1921.
    Medium voices (e1–e2); 0:45; Fast and noisily, then slower; conversational; tricky, fun; a favorite; recorded by Alexander (2), Bauman, Boatwright (Overtone), Curry, DeGaetani (Nonesuch), Fischer-Dieskau, Herford (1), Ingham, Nixon, Puffer (2).

At Sea, Robert Underwood Johnson; *34S* and *114S;* also incl. *AAS;* comp. 1921.

Lower voices (c1–d2); 1:15; Slowly; sustained over chords; recorded by Alexander (2), Herford (2).

At the River, text and tune from "Shall We Gather at the River?" by Robert Lowry; *34S* and *114S;* comp. 1916.

All voices (e♭1–e♭2); 1:15; Allegretto; a quirky but moving adaptation of this lilting, famous hymn; recorded by Alexander (2), Boatwright (Overtone) DeGaetani (Nonesuch), Fischer-Dieskau, Cleo Laine on RCA (LRL1-5058), Nixon, Ramey, Stewart.

August, Folgore da San Geminiano; *12S* and *114S;* comp. 1920.

Medium voices (c1–e2); 2:30; Con grazia; lyrical declamation; follows and illustrates the changing imagery; evocative; unusual; can group with *September* and *December;* recorded by Herford (2).

Autumn, Harmony T. Ives; *9S* and *114S;* comp. 1908.

Medium voices (b♭–f2); 3:00; Adagio; quiet; tonal; vocal and piano lines intertwine over muted chords; romantic, haunting; recorded by Alexander (1), Boatwright (Overtone), Fischer-Dieskau, Herford (2), Stewart.

Berceuse, Charles E. Ives; *13S* and *114S;* comp. 1900.

Medium voices (b#–e2); 1:30; Adagio; tonal; sustained; hushed; affecting; recorded by Alexander (1), Boatwright (Overtone), Herford (1), Upshaw on MusicMasters CD (60128L).

The Cage, Charles E. Ives; *14S* and *114S;* comp. 1906.

All voices (d1–e2); 0:45; evenly and mechanically; recitando over building chords; the singer contemplates the leopard's caged existence; humorous; abrupt; recorded by Alexander (1), Curry, DeGaetani (Nonesuch), Herford (2), Ingham, Nixon, Puffer (1), Carolyn Watkinson on Etcetera CD (KTC 1007).

The Camp Meeting, Charlotte Elliot; *13S, 114S,* and *SS;* der. from Symphony No. 3; comp. 1912.

Low voices (a♭–e2); 4:00; Largo cantabile; tonal; chromatic; sustained over a complex accompaniment; moving; recorded by Alexander (2), Herford (2), Ingham, Parker.

Canon, Thomas Moore; *19S* and *114S;* comp. 1894.

All voices (d1–f#2); 1:30; Allegro; tonal, lyric; recorded in an unpublished early version by Boatwright (Columbia), and, in the later version, by Hanks on DWR 6417, Puffer (1), and Sperry.

Chanson de Florian (Florian's Song), J. P. Claris de Florian; *114S;* also pub. separately Mercury c1950; comp. 1901.

Lower voices (b–d2), woman's text; 2:00; Allegro (Tempo di Scherzo); in French; tonal; lilting; recorded by Alexander (2), Hart, and Parker.

Charlie Rutlage, from Cowboy Songs; *7S* and *114S;* comp. 1920/21.

Any voice that can cut the dense piano writing (d1–d2), best for men; 3:00; In moderate time; colloquial; declamatory; some speaking in rhythm; tuneful, over a vamping piano, becoming fast, loud, and wild as narration builds to Charlie's death; then a recalling of the first motive with the final wish that Charlie meet his loved ones in eternity; Alexander (1), Bauman, Hanks (DWR 6417), Herford (2), Ingham, Nixon, Puffer (2), Ramey, Stewart.

The Children's Hour, Henry Wadsworth Longfellow; *34S* and *114S;* comp. 1901.

Middle and lower voices (d1–d2); 2:15; Adagio sostenuto; a silken recitando over hushed, liquid sixteenths frames a più mosso section; evocative, magical; recorded by Alexander (2), Boatwright (Overtone), Fischer-Dieskau, Herford (1), Lear, Puffer (1), Ramey.

A Christmas Carol, Charles Ives; *19S* and *114S;* comp. 1898.

Lyric voices (d1–c2); 2:00; Larghetto; tonal, subtle syncopations; strophic; simple; pretty; recorded by DeGactani (Nonesuch), Fischer-Dieskau, Nixon, Puffer (1), and Sharp.

Christmas Carol, words and tune by Edith Ives;[14] *11S2H;* comp. 1925.

All voices (d1–d2); 2:00; Andante; tonal; traditional; strophic with a refrain.

The Circus Band, Charles Ives; *10S* and *114S;* also incl. *AASTC;* der. early brass piece; comp. 1894.

Any voice that can cut through the piano writing (c#1–f#2); 2:00; In quickstep time; tonal; colorful dissonances; infectious syncopations; major piano part with crashing chords; nostalgic evocation of childhood; exuberant, tuneful; fun; recorded by Alexander (2), DeGaetani (Nonesuch), Herford (1), Cleo Laine on RCA (LRL1-5058), Lear, Ramey, and Sharp.

The Collection, stanzas from old hymns; *13S, SS,* and *114S;* comp. 1920.

Medium voices (e1–f#2); 2:30; In moderate time; tonal; two hymn-like verses.

Cradle Song, A. L. Ives; *19S* and *114S;* comp. 1919.
All voices (e#1–c#2); 2:00; Sognando; bitonal, but with a feeling of tonality; three verses of eight measures alternating 6/8 and 2/4; slow, quiet.

December, Folgore da San Geminiano; *34S* and *114S;* arr. voice/piano 1920.
Lower voices that can cut the dense piano writing (c#1–d2); 1:00; Allegro con spirito; Roughly and in a half-spoken style; crashing chords and clusters; even a cluster for the voice (a fat non-tone perhaps); rhythmically terrifying; loud, crazy, even ugly, but effective; can pair with *August* and *September;* recorded by Herford (2), Ingham.

Die Alte Mutter, see *The Old Mother.*

Disclosure, Charles E. Ives; *12S, SS,* and *114S;* comp. 1921.
Higher voices (e♭1–g2); 1:00; Andante moderato; broad; chordal; philosophical; recorded by Boatwright (Overtone), Fischer-Dieskau.

Down East, Charles Ives; *13S, SS,* and *114S;* comp. 1919.
All voices (c1–d2); 2:45; Very slowly; the hushed, impressionistic opening becomes tonal and tuneful; a recalling of *Nearer My God to Thee;* nostalgic; recorded by Alexander (1), Boatwright (Columbia), DeGaetani (Bridge).

*Dreams, Porteous; *9S* and *114S;* comp. 1897.
Higher voices (c1–f2); 3:30; Moderato; tonal; strophic; lyrical over a fluid accompaniment; a sentimental ballad; recorded by Alexander (1).

Duty, Emerson; (combine with *Vita*);[15] *34S, 4S,* and *114S;* arr. for piano 1921.
Any voice (e1–e2); 0:30; declamatory; big chords; recorded by Herford (2), Lear.

An Election, see *It Strikes Me That.*

Elégie, Gallet; *9S* and *114S;* comp. 1901.

Medium and lower voices (a–f2); 4:00; Largo sostenuto; tonal; sustained; romantic; a gorgeous example of French style; recorded by Alexander (2), Fischer-Dieskau, Parker.

Evening, John Milton; *7S* and *114S;* also incl. *AAS;* comp. 1921.
Medium voices (c#1–d2); 1:45; Largo; lyrical; gently flowing; some exquisite moments in this peaceful contemplation; recorded by Alexander (1), Bauman, Boatwright (Overtone), Nixon, Puffer (1).

Evidence, Charles Ives; *9S* and *114S;* comp. 1910.
Medium and lower voices (b♭–e♭2); 1:30; Andante tenuto; tonal; lyrical over flowing sextuplets and a right hand melody; warm and reflective; recorded by Alexander (2).

Far from my heav'nly home, Rev. H. F. Lyte; *11S2H;* comp. 1890-92.
Spec. contralto (g-b1); 3:00; Andante; tonal; many very low notes; a sacred solo; recorded by Hart.

A Farewell to Land, George Lord Byron; *19S;* comp. 1925.
Any voice that can can control the line and handle the range (g#–g2); 1:45; Adagio; quiet; a slow, sinuous, descending line for both piano and voice; a faster, melismatic central section; intricate rhythms; eerie and haunting; recorded by Alexander (2), Curry, DeGaetani (Nonesuch), Fischer-Dieskau, Nixon, Puffer (2).

La Fède (The Faith), Ariosto; *19S* and *114S;* comp. 1920.
Lower voices (c1–d2); 0:45; Lento maestoso; in Italian; declamatory over pungent chords.

Feldeinsamkeit (In Summer Fields), Almers; *19S* and *114S;* comp. 1898.
Medium voices (c1–f2); 3:00; Allegretto molto tranquillo; in German; tonal, warm and lyrical over rippling piano figures; romantic; recorded by Alexander (2), Boatwright (Columbia), Fischer-Dieskau, Hampson, Herford (2), Marcoulescou on Orion (OC685).

Flag Song, Henry S. Durand; Peer c1968; comp. 1898.
Medium voices (c1–c2); 2:00; Maestoso; tonal; strophic; straightfoward; patriotic.

Forward into Light, Henry Alford from Bernard (from the cantata "The Celestial Country"); *10S, SS,* and *114S;* comp. 1898.

Aria for Tenor (or Soprano) (c1–a2); 4:00; Allegretto; tonal; romantic; recorded by Douglas Perry, with orchestra, on Columbia M432504.

from "Amphion," Alfred Lord Tennyson; *10S* and *114S;* comp. 1896.
Medium voices (d1–g2); 1:00; Allegretto con spirito; tonal; happy; dainty; charming; recorded by Hart.

from "The Incantation," Lord Byron; *34S* and *114S;* arr. voice/piano 1921.
Medium voices (e♭1–d2); 1:30; Allegretto moderato; same vocal phrase repeated over elaborate piano figurations; treacherous meter changes; mystical; rarely heard; recorded by Boatwright (Columbia), Herford (2).

from "Lincoln, the Great Commoner," Edwin Markham; *114S;* also pub. separately Peer c1952; comp. 1921.
Big medium voices (c1–e2); 3:45; Maestoso but not too slowly; sustained declamation over mammoth chords; a big, difficult, patriotic song; recorded by Herford (2), Puffer (1).

from "Night of Frost in May," George Meredith; *19S* and *114S;* comp. 1899.
Low voices (b♭–e♭2); 1:30; Andante con moto; tonal; quiet; flowing; lyric; contemplative; recorded by Alexander (2).

from "Paracelsus," Robert Browning; *19S* and *114S;* comp. 1921.
Dramatic voices (c♭1–f#2); 3:15; Allegro; tempo changes; imposing piano introduction; expansive; dense; difficult; philosophical; commanding; recorded by Alexander (2), DeGaetani (Nonesuch), John Hanks on Duke, Vol 2 (DWR 6417), Herford (1), Ingham, Puffer (1).

from "The Swimmers," Louis Untermeyer; *34S* and *114S;* comp. 1915-21.
Medium voices that can cut the dense piano writing (c#1–e2); 1:30; Alternately fast and slower; the quiet opening gradually grows to a monumental ending; difficult singing over intricate piano figurations and clusters evoking water sounds; exalted; unusual; recorded by Boatwright (Overtone), Fischer-Dieskau, Herford (1), Ingham, Nixon, Puffer (1).

General William Booth Enters Into Heaven, Vachel Lindsay;[16] *19S;* comp. 1914.

Big voices that can cut the dense piano writing (b–e2); 4:45; Allegro moderato (March time); many tempo changes; shouts, declamation, and cantabile; tone clusters; rhythmically complex; a powerful, dramatic narrative; one of the most difficult, famous, startling, and stunning of all Ives; recorded by Boatwright (Overtone), Curry, Gramm on Desto (411/412); Herford (1), Ingham, Pazmor on New World (247) or CRI (SRD 390),[17] Nixon, Puffer (1).

God Bless and Keep Thee, poet unknown; incl. *11S2H;* comp. 1897?
Rec. lower voices ([ab]bb–b1); 1:45; Andante sostenuto; tonal; warm.

Grantchester, Rupert Brooke; *9S* and *114S;* comp. 1920.
Lower and medium voices (c1–c2); 2:15; Adagio non tanto; lyrical; contemplative; follows nature imagery; impressionistic; recorded by Lear, Herford (2), Ingham, Puffer (2), Carolyn Watkinson on Etcetera CD (KTC 1007).

The Greatest Man, Anne Collins; *3S, 34S,* and *114S;* comp. 1921.
All voice (e1–g2); 1:30; Allegro moderato; a boy boasts about his father; jaunty, with dotted rhythms; fun, popular; recorded by Alexander (1), Boatwright (Overtone), Bauman, Herford (2), Cleo Laine on RCA (LRL1-5058), Nixon, Stewart.

Harpalus (An Ancient Pastoral), Thomas Percy; *34S* and *114S;* comp. 1902.
Higher voices (f1–g2); 1:15; Allegretto; strophic; tonal, melodic over bright, busy piano figurations; recorded: Alexander (2), Boatwright (Overtone).

He is There! see *They are There!*

His Exaltation, Robert Robinson; *9S, SS,* and *114S;* comp. 1913.
Lower voices (a–e2); 2:15; Slowly (maestoso); long piano introduction; based on a hymn; lyrical; alternately exuberant and tender; recorded by Alexander (2), Ingham, Parker.

Housatonic at Stockbridge, Robert Underwood Johnson; *12S* and *114S;* comp. 1921.
Lower voices (db1–f2); 3:15; Slowly and quietly; sustained and lyrical over a murmuring, undulating piano score; builds to a resounding ending; atmospheric; haunting; recorded by Alexander (1), DeGaetani (Nonesuch), Herford (1), Ingham, Stewart, Villamil.

Hymn, Gerhardt Tersteegen; *34S* and *114S;* comp. 1904; arr.
voice/piano 1921.
    Medium voices (c#1–e2); 2:00; Largo; warm and sustained over a
fluid piano score; rarely heard; recorded by Alvin Brahm, with string
quartet, on Columbia (M4 32504).

I Travelled among Unknown Men, William Wordsworth; *10S* and
114S; comp. 1901.
    Medium voices (c1–f2); 1:15; Andante con moto; tonal; tuneful.

Ich grolle nicht (I bear no grudge), Heinrich Heine; *34S* and *114S;*
comp. 1899.
    Full voices (d1–f2); 2:45; Adagio; in German; tonal; strophic;
romantic; recorded by Alexander (2), Curry, Fischer-Dieskau,
Hampson, Marcoulescou on Orion (OC 685).

Ilmenau (Over all the Treetops), von Goethe; *114S;* also pub. separately Peer c1952; comp. 1902.
    Medium voices (d#1–f#2); 1:45; Lento ben tenuto; in German;
tonal; quiet; warm; romantic; recorded by Alexander (2), Hampson,
Marcoulescou on Orion (OC 685).

Immortality, 34S and *114S;* comp. 1921.
    Medium voices (c1–d2); 1:45; Adagio; sustained; dissonant, but
ends tonally; quiet; agitated central section; on the death of a child;
recorded by Alexander (1), Herford (1), Puffer (2).

Incantation, see *from "the Incantation."*

The Indians, Charles Sprague; *19S* and *114S;* arr. voice/piano 1921.
    Medium voices (d♭1–d2); 2:15; Very Slowly; a lament over rolled
chords; poignant and strange; recorded by DeGaetani (Nonesuch),
Herford (1), Puffer (1).

In Flanders Fields, John McCrae; *14S* and *114S;* comp. 1919.
    Medium voices (d1–e2); 2:15; Maestoso (but with energy and not
too slowly); marchlike in parts, with patriotic song quotations;
chordal; builds, then subsides with a sinister abruptness; recorded by
Boatwright (Overtone), Fischer-Dieskau, Herford (1), Stewart.

The Innate, Ives; *19S* and *114S;* comp. 1908; arr. voice/piano 1916.
    Lower voices (d♭1–e2); 2:30; Slowly; quiet and reflective; builds
and broadens; recorded by DeGaetani (Nonesuch).

In Summer Fields, see *Feldeinsamkeit.*

*In the Alley, Charles Ives; *13S* and *114S;* comp. 1896.
All voices (c#1–e2); 2:30; Moderato; tonal; Ivesian fun and games; a sharp parody of turn-of-the-century practices; recorded by Herford (2), Ramey, and Sharp.

In the Mornin', Negro spiritual; *11S2H;* arr. 1929.
Medium voices (d1–f#2); 2:15; Slowly; tonal; Ives's one arrangement of a spiritual is very moving; recorded by DeGaetani (Nonesuch), Herford (1).

It Strikes Me That, Charles Ives; pub. separately Mercury c1935; also under the title *An Election* in *19S* (with slightly different words) and as *Nov. 2, 1920* in *114S;* comp. 1920; arr. voice/piano 1921.
Medium voices (c1–f#2); 3:45; Slowly; tempo changes; wordy and declamatory; many twists and turns in this discourse on the election of 1920; big, sustained ending evokes the spirit of Lincoln; difficult; recorded by Curry, Herford (2), Ingham, Puffer (2).

Kären, Anonymous; *12S* and *114S;* comp. 1894.
Medium voices (d♭1–g♭2); 1:00; Allegro moderato; tonal, lyric, sweet.

The Last Reader, Oliver Wendell Holmes; *34S* and *114S;* comp. 1911; arr. voice/piano 1921.
Medium voices (d1–d2); 1:45; Andante con moto; lyric; contemplative; recorded by Ingham, Lear.

The Light that is Felt, John Greenleaf Whittier; *114S;* also pub. separately Mercury c1950; also incl. *CAAS;* comp. 1904.
Lower voices (b–c#2); 2:15; Slowly; tonal; hushed, warm and lyrical over lightly falling piano figurations; recorded by Lear (in a higher key).

Like a Sick Eagle, John Keats; *34S* and *114S;* comp. 1920.
Medium voices (c1–d♭2); 2:15; Slowly...in a weak and dragging way; hushed; unbarred; moves in semitones; restraint and control required; difficult; eerie, unearthly, haunting; recorded by Alexander (1), DeGaetani (Nonesuch), Puffer (1).

Lincoln, the Great Commoner, see *from "Lincoln, the Great Commoner."*

Luck and Work, Robert Underwood Johnson; *4S, 34S* and *114S;* comp. 1916; arr. voice/piano 1920.

Medium voices (d1–e2); 0:30; Fast and hard, then slower and easily; an epigram; succinct and humorous; recorded by Boatwright (Columbia), Herford (2), Ingham.

Majority, text probably by Ives; *19S* and *114S;* comp. 1915; arr. voice/piano 1921.

Big voices that can cut the dense piano writing (c#1–f2); 6:45; Slowly; long introduction with massive clusters; then, changing tempos, quieter dynamics, and lyrical passages; sustained; a dramatic tribute to the masses; very difficult; recorded by DeGaetani (Nonesuch), Ingham, Puffer (2).

Maple Leaves, Thomas Bailey Aldrich; *7S* and *114S;* comp. 1920.

Medium voices (c1–b1); 1:00; Andante; lyrical, quiet nature contemplation over flowing piano figures; recorded by Alexander (1), Boatwright (Overtone), Herford (2), Lear, Puffer (2).

Marie, Rudolf Gottschall; *14S* and *114S;* comp. 1896.

Lower voices (c1–d2); Poco andante; tonal; a sentimental ballad; recorded by Sharp.

Memories (a. Very Pleasant, b. Rather Sad), Charles Ives; *10S* and *114S;* comp. 1897.

Medium voices (b–e2); 2:45; tonal; in two totally contrasting tuneful sections: A. Presto; excited over a vamping piano part; fast articulation and whistling; B. Adagio; hushed; a nostalgic melody melting into a final hum over dreamy arpeggios; an enchanting song; recorded by Alexander (1); DeGaetani (Nonesuch), Herford (1), and Ohrenstein.

Mirage, Christina G. Rossetti; *10S* and *114 Songs;* comp. 1902.

Medium voices (c1–f2); 1:00; Moderato; tonal; warm and lyrical over a fluid piano score; rarely heard; a nice, small song; recorded by Alexander (2), Herford (2), and Sperry.

Mists, Harmony T. Ives; *34S* and *114S;* comp. 1910.

Higher voices (e1–g2); 1:45; Largo sostenuto; subdued over eerie chords; briefly animated with memory of happier days; recorded by Boatwright (Columbia), Puffer (1).

My Native Land, Traditional; *12S* and *114S;* comp. 1897.

Medium voices (d1–c2); 1:30; Adagio; tonal; warm; nostalgic; recorded by Sperry.

Nature's Way, Charles Ives; *14S* and *114S;* comp. 1908.
Higher voices (d1–f2); 1:00; Adagio Moderato; tonal; lyrical; quaint; recorded by Ohrenstein.

Naught that Country Needed, Alford from Bernard (from the cantata "The Celestial Country"); *14S, SS,* and *114S;* comp. 1899.
Aria for Baritone (A–f1); 3:45; Moderato; tonal, lyric; flowing; recorded by Bruce Fifer, with orchestra, on Columbia (M4 32504).

The New River, Charles Ives; *34S* and *114S;* comp. 1912; arr. voice/ piano 1921.
Medium or high voices (d♭1–d#2 [a#2]), the optional higher line helps cut through the percussive piano score; 1:00; Fast and Rough; dramatic; a protest against industrialization; difficult; rarely heard; recorded by Boatwright (Columbia), Herford (1), Ingham.

Night of Frost in May, see *from "Night of Frost in May."*

A Night Song, Thomas Moore; *13S* and *114S;* comp. 1895.
Higher voices (e♭1–e♭2); 1:00; Allegretto vivace; tonal; lyrical over staccato chords; spirited and charming; recorded by Alexander (2), Hart, and Ramey.

A Night Thought, Thomas Moore; *34S* and *114S;* comp. 1895.
Medium voices (b–d#2); 1:00; Adagio; tonal, lyrical, reflective.

No More, William Winter; *11S2H;* comp. 1897.
Medium voices (c#1–e2); 3:30; Moderate; tonal; in two sections; narrative; a sentimental ballad; recorded by Boatwright (Columbia).

Nov. 2, 1920, see *It Strikes Me That.*

*An Old Flame, Charles Ives; *13S* and *114S;* comp. 1896.
Medium voices (c1–f2); 2:15; Con moto; tonal; lyric; sentimental love ballad; recorded by Alexander (2), Ramey, and Sharp.

Old Home Day, Charles Ives; *13S* and *114S;* comp. 1920.
Medium voices (d1–e2); 4:00; Slowly, then moderately and with even rhythm; a hushed, lyric, misty evocation followed by two spirited verses with a march-like refrain and optional obbligato; wonderful Americana; recorded by Boatwright (Columbia).

The Old Mother (Die Alte Mutter), Aasmund Olafsen Vinje; *13S* and *114S;* comp. 1900.

Medium voices (d1–e2); 1:45; Andante con moto, quasi allegretto; tonal; Brahmsian; recorded, in German, by Alexander (2) and Marcoulescou on Orion (OC 685).

*Omens and Oracles, *10S* and *114S;* comp. about 1900.

Medium voices (c1–f2); 2:00; Andante, with tempo changes; tonal; lyrical; sentimental.

On Judge's Walk, see *Rough Wind.*

On the Antipodes, Charles Ives; *19S;* for two pianos and optional organ or other low instrument; comp. 1915–1923.

Higher voices (a–a2); 2:30; many short sections, each with an abrupt tempo, dynamic, and timbral change; depicts the many faces of Nature; imposing opening and closing; difficult; a big piece; rarely heard; recorded by Puffer (2), Ingham, Villamil.

*On the Counter, Charles Ives; *14S* and *114S;* comp. 1920.

Medium voices (d1–e2); 1:15; Andante; tonal; lilting; an amusing parody of the sentimental ballad (see Cadman Footnote 4); recorded by Alexander (1).

1, 2, 3, Charles Ives; *4S* and *114S;* comp. 1921.

Medium voices (f1–d2); 0:30; Fairly fast; a spirited, tricky, humorous teaser; recorded by Alexander (1), Boatwright (Overtone), Curry, Ingham, Puffer (2).

The One Way, Charles Ives; *11S2H;* comp. 1923.

Higher voices (f1–g2); 2:45; Andante; tonal; a parody of conservatory training; lyric verses with faster marchlike refrains; recorded by Boatwright (Columbia).

Paracelsus, see *from "Paracelsus."*

Peaks, Henry Bellaman; *11S2H;* also incl. *AAS;* comp. 1923.

Medium voices (d1–e2); 1:30; Andante con moto; hushed; lyrical; mystical; recorded by Boatwright (Columbia), Herford (1).

Pictures, Monica Peveril Turnbull; *11S2H;* also incl. *AAS;* comp. 1906.

Medium voices (c#1–e2); 2:30; Con moto; tonal, lyrical; four connecting settings about nature; animated central section; recorded by Boatwright (Columbia), Herford (1).

The Pond, see *Remembrance.*

Premonitions, Robert Underwood Johnson; *34S* and *114S;* comp. 1917; arr. voice/piano 1921.
Medium voices (c#1–f2); 1:30; Slowly; subdued, then accelerates and builds to a dramatic ending; recorded by Herford (2).

Qu'il m'irait bien (How It Becomes Me), Anonymous; *12S* and *114S;* comp. 1901.
Medium voices (d♭1–f), 1:00; Allegretto vivace; in French; tonal; bright; a sophisticated bergerette; recorded by Alexander (2), Ohrenstein, and Parker.

The Rainbow (So May It Be), William Wordsworth; *34S* and *114S;* comp. 1914; arr. voice/piano 1921.
Medium voices (c1–f2); 1:15; Moderately fast; becomes slow and quiet; rhythmic difficulties; recorded by Herford (2).

Religion, James T. Bixby; *12S* and *114S;* comp. 1920.
Medium full voices (d♭1–e♭2); 1:30; Andante; chordal, broad, sustained; recorded by Curry; Herford (2).

Remembrance (The Pond), Charles Ives; *12S* and *114S;* comp. 1921.
Medium voices (g1–e2); 0:45; Slowly; hushed; sustained; a haunting evocation of Ives's father; recorded by Alexander (2), Curry, and with violin obbligato, Schonbrun.

Requiem, Robert Louis Stevenson; *19S;* comp. 1911.
Big higher voices (d♭1–f#2); 1:45; Allegro moderato; dynamic and tempo changes; massive, dissonant chords; complex rhythms; different; recorded by Boatwright in a higher key (Columbia), Ingham, Puffer (1).

Resolution, Charles Ives; *19S* and *114S;* comp. 1921.
Medium voices (c1–c2); 0:30; Moderately; straightforward, chordal; recorded by Boatwright in a higher key (Columbia).

Rock of Ages, Augustus Montague Toplady; *11S2H;* comp. 1889–92.
Sacred Solo for Contralto and Organ (or piano); a quirky arrangement of the famous hymn; recorded by Hart.

Romanzo di Central Park, Leigh Hunt; *14S* and *114S;* comp. 1900.
Low voices (c1–a1);[18] 2:00; Andante con grazia, con espressione e con amore; in English; tonal; a melodious, flowing spoof on rhymes

in poetry; recorded by Alexander (1), Herford (2), Ramey.

Rosamunde, Helmine von Chézy, trans. Bélanger; *14S* and *114S;* comp. 1898.

Medium voices (d1–f♭2); 2:15; Andante; in French; tonal, lyric; lilting; a lament; recorded by Alexander (2), Ohrenstein (under the title *Ballad from Rosamunde),* and Parker.

Rough Wind (adapted from *On Judge's Walk,* Arthur Symons), Percy B. Shelley; *34S* and *114S;* comp. 1898; arr. voice/piano 1902.

Higher voices (e♭1–a2); 1:00; Allegro; tonal; excited, active; builds to a big ending; difficult; (*On Judge's Walk* is recorded by Boatwright on Columbia).

A Scotch Lullaby, Charles Edmund Merrill Jr.; incl. *11S2H;* comp. 1896.

Rec. medium and higher voices (c#1–f#2); 1:30; Andante sostenuto; tonal; in dialect; recorded by Ohrenstein.

A Sea Dirge, William Shakespeare; *11S2H;* comp. 1925.

Medium voices (c1–e2); 1:45; In a slow swaying way; dramatic opening; sustained; eerie; a fascinating setting of "Full fathom five..."; recorded by Boatwright (Columbia), Ingham.

The See'r, Charles Ives; *7S* and *114S;* also incl. *AAS;* comp. 1913/20?

Medium voices (c1–d2); 0:45; Moderately fast; tricky, off-balance rhythms; melismas; crazy, good fun; recorded by Alexander (1), DeGaetani (Bridge), Herford (1), Ingham.

September, Folgore da San Geminiano; *34S* and *114S;* comp. 1920.

All voices that can cut through the piano writing (d1–g#2); 0:45; Presto; fast, spitting declamation over intricate, dense piano figurations; rhythmically complex; very difficult; can group with *August* and *December;* recorded by Boatwright, with changes, (Columbia), Herford (2), Ingham, Puffer (2).

Serenity, John Greenleaf Whittier; *7S* and *114S;* also incl. *AAS* and *CASS;* comp. 1919.

Lyric medium voices (f1–e2); 2:15; Very slowly, quietly and sustained, with little or no change in tempo or volume throughout; minimal, sustained vocal movement over ostinato chords; superb control needed; mesmerizing; haunting; an exquisite song; recorded by

Alexander (1), Boatwright (Overtone), DeGaetani (Nonesuch), Lear, Puffer (2).

The Side Show, Charles Ives; *12S* and *114S;* comp. 1921.
      Medium voices (d1–f2); 0:45; In a moderate waltz time; this out of kilter waltz is a favorite with audiences; tricky but fun; recorded by Alexander (1), Boatwright (Columbia), DeGaetani (Bridge), Herford (1), Lear, Nixon, Puffer (2), Carolyn Watkinson on Etcetera CD (KTC 1007).

Slow March, Charles Ives; *10S* and *114S;* comp. 1888.
      Lower voices (c1–c2); 2:00; Largo; tonal; a solemn march, based on Handel, for the burial of the family pet; Ives first song; recorded by Alexander (1), Boatwright (Columbia), Puffer (2), Ramey, and Sharp.

Slugging a Vampire, Charles Ives; *19S;* comp. 1902.[19]
      All voices that can cut the dense piano writing (b–f2); 0:30; Allegro con fuoco; tonal; rhythmic; a funny, crazy song; recorded by Alexander (1), Ingham.

So May It Be! see *The Rainbow.*

Soliloquy (Or a Study in 7ths and Other Things), Charles Ives; *34S;* comp. 1907.
      High voices that can be heard over the racket (d♭1–b2); 0:45; Adagio (chant, half-spoken over quiet chords), then Allegro; accelerates; disjunct; comprehensability and ensemble are virtually impossible, but the effect of this off-the-wall contemplation of nature is stunning; the audience will either gasp or laugh nervously; recorded by Ingham, Nixon, Villamil.

A Son of a Gambolier, Anonymous; *9S* and *114S;* comp. 1895.
      High voices (g1–a2); 2:45; In a fast two-step time; high tessitura; requires obbligato instruments; long piano solos; a street song; recorded by Sperry.

*A Song—for Anything, Charles Ives; *14S* and *114S;* comp. 1892.
      Lower voices (a–e2); 1:00 (for each verse); Andante moderato; strophic with three types of texts, including sacred; a sentimental ballad; recorded by Sharp.

Songs My Mother Taught Me, Heyduk;[20] *14S* and *114S;* comp. 1895.
Lower voices (b♭–c2); 2:00; Largo; tonal; hushed; rocking, with a melting melody; recorded by Alexander (1), DeGaetani (Bridge), and Hart.

The South Wind, Charles Ives; *34S* and *114S;* comp. 1899.
Medium voices (b–f2); 2:00; Andante con moto; tonal; lyrical; strophic.

Spring Song, Harmony T. Ives; *12S* and *114S;* also incl. *AASTC;* comp. 1904.
Higher voices (c1–g2); 1:15; Allegretto; tonal; lyrical; recorded by Alexander (1), Herford (2).

The Swimmers, see *from "The Swimmers."*

Tarrant Moss, Rudyard Kipling; *13S* and *114S;* comp. 1898.
See footnote to *Slugging a Vampire;* recorded by Boatwright (Overtone), Herford (2).

There is a certain garden, poet unknown; *11S2H;* comp. 1893.
Lower lyric voices (a–e2); 1:45; Allegretto con moto; tonal, light, Victoriana, with a hint of later Ives; recorded by Boatwright (Columbia), Hart, and Herford (1).

There is a Lane, Harmony T. Ives; *9S* and *114S;* comp. 1902.
Medium voices (c1–f2); 1:45; Adagio sostenuto; tonal; quiet; nostalgic; recorded by Alexander (2), Boatwright (Columbia); Lear.

They are There! Charles Ives; *9S;* also pub. separately Peer c1961 (ed. Lou Harrison); the original, *He is There!* is found in *114 Songs;* comp. 1917.[21]
Medium voices (d1–g2); 2:45; In march time; optional high obbligato instrument; tonal; spirited; patriotic, but rather wild; recorded by Alexander (2), Boatwright (Overtone, *He is There!*), Herford (1), Ives (not to be missed), Ramey.

The Things Our Fathers Loved, Charles Ives; *14S* and *114S;* comp. 1917.
Medium voices (c1–d#2); 1:45; Slowly and sustained; a more excited central section; follows the imagery of things past; emotional; warm; recorded by Alexander (1), Boatwright (Columbia), DeGaetani (Nonesuch), Herford (1), Ingham, Stewart.

Thoreau, Charles Ives after Henry David Thoreau; *34S* and *114S;* comp. 1915.

Clear, lower voices (c#1–d2); 2:30; a spoken introduction from *Walden* over misty chords; then sustained declamation over a fluid piano score; hushed throughout; philosophical; recorded by DeGaetani (Nonesuch), Herford (2), Stewart (without spoken text).

Those Evening Bells, Thomas Moore; *14S* and *114S;* comp. 1907.

Medium voices (c1–e♭2); 1:45; Moderato con moto; tonal; hushed; lyrical; recorded by Boatwright, with some differences, as *The Sea of Sleep* (Columbia).[22]

To Edith, Harmony T. Ives; *3S, 10S,* and *114S;* comp. 1892; rev. 1919.

Medium voices (e♭1–e♭2); 1:00; Andante moderato; tonal; delicate; charming.

Tolerance, Rudyard Kipling (as quoted in Pres. Hadley's lectures); *34S* and *114S;* comp. 1909.

Medium voices (d#1–f2); 0:45; Slowly; declamatory over chords; builds to final climax.

Tom Sails Away, Charles Ives; *2S, 19S,* and *114S;* comp. 1917.

Medium voices (c1–d2); 3:00; Slowly and quietly; stream of consciousness; builds to a more excited central section as blurred childhood memories of Tom, who is now at war, appears to become real; many evocative song quotations; atmospheric; nostalgic; poignant; recorded by Alexander (1), DeGaetani (Bridge), Fischer-Dieskau, Herford (1), Ingham, Lear, Puffer (2), Carolyn Watkinson on Etcetera CD (KTC 1007).

Two Little Flowers,[23] Harmony Ives; *3S, 19S,* and *114S;* comp. 1921?

Lyric voices ([b♭]d1–e2); 1:30; Allegretto; tonal, quiet; tuneful over flowing piano figures; striking for its affecting simplicity; recorded by Alexander (1), Bauman, Boatwright (Overtone), DeGaetani (Bridge), Fischer-Dieskau, Herford (1), Lear, Puffer (2).

Vita, Manlius; see *Duty; 4S* and *34S;* comp. 1921.

Medium voices (a1–e2); 0:30; Adagio; in Latin; sustained.

Vote for Names, Charles Ives; pub. separately Peer c1968; also incl. *VN;* comp. 1912.

Higher voices (b–a2); 0:45; Freely; the independent vocal line is spoken and sung without reference to the piano; unbridled political sarcasm.

The Waiting Soul, William Cowper; *12S, SS,* and *114S;* comp. 1908.
Low voices (b-e2); 2:00; Andante; tonal; sustained declamation; builds; meditative.

Walking, Charles Ives; *7S* and *114S;* comp. 1900/02?
Medium voices (d1–f#2); 1:45; Allegro con spirito; follows the imagery; complex, but wholesome; recorded by Boatwright (Overtone), Herford (2), Ingham, Lear, Puffer (1), Carolyn Watkinson on Etcetera CD (KTC 1007).

Walt Whitman, from "Leaves of Grass"; *34S* and *114S;* comp. 1921.
Big medium voices (c1–f2); 0:45; Fast and in a challenging way; declamatory over powerful chords; aggressive; recorded by Herford (2), Ingham, Puffer (1), Stewart, Elizabeth Suderburg (OLY-104).

Waltz, Charles Ives; *12S* and *114S;* comp. 1895.
Lower voices (b–d2); 1:15; tonal; tuneful; spirited, old-time wedding waltz; recorded by Herford (2) and Sharp.

Watchman! John Bowring; *14S, SS,* and *114S;* comp. 1913.
Medium voices (d1–f#2); 1:45; Andante con moto; atonal introduction; then, a tonal, but off-kilter, setting of a familiar hymn; recorded by Alexander (2), Parker.

Weil' auf mir, Nikolaus Lenau; *14S* and *114S;* comp. 1902.
Medium voices (d♭1–f2); 2:00; Moderato sostenuto; in German; tonal; sustained over fluid piano figures; a gorgeous romantic lied; recorded by Alexander (2), Fischer Dieskau, Yolanda Marcoulescou on Orion OC685.

West London, Mathew Arnold; *34S* and *114S;* arr. voice/piano 1921.
Medium voices ([b]c1–f2); 3:15; Moderato; narrative; depicts the dignity of a woman struggling against poverty; a stirring climax; a hushed ending; philosophical; intense and moving; recorded by Boatwright (Columbia), DeGaetani (Bridge), Fischer-Dieskau, Herford (1), Nixon, Puffer (1).

When Stars are in the Quiet Skies, Bulwer Lytton; *34S* and *114S;* comp. 1891.
Medium voices (d1–d2); 3:00; Adagio; tonal; strophic; sustained; melodious; quiet; recorded by Hart.

Where the Eagle, Monica Peveril Turnbull; *3S* and *114S;* also incl. *CC;* comp. 1900.

Medium voices (d1–e2); 1:45; Adagio molto; tonal; chromatic; lyrical over fluid piano figures; philosophical; recorded by Boatwright (Overtone), Fischer-Dieskau, Herford (1).

The White Gulls, from the Russian, trans. Maurice Morris; *34S* and *114S;* comp. 1921.

Medium voices (b–e2); 2:15; Largo; sustained and quiet; briefly animando; evokes the gull's leisurely flight; philosophical; recorded by DeGaetani (Bridge), Fischer-Dieskau, Herford (1), Puffer (2), Elizabeth Suderburg (OLY-104).

*The World's Highway, Harmony T. Ives; *13S* and *114S;* comp. 1893.

Higher lyric voices (d1–g2); 2:30; Allegretto; tempo and dynamic changes; tonal, flowing; melodious; recorded by Upshaw on MusicMasters CD (60128L).

The World's Wanderers, Percy B. Shelley; *10S* and *114S;* comp. 1895.

Medium voices (e♭1–e♭2); 2:00; Adagio sostenuto; tonal; lyrical; strophic; recorded by Ohrenstein.

Yellow Leaves, Henry Bellaman; *11S2H;* comp. 1923?

Low voices (a–e2); 2:00; Slowly; an arresting central section; sustained low notes; pictorial; atmospheric; recorded by Boatwright, in a higher key, (Columbia), Herford (1).

Also of interest:

Sunrise, Charles Ives; Peters c1977; comp. 1926; for medium voices, with violin; Very slowly and quietly; an agitated middle section; long, minimal and spare; a haunting reflection; possibly Ives's last original work; recorded by DeGaetani on Elektra/Nonesuch CD (79248-2-ZK), Parker, Schonbrun.

BIBLIOGRAPHY

AmerGroves, Baker, Ewen, Friedberg (I), Goss, Greene, Hall, Ivey, Mellers, Nathan, Thompson.

Bellaman, Henry. "Charles Ives: The Man and His Music." *The Musical Quarterly* 19 (January, 1933): 45–58.

Block, Geoffrey. *Charles Ives: A Bio-Bibliography*. Westport, Connecticut: Greenwood Press, 1988.

Boatwright, Howard. "The Songs," *Music Educator's Journal* 61 (October 1974); 42–47.

Carr, Cassandra I. "Charles Ives's Humor as Reflected in His Songs," *American Music* 7 (Summer 1989): 123–139.

Copland, Aaron. "One Hundred and Fourteen Songs," *Modern Music* 11 (January-February, 1934): 59–64; reprinted as "The Ives Case" in *Our New Music*. New York: McGraw-Hill, 1941.

Cowell, Henry and Sidney Cowell. *Charles Ives and His Music*. Paperback ed. New York: Oxford University Press, 1969.

Hitchcock, H. Wiley. *Ives*. London: Oxford University Press, 1977. The first chapter offers an excellent analysis of the songs.

Ives, Charles E. *Memos*. Edited by John Kirkpatrick. New York: W.W. Norton & Company, Inc., 1972.

————. "Postface," *114 Songs*. West Redding, Connecticut: C. E. Ives, 1922.

Perlis, Vivian. *Charles Ives Remembered*. New Haven: Yale University Press, 1974. Wonderful for getting to know Charles Ives, the man.

Rossiter, Frank R. *Charles Ives and His America*. New York: Liveright, 1975.

Walker, Donald R. "The Vocal Music of Charles Ives," *Parnassus: Poetry in Review* 3 (Spring-Summer 1975): 329–344.

Warren, Richard. *Charles E. Ives: Discography*. New Haven: Historical Sound Recordings, Yale University Library, 1972.

Wooldridge, David. *From the Steeples and Mountains*. New York: Alfred A. Knopf, 1974. A comprehensive, but controversial biography and study.

Yates, Peter. "Charles E. Ives: An American Composer," *Parnassus: Poetry in Review* 3 (Spring-Summer, 1975): 318–328.

---

[1] It was printed by G. Schirmer, who took Ives's money but otherwise, refusing to put their name on the project, disassociated themselves.

[2] Aaron Copland, *Modern Music*, 61.

[3] Donald Walker, *Parnassus*, 342.

[4] *Memos*, 126. He cites *Evidence*, *Spring Song*, and *Autumn* as samples.

[5] Peter Yates, "Charles Ives: An American Composer," *Parnassus*, Spring/Summer 1975, p. 325.

[6] *Memos*, 127.

[7] Vivian Perlis, *Charles Ives Remembered*, 82.

[8] One may also hear mention of *50 Songs* (C. E. Ives c1922), a drastic editing by Ives of *114 Songs*. This album, however, has never been reprinted.

[9] Peer-Southern expects this album to be published by the end of 1993.

[10] This long out of print LP, with John Kirkpatrick at the piano, was the first recording comprised exclusively of Ives songs.

[11] This interesting recording has Henry Brant as its pianist. Brant, who became an important experimental composer himself, was an early enthusiast of a yet unknown Ives. This author feels the performances on this recording, despite Ingham's vocal shortcomings, are as close to what Ives would have wanted as any in existence. Liner notes indicate Ingham and Brant intend to record many more of the Ives catalogue.

[12] Ives performs *He is There* and other pieces. There are also reminiscences by people who knew him.

[13] Postscript to *114 Songs*.

[14] Ives's adopted daughter.

[15] Also known as *Two Slants (Christian and Pagan)*.

[16] For more on this poem and General William Booth, see entry for the same song under Sidney Homer.

[17] Though somewhat restrained compared to later interpretations, this is a historic recording. Pazmore was a friend of Ives and, according to Philip Miller in the liner notes of the New World issue, this is the first recording ever made of an Ives song.

[18] In a note to this song, Ives declares it can be sung an octave higher.

[19] The song *Tarrant Moss* uses the same tune, and attempts to use Rudyard Kipling's words. But because permission to use this poem was not given, Ives gives the singer the first four words and refers him to the poem for the rest. Out of spite he then writes *Slugging a Vampire*.

[20] Ives uses the same translation as the famous Dvorak setting.

[21] *They are There!* is the updated version (for World War II) of *He is There!* It was Ives preferred version.

[22] *The Sea of Sleep* will appear in *40 Earlier Songs*.

[23] The two little flowers to which this song is dedicated are their six-year-old adopted daughter and her friend Susan, who played together near New York's Grammercy Park. It was Ives's last collaboration with his wife.

FREDERICK JACOBI
b. May 4, 1891, San Francisco, CA; d. Oct. 24, 1952, New York, NY

Though Frederick Jacobi was best known for his compositions derived from American Indian and Hebraic sources, much of his music, including his songs, was eclectic.

When Jacobi was a boy his family moved to New York, where he studied with Rubin Goldmark. He also studied with Paul Juon at Berlin's Hochschule für Musik and, again in New York, with Ernest Bloch, who inspired his interest in Hebrew influences. From 1913 to 1917 Jacobi was an assistant conductor at the Metropolitan Opera but, during World War I, played saxophone for the army band. Then, in the 1920s, he immersed himself in the music of the Pueblo Indians. Jacobi taught at the Master School of the Arts (1924–1936), and at the Juilliard School of Music (1936–1950). He also lectured at Hartt College, Mills College, and the University of California at Berkeley. He was married to pianist Irene Schwarz, with whom he had three children.

THE SONGS

Jacobi's handful of published—but virtually unperformed—songs are primarily romantic and lyrical. Unfortunately, they are also uneven. Several smaller songs are first-rate, but big songs tend to ramble and become inflated. Except for the stamina required for some of the latter, musical and technical problems are minimal. An appealing grouping might be made by extracting songs from various sets. The following comprise the greater part of Jacobi's published output.

The Look, Sara Teasdale; G. Schirmer c1915.
> Rec. high voices (c#1–g#2), best for women; 0:45; Gaily; light and lyrical.

Paradox, Frank L. Koch; G. Schirmer c1915.
> Rec. high voices (c1–g2), best for men; 1:00; Simply and not too quickly; lyrical.

Three Songs, Philip Freneau; Valley c1955; ded. to various singers.
> Rec. high voices (d1–bb2); 7:30; titles are: *On the Sleep of Plants; Elegy; Ode to Freedom;* clearly intended as a set; in response to the poetry, these songs are unabashedly eighteenth-century English in style.

Three Songs to Poems by Sarojini Naidu, G. Schirmer c1918.
> Spec. medium voices (c#1–a2), rec. full high voices; 10:00; titles are: *The Faery Isle of Janjira; In the Night; Love and Death;* though clearly intended as a set, *Love and Death* is too long and tediously emotional to be programmed; the first two are attractive, romantic, pseudo Eastern settings. William Treat Upton liked them all but "treasured" *The Faery Isle of Janjira.*[1]

Two Poems by Geoffry Chaucer, G. Schirmer c1923.
  Rec. medium and higher voices (c#1–a2), best for men; 4:30; in
  middle English; make a good pair, but can be used individually.
  Roundel, (d1–e♭2); 1:45; Not quickly; cantabile over a delicate, supple, fluid accompaniment; a lovely, tender song.
  Ballade, (c#1–a2); 2:45; Very quickly and with humor; starts well but
  becomes a little long-winded.

BIBLIOGRAPHY
AmerGroves, Baker, Ewen, Greene, Thompson, Upton.

---

[1] William Treat Upton, *Art Song in America,* 145.

SERGIUS KAGEN
b. Aug. 22, 1909, St. Petersburg, Russia; d. March 1, 1964, New York, NY

Sergius Kagen's impressive career as voice teacher, coach, accompanist,
writer, and editor, has somewhat overshadowed his achievements as a
composer.
  Kagen was the third son of well-off, intellectual parents. His father
was a Lithuanian Jew; his mother a Russian atheist. When his older
brother, who was studying to be a pianist, died in the Revolution, Kagen,
aged nine, began piano lessons and soon entered the St. Petersburg
Conservatory. But in 1920 the family, shattered by the events of the
Revolution, fled to Berlin, where Kagen studied with Leonid Kreutzer
and Paul Juon. Following his family to the United States, in 1930 Kagen
entered the Juilliard School. There, while earning his bachelor's and
graduate degrees, he accompanied the students of the great soprano
Marcella Sembrich, who became an important mentor. After Sembrich's
death in 1935 many of her students—including soprano Genevieve
Greer, who became his wife in 1937—continued to study with Kagen.
Joining the Juilliard faculty in 1940, he gave vocal literature classes and
earned a major reputation as a voice teacher. He also became a highly
regarded coach and accompanist, not only for students but for established artists like Povla Frijsh, Ezio Pinza, and Mack Harrell. In 1949,
the year he began to compose his own songs, his first book, *Music for
the Voice,* was published.[1] A second book, *On Studying Singing,* appeared the following year.[2] Kagen also edited 39 volumes of songs and
arias for International Music Company. These editions and both books

are still in print and widely used today. When he died from a heart condition, he was in the midst of writing two operas.

THE SONGS

Coming to composition rather late in life, Kagen's 48 songs, mostly composed in 1949 and 1950, were primarily a response to contemporary music's abuse of the art song genre. It was a situation where, with his wife's encouragement, he felt he could make a difference.[3] But, although his songs meet all the requirements of good composition, including originality and style, they are surprisingly mild-mannered and fail to make much of an impression. Excessive chromaticism, mixing of tonalities, and constantly changing meters all seem a self-conscious effort to prove song can be different and modern, yet still be singable.

Kagen was not a singer himself, but his long experience in working with voices certainly made him cognizant of their strengths and limitations. His desire to express the text, however, seems to take precedence over everything. Vocal lines are drawn in a distinctive declamatory style. Tune is of little account and accompaniments are evocative but restrained. Both poetry and subject matter are predominantly American, and—despite his cosmopolitan background— some songs actually have a homespun quality. Jan DeGaetani has recorded one that was never published, *The Junk Man,* on Elektra/Nonesuch CD (79248-2-ZK).[4] A selection of this author's preferences follows.

All Day I Hear the Noise of Waters, James Joyce; Weintraub c1950.
    Rec. medium voices (f1–f#2); 1:30; Agitato; dramatic singing over accompanimental figures depicting water.

I'm Nobody, Emily Dickinson; Weintraub c1950; to Mme. Povla Frijsh.
    Rec. medium and high lyric voices (d1–g2); 1:15; With humor; declamatory; light and busy; yet another good setting of this poem.

Mag, Carl Sandburg; Weintraub c1950; to Howard Swanson.
    Spec. low voices, in bass clef (B♭–e1); 2:30; Slowly and heavily; declaimed over an accompaniment that builds in piquancy to match the despair poverty has wrecked on one man's marriage; poignant but somewhat ponderous.

Maybe, Carl Sandburg; Weintraub c1950.
    Rec. lyric voices (d1–g2), text suggests women; 1:00; With great simplicity; musing on a possible marriage proposal; light and spare.

A June Day, Sara Teasdale; Weintraub c1950.

Rec. high lyric voices (f#1–b♭2); 1:15; Gently, not too slowly; a clear, flutey voice is needed to sustain the tessitura and cut the busy warbling piano figures, which are entirely set in the treble clef; intricate, quiet, and delicate.

Let It Be Forgotten, Sara Teasdale; Weintraub c1950.
Rec. medium lyric voices (f1–f2); 1:15; Andante; short phrases; reflective; hushed.

Sleep Now, O Sleep Now, James Joyce; Leeds c1951.
Rec. low voices (a–e2); 1:30; Andante; lovely melody over a pulsing, syncopated accompaniment, effectively evoking the "unquiet heart."

Also of interest:

Because I Could Not Stop For Death, Dickinson, Andante, parlando; ***Drum,*** Hughes, lower voices, Allegro, rhythmic and spare; ***Miss T,*** De la Mare, Allegretto, cute; ***3 Satires,*** different poets, orig. pub. separately in high and low keys, also available as a cycle, somewhat amusing; ***Upstream,*** Sandburg, for big voices, Maestoso.

BIBLIOGRAPHY

Quillian, James W. "Howard Swanson and Sergius Kagen: New Songs to Sing," *Repertoire.* (November, 1951).
Starer, Robert. *Continuo: A Life in Music.* New York: Random House, 1987. The chapter "Juilliard and Accompanying" is primarily about Kagen.
Woods, Billy Jon. "The Songs of Sergius Kagen," *NATS Bulletin* 27 (February/March 1971). This includes a complete listing of his songs.

---

[1] *Music for the Voice.* New York: Rinehart & Company Inc., 1949; (revised) Bloomington: Indiana University Press, 1968.

[2] *On Studying Singing.* Reprint edition. New York: Dover, 1960.

[3] Some of Kagen's views on the state of the genre are given in his article, "The American Concert Song," *The Juilliard Review* 1 (Fall, 1954).

[4] Fewer than 20 songs were published.

JOHN KOCH
b. March 17, 1928, Haverhill, NH

John Koch studied at Johns Hopkins University, the Peabody Conservatory and, with Bernard Wagenaar and Peter Mennin, at the Juilliard School. In 1960 he studied with Nadia Boulanger on a Fulbright grant. Koch has written symphonies, concertos, chamber music, and a handful of attractive songs. He is also a pianist, who has both concertized and accompanied. He currently lives in Norwich, Vermont.

THE SONGS
Koch has written a handful of light, lyrical, appealing songs. Vocal lines are graceful and tuneful. Accompaniments never press the voice and convey the mood with a minimum of fuss. Four songs are recorded by John Reardon on Serenus (SRE 1019). Some recommendations follow.

Silver, Walter de la Mare; General c1965.
    Rec. medium voices (e1–f#2); 3:00; Freely and smoothly; sustained vocalism; impressionistic harmonies; a highly evocative setting of this beautiful poem about the moon; recorded by Reardon.

Tame Cat, Ezra Pound; General c1965; also incl. *AAS.*
    Rec. medium voices (e♭1–e♭2); 1:15; Andante; conversational with a descriptive accompaniment; a cat's whimsical musings on beautiful women; recorded by Reardon.

Also of interest:
Calico Pie, Lear, also incl. *AAS,* a pretty, light waltz; *An Epitaph,* De la Mare, delicate, sustained; *An Immorality,* Pound, also incl. *AAS,* a cantabile lovesong, recorded by Reardon; *O My Luv Is Like a Red, Red Rose,* Burns, straightforward, folklike; *The Tea Shop,* Pound, sustained, recorded by Reardon; *New Songs of Old Mother Goose,* six diverse settings—imaginative, skillful, and, when appropriate, very pretty.

BIBLIOGRAPHY
Batsford, J. Tucker. Liner notes. "John Reardon Sings Contemporary Art Songs." Serenus 1019.

A. WALTER KRAMER
b. Sept. 23, 1890, New York, NY; d. April 8, 1969, New York, NY

A. Walter Kramer was better known as a music critic, editor, and administrator, than as a composer. His father was a musician who had emigrated from Moravia. Kramer studied the violin for many years, but concerned that life as a concert violinist might be too confining, he also explored other areas of the music world. From 1910 to 1922 he was a critic on *Musical America*. Then, for a while he lived abroad, where he did some composing and studied with Gian Francesco Malipiero. In 1927 he became Music Supervisor for CBS Radio but, two years later, returned to *Musical America* as its editor-in-chief, remaining until 1936. From 1936 to 1956 he was Managing Director of Galaxy Music. He also helped found and was later president of the Society for Publication of American Music.

THE SONGS
Though Kramer composed in many idioms, his numerous well-crafted, eclectic songs probably received the most attention. Working his way through German influences and a subsequent French impressionistic period, he eventually found his own style, but his penchant for sentimental texts undermined the possibility of lasting success for most of his songs. Nevertheless, some have genuine personality and mood. Scrupulously attentive to the poem and exercising considerable restraint, Kramer usually wrote in a lyrical declamatory style with a sprinkling of romantic and recitative-like passages set over colorful, illustrative accompaniments. The following are recommended and representative.

The Faltering Dusk, Op. 45, No. 1, Louis Untermeyer; Ditson c1919.
     Pub. high and low (high, eb1–gb2); text suggests women; 2:30; Slowly, alternately intense and simple; folklike melody rises briefly to a climax; reminiscent of Brahms; a restrained but dramatic little dialogue between mother and daughter.

I Have Seen Dawn, Op. 48, No. 1, John Masefield; G. Schirmer c1922; also incl. *NAAS*.
     Pub. low and high (low, b#–d2), text suggest men; 2:30; Freely declaimed, ardently; descriptive; impressionistic; lyrical.

The Last Hour, after a poem by Jessie Christian Brown; Church c1914.
     Pub. high, medium, low (low, b–eb2); 3:00; Slowly—passionately. Kramer gives this maudlin poem (which asks how two lovers

would spend their last hour together if that was all the time they were given) dignity and pathos; restrained but warm declamation over more fervent piano gestures; an affecting song and one of Kramer's most popular.

Now Like a Lantern, Op. 44, No. 5, Alice Raphael; Ricordi c1919.
   Rec. medium voices (f1–f2[ab2]); 2:15; Slowly - with warmth; sustained declamation; much description, atmosphere, and word-painting; ends romantically.

Swans, Op. 44, No.4, Sara Teasdale; Ricordi c1917/1953.
   Pub. medium and two high keys (highest, eb1–bb2); rec. lyric voices; 2:15; Slowly, very calmly; elastic recitative-like passages alternate with sustained lyrical ones; floating high pianissimos; quiet, impressionistic; recorded with unearthly high notes by McCormack on New World (247).

BIBLIOGRAHY
AmerGroves, Baker, Thompson, Upton.
Howard, John Tasker, "A. Walter Kramer: the Early Years," *The Music Journal* (March 1972).
———. A. Walter Kramer. New York: J. Fisher, 1926.

EZRA LADERMAN
b. June 29, 1924, New York, NY

Laderman's large catalogue contains a sizable amount of vocal music, including three commanding cycles for solo voice and piano.
   Laderman studied at the High School of Music and Art in New York. After serving in World War II, he studied privately with Stefan Wolpe, and with Miriam Gideon at Brooklyn College, graduating in 1949. Two years later he received a master's degree from Columbia University, where his teachers were Douglas Moore and Otto Luening. Laderman has taught at Sarah Lawrence and SUNY (Binghamton), and headed the music division of the National Endowment for the Arts. In 1989 he became dean of the Yale School of Music. He is married with three children.

THE SONGS
Carefully thought out and notated in the minutest detail, Laderman neither cuts corners nor spares his performers in conveying the drama of the

vivid, profound, and intellectually provocative texts he chooses to set. Although no unconventional vocal devices are called for, in the soprano cycles the extremes of range, tempo, and dynamic, the wide intervals, the complex rhythms, and the variety of vocal styles (florid, declamatory, lyrical, dramatic) all indicate that only those blessed with stamina, emotional fortitude, a secure vocal technique, and solid experience in the twentieth-century idiom should invest the time. Similar demands are required of the pianist. The cycle for baritone, on the other hand, is considerably more manageable and accessible. Judith Raskin recorded the two cycles for soprano with impressive skill, artistry, and tonal beauty on Desto (DC 7105).

From the Psalms, from Psalms 7, 9, 22, 39, 57, 61, 69, 103, 104, and 119; Oxford c1970; comm. by Desto Records for Judith Raskin.

Spec. soprano (b–a2); 11:00; titles are: *What I did not steal; Behold the wicked man; From the end of the earth; Look away from me; Thou didst set the earth;* fragments from the psalms are strung together to make "an impassioned plea for the survival of man";[1] compared with *Songs for Eve* the range is modest, but exceptional stamina is nevertheless required, mainly because the emotion is even more intense and the tessitura is high (for example, the last four braces are nothing but sustained high Gs); atonal and highly dissonant; very difficult; both the anguish and the intensity of this shattering cycle can be overwhelming; recorded by Raskin.

The Riddles, Archibald MacLeish (from *Songs for Eve*); Oxford c1968.

Rec. sopranos (bb–a2); Allegretto; tonal; shifting meters; a sprightly, tuneful, accessible excerpt (pub. separately) from *Songs for Eve.*

Songs for Eve, Archibald MacLeish; Oxford c1968; commissioned by and dedicated to Judith Raskin.

Spec. soprano (bb–c#3[c3]), rec. high sopranos with dramatic capabilities; 29:00; titles are: *What Eve Sang; Eve's Exile; Eve's Now-I-Lay-Me; Eve in the Dawn; The Riddles* (see above entry for this song which has been published separately); *Eve's Rebuke to Her Child; Eve Quiets Her Child; Eve Explains to the Thrush Who Repeats Everything.* Although the cycle is carefully contoured for a full dramatic and musical effect, certain individual songs could be used or smaller groups made; the first five songs are more lyrical, less demanding, and more accessible to the listener than the latter three; the mix of vocal styles includes playful lyricism, sustained cantabile, and stark declamation; all the difficulties previously described with the addition of high notes left hanging; a vocal tour de force and an equally challenging and virtuosic piano score; dissonant and atonal with occasional, unexpected forays into tonality; irregular meters and other rhythmic complexities; primal, emotional, spiritual; an important, cogent, powerful cycle; recorded by Raskin.

Songs from Michelangelo, trans. by Joseph Tusiani; Oxford 1975; first performed by Sherill Milnes (1973).

Spec. baritone (F–e1); though Laderman provides higher options for the lowest lines (most prevalent in the last song), this work is recommended for bass-baritones; 23:00; titles are: *Who is the one that draws me to you; O sweeter a sudden death would be; Your face is sweeter than mustard; The more you see the torment on my face; If in a woman a part is beautiful; For all this anguish; Alas, for I am now betrayed.* Despite its length, this is a more manageable cycle than the other two; melodic, vocally lush; good variety of mood and tempo; Michelangelo's amazingly modern sentiments about his loved one are alternately raunchy, witty, lyrical, and poignant; the final song, which ties the work together, is a stirring monologue on time and eternal death; a strong cycle.

BIBLIOGRAPHY
AmerGroves, Baker, Ewen, Greene.
Liner notes. *Ezra Laderman: Songs for Eve/From the Psalms.* Desto (DC 7105). It would appear that Laderman himself wrote these explanatory notes.

---

[1] Liner notes, Desto (DC7105).

FRANK LA FORGE
b. Oct. 22, 1879, Rockford, IL; d. May 5, 1953, New York, NY

Frank La Forge was the composer and arranger of a large catalogue of songs. He was also a teacher, coach, and accompanist to countless vocal stars, including Marian Anderson, Lawrence Tibbett, and Lucrezia Bori. His custom of accompanying entirely by memory—in performance— was a feat of legendary proportions.

A boy soprano of local fame, La Forge first learned piano from his older sister. In 1900 he went to Vienna to study with Leschetizky; then toured Europe, Russia, and the United States as accompanist to Marcella Sembrich. In 1920 he settled in New York where he maintained a busy studio. He died while performing at a Musician's Club dinner.

Of La Forge's many original songs, a number of early efforts were written in German in a conventional *lied* style. *Spuk* (Spooks), *An Einen Boten* (To a Messenger), and *Schlupfwinkel* (Retreat)—often heard in their very workable English translations—are all excellent examples. Most, however, were written in the accessible concert ballad style, which was so popular in America at the time. And, as a result of La Forge's close acquaintance with so many top singers, they were often designed to show the voice of specific artists. *Come Unto These Yellow Sands* (for Sembrich's coloratura) and *Song of the Open* (for Frances Alda's full soprano) were especially popular. Despite some excesses (usually in the accompaniments), La Forge's songs are tasteful and well-crafted, but few are memorable. He was perhaps more successful as an arranger—his excellent set of Mexican folk songs is notable— and as the compiler of the popular anthology for students, *Pathways of Song*.

BIBLIOGRAPHY
AmerGroves, Baker, Howard (OAM), Thompson.
"Rare Versatility Marks Musical Activities of Frank La Forge," *Musical America* (September 1930).

JOHN LA MONTAINE
b. March 17, 1920, Oak Park, IL

His large output includes three operas, a great deal of choral music, but only a few art songs. This is unfortunate, for John La Montaine writes music that sings and invites the ear.

For many years he was a diligent student of the piano, but La Montaine always wanted to be a composer. He studied at the American Conservatory in Chicago; then, at the Eastman School with Bernard Rogers and Howard Hanson. After five years service in the U.S. Navy during World War II, he resumed his studies, this time with Bernard Wagenaar at the Juilliard School, and Nadia Boulanger at the American Conservatory in Fontainebleau. From 1950 to 1954, he was the pianist for Toscanini's NBC Orchestra. In 1956 Leontyne Price and the National Symphony premiered his *Songs of the Rose of Sharon,* bringing him considerable recognition. In 1959 he received a Pulitzer Prize for his first Piano Concerto, and the following year, on an invitation from President and Mrs. John F. Kennedy, he became the first composer commissioned to write for a presidential inauguration. Though hindered by a chronic eyesight problem, La Montaine continues to be the recipient of a steady stream of awards and commissions.

THE SONGS

La Montaine writes lovely songs, modern but accessible. In his ample catalogue, mostly of large forms, he has responded to a variety of influences ranging from medieval to serial, and even including exotic bird song. Although his solo songs are tonal and in a conventional idiom, his inventive musical ideas and imaginative response to the poetry set them apart from the routine, giving them a fresh and individual character. In addition, his light touch, sensitivity for word setting, and extravagant lyricism make him a natural for the genre. Intelligently crafted for the voice, La Montaine's songs make only moderate demands on the singer, and the same can be said of his lucid, often illustrative, accompaniments. Musical problems also are modest. *Songs of the Rose of Sharon,* the acclaimed biblical cycle for soprano and orchestra is available—but not recommended—in piano reduction. Polly Jo Baker, with La Montaine at the piano, has recorded *Six Sonnets of Shakespeare* on Fredonia Discs (8), and Eleanor Steber sings *Stopping by Woods* on Desto (411/412). The following is a virtually complete listing of his published art songs.[1]

Six Sonnets of Shakespeare, Op. 12; Fredonia c1962; comp. 1957.
> Rec. high lyric voices (b–a2); 15:30; titles are: *Let not my love be called idolatry; From you have I been absent; Take all my loves; No longer mourn; Shall I compare thee; Not from the stars;* beautifully contoured as a cycle and best kept as one, though some songs might be used individually; the poignant *No longer mourn* and the sustained, but soaring *Shall I compare thee* are especially compelling; an excellent set; recorded by Baker.

Stopping By Woods on a Snowy Evening, Robert Frost; Galaxy c1963.
> Spec. medium voice (c1–eb2); Simply and rhythmically; 2:00; a lovely melody over piano figures evoking the ride through the woods; pauses only for a moment's profound reflection on the scene; recorded by Steber.

Three Poems of Holly Beye, Op. 15; Cordon Press c1954.
> Spec. medium voice (b–f#2), best for women; 4:30; titles are: *Definition of the Highest; The Happiness; Song from the Bamboo Cycle;* spare piano; not difficult; opens lightly and lyrically; closes

with a quiet, poignant *quasi recitativo;* an appealing set of love songs—reflective and, in their delicate expression, feminine.

BIBLIOGRAPHY
AmerGroves, Baker, Ewen, Greene, Thompson

---

[1] At this time, Fredonia Press – Discs appears to be the principal source for anything regarding La Montaine's music.

MARGARET RUTHVEN LANG
b. Nov. 27, 1867, Boston, MA; d. May 29, 1972, Boston, MA

The consummately crafted, comely songs of Margaret Ruthven Lang are happy reminders of an innocent age.

She was the daughter of Benjamin Lang, one of Boston's busiest musicians and Margaret's first teacher. Her mother was an amateur singer. After a year of study abroad, in 1887 Lang returned to Boston to complete her education with George Chadwick and Edward MacDowell. She never married, but devoted herself to composition, and enjoyed regular performances of her works.[1] Before she was even 50, however, she stopped composing altogether. Her next 54 years were spent involved in her community's musical affairs. Lang's lifelong attendance at the Boston Symphony concerts inspired the orchestra, under Erich Leinsdorf, to perform the "Old Hundredth" in honor of her 100th birthday.

THE SONGS
Unlike the sentimental parlor song we generally associate with the period, Lang's many songs are intelligent and sophisticated settings of tasteful poetry. Lang had imagination and a remarkable melodic gift. Never at a loss for ideas, her songs often develop in unexpected ways, rarely following the usual repetitious strophic patterns and often employing unusual harmonies. What's more, they are eminently singable. Recital Publications has done a real service in reprinting three sets. Though *5 Songs,* Op.15 (to the inconsequential poetry of Lizette Woodworth Reese) is less successful, *Nonsense Rhymes and Pictures* (Edward Lear) and *10 Songs* (for medium voice) make an excellent introduction to Lang's work. Some recommendations follow.

Ghosts, Munkittrick; incl. *10 Songs* (Recital Pub. Reprints).
        Spec. medium voice (f1–f2); 0:45; Allegretto; delicate; light; pretty.

An Irish Love Song, Schmidt c1895; also incl. *LF (1)*.
   Pub. three keys (high, c1–g2), a man's text; 1:45; Andantino; a lovely, strophic Irish ballad; Lang's most popular song.

Lament, S. Galler (1535); incl. *10 Songs* (Recital Pub. Reprint).
   Rec. medium voices (d1–d2); 2:00; Andante con espressione; in French; plaintive.

Night, Louise Chandler Mouton; incl. *10 Songs* (Recital Pub. Reprint).
   Rec. higher voices (d#1–g2); 2:30; Con moto; lyrical and sustained over undulating triplets; a warm, rather big song.

Nonsense Rhymes and Pictures, Edward Lear; Recital Pub. Reprint c1985.
   Rec. any voice (g–c3), this extreme range only applies to the final song; a range of timings from 0:30 to 1:30 each; 12 delightful settings, each accompanied by a little drawing and each beginning "There once was a...," best to select a smaller group; despite the sameness of meter, each song gets a totally original treatment; full of delightful surprises; clever, witty, and fun.

Also of interest:

In the Twilight, Bowman, incl. *10 Songs,* Andantino con moto, hushed and unvarying but rather magical; ***Song in the Songless,*** Meredith, Andante, an unusual mournful song.

BIBLIOGRAPHY
AmerGroves, Ammer, Baker, Greene, Hughes, Thompson.

---

[1] Lang also wrote orchestral pieces but most of her work was devoted to choral music and songs.

BENJAMIN LEES
b. Jan. 8, 1924, Harbin, Manchuria

A highly regarded composer of instrumental music, Benjamin Lees has also written three compelling sets of songs.

   Born to Russian parents (with the last name, Lysniansky), Lees was a baby when the family immigrated to San Francisco (moving to Los Angeles in 1940). Through the naturalization of his parents he became an American citizen in 1931. A serious student of the piano, after serving in the U.S. Army (1942–1945), Lees decided on a career in music. Working his way through UCLA, he studied with Ingolf Dahl, Richard Donovan, and Halsey Stevens; then spent four more years studying privately with George Antheil. In 1954, with the help of fellowships and awards, Lees went to Europe, where he studied and composed, living for various periods in Finland, Paris, Vienna, and Genoa. Returning to America in 1961, he taught at Peabody Conservatory, Manhattan School, Queens College, and the Juilliard School. In 1948 Lees married Leatrice Banks and they have a daughter.

THE SONGS

Lees has written three colorful, imaginative, evocative sets of songs entirely (with the exception of a single William Blake poem) to the poetry of Richard Nickson, for whose magical nature imagery Lees seems ideally suited. These are beautiful, even romantic songs, and they can be rewarding for the right voice type. But be forewarned, for despite the rich expressivity, the vocal writing often seems to have been instrumentally conceived. Over a dizzying array of atmospheric piano figurations, sustained vocal lines, mainly comprised of long tones moving conjunctly in a very specific tessitura, fill the pages. Though Lees does not use key signatures, he works within a traditional, primarily tonal framework. Changing meters and some rhythmic irregularities present the only real musical difficulties. Despite the technical challenges of the vocal writing, these songs, presumably the only ones that have been published, are strongly recommended.

Cyprian Songs, Richard Nickson; Boosey c1960.
    Spec. baritone, in bass clef (A–f#1); 10:00; titles are: *From what green Island; Wake! for the night of shadows; Still is it as it was; Over me like soft clouds;* all are in moderate or slow tempos, but with such good movement and variety of accompanimental figures that they easily sustain interest; much legato singing; some dramatic moments but generally lyrical, subdued, and dreamy; a beautiful love cycle for the quieter part of a program.

Songs of the Night, Richard Nickson; Boosey c1958.
    Rec. high lyric voices (f1–bb2), best for tenors; 11:00; titles are: *O Shade of Evening; A Star Fell in Flames; The Enemies; A Whisper of Rain; Fall to the Night Wind; On Eastern Hills;* high tessitura in many of the songs; some difficult approaches to high notes; dramatic, declamatory, and recitative-like passages but also much sustained

singing; tempo markings are all on the moderate side, but (as with
Cyprian Songs) these diverse nocturnal images are set with such a
variety of descriptive accompaniments there is no sense of sameness;
the cycle opens with a lyric love song, and closes hailing the approach of day with a climactic ending; an effective work for voices
comfortable with the technical challenges.

Three Songs; Boosey c1968; first perf. by Maureen Forrester.
   Spec. contralto (f–f2); three very different songs concerning
youth, love, and the passage of time; an excellent set, but songs could
be used individually; once again, despite the similarity in tempo
markings, each song has a totally separate and very definite kind of
motion; some difficult, very low, sustained tones.
   The moonlit tree, Richard Nickson; (g#–c2); 3:00; Adagio; evocative, sustained.
   Close all the doors, Richard Nickson; (g–e2); 2:15; Moderato; similar to W. H. Auden's wonderful *Stop All the Clocks;* intense and
sustained over a taut, rhythmic accompaniment; interesting
dynamics; dramatic and effective.
   The Angel, William Blake; (f–f2); 3:00; Andante con moto with
tempo and textural changes; a variety of vocal styles; an unusual,
dramatic song.

BIBLIOGRAPHY[1]
AmerGroves, Baker, Ewen, Greene, Thompson.

---

[1] Four major articles (1959, 1963, 1964, and 1975) on Lees appear in *Tempo*
magazine, but they are all highly analytical assessments of instrumental
works, and do not discuss either his life or his vocal writing.

SVEN LEKBERG
b. Aug. 7, 1899, Chicago, IL; d. Jan. 11, 1984, Indianola, IA

The son of a Swedish lithographer, Sven Lekberg graduated from
Northwestern University, then studied piano with Alfred Cortot, and
composition with Vincent D'Indy and Paul Dukas in Paris. He also stud-
ied at the Eastman School of Music (composition with Howard Hanson),
Columbia University, Union Theological Seminary, and Illinois
Wesleyan University. Though Lekberg did some performing as a pianist,

for 25 years he taught composition and piano at Simpson College in Indianola, Iowa, where his wife, a singer, was also on the faculty.

Best known for his choral music, Lekberg's special affinity for the voice is also heard in his few published songs. These lyrical, conventional pieces are warmly expressive, and make wonderful vehicles for bigger voices that can soar over the lavish accompaniments. For Lekberg, such a singer was the full-throated soprano Carol Stuart, to whom he dedicates several songs. High notes are not always easily approached, and stamina is imperative. Lekberg's few published songs are: *Birds Singing at Dusk* (incl. in *CAS), A Ballad of Trees and the Master*, and four settings of Edna St. Vincent Millay. Originally issued individually, all four Millay were recently reprinted in *RAAS*. Of these, *The Spring and the Fall* (recorded by Cynthia Haymon on Argo CD 436 117-2ZH) and *The Road to Avrillé* are notable.

BIBLIOGRAPHY
Information for this entry was provided by the Department of Music at Simpson College.

CHARLES MARTIN LOEFFLER
b. Jan. 30, 1861, Mulhouse, Alsace;[1] d. May 19, 1935, Medfield, MA

Recent scholarship has stimulated new interest in Charles Loeffler, who many thought to be a mystic, and whose bold, imaginative music both fascinated and bewildered Americans in the early twentieth century.

Loeffler was the son of German parents. His father, once imprisoned by the Prussian government for political reasons, was an agricultural scientist, who also wrote poetry and novels under a pseudonym.[2] When Loeffler was still a boy, he studied violin in Russia, where his family lived before moving to Hungary. Later he studied composition with Ernest Guiraud in Paris, and violin with the great Joseph Joachim in Berlin. In 1881 Loeffler went to America to pursue a career as a violinist, and in 1887 he became an American citizen. For 20 years he was assistant concertmaster of the Boston Symphony Orchestra, which later premiered many of his works, and a local favorite as violin soloist. Retiring from the orchestra in 1903, Loeffler spent two years in Paris, then returned to his farm in Medfield, Massachusetts, where he lived a reclusive life devoted to teaching, composing, and raising thoroughbred horses. In 1910 he married Elise Fay Burnett.

THE SONGS

Influences from his diverse cosmopolitan background (Slavic, German, and especially French), a fascination with the metaphysical world, and intense personal introspection make up Loeffler's confusing musical profile. If his songs are uneven and a bit desultory, the best are poetic, imaginative, and at times, quite striking and beautiful. In the three sets that fall within the guidelines of this book[3] one finds him drawn to a variety of occult subjects by French, British, and American poets—most particularly, the Symbolists. Expansive and opulent, with dense textures, sensual, exotic harmonies, brilliant colors, and sweeping motion, critics of the time differed as to whether they were ultra-modern or just decadent.

Loeffler was not afraid to take risks or to make extravagant demands on his performers. Though singers will luxuriate in the melodic and lush vocal writing, they must be full-throated to be heard over the elaborate accompaniments, which can be musically complex and technically formidable. An excellent recording by mezzo-soprano D'Anna Fortunato features Loeffler's songs on Northeastern (NR 207). The *Five Irish Fantasies* are recorded in their orchestral version by Neil Rosenshein on New World CD (332-2). The gorgeous settings for voice, piano, and viola (Op. 5) do not meet the guidelines of this book, but should be considered by all plummy voices who are fortunate in having a violist on hand.[4] The following list is comprised of Loeffler's most important published songs.

Five Irish Fantasies,[5] G. Schirmer c1934 (piano version).[6]
    Rec. high voices (d1–b2); 28:00;[7] titles are: *The Host of the Air; The Hosting of the Sidhe; The Fiddler of Dooney; Ballad of the Foxhunter; Caitilin ni Uallachain.* Though Loeffler provided a piano version, everything about these songs, in particular the last two, suggest the orchestral version would be preferable. Considerable range, weight, stamina, and in the last two, high tessitura, are required of the singer; the virtuosic, descriptive, rhapsodic accompaniments are every bit as important and challenging as the vocal writing; recorded in their entirety by Rosenshein with orchestra, and the first three— with the first two in the original 1908 version—by Fortunato with piano.

Four Songs, Op. 15; G. Schirmer c1906; also Recital Pub. Reprint.
    Spec. medium voice (c1–f2); best for men; 10:00; though there is a cohesion to the style (not so flagrantly French as Op. 10), there is no need to keep these songs together; comfortable vocal writing.

Sudden Light, Dante Gabriel Rossetti; (d♭1–e2); 2:30; Adagio; quietly; a final very light and fast section; mystical; quite effective.

A Dream Within a Dream, Edgar Allen Poe; (c1–e2); 3:00; Andante moderato; subdued with animation in the central section.

To Helen, Edgar Allen Poe; (d♭1–f2); 2:00; Andante, un poco allegretto; a relaxed, conversational vocal line over flowing accompaniment; a lovely song, the best of the set.

Sonnet, G. C. Lodge; (d♭1–f2); 2:30; Andante; the weakest of the four.

Quatre Mélodies, Op. 10, Gustave Kahn; G. Schirmer c1903; also Recital Pub. Reprint and Masters Music.

Spec. medium voices (b♭–f2); no need to keep these atmospheric, heavily French, songs as a set.

Timbres oubliés (Forgotten Sounds), (a♭1[c♭1]–e♭2); 4:00; Andante; flowing.

Les soirs d'automn (Autumn Evenings), (b♭–d#2); 4:00; Andante; quiet with animated sections; recorded by Fortunato.

Adieu pour jamais (Farewell Forever), also incl. *50AS;* (b♭–f2); 3:45; Moderato; a gentle melody over a flowing accompaniment; recorded by Fortunato.

Les Paons (The Peacocks), also incl. *50AS;* (d1–f2); 4:30; Lento; somewhat declamatory; glissando-like figures depict the peacock displaying his plumage.

The Wind Among the Reeds, see *Five Irish Fantasies* and footnote 6.

BIBLIOGRAPHY

AmerGroves, Baker, Ewen, Greene, Friedberg (I), Howard, Thompson, Upton.

Engel, Carl. "Charles Martin Loeffler," *Musical Quarterly* 11 (July 1925): 311–329.

Knight, Ellen. "Charles Martin Loeffler." Liner Notes, *Charles Martin Loeffler: Songs* (Northeastern NR 207).

---

[1] There is a question as to whether Loeffler was born in Schoneberg near Berlin or, as he claimed, in Mulhouse, which was then the French province of Alsace.

[2] The pseudonym was "Tornow." Charles Loeffler later used it as a middle name.

[3] Other works for solo voice include additional instruments.

[4] In addition to the *Quatre Poèmes,* Op. 5, published by Schirmer in 1905, one should consider *Selected Songs with Chamber Accompaniment,* ed. by Ellen Knight. (Recent Researches in American Music, XVI) Madison: A-R Editions, Inc., 1988. This volume contains ten previously unpublished songs.

[5] William Butler Yeats is the poet for all texts except *Caitilin ni Uallachain,* which is a translation from the Gaelic of William Heffernan.

[6] The first two of these five songs were originally issued in 1908 as *The Wind Among the Reeds,* which is the title of the William Butler Yeats volume from which the poems are drawn. In 1920 Loeffler revised and orchestrated these two songs, added three more (which John McCormack performed), and changed the title to *Five Irish Fantasies.* The piano version was not created until 1934.

[7] Timing is based on the recording with orchestra. A piano version would naturally be shorter.

OTTO LUENING
b. June 15, 1900, Milwaukee, WI

Of German ancestry, Luening studied music abroad, primarily in Zurich, Switzerland, where his compositional efforts were encouraged by Busoni. Returning to the United States in 1920, he composed, conducted, performed as a flutist, and taught (primarily at Bennington College and Columbia University). A moving force in promoting contemporary American music, he helped found the American Composers Alliance, the American Music Center, and Composers Recordings Incorporated. In 1927 he married soprano Ethel Codd. Divorced in 1956, he later married Catherine Brunson, a musicologist and teacher.

Luening's huge reputation for his pioneer work in the field of electronic music has overshadowed his work in other idioms, including song. Though they play but a tiny part in his mammoth catalogue, Luening wrote songs at various times in his life. During the years of his marriage to Ethel Luening, he unleashed a small deluge, which he and his wife performed. Their lyricism and conventionality will surprise those who only know his more experimental music.

Despite their numbers, Luening's songs are hard to find. Several are available from the American Composers Alliance. Of these, *Ah! Sunflower* and *Sun of the Sleepless* have nice feeling, but most are sketchy, inconsistent, and generally disappointing. In his autobiography, Luening credits Highgate Press with having published the majority of his songs, but at the author's request, E. C. Schirmer, distributor for

Highgate, could only produce a few in archive reprint. The best of these are the lyrical *Nine Songs to Poems of Emily Dickinson,* several of which would make a nice contribution to a Dickinson group. Two Walt Whitman settings, the odd, jaunty *A Farm Picture* (also incl. *AAS*) and the lovely *Here the Frailest,* were published by Associated. From *Three Songs* for high voice, published by G. Schirmer, *Gliding o'er all* (Whitman) is fleeting, but effective. Two Blake settings, the hymnlike *Divine Image* and folklike *Love's Image,* are published by Marks and recorded by Mildred Miller on Desto (411/412).

BIBLIOGRAPHY
AmerGroves, Baker, Ewen, Greene, Thompson.
Luening, Otto. *The Odyssey of an American Composer: The Autobiography of Otto Luening.* New York: Charles Scribner's Sons, 1980.

EDWARD MACDOWELL
b.Dec. 18, 1860, New York, NY; d. Jan. 23, 1908, New York, NY

Edward MacDowell was America's first internationally recognized composer, though in hindsight his brief career seems somewhat overrated. His catalogue favors small forms, but his songs are neither as distinctive nor as technically sound as the moody descriptive piano pieces for which he is justly renowned. All the same, a small handful rank among the best of his day.

His parents were cultured, well-off Quakers, who encouraged their son in all his artistic endeavors. MacDowell began piano lessons at age eight and, at 16, his mother took him to Paris for further study. Later he studied composition with Joachim Raff in Frankfurt, Germany. In Weimar, he performed his own piano concerto for Franz Liszt, who recommended him to the publishers Breitkopf and Härtel.

Married in 1884 to his young piano student from Connecticut, Marian Nevins, the couple lived in Frankfurt until their return to America in 1888. Settling in Boston, MacDowell taught and performed while his compositions were heard with increasing regularity on both sides of the Atlantic. In 1895 he bought a farm in Peterborough, New Hampshire, which, as the famed MacDowell Colony, would later fulfill its namesake's dream of a summer sanctuary for composers, writers, and artists to work surrounded by nature.[1] In 1896 Columbia University hired him as its first professor of music, but in 1904, after a dispute with the University, MacDowell resigned that position. From then on his health and mental state went into a rapid decline, and by the time of his death he was described as childlike and totally insane.

THE SONGS

Integrity, good taste, and poetic sensibility distinguish many of Mac-Dowell's 42 romantic, lightweight songs from the vast majority of American songs of the period. Others can be quaint or sentimental, but a greater problem arises from his insistence that in songwriting text takes precedence over all else.[2] And, as he was never comfortable with the idea that other people's poems be turned into music, his solution for achieving perfect unity was to write the poem himself. Carrying these concerns to extreme, MacDowell's style became pedantic and inhibited, lacking the depth or evocative powers of his famous piano pieces.

Lyric voices are generally best for spinning the delicate melodies and ensuring that the words are kept clear and unweighted.[3] Piano writing, in keeping with his avowal that "accompaniment should be merely a background for the words,"[4] is spare and unobtrusive with few solo passages. Though experts speak well of late songs in which MacDowell was searching for his personal voice, this author finds them flawed and self-conscious, preferring many of the earlier, more imitative ones in the 'genteel' tradition. These, if kept to a carefully chosen few, can be a bonus on a song recital.

For the best general selection one should obtain *Edward MacDowell: Songs (EMS),* a reprinting of his best known opuses—40, 47, 56, 58, and 60—by Da Capo Press (New York, 1972) with an introduction by H. Wiley Hitchcock. Opus 56 is also published by Masters Music. *Six Selected Songs,* Schmidt c1912 (low and high voice with some changes between the two) includes *To a Wild Rose* (an adaptation of the ever popular piano piece) and other songs not found in the Da Capo album. There are recordings by Alma Gluck on New World (247), John Hanks on Duke, Vol. 1 (DWR 6417), Alexandra Hunt on Orion (ORS 77272), and John McCollum on Desto (411/412). Also, three attractive, early German settings (Op. 33) are recorded by Yolanda Marcoulescou on Orion (OC 685), and five (Op. 11 and 12) by Thomas Hampson on Teledec CD (9031-72168-2). The following list includes MacDowell's best known songs as well as the author's personal recommendations. Virtually all are available in *EMS* (see above). With the exception of Opus 56, most were published in one key only.

As the Gloaming Shadows Creep, Op. 56, No. 4, Edward MacDowell; Jung c1898; also incl. *EMS.*

Pub. high and low voices (low, c1–eb2); 2:00; tenderly; sustained; recorded by Hunt under the title *Fra Nightingale.*

Long Ago, Op. 56, No. 1, Edward MacDowell; Jung c1898; also incl. *EMS.*

Pub. high and low (low, bb–eb2); 1:30; Simply, with pathos; folk-like, arching, sustained melody; a sentimental favorite; recorded by Gluck and Hanks.

Midsummer Lullaby, Op. 47, No. 2, after Goethe; Breitkopf c1893; also incl. *EMS.*

Rec. medium and lower lyric voices (e1–c#2); 1:30; Dreamily; a simple, lilting melody over pulsing chords; recorded by Hunt.

The Sea, Op. 47, No. 7, William Dean Howells; Breitkopf c1893; also incl. *EMS.*

Rec. medium voices (d1–d2); 2:00; Broadly, with rhythmic swing; a quietly dramatic song of the aftermath of a shipwreck; descriptive; unusual; one of MacDowell's best; recorded by Hanks and McCollum.

Thy beaming eyes, Op. 40, No. 3, W. H. Gardner; Schmidt c1890; also incl. *EMS.*

Rec. lyric or heavier voices (c1–f2); 1:30; With sentiment, passionately; very sustained; recorded by Hanks.

Tyrant Love, Op. 60, No 1; Edward MacDowell; Schmidt c1902; also incl. *EMS* and *AASTC.*

Rec. higher lyric voices (d1–g2); 1:15; Lightly, yet with tenderness; the delicate opening and close frame a more impassioned outpouring; a charming song.

Also of interest:

Fair Springtide, MacDowell, also incl. *EMS,* Very slow, with pathos; **Folksong,** Howells, also incl. *EMS,* Slowly and simply, with pathos, recorded by Hunt; **In the Woods,** after Goethe, also incl. *EMS,* Moderately, lightly; **A Maid Sings Light,** MacDowell, also incl. *EMS,* Brightly, archly, recorded by Gluck; **O Lovely Rose,** Gardner, also incl. *EMS,* Slowly, with great simplicity; **The Swan Bent Low to the Lily,** MacDowell, also incl. *EMS,* With much feeling, recorded by Hunt; **To a Wild Rose,** Hagedorn, incl. *Six Selected Songs,* an arrangement of the enduring piano piece of the same name, recorded by Hunt; **The West**

Wind Croons in the Cedar Trees, MacDowell, also incl. *EMS,* Not fast, with much character.

BIBLIOGRAPHY

AmerGroves, Baker, Ewen, Friedberg (I), Greene, Hall, Nathan, Thompson, Thorpe (on *The Sea),* Upton.

Finck, Henry T. "MacDowell's Songs and Piano Pieces," *The Musician* (March 1906).

Gilman, Lawrence. *Edward MacDowell: A Study.* 1908. Reprint. New York: Da Capo Press, 1969.

MacDowell, Edward. *Critical and Historical Essays.* Boston: Arthur P. Schmidt, 1912.

Porte, John F. *Edward MacDowell.* London: Kegan Paul, Trench, Trubner and Co., 1922.

Summerville, Suzanne. "The Songs of Edward MacDowell," *NATS Bulletin* 35 (March/April, 1979): 36–40.

---

[1] The MacDowell Colony was officially founded in 1907. It was faithfully run by MacDowell's widow until her death in 1956, but is still a favorite retreat for artists today.

[2] These beliefs were originally voiced in a 1904 interview in *Etude,* but are reprinted in both books by Lawrence Gilman. See bibliography.

[3] For these same reasons, MacDowell provides endless breath marks, a practice more confusing than it is helpful.

[4] This quote from an *Etude* interview is cited in Gilman, *Edward MacDowell: A Study,* 163.

MANA-ZUCCA[1]

b. Dec. 25, 1887,[2] New York, NY; d. March 8, 1981, Miami Beach, FL

Mana-Zucca was a pianist, singer, and composer of some of the most popular songs of her era. Born (Gisella) Augusta Zuckermann, she was a child prodigy, who impressed her piano teacher, Alexander Lambert, with her own compositions. She spent several years in Europe, where she studied, concertized as a pianist, and did some professional singing. Returning to the United States in 1915, she performed, began to publish her compositions, and effected her name change. For over a decade she was the darling of audiences and the media. Marrying Irwin M. Cassel in 1921, the couple eventually settled in Miami.[3]

As a composer, Mana-Zucca built an enormous catalogue in all idioms, including opera. It was, however, her songs that brought her the greatest renown. These zesty numbers, melodious and rhythmically infectious, were performed regularly by top classical artists and still show up on light programs or as encores. Whether charming trifles *(The Big Brown Bear)* or deeply felt espousals of life for full-bodied voices *(I Love Life* and *There's Joy in My Heart),* despite their old-fashioned sentimentality, they somehow maintain integrity and good taste. Maryanne Talese has recorded *Nichavo,* one of several popular Hebraic settings, and *I Love Life* on Premier (002). The latter is also recorded by John Charles Thomas on Nimbus CD (7838).

BIBLIOGRAPHY
AmerGroves, Baker, Howard, Thompson.
Ross, Claire. "The Voice of Youth," *Musical Courier,* Jan. 24, 1918.

---

[1] The use of a hyphen in the name varies from source to source. Periodicals of the time refer to her as Miss Zucca, but as virtually all reference works include the hyphen and list her alphabetically under 'M,' the author has reluctantly chosen to follow suit.
[2] The date of Mana-Zucca's birth has also been given as 1885, 1891, and 1894. The author chose the year given by the most recent source: Baker (Eighth Edition).
[3] Dade County declared 1979 Mana-Zucca Year in appreciation of her musical services to the community.

KATHLEEN LOCKHART MANNING
b. Oct. 24, 1890, Hollywood, CA; d. March 20, 1951, Los Angeles, CA

A singer, pianist, and composer, Kathleen Manning studied piano with Moritz Moszkowski in Paris. She made her operatic debut at Covent Garden and then performed with the Hammerstein Opera Company in London for the 1911–12 season. Although she did some concertizing on her return to the United States, most of her life was spent with her husband, a telephone company executive, in the Los Angeles area, where she composed operas, symphonic poems, piano pieces, and countless pretty songs. Often set to her own deft poetry, her quaint song cycles time and time again evoked foreign places. The best known of these was *Sketches of Paris,* which includes the lovely *In the Luxemburg Gardens.* But there were also *Sketches of London, Sketches of New York, Songs of Egypt,*

Chinese Impressions, and *Japanese Ghost Songs.* The delicate, charming *Shoes,* included in *NAAS* and recorded by Nancy Tatum on London (OS 26053), was also very popular. Far too sentimental for today's audiences, Manning's songs are, nevertheless, colorful and skillfully crafted.

BIBLIOGRAPHY
Baker, Thompson, Upton (Sup).
Obituary, *Musical Courier,* April 15, 1951.

DONALD MARTINO
b. May 16, 1931, Plainfield, NJ

Donald Martino first aspired to be a clarinetist, and playing the instrument in jazz concerts has been a source of both recreation and income at various times in his life. But while at Syracuse University, he studied composition with Ernst Bacon, who strongly encouraged him in that direction. At Princeton University, Martino did graduate work with Roger Sessions and Milton Babbitt. Then, on a Fulbright scholarship, he studied with Luigi Dallapiccola in Florence. Martino has lectured and taught at Princeton, Yale, and Harvard universities. And, from 1970 to 1980, he was chairman of the composition department at the New England Conservatory. Since then he has been a full professor of music at Brandeis University. In 1979, to circumvent the problems of the publishing world, he founded Dantalian, Inc., where he copies, publishes, and promotes his own music. Martino has won many awards, including the 1981 Pulitzer Prize for a chamber work, *Notturno.*

THE SONGS
Martino's songs fall into two contrasting categories. The first, written while still at Syracuse, are in a conventional idiom. The second, written only a few years later, reflect his studies with mathematically oriented teachers and strongly evoke the Second Viennese School. Though the former are only moderately difficult, the latter are rhythmically complex and incur the usual pitch difficulties inherent in twelve-tone writing. In common with all are invention, lyricism, and strong personality. Otherwise, the songs of the two periods might have been written by different composers. All four sets are in print.

From "The Bad Child's Book of Beasts," Hilaire Belloc; Dantalian c1978; comp. 1952.

Spec. high voice (c1–a2); 4:30; titles are: *The Lion, the Tiger; The Frog; The Microbe;* various vocal styles; some high tessitura in the second song; not as conventional as they first appear, but these colorful, witty songs make a winning set.

Separate Songs, Dantalian c1978; comp. 1951.
Spec. high voice (c1–a2[c3]); 4:30; these early songs can be programmed as a pair or (as the title states) separately; not in any key; both are lyrical, melancholy, atmospheric; good songs.
All day I hear the noise of waters, James Joyce; (c1–g2); 1:30; Adagio, tranquillo; broad, arching melodic line over fluid arpeggios.
The half-moon westers low, my love, A. E. Housman; (d1–a2[c3]); 3:00; Moderato; straightforward and ballad-like, but difficult with a long sustained high A and complex cross rhythms over ostinato piano figures.

Three Songs, James Joyce; Ione c1970; comp. 1955.[1]
Spec. soprano or tenor (b♭–b♭2), or bass (F#–f#1); some texts suggest men; 6:00; titles are: *Alone; Tutto è Sciolto* (in English); *A Memory of the Players in a Mirror at Midnight;* atonal; rhythmically complex, especially in matters of ensemble; frequently changing dynamics; often fragmented; disjunct with melismatic passages; some whispering; independent piano writing; the first two songs are more contemplative with moments of passion; the last is intense and ends dramatically; extremely difficult; performers must be both technically and musically advanced, as well as proficient in the contemporary idiom.

Two Rilke Songs, Ione c1970; comp. 1961.
Spec. mezzo-soprano (f–a2); 4:00; titles are: *Die Laute* (The Lute); *Aus einer Sturmnacht VIII* (On a Stormy Night VIII); atonal; rhythmically complex; many dynamic and tempo fluctuations; disjunct with some very wide intervals; declamatory (some sprechstimme) with cantabile passages; performers must be advanced.

BIBLIOGRAPHY
AmerGroves, Baker, Ewen, Greene, Manning (on *Three Songs*).
Scanlan, Roger. "Spotlight on Contemporary American Composers: Donald Martino," *NATS Bulletin* 36 (May/June 1980).
Tassel, Janet. "Donald Martino at Sixty," *Musical America* (May 1991).

Various authors. "A Tribute to Donald Martino," *Perspectives of New Music* 29 (Summer 1991): 212–503. This tribute includes a conversation with Martino and an analysis of his song *Alone.*

---

[1] A revised version (1961) for bass voice is also published by Ione.

DOUGLAS MOORE
b. Aug. 10, 1893, Cutchogue, NY; d. July 25, 1969, Greenport, NY

Douglas Moore is best known for his operas on American themes. His family had roots on Long Island going back over 250 years; his father was publisher of the magazine *Ladies World,* and his mother, a descendant of Miles Standish and John Alden, was an editor. At Yale University, Moore studied with Horatio Parker and wrote some light songs. After serving in the Navy during World War I, he remained in Paris to study with Vincent D'Indy.[1] Later, he studied with Ernest Bloch in Cleveland and then, back in Paris, with Nadia Boulanger. In 1926 Moore joined the music faculty at Columbia University and, from 1940 until his retirement in 1962, headed the department. He also wrote two books on music.[2] Though his opera *Giants in the Earth* won a Pulitzer Prize in 1951, his greatest triumph was *The Ballad of Baby Doe,* which premiered in 1956.[3] Moore was married in 1920, and had two daughters. He lived most of his life on Long Island.

THE SONGS
A friend to many poets, including Archibald MacLeish, Vachel Lindsay, and Stephen Vincent Benét, Moore had an affinity for setting words to music. His small catalogue of songs is uneven, but the best of them— like his operas—are tuneful and candid. Though not difficult musically, they often require bigger voices. The following are recommended.

Adam Was My Grandfather, Stephen Vincent Benét; Galaxy c1938.
> Spec. medium voices (c1–f#2), best for men; 2:00; Allegro moderato; rhythmically spirited; good variety in the treatment of the four stanzas; jaunty; like an American folk ballad.

Old Song, Theodore Roethke; Fischer c1950; also incl. *CSE.*
> Spec. medium voice (c1–f2); 2:30; Andante; a wistful, sustained melody over quietly moving piano figures; like a folk ballad.

Under the Greenwood Tree, William Shakespeare; Fischer c1950; also incl. *CSE.*

   Pub. high voice (f1–a2);[4] 2:00; Andantino; lyrical and lilting over a fluid piano part; an especially romantic, appealing setting of this famous poem.

Also of interest:

Come Away Death, Shakespeare, for bass-baritones, unaccompanied, recorded by Gramm on Desto (411/412);[5] *Three Sonnets by John Donne,* also incl. *RAAS,* for big high voices, dramatic, weighty, melodically pedestrian, *Death, Be Not Proud* has been recorded by Eleanor Steber on Desto (411/412).

BIBLIOGRAPHY
AmerGroves, Baker, Ewen, Friedberg (I), Goss, Greene, Thompson.
Hardee, Lewis J. Jr. "The Published Songs of Douglas Moore," *NATS Bulletin* 29 (May/June 1973).

---

[1] During the war, Moore met John Jacob Niles and they collaborated on a humorous collection *Songs My Mother Never Taught Me.*
[2] *Listening to Music* (1932), and *From Madrigal to Modern Music* (1942).
[3] *The Devil and Daniel Webster, The Wings of the Dove,* and *Carrie Nation* were other successful operas.
[4] Available in a low key (*CSE* for low voice).
[5] The author has been unable to locate this song, but according to the Desto recording, it was published by Mills Music.

MARY CARR MOORE
b. Aug. 6, 1873, Memphis, TN; d. Jan. 9, 1957, Inglewood, CA

Raised on the West Coast, Mary Carr Moore studied voice with Henry Bickford Pasmore and composition with John Haraden Pratt in San Francisco. Later she settled in the Los Angeles area, where she became a respected figure of the musical community. Her career was thwarted by her distance from East Coast musical centers as well as by prevailing Victorian notions about artists, especially women. Nevertheless, despite these obstacles and others in her personal life (loss of family finances, two divorces, raising children as a single parent, and serious illness), music was her livelihood. Moore performed as a singer, taught singing, and produced a sizable catalogue of compositions in a variety of idioms.

With her mother as librettist, her opera, *Narcissa,* was produced several times on the West Coast and gave her national recognition.

Though some of Moore's approximately 250 songs are of the parlor variety, most are serious, lyric works. Their forthright, thoughtful expression and their beautifully sculpted vocal lines explain much of their appeal. The majority remain in manuscript, but quite a few, such as the exuberant *May,* the vigorous *Call of the Sea,* and the very popular *Lullabye,* were published individually and are well worth tracking down in libraries. A recent recording with soprano Evelyn De La Rosa and tenor David Rudat on Cambria (C 1022) offers an impressive selection. Da Capo Press is preparing a collection of Moore's songs, which will include those heard on the recording.

BIBLIOGRAPHY

AmerGroves, Ammer, Baker, Thompson.

Smith, Catherine Parsons and Cynthia S. Richardson. *Mary Carr Moore: American Composer.* Ann Arbor: The University of Michigan Press, 1987. This carefully researched, thoughtful biography provides a vivid picture of the artist struggling to make a livelihood in an, as yet, undeveloped area of the United States. It also provides a full listing of Moore's works.

_____"Mary Carr Moore and the American Music Movement," *American Music Teacher* 38 (February/March 1989).

CHARLES NAGINSKI

b. May 29, 1909, Cairo, Egypt; d. Aug. 4, 1940, Lenox, MA

Charles Naginski's brief career produced a small handful of striking songs.[1]

Naginski came to America as a child with his Russian father (who taught him piano) and his Greek mother. He studied with Rubin Goldmark on a fellowship from the Juilliard School of Music, graduating in 1933. He also worked with Roger Sessions and, in 1938, won a fellowship to the American Academy in Rome. On the threshold of what appeared to be a promising career, Naginski, attending the Berkshire Music Center at Tanglewood as a composition student of Paul Hindemith, drowned in the nearby lake.

THE SONGS

Whether a comical narrative in Italian dialect or a haunting evocation by Walt Whitman, Naginski had a remarkable ability to capture and convey the essence of a poem. Every one of his seven published songs is distinctive, fresh, and full of personality. All are eminently singable but tend to be best for medium and lower range voices. An excellent pianist himself, Naginski's accompaniments are especially colorful. Despite the wide variety of subject matter, an effective group could easily be put together. The following is believed to be a complete listing of his published songs. All are warmly recommended.

Look Down, Fair Moon, Walt Whitman; G. Schirmer c1942.

Pub. medium voice (d1–e2); 2:30; Lento; an eerie piano introduction and postlude frame a haunting exhortation asking the moon to light the ghastly faces of the dead soldiers; an intense, moving song.

Mia Carlotta, T. A. Daly; G. Schirmer c1940.

Pub. medium voice (d1–e2); 1:30; Allegretto; a patter narrative about "Giuseppi, da barber," who "gotta da seely young girls...but notta Carlotta"; easy, charming, and fun.

Night Song at Amalfi, Sara Teasdale; G. Schirmer c1942.

Pub. medium voice (d1–e2); 1:30; Lento; lightly declaimed over a few spare chords; hushed; poignant.

The Pasture, Robert Frost; G. Schirmer c1940; also incl. *S22A;* to Mme. Povla Frijsh.

Pub. medium voices (b♭–e♭2); 1:15; Comodo; some low singing; a cheerful, jaunty figure in the piano carries this simple, charming song.

Richard Cory, Edward Arlington Robinson; G. Schirmer c1940; to Mme. Povla Frijsh.

Pub. low or medium voices (a–e2[g2]); 1:30; Allegretto, very slick; a quasi parlando, much of which sits low; Robinson's startling portrait is eloquently depicted.

The Ship Starting, Walt Whitman; G. Schirmer c1942.

Rec. medium and low voices (b♭–c2); 1:15; Moderato; over huge waves of sweeping piano figurations, the voice recalls the thrill of the ship as it gathers momentum for its voyage; breathtaking; different.

Under the Harvest Moon, Carl Sandburg; G. Schirmer c1940.

Pub. medium voice (d1–e2); 2:00; Moderato; an improvisatory piano with many evocative figurations; poignant, reflective vocalism.

BIBLIOGRAPHY
Baker, Friedberg (II), Greene, Thompson.

---

[1] In addition to the songs, Naginski wrote two symphonies, a ballet suite, and other instrumental music.

WILLIAM HAROLD NEIDLINGER
b. July 20, 1863, Brooklyn, NY; d. Dec. 5, 1924, East Orange, NJ

A composition student of Dudley Buck, W. H. Neidlinger was also an organist and conductor of choral groups. In 1896 he left for Europe, where he continued his studies while teaching voice in Paris and London. Returning to the United States in 1901, he settled in Chicago. With the success of his *Small Songs for Small Singers,* a collection used in kindergartens, he became interested in child psychology and subsequently founded and ran the Neidlinger School for the Unusual Child in East Orange, New Jersey. In addition to his songs for children, Neidlinger also wrote Christmas pieces, in particular the popular *Birthday of a King,* two comic operas, a successful cantata, and a large catalogue of solo songs. Though generally too simplistic for today's audiences, such songs as the charming *My Laddie,* the romantic *Crossing the Bar,* and his best known song, the lovely *Serenade,* are straightforward, tuneful, and refreshingly unaffected. *Memories of Lincoln,* a long song set to selections from Walt Whitman's *Leaves of Grass,* is impressive for its depth of feeling and controlled drama. Classical Vocal Reprints has a large collection of Neidlinger.

BIBLIOGRAPHY
Hughes, Thompson.

ETHELBERT NEVIN
b. Nov. 25, 1862, Edgeworth, PA; d. Feb. 17, 1901, New Haven, CT

One of the most popular of the turn-of-the-century American composers, Ethelbert Nevin[1] won the public's fancy with his charming piano and vocal miniatures.

The son of musical parents of Scotch and Irish descent, Nevin was born at "Vineacre," his family's estate near Pittsburgh. He studied music in Boston and subsequently in Germany, then for several years maintained a busy career as a pianist, teacher, and composer. In 1887 he married his childhood sweetheart with whom he had two children. For a while the family lived abroad, mostly in Italy, where they hoped the milder climate would improve Nevin's poor health, but in 1897 they returned to live in New York. In 1900 they settled in New Haven. The following year Nevin's untimely death from a stroke stunned the nation.

Nevin's large catalogue of songs, several of which were best sellers, are considered his most important contribution. One cannot help but appreciate the lilting lyricism of *A Nightingale's Song, 'Twas April,* or the little cycle, *Un Giorno in Venezia,* but in great part due to the old-fashioned lyrics, most are untenable by today's standards. However, even into the 1920s, well known concert artists included them on their programs, while the beloved contralto Elizabeth Schumann-Heink single-handedly made a classical "hit" of *The Rosary.* The public's passion for this one song—attributable as much to its maudlin message as to the music—has, in fact, obfuscated better examples of Nevin's work.

Paul Sperry has recorded five songs, including the popular *Oh! That We Two Were Maying* and the arrangement for voice of the alluring *Narcissus* [2] on Albany CD (TR0Y034–2). These and others are included in *SIA* and *AASTC. Ethelbert Nevin: 26 Favorite Compositions for Voice and Piano,* Schirmer c1943, has long been out of print, but there are two reprint editions from Recital Publications. One, the *Album of Nine Songs* (for low voice) is primarily comprised of Nevin's early, skillful, but imitative French and German songs. The other, *Song Album Two,* which includes *The Rosary* and the lovely *At Twilight,* is generally more representative of Nevin's quaint idiom.

BIBLIOGRAHY
AmerGroves, Baker, Greene, Hall, Howard, Nathan, Thompson, Upton.
Howard, John Tasker. *Ethelbert Nevin.* New York: Thomas Y. Crowell Company, 1935. Preferable to the sentimental Thompson biography, Howard also includes a full listing of Nevin's works and a comprehensive bibliography.
Thompson, Vance. *The Life of Ethelbert Nevin.* Boston, Mass.: The Boston Music Co., 1913.

---

[1] Not to be confused with Arthur (a brother), George (a cousin) or Gordon (a nephew)—all Nevins, all composers.

[2] Nevin often got extra mileage from his more successful melodies by arranging them for a variety of instrumentation or other voices. For example, the cover to *Narcissus* lists 20 other available arrangements of the piece, including mandolin, cornet, two different saxophones, and even piano 6-hands. Originally, *Narcissus* (the piece that made him instantly famous) was part of his piano cycle, *Water Scenes* (1891).

JOHN JACOB NILES
b. April 28, 1892, Louisville, KY; d. March 1, 1980, Lexington, KY

John Jacob Niles is so well known as an arranger and performer of folk music, few realize his classical training and considerable contribution to art song.

Born into a musical family, his mother, a church organist, taught Niles theory and keyboard. Subsequently, he studied at the Cincinnati Conservatory of Music, the University of Lyons, and the Schola Cantorum in Paris. His varied career included teaching positions at the Curtis Institute and Juilliard School. He was also an accomplished poet and, in 1920, even made an operatic debut singing in Massenet's *Manon* with the Cincinnati Opera. But mostly he arranged folksongs (especially those of the Southern Appalachia) and sang them in concert, accompanying himself with dulcimers and lutes. Niles lived most of his life on a farm outside Lexington, Kentucky. In 1936 he married Rena Lipetz, a writer, with whom he had two sons.

THE SONGS
Niles is best known for his adaptations, arrangements, and original folk ballads and carols. The latter, though classically composed, so perfectly evoke the folk idiom that they are often mistakenly considered to be in the public domain. It is, in fact, the unusual combination of traditional sounding melody and full compositional treatment that is the Niles hallmark. And it has made his beautiful songs a refreshing change of pace on both popular and classical concert stages. But Niles also left a number of original *art* songs. Some, especially the sophisticated Merton settings, show virtually no folk overtones, and can be difficult musically and technically. Others, often to Niles's own poetry, are more balladlike and tuneful, but can surprise with expansive vocal lines that rise to lusty

high notes. Late in his life, Niles met a fine lyric soprano, Jacqueline Roberts, who performed many of these songs and, under his supervision, made several tapes.[1] Listening to them, it is clear he encouraged a fairly free performance style, employing enough rubato to create an almost improvisatory quality.

Originally, most songs were published individually, and many of the best known are still available in that form. However, there are also two albums from G. Schirmer, each titled *The Songs of John Jacob Niles (SJJN)*. Issued in one key only and with emphasis on the folk ballads and arrangements, they are identical (even with the same preface by Niles) except that the 1990 edition contains eight songs not included in the 1975 edition. As these new songs are all excellent, the more recent album is especially recommended. Three of the Merton settings have been recorded (transposed) by William Parker on New World (305); four of the colorful *Gambling Songs* (adapted by Niles) by Mack Harrell on Remington (199-140).[2] The following recommendations are taken from Niles's output of art songs and have little or no folk orientation. (The songs in folk ballad tradition are generally outside the guidelines of this book, but because they represent the best of Niles and are so focal to his catalogue, the most famous are listed under *Also of interest*.)

The Blue Madonna, John Jacob Niles (suggested by a Medieval Spanish Folk Tale); G. Schirmer c1948; also incl. *RAAS;* for Gladys Swarthout.
  Rec. high lyric voices (g1–b♭2); 1:30; In the stately manner of the Pavanne; the nativity story in three short stanza, each followed by a Tra la la refrain in the more rapid tempo of a Spanish Waltz; sustained final high B flat; evocative of Spain.

Calm Is the Night, John Jacob Niles; Schirmer c1956; also incl. *RAAS*.
  Rec. medium and lower voices (b–e2); 1:45; Tranquillo; the voice spins a haunting melody over undulating chords; strophic; hushed; a beautiful song.

Careless Love, John Jacob Niles; G. Schirmer c1955; also incl. *RAAS*.
  Pub. high and low (high, d1–a2); 3:15; lilting; like a traditional ballad but with some operatic-like passages.

Evening, Thomas Merton, Op. 171; G. Schirmer c1972; also incl. *The Niles–Merton Songs* (Mark Foster) and *SJJN*.
  Rec. high voices (d1–a2); 2:45; quietly flowing; lyrical declamation with some high phrases; based on the call of the whippoorwill,

which is heard in the first measure and repeated throughout; recorded by Parker.

The Lotus Bloom, Anonymous adaptation from the Chinese; G. Schirmer c1952; also incl. *SJJN.*
Rec. high voices (f1–b♭2); 2:00; Slowly, with resignation; big, sustained vocal lines, that often ascend to long high notes; spare chords; desolate, yet emotional.

Merton Songs, Op. 171 and 172; Foster c1981.
Rec. high voices (b–b♭2); not all are original poems of Merton but rather his translations of other poets; expansive, operatic in scope, vocally and interpretively demanding; too often long syllabic lines meander; of the 22 songs, the following are recommended.
Evening, see separate entry.
For My Brother: Reported Missing in Action, 1943, Op. 172, No. 5; (c1–g2); 4:45; Adagio; a big song ending with a funeral march; recorded by Parker.
Love Winter When the Plant Says Nothing, Op. 171, No. 9; (d1–g2); 1:45; lyrical.
The Weathercock of the Cathedral of Quito, Op. 171, No. 6; (e1–a2); 2:30; Marcato - very deliberately; alternately buoyant and lyrical.

Reward, John Jacob Niles; G. Schirmer c1963; also incl. *RAAS.*
Rec. higher voices (e♭1–g2); 2:15; Tenderly and with feeling; flowing; shifting meters; ends big; a warm, lyric, love song.

The Silent Stars, John Jacob Niles; Fischer c1948; to Gladys Swarthout.
Spec. medium voices (e1–e2); 2:30; Allegretto; strophic, employing a variety of accompanimental figures; a lovely folklike melody set to a Christmas text.

Also of interest:

(Most of the following give the impression of being folksongs but are, in fact, original Niles. Those based on already existing fragments of melody, such as *I Wonder as I Wander* are not included. All appear in both editions of *SJJN.* The eight new titles included in *SJJN* [1990] are also recommended.) ***The Black Dress,*** text adapted by Niles, Andante con moto; ***Black Is the Color of My True Love's Hair,***[3] text adapted by Niles, With great tenderness; ***Carol of the Birds,*** Niles, In graceful, pastoral style; ***Go 'way from My Window,*** text adapted by Niles; Andante con moto; *The Lass from the Low Countree,* text adapted by Niles, Andante espressivo; *Sweet little boy Jesus,* Niles, Very Gently; *What Songs Were Sung,* Niles, a Christmas text, Tenderly.

BIBLIOGRAPHY

AmerGroves, Baker, CBY (1959), Greene, Howard, Thompson.
Coppage, Noel. "John Jacob Niles," *Stereo Review* (January 1975).
Johnson, Helen Shea. "John Jacob Niles: The Minstrel of Boone Creek," *Musical Journal* (January/February 1980): 13–18.

---

[1] These tapes were provided by the special collections and archives of the University of Kentucky Libraries in Lexington, Kentucky.

[2] Niles himself has recorded assorted American folk and gambling songs on Camden (CAL 219). His singing was high and thin, with pure intonation and exemplary enunciation.

[3] See Preface to *Songs of John Jacob Niles* (Schirmer) for Niles's explanation that this famous tune did, in fact, originate with him.

PAUL NORDOFF[1]

b. June 4, 1909, Philadelphia, PA; d. Jan. 18, 1977, Herdecke, Germany

Paul Nordoff is mainly remembered for his pioneering work in music therapy, but his compositions, especially the large forms, once enjoyed a fine reputation. His lifelong affinity for song, however, was not so well known, and though he was prolific in that medium, only a few ever reached publication.

Born into a theatrical family, Nordoff exhibited musical gifts at an early age. At the Philadelphia Conservatory of Music he earned bachelor's and master's degrees in piano, then went to the Juilliard School, where his principal teachers were Olga Samaroff for piano[2] and Rubin Goldmark for composition. With a Bearns prize and the first of two Guggenheim fellowships, in 1933 Nordoff traveled to Europe, settling in Germany, where he composed and did some vocal accompanying. In 1938 he became head of the composition department at the Philadelphia Conservatory, resigning in 1942. In 1945 he took a teaching position at Michigan State College and, that same year, married eurythmist, Sabina Zay, with whom he had two sons and a daughter. In 1948 he joined the music faculty at Bard College. Although his recognition as a composer was steadily rising, during this time he became increasingly interested in the education of handicapped children, and in 1959 he resigned from

Bard to study the subject. In 1960 he received the degree of Bachelor of Musical Therapy from the Combs College of Music in Philadelphia. From this point on, he taught, wrote books, and composed music, all targeted to the concerns of handicapped children, especially the brain damaged and mentally retarded. He also founded the Nordoff Music Therapy Center at the Goldie Leight Hospital in London, and was working to develop a similar facility in West Germany when he died of cancer.

THE SONGS

Twelve songs published by Schott form the backbone of what is known of Nordoff's songs today, but dozens of others have never been published. According to Ruth Friedberg,[3] an English publishing firm has shown interest in a large number of Nordoff's settings of E. E. Cummings, but as Nordoff is a fairly obscure composer, it seems unlikely this project will ever materialize. The few songs that are available are of a perplexing variety. Ranging from the folk inspired to sophisticated settings of modern and Elizabethan poetry, some are abstract and dissonant, others romantic and consonant; some are just pretty. For the most part, however, they are finely wrought, beautifully proportioned, and thoughtful songs, all sharing Nordoff's uncommon refinement and poetic sensibility.

Although ranges are usually modest, vocal lines are so delicate and slender that lyric voices are generally more appropriate. Nordoff was a fine pianist, and his clean, independent piano writing, often with intricate solo passages, is often a prominent feature. All songs are currently out of print but, since they went through several printings, should be quite easy to find in libraries. Virtually all published songs are listed.[4]

Beautiful City, Associated c1948.
Spec. medium voice (d1–g2); 1:30; Moderato; a vigorous setting of the well-known spiritual; much rhythmic and dynamic interest; full ending.

Can Life Be a Blessing, John Dryden; Schott c1938.
Rec. high lyric voices (d1–g2); 1:45; Moderato; a sprightly parlando melody in a high tessitura over running triplets.

Dirge for the Nameless, Walter Prude;[5] Associated c1945.
Rec. medium and high weightier voices (b♭–g♭2); 2:15; Largo; one of the most difficult of Nordoff's songs; a ponderous vocal line; severe harmonies.

Elegy, Elinor Wylie; Schott c1938.
　　Rec. lyric voices (c1–f2); 1:00; Slowly; a hushed, unadorned, lovely miniature.

Embroidery for a Faithless Friend, Walter Prude; Associated c1945; also incl. *AAS.*
　　Spec. medium voice (c1–a2), rec. big high voices; 1:15; Allegro; disjunct over a bizarre waltz accompaniment; sustained high notes; a strange poem on the symbolism of colored yarns; uncharacteristically astringent and stark; recorded by Cynthia Haymon on Argo CD (436 117 2ZH).

Fair Annette's Song, Elinor Wylie; Schott c1938.
　　Rec. higher lyric voices (c1–f2); 0:30; Quickly; a charming, light song about the passing of the seasons.

Jour des Morts: Cimitière Montparnasse, Charlotte Mew; Schott c1938.
　　Rec. higher lyric voices (d#1–g#2); 1:15; Slowly; in English (despite title); a touching poem, set with warmth and simplicity; a lovely song.

Lacrima Christi, Marya Mannes; Mercury c1947; comp. 1932.
　　Rec. medium voices (c1–f2); 2:15; Very slowly; Christ's anguish on the cross; linear; sustained; austere; intense.

Music I Heard With You, Conrad Aiken; Schott c1938.
　　Rec. medium and high voices (d#1–f#2); 2:00; Slowly; warm, legato melodic line over a flowing accompaniment; much rubato and harmonic color.

Serenade, Kathleen Millay; Schott c1938.
　　Rec. higher lyric voices (c#1–f#2); 1:15; the waltzlike movement makes the serenade to the dead lover all the more poignant.

Song,[6] Anonymous; Schott c1938.
　　Rec. higher lyrical voices (db1–a2); 2:45; Andante; a lovely, plaintive melody; generally subdued.

Song of Innocence, William Blake; Fischer c1952; also incl. *SE.*
　　Rec. medium lyric voices (d1–f#2); 2:00; Allegro; lively; sparse; a poignant central section.

Tell Me, Thyrsis, John Dryden; Schott c1938.

Rec. higher voices (e1–g2); 1:15; Allegro; a straightforward tune over triplets.

There Shall Be More Joy, Ford Maddox Ford; Schott c1938.
Rec. lyric voices (c#1–f#2); 1:30; Allegro; a modest, graceful song despite elaborate piano writing.

This Is the Shape of the Leaf, Conrad Aiken; Schott c1937.
Rec. medium lyric voices (b–e2); 3:30; Slowly; several segments; undulating triplets; cross rhythms; in a lyrical parlando; delicate; hypnotic, even static, but with a haunting beauty.

Time, I Dare Thee to Discover, John Dryden; Schott c1938.
Rec. higher lyric voices (d#1–g2); 2:00; Adagio; tessitura on the high side; two poignant motifs; an affecting song.

White Nocturne, Conrad Aiken; Ditson c1942.
Pub. medium voice (e1–e2); 2:15; Andante; subdued over a spare piano; recorded by John Hanks on Duke, Vol. 1 (DWR 6417).

Willow River, Marjorie Allen Seifert; Schott c1938.
Rec. lyric voices (d1–g2); 2:15; Lazily; a rocking 6/8; balladlike, but with some sting.

BIBLIOGRAPHY

AmerGroves, Baker, Ewen, Friedberg (II), Greene, Nathan, Thompson.

---

[1] Born Paul Bookmeir, Olga Samaroff persuaded him to change his name. He chose Nordoff simply because he liked the sound of it.
[2] Samaroff was also Nordoff's teacher at the Philadelphia Conservatory.
[3] Ruth C. Friedberg, *American Art Song and American Poetry, Vol. II,* 183.
[4] The principal exception would be *Anthony's Song Book,* G. Schirmer c1950, a set of simple songs with texts by Nordoff, written for his son, Anthony, but of little interest to either adults or children.
[5] Walter Prude was married to Agnes de Mille, the dancer and choreographer for whom Nordoff wrote ballet scores.
[6] Text also known as *The Baily Beareth the Bell Away.*

RICHARD OWEN
b. Dec. 11, 1922, New York City, NY

As a child, Richard Owen, whose father was an opera-loving lawyer, studied piano and regularly attended the Metropolitan Opera. After graduating from Dartmouth College and Harvard Law School, Owen followed in his father's footsteps and entered the legal profession. Establishing himself in private practice, he later went into government service. But Owen had dabbled in music all his life, and while continuing with his law career, at age 29, he began to study piano again. A year later he attempted to write an opera for a competition, but realizing his lack of basic technical tools, decided to study composition. His teachers have included Vittorio Giannini and Robert Starer. His first opera was performed in 1956 by the local Bar Association. Four years later he married one of the singers from that production, a soprano from the Juilliard School, Lynn Rasmussen, who, as Lynn Owen, pursued a successful career of her own. Together they raised three sons and were active in the Maine Opera Association. Although Owen was appointed a federal judge in 1974, he has continued to compose.

THE SONGS

Owen's music is primarily vocal and includes several operas. Best known is the religious work, *A Fisherman Called Peter*. Though the subject matter and titles of his few published songs are philosophical and unusual, he makes conventional use of the modern idiom. Nicely crafted for the voice, his songs have a good feeling for the mood and drama of the texts. Two are recorded by baritone John Reardon on Serenus (1019). The following is believed to be a complete list of Owen's published songs.

I Saw a Man Pursuing the Horizon, Stephen Crane; General c1966.
    Rec. medium and higher voices (g1–g2); 0:30; Allegro; declamatory over a disjointed running accompaniment; philosophical; recorded by Reardon.

The Impulse, Robert Frost; General c1966.
    Rec. medium voices (e♭1–f2); 2:45; Andante, con moto; declamatory; quasi recitative in places; spare; a strange scene of a man's 'impulse' towards a woman who then disappears.

Patterns, Amy Lowell; General c1973; to my wife.
    Rec. medium women's voices (b♭–a2); 7:15; Andante; a monologue reflecting on life's patterns; mostly declamatory with some recitative; many sections, some quite intense; moderately difficult; slow getting started.

Till We Watch the Last Low Star, Witter Byner; General c1962; to Lynn.

Rec. most lyric voices (c1–g♭2); 0:45; Andante; lyrical, over moving eighths; a nice song.

There Were Many Who Went in Huddled Procession, Stephen Crane; General c1966.

Rec. any medium voice (c♭1–f#2); 2:00; Andante; declaimed philosophical text over dirge-like chords; a more active, lyrical central section; recorded by Reardon.

BIBLIOGRAPHY

Friedberg (III).

"Husband, Father, Attorney, Composer," *Music Journal*, 25 (April 1967).

Ross, Mary Bishop. "Richard Owen sits on two benches: judicial and piano," *Dartmouth Alumni News* (March 1983).

HORATIO PARKER

b. Sept. 15, 1863, Auburndale, MA; d. Dec. 18, 1919, Cedarhurst, NY

Though Horatio Parker is best known for his choral music, his numerous songs, at one time, also enjoyed some success.

Of British descent, his father was an architect; his mother an organist and writer. Though as a young child Parker disliked music, as a teenager he developed an insatiable appetite for it. He began by studying piano and theory with his mother, but soon commuted to Boston where his principal teacher was George Chadwick. In 1882 he went to Munich and studied for three years with Josef Rheinberger. Married in 1886 to a German piano student, the couple settled in New York City and raised three daughters. In 1893 the oratorio *Hora Novissima,* which remains Parker's most important work, brought him international fame. Though his opera *Mona* (1910) was judged a failure, it was only the third by an American to be produced by the Metropolitan Opera. In 1894 Parker became a professor of music at Yale University, and in 1904, Dean of the School of Music, a position he held until his death.[1]

THE SONGS

Although Parker's first compositions, written when he was 15, were songs (50 settings of nursery rhymes by Kate Greenaway), he does not seem comfortable with either the intimacy or lyricism of the genre.

Overly elaborate, with a tendency to ramble through endless modula-
tions and constantly changing textures, they lack cohesion. Lovely
moments—of which there are many—are undone by too many new
ideas. Pianists can generally enjoy the skillful and imaginative piano
writing, but singers must contend with haphazard shifts of tessitura,
graceless turns of phrases, and stilted prosody. The few songs that overcome these problems, however, are commendable examples of
Germany's training of and influence on the eager young Americans of
Parker's generation. Some recommendations follow.

The Lark Now Leaves His Watery Nest, from *Six Old English Songs,*
    Op. 47, No. 6, William Davenant; Church c1899.
        Pub. high and low (high, c1–b♭2); 2:00; Allegro; a bright melody
    with florid passages; a favorite in its time and still a delight; record-
    ed by Emilio de Gogorza on New World (247).

Love in May, Op. 51, No. 1, Ella Higginson; Church c1901.
        Rec. high voices (d♭1–g♭2[a♭2]); 1:30; Moderato; exuberant love
    song, recorded at top speed by Emma Eames on New World (247).

Night-fall, Martin Schütze; Boston c1914.
        Rec. high voices (d1–a♭2); 1:30; Moderato tranquillo molto; a sus-
    tained 4/4 vocal melody over flowing 10/8 accompaniment; a lovely,
    unusual song.

Seven Songs, Op. 70, Brian Hooker;[2] Church c1910; also a Recital Pub.
    Reprint; two songs are dedicated to George Hamlin.
        Pub. low and high voice; of the seven songs, the following are rec-
    ommended, though with some reservation.
    I shall come back, (high, d1–g2); 1:30; Con fuoco; impassioned.
    A Man's Song, (high, d1–f2), man's text; 1:30; Moderato; quiet; lyri-
        cal.
    Only a little while, (high, c1–g2); 2:15; Moderato; lyrical.
    A Robin's Song, (high, d1–a2), rec. light voices; 1:45; Allegro mod-
        erato; bright with some florid passages.

Six Old English Songs, Op. 47, various Elizabethan poets; Church
    c1899; also a Recital Pub. Reprint.
        An evocation of eighteenth-century style; each song is in two vers-
    es of varying size and difficulty; more cohesive than many of Parker's
    songs; notable among the six is *The Lark Now Leaves His Watery
    Nest* (see above entry).

Also of interest:

The Blackbird, Henley, also incl. *AASTC,* moderato; ***Lute-Song,***
Tennyson, also incl. *AASTC,* Rather slow.

BIBLIOGRAPHY

AmerGroves, Baker, Ewen, Greene, Hughes, Tawa, Thompson, Upton.

Kearns, William K. *Horatio Parker, 1863-1919: His Life, Music and
Ideas.* Metuchen, NJ & London: Scarecrow Press, 1990.

Semler, Isabel Parker.[3] *Horatio Parker: A Memoir for his Grandchildren
compiled from Letters and Papers.* New York: G.P. Putnam, 1942;
reprint, New York: Da Capo, 1973.

Smith, David Stanley. "A Study of Horatio Parker," *Musical Quarterly*
16 (April 1930): 153–169.

---

[1] Though many of his students, including Roger Sessions and Quincy Porter,
went on to successful careers, Parker is especially well known for having
been the only formal composition teacher of Charles Ives, whose radical
views seriously conflicted with Parker's own conservative instruction.

[2] Brian Hooker was a colleague of Parker at Yale and later the librettist for his
opera, *Mona.*

[3] His daughter.

THOMAS PASATIERI
b. Oct. 20, 1945, Flushing, NY

In the early 1970s Thomas Pasatieri became the darling of singers by
writing accessible, singable music in a romantic vein. Commissions for
his operas abounded and many recitals included a Pasatieri song.
Though his music generated as much negative criticism as accolades,
and though in recent years his output has noticeably slackened, like him
or not, he made a mark.

The son of second generation Sicilians with no trace of music in the
family tree, Pasatieri was, nevertheless, fascinated by music and theater
from an early age. He began studying piano at age seven and, within two
years, was playing publicly in New York City. He also took up conducting and involved himself in his school's theatrical productions. At
14, without any instruction, he began writing music, and a year later,
after hearing Nadia Boulanger give a lecture, he sent the great teacher
his compositions. Boulanger encouraged him, and for over a year, he
studied with her by means of a trans-Atlantic correspondence.

In 1961, on a scholarship from the Juilliard School, Pasatieri began formal studies under Vincent Persichetti and Vittorio Giannini. The vocally oriented Giannini opened Pasatieri's eyes to the world of opera, but insisted on careful theoretical study and the composition of several hundred songs before permitting his young protégé to attempt one. In 1965, as a student of Darius Milhaud at the Aspen Music School, Pasatieri won the Aspen Festival Prize with his one-act opera, *The Women*. A deluge of operas followed, including *The Trial of Mary Lincoln, The Black Widow,* and *The Seagull,* all of which were commissioned and given first-rate premieres. Pasatieri has taught at the Juilliard School, the Manhattan School, and the University of Cincinnati Conservatory of Music. He has also been Artistic Director of the Atlanta Opera and, more recently, the president of Topaz Productions, his own film production company.

THE SONGS

Pasatieri has been a friend to many singers, and some of the best American artists have premiered his works—Frederica Von Stade, John Reardon, Catherine Malfitano, to name a few. Clearly an opera singer's composer, he likes to fill his songs with grand gestures and lush vocalism. Unfortunately, the result is that they often wander aimlessly, swamped by an excess of notes, riddled with cliches, and crippled by an unwillingness to curb inflated emotions and suffocating seriousness. It is, therefore, primarily for their sincerity and naturalness that the author prefers Pasatieri's smaller, earlier, lighter songs, where his gift for writing smoothly flowing vocal lines and graceful prosody is more in evidence. Musically there are few problems in any of Pasatieri's songs. Rhythms are conventional and pitches, regularly doubled by the piano, are easily found in the predominantly tonal haze.

Though they were generally regarded as exercises, Pasatieri has estimated that he composed some 400 songs before the age of 18.[1] The majority—and the best—of his published songs, however, were composed in the 1970s. Only available in collections or as sets, these are primarily found in the following albums: *Pasatieri Songs Volume One (PS1)* and *Pasatieri Songs Volume Two (PS2),* both published by Belwin Mills, 1977 and 1980 respectively; and *Selected Songs: Thomas Pasatieri (SS)* from Southern. Though the author cannot recommend the three cycles and one collection that appeared in the late 1980s and early 1990s, as major works by a popular composer, they are listed under *Also of interest. Three Poems of James Agee* have been recorded by Theresa

Treadway on Orion (ORS 84476) and Sharon Mabray on Owl (28). The list that follows combines personal preferences with those that have been especially popular with singers.

The Kiss, Martin Dulman; incl. *PS1;* comp. 1976; to Catherine Malfitano.
Rec. high lyric voices (g1–ab2); 2:30; Adagio fluido e cantabile; many melismatic passages.

Overweight, Overwrought Over You, Shiela Nadler; incl. *PS2.*
Rec. lusty medium voices (bb–g2); 1:45; Allegro; a catchy melody which reprises several times; final florid cadenza; the title of this clever, hilarious poem by the mezzo-soprano Shiela Nadler tells it all; a genuinely funny song.

These Are the Days, Emily Dickinson; incl. *PS2;* comp. 1973.
Rec. medium and high lyric voices (db1–gb2); 2:15; Andante moderato; tender and lyrical with a few melismatic passages; a più mosso central section swells to a *ff* appassionato.

Three Poems of James Agee, Belwin-Mills c1974; to Shirley Verrett.
Rec. big mezzo or soprano voices (db1–a2); 7:30; titles are: *How Many Little Children; Lullaby* (the best of the three); *Sonnet;* definitely conceived as a cycle, these are three of Pasatieri's better romantic songs; not difficult musically; they begin simply and end dramatically; opulent piano writing; some good melodies, interesting ideas, and lush (if inflated) vocalism; recorded by Mabray and Treadway.

Three American Poems, Louis Phillips; incl. *SS;* comp. 1969.
Rec. medium and high lyric voices (c1–a2); 3:30; these three short songs, which need not be kept as a group, are a pleasure— light in texture, fresh, and natural.
Boundaries, to Robert Holton; (d1–e2); 1:00; Andantino; a light parlando melody contemplates "Which is you and which is me?"
Haiku, to Evelyn Lear; (db1–a2); 1:45; Adagio; più mosso sections; delicate.
Critic's Privilege, to Evelyn Mandac; (c1–f2); 0:45; Allegretto buffo; light and genuinely charming.

Two Shakespeare Songs, incl. *SS;* comp. 1965.
Rec. medium and higher voices; do not go well together.

Parting, (text from *Romeo and Juliet*); to my parents; (e1–f2); 1:15;
   Andante mosso; simple and delicate.

That Time of Year (Sonnet 13), to Jennie Tourel; (c#1–ab2); 2:15;
   Molto lento; not tonal; declaimed; accelerates and builds to a central *fff*; dramatic and strong; different from other Pasatieri.

Also of interest:

Day of Love, Van Cleave, G. Schirmer c1983, called a cycle, but in actuality, one continuous, long song, for high medium voice; *Sieben
Lehmannlieder,* Lotte Lehmann,[2] Presser c1991, in German, more restrained, but routine; *Three Coloratura Songs,* various poets, incl. *SS,*
long and ambitious, but different; *Three Sonnets from the Portugese,*
Elizabeth Barrett Browning, G. Schirmer c1984, for medium and higher voices, songs connect; *Windsongs,* various poets, G. Schirmer c1989;
a collection for soprano, one song includes viola.

BIBLIOGRAPHY
AmerGroves, Baker, Ewen, Greene.
Davis, Peter G. "They Love Him in Seattle." *New York Times Magazine,*
   March 21, 1976.
Pasatieri, Thomas, "The American Singer: Gold Mine for Composers,"
   Music Journal 32 (January 1974).
Scanlan, Roger. "Spotlight on American Composers: Thomas Pasatieri,"
   NATS Bulletin 31 (December 1974).
Sperber, Ann. "Let Me Entertain You," *Opera News,* March 4, 1972.

---

[1] Peter G. Davis. "They Love Him in Seattle," *New York Times Magazine,*
   March 21, 1976, 46.
[2] The great soprano Lotte Lehmann also painted, sculpted, and wrote poetry.

RONALD PERERA
b. Dec. 25, 1941, Boston, MA

Though many of Perera's works for solo voice use instruments, tape, or
orchestra, his two cycles for voice and piano make an impressive contribution to the contemporary repertoire.

   Perera received both his bachelor's and master's degrees from
Harvard University, where he studied with Leon Kirchner and three
times received the University's award for choral writing. He also studied
electronic music abroad with Gottfried Michael Koening. A recipient of

numerous grants and awards, Perera has co-authored a book on electronic music, and taught briefly at Syracuse University and Dartmouth College. Since 1971 he has lived with his wife and three children in Northampton, Massachussetts, where he teaches at Smith College.

THE SONGS

Perera's two published cycles, though composed but a few years apart, are very different from each other.[1] Yet neither reveals the composer's background in electronic music, and both demonstrate an expressive, sympathetic use of the voice, and colorful, evocative, often virtuosic piano writing. Both are highly recommended. Gretchen D'Armand has recorded *Apollo Circling* on Opus One (27).

Apollo Circling, on a poem by James Dickey;[2] E. C. Schirmer; comp. 1971/72.

  Spec. high voice (c1–c3); 14:30; titles are: *So Long; The Moon Comes; You Lean Back; You Hang Mysteriously;* although Perera describes these as "four lyric songs," there is considerable drama here; primarily declamatory; disjunct with many difficult high notes; technically, musically, and interpretively difficult; atonal, with tonal areas; stark and intense, with a cold, eerie opening and impassioned close; on the experience of the astronauts visit to the moon; an evocative, unusual, powerful contemporary cycle; recorded by D'Armand.

Five Summer Songs, Emily Dickinson; E. C. Schirmer c1976; comp. 1969/72.

  Rec. lyric medium voices (b–f#2); 12:00; titles are: *New Feet Within My Garden Go; South Winds Jostle Them; I Know a Place; To Make a Prairie; The One That Could Repeat the Summer Day;* best kept as a set; excellent variety of mood and color; atonal, but with a strong feeling of tonality throughout; gentle dissonances; not difficult for the voice, but the colorful piano writing is intricate and requires dexterity; elegant, lyrical, compelling songs.

BIBLIOGRAPHY

AmerGroves, Baker, Manning (on *Five Summer Songs*).

---

[1] A listing of his work shows that Perera has written several other works for voice and piano, which have not, as yet, been published.

[2] Taken from Dickey's commemorative poem *For the First Manned Moon Orbit*.

GEORGE PERLE
b. May 6, 1915, Bayonne, NJ

A student of Wesley LaViolette and Ernst Krenek, George Perle's early interest in serialism became a search for the tonality he believed inherent in the twelve-tone system. He has authored several books (including *Twelve-Tone Tonality)* and held numerous teaching positions.

Thirteen Dickinson Songs, Emily Dickinson; in three volumes, Gunmar c1981, c1983, c1984 respectively; comp. 1977-78; comm. for Bethany Beardslee by the National Endowment for the Arts.

Spec. sopranos (f#–c#3), rec. lyric voices; 36:00; though ideally heard in its entirety, because of its length and the demands it makes on both performers and listeners, programming either a single volume or a selection from the three might be wiser; primarily lyrical declamation over virtuosic, independent piano writing; difficult ensemble; singers require exceptional range and flexibility to cleanly and quickly negotiate the difficult intervals (for example, the extremes of range are exercised on the first page alone); some of the higher placed words are virtually impossible to enunciate, but clarity of delivery in every area is of prime importance; a few songs settle in certain tessituras (including some appropriate for mezzos), but these are the exception; atonal; the meticulously notated rhythmical complexities include cross rhythms, shifting and uneven meters, unmetered or unbarred sections, and a plethora of hairsplitting irregularities; emotions range from fanciful and wistful to melancholic and mystical, and Perle has given each volume a subtitle that captures its overall mood, with the final song of Vol. III designated *Closing Piece;* though only for the most advanced technicians and musicians, this is, nonetheless, an exceptionally poetical, expressive, and altogether moving set of songs; brilliantly recorded by Bethany Beardslee on CRI (403).

Vol. 1 (From a Childhood); (f#–c#3); 10:30; titles are: *Perhaps you'd like to buy a flower; I like to see it lap the miles; I know some lonely houses off the road; There came a wind like a bugle.*

Vol. II (Autumn Day); (a–b2); 11:30; titles are: *Beauty—be not caused—it is; The Wind—tapped like a tired man; These are the days when birds come back; The Hearts asks pleasure—first.*

Vol. III (Grave Hour); (g–c#3); 14:00; titles are: *What if I say I shall not wait; If I'm lost—now; The loneliness one dare not sound;*

Under the light, yet under; and *(Closing Piece) She bore it till the simple veins.*

BIBLIOGRAPHY
AmerGroves, Baker, Ewen, Greene, Thompson.

VINCENT PERSICHETTI
b. June 6, 1915, Philadelphia, PA; d. Aug. 14, 1987, Philadelphia, PA

Vincent Persichetti composed for practically every idiom but never aligned himself with any particular compositional school. Innate refinement and lyricism, however, are heard throughout his body of work and show particularly well in his elegant songs.

Persichetti was raised in the predominantly Italian neighborhood of South Philadelphia. Though neither his Italian father or German mother were musical, they recognized their eldest son's potential. At the age of five he began piano lessons, and then went on to study organ, double bass, theory, and composition (the last with William King Miller) at nearby Combs Conservatory. After graduating from Combs in 1936, Persichetti became the head of its composition department. Meanwhile, he continued piano studies with Olga Samaroff and composition— briefly and not too satisfactorily—with Paul Nordoff. From 1941 until 1961 Persichetti headed the Philadelphia Conservatory's theory and composition departments. In 1947 he also joined the faculty of the Juilliard School, commuting to New York until his retirement in 1987. In these same years he wrote regularly for a variety of publications, authored the highly regarded textbook *Twentieth-Century Harmony,* and was director of publications at Elkan-Vogel.

In 1941 Persichetti married Dorothea Flanagan, a fine pianist from Kansas, who promoted her husband's music, played in concerts with him, and became widely known as a teacher. Together, they raised two children and enjoyed what was, by all accounts, a virtually idyllic existence until his death from lung cancer.

THE SONGS
Persichetti, who tended to compose for one medium at a time, wrote most of his sensitive, lucid songs in the 1950s. Probably because they are a relatively small segment of his mammoth catalogue, they have received scarce attention, with the exception of the Dickinson settings,

which are popular in teaching circles. But Persichetti loved singing and poetry, and served them both without sacrificing his personal voice.[1]

Persichetti can as easily spin a conjunct line of limpid, melting beauty as he can construct one of taut angularity and wide intervals. In either case, he never presses the voice and his declamation is flawless, with every syllable weighted perfectly. Accompaniments are lean, using only the minimum of notes to evoke and define. Most move in or around a tonal area and are only mildly dissonant—*Harmonium* being the exception. Again excepting *Harmonium,* none of his songs are difficult for the singer or the pianist. Isolated recordings are noted with the song entries. The following is believed to be a complete listing of Persichetti's published songs.

Emily Dickinson Songs, Op. 77; Elkan-Vogel c1958; pub. separately.
> Rec. medium lyric voices (d♭1–f2); 5:15; though conceived as a set with a specific order, these little gems can be used individually; not difficult; slender vocal lines and spare accompaniments; tuneful; fresh and charming.
> **Out of the Morning,** (d1–e2); 1:15; Andante; a limpid melody over broken chords.
> **I'm Nobody,** (d1–e2); 1:00; Allegretto; a variety of rhythmic twists make this a favorite; conversational; light and lively.
> **When the Hills Do,** (d1–d2); 1:00; Slowly; short phrases; tender, spare.
> **The Grass,** (d♭1–f2); 2:00; Andante affettuoso; tuneful, flowing; recorded by Hanks on Duke Vol. 2 (DWR 7306).

Harmonium, Op. 50, Wallace Stevens; Elkan-Vogel c1959.
> Spec. soprano (c1–c3), singers should not be deterred by the high C, for most of the songs lie in a moderate range and tessitura, and all high notes are intelligently approached; 60:00; since a full performance is obviously impractical, despite the use of recurring themes and the designation "cycle," smaller groupings are strongly recommended and were approved by the composer;[2] titles are too many to list, but a few of the author's particular preferences are: *Lunar Paraphrase; The Wind Shifts; Six Significant Landscapes; In the Clear Season of Grapes; Tea; Infanta Maria; Domination of Black; and Of the Surface of Things.* This is evocative music in which the sympathetic, vivid writing for the voice is often offset by a cool, assertive piano. As with much of Persichetti's music, this creates a rather unusual sonority, which needs more than one hearing to assim-

ilate. Performers will quickly realize the greatest preparation time will go into ensemble. Despite its intellectual look, *Harmonium* is a deeply felt, moving, and, at times, breathtakingly beautiful work. It is also one of our most important cycles. John Hanks has recorded *The Death of a Soldier, The Snow Man,* and *Of the Surface of Things* on Duke, Vol. 2 (DWR 7306) and Mildred Miller has recorded *Sonatina to Hans Christian Andersen* on Desto (411/412).

Hilaire Belloc Songs, Op. 75; Elkan-Vogel c1965; pub. separately.

Rec. medium, lyric voices (c1–e2); 2:45; simple, spare, melodic, appealing.

Thou Child So Wise, also incl. *CAAS;* (c1–e♭2); 1:30; Slowly; sustained over delicate broken chords; quiet; recorded by Hanks, transposed up, on Duke Vol. 2 (DWR 7306).

The Microbe, (c1–e2); 1:15; Innocente; moves fleetingly; lightly humorous.

James Joyce Songs, Op. 74; Elkan-Vogel c1959; pub. separately.

Rec. medium voices (c1–f#2); 5:15; more densely textured and dissonant than the Dickinson or Belloc settings; a somber set.

Unquiet Heart, also incl *CAAS,* (d#1–f#2); 1:45; Doloroso; sustained over throbbing chords; restless.

Brigid's Water, (c1–d2); 1:30; Sostenuto; bell effects, like a dirge.

Noise of Waters, (c#1–e2); 2:00; Andante; sustained over a lamenting piano; uneasy; recorded by Myron Meyers on Musical Heritage (912016M).

A Net of Fireflies, Op. 115, various Japanese Haiku poets, trans. Harold Steward; Elkan-Vogel c1972; comp. 1970; comm. by Carolyn Reyer.

Rec. medium voices (c1–g2); 19:00; 17 settings of Haiku, approximately a minute each; recurring motifs clearly establish this work as a cycle, but a smaller group could be made and might be more effective; atonal; fragmented; nicely crafted but probably the least distinguished of Persichetti's songs.

Two Chinese Songs, Op. 29; traditional Chinese texts, trans. Arthur Waley; Elkan-Vogel c1979; comp. 1945.

Rec. low, lyric voices (a♭–d2); 1:15; titles are: *All Alone; These Days;* the first is slow and subdued, the second spirited; two tiny songs in which the piano is but a single line.

BIBLIOGRAPHY

AmerGroves, Baker, Ewen, Friedberg (III), Greene, Thompson.
Chrisafides, Peter. "Roxborough's Persichetti: Top Composer Prepares Debut of His 'Best Work'," *Philadelphia Sunday Bulletin,* April 12, 1970. This article gives an excellent overall picture of the man.
Patterson, Donald L. and Janet L. Patterson. *Vincent Persichetti: A Bio-Bibliography.* Westport, Connecticut: Greenwood Press, 1988.
Scanlan, Roger. "Spotlight on Contemporary American Composers: Vincent Persichetti," *NATS Bulletin* 34 (February 1978).

---

[1] Persichetti was especially well known for his choral music and occasionally wrote the words himself, anonymously.

[2] Author's telephone conversation with Persichetti (August, 1980).

DANIEL PINKHAM
b. June 25, 1923, Lynn, MA

Daniel Pinkham is highly regarded both as a composer and as a specialist in and performer of early music. Though he is best known for choral music, his sizable catalogue also contains a choice handful of sensitive art song.

Pinkham's great-grandmother was Lydia E. Pinkham—famed for her medical remedies—and his father was president of the company that bore her name. As a little boy Pinkham studied the piano and began to compose. While attending Phillips Academy in Andover, the pure, spare sounds of the singing and instruments he heard during a visit from the Trapp family[1] inspired an interest in early music. At Harvard University, where he earned his master's degree in 1944, he studied composition primarily with Walter Piston. Elsewhere, his teachers include Arthur Honegger, Nadia Boulanger, and Samuel Barber. Pinkham has been on the faculties of Harvard, Boston Conservatory, Simmons College, and since 1957, the New England Conservatory. Concurrently, he composed, conducted, and performed as a harpsichordist and organist.

THE SONGS
In the 1940s and early 1950s, Pinkam wrote some compelling songs, which he invested with his clear, sensitive personal voice, and filled with lovely, lyric melodies, beautifully turned phrases, and imaginative rhythms. Later, like Igor Stravinsky, whom he greatly admired, not wanting to repeat himself, he purposefully set out to solve new prob-

lems.[2] But in exploring more experimental compositional techniques, the fresh, graceful lyricism of the early songs was forfeited. By comparison, his more recent songs, generally to Biblical texts, seem stiff and uninspired. Most disappointing of all, they no longer sing.

A practical composer and an experienced performer himself, most Pinkham songs do not present many technical or musical difficulties.[3] With the text always rendered to be intelligible, vocal lines of the early songs flow easily and gracefully, usually within a very moderate range, often in the style of a lyrical, even tuneful, recitative. Later songs extend the range somewhat. Lines become more disjunct and tonal centers less evident, though Pinkham is always generous in providing the pitch somewhere in the accompaniment. In both compositional periods the piano writing is primarily accompanimental and rather spare. The many songs with instruments (including electronic tape) are not considered here. Recommendations, with emphasis on those appropriate for recital rather than church use, follow.

Elegy, Robert Hillyer; Ione c1964; comp. 1949; to Nell Tangeman.
   Spec. medium voice (b–e2); 1:30; Andante; the tessitura is low, but the vocal line is light and smooth; quiet and tender; a gem.

The Faucon, Anonymous; Row c1949; comp. 1945.
   Rec. high lyric voices (e♭1–a♭2); 2:15; Andante con moto, ma flessibile; a poignant modal melody; a refrain and four stanzas with variations; melismatic passages; a lovely setting of this haunting, mystical narration in Middle English.

Heaven-Haven (A Nun Takes the Veil), Gerard Manley Hopkins, with a second stanza *World-Welter* (A Nun Removes the Veil), Norma Farber; Ione c1983; comp. 1947.[4]
   Spec. medium voice (c#1–f2), rec. higher lyric voices; 2:15; Andante semplice; a sad, rocking melody.

The Hour Glass, Ben Jonson; Ione c1964; comp. 1956.
   Rec. higher lyric voices (c1–g2); 1:30; Andante, mesto; lyrical declamation over a spare accompaniment; subdued and reflective.

Music, Thou Soul of Heaven, Anonymous; Ione c1978; comp. 1953, rev. 1977; to Ned Rorem.
   Spec. medium voices (c1–g2); 1:15; Con moto; vocally warm and full; affirmative, even buoyant, but with a quiet ending.

A Partridge in a Pear Tree, Old English, Anonymous; Row c1948; comp. 1945.

Rec. high voices (d1–b♭2); 0:45; Allegro leggiero e scherzando; a solid middle voice is needed to cut the brassy, exuberant accompaniment; fun setting of the last verse of this famous Christmas song.

Sing Agreeably of Love, W. H. Auden; Row c1949; comp. 1948.

Rec. medium and higher lyric voices, (e1–e2); 2:15; In the manner of a folksong; lilting; tuneful; strophic, with a refrain; a good poem and an appealing song.

Slow, Slow Fresh Fount, Ben Jonson; Peters c1961; comp. 1949.

Pub. high, medium, low (high, f#1–g♭2); 2:15; Andantino; sustained; tessitura stays high; sad and subdued; recorded by John McCollum on Desto (411/412).

Stars I Have Seen Them Fall, A. E. Housman; Ione c1983; comp. 1946, rev. 1973.

Spec. medium voice (d1–f2); 1:30; Flexible; an introspective, musing, lyrical recitative; quite beautiful.

Also of interest:

Letters from Saint Paul, six Biblical texts, each of which is generally short and declamatory, for high voice; *Now the Trumpet Summons Us Again,* one line from the Inaugural Address of John F. Kennedy, high voice, long and declamatory; *Three Songs from Ecclesiastes,* for high voice, generally declamatory with lyrical passages.

BIBLIOGRAPHY

AmerGroves, Baker, Ewen, Greene, Thompson.

DeBoer, Kee and John B. Ahouse. *Daniel Pinkham: Bio-Bibliography.* Westport, Connecticut: Greenwood Press, 1988.

Scanlan, Roger. "Spotlight on Contemporary Composers," *NATS Bulletin* 33 (December 1976).

Smith, Warren Storey. "Daniel Pinkham," *American Composers Alliance Bulletin* 10 (1961): 9–15.

---

[1] The Austrian ensemble. Much later, the family was the subject of Rodgers and Hammerstein's *The Sound of Music.*

[2] See Pinkham's article, "New Problems Enlarge Horizons," *Music Journal* (April, 1965), for his philosophy about change.

[3] Warren Storey Smith points out that Pinkham's practicality includes composing only with the knowledge it will be performed.

[4] The Farber setting was added in 1975.

SAM RAPHLING
b. March 19, 1910, Fort Worth, TX; d. Jan. 8, 1988, New York, NY

Little has been written about this eclectic but highly individualistic composer, who produced a large catalogue in a variety of idioms. Raphling grew up in Chicago, where he studied piano and received a master's degree from the Chicago Musical College. As an exchange student, he went to Germany and studied with Artur Schnabel. On returning to Chicago, he was active for many years as a teacher, pianist, and composer. Later, he settled in New York, where he taught at the Greenwich House Music School.

THE SONGS
Raphling's several sets of songs are wildly uneven in quality and written in an assortment of styles. The earliest, dating from the 1950s, are rugged, folksy portraits of American characters, while later settings, from the 1970s, are lyrical, sophisticated, and imbued with an aura of atonality. Some work and some don't, but Raphling's idiosyncratic panache is common to them all.

Performers are advised not to look for anything pretty in Raphling's generally stark expression. With the notable exception of *Shadows in the Sun,* there is little opportunity to show off vocal riches. Ranges are always modest and tend to favor low voices. The better known songs, a few of which are recommended, are listed.

Poems by Carl Sandburg, Musicus c1952; pub. separately.[1]
    Rec. low voices (b♭–g2), several texts suggest men; 11:00; titles are: *Cool Tombs; Fog; Gone; Mag;* possibly the most unusual of all Raphling's unusual songs; folklike, almost primitive; square rhythms; considerable dissonance; declamatory over spare piano textures; of the four, the mysterious *Fog* and somber *Gone* are recommended.

Shadows in the Sun, Langston Hughes; General c1971.
    Rec. medium and high voices (c♭1–g♯2); 15:00; titles are: *Beggar Boy; Troubled Woman; Suicide's Note; Sick Room; Soledad (A Cuban Portrait); To the Dark Mercedes of "El Palacio de Amor"; Mexican Market Woman; After Many Springs; Young Bride; The Dream*

Keeper; Poem; should only be sung as a cycle. These are sad, tender, evocative, deeply felt portraits, which also retain Raphling's personal stamp. Unlike his other songs, however, dissonances are softened, and the vocal writing warm, pliable, and lyrical. Despite the use of key signatures, there is only an occasional feeling of tonality; moderately difficult; Raphling's best songs; warmly recommended.

Spoon River Anthology, Edgar Lee Masters; Musicus c1952; pub. separately.[2]

Rec. lower voices; more of Raphling's spartan declamation; could make a nice group or might be combined with some of the Sandburg settings.

Anne Rutledge, (b–f2); 4:15; Very slow; spare, quiet, declamatory; about Abraham Lincoln's early love, who died young; difficult to sustain dramatically, but affecting.

Lucinda Matlock, (b♭–a2); 2:45; Very moderately lively; many sections; an old woman's recounting of her tough but positive life; uneven and a bit rambling.

Penniwit, the Artist, (d1–a1[e2]); 1:30; Moderately lively (with humor); an amusing and well drawn portrait of a photographer at work.

Also of interest:

Animal Joker, Esar, ten little songs; **Fugue on "Money,"** Armour, incl. *CAS,* moderately lively, no fugue here, mildly humorous; **John James Audubon,** Benét, higher voices, somewhat lively; **New Songs on Four Romantic Poems,** various poets, disjunct, dissonant, difficult; **Shine, Great Sun,** Whitman, for baritones, Lively-agitated-brilliantly, **Washington Monument by Night,** Sandburg, moderately.

BIBLIOGRAPHY
Baker, Thompson.
Boyd, Mullen. Liner notes. "The Music of Sam Raphling - Vol. 1." Serenus 12061. This recording does not include any vocal music.
Obituary, "Sam Raphling Dies; Composer and Pianist," *New York Times,* January 14, 1988.

---

[1] Though two other titles appear on the cover of these songs, it seems they were never published.

[2] Though six songs are listed on the cover of the songs, only three seem to have been published.

GARDNER READ
b. Jan. 2, 1913, Evanston, IL

Overshadowed by his achievements in instrumental forms, Gardner Read's wonderful, atmospheric songs go virtually unnoticed.

His father, an insurance broker, loved music and his mother was a concert pianist, but Read did not begin to study music until he was 15. In 1932, after studies at Northwestern University, he entered the Eastman School of Music on scholarship, where his composition teachers included Howard Hanson and Bernard Rogers. Later he studied abroad with Ildebrando Pizzetti and Jean Sibelius, and at the Berkshire Music Center with Aaron Copland. After heading composition departments in several Midwestern schools, from 1948 until his retirement in 1978, Read was a professor at the School for the Arts at Boston University. A prolific composer and a winner of several awards, his orchestral works have received considerable acclaim. He has also authored many theoretical books on music. Married to Margaret Vail Payne, with whom he had one daughter, Read lives in the coastal town of Manchester, Massachusetts.

THE SONGS
With their gracious, comfortable melodic lines, Read's lovely, sensitively crafted, unpretentious songs should be a boon to singers looking for something fresh and unhackneyed. For the most part, he has set first-rate lyric poems by lesser known American poets, and interpreted them with sensibility, imagination, and an exceptional gift for evoking their mood. With the notable exceptions of his 1986 prize-winning *Nocturnal Visions* and his propensity for setting vocal lines over irregular accompanimental patterns, one encounters few technical or musical difficulties. The following is believed to be a complete listing of Read's published songs.

All Day I Hear, Op. 48, No. 2, James Joyce; Boosey c1950.
> Rec. bigger medium or lower voices (b–e2); 2:00; Flowingly, with liquid motion; mournful, sustained vocal lines over hushed, but sweeping, piano figurations; ends on a somber recitative passage; a beautiful evocation of the sea.

From a Lute of Jade, Op. 36, various Chinese poets (5th, 6th, and 7th centuries); Composers Press c1943.
> Spec. medium voices (c1–f#2); 6:00; titles are: *Tears; The River and the Leaf; Ode;* generally moderate tempos; sustained and lyrical

over a colorful piano score; big ending; moody and impressionistic; an effective small set.

It Is Pretty in the City, Op. 84, No.4, Elizabeth Coatsworth; Southern c1953.

Rec. medium or high lyric voices (b–g2); 1:30; Flowing, somewhat rubato; brief phrases; a lovely, delicate, ingenuous song.

Lullaby for a Man-Child, Op. 76, No. 1, Jean Starr Untermeyer; Galaxy c1957.

Spec. medium voice (c1–f2); 4:30; Slowly, with quiet feeling; a steady rocking; mournful, tender, and affecting; unusual.

Nocturnal Visions, Op. 145, various poets; Boosey c1989; comp. 1985; Winner of the 1986 NATS Art Song Composition Contest.

Spec. baritone, in bass clef (B–a1[g1]), rec. high baritone or tenor; 15:00; titles are: *Night of All Nights; The First Jasmines; I Hear an Army;* first two songs generally tonal; no sense of key in the last, especially chromatic song; long, expansive phrases for both performers; some beautiful cantabile in the first two songs and exciting dramatic writing in the last, but the tessitura is high; an accomplished pianist is needed and the ensemble abounds in complex cross-rhythms; altogether difficult, but if one can get past the challenges, an impressive romantic set.

Nocturne, Op. 48, No. 1, Frances Frost; Associated c1946; also incl. *AAS* and *RAAS.*

Rec. high and medium lyric voices (eb1–f2); 2:30; Slowly, with nostalgia; in an unusual 11/8 throughout; sustained over fluid accompaniment; a brief recitative central section; warm and evocative.

Piping Down the Valleys Wild, Op. 76, No. 3, William Blake; Galaxy c1950.

Spec. medium or low voices (d1–e2), also rec. high voices; 1:30; Lightly, with simplicity; a lilting, clean vocal line answers the piping figures in the piano; a delightful setting of this lovely poem.

The Unknown God, Op. 23, No. 2, George W. Russell; Associated c1946; also incl. *RAAS.*

Spec. medium voices (d1–e2); 1:30; Misterioso e poco lento; a warm vocal line over silvery piano figurations; becomes animated, but ends on a subdued tone; good mood and some lovely writing.

Also of interest:

At Bedtime, Beyers, Quietly, with gentle motion, a nice lullaby; *Lullaby for a Dark Hour,* Kreymborg, for lower voices, With a steady, relentless beat; *The Moon,* Davies, Moderato con moto; *Pierrot,* Teasdale; for high lyric voices, Grazioso; *When Moonlight Falls,* Conkling, for lower voices; Moderato; *A White Blossom,* Vail Read, incl. *CAS,* Tranquilly, sustained.

BIBLIOGRAPHY
AmerGroves, Baker, Ewen, Thompson.

PAUL REIF
b. March 23, 1910, Prague, Czechoslovakia; d. July 7, 1978, New York, NY

Versatile in both popular and classical music, Reif used such a dizzying variety of styles that his songs are difficult to categorize.

A child prodigy on the violin, Reif went on to study composition with Franz Schmidt and Richard Stöhr at the Vienna Academy, and with Richard Strauss. Teachers in conducting included Bruno Walter. In 1941 Reif immigrated to the United States, and in 1943 became a citizen. He joined the U.S Intelligence Corps and received a Croix de Guerre and a Purple Heart. While serving in North Africa he wrote *Dirty Gertie from Bizerte,* a song for the troops, which was introduced by Josephine Baker. In 1945 he returned to the United States and settled in Hollywood, where he established himself as an arranger.

THE SONGS
Reif's different compositional styles meet with varying degrees of success. The best songs, benefitting from the composer's theatrical flair, are apt to be clever, entertaining, spirited, and colorful. Less successful are those, usually on serious themes, which elicit an atonal, chromatic, and severely dissonant palette. With few exceptions, a Reif song requires both musical and technical proficiency. Vocal lines, which often favor a cruelly high tessitura, can be disjunct and pitches elusive. Piano parts, rife with dense, accidental-laden chords, can be extremely difficult. Performers may be called upon to employ contemporary techniques such as sprechstimme or special piano effects.

Other than the few pieces published by General in the late 1950s and early 1960s, the bulk—and the more assured, imaginative, and sophisticated—of Reif's vocal output was published by Seesaw in 1970 and 1971, in a manuscript which is quite difficult to read. John Reardon has recorded *Five Finger Exercises* on Serenus (SRE 1019).[1] Though there is much of interest in many of Reif's songs, many seem overdone and wearying. The following are recommended with confidence; those under *Also of interest,* with reservation.

Five Finger Exercises, T. S. Eliot; General c1957.

Rec. medium or high voices (b♭–g2, c3 in falsetto); 9:30; titles are: *Lines To A Persian Cat; Lines To A Yorkshire Terrier; Lines To A Duck In The Park; Lines to Ralph Hodgson, Esqre.; Lines For Cuscuscaraway And Mirza Murad Ali Beg;* designated a cycle; traditional keys and rhythms; though the first three are more sober reflections, the overall effect is fairly lightweight and humorous; recorded by Reardon, who improves the order by putting *Lines to Ralph Hodgson* first.

German for Americans, Paul Reif; Seesaw c1971.

Rec. high voices (c1–b2); 12:00; primarily in English with some simple German phrases; seven humorous vignettes about traveling in Germany, to be sung without interruption; Reif encourages the singer to do some acting out of the little scenes; of only moderate vocal or musical difficulty; familiar musical quotations; spoken dialogue; opens "Here we go - fasten your seat belt - no smoking - Germany, here I come" and closes "Call from overseas? - For me? Ich komme schon... I'm coming." Entertaining.

Richard Cory, E. A. Robinson; Seesaw c1971.

Rec. high voice, probably best for tenor (b–a2); 3:15; a variety of tempos but generally moves along; high tessitura; primarily lyrical; descriptive, difficult piano score; highly dissonant and chromatic; a wonderful narrative poem, effectively interpreted.

Also of interest:

The Circus, Koch, coloratura sopranos, nine songs, long and very difficult, the lighthearted humor of the opening turns black; **The Fishes and the Poet's Hands,** Yerby, high voices, a cycle of three songs to be sung without interruption, macabre revelations stemming from the death of Shelley, very difficult; **O You Whom I Often and Silently Come,** Whitman, high lyric voices, slow and sustained, dissonant, difficult. (All the above are available from Seesaw.)

BIBLIOGRAPHY
Baker, Greene.

---

[1] Reif's *Four Songs on Words of Kenneth Koch* also appears on Serenus (12022). Though liner notes give General as the publisher, General has told this author that it never published these songs.

WALLINGFORD RIEGGER
b. April 29, 1885, Albany, GA; d. April 2, 1961, New York, NY

Riegger, who spent most of his life in New York City, is best known for his compositions based on twelve-tone techniques. Unfortunately, he wrote few songs. Referring to *The Dying of the Light,* Hans Nathan wrote: "Riegger's artistic integrity confirms a standard of song writing that will eventually discourage its facile representatives."[1]

The Dying of the Light,[2] Dylan Thomas; Associated c1956; also incl. *AAS;* comm. by and ded. to the Juilliard School of Music.[3]

Rec. high voices with some weight (b–a2); 5:00; Slowly and with expression; many tempo changes; lyrical declamation, punctuated with dramatic passages; one spoken passage; some difficult intervals; generally linear, occasionally contrapuntal, piano writing; cluster chords; atonal; moderately difficult; an exhortation that man must rage against approaching death; evocative, intense, and profoundly moving.

BIBLIOGRAPHY
AmerGroves, Baker, Ewen, Greene, Nathan, Thompson.

---

[1] Hans Nathan, "United States of America," *A History of Song* (ed. Denis Stevens), 454.

[2] Thomas's title is *Do not go gentle into that good night.* Perhaps Thomas's most famous poem, it was written during his father's last illness.

[3] Riegger was a member of the Juilliard's first graduating class. At that time (1907), it was called the Institute of Musical Art.

VITTORIO RIETI
b. Jan. 28, 1898, Alexandria, Egypt

Though best known for his prodigious instrumental catalogue, it would be a mistake to overlook Rieti's colorful, distinctive songs.

Despite his chance birth in Egypt, his parents were from Italy, where Rieti grew up and was educated. While studying the piano, he considered a career in economics. Then, after serving in World War I, he settled in Rome for two years of study with Ottorino Respighi. His compositions caught the attention of Alfredo Casella, who became instrumental in promoting them. In the late 1920s Rieti often visited Paris, where his association with the great choreographers Balanchine and Diaghilev led him to compose ballet scores. With the outbreak of World War II, Rieti joined the exodus of European composers to the United States and, in 1944, became an American citizen. Rieti has taught at the Peabody Conservatory, Chicago Musical College, Queens College, and the New York College of Music. A widower, he retired from teaching but continued to compose, dividing his time between New York, Rome, and Paris.

THE SONGS
With neoclassicism as their primary influence, Rieti's beautifully proportioned songs are sparkling, crisp, light, and fluent. The generally happy, often humorous texts suggest brisk tempos, but even the slower or more serious songs have an intrinsic vitality. Reflecting his cosmopolitan life style with a set each in French and Italian, and three in English, Rieti easily absorbs the distinguishing characteristics of any language or poet, and renders each anew in a modern, but personal, idiom. Singers should have no trouble negotiating the active lines or communicating the words. Musically, Rieti's tonal songs with their spicy dissonances are tricky, but not problematic. Some unusual intervals, a plethora of accidentals, and frequent meter changes are about the extent of the difficulties for the singer. The colorful piano writing, on the other hand, can be fairly intricate.

Though a song here or there might be extracted for some other use, each set has such a distinctive personality it is probably kept intact. All are available from General, whose recording label (Serenus) has included several Rieti works in their catalogue. *Quattro Lyriche Italiane* is recorded by John Reardon on Serenus (12019) and *Quatres Poèmes de*

Max Jacob by Paul Sperry on Serenus (12078). The following is believed to be a complete listing of Rieti's published songs.

Five Elizabethan Songs, various poets; General c1968; comp. 1967.

Spec. medium-high lyric voices (a#[c]–a#2[g#2]), texts suggest men; 8:30; titles are: *Madrigal* (Anonymous); *Montanus' Sonnet* (Thomas Lodge); *Fain Would I Have a Pretty Thing* (Anonymous); *To His Lady, Of Her Doubtful Answer* (Thomas Howell); *Love Me Little, Love Me Long* (Anonymous); generally linear; a mix of declaimed and sustained vocal styles over generally fluid accompaniments; these crisp, neoclassical songs on light-hearted matters of love evoke the Elizabethan spirit; clever, elegant, delightful.

Four D. H. Lawrence Songs, General c1964; comp. 1960.

Rec. medium voices (d1–f#2), texts mostly suggest men; 6:15; titles are: *Aware; Thomas Earp;*[1]*December Night; Quite Forsaken;* generally serious songs about love; descriptive; an unusual small set.

Quatres Poèmes de Max Jacob, General c1975; comp. 1933.

Rec. medium lyric voices (b♭–g2); 7:00; in French, titles are: *La Crise; Le Noyer Fatal; Soir d'été; Monsieur le Duc;* metronome markings appear to be doubled throughout; French in feeling; employs the semi-popular style of certain members of Les Six; a charming, light, little set of excellent variety; recorded by Sperry.

Quattro Lyriche Italiane, various 15th- and 13th-century poets; General c1966; comp. 1945.

Rec. higher lyric voices (c#1–a♭2), texts suggest men; 9:15; in Italian (with English translations), titles are: *E Per Un Bel Cantar* (Because a Bird Was Sweetly Singing); *La Non Vuol Esser Più Mia* (She No Longer Will Be Mine); *E Lo Mio Cor S'Inclina* (To Thee My Heart Is Leaning); *Canti Ognun* (Let Us Sing); brisk tempos; light, fluent singing; active piano; bright songs in Rieti's customary neoclassical style, perfectly suited to the charming, archaic poems concerning men's problems with women; recorded by Reardon.

Two Songs Between Two Waltzes, W. B. Yeats; General c1964; comp. 1957; to Alice Esty.

Rec. medium voices (c1–f2), texts suggest men; 9:30; titles are: *The Fiddler of Dooney* (A Waltz); *When You Are Old* (A Barcarolle); *Maid Quiet* (A Madrigal); *Brown Penny* (Another Waltz); this little set must remain intact for the title to be valid; otherwise, there is no central theme; a mix of declamation and lyricism with an especially lovely cantabile barcarolle; colorful; different.

BIBLIOGRAPHY
AmerGroves, Baker, Greene, Thompson.
Ericson, Raymond. "No Memoirs from Rieti, " *New York Times,* January 14, 1973.

---

[1] T. W. Earp, the subject of this poem, was an art critic who had criticized Lawrence's paintings.

GEORGE ROCHBERG
b. July 5, 1918, Paterson, NJ

As one who abandoned a career built on serialism and then embraced tradition, Rochberg has met with both derision and praise. But in several of his song cycles avant-garde and conventional idioms coexist with considerable success.

The son of immigrants from the Ukraine, Rochberg grew up in Passaic, New Jersey, where he studied piano, took part in various jazz groups, and attempted some composing. In 1939 he graduated from Montclair State Teachers College and subsequently won a scholarship to the Mannes School of Music in New York, where he studied theory and composition with George Szell, Leopold Mannes, and Hans Weisse. Inducted into the army, Rochberg was wounded in Europe during World War II. On discharge, he studied at the Curtis Institute with Rosario Scalero and Gian Carlo Menotti. In 1949 he received a master's degree from the University of Pennsylvania, then studied in Rome with Luigi Dallapiccola, who urged him into twelve-tone composition. Returning to the United States in 1952, Rochberg taught at Curtis and became Director of Publications for the Theodore Presser Publishing Company. In 1960 he became chairman of the composition department of the University of Pennsylvania, resigning the chair in 1968, but continuing on the faculty. In 1941 Rochberg married Gene Rosenfeld and the couple had two children. But in 1964, the death of their son, Paul, due to a brain tumor, so shattered Rochberg that he ceased to compose. During this time, however, he realized his dissatisfaction with serialism, and when, two years later, he returned to composition, he began to search for simpler ways to express complicated things. In 1983 Rochberg resigned

from the University to devote himself to composition. The Rochbergs
live in Newtown Square, Pennsylvania.

THE SONGS

Rochberg's strong affinity for the mythical, fantastic, and spiritual, give
his songs a distinctive aura. He has found his texts primarily in poems
by his son or in spiritual writings, primarily those of eastern religions.
For the most part, his scores are spare and evocative, and as they often
give a sketchy or improvisatory impression, the listener barely realizes
their meticulous detail and exacting craftsmanship. *Songs of Solomon*
and *Seven Early Love Songs,* written before he became involved in serialism, are romantic and tonal; the remainder of his songs combine both
tonal and atonal characteristics. Rochberg's vocal writing is generally in
a natural, lyrical declamation, though some especially ambitious songs
call for avant-garde techniques and a wide selection of colorful vocal
timbres. Piano writing tends to be lean in texture but intricate in detail.
Musically, the scores can be complex, requiring long and careful study.
Sharon Mabry has recorded *Eleven Songs* on Owl (28) and Neva Pilgrim, with Rochberg at the piano, *Songs in Praise of Krishna* on CRI
(360). The following is believed to be a complete listing of Rochberg's
published songs.

Eleven Songs, Paul Rochberg; Presser c1973; comp. 1969.
    Spec. mezzo soprano (g#–b♭2), rec. higher voices; 21:00; titles
    are: *Sunrise, a morning sound; We are like the mayflies; I am baffled
    by this wall; Spectral butterfly; All my life; Le Sacre du Printemps;
    Black tulips; Nightbird berates; So late; Angel's wings (Ballad); How
    to explain (Ballad);* good diversity; possibly a smaller group could be
    made; difficult for both performers; atonal; often unmetered; many
    avant-garde effects; the singer must deal with quarter-tones, sprech-
    stimme, elongation of consonants, and singing into the piano; detailed
    written instructions as to timbre call for everything from a white,
    heady tone to a wide vibrato; piano effects include clusters, and play-
    ing inside the piano; colorful, pictorial, with a prevailing feeling of
    the mystical; recorded by Mabry.

Fantasies, Paul Rochberg; Presser c1975; comp. 1971.
    Rec. medium and higher voices (b♭–a♭2); 5:00; titles are: *The
    toadstools in a fairy ring; There were frog prints in the rime; The
    frogs hold court; Five chessman on a board;* good variety of mood
    and tempo; the pictorial piano part dominates this mini-cycle as it

describes the fantastical (both humorous and mysterious) little scenes; fragmented vocal part; a good primer in contemporary techniques.

Four Songs of Solomon, orig. pub. separately by G. Schirmer c1949; reissued 1975 under one cover, Presser c1949; also incl. *RAAS.*

Rec. high strong voices (c#1–b2[b♭2]), probably best for tenor; titles are: *Rise up, my love; Come, my beloved; Set me as a seal; Behold! Thou art fair;* high tessitura; tonal; largely chordal and loud; rhythmically driving; uncharacteristically opulent; the first two of these joyful love songs are quite nice, but taken as a whole, the set is pedantic and overwrought.

Songs in Praise of Krishna, texts are translations from the Bengali;[1] Presser c1981; written for and first performed by Neva Pilgrim in 1971.

Spec. soprano (a♭–b2); 33:00; 14 songs, which clearly must remain a cycle due to the intermingling of themes and the narrative thrust; the soprano takes on three characters: Radha (a beautiful girl), Krishna (the god), and an old woman (Krishna's messenger, sent to plead with Radha); chromatic; atonal; disjunct; styles range from free, unmetered quasi-recitative to metrically structured full-throated singing; deals with the anguish, ecstasy, sensuality, and spirituality of love; avant-garde techniques are not employed, but performers must be well schooled in the contemporary idiom; recorded by Pilgrim.

Songs of Inanna and Dumuzi, based on Ancient Sumerian texts; Presser c1983; comp. 1979.

Spec. contralto (g–g2), also suitable for mezzo-soprano; 25:00; two songs are entirely in Sumerian (a glossary of pronunciation is provided), the rest in English with occasional phrases in Sumerian; titles are: *sa lam-lam-ma* (Luxuriant Heart); *He blossoms, he abounds; She calls for the bed; he-tum-tum* (May he bring); *lu-bi-mu lu-bi-mu* (My lubi, my lubi); *May the Tigris and the Euphrates; Luxuriant Heart;* only a few notes dip below the staff; disjunct but often lyrical, even melodious; colorful piano score; some songs are rhythmically incisive and metrically strict, others are in a free *senza misura* style; atonal; much repetition of motifs; on the ecstatic love (occasionally overtly erotic) between Inanna, a Sumerian goddess of love, and Dumuzi, a shepherd god; singable and accessible but very long and repetitious.

2 Songs from Tableaux, Paul Rochberg; Presser c1971; comp. 1968.[2]

Rec. medium or high lyric voices (a♭–g#2); titles are: *Ballad* and *Night Piece;* special effects in piano; the voice is disjunct and requires a variety of timbres and contemporary techniques; fragmented, spare, and filigreed; evocative miniature sketches.

Also of interest:

Seven Early Love Songs, various poets, Presser c1992, for high voices, very old-fashioned and not recommended.

BIBLIOGRAPHY

AmerGroves, Baker, CBY (1981), Ewen, Greene, Manning (on *Songs in Praise of Krishna),* Thompson.

Dixon, Joan DeVee. *George Rochberg: A Bio-Bibliographic Guide to his Life and Works.* Stuyvesant, New York: Pendragon Press, 1991.

LaFave, Kenneth. "Odyssey to Opera," *Opera News* (July 1982).

Scanlan, Roger. "Spotlight on Contemporary American Composers: George Rochberg," *NATS Bulletin* 33 (October 1976).

---

[1] Taken from lyrics by Vaishnava poets of Bengal, written between the fourteenth and seventeenth centuries.

[2] Rochberg transcribed these two miniatures from the larger *Tableaux* (for soprano with instruments), a work which has been recorded by Jan DeGaetani.

CLARA KATHLEEN ROGERS
b. Jan. 14, 1844, Cheltenham, England; d. March 8, 1931, Boston, MA

Despite her English roots, Clara Rogers is considered to be an early and distinguished representative of the American woman composer.

The daughter of composer John Barnett, she studied theory, piano, and singing, graduating from the Leipzig Conservatory with honors. In 1863, under the stage name of Clara Doria, she made her operatic debut in Turin, Italy, then, in 1871, went to New York with the Parepa-Rosa Opera. In 1878 she married Henry Rogers, a lawyer from Boston, and automatically became an American citizen. In Boston she helped to found the Bach Club, joined in the Manuscript Club's activities to help unknown composers, and embarked on a distinguished career as a voice teacher, becoming a professor at the New England Conservatory of Music in 1902. She also wrote several treatises on singing (stressing diction)[1] and an autobiography. Meanwhile, she composed some small chamber pieces and many songs. Set to choice classical poetry, influenced by the German romantic school (but without any of its excess), these clean, fresh songs are notable for their taste, craftsmanship, and vitality. *Sudden Light* and *Overhead the Treetops Meet* were especially admired by William Treat Upton. The song *Confession* and several sets to the poetry of the Brownings are also recommended.

BIBLIOGRAPHY
AmerGroves, Ammer, Baker, Thompson, Upton.
Rogers, Clara Kathleen. *Memories of a Musical Career.* Little, Brown, and Company, 1919.
————. *The Story of Two Lives.* Henry Munroe Rogers, 1932.

---

[1] These are: *The Philosophy of Singing; My Voice and I; Your Voice and You; The Voice in Speech;* and *English Diction in Song and Speech.*

JAMES H. ROGERS
b. Feb. 7, 1857, Fair Haven, CT; d. Nov. 27, 1940, Pasadena, CA

The son of an Episcopalian minister, James Rogers studied music in Berlin and Paris. In 1881 he settled in Cleveland, Ohio, where he taught, composed, and for 50 years served as organist for the Euclid Avenue Temple. For 17 of those years, he was also a noted music critic for the Cleveland *Plain Dealer.* In 1932 he retired to Pasadena.

Though Rogers was well known for his organ music and also published sacred songs,[1] it was his romantic concert songs that brought him deserved popularity. Marcella Sembrich, Lillian Nordica, Geraldine Farrar, and Louise Homer are but a few of the opera stars who regularly included them on their programs. The warm lyricism and melodiousness of the vocal writing as well as the lovely, fluid accompaniments certainly make them gratifying to perform. If a bit old-fashioned, with "their air of health and well-being,"[2] they are, on the whole, admirable representatives of the era's concert song. All songs are in a minimum of two keys. Though none are truly distinguished, of the best known, *At Parting; The Time for Making Songs Has Come* (recorded by Dale Moore on Cambridge CRS 2715); and *Cloud-Shadows* can still be recommended. *The Star* and *The Last Song,* once runners up in popularity, seem pedestrian and inflated by comparison. Forgotten, but lovely, are: *Wind Song; Love Has Wings;* and *Fly, White Butterflies, Fly.* A set of four songs to poems of Walt Whitman, *In Memoriam* (for medium voice only), is perhaps his most ambitious work. Dedicated to his son, recently killed in World War I, though his sincerity is indisputable, in these songs Rogers seems awkward and over his head. Most Rogers songs are standard library items.

BIBLIOGRAPHY
Hall, Howard (OAM), Hughes, Thompson, Upton.
Bradley, Alice. "Cleveland's Well Loved Composer," *Musical America,*
    October 28, 1911.
Obituary, *Musical America,* December 10, 1940.

---

[1] Many of these were published under the pen name of Edward Campion.
[2] Hall, *The Art Song,* 265.

NED ROREM
b. Oct. 23, 1923, Richmond, IN

Ned Rorem is generally considered to be America's foremost composer of art song, and—remarkably—from his achievements in that over-looked and diminutive idiom he has also gone on to build a major career in all forms.

The family moved to Chicago when Rorem was an infant. Of Norwegian descent, his father, a prominent medical economist and co-founder of Blue Cross, and his mother, an activist in pacifist movements, raised Rorem and his older sister as Quakers. Though not musical themselves, they exposed their children to the best in music. As a child Rorem attempted some composition and began to study piano. Two of his early teachers, Margaret Bonds and Nuta Rothschild were especially influential: Bonds, a composer herself, taught him notation and introduced him to American music; Rothschild opened the doors which would turn Rorem into an avowed Francophile. Studies at the School of Music at Northwestern and with Leo Sowerby at the American Conservatory were followed by an unsatisfactory year with Rosario Scalero at the Curtis Institute. Moving to New York, Rorem studied with Bernard Wagenaar at the Juilliard School and graduated with a master's degree in 1948. He also studied privately with Aaron Copland at the Berkshire Music Center, and with Virgil Thomson in New York.

In 1948 Rorem won both the Music Library Association's award for the year's best published song *(The Lordly Hudson)* and the $1,000 George Gershwin Memorial Prize, which enabled him to make his first trip abroad. For two years in Morocco and another seven in Paris, he combined a generally dissolute life of drinking, drugs, and sexual promiscuity with hard work. And, under the patronage of Viscountess Marie Laure de Noailles, who provided him with a place to work, introduced him to prominent people, and sponsored opportunities for his music to be heard, he produced some important compositions. By the time he returned to America in late 1957, he had achieved significant recognition.

Rorem is also well known for his prose writing. In 1966 *The Paris Diary*, the first of several gossipy, self-absorbed, but engaging journals, which record not only the everyday concerns of a professional life but also the very intimate affairs of an avowed homosexual, was published to considerable critical acclaim. In addition, he has published numerous intelligent, provocative, and stylish articles on music, which over the years have been gathered into collections. For a long time Rorem has lived with organist James Holmes in Manhattan, spending summers in Nantucket. He often performs as an accompanist (primarily of his own music) and has does some teaching, most recently at the Curtis Institute. His numerous awards include the 1976 Pulitzer Prize for *Air Music*.

THE SONGS

It is by virtue of its consistently superior quality that Rorem's catalogue of several hundred art songs has earned its sterling reputation. One is less likely to be awed by an individual song as to be admiring of the total corpus. Unconcerned with novelty for novelty's sake and content to be labelled mainstream, over the decades Rorem's vocal writing has evolved and matured more than it has actually changed. The simple, lyric, contained utterance of the 1940s and early 1950s, in the 1960s extends into a more sophisticated, complex, ranging, and graphic expression. Single songs give way to the cyclic form and often include other instrumentation. More demanding of the listener—textually as well as musically—these works of his maturity, though forfeiting much of the endearing intimacy of the earlier songs, can be compelling. After 1976, however, with the exception of two 1989 lyrical settings of Whitman, Rorem's published songs for voice and piano, temporarily at least, cease.

With exquisite literary taste and verbal sensibility, and with absolute command of his craft, Rorem sets only choice texts. Favorite poets have been Walt Whitman, Theodore Roethke,[1] and his friend Paul Goodman, but his tastes also include British and French poetry. Singers will generally find the vocal writing so idiomatic, gracious, and clean that there should be no difficulty clearly enunciating the text. Keep in mind, however, that the supple, tuneful works of Rorem's younger days are far less demanding for the voice than those of his maturity. Usually conceived for specific artists, and often responding to a more abstract poetry, vocal lines in the large-scale later works assume angular contours and stretch the range and technique of the average singer. Finding good breathing places to ensure the best phrasing in some of the longer lines requires thought. Rhythms also take on greater complexity and piano parts become increasingly independent and virtuosic. Though, in various writings, Rorem often describes the origins of his songs, he never analyzes or interprets them for others, cognizant that, once published, the song is no longer under his control. In that same spirit (though with so many songs to choose from he wonders why it is necessary), he is open to both transposition and excerpting songs from cycles.[2]

The following recordings make up the greater part of the Rorem song discography. With the exception of *War Scenes,* all have Rorem at the piano. Gianna D'Angelo, Phyllis Curtin, Regina Safarty, Charles Bressler, and Donald Gramm, sing various songs on Columbia (ML-5961/MS-656), reissued on Odyssey (32 16 0274) and excerpted on New World (229); Phyllis Bryn-Julson, *The Nantucket Songs* on CRI CD (ACS 6007); Katherine Ciesinski, *Women's Voices* on CRI (485); Phyllis Curtin, Beverly Wolff, and Donald Gramm, various songs on CRI CD (238); Donald Gramm, *War Scenes* and other songs on Phoenix CD (116); Rosalind Rees, various songs on GSS (104); Regina Safarty, *Poems of Love and the Rain* on CRI (202); Beverly Wolff, *Poems of Love and the Rain* on Phoenix CD (108). Other isolated recordings are listed with the appropriate song entry.

Virtually all the songs were originally published separately, but four albums of selected songs by Ned Rorem are also available: *Song Album: Volume One,* Boosey c1980 *(SA1); Song Album: Volume Two,* Boosey c1982 *(SA2); Song Album: Volume Three,* Boosey c1992 *(SA3);* and *14 Songs on American Poetry,* Peters *(14SAP).*

Despite its size, the overall distinction of and interest in the Rorem catalogue warrants the identification of virtually every published song. (Singers will also want to consider many of the sets and cycles that employ more than one voice or other instruments.) Only the three 1947 songs to poems of Paul Goodman, *Paul's Blues,* because they were published in a limited edition (Red Ozier Press c1984), are knowingly omitted. Of the piano reductions which have been made of some of the song cycles with orchestra, only *Six Songs for High Voice* is included here, since these songs have a history of being sung with piano. Some early songs, originally published separately, were later reissued under one cover with other songs of the same poet. These are listed below in the form that they first appeared.

Absalom, Paul Goodman; Boosey c1972; also incl. *SA1;* comp. 1946.
Rec. higher full voices (d1–f#2); 2:30; Andantino lamentoso; declamatory with dramatic passages; a moving song.

Alleluia, Hargail c1949; also incl. *SA3;* comp. 1946; to Jennie Tourel.
Rec. high voices (b–g#2); 2:15; Fast and somewhat hysterical; various deliveries of the word "alleluia"; rhythmically complex; spirited, catchy, fun; a favorite with audiences; recorded by Rees, and Eleanor Steber on Desto (411/412).

An Angel Speaks to the Shepherds, St. Luke 2:9-15; Southern c1956; comp. 1952.
Rec. high voices (d1–ab2); 5:00; Largo e molto sostenuto; subdued, sustained; animated central section; a tedious narrative.

Are You the New Person? Walt Whitman; incl. *SA3;* comp. 1989; to Phyllis Curtin.
Rec. high voices (c#1–a2); 3:15; Easily; recalls the lyricism of the younger Rorem, but without quite the same suppleness in the vocal writing.

As Adam Early in the Morning, Walt Whitman; Peters c1961; also incl. *14SAP;* comp. 1957.
Rec. medium voices (c#1–e2); 1:15; Maestoso; sustained over chords; recorded by Gramm (Phoenix).

The Call, Elkan-Vogel c1953; comp. 1957; see *From an Unknown Past* (My Blood Is So Red).

Catullus: On the Burial of His Brother, trans. by Aubrey Beardsley; Boosey c1969; also incl. *SA2;* comp. 1947; to David Lloyd.
Rec. high voices (cb–ab2), text suggests men; 1:45; Sombre and steady; sustained; poignant.

A Child Asleep in Its Own Life, Wallace Stevens; Boosey c1974; from *Last Poems of Wallace Stevens;*[3] also incl. *SA2*.
Rec. medium and higher voices (b–f#2); 1:45; Intense and gentle; lyrical over a spare piano part.

A Christmas Carol, about 1500 A.D.; Elkan-Vogel c1953.
    Rec. medium-high voices (c1–f2); 1:45; Allegretto; lyrical; unac-
companied passages; recorded by Bressler (Columbia), Hanks on
Duke Vol. 2 (DWR 7306), and Rees.

Clouds, Paul Goodman; Boosey c1968; also incl. *Three Poems of Paul
Goodman* and *SA2;* comp. 1953; to David Diamond.
    Rec. higher voices (e1–f#2); 2:30; Infinitely slow, pale; in a "half-
voice," sustained, over "drifting" chords; evocative; impressionistic;
recorded by Hanks on Duke Vol. 2 (DWR 7306), and Rees.

Confitebor tibi, Isaiah 12; Boosey c1972; also incl. *SA2;* to James
Holmes.
    Rec. high voices (c1–a2); 2:15; Flexible; an unaccompanied
prayer.

Conversation, Elizabeth Bishop; Boosey c1969; comp. 1957; to James
Holmes.
    Rec. high full voices (d1–g2); 2:15; Extremely slow; dramatic;
harsh chords; recorded by Rees.

Cradle Song, see *Six Songs for High Voice.*

Cycle of Holy Songs, from the Psalms; Southern c1955; comp. 1951.
    Rec. full, high voices (b–a2); 9:00; can be used individually; long
lines and full accompaniment necessitate stamina and security
throughout the range; all but *Psalm 142* are recorded by Curtin
(Columbia).
    Psalm 134; (d1–g#2); 2:00; Allegro moderato maestoso.
    Psalm 142; (b–g2); 2:00; Andante; relatively subdued.
    Psalm 148; (c1–g2); 2:00; Allegro con brio; pressing forward; jazz-
like syncopation.
    Psalm 150; (d1–a2); 3:00; Maestoso; broad; demanding; big ending;
the most effective of the four.

Doll's Boy, E. E. Cummings; incl. *SA3;* comp. 1944.
    Rec. high voices (d1–g2); 2:00; Adagio; lyrical declamation in small
note values; a winsome, enigmatic little song.

Early in the Morning,[4] Robert Hillyer; Peters c1958; also incl. *14SAP;*
comp. 1955.
    Rec. medium voices (d1–f2); 1:45; Moderato; a tuneful, nostalgic
waltz; musings of an American visiting Paris; recorded by Gramm

(Phoenix, Columbia, NW), Cynthia Haymon on Argo CD (436 117-2ZH), and Rees.

Echo's Song (Slow, slow, fresh fount), Ben Jonson; Boosey c1953; also incl. *SAI;* comp. 1948.

Rec. medium and higher voices (e♭1–f2); 2:00; Andantino; plaintive, tender, and lovely; rarely heard; recorded by Bressler (Columbia).

Epitaph, Anonymous 15th Century; Elkan-Vogel c1953; pub. with *To You;* comp. 1953.

Rec. medium and higher lyric voices (d1–f2); 0:45; Very slowly; sustained over a single piano line.

Five Poems of Walt Whitman, Boosey c1970; comp. 1957 (*Reconciliation* in 1946).

Rec. medium voices, (b–f#2); any one of these songs can be used individually.

Sometimes with One I Love, also incl. *SAI;* ded. to Beverly Wolff. (b–e♭2); 1:30; Lento; intense declamation, then "tranquillo"; recorded by Rees.

Look Down, Fair Moon, also incl. *SAI;* ded. to Donald Gramm. (d1–e2); 1:30; Very slow; sustained over chords; a stark lament; recorded by Gramm, transposed down, (Phoenix).

Gliding O'er All, ded. to Phyllis Curtin. (b♭–e♭2); 0:30; Allegro; lyrical; philosophical; recorded by Gramm (Phoenix).

Reconciliation, ded. to Adele Addison. (d1–f#2); 2:00; Quietly; delicate, poignant declamation.

Gods, ded. to Patricia Neway. (c1–f2); 2:30; Declamatory; unaccompanied opening; philosophical and intense.

Flight for Heaven, Robert Herrick; Mercury c1952; comp. 1950; to Doda Conrad.[5]

Spec. bass voice (F#–e♭1), rec. baritones as tessitura (though it varies within the cycle) seems high for bass; 14:00; titles are: *To Music, to becalm his Fever; Cherry-Ripe; Upon Julia's Clothes; To Daisies, not to shut so Soon; Epitaph; Another Epitaph; To the Willow-Tree; Comfort to a Youth that had lost his Love; To Anthea, who may command him Anything* (this last song is dedicated to Marie Laure); nine songs on a variety of themes (mostly love and death) with a piano interlude; several are quite difficult; an interesting though uneven set, and with the added problem of shifting tessituras, it might be best to exclude a few numbers; *To a Willow Tree* and *Upon Julia's Clothes* are recorded by Gramm (Columbia, NW).

For Poulenc, Frank O'Hara; E. C. Schirmer c1968; comp. 1963; also incl. *Four Songs;* comm. by Alice Esty for memorial concert to Poulenc.

　　Spec. medium high (c1–f#2); 2:45; Like a Gymnopodie; sustained; subdued; evocative; recorded by Curtin (CRI).

For Susan,[6] Paul Goodman; Boosey c1968; comp. 1953; also incl. *Three Poems of Paul Goodman* and *SA1*.

　　Rec. high voices (e1–g2); 1:00; Easily; flowing; lyrical; recorded by Hanks on Duke Vol. 2 (DWR 7306), and Rees.

Four Poems of Tennyson, Boosey c1969; comp. 1963 (*The Sleeping Palace* in 1949); comm. by and ded. to Ellen Faull.

　　Rec. high lyric voices (b–a2); 10:30; can be used individually but also a good set, though the last song is weak and could be dropped; the cantabile writing requires considerable vocal flexibility and suppleness; these magical songs perfectly capture Tennyson's evocative imagery and bask in fluid lyricism; wonderful to show the voice, and ever so inviting to the ear.

　　Ask Me No More, also incl. *SA2;* (b–a2); 3:00; Passionate, smooth, and supple; a curving, sinuous vocal line builds to a climax before the exquisite restraint of the final page; a beautiful song; recorded by Rees.

　　Now Sleeps the Crimson Petal, also incl. *SA1;* (b–a2); 3:00; Allegretto scherzando with several changes; fanciful; intimate; light; recorded by Rees.

　　Far—Far—Away, also incl. *SA1;* (d–g2); 1:45; Fast and poignant; breathless parlando; some sustained passages; recorded by Rees.

　　The Sleeping Palace, (d1–d2); 2:45; Quietly; evocative melody over chords; not as inspired as the other songs in this set.

Four Songs, E. C. Schirmer c1986; pub. separately and together; see separate entries for: *For Poulenc, The Midnight Sun, The Mild Mother,* and *The Tulip Tree.*

From an Unknown Past, various 16th-century poets; Southern c1953/1963; (arr. by Rorem from the orig. version for mixed chorus a cappella).

Rec. medium and lower voices (g#–f#2); 8:00; titles are: *The Lover in Winter Plaineth for Spring; Hey Nonny No!; My Blood So Red* (also pub. separately and recorded by Donald Gramm under the title *The Call); Suspiria; The Miracle; Tears; Crabbed Age and Youth;* mostly short songs that are best kept as a set; good variety of tempo and mood; opens, Lonely and smooth; closes, Allegro con spirito; not difficult; tastefully evocative of the madrigal; a colorful, attractive set.

Full of Life Now, Walt Whitman; Boosey c1990; incl. *SA3;* comp. 1989.

Rec. high voices (c#1–g2); 1:30; Rambunctious; waltz-like; joyous; big ending.

Hearing, Kenneth Koch; Boosey c1969; to Carolyn Reyer; comp. 1965/1966.

Spec. medium-low voices (f#–a2); the 26:00 indicated seems too long;[7] individual songs could be used or the set shortened; diverse vocal styles; very demanding at times; numerous musical, especially rhythmical, intricacies; a wordy set, mostly about love, in which Koch's sometimes obscure but always dazzling imagery provides a perfect vehicle for Rorem's virtuosic, imaginative word-setting; a splendid set, too often overlooked in favor of Rorem's more dramatic cycles.

In Love With You (Three songs in One), (g#–g2); 5:30; the three parts are: Large, free, enthusiastic; Allegretto semplice; Straightforward, not too slow; excited declamation frames the lyrical center.

Down at the Docks, (bb–gb2); 2:00; Moving, like a Barcarolle but more animated; lyrical, tuneful.

Poem, (g#–g2); 2:30; Conversationally; over occasional chords.

Spring (Let's Take a Walk), also incl. *SA1;* (a–g2); 2:15; Rather fast strict tempo, yet casual and gracious; recorded by Rees.

Invitation, (b–g#2); 2:15; Quite slow; cantabile over a richly textured piano score; especially recommended.

Hearing, (f#–a2); 8:30; Madly Exuberant! a fast, crisp recitando; intricate rhythms; exquisite detail; a kaleidoscopic depiction of sound imagery; requires endurance and vocal flexibility; especially recommended.

I am Rose, Gertrude Stein; Peters c1963; comp. 1955; also incl. *14SAP.*
  Spec. medium voice (c#1–f#2); 0:20; Allegretto; a coyly arching tune; deftly artless and charming; always a winner; recorded by Rees and Safarty (Columbia, NW).

I Will Always Love You, Frank O'Hara; comp. 1957; incl. *SA3.*
  Rec. high voices (c#1–a2); 2:00; in a moderate tempo; flowing, warm and lyrical.

In a Gondola, see *Six Songs for High Voice.*

Jack L'Eventreur (Jack the Ripper), Marie Laure de Noailles; Boosey c1972; also incl *SA2;* comp. 1953.
  Rec. dramatic sopran (b–c#3); 4:30; Lent et sombre; sustained; a recurring theme builds over chords to a central climax (*ffff* high C); eerie.

A Journey, Andrew Glaze; Boosey c1977; comp. 1976; ded. to Alice (Esty).
  Rec. medium voices (d1–eb2); 1:30; moves quickly; a child's narrative; recorded by Rees.

Let's Take a Walk, Kenneth Koch, see *Spring* from the cycle *Hearing.*

Little Elegy, Elinor Wylie; pub. with *On a Singing Girl* under the title *Two Songs;* Hargail c1952; also incl. *SA2;* to Nell Tangman.
  Rec. medium voices (c#1–e2); 1:00; Andante; supple and tuneful over simple chords; recorded by Curtin (CRI).

The Lordly Hudson,[8] Paul Goodman; Mercury c1947; comp. 1947; to Janet Fairbank.
  Rec. higher full voices (db1–g2); 2:15; lyrical, at times dramatic, over a flowing, richly textured piano score; sweeping and broad; wonderful to sing; Rorem has perfectly conveyed both the urgency and the nobility inherent in this moving poem; recorded by Rees and Sarfaty (Columbia).

The Lord's Prayer, Peters c1957; comp. 1957.
  Rec. higher voices (c1–g2); 1:45; Moderato; a routine setting.

Love, Thomas Lodge; Boosey c1969; also incl. *SA2;* comp. 1953.
  Rec. medium and high voices (c#1–g2); 1:45; Calm and nervous; a lovely, sinuous melody over chords; an appealing song.

Love in a Life, Robert Browning; Boosey c1972; also incl. *SA1;* comp. 1951.

   Rec. medium voices (c1–f#2), text suggests men; 4:00; Depressing, nostalgic, intense, but never heavy; lyrical declamation over a busy, thick piano score; unusual and interesting, but could be tedious without a first-rate interpreter.

Lullaby of the Woman of the Mountain, Padraic Pearse, trans. Thomas MacDonagh; Boosey c1956; also incl. *SA2;* comp. 1950.

   Rec. medium voices (c#1–f#2); 2:00; Easily; rocking, lyrical and tender; recorded by Bressler (Columbia, NW).

Memory, Theodore Roethke; Peters c1961; comp. 1959; also incl. *14SAP;* to Alice Esty.

   Rec. medium voices (d1–e2); 1:00; moderately moving; a simple, evocative melody set three times; spare; dreamlike.

The Midnight Sun, Paul Goodman; E. C. Schirmer c1968; also incl. *Four Songs;* comp. 1953.

   Spec. medium high voices (d#1–e2); 1:30; Hollow and quite freely; floating declamation over spare, occasional chords; evocative; mystical.

The Mild Mother, Anonymous, 15th century; E. C. Schirmer c1968; also incl. *Four Songs;* comp. 1952; to Rosemarie Beck.[9]

   Spec. medium high (c1–f2); 1:00; Restrained and passionate; religious text; spare; warm.

My Papa's Waltz, Theodore Roethke; Peters c1963; comp. 1959; also incl. *14SAP;* to Alice Esty.

   Rec. medium voices (b–f#2), text suggests men; 1:15; Very fast but joyless, breathless, crude and free; an energetic waltz; elaborate solo piano passages; recorded by Gramm (Columbia, NW).

Nantucket Songs, various poets; Boosey c1981; comp. 1978/79, commissioned by the Elizabeth Sprague Coolidge Foundation.

   Rec. high voices (b♭–c3); 18:00; titles are: *From Whence Cometh Song* (Theodore Roethke); *The Dance* (William Carlos Williams); *Nantucket* (William Carlos Williams); *Go, Lovely Rose* (Edmund Waller); *Up-Hill* (Christina Rossetti); *Mother, I Cannot Mind My Wheel* (Walter Savage Landor); *Fear of Death* (John Ashbery); *Ferry Me Across the Water* (Christina Rossetti); *The Dancer* (Edmund Waller); an excellent set, but smaller groups could be made. The title comes from the fact that they were all composed on Nantucket. Otherwise there is no particular thematic thread. Rorem's introductory note suggests *"Popular Songs"* as an apt subtitle because he considers them to be "entertaining" and "emotional rather than intellectual." But do not be misled; these are serious songs and a far cry from the traditional use of the word "popular." Several are musically and technically very demanding, requiring virtuoso performances from voice and piano; recorded by Phyllis Bryn-Julson.

Night Crow, Theodore Roethke, Peters c1963; comp. 1959; also incl. *14SAP.*

Rec. medium voices (c1–g2); 2:00; Molto Lento - quasi recitativo; declamatory and quite dramatic; bleak imagery; reflective; a strong, different song; recorded by Gramm (CRI).

The Nightingale, about 1500 A.D.; Boosey c1956; comp. 1951; also incl. *SA1.*

Rec. medium or higher lyric voices (c#1–f#2), text suggests men; 1:00; Fast and delicate and supple; parlando over staccatos and other lively piano figures; flexibility and easy articulation needed; charming; recorded by Curtin (Columbia), and Rees.

O Do Not Love Too Long, William Butler Yeats; incl. *SA3;* comp. 1951.

Rec. medium voices (bb1–db2); 1:30; Molto Lento; languidly flowing; melodic; melancholy.

O You Whom I Often and Silently Come, Walt Whitman; Peters c1961; comp. 1957; also incl. *14SAP.*

Rec. medium voices (c#1–e2); 0:20; Supple; parlando over light chords; graceful; fleeting; recorded by Gramm (Desto), Cynthia Haymon on Argo CD (436 117-2ZH), Rees, and Safarty (Columbia).

On a Singing Girl, Elinor Wylie; pub. with *Little Elegy* under the title *Two Songs;* Hargail c1952; comp. 1946; also incl. *SA2;* ded. to Daniel Pinkham.

Rec. high voices (f1–f2); 1:00; Calm and Moderate; lyrical declamation over chords; warm.

Philomel, Richard Barnefield; Hargail c1952; comp. 1950.

Rec. medium voices (b–e2); 3:00; Melancholy; a parlando narrative; subdued.

Pippa's Song, see *Six Songs for High Voice.*

Poèmes pour la paix (Poems for Peace), 15th- and 16th-century poets; Boosey c1970; comp. 1953.

Spec. medium voice (b–a♭2); 13:00; in French; titles are: *Lay* (Jehan Regnier); *Ode* (Pierre de Ronsard), also incl. *SA2; Sonnet 1* (Olivier de Magny); *Sonnet 11* (Olivier de Magny); *Sonnet* (Jean Durát); *L'hymne de la paix* (Jean-Antoine de Baif); a smaller group could be made; reflections on war and peace; good diversity; deep feeling and spare, archaic sonorities combine to create a rare and moving effect; seldom performed, but special.

Poems of Love and the Rain, various poets; Boosey c1965/86; comp. 1962; to Regina Safarty.

Spec. mezzo-soprano (f#–a2); 28:00; titles are: *Prologue: from "The Rain"* (Donald Windham); *Stop All the Clocks* (W. H. Auden); *The Air Is the Only* (Howard Moss); *Love's Stricken "Why"* (Emily Dickinson); *The Apparition* (Theodore Roethke); *Do I Love You: Part 1* (Jack Larson); *In the Rain* (E. E. Cummings); *Song for Lying in Bed During a Night Rain* (Kenneth Pitchford); and *Interlude* (Theodore Roethke). Contrasting versions of these poems are then set, but in reverse order (and using Part II of the Jack Larson poem), until it reaches the *Epilogue*, which is exactly the same as the *Prologue* but a half tone lower. The result is a mirror-image effect that is truly provocative. Difficult in every respect; a major cycle and Rorem's most innovative contribution to the song literature; recorded by Wolff (Phoenix) and Safarty.

A Psalm of Praise, Psalm 100; Associated c1946; comp. 1945; to David Diamond.

Rec. medium and higher voices (c1–g2); 3:00; Rather fast and nervous; tempo changes; shifting meters and some jazz-like rhythms; similar to *Alleluia* but less inspired.

Rain in Spring, Paul Goodman; Boosey c1956; comp. 1949; also incl. *SA1*.

Rec. lower voices (a–e♭2); 1:30; Very languid; tuneful over evocative piano figures; a wonderful song; recorded by Rees and Safarty (Columbia).

Requiem, Robert Louis Stevenson; Southern c1956; comp. 1948.

Rec. medium voices (c#1–f#2); 2:00; Very quietly; lyrical; recorded by Bressler (Columbia).

The Resurrection, St. Matthew 27: 62–66; 28; Southern c1965; comp. 1956; to Virgil Thomson.

Rec. higher voices (b♭–a♭2); 12:00; Allegro; many tempo and mood changes; ends quietly after a dramatic climax; a narrative with limited usage due to its length and subject matter; well crafted, spirited, and with good variety, but routine and predictable.

Rondelay, see *Six Songs for High Voice.*

Root Cellar, Theodore Roethke; Peters c1963; comp. 1959; also incl. *14SAP;* to Alice Esty.

Rec. medium and high dramatic voices (b♭–g2); 2:00; Intensely slow, declamatory and strong; severe chords; austere nature imagery; unusual; effective; recorded by Gramm (Columbia, NW), and Rees.

Sally's Smile,[10] Paul Goodman; Peters c1957; comp. 1953; also incl. *14SAP*.

Rec. medium voice (e1–f#2), best for men; 0:45; Fast and delightful; breathless, exuberant love song; recorded by Gramm (Columbia), and Rees.

See How They Love Me, Howard Moss; Peters c1958; comp. 1956; also incl. *14SAP*.[11]

Rec. high lyric voices (e♭1–a2); 1:45; Quietly; lilting; builds to a central climax; tender and sad; recorded by Bressler (Columbia), Cynthia Haymon on Argo CD (436 117-2ZH), and Rees.

The Serpent, Theodore Roethke; Boosey c1974; comp. 1972; also incl. *SA1;* to Phyllis Curtin.

Rec. high voices (b♭–a2); 2:00; Very fast; a chipper narrative with dialogue over slithery piano figurations; both performers need flexibility; witty; recorded by Rees.

The Silver Swan, Orlando Gibbons; Peer c1950; comp. 1949; also incl. *VN*.

Rec. very high voices (e1–c3); 3:00; Largo; sustained with melismatic passages over a spare modal piano texture; plaintive; recorded by D'Angelo (Columbia).

Six Songs for High Voice, Peters c1963; orig. for voice and orchestra; also pub. for voice and piano, both separately and as a set.

Rec. very high sopranos (c1–f3); 12:45; a cycle only by dint of having been composed for the same singer—Virginia Fleming; varying degrees of vocal difficulty; songs can be used individually.

Pippa's Song, Robert Browning; (d1–d3); 2:00; Rustling and unhurried; the gorgeous, sustained vocal line, imitated by the piano and suspended amidst tremolos, would definitely sound better with instruments, but still holds one enthralled; recorded by d'Angelo (Columbia, NW).

Cradle Song, Anonymous 16th century; (f1–c♭3); 1:15; Andante; in old English; in a high tessitura; lyrical with melismatic decoration; a lovely song.

Song for a Girl, John Dryden; to Virginia Fleming; (e1–e3); 1:00; Fast, light; a sprightly parlando over chords; recorded by D'Angelo (Columbia).

Rondelay, John Dryden; (e♭1–c3); 2:45; Simply, sadly; difficult wide intervals for the voice; a narrative with some drama.

In a Gondola, Robert Browning; to Gianna d'Angelo; (f♯1–c3); 2:00; Smooth; opens in a half-voice and builds to a central climax over rising ostinato chords; recorded by d'Angelo (Columbia).

Song to a Fair Young Lady, Going Out of Town in the Spring, John Dryden; (c1–f3); 3:45; Allegro moderato; better for orchestra; some sustained singing but mostly a ranging parlando with coloratura passages; an aria.

Snake, Theodore Roethke; Peters c1963; comp. 1959; also incl. *14SAP;* to Alice Esty.

Rec. medium and higher voices (e1–f2); 1:00; Presto; a straightforward melody over scurrying triplets; melismatic passages; recorded by D'Angelo (Columbia, NW), and Rees.

Song for a Girl, see *Six Songs for High Voice.*

A Song of David, Psalm 120; Associated c1946; comp. 1945; also incl. *CASS* and *AAS.*

Rec. medium voices (d1–g2); 2:00; Andante serioso; sustained over steady chords; a more agitated central section.

Song to a Fair Young Girl, Going Out of Town in the Spring, see *Six Songs for High Voice.*

Spring (Nothing Is So Beautiful As Spring), Gerard Manley Hopkins; Boosey c1953; comp. 1947; also incl. *SA2;* to Marie Laure de Noailles.

Rec. high voices (c#1–a2); 1:45; Allegretto con moto; lyrical parlando; a central climax; a sparkling song recorded by Curtin (Columbia, NW).

Spring (Let's Take a Walk), Kenneth Koch; see *Hearing.*

Spring and Fall (to a young child), Gerard Manley Hopkins; Mercury c1947; comp. 1946; also incl. *CAAS;* to Mme. Eva Gauthier.

Rec. medium lyric voices (d#1–f#2); 2:00; the supple, lyrical declamation is fraught with tenderness and pain; a lovely, poignant song; recorded by Gramm (Columbia, NW).

Stopping by Woods on a Snowy Evening, Robert Frost; incl. *SA3;* comp. 1947; for my father.

Rec. high voices (d1–f#2); 2:15; Andantino; lyrical; a routine but sympathetic setting.

Such Beauty as Hurts to Behold, Paul Goodman; Peters c1961; comp. 1957; also incl. *14SAP;* to Marc Blitzstein.

Rec. medium and higher voices (d1–g♭2); 2:30; Very slow, very free; declamatory; introspective; taut emotion; recorded by Rees and Safarty (Columbia).

That Shadow, My Likeness (from *Whitman Cantata),* Walt Whitman; Boosey c1983; incl. *SA3.*

Rec. medium voices (c1–c2); 1:30; Smooth; an undulating vocal line with melismatic passages over spare chords.

Three Calamus Poems, Walt Whitman; Boosey c1982; comp. 1982; to Donald Collup (who commissioned the work).

Spec. medium voice (a–g2); 10:00; titles are: *Of Him I Love Day and Night; I Saw in Louisiana a Live Oak Growing; To a Common Prostitute;* Calamus (Whitman's symbol for "love of comrades") is the theme for this set, which should be kept intact; although a late work, the vocal writing is fluid and supple and does not make any unusual musical or vocal demands; some difficult piano figurations; deeply felt, very moving, exceptionally beautiful, but rarely performed; a special set.

Three Poems of Demetrios Capetanakis, Boosey c1968; comp. 1954.
> Rec. full medium or higher voices (c1–a2); 9:00; best as a set but can be sung individually; similar in mood and motion; serious, dark subject matter; a strong set.
>
> ***Abel,*** (d1–a2); 2:45; Rigidly calm; warm and somewhat conversational; grows in intensity.
>
> ***Guilt,*** (c1–g2); 2:45; Slow, free, stark; recorded by Hanks on Duke Vol 2 (DWR 7306).
>
> ***The Land of Fear,*** also incl. *SA2;* to Betty Allen; (d1–ab2); 2:30; Intense; warm and broad, building to an impassioned central climax, ending simply.

Three Songs of Paul Goodman, Boosey c1968; see separate entries for *For Susan, Clouds,* and *What Sparks and Wiry Cries;* though these three songs first appeared individually, they make an excellent, well contrasted set; recorded as a set by Hanks.

To a Young Girl, William Butler Yeats; Boosey c1972; comp. 1951; also incl. *SA1.*
> Rec. medium voices (cb1–eb2); 1:30; Largo (delicate and intense); hushed, lyric declamation; builds in intensity before fading; supple; affecting.

To Jane, Percy B. Shelley; Boosey c1976; comp. 1974.
> Rec. medium voices (b–d2); 1:30; Smoothly waltzed; lyrical with recurring theme over thin accompaniment; unusually simple for a later Rorem song.

To You, Walt Whitman; Elkan-Vogel c1965; comp. 1957; pub. with *Epitaph.*
> Rec. medium voices (db1–eb2); 0:30; Moderato; conversational; lyrical and affecting; recorded by Gramm (Columbia, NW, and Phoenix).

The Tulip Tree, Paul Goodman; E. C. Schirmer c1968; comp. 1953; also incl. *Four Songs.*
> Spec. medium high voices (c1–ab2); 1:30; Moving; an eerie childhood scene narrated in a lyrical parlando with some dialogue and drama; recorded by Curtin (CRI).

Two Poems of Edith Sitwell, Boosey c1982; comp. 1948.
> Spec. medium-high voices (c1–g2); despite similarities they can be sung together or individually; both are in a warm lyric parlando

over flowing accompaniments; melodic and haunting; excellent songs; recorded by Rees.

You, the Young Rainbow, (c1–g2); 2:15; to Rosalind Rees; in a moderate tempo; sad and subdued.

The Youth with the Red-Gold Hair, also incl. *AAA;* (d1–g2); 2:15; Calm and distant; nostalgic.

Two Poems of Theodore Roethke, Boosey c1969; comp. 1959; to Alice Esty.

Rec. medium voices (c1–g2); 3:30; a good contrasting pair but can be used individually; recorded by Teresa Treadway, in a "pop" style, on Orion (ORS 84476).

Orchids, also incl. *SA1;* (c1–e2); 2:15; Sinister, languid and floating; declamatory over occasional chords; hushed; eerie; impressionistic.

I Strolled Across an Open Field (The Waking); also incl. *SA2;* (d1–g2); 1:15; Quite fast and exuberant; a spirited vocal line over a busy piano.

Two Songs, see *Little Elegy* and *On a Singing Girl.*

Visits to St. Elizabeth's (Bedlam);[12] Elizabeth Bishop; Boosey c1964; comp. 1957.

Spec. medium voice (d1–g2);[13] 3:15; Allegro; the tempo never changes; lyric moments but mostly parlando over a percussive piano; incisive and rhythmic; stamina and good memorization skills needed; mimics the cumulative effect of the nursery rhyme "This is the house that Jack built," building up to a twelve-line finale of vivid, desperate images of the asylum; startling and unforgettable; recorded by Mildred Miller, under the title *Bedlam,* on Desto (411/412), Rees, and Safarty (Columbia).

The Waking, Theodore Roethke; Peters c1969; also incl. *14SAP;* comp. 1959; to Alice Esty.

Rec. medium and high voices (d1–g2); 2:30; Andante sostenuto; a beautiful, taut, arching melody repeated with subtly shifting contours, harmonies, and textures; difficult to maintain the interest and intensity, but a compelling song if done well.

War Scenes, Walt Whitman; Boosey c1971; designed for Gerard Souzay who first performed it with Dalton Baldwin in Washington, D.C.; dedicated to those who died in Vietnam during the composition: 20-30 June, 1969.

Spec. medium-low voice (g–g♭2), best for men; 12:00; titles of this anti-war cycle are: *A Night Battle; Specimen Case; An Incident; An Inauguration; The Real War Will Never Get in the Books;* excerpts from Whitman's Civil War Diary *(Specimen Days);* some lyrical passages but primarily declamatory, often in a recitative style; requires range and flexibility; descriptive piano score; opens *ffff*, closes *ppp;* stark, dramatic, intense; recorded by Gramm, with Eugene Istomin at the piano (Phoenix).

What If Some Little Pain, Edmund Spenser; Hargail c1952; also incl. *SA2.*

Rec. medium and higher voices (c1–f2); 1:45; Lento; sustained; reflective; intense; recorded by Safarty (Columbia).

What Sparks and Wiry Cries, Paul Goodman; Boosey c1968; comp. 1952-56; also incl. *Three Poems of Paul Goodman.*

Rec. high voices (c1–b♭2); 2:00; Sharp and intense; pressing forward, declamatory over chords; sudden dynamic changes; recorded by Curtin (CRI), Hanks on Duke Vol. 2 (DWR 7306), and Rees.

Where We Came, Jean Garrigue; Boosey c1976; comp. 1974; for Ben Weber.

Rec. high voices (d1–g#2); 2:15; Floatingly; unaccompanied opening, then a spare staccato accompaniment; flexibility required for the difficult, rather disjunct, lyrical declamation and melismatic passages; the experience of a magical moment in nature; somewhat odd, but a beautiful song.

Women's Voices, various poets; Boosey c1979; comp. 1975/76; comm. by and ded. to Joyce Mathis.

Spec. sopranos (b♭–b2), rec. dramatic sopranos; 22:00; titles are: *Now let No Charitable Hope* (Elinor Wylie); *A Birthday* (Christina Rossetti), also incl. *SA3; To My Dear and Loving Husband* (Anne Bradstreet); *To the Ladies* (Mary Lee, Lady Chudleigh); *If Ever Hapless Woman Had a Cause* (Mary Sidney Herbert, Countess of Pembroke); *We Never Said Farewell* (Mary Elizabeth Coleridge); *The Stranger* (Adrienne Rich); *What Inn Is This* (Emily Dickinson); *Defiled Is My Name* (Queen Anne Boleyn); *Electrocution* (Lola Ridge); *Smile, Death* (Charlotte Mew); no common theme other than that the poetry is by women and mostly concerns the female experience; a smaller group could be made; a big, dramatic, flexible, wide-ranging voice is needed for these difficult songs; formidable piano writing; dramatic opening, quietly intense close; good variety of tempos and colors but little relief from the otherwise dark emotions; a profound, dramatic set; recorded by Ciesinski.

Youth, Day, Old Age, and Night, Walt Whitman; Peters c1958; comp. 1954; also incl. *14SAP*.

Rec. high voices (c1–a2); 1:30; Rather slŏw; declamatory; chordal with ornamental passages; strong contrasts; opens broad and exuberant; closes quietly; philosophical; a strong, interesting song; recorded by Bressler (Columbia).

BIBLIOGRAPHY

AmerGroves, Baker, CBY (1967), Ewen, Friedberg (III), Greene, Gruen, Thompson.

Gruen, John. "'Now I Can Die Official,' Says Pulitzer-Winner Ned Rorem." *The New York Times,* May 30, 1976.

McDonald, Arlys L. *Ned Rorem: A Bio-Bibliography.* Westport, Connecticut: Greenwood Press, 1989.

Middaugh, Bennie. "The Songs of Ned Rorem: Aspects of Musical Style." *NATS Bulletin* 24 (May 1968).

Miller, Philip L. "The Best in American Song: Ned Rorem." *American Record Guide* 30 (May 1964).

————."The Songs of Ned Rorem." *Tempo* 127 (December 1978).

"The NATS Bulletin Interviews Ned Rorem." *The NATS Bulletin* 39 (Nov/Dec 1982).

Peyser, Joan. "Ned Rorem Delivers a Solo on the State of Music." *The New York Times,* May 3, 1987.

Rorem, Ned.[14] *Music from Inside Out.* New York: George Braziller, 1967. Includes: "Writing Songs," "Anatomy of Two Songs," and "Song and Singer."

————. *The Nantucket Diary of Ned Rorem: 1973–1985.* San Francisco: North Point Press, 1987. Recommended by this author as the most interesting of the diaries.

————. *Setting the Tone: Essays and a Diary.* New York: Coward-McCann, Inc., 1983. Includes: "The American Art Song," "More Notes on Song," "Writing Songs," "Song and Singer."

————. *Settling the Score: Essays on Music.* New York: Harcourt Brace Jovanovich, Publishers, 1988. Includes: "Poetry of Music," "Some Singing in America," "Anatomy of Two Songs," "A Postscript on Whitman."

[1] Rorem set eight of the Roethke poems at the suggestion of the soprano Alice Esty, to whom they are dedicated.

[2] "The NATS Bulletin Interviews Ned Rorem," *NATS Bulletin* (Nov/Dec 1982), 6.

[3] This is a suite for voice, cello, and piano.

[4] John Duke set this poem as *Morning in Paris*.

[5] Conrad, the son of the Polish-born French soprano Marya Freund, was a bass-baritone.

[6] Susan is Paul Goodman's daughter.

[7] The times given with the individual songs are, therefore, those of the author's experience.

[8] The Music Library Association's "best published song of the year."

[9] Rorem's sister.

[10] Sally is Paul Goodman's wife.

[11] This song is also included under the title *A Princess' Song* in Rorem's cantata for voices and piano *King Midas* (1970).

[12] The poem is based on a visit to Ezra Pound who for many years had been incarcerated by the U.S. Government in the St. Elizabeth's mental institution. Bishop's own mother had also once been confined in an asylum.

[13] In a letter to Rorem after the recording was released, Bishop questioned the use of a soprano as well as the fast tempo and hysteria. See *Settling the Score*, 294.

[14] As books and articles by Ned Rorem are too numerous to list in entirety, only those believed to be of most interest to singers are included here.

MARY TURNER SALTER
b. March 15, 1856, Peoria, IL; d. Sept. 12, 1938, Orangeburg, NY

The songs of Mary Turner Salter are as representative of her period as any, and yet as a composer she was virtually untrained. Born to musical parents, Salter performed as a singer at an early age. A mezzo-soprano, she studied voice in Iowa, at the New England Conservatory, and privately in New York. She had a modest career in concert and oratorio, and was a soloist at major churches on the East Coast. She also taught singing for two years at Wellseley College. In 1881 she married organist and music teacher Sumner Salter, with whom she had five children. Eventually settling in Williamstown, Massachusetts, to better perform her domestic duties, Salter gave up singing and teaching, and turned instead to composing, which she continued to do into her eighties.

THE SONGS

Salter's approximately 80 published songs were composed primarily from instinct and love of good melody, and with help from her husband. But to study them one would not suspect her almost total lack of theoretical education. Though somewhat quaint, Salter's songs are tasteful, tuneful, and genuinely charming. A few are surprising for their dramatic and expressive power. Three of Salter's cycles are reprints from Recital Publications. Some songs appear in anthologies. A sampling of her better known work follows.

The Cry of Rachel, Lisette Woodworth Reese; G. Schirmer c1905/1933.
Pub. high and low (high, c1–a2), rec. dramatic women's voices; 3:15; Risoluto, then Allegro appassionato; pulsing chords support a big vocal line; highly dramatic and intense; a mother's plea to join her dead child; somewhat dated, but sincere and strong.

Lyrics from Sappho, trans. Bliss Carman; Recital Pub. Reprint.
Pub. medium voice (d1–f2); 12:00; eight songs of good variety; lyrical; in a narrow vocal range; natural and expressive; a bit long, but a few songs could be cut; the most interesting of Salter's cycles.

Requiem of the Sea, Anonymous, from "The Bookman"; Schmidt c1913; to Madam Schumann-Heink.
Pub. low and high (low, bb–d2), rec. voices with some weight; 2:30; Grave; sustained low notes alternate with lyrical passages; big ending; unusual and effective.

Also of interest:

From Old Japan, Hyatt, Recital Pub. Reprint; six pretty songs for high voice, quaint; *A Night in Naishapur,* Dole, Recital Pub. Reprint; six short songs for low voice, exotic, *The Moon has long since wandered* (from this set) is quite unusual; *The Pine Tree,* Salter, also incl. *ASA,* Lento, one of her most popular songs.

BIBLIOGRAPHY[1]

Ammer, Baker, Hughes, Thompson.
Kinscella, Hazel Gertrude. "How Mary Turner Salter Composes Her Songs," *Musical America,* March 1, 1919.

---

[1] According to a note in Ammer, a book about Mary Salter called *In Memoriam* (author unknown but assumed to be her husband) was privately published in 1939, and can be found in the New York Public Library Music Division.

WILLIAM SCHUMAN
b. Aug. 4, 1910, New York, NY; d. Feb. 15, 1992, New York, NY

Best known for his orchestral works, including 10 symphonies, William Schuman's vocal catalogue is largely choral, and includes a few operas.[1] His songs are few in number, but rank with the best.

In public school Schuman, of German-Jewish descent, studied violin and bass, organized a jazz band, and wrote popular songs. Though he contemplated a career in business, he was overwhelmed on hearing his first New York Philharmonic Concert and abruptly turned to classical music studies. Married with two children, he conscientiously prepared himself for a teaching career, earning a master's degree in 1937 from Teachers College at Columbia University. From 1933 to 1945 Schuman taught music at Sarah Lawrence College, and during that time (1936 to 1938) studied composition with Roy Harris. In 1942 he received the first Pulitzer prize ever awarded for music.[2] One of the most influential and popular arts administrators of our time, Schuman helped found and then presided over both the Juilliard School of Music (1945-1962) and the Lincoln Center for the Performing Arts (1962-1969).

THE SONGS
Schuman's handful of published songs are consistently excellent but in such diverse styles that each must be considered on an individual basis. All are vocally idiomatic and, in their different ways, extremely rewarding. Rosalind Rees sings *time to the old* on a recording of Schuman's chamber works with solo voice on CRI (S-439). The following songs are warmly recommended.

Holiday Song, Genevieve Taggard; G. Schirmer c1942; incl. *CAS28.*
>   Rec. medium voices (c1–f2); 2:00; Moderato with changing tempos; tuneful, rhythmic; some humming and "deedelee dees"; spirited, fun, and different.

Orpheus with His Lute, William Shakespeare; G. Schirmer c1944; also incl. *20CAS;* comp. 1944.
>   Spec. medium voice (c1–f#2), rec. lyric voices; 2:00; Slowly; a compelling melody over quiet chords; simple and eloquent; an exquisite song in praise of music.

time to the old, Archibald MacLeish; Merion c1980; comp. 1979; for Rosalind Rees.

Rec. medium voices (b–g#2); 11:15; titles are: *The Old Gray Couple; Conway Burying Ground; Dozing on the Lawn.* Schuman's directions state that the three songs be performed without pause; thus, the feeling is of one long song. Slow tempos throughout; chordal; atonal; strongly dissonant in places; singer's pitches are often hidden in the dense chords; a sustained, expressive, but disjunct vocal line; generally subdued with some dramatic moments; reflections on old age, time running out, companionship, and death; not depressing, but intense and poignant; recorded by Rees; *Dozing on the Lawn* is also recorded by Jan DeGaetani on Elektra/Nonesuch CD (79248-2-ZK).

BIBLIOGRAPHY
AmerGroves, Baker, Ewen, Goss, Greene, Thompson.
Peyser, Joan. "A Life Spent on One Musical Path," *New York Times,* August 12, 1990.

---

[1] One of his operas, the successful *Casey at the Bat,* reflects his lifelong passion for baseball.

[2] Given to Schuman for *A Free Song,* his second secular cantata.

ROGER SESSIONS
b. Dec. 28, 1896, Brooklyn, NY; d. March 16, 1985, Princeton, NJ

Roger Sessions was a distinguished composer, whose intellectual and highly complex style also contained an expressive, lyrical voice. His vast catalogue includes opera and choral music but, regrettably, only one published song—the exquisite *On the Beach at Fontana.*

On the Beach at Fontana, James Joyce; incl. *CC* and *NVS;* comp. 1929.
Rec. high voices (c1–a♭2); 2:00; Un poco inquieto; musically intricate; tonal but highly chromatic; cross rhythms and changing meters; sustained, intensive declamation over fluid sixteenths that ebb and flow with the "whining wind"; builds to a final anguished climax; word painting with many sibilants; mournful and despairing; a remarkable song that delivers on many levels; recorded by Bethany Beardslee on New World (243) and Myron Myers on Musical Heritage Society (912016M).

BIBLIOGRAPHY
AmerGroves, Baker, Ewen, Goss, Greene, Manning, Thompson, Upton (Sup).

ARTHUR SHEPHERD
b. Feb. 19, 1880, Paris, ID; d. Jan. 12, 1958, Cleveland, OH

Though his idiom is conventional, Arthur Shepherd's strict musical conscience prompted an expression that is not readily accessible.
Nevertheless, several of his seldom heard songs are superb.

His English parents arrived in the small Mormon town of Paris,
Idaho, in 1877.[1] Both were musical, and three of their ten children
became professional musicians. Shepherd's exceptional gifts were evident at an early age, and when he was only 12, he was sent East to the
New England Conservatory of Music. There he studied composition
with Percy Goetschius, who became a lifelong friend and mentor.
Graduating with honors at age 17, Shepherd moved to Salt Lake City,
where he established himself as a conductor, pianist, and teacher. In
1905, while in New York for rehearsals of a prizewinning overture,[2] he
met Arthur Farwell, who published some of Shepherd's songs and piano
pieces in his Wa-Wan Press. For a while, Shepherd was drawn into
Farwell's crusade for a nationalist school of music, but eventually found
he could not agree with Farwell's extreme views.

In 1909 Shepherd took a teaching position at the New England
Conservatory and brought his wife, two sons, and daughter to Boston.
But after serving as an army bandleader in World War I, he returned to
a divorce in which he was given custody of his sons. In 1920 he became
assistant conductor of the newly formed Cleveland Orchestra and, two
years later, married his second wife with whom he had another son. He
remained with the orchestra until 1926, then from 1928 to 1931 served
as music editor of the *Cleveland Press,* and from 1928 until his retirement in 1950 taught at Western Reserve University. Shepherd died
unexpectedly from complications following routine surgery.

THE SONGS
Shepherd's approximately 30 songs were composed in bunches at different stages of his career. Some are routine and suffer from a certain
sameness, but the good ones are very fine indeed. Lean and introspective, with their sensitive craftsmanship, unerring prosody, clean lines,
elegant proportions, and intimate, personal style, they draw the listener
into a poetic and rarefied world.

The considerable intricacy, detail, and counterpoint in these tonal,
but highly chromatic songs create special work for the ensemble. There
is also little doubling of the vocal line by the piano and, as a result of

Shepherd's fastidious attention to word setting, a considerable amount of meter changing. Otherwise, these songs are not especially difficult. Shepherd believed in the importance of good, tuneful melodies and performers will enjoy the lyrical, singing lines. The piano writing, though idiomatic, can be quite involved, especially in the animated songs. In addition to those that were commercially published, many of Shepherd's songs are available, in manuscript form, in Richard Loucks's *Arthur Shepherd—American Composer.* Henry Herford has recorded three on New World (327). Many others are recorded, with a faltering technique but pure tone, by Marie Simmelink Kraft on *Songs of Arthur Shepherd* issued by the Department of Music of Western Reserve University.[3] Most of Shepherd's commercially published songs are listed below. Only a few from the Loucks album are noted, both because the volume is difficult to obtain and because the songs are less consistently good. All are in one key only.[4]

April, Sara Teasdale; incl. Loucks; comp. 1941.
> Rec. medium lyric voices (d1–e2); 1:30; Andantino; a simple, warm melody over a lilting accompaniment; quiet dynamics; recorded by Kraft.

Bacchus, Frank Dempster Sherman; incl. Loucks; comp. 1932; to Marie Simmelank Kraft.
> Rec. high lyric voices (d1–b2); 2:15; Allegro leggeremente; a light spirited melody over running sixteenths; staccato effects; some high legato passages; recorded by Kraft.

The Fiddlers, Walter de la Mare; Valley c1948; to Marie Simmelink Kraft.
> Rec. medium and high voices (d1–g2); 2:15; Allegro alla giga; rhythmic and vital, with an Elizabethan flavor; describes good Queen Bess dressing to the animated playing of nine fiddlers; amusing and different.

The Gentle Lady, John Masefield; incl. Loucks; comp. 1915.
> Rec. medium lyric voices (b–f2); 2:45; Tempo di minuetto; quiet; a beguiling little motif develops differently in the three strophes; recorded by Kraft.

Golden Stockings, Oliver St. John Gogarty; from *Seven Songs,* Valley c1961; comp. 1937.

Rec. high lyric voices (d1–g2), text suggests men; 2:00; Allegretto giojante; light and buoyant with a slower, more declamatory middle section; recorded by Kraft and, transposed down a step, by Herford.

Morning Glory, Siegfried Sassoon; from *Seven Songs,* Valley c1961.

Rec. high lyric voices (f1–g2); 2:30; Andante semplice; sustained; quite chromatic; an unusual song describing the nativity scene; recorded by Kraft.

Reverie, Walter de la Mare;[5] from *Seven Songs,* Valley 1961; also incl. Loucks; comp. 1932.

Rec. medium and lower voices (c1–g2); 3:30; Allegretto; delicate, lyrical, parlando over staccato eighths in the piano, representing the hypnotic pacing of Sophia's horse; a brief recitative-like central section; reflective; evocative; recorded by Kraft.

Seven Songs, see *Golden Stockings; Morning-Glory; Reverie; Softly Along the Road of Evening; To a Trout;* and *Virgil.* The last of the seven, *Serenade,* includes viola and is not listed.

Softly Along the Road of Evening, Walter de la Mare; incl. *Seven Songs,* Valley c1961; comp. 1932.

Rec. medium lyric voices (bb–g2); 2:30; Andante tranquillo; lyrical declamation over a flowing accompaniment describes the pastoral scene; warm, hushed, and delicate; an exquisite song.

The Starling Lake, Seumas O'Sullivan; Valley c1948; comp. 1944; to Marie Simmelink Kraft.

Rec. medium and high lyric voices (c1–f2); 3:30; Andante tranquillo; a plaintive vocal melody over moving piano figures; subdued declamatory sections; atmospheric; recorded by Kraft.

To a Trout, Oliver St. John Gogarty; from *Seven Songs,* Valley c1961; comp. 1941.

Rec. medium and low voices (c1–f2); 1:45; animated; lyrical declamation over rippling, water figurations; a charming scherzando section; a cheerful appreciation—with a nod to Schubert—of the trout by the fisherman with a hookless bait; recorded by Kraft and Herford.

Virgil, Oliver St. John Gogarty; from *Seven Songs,* Valley Music c1961; comp. 1941.

Spec. baritones, in bass clef (c–fb1); 4:45; Andante espressivo e con ampiezzo; highly chromatic; expansive and dramatic with recitando sections; an eloquent postlude; a moving tribute to the great Roman poet; recorded by Herford.

Also of interest:

Five Songs, James Russell Lowell, incl. *Wa-Wan (5),* also Recital Pub. Reprint, for high voice, in the more lush German romantic tradition, fuller in texture than later songs.

BIBLIOGRAPHY

AmerGroves, Baker, Ewen, Greene, Thompson, Upton.

Loucks, Richard. *Arthur Shepherd: American Composer,* Provo, Utah: Brigham Young University Press, 1980.

Newman, William S. "Arthur Shepherd," *Musical Quarterly* 36 (April 1950): 159–179.

---

[1] Shepherd grew up as a Mormon but later abandoned the church.

[2] In 1905 Shepherd's *Overture Joyeuse* won the Paderewski Prize of $500 and a performance with the New York Symphony under Walter Damrosch.

[3] Shepherd's best known work, *Triptych* (for high voice and string quartet) has been recorded by Betsy Norden on New World (218).

[4] Since Shepherd reworked certain songs many times, other keys may be in existence. (Loucks, 40).

[5] Also set under the title *When Slim Sophia Mounts Her Horse* by John Duke.

ELIE SIEGMEISTER

b. Jan. 15, 1909, Harlem, NY; d. March 10, 1991, Manhasset, NY

Throughout his diverse and colorful catalogue, Elie Siegmeister freely employed a wide—sometimes confusing—variety of compositional styles. All are heard in his large and vigorous corpus of songs.

Siegmeister's father was a surgeon, and both his parents were of Russian-Jewish ancestry. When he was five, the family moved to Brooklyn, and Siegmeister began to study piano. Unusually bright and energetic, at the age of 15 he entered Columbia University, where he studied composition with Seth Bingham and, on the side, with Wallingford Riegger. Three years later he graduated *cum laude* and left for Paris and four years of study with Nadia Boulanger.[1]

Siegmeister returned home in 1932 convinced that American music was too dominated by European influences to ever reach the mainstream public. As a result, he joined groups of composers devoted to national-

ist and social concerns,[2] helped found the American Composers
Alliance, organized concerts, and conducted working people's choruses.
Inspired both by American folk music and Charles Ives's use of the vernacular, Siegmeister incorporated folk materials into his own works. He
also compiled and supplied accompaniments for several important collections of folk songs,[3] and organized the American Ballad Singers. In
1945 his own compositions came into prominence when Arturo
Toscanini premiered his *Western Suite* with the NBC Symphony.

 After holding a variety of teaching positions, in 1949 Siegmeister
joined the music faculty at Hofstra University in Long Island, New
York, where he remained until his retirement in 1976. From his home in
Great Neck, Long Island, he continued to write,[4] perform, organize, and
compose until his death from a brain tumor. Married to Hannah Mersel,
an educator he met while a student in Paris, he had three daughters.[5]

THE SONGS
As evidence of his astonishing versatility, Siegmeister's unorthodox catalogue includes opera, Broadway musicals, symphonies, chamber and
choral music, children's pieces, film scores, band music, folk and art
songs. But vocal music, above all else, was a constant.[6] His approximately 100 songs (he destroyed another 100) range from the folksy,
tuneful *Johnny Appleseed* to the brutal, ultra-modern *Strange Funeral at
Braddock*. Aligning himself with no prescribed method of composition,
he may employ tonality or atonality, lush romantic harmonies or pungent
dissonances, conventional lyricism or taut angularity. And while he may
incorporate any vernacular source, especially folk, jazz, and the blues,
he may just as easily compose purely in the abstract. The character of the
text determines the setting, and most often he turns to American poets.
The urban lyricism of his long time friend, the great black poet Langston
Hughes, is a special inspiration.

 Siegmeister professed a hearty love of singers, but cautioned that
the key to song is through diction, vocal color, and character portrayal.[7]
When writing in a folklike or otherwise conventional vein, his songs are
lyric and even tuneful, but in his more ambitious style, vocal lines
become disjunct and declamatory. Piano writing is similarly varied and
can be difficult. *Songs of Elie Siegmeister (SES)* was published by the
Alfred Publishing Company in 1978. Bass-baritone Herbert Beattie and
soprano Elizabeth Kirkpatrick share a recording devoted to Siegmeister
songs on Orion (ORS 76220). Kirkpatrick has also recorded *Songs of
Innocence* and *City Songs* on Gasparo CD (GS-253). Soprano Esther

Hinds has recorded the cycles *Madam to You* and *The Face of War* on CRI (SD 416). Several cycles for voice with chamber ensemble have also been recorded. A sampling of better known and recommended songs are listed.

Elegies for Garcia Lorca, Antonio Machado; incl. *SES;* comp. 1938.
   Rec. medium and low voices (a–f#2); 5:15; titles are: *The Crime; The Poet and Death; Elegy;* in conventional, straightforward, lyrical language, Siegmeister has movingly set these spare laments on the murder of the great Spanish poet; an excellent small, serious, and, sometimes, haunting cycle; recorded by Beattie.

The Face of War, Langston Hughes; Fischer (facsimile edition) c1978; comp. 1967.[8]
   Spec. low voice (g–f♭2);[9] 8:30; titles are: *Official Notice; Listen Here, Joe; Peace; The Dove; War;* the steely, disjunct vocal writing is in a low tessitura; generally atonal; taut, occasional jazzlike rhythms; good variety in tempo; grim, intense anti-war songs; a potent, painful cycle; recorded by Hinds in what must be the medium key.

Five Cummings Songs, incl. *SES;* comp. 1970.
   Rec. medium and high lyric voices (a#–a♭2); 10:30; titles are: *in spite of everything; the first of all my dreams; raise the shade; up into the silence; because it's spring;* much slow, sustained singing with some *pp* high notes; difficult musically and vocally; not in any key; very chromatic; shifting meters; disjunct vocal phrases; nonetheless, lyrical and affecting; recorded in a different order by Kirkpatrick.

Johnny Appleseed, Rosemary Benét; Mercury c1949.
   Rec. medium and low voices (b–e2); 3:00; Slowly, with a drawl...Lively, rhythmical; three stanzas with a vampish accompaniment and playful changes in tempo; tasteful and charming; a possible encore; recorded by Beattie.

Lazy Afternoon, Leo Paris (from "Ozark Set"); Marks c1947.
   Rec. medium voice (d1–d2); 3:15; Moderately; a warm, infectious, folklike melody in three stanzas; could be an encore; recorded by Beattie.

Madam to You, Langston Hughes; Peters c1975.
   Rec. full medium or high women's voices (a–a♭2); 13:00; titles are: *Madam and the Census Man; Madam and the Minister; Mama and Daughter; Madam and the Rent Man; Madam and the Fortune*

Teller; Madam and the Number Runner; Madam and the Wrong Visitor; generally tonal; dissonant; jazzlike; frequently shifting meters; mostly declamatory; in each of these songs Madam Alberta K. Johnson, a black woman of strong character from the Harlem tenements, successfully takes on a different character who is confronting her; occasionally humorous; recorded by Hinds.

Nancy Hanks, Rosemary Benét; Marks c1947; comp. 1933; for Hannah, on her birthday.

Rec. medium or high voices (d♭1–f2); 2:45; Moderately; a straightforward, conventional setting of this fine poem about Lincoln's mother returning, as a ghost, to inquire about her son; recorded by Kirkpatrick.

The Strange Funeral at Braddock, Michael Gold; Presser c1936; comp. 1933.[10]

Spec. baritone (g#–e2); 7:30; Andante con moto; this social satire "depicting the death of a steel-worker in a flow of molten steel, contains sharp dissonances, tone clusters, crashing chords, wild rhythms, and jagged vocal leaps, shouts and cries."[11] A tremendous work for a singer with strong dramatic instincts (including many spoken sections) and a high level of musical sophistication; recorded by Beattie.

Also of interest:

Evil, Eberhart, incl. *SES,* low voices, in bass clef, long, difficult, recorded by Beattie; *For My Daughters,* Rosten, incl. *SES,* in a conventional style, much mother and daughter dialogue, five of the eight songs are recorded by Kirkpatrick; *Lonely Star,* Siegmeister, Southern c1952, Moderately slow, a combination of folk, pop, and classical; *Two Songs of the City,* Hughes, incl. *SES,* conventional, lyrical, recorded by Kirkpatrick.

BIBLIOGRAPHY
AmerGroves, Baker, Ewen, Greene Thompson.
"Elie Siegmeister: Interview," *The Music Journal* 35 (April 1977).
Oja, Carol J. "Composer with a Conscience: Elie Siegmeister in Profile," *American Music* 6 (Summer 1988): 158–180.
Scanlan, Roger. "Spotlight on Contemporary American Composers," *NATS Bulletin* 35 (Jan/Feb 1979).

Siegmeister, Elie. "The Composer and the Singer." Address to the 1980 National Convention of NATS held in Denver, Colorado. Printed in *NATS Bulletin* 37 (May/June 1981).

Siegmeister, Elie, ed. *The Music Lover's Handbook*. New York: William Morrow, 1943. This delightful compendium of musical miscellany contains several articles by Siegmeister, including an autobiographical sketch.

---

[1] In "Composer with a Conscience," *American Music* (Summer, 1988), Siegmeister credits Boulanger's ability in certain areas, but is very critical of her effete ways and plainly did not like the illustrious teacher.

[2] The Young Composers Group and Composers' Collective.

[3] Best known of these is *A Treasury of American Folk Song* (1940).

[4] One of his best known books is *The Music Lover's Handbook* (1943), which he expanded in 1973.

[5] One of his daughters, Nancy, became a concert violinist. With her husband, pianist Alan Mandel, they have performed much of Siegmeister's work. Alan Mandel is the accompanist on most of Siegmeister's vocal recordings.

[6] The first piece Siegmeister ever completed was a song to the poetry of Wallace Stevens called *Rosenbloom is Dead* (also referred to as *Cortege for Rosenbloom*). It pleased Siegmeister that, even at age 17, he revealed a personal voice. His first published work was the song *The Strange Funeral at Braddock*.

[7] Elie Siegmeister, "The Composer and the Singer." Reprinted in *NATS Bulletin* (May/June 1981), p. 18.

[8] First performed, in its orchestral version, by William Warfield in 1968, according to Siegmeister's liner notes (CRI SD 416), these songs were written for an anti-Vietnam war concert, organized by Siegmeister, in Carnegie Hall. *The New York Times* review of this concert (May 25, 1968), however, refers to it as a concert in honor of Martin Luther King. On the same recording Siegmeister also gives the date of their composition as 1966, but the sheet music gives 1967 for both music and poetry.

[9] The score, however, states that medium and high voice are available from publisher

[10] This song so impressed Henry Cowell that he included it in his *New Music Quarterly*.

[11] "The Composer and the Singer," *NATS Bulletin,* (May/June 1981), p. 18.

HALE SMITH
b. June 29, 1925, Cleveland, OH

African-American composer Hale Smith began studying piano as a boy. After serving in the army, he studied composition with Marcel Dick at the Cleveland Institute of Music, receiving degrees in 1950 and 1952. In 1958 Smith moved to New York, where he worked as a music editor and consultant for major publishers, including E. B. Marks and C. F. Peters. He also made arrangements for jazz performers and taught at local colleges. From 1970 until his retirement in 1984, Smith taught at the University of Connecticut (Storrs). His large catalogue includes many functional compositions such as film scores and band music.

THE SONGS
Mood, desolate and philosophical, is the predominant feature of Smith's thoroughly modern, atonal songs. Cool, but expressive vocal lines, primarily in a sustained declamatory style, are set over spare, linear, widely spaced textures. Though not especially disjunct, intervals can be difficult and the singer gets little help from the independent piano writing. Two of Smith's cycles date from the early 1950s. Three decades later, in much the same style but with more complex rhythms, the Raymond Patterson settings completed the list of his published songs.

Beyond the Rim of Day, Langston Hughes; Marks c1970; comp. 1950.
Spec. high voice (c1–b♭2); 7:45; titles are: *March Moon; Troubled Woman; To a Little Lover-Lass, Dead;* alternately lyrical, declamatory, and dramatic; of only moderate difficulty; beautifully crafted; expressive and evocative; an affecting cycle.

Three Patterson Lyrics, Raymond Patterson; Merion c1986.
Spec. soprano (c1–a♯2), also rec. for lyric mezzos; 14:00; titles are: *Night Piece; To a Weathercock; The World Bows Down to Beauty (Sonnet I);* the long vocal lines are somewhat disjunct and drift between a quasi recitative and a lyrical declamatory style; linear, evocative piano writing; slow to moderate tempos; atonal; strongly united in their mood of desolation brought on by unfulfilled searching, these songs are unremittingly serious, but beautiful and effective.

The Valley Wind, various poets; Marks c1974; comp. 1952-55.
Spec. medium voice (b–g2); 15:00; titles are: *The Valley Wind* (Lu Yün); *Spring* (William Shakespeare); *Envoy in Autumn* (Tu Fu); *Velvet Shoes* (Elinor Wylie); a variety of moods and subjects, but

structurally strong as a set; lyrical; linear; many tempo fluctuations; recorded by Harris.

BIBLIOGRAPHY
AmerGroves, Baker, Southern.
Scanlan, Roger. "Spotlight on American Composers: Hale Smith," *NATS Bulletin* 33 (May 1977).

JULIA SMITH
b. Jan. 25, 1911, Denton, Texas; d. Apr. 27, 1989, New York, NY

After graduating from North Texas State University in 1930, Julia Smith proceeded to New York City, where she studied piano and composition with Frederick Jacobi and Rubin Goldmark at the Juilliard Institute. Subsequently she received both her master's and doctor of philosophy degrees at New York University,[1] where Marion Bauer was among her teachers. Also a concert pianist, Smith's lecture-recitals on the piano music of Aaron Copland were popular events throughout the United States. In the 1940s she founded the Music Education Department at Hartt College of Music, and also taught at Juilliard and the New Britain Connecticut Teachers College. A vigorous promoter of women's music, in the 1960s she compiled *A Directory of American Women Composers*. She was married to an inventor and engineer, Oscar A. Vielehr.

THE SONGS
Smith's accessible songs are rich in feeling and atmosphere. Not always as conservative as they first appear to be, the tuneful, idiomatic vocal lines are straightforward, but the colorful accompaniments make some unexpected harmonic digressions. Sensibly written for the voice, they are excellent material for students, who will also enjoy their imagination and vitality.

Prairie Kaleidoscope, Ona Mae Ratcliff; Mowbray c1981.
　　　Rec. high voices (d1–a2); 10:15 is specified, but if one follows the metronome markings 7:00 would be more accurate; titles are: *Autumn Orchestra; Captive; Prairie Wind; Answer; Wakening;* best kept as a set; good variety; illustrative accompaniments; these lyrical, vivid evocations of nature on the prairie culminate in an intense and personal final song; sensitive and straightforward; a good set.

Three Love Songs, Karl Flaster; Mowbray c1954.

Pub. high, medium, and low voices (med., c1–g#2); 5:00; titles
are: *I Will Sing the Song; The Door That I Would Open; The Love I
Hold;* two flowing lyrical songs surround the more dramatic center-
piece; a nice, romantic set.

BIBLIOGRAPHY
AmerGroves, Ammer, Baker.
Craig, Mary. "Julia Smith: Composer and Ambassadress of U.S. Music,"
  Musical Courier (July 1959).

---

[1] Her doctoral dissertation was published in 1955 as *Aaron Copland* (New
  York, E. P. Dutton).

OLEY SPEAKS
b. June 28, 1874, Canal Winchester, OH; d. Aug. 27, 1948, New York, NY

For a period of time Oley Speaks was as well known for his baritone
voice as for his composition. Growing up in Columbus, Ohio, he stud-
ied piano, sang in church, and tried writing music. In 1898 he went to
New York City to study singing with, among others, the famous
American soprano Emma Thursby. As he became more interested in
composing, he also studied with Will Macfarlane and Max Spicker.
Meanwhile, in a concert career that took him throughout the country,
Speaks often programmed his own songs. Several of these, such as
Morning, the burly *On the Road to Mandelay* (recorded by Thomas
Hampson on EMI CD [7 54051 2] and Dale Moore on Cambridge [CRS
2715]), and the tender *Sylvia* (the latter two are incl. *AASTC),* became
immensely popular. Speaks's genre borders on the popular ballad style,
but the vocal demands are such that classically trained singers are generally required. In fact, because accompaniments can be very dense, big,
sturdy voices are often best. *To You, The Bells of Youth, Star Eyes,* and
The Perfect Prayer are other good examples of his style and (along with
the songs mentioned above) can all be found in *Album of Songs by Oley
Speaks* (G. Schirmer c1944). Exclusively a composer of song and choral
music, for 15 years Speaks served on the board of ASCAP. Radio and
concert singer Margaret Speaks was his niece.

BIBLIOGRAPHY
AmerGroves, Baker, Ewen (PAC), Thompson.
"America's Popular Composers: Oley Speaks," *Music Journal* (Novem-
  ber 1956).

ALEXANDER STEINERT
b. Sept. 21, 1900, Boston, MA; d. July 7, 1982, New York, NY

Alexander Steinert worked in many areas of the music world, but as a composer in the classical idiom he is almost entirely forgotten. His art songs, however, have beauty and imagination.

The son of a piano manufacturer, Steinert graduated from Harvard University with high honors in 1922. Subsequently he studied composition privately with Charles Loeffler in Boston, then with Charles Koechlin and Vincent d'Indy in Paris. In 1927 Steinert won the American Prix de Rome and spent three years at the American Academy in Rome. In 1937, in a performance with the Boston Symphony, he was the pianist for his own concerto. On Broadway, he was the leading coach for the original *Porgy and Bess* and conducted many performances. He also assisted Cole Porter on his last four shows. In 1940 Steinert moved to Hollywood, where he conducted, composed, and arranged film music. During the war he served in the U.S. Army Air Forces, composing for documentaries and training films. Later, he wrote for radio and television. He spent his last years teaching privately in New York City.

THE SONGS
Steinert composed into the 1950s, but publication of nearly all his classical works—orchestral pieces, sonatas, and art songs—seems to have ended in the 1930s. Though at first barely acknowledging him, Upton eventually commended the "outstanding quality"[1] of Steinert's later songs and wrote of their peculiar position "at the dividing line between the old and the new...."[2] Steinert's songs are heavily influenced by the French modern school, but in the harmonies of the last songs, one hears traces of a jazz influence. One consequence of this unusual harmonic palette is that pitches may briefly be elusive for the singer. Otherwise, the only difficulty is one of ensemble caused by the frequent use of cross rhythms over an already intricate piano score. Virtually all of Steinert's published songs are listed.

Four Lacquer Prints, Amy Lowell; Senart c1932; to Eva Gauthier.
Rec. lyric medium voices (c#1–e2); 4:30; titles are: *Vicarious; Temple Ceremony; Storm by the Seashore; A Burnt Offering;* lyrical declamation; the voice in its lower range may have trouble cutting through the intricate piano texture; impressionistic, delicate, evocative miniatures; a beautiful, small set.

Three Poems by Shelley, Senart c1932.
> Rec. high voices with some weight (b♭–b♭2);[3] 8:00; expansive, exotic songs, full of color and interest; an effective set; *Ozymandias* could be extracted.

The Waning Moon, (e1–g2); 1:45; Molto lento; quietly declaimed over changing figurations; atmospheric.

Ozymandias, (b♭–b♭2); 3:30; Lento; tempo changes; a soaring climax and subdued ending; a strong setting of this wonderful poem.

To the Nile, (b♭–a2[g♭2]); 2:45; Allegro moderato; sustained over flowing water figures; powerful ending.

Two Songs, Lilian Gertrude Shuman; Boston c1921.
> Spec. high voice (d♭1-b♭2[a2]), tenors best; 4:00; more romantic than the other sets; can be sung individually.

Snow at Twilight, (e1–a2); 1:45; Tranquillo; high tessitura; lyric and sustained over an elaborate accompaniment.

My Lady of Clouds, (d♭1-b♭2[a2]); 2:15; Andante, ma non troppo; lyric and sustained over fluid piano figures; builds to a big central climax; a lovely song.

BIBLIOGRAPHY
Baker, Howard (OAM and OCC), Thompson, Upton (Sup).

---

[1] William Treat Upton, *Art Song in America: Supplement,* 10.

[2] Ibid.

[3] The original orchestral version specified soprano, but a tenor might be best.

WILLIAM GRANT STILL
b. May 11, 1895, Woodville, MS; d. Dec. 3, 1978, Los Angeles, CA

William Grant Still is generally considered to be the dean of African-American composers. His mother was a teacher; his father, a teacher and a musician, died when Still was a baby. The family moved to Little Rock, Arkansas, where his mother remarried a man who sang, played opera recordings, and took his stepson to concerts. Though as a child Still took violin lessons, he entered Wilberforce College to study medicine, only to drop out when he found himself too busy with musical activities. He returned, however, in 1915 to earn a bachelor of science degree, and then studied music briefly at the Oberlin College Conservatory. After serving in World War I he went to New York City, where he made arrangements for W. C. Handy, Paul Whiteman, and Sophie Tucker, played violin, cello, and oboe in various orchestras, and oversaw the radio show "Deep River Hour." In addition, he studied with the avant-garde composer Edgar Varèse and also took some lessons with the conservative George Chadwick. Although Still never thought of himself as a black composer, it was his *Afro-American* Symphony, the first symphony by a black composer to be played by a major orchestra (Rochester Philharmonic) that, in 1931, brought him national recognition. In 1934 he moved to Southern California. A youthful marriage, which produced three children, had ended in divorce. In 1939 Still married again, this time to the journalist, pianist, and librettist of his operas, Verna Arvey, with whom he had two more children.

THE SONGS

In his handful of expressive, deeply felt art songs, one hears the kind of grandness and drama that Still had heard in the opera he loved as a child. Tonal and only mildly dissonant, with straightforward rhythms and rich, mostly homophonic accompaniments, singers with full-bodied voices and a passionate temperament should have little difficulty with these well written songs. *Songs of Separation* is recorded by mezzo-soprano Claudine Carlson on Bay Cities CD (1033), by baritone Robert Honeysucker on New World CD (80399-2), and by mezzo-soprano Cynthia Bedford on Desto (DC-7107). The following is believed to be a complete listing of Still's regrettably few published songs.

Breath of a Rose, Langston Hughes; also incl. *NAAS* and *RAAS*.
    Pub. high and low (high, e♭1–f#2); 2:30; Slowly; many tempo changes; the same theme takes on different guises as it describes the many faces of love; sustained over various accompanimental effects; difficult to connect the many changes, but a strong, emotive song.

Grief, LeRoy V. Grant; also incl. *AASBAS* and *RAAS*.
    Rec. medium voices (f1–g2); 3:15; Freely; a quiet chantlike recitando, over slowly rolled chords, frames a central full-throated, lushly accompanied cantabile; effective; recorded by Susan Mathews on BOMC (91-6674).

Songs of Separation, various Afro-American poets; Leeds c1949.
    Rec. full higher voices (d1-a2), two texts suggest men; 7:30; titles are: *Idolatry* (Arna Bontemps); *Poème* (Philippe Thoby Marcelin, in French); *Parted* (Paul Lawrence Dunbar); *If You Should Go* (Countee Cullen); *A Black Pierrot* (Langston Hughes); best kept as a set;

though in a variety of moods, each song deals with lovers who are separated; much sustained and some dramatic singing; an important and effective cycle; recorded by Carlson, Bedford, and Honeysucker (transposed down).

Winter's Approach, Paul Lawrence Dunbar; G. Schirmer c1928; also incl. *RAAS.*
　　Rec. high voices (e♭1–a♭2); 1:45; Animated and humorous; in dialect; like a spiritual.

BIBLIOGRAPHY
AmerGroves, Baker, Ewen, Goss, Greene, Southern, Thompson.
Haas, Robert Bartlett, Ed. *William Grant Still and the Fusion of Cultures in American Music.* Los Angeles, California: Black Sparrow Press. This work provides biography, discussion of Still's music, many of Still's writings, a discography, and a bibliography.
Hains, Frank. "William Grant Still...An American composer who happens to be black," *Musical America* (March 1975).
Lippey, Joyce and Walden E. Muns. "William Grant Still," *Music Journal* (November 1963).

LILY STRICKLAND
b. Jan. 28, 1887, Anderson, SC; d. June 6, 1958, Hendersonville, NC

From a musical family, in which both her mother and grandmother were singers, Lily Strickland studied at Converse College in Spartanburg, South Carolina. In 1910 she went to New York to continue her studies at the Institute of Musical Art with Dr. Percy Goetchius. Though she also wrote piano and choral works, Strickland is remembered for her many songs for which she often wrote the words. In them, she fashioned the native melodies she heard in her frequent travels into a quasi-popular style of concert ballad. Her first songs, such as the popular *Mah Lindy Lou* (recorded by John Charles Thomas on Nimbus CD [7838]) were drawn from her Southern roots. Subsequently she turned to American Indian influences, and in the 1920s, as a result of her experiences living in India with her husband, she composed numerous settings on Eastern themes, including *Songs of India* and *Himalayan Sketches.*[1] Despite their former popularity, by today's standards Strickland's songs are naïve and old-fashioned. The *Bayou Songs* and *My Lover Is a Fisherman* are some

352 A Singer's Guide to the American Art Song

of the best, while *I Remember*, recorded by Maryanne Telese on Premier (PRLP 002), is an excellent example of her style.

BIBLIOGRAPHY
AmerGroves, Ammer, Baker, Howard (OAM), Thompson.
"Women Composers of America: 20," *Musical America*, October 16, 1909.

---

[1] She also wrote articles about Indian music, including "Rabindranath Tagore–Poet-Composer" for *Musical Quarterly* (1929).

ANTHONY STRILKO
b. July 4, 1931, Philadelphia, PA

Anthony Strilko is not yet a well known composer, but his small catalogue of distinctive, expressive songs make a valuable contribution to the repertoire.

Strilko graduated from the Juilliard School of Music, where he studied composition with William Bergsma, Vincent Persichetti, and Vittorio Giannini. He also studied on a Fulbright Scholarship with Darius Milhaud at the Paris Conservatoire. He has won several awards, including the Elizabeth Sprague Coolidge Prize and a Joseph H. Bearns Prize, and he was twice a winner of the Marion Freschl Song Prize. His diverse catalogue includes a one-act opera and many settings of William Blake. When not composing, Strilko edits musical manuscripts for various publishers in New York.

THE SONGS
Strilko's early songs—regrettably the only ones published from an otherwise large catalogue of songs—are thoroughly modern but in no way experimental. Employing a rather spare palette, he is deft at creating the diverse moods and atmospheres of the choice but unusual little poems he is adept at finding. Most impressive, however, is the restraint and economy with which he conveys a notable depth of feeling. Exceedingly well written for the voice, the songs move in and out of tunefulness—a commodity Strilko has in abundance when he chooses to use it. Piano parts are lucid and descriptive. Rarely in a particular key but usually working around a central note, Strilko's songs present few serious musical difficulties. The following is a complete listing of those that have been published.

The Canal Bank, James Stephens; Mercury c1962; comp. 1959.
Rec. high lyric voices (f1–g2); 0:45; Andantino; light and bright; a charming song.

Canticle to Apollo, Robert Herrick; Mercury c1963; comp. 1960.
Rec. medium voices (e♭1–f♭2); 1:30; Straightforward; in a moderate tempo; sustained with melismatic passages over a broad ostinato and counter-melody; a good song about music.

David's Harp, Victor E. Reichert; Mercury c1968; comp. 1965.
Rec. medium voices (d1–e2); 1:45; Moderato con moto; fluid declamation over rolled chords; builds and recedes; a strong, poignant song.

The Fiddler's Coin, Patricia Benton; Mercury c1966; comp. 1965.
Rec. lower voices (d♭1–e2); 1:45; Moderately - with motion; sustained over the piano score's desolate evocation of a lonely street fiddler; spare and affecting.

From Autumn's Thrilling Tomb, Edgar Bogardus; Mercury c1967; comp 1955-67.
Rec. high voices (e♭1–a2); 3:15; Lento; sustained declamation over a spare piano part; a bleak song on death.

Little Elegy, Elinor Wylie; Mercury c1962; comp. 1958.
Rec. high voices (c1–a♭2); 1:45; Very slowly; a warm expressive melody over a simple accompaniment; builds then recedes; a touching, tender song.

Ophelia, Elinor Wylie; Mercury c1965; comp. 1963; for Shirley Verrett.
Rec. medium voices (d1–g2), woman's text; 3:00; Lento; broad, sustained declamation over a spare, independent piano; profoundly sorrowful.

Point Charles, Ronald Perry; Mercury c1967; comp. 1957.
Rec. medium and higher voices (c#1–g#2, with many opts. [d1-e2]); 1:15; Leisurely; vivid, unorthodox imagery of a town remembered from childhood; whimsical and with a tinge of nostalgia; light and lyrical.

Songs from "Markings" I and II, Dag Hammarskjöld; Mercury c1966; comp. 1965.
Rec. higher weightier voices (d1–a♭2); 5:30; both songs are fairly slow moving; the first is declamatory and assertive; the second more

lyrical, building to a big climax; on philosophical themes; intense, stirring songs.

BIBLIOGRAPHY

Folkman, Benjamin. Program notes to "Music for the Voice by Anthony Strilko." Merkin Concert Hall, Abraham Goodman House, New York, NY. (November 12, 1990).

Brant, Henry. "Six Young Composers," *The Juilliard Review* (Spring 1954); gives some idea of Strilko's compositional thinking when he was still a student, but little else.

HOWARD SWANSON
b. Aug. 18, 1907, Atlanta, GA; d. Nov. 12, 1978, New York, NY

One of America's first important black composers of classical music, in the late 1940s and early 1950s, Howard Swanson wrote highly individual songs, which were performed by noted artists and singled out by the critics.

Though his father, a farmer, was poor and illiterate, his mother, a country school teacher, was well educated and musical. When Swanson was nine the family moved to Cleveland, where he began piano lessons. Beginning in 1927, and for more than a decade, he worked on the railroad and as a postal clerk while taking evening classes at the Cleveland Institute of Music. Encouraged by his composition teacher, Herbert Elwell, Swanson applied for and, in 1938, received a Rosenwald Fellowship to study in Paris with Nadia Boulanger. Forced by the war to return to America in 1941, he worked for the Internal Revenue Service by day, and at night composed in his Harlem walk-up. Artists such as Everett Lee, Marian Anderson, William Warfield, and Helen Thigpen began to program his songs, and in 1950 Dimitri Mitropoulos successfully premiered *Short Symphony,* which won a Music Critics' Circle Award.[1] From 1952 to 1966 Swanson again lived in Paris. Ultimately, he settled down in New York but never quite regained the recognition he had held earlier.

THE SONGS
Though written in a conventional idiom, Swanson's songs are modern and distinctive. Some, to more abstract texts, employ spare, dissonant harmonic textures, in which critics have often noted a French influence.[2] Others are more generally accessible, and in their expression of the

underlying sadness of the human condition and occasional introduction
of jazz elements, convey a nostalgic American flavor. But no matter the
text or approach, Swanson's poetic and intensely personal voice makes
a profound impression.

Since such highly individual and predominantly serious songs are
not easily absorbed or communicated, advanced performers are required.
Moreover, though vocal lines are decidedly assured and very expressive,
they are rarely tuneful, tend to be fragmented, and can be demanding.
There are songs for a variety of voices here, but with the dark themes of
Swanson's chosen texts and the inspiration of such deep throated singers
as Marian Anderson and William Warfield, low voices are favored.
However, though black singers have a history of performing these songs,
there is no reason white singers should avoid them. Accompaniments—
often with big solo passages— are imaginative and involved, but the
profusion of accidentals, thick harmonic textures, and complex rhythms
create considerable work for both performers. Though long out of print
Swanson's songs are quite easily found in libraries. (The American
Music Center in particular has an excellent collection.) There are recordings by Helen Thigpen on Desto (6422) and Willis Patterson on BOMC
(91-6674). Virtually all Swanson's published songs are noted.

Cahoots, Carl Sandburg; Weintraub c1951; to William Warfield.

Rec. low voices (b♭–e♭2), best for men; 3:30; Moderately - not too
fast; short declamatory phrases follow the vernacular of street low-
life; dissonant; some blues-like passages; difficult to hold together,
but could be effective and different.

A Death Song (Lullaby), Paul Lawrence Dunbar; Leeds c1951; also incl.
AASBAC; to Lawrence Winters.

Rec. low voices (b♭–e♭2); 3:45; Andante moderato; Swanson provides a straight version of the text, indicating it need not be sung in
dialect; a recurring, haunting piano figure; a hushed, spiritual-like lullaby; unusual and very beautiful; recorded by Patterson.

Ghosts in Love, Vachel Lindsay; Weintraub c1950.

Rec. medium voices (f1–e♭2); 1:45; Lento; lyrical declamation
over a delicate, provocative, piano figure, evoking eeriness; recorded
by Thigpen.

In Time of Silver Rain, Langston Hughes; Weintraub c1950.

Rec. high lyric voices (d1–a2); 3:00; Moderato; atonal; warm and
lyrical in a high tessitura over strange harmonies.

Joy, Langston Hughes; Weintraub c1950; to Edward Lee Tyler.

  Rec. medium voices (b♭–e2); 0:45; Allegro; lyrical declamation with sustained final notes; bright and spirited; recorded by Thigpen (transposed up).

The Junk Man, Carl Sandburg; Weintraub c1950.

  Rec. higher voices (e1–g2); 2:45; Moderato; declamatory; dissonant; the junk man, symbolizing death, carries away the worn out clock; the striking imagery is powerfully communicated; dramatic; recorded by Thigpen.

The Negro Speaks of Rivers, Langston Hughes; Weintraub c1950; also incl. *AASBAC;* to Marian Anderson.

  Rec. low voices (g–e♭2); 4:15; Moderato (with steady rhythm); a soothing melodic refrain over rocking chords conveys the expansiveness and antiquity of rivers; a central dramatic section with recitative passages; many low notes; evocative and strong; recorded by Patterson and Thigpen (transposed up).

Night Song, Langston Hughes; Weintraub c1950; to Helen Thigpen.

  Rec. medium and high lyric voices (d1–g2); 2:15; Andantino; sustained over a flowing but independent accompaniment; warm and magical; recorded by Thigpen.

Pierrot, Langston Hughes; Weintraub c1950.

  Rec. low voices (a#–d2); 2:45; Allegro; hefty voices with excellent articulation are essential to be heard over the spirited, rhythmic accompaniment, which dominates this odd, but fun, narrative of the Pierrot theme; somewhat tuneful but very dissonant.

Saw a grave upon a hill, May Swenson; Weintraub c1952.

  Rec. very low voices (d–b♭1); 2:45; Slow and grave; sustained over chords and chilling piano figurations; difficult to communicate; serious and somber.

Still Life, Carl Sandburg; Weintraub c1950.

  Rec. medium voices (d♭1–g2); 1:30; Moderately fast; this is anything but the quiet song the title suggests; a busy accompaniment evokes the motion of the train; jazzlike with syncopations; recorded by Thigpen.

The Valley, Edwin Markham; Weintraub c1950; to Sergius Kagen.

Pub. medium and low (low, b♭–d♭2); 1:45; Andante; hushed, lyrical declamation over a steadily moving, spare accompaniment; a
lovely, poetic song; recorded by Thigpen.

Also of interest:

Four Preludes, Eliot, high lyric voices, abstract songs with little diversity; *I Will Lie Down in Autumn,* Swenson, also incl. *AASBC,* for lower
voices, Andante, somber, recorded by Patterson; *Snowdunes,* Swenson,
for high voices, Adagio; chordal; *Songs for Patricia,* Rosten, four songs
for high voices; *To Be Or Not To Be,* Anonymous, Moderato - in a casual manner, mildly humorous.

BIBLIOGRAPHY
AmerGroves, Baker, Greene, Southern, Thompson.
Baker, David N., Lida M. Belt, and Herman C. Hudson, eds. *The Black
    Composer Speaks.* Metuchen, New Jersey: Scarecrow Press, 1978.
Quillian, James W. "Howard Swanson and Sergius Kagen: New Songs
    to Sing," *Repertoire* (November 1951).
Spearman, Rawn Wardell. "The 'Joy' of Langston Hughes and Howard
    Swanson," *Black Perspectives in Music 9* (1981). In addition to an
    analysis of the song *Joy,* and a discussion of Langston Hughes, this
    interview probes Swanson's background and his feelings about the
    black experience in music.

---

[1] This award, given in 1952, brought Swanson unusual recognition in a small
    column headed "The Year's Best" in *Time* magazine (January 21, 1952).

[2] See Virgil Thomson's review of Helen Thigpen's Town Hall recital in the
    Herald Tribune (Nov. 17, 1949), reprinted in *Music Left and Right;* also
    Henry Cowell in *Musical Quarterly* (1950) p. 453.

RANDALL THOMPSON
b. April 21, 1899, New York, NY; d. July 9, 1984, Boston, MA

Best known for his forthright, accessible choral compositions, Randall
Thompson's handful of songs have a similar appeal.

Thompson, who came from an old New England family, attended
Harvard University, where he studied music with Edward Burlingame
Hill, Walter Spalding, and Archibald T. Davison, and graduated in 1922
with a master's degree. He also studied privately with Ernest Bloch. As
winner of an American Prix de Rome, Thompson lived in that city for

three years. On his return he held positions at various universities, including Wellesley College, the Curtis Institute (where he was director for two years), the University of Virginia, Princeton University, and from 1948 until his retirement in 1965, Harvard University. In 1927 Thompson married Margaret Quayle Whitney, with whom he raised four children.

THE SONGS

Although Thompson's songs are set in an unabashedly conventional idiom, they are notable for their sincerity, poetic sensibility, and quiet elegance. His writing for the voice is, both musically and technically, so simple and straightforward that much of it could be managed by beginners. The same holds true for the accompaniments. In a sophisticated, stimulating recital program the ingenuousness of these songs might provide a welcome respite. Povla Frijsh's exquisite recording of *Velvet Shoes* is available on New World (247). A list of Thompson's best known published songs follows.

My Master Hath a Garden, Anonymous; E. C. Schirmer c1938.
>   Rec. any voice (e♭1–e♭2); 1:45; Allegretto...Moderato (alternately); a warm, straightforward lyric line; bright piano interludes.

The Passenger, M. A. DeWolfe Howe; E. C. Schirmer c1961; to Gerard Souzay.
>   Spec. baritone, in bass clef (G–f1); 6:30; Lento tranquillo; expansive vocal lines over steady chords; piano interlude; dangerously close to being tedious and sentimental but could be effective if delivered with imagination and dignity; more ambitious than most Thompson; a reflection on death.

Siciliano, Philip H. Rhinelander; E. C. Schirmer c1980.
>   Spec. baritone (c#1–f2), rec. any medium high lyric voice; 1:45; Poco allegretto; melodious and lilting; images of love.

Tapestry, William Douglas; E. C. Schirmer c1986; comp. 1925.
>   Spec. mezzo-soprano (b–e2); 2:15; Con moto tranquillo; long, sustained vocal lines over a flowing accompaniment; a bit stiff and static.

Velvet Shoes, Elinor Wylie; E. C. Schirmer c1938.
>   Spec. medium voices (c1–e2); 3:15; Quasi una marcia in lontananza; muted march-like piano solos alternate with a warm, compelling vocal melody; a lovely song, treasured for its disarming simplicity; recorded by Frijsh.

BIBLIOGRAPHY
AmerGroves, Baker, Ewen, Greene, Thompson.

VIRGIL THOMSON
b. Nov. 25, 1896, Kansas City, MO; d. Sept. 30, 1989, New York, NY

He traveled in the most cosmopolitan and sophisticated circles, but Virgil Thomson never lost touch with the plain language of his Midwestern roots. Though his vocal music is a curious offspring of these disparate worlds, and can as easily perplex and infuriate as it can disarm and enchant, no one disputes that it boasts some of the most felicitous musical declamation in the song repertoire.

Of Scotch, Irish, and Welsh descent, Thomson's grandparents came from Kentucky and Virginia. Though his family had a long history of farming, his father failed in that business and took up work as a post office administrator. Thomson grew up in a happy Baptist home where relatives came to make music. At age five he began piano lessons with a cousin and, at 12, began to study more formally. Before long he was earning money as an accompanist for both singers and silent movies. Entering Harvard University in 1919, his principal teachers were Edward Burlingame Hill, Archibald T. Davison, and S. Foster Damon, who were all French influenced. In 1921 Thomson toured Europe with the Harvard Glee Club, then remained a year in Paris to study with Nadia Boulanger before returning to finish his degree at Harvard. From 1925 until 1940 he again lived in Paris. There he met the two artists who would most influence his work: Eric Satie, the French composer who sought to purge music of its nineteenth-century excesses; and Gertrude Stein, the American expatriate poet who gave more importance to the sound and association of words than to their meaning. The opera *Four Saints in Three Acts,* just one of Thomson's brilliant collaborations with Stein, premiered in 1934 and was focal to establishing his reputation.

In 1940 Thomson returned to the United States and moved permanently into the Chelsea Hotel on Manhattan's West 23rd Street. From 1940 to 1954 he was chief music critic for the *Herald Tribune,* and became as well known for his clean, elegant prose, and astute, provocative opinions as for his own compositions. In the years that followed Thomson continued to write (notes and words), conduct, and lecture. Deafness slowed these activities in his last years and he died quietly in his hotel apartment.

THE SONGS

Thomson knew that, ultimately, his fame rested with his three operas.[1] He spoke less positively of his approximately 70 published songs.[2] Composed between 1926 and 1980,[3] they make unquestionably an uneven catalogue. The best songs are jewels fashioned out of finely etched melodies, subtle harmonies, sparkling rhythmic invention, a frugality of notes, and—more often than not—wit. The poorest are dead weights, comprised of pedestrian melodies, unforgiving ostinato accompaniments, and aimless ramblings. The majority lie somewhere in between—pleasing, amusing, serviceable, but not compelling.

The inimitable Thomson style is a cross between provincialism and worldliness, American square-shooting and French refinement. His fresh, lucid idiom has a rare ability to cleanse the palate making it a boon to good programming. Many of his songs make excellent opening or closing numbers (perfect for warming up or winding down) or else provide a welcome respite between weightier courses. It is Thomson's legacy that, if set correctly, vocal music *can* be understood. Therefore, in great part due to the ease and naturalness of his prosody, with the exception of some of the bigger songs, any singer with a free vocal production will have little trouble, while those burdened with constricted cords or tongue should benefit from the easy conversational style. Accompaniments are mostly supportive, often vamplike or with ostinato characteristics. However, as simple as Thomson's songs appear on the surface, more often than not, performers can be in for some nasty rhythmic fun-and-games.

Thomson wrote many songs in French, which date from the years he lived in Paris. He was fluent in the language and proud of his settings. Most translations were commissioned from friends (first Sherry Magnan and later Donald Sutherland) and overseen by Thomson himself. He also carefully provided optional notation to accommodate the translations, suggesting he approved their use in performance.

Many Thomson songs still remain in manuscript, but the majority have been published and are in print from a variety of publishers. Principal recordings are: Betty Allen, with Thomson at the piano, on CRI (SRD 207); Meriel Dickinson on Unicorn (UN1-72017); Mack Harrell on CRI (398); Martha Herr on New Albion CD (034); Ellen Lang on Musical Heritage CD (MHS 512622K); William Sharp on New World CD (369-2); Paul Sperry on Albany CD (TROY043). Singers will want to consider other Thomson works such as duets, chamber works, and arias from the operas. The following is a list of recommendations and better known songs. Those under *Also of interest* are of lesser merit but virtually complete the published Thomson catalogue.

Air de Phèdre (Phaedra's Farewell), Jean Racine, trans. by Donald Sutherland; Southern c1974; comp. 1930.

Spec. soprano (d1–b♭2); 6:00; in an unfluctuating moderate tempo; recitando with a few sustained phrases; more difficult than most Thomson; despite the dramatic content of the Queen's narration, in which she describes what has brought her to suicide, the music maintains a quiet dignity; a concert monologue for mature artists.

At the Spring, Jasper Fisher; Gray c1965; comp. 1955.

Spec. medium voice; (d1–g2), rec. higher lyrics; 1:00; allegretto; clever rhythms; dynamic contrasts; charming, playful, pretty, and cheerful; a nice opener; recorded by Sharp (transposed down).

The Courtship of Yongly Bongly Bo, Edward Lear; G. Schirmer c1977; comp. 1973/74.

Rec. medium and higher lyric voices (e♭1–f2); 7:00; flowing, in a moderately fast tempo; tuneful; various illustrative piano figurations; a whimsical, humorous, but touching little narrative by the master of nonsense verse; needs a good storyteller more than a pretty voice to hold the interest; recorded by Herr.

Five Songs from William Blake, Southern c1953; orig. for baritone and orchestra (Southern c1951); comp. 1951.

Rec. high baritones, in bass clef (A–g1); 18:00; titles are: *The Divine Image; Tiger! Tiger!; The Land of Dreams; The Little Black Boy; And Did Those Feet;* best kept as a cycle; broad phrases and hefty high notes call for an operatic approach; even in piano reduction, these are notable Thomson; unabashedly eclectic, emotional, but forthright settings of Blake's beautiful, mystical verses; all but *The Little Black Boy* (a text that some find distasteful in twentieth-century America) are recorded with orchestra by Harrell.

If Thou a Reason Dost Desire to Know, Sir Francis Kynaston; Southern c1962; comp. 1955.

Rec. medium voices (c1–f2), text suggests men; 2:00; conversa-
~ tional; quiet throughout; a love song; subtle and seductive; recorded by Sharp (transposed down).

John Peel, John Woodcock Graves; Southern c1962; comp. 1955.

Rec. baritones, in bass clef (B–e1); 3:15; not too fast, but vigorous; based on the well-known traditional tune, with variations on the hunting horn call; ends abruptly; different; recorded by Sharp (transposed down).

Jour de chaleur aux bains de mer (Hot Day at the Seashore),[4] Duchesse de Rohan, trans. by Sherry Mangan; Boosey c1963; comp. 1928.

 Rec. high voices (c1–g2); 1:00; the voice carries the cheerful tune in duple meter over a vamping piano, misbarred to effect a waltz (a favorite Thomson device); rhythmic pranks and unmitigated charm make this a winner.

Mostly About Love, Kenneth Koch; G. Schirmer c1964; comp. 1959; to Alice Esty; pub. separately.

 Rec. medium or higher voices (c1–g2); 13:00; humorous, contemporary reflections on love; can be used individually or as a set.

Love Song, (c1–g2); 2:15; the rapid conversational opening broadens into a more sustained lyricism; a progression of love images.

Down at the Docks, (d1–g2); 2:15; lyrical, building over various chordal figurations.

Let's Take a Walk, (d1–g2); 2:15; conversational becoming sustained over a flowing accompaniment; recorded by Nancy Tatum on London (OS 26053).

A Prayer to St. Catherine, (e♭1–f2); 2:30; conversational, over chords; subdued opening builds; recorded by Sharp, Sperry, and by Federica Von Stade on CBS (37231).

Praises and Prayers, G. Schirmer c1963; comp. 1963; commissioned by the Ford Foundation for Betty Allen; pub. separately.

 Rec. big medium voices (c#1–g2); 18:15; primarily declamatory; colorful accompaniments; the weighty middle tessitura can be wearying for any but the right voice; conceived as a cycle, but songs may be programmed singly or in smaller units; recorded by Allen and Lang.

From the Canticle of the Sun, St. Francis of Assisi; (c#1–e2); 5:45; declamatory; stately.

My Master Hath a Garden, Anonymous; (f1–e♭2); 1:45; Tempo commodo; delicate, pretty.

Sung by the Shepherds, from "A Hymn of the Nativity" by Richard Crashaw; also incl. *CASS;* (d1–g2); 4:30; various textures and tempos; builds to final *fff*.

Before Sleeping, Anonymous; (d1–d2); 2:15; a prayer; simple and spare; can be sung almost in a "white voice";[5] recorded by Nancy Tatum on London (OS 26053).

Jerusalem, My Happy Home, from "The Meditations of St. Augustine"; (d1–f#2); 4:00; Molto ritmico; chordal; buoyant.

Preciosilla, Gertrude Stein; G. Schirmer c1948; also incl. *S22A* and *RAAS;* comp. 1927.

Pub. high and low (high, e♭1–a2);[6] 5:00; a recitative and aria; Thomson's use of eighteenth-century operatic style is the antithesis of Stein's thoroughly modern poem, making her words seem even more nonsensical; recorded by Herr and Sperry.

Shakespeare Songs, Southern c1961; comp. 1956/57; pub. separately and as a set.

Rec. medium and higher lyric voices (d1–a2[g2]); 11:30; these lyrical and Elizabethan sounding songs can be used individually or in any grouping, but—if the same voice feels right for all—they also make an excellent set; recorded by Herr.

Was This Fair Face the Cause? (f1–f2); 2:15; Lazy and lackadaisical; cantabile over a moving, staccato accompaniment; repeated, humming.

Take, O, Take Those Lips Away; also incl. *VN;* (e1–f2); 2:30; Very slowly; a slender, tender melody over a lutelike accompaniment; repeated *ppp;* a gorgeous song; also recorded by Sperry.

Tell Me Where Is Fancy Bred; (f1–g2); 1:30; a warm melody over bell-like chords; also recorded by Yolanda Marcoulescou-Stern on Gasparo CD (287).

Pardon, Goddess of the Night; (d1–e♭2); 2:15; Lento molto espressivo (after a piano introduction); sustained chords.

Sigh No More, Ladies; (d1–a2[f2]); 3:00; crisp and rhythmic; ends in a fandango; also recorded by Marcoulescou-Stern on Gasparo.

Susie Asado, Gertrude Stein; incl. *CC;* comp. 1926.

Rec. high lyric voices (d1–g2); 1:30; Thomson's first Stein setting and his first published song; interesting rhythmic play; parlando; nonsensical text; Thomson has written that the "music-idea in both voice and piano is an evocation of bird sounds."[7]

The Tiger, William Blake;[8] G. Schirmer c1967; also incl. *CAS28;* comp. 1926.

Rec. high voices (d1–g2); 3:00; declaimed over a hair-raising ostinato; a brief lyrical section; powerful and arresting; recorded by Eleanor Steber on Desto (411/412).

Two by Marianne Moore,[9] G. Schirmer c1966; comp.1963; pub. separately; in memory of Francis Poulenc.

    Rec. medium voices (d1–f2); 4:00; can be sung separately or as a
unit; recorded by Lang, Sharp, and Meriel Dickinson on Unicorn
(UN1 72017).

English Usage, or "Strike till the iron is hot"; also incl. *CAS28;*
    (d1–e2); 2:00; short declamatory phrases; text spoofs affectation
in language; "A free recitative punctuated by short major
chords."[10] Also recorded by Sperry.

My Crow Pluto, or "Even when the bird is walking we know that it
has wings"; also incl. *20CAS;* (d1–f2); 2:00; this absurdly erudite
poem, replete with Italian phrases, is set with mock passion over
lush and rippling piano figures.

La Valse Grégorienne, Georges Hugnet, trans. by Donald Sutherland;
Southern c1940/80; comp. 1927.

    Spec. medium voice (d1–a2); 2:15; four small songs depicting
"the waking dreams of a very young man."[11] To be sung without
pause; cantabile; basically a waltz with some misplaced barring;
recorded by Herr.

Also of interest:

The Bell Doth Toll, Heywood, also incl. *VN,* for lower voices, eerie;
La Belle en dormant (Beauty Sleeping), Hugnet, four small lyric songs;
Le Berceau de Gertude Stein, Hugnet, eight small songs to be sung
without pause; unchanging tempo, recorded by Marcoulescou on Orion
(OC 685); ***Consider Lord,*** Donne, for low voices, slow and majestic,
Dirge, Webster, broad over rolled chords; ***Film: Deux Soeurs qui ne
sont pas soeurs*** (Two Sisters Not Sisters), Stein, about Stein and her
poodle; ***Four Songs to Poems of Thomas Campion,*** also arr. with clarinet, viola and harp, love songs, recorded with instruments by Lang,
There is a Garden in Her Face with piano by Sperry; ***Look, How the
Floor of Heaven,*** Shakespeare, for high voices, hushed, spare; ***My
Shepherd Will Supply My Need,*** Watts (paraphrase of Psalm 23), also
incl. *Folk Songs by Master Composers* (Da Capo), Allegro ma sostenuto; ***Portrait of F.B.,*** Stein, for higher voices, Tempo commodo, recorded by Dickinson; ***Remember Adam's Fall,*** Anonymous, builds to a
stirring finale; ***Le Singe et le Léopard*** (The Monkey and the Leopard),
de La Fontaine, many changes; ***Tres Estampas de Niñez*** (Three

Sketches from Childhood), Rivas, *What Is It?* Campion, also arr. with guitar accompaniment, in Elizabethan style.

BIBLIOGRAPHY

AmerGroves, Baker, Ewen, Friedberg (II), Goss, Greene, Manning (on Blake songs), Mellers, Stevens, Thompson.

Hoover, Kathleen and John Cage. *Virgil Thomson: His Life and Music.* New York: Thomas Yoseloff, 1959.

Meckna, Michael. *Virgil Thomson: A Bio-Bibliography.* Westport, Connecticut: Greenwood Press, 1986.

Ramey, Phillip. "Virgil Thomson at 85: A Candid Conversation," *Ovation* (November 1981).

Thomson, Virgil. *Music with Words: A Composer's View.* New Haven and London: Yale University Press, 1989.

———. *Virgil Thomson.* New York: A. A. Knopf, 1966. Reprint. New York: Da Capo Press, 1977.

———. *A Virgil Thomson Reader.* Boston: Houghton Mifflin Company, 1981.

Various authors. "A Tribute to Virgil Thomson on his 81st Birthday," *Parnassus: Poetry in Review* 5 (Spring/Summer 1977): 405–531.

---

[1] *Four Saints in Three Acts* (1927), *The Mother of Us All* (1947), and *Lord Byron* (1967).

[2] Phillip Ramey, "Virgil Thomson at 85," *Ovation,* 12.

[3] The earliest, *Vernal Equinox* (to a poem by Amy Lowell) dates from 1920 but remains unpublished.

[4] This is the second in a set called *Trois Poèmes de la Duchesse de Rohan.* The other two songs (*A Son Altesse le Princesse Antoinette Murat* and *La Seine)* remain unpublished, though *La Seine* was reproduced in the Parnassus tribute to Thomson (see bibliography). They are wonderful songs that should be published.

[5] Virgil Thomson, *Music with Words,* 89.

[6] The low version is only found in collection.

[7] *Music with Words,* 85.

[8] This is a completely different setting from Thomson's 1951 version in *Five Songs from William Blake.*

[9] A good study of these songs is found in Friedberg's *American Art Song and American Poetry: Vol. II,* 26–39.

[10] *Music with Words,* 88.

[11] Ibid, 79.

GEORGE WALKER
b. June 27, 1922, Washington, D.C.

For decades the distinguished black composer George Walker has been producing potent, personal songs strongly rooted in the traditions of classical art song.

The son of a physician, Walker studied music as a young boy. Subsequently, his considerable education, especially in piano and composition, included studies at Oberlin College Conservatory, the Curtis Institute, the American Conservatory at Fontainebleau, the Eastman School, and private studies with Nadia Boulanger. In 1945 Walker gave his debut piano recital in New York and also won the Philadelphia Orchestra Youth Audition, which included an appearance with the orchestra. With his career as a concert pianist assured, in the late 1940s he began to receive attention for his compositions as well. In 1960 he married pianist Helen Siemens and the couple settled in New York City, where Walker taught at the Dalcrose School of Music and at the New School for Social Research. They had two children but were divorced in 1975. Since 1969 he has been on the faculty of Rutgers University.

THE SONGS
Walker imbues each of his luminous songs with poetic sensibility and an expressivity notable for its restraint. Frugal with notes, his textures are spare and pure. Early songs are generally in a traditional idiom and, despite the telling dissonances, present few musical problems for either performer. Later songs, however, are more abstract and severe. Atonal and rhythmically complex, they require intensive study. Though Walker has arranged some spirituals, in his art songs only the compelling singing quality and occasional rhythmic and jazz elements reveal anything of his black heritage. In the diverse poetry he chooses to set the underlying melancholy seems to stem from no particular human situation.

Walker's writing for the voice shows a real appreciation of many of its singular characteristics. His taut lyricism, however, occasionally requires stamina and control to handle long legato lines, passages of unremitting high tessitura, and *pianissimos* that must be plucked from the atmosphere. A good selection of Walker songs is in print. A fine recording by Phyllis Bryn-Julson on CRI (SD 488), one side of which is devoted to his songs, provides a comprehensive view. The following is believed to be a complete listing of Walker's published songs.

The Bereaved Maid, Anonymous; General c1971; also incl. *AAS.*

Rec. medium and high voices (d♭1–f2); 4:00; changing tempos and dynamics; yet another superb setting of this amazing, mystical poem;[1] haunting; bleak; stunning; recorded by Bryn-Julson.

Emily Dickinson Songs, Southern c1986.

Spec. high voice (d1–c2); 6:45; the singer needs some weight to the voice, an easy command of high tessitura, and superior musicianship; good as a set but no reason not to use the songs individually; the last three about death form a strong grouping and are recorded by Bryn-Julson.

Wild Nights, (f1–c3); 1:00; Agitated; dramatic.

What If I Say I Shall Not Wait, (d1–b2); 2:45; Dramatically; unmetered until the final passage; declamatory with some sprechstimme; many contrasting elements; very difficult; powerful.

I Have No Life But This, (e1–a2); 1:30; Very slowly; dramatic declamation.

Bequest, (e1–a2); 1:30; Very slowly; parlando.

Hey Nonny No, Anonymous; General c1975.

Rec. medium voices (e1–d2); 1:00; quiet, moving, delicate, rhythmic; appealing; recorded by Bryn-Julson.

I Went to Heaven, Emily Dickinson; General c1971; also incl. *AAS.*

Rec. higher voices (f#1–e2); 1:00; Playfully; light and graceful with mischievous rhythms; a charming song; recorded by Bryn-Julson.

Lament, Countee Cullen; General c1975; also incl. *AASBAS.*

Rec. lower voices (a–d2), text suggests men; 3:15; quiet and subdued; lyrical declamation; recorded by Willis Patterson on BOMC (91-6674).

Nocturne, Donald S. Hayes; Southern c1987; incl. *VN.*

Rec. medium and high voices (c#1–g#2); 2:15; Quietly; vocal and piano lines intertwine; warm and lyrical.

A Red, Red Rose, Robert Burns; General c1975; also incl. *AASBAS.*

Rec. full medium voices (a#–g2); 4:15; disjunct and melismatic over an elaborate, intricate piano score; an improvisatory effect with a blues influence; quiet opening builds to big ending; many rhythmic difficulties; different from other Walker songs; atonal; dissonant; aggressive; recorded by Bryn-Julson, and Laura English Robinson on BOMC (91-6674).

Response, Paul Lawrence Dunbar; General c1971.
    Rec. medium and higher voices (e♭1–e2), text suggests men; 2:15; slowly moving; somewhat dissonant chords accompany the long sustained lyric lines; plaintive; recorded by Bryn-Julson.

So, We'll Go No More A Roving, Lord Byron; General c1971.
    Rec. high lyric voices (d1–g2); 2:00; Moderately; an evocative melody; subdued opening and closing; a stirring, full, central section; excellent song; recorded by Bryn-Julson.

Sweet, Let Me Go, Anonymous; General c1971; also incl. *AAS.*
    Rec. high lyric voices (d1–g#2); 1:45; slow, hushed; a plaintive melody over a rocking accompaniment, increasing in drama; recorded by Bryn-Julson.

With Rue My Heart Is Laden, A. E. Housman; General c1972.
    Rec. medium and higher lyric voices (d1–f#2); 2:45; Rather slowly; a delicate, spare piano line intertwines with the sustained vocal melody; agitated central section; profoundly melancholy; contained and compelling; recorded by Bryn-Julson.

BIBLIOGRAPHY
AmerGroves, Baker, Ewen, Southern.
Walker, George. "Make Room for Black Classical Music," *The New York Times,* November 3, 1991.

---

[1] Daniel Pinkham and John Edmunds have each made settings under the title *The Faucon.* Ramiro Cortès called it *The Falcon.*

ROBERT WARD
b. Sept. 13, 1917, Cleveland, OH

Best known for his operas, especially *The Crucible,* which won a Pulitzer Prize in 1962, Robert Ward has written a handful of romantic songs.
    As a child, Ward studied piano, sang in church, heard opera (when the Metropolitan came to town), and wrote his first compositions. At the Eastman School of Music he studied with Howard Hanson and Bernard Rogers. After graduation he moved to New York and, in 1939, entered the Juilliard School of Music, where he studied composition with Frederick Jacobi. During World War II, as conductor of the Seventh

Infantry Band, Ward toured the Pacific. Joining the Juilliard faculty in 1946, he remained there until 1956, the year his first opera, *He Who Gets Slapped,* premiered.[1] Since then he has held administrative positions at Galaxy Music, Highgate Press, and the American Composers Alliance. From 1967 to 1972 he was chancellor of the North Carolina School for the Arts, and from 1977 to 1987 professor of music at Duke University. Ward married Mary Benedict in 1946 and the couple raised five children.

THE SONGS

Ward's best successes have been in large forms, especially opera, and his published songs all have an an operatic thrust. Unabashedly romantic, Ward enhances their inherent drama with telling dissonances, rich accompanimental support, and searing vocal lines. Whether spinning a limpid melody or building to a powerful climax, he clearly loves the voice and knows how to display the singer's riches. Big, opulent voices are especially well served. *Songs for Pantheists* is recorded by Sylvia Stahlman on CRI (206) and *The Sorrow of Mydah* by John McCollum on Desto (411/412). William Stone sings arias and songs (transposed down) on Bay Cities CD (1029). Though all are published in only one key, Stone's recording, overseen by Ward, indicates that transposition is acceptable.

As I Watched the Ploughman Ploughing, Walt Whitman; Peer c1951; comp. 1940.
> Rec. high full voices (c1–a2); 2:00; Adagio; the subdued pastoral opening quickly turns to heavy drama; sustained over a moving accompaniment; recorded by Stone.

Rain Has Fallen All the Day, James Joyce; Peer c1951; comp. 1940.
> Rec. high full voices (c1–a2); 1:30; Moderato; simple, translucent opening; builds to an expansive climax; recorded by Stone.

Sacred Songs for Pantheists, Highgate c1966; comp. 1951; with orchestra or piano.
> Spec. soprano; 14:15; titles are: *Pied Beauty* (Gerard Manley Hopkins); *Little Things* (James Stephens); *Intoxication* (Emily Dickinson); *Heaven-Haven* (Gerard Manley Hopkins); *God's Grandeur* (Gerard Manley Hopkins). With Pantheism, the doctrine that everything in the universe is a manifestation of God, as its unifying theme, this work is best kept as a cycle. Certain songs, however, could be performed individually; in particular, *Little Things* and *Heaven-Haven.* Vocally challenging; requires stamina, a good legato

and generally hefty, operatic singing; tessituras tend to be high; for these reasons and because much of the accompaniment sounds overblown on the piano, the orchestra rendition is preferable; highly charged and a bit melodramatic; nevertheless, a solid cycle abounding in warm lyricism and grand effect; recorded by Stahlman.

Sorrow of Mydah, John Masefield; Peer c1952; comp. 1939.

Rec. dramatic high voices (e1–a2); 3:45; Adagio; long, sustained lines over an active piano; dramatic climaxes; evocative and intense; a big, important song—definitely Ward's best; powerfully recorded by McCollum and Stone.

Vanished, Emily Dickinson; Peer c1951; comp. 1941.

Rec. medium and high lyric voices (d1–g2); 1:45; Andante; subdued; on death; recorded by Stone.

BIBLIOGRAPHY
AmerGroves, Baker, CBY(1963), Ewen, Greene, Thompson.
Kozinn, Allan. "American Eclectic," *Opera News* (June 1982).
Kreitner, Kenneth. *Robert Ward: A Bio-Bibliography.* Westport, Connecticut: Greenwood Press, 1988.

---

[1] The ballad from this opera, originally called *Pantaloon,* is recorded by William Parker on New World (300).

HARRIET WARE
b. Aug. 6, 1877, Waupun, WI; d. Feb. 9, 1962, New York City, NY

During the first two decades of the twentieth century, Harriet Ware stood at the forefront of American women composers. Growing up in St. Paul, Minnesota, she studied music with her father and performed as a concert pianist. When she was 15 she went to New York, where she took piano and composition with William Mason. Two years later she continued these studies first in Paris with Sigismund Stojowski; then, in Berlin, studying piano with Mme. Gruenwald, and composition with Hugo Kaun. Returning to New York, Ware married Hugh Krumbhaar, an engineer, and built an impressive reputation as a pianist, teacher, and composer. Though Ware's style is totally conventional, her melodious songs have personality. She had excellent taste in poetry and was especially known for her many settings of Edwin Markham. *Joy of the Morning* (also incl. *AAS), The Boat Song, The Call of Radha, Fairy*

Bark, Stars, Hindu Slumber Song, and *The Last Dance* are all representative of her solid, attractive writing.

BIBIOGRAPHY

Ammer, Baker, Howard (OAM), Thompson.

Crothers, Stella Reid. "Women Composers of America—44," *Musical America,* April 2, 1910.

Martens, Frederick H. "(Ware) Champions American Poetry as Inspiration to Composers," *Musical America,* April 3, 1915.

ELINOR REMICK WARREN[1]
b. Feb. 23, 1900, Los Angeles, CA; d. April 27, 1991, Los Angeles, CA

For a conservative composer of limited renown, Elinor Remick Warren has received an impressive amount of attention in recent years. The only child of musical parents (her father made a living in business but was also a singer and choral conductor; her mother was a pianist), Warren began composing little pieces at the piano when she was three. As a young woman, she went to New York City, where she studied piano with Olga Steeb, organ with Clarence Dickinson, and interpretation with Frank La Forge.[2] La Forge encouraged her to perform her songs for his vocal students (many future stars among them) as well as for major publishers. He also recommended her as an accompanist to such celebrated singers as Lucrezia Bori and Lawrence Tibbett. By following these channels, Warren's songs were not only published but also received wide exposure. After an unhappy marriage ended in divorce, Warren married Z. Wayne Griffin, a motion picture producer, and raised three children. But she continued her musical activities and, as a very old woman, oversaw a recording and an album devoted to her songs. She was also the subject of a full-length biography.

THE SONGS
In the concert hall and on the radio, Kirsten Flagstad, Helen Traubel, Jeanette MacDonald, and Richard Crooks are but some of the major artists who sang Warren's 65 published songs. Other than as a showcase for big voices, it is difficult for this author to understand their appeal, and yet their success, at least at one time, was authentic. Though written in a romantic style with overtones of French impressionism, they generally want for imagination and poetic sensibility. Sturdy voices and plenty of stamina are required to scale the grand, but pedestrian vocal lines

and inflated accompaniments. Lighter songs tend to be precious and sentimental. In 1982 Carl Fischer published *Selected Songs by Elinor Remick Warren (SSERW)*. Though originally issued in two or more keys, the 12 included in this album are for high voice. Warren, however, has re-edited some, adding optional notes to make them adaptable for lower voices. Shortly before Warren's death, Marie Gibson, with Warren accompanying and an occasional flute obbligato, recorded 26 songs on Cambria CD (1028). A few recommendations follow.

Lady Lo-Fu,[3] Mona Modini Wood; Fischer c1927; also incl. *SSERW*.
   Pub. high and low (high, d#1–g#2); 3:00; Moderate and even time; lyrical; nice melismatic passages; wistful; evocative; recorded by Gibson.

Silent Noon, Dante Gabriel Rossetti; Ditson c1928.
   Pub. high and low (high, eb1–ab2); 3:15; Slowly and tranquilly; subdued but broadens and intensifies; final *p* high note; good impressionistic song; recorded by Gibson.

Snow Towards Evening, Melville Cane; G. Schirmer c1937; incl. *S22A*.
   Pub. high and low (high, eb1–ab2); 2:15; Andante tranquillo; some quasi recitative passages; otherwise, sustained; word painting; delicate; recorded by Gibson.

Also of interest:

By a Fireside, Jones, Slowly, dreamily, recorded by Gibson; *White Horses of the Sea,* Hendry, also incl. *SSERW,* Fast, with abandon, one of her best known songs, big singing, recorded by Gibson.

BIBLIOGRAPHY
AmerGroves, Ammer, Baker, Greene, Thompson, Upton (Sup).
Bortin, Virginia. *Elinor Remick Warren: Her Life and Her Music.* Composers of North America, No. 5. Metuchen, New Jersey: Scarecrow Press, 1987.
"Elinor Remick Warren Has Busy Musical Life," *Musical Courier* (June 1953).

---

[1] Usually referred to by these three names, none of them is her married name. Remick was her mother's name; Warren, her father's.
[2] In 1959 she also studied for a few months with Nadia Boulanger in Paris.
[3] Originally titled *My Lady Lo-Fu.*

WINTTER WATTS
b. March 14, 1884, Cincinnati, OH; d. Nov. 1, 1962, Brooklyn, NY

Though his catalogue is frustratingly inconsistent, Wintter Watts could write songs of such compelling poetic beauty that the best are still recalled with real affection.

Watts came from an artistic family on both sides. His father was a painter and poet; his mother's family (the Wintters) were painters and architects. Watts studied art and began an apprenticeship in architecture. He also sang in church choirs, and studied piano, organ, and eventually voice. As he became increasingly interested in becoming a composer, he studied at the Conservatory of Music in Cincinnati, then at the Institute of Musical Art (later incorporated into the Juilliard School), where he worked with Dr. Percy Goetschius. Graduating in 1914, Watts took a brief teaching job in California, then taught privately in New York. In 1919 he won the Morris Loeb prize for a symphonic poem. Aided by a Pulitzer scholarship and the Rome Prize, he made trips to Europe and eventually settled in Italy, remaining there until 1931 when he returned to live in Brooklyn. Despite the interest of a number of singers, especially Eva Gauthier, and a program devoted to his songs at the New York Public Library, he gradually disappeared from the musical scene.

THE SONGS
Most of Watts's approximately 80 songs were published between 1908 and 1925.[1] At first they flowed a bit carelessly from his pen, but with maturity they became expert and eloquent. Unquestionably, the best are those of the middle years—approximately 1918 through 1921—when to his effusive and spontaneous lyric voice he gradually added the craft that had been lacking. Extrovert, colorful, evocative, and unabashedly romantic, these are vintage Watts and the songs for which he is justly remembered. Unfortunately, though his late songs were admired (albeit with reservation) by William Treat Upton, this author finds them totally defeated by the cloying opulence of their harmonies.

Referring again to the best songs, singers can expect to find some awkward moments in the vocal writing. However, putting aside these occasional lapses, they can also anticipate lustrous, searing lines, replete with floating pianissimos and full-throated high notes. Similarly, pianists will relish the lavish (accidental-laden) piano scores. Reserve extra reheasal time, however, to settle the detailed expression markings and endless, subtle tempo adjustments. Except for Eva Gauthier singing *The*

Wings of Night on Town Hall Records, there appear to be no recordings. Recommendations are primarily selected from the better known works. Most are available in two or more keys.

A Little Page's Song, William Alexander Percy (XIII Cent.); Ditson c1920.

Rec. lyric voices (high, g1–a♭2); 1:45; Serene; clean vocalism over a mellifluous piano; a lovely, happy song for light, fresh voices; pairs well with *A Little Shepherd's Song.*

A Little Shepherd's Song, William Alexander Percy (XIII Cent.); G. Ricordi c1922.

Rec. lyric voices (high, g1–b♭2); 2:00; Moderato (short piano prelude), then allegro; a bright, lilting melody; once very popular, especially with students;[2] pairs well with *A Little Page's Song.*

The Poet Sings, Richard Le Gallienne; Ditson c1919; also incl. *CAAS;* to Mr. John McCormack.

Rec. lyric voices (e♭1–a♭2); 1:15; Serenely flowing; an ardent, arched melody over surges of broken chords; a favorite with singers.

Vignettes of Italy, Sara Teasdale; Ditson c1919; some also pub. separately.

Pub. high voice only (d1–b♭2), though traditionally associated with sopranos, men have sung many of these songs; 18:00; in cyclic form, but groups can be made up or individual songs extracted; the poet departs from her—though gender is never very clear—loved one in the first song; the remaining songs are reflections on places in Italy; the last recalls the original theme of parting; some demanding and unidiomatic passages for the singer; a flawed but gorgeous cycle fraught with emotion and reflection, as well as opportunities for romantic pianists and singers to display their gifts in the luminous, expansive writing.[3]

Addio, (f1–a♭2); 2:45; Moderato con moto; generally flowing.

Naples, (e1–g2); 1:45; Con brio; light and bright.

Capri, also incl. *SSSR,* (e1–g2); 2:00; Well sustained; contemplative; difficult.

Night Song at Amalfi, (f1–g2); 2:00; Rubato; lightly moving; many changes.

Ruins of Paestum, (e♭1–g♭2); 1:30; Andante sostenuto; declamatory; subdued.

From a Roman Hill, (e♭1–g♭2); 1:45; Con moto; a flowing 7/4.

Ponte Vecchio, Florence, (d1–f#2); 1:30; Andante; lush; vivid bell effects.

Villa Serbelloni, Bellaggio, (g#1–g#2); 1:15; Con moto; graceful; lyrical; difficult ending.

Stresa, (d1–bb2); 3:45; Andante tranquillo; piano prelude; vocally demanding; expansive; an exquisite song.

The Wings of Night, Sara Teasdale; G. Schirmer c1921; also incl. *NAAS.*

Rec. lyric voices (high c#1–g2); 1:30; Con moto tranquillo; arching over a lush fluid accompaniment; some sustained *p* high notes; colorful harmonies; contemplative; recorded by Gauthier.

With the Tide, Edward J. O'Brien; G. Schirmer c1922.

Pub. high voices only (db1–a2); 1:00; With splendid sweep; full throated cantabile over a lush, flowing accompaniment; big ending.

Also of interest:

The Boat of My Lover, Craik, Moderato; *Dark Hills,* Robinson, Andante Sostenuto, for low voice only; *Green Branches,* MacLeod, Andante con moto; *Joy,* Teasdale, Flowing rapturously; *Pierrot,* Teasdale, Bright; *Transformation,* Rittenhouse, Lento, chordal; *Wood Song,* Hamilton, also incl. *Julia Culp's Collection of Her Favorite Songs,* Moderato.

BIBLIOGRAPHY

AmerGroves, Baker, Greene, Hall, Hughes, Thompson, Upton, Upton (Sup).

Mathew, Gladys Hagee. "Wintter Watts: American Song Composer," *NATS Bulletin* 38 (Jan/Feb 1982).

Peyser, Herbert F. "Wintter Watts's New Cycle a 'Contribution of Permanent Value to American Song Literature'," *Musical America,* March 13, 1920.

---

[1] AmerGroves calculates over 200 Watts songs, but they must be including everything. The figure of 80 published songs by the time he returned to the United States, is offered by Gladys Mathew in the *NATS Bulletin* article. A 1923 *Musical America* profile on Watts notes 60. One finds few copyright dates later than 1930.

[2] Eleanor Steber recalls how performing this song always brought back childhood memories of wandering in the hills behind her home in West Virginia.

(Eleanor Steber and Marcia Sloat, *Eleanor Steber: An Autobiography*, Ridgewood, New Jersey: Wordsworth, 1992, p. 8.)

[3] See Herbert Peyser in *Musical America* for a rare (for American song) rave review.

BEN WEBER[1]

b. July 23, 1916, St. Louis, MO; d. May 9, 1979, New York, NY

Not well known by the general public but highly regarded by his colleagues, Ben Weber wrote twelve-tone compositions in small forms. These include a handful of expressive songs.

Raised in Louisville, Kentucky, the family moved to Chicago when Weber was seven. While preparing for a career in medicine at De Paul University, he also studied voice, piano, and theory. With the encouragement of Arnold Schoenberg, whom he met in 1940, Weber subsequently pursued a career in composition with virtually no further instruction. In 1945 he settled in New York, where he made a living copying music, teaching privately, and working in the recording industry. In the 1950s, he received a number of awards, and his compositions began to be performed by major artists and orchestras. He lived most of his life alone in Manhattan.

THE SONGS

In Weber's art songs one hears little of the fragmentation usually associated with twelve-tone composition. Moreover, his vocal lines, when taken by themselves, can be so lyrical and expansive that to the singer they feel quite tonal.[2] Only in their interaction with the highly independent piano writing is one reminded of the strong atonal language which Weber employs in degrees that range from almost serial to very chromatic. Weber's several vocal works with instrumentation other than piano include his widely admired *Concert Aria After Solomon,* which has been recorded by Bethany Beardslee, and *Four Songs* for voice and solo cello. The following is believed to be a complete list of his published songs for solo voice and piano alone. Those published by the American Composers Alliance are in a clear manuscript.

A Bird Came Down the Walk, Op. 57, Emily Dickinson; ACA; comp. 1963; comm. by Alice Esty.

Rec. medium voices (c1–f2); 3:15; Animando, rubato; traces of serialism; difficult pitches and rhythms; declamatory over an intricate piano part; much pictorializing by voice and piano; light humor.

Five Songs, Op. 15, Adelaide Crapsey; ACA c1955; comp. 1941.

Spec. sopranos (b♭–g2); 5:00; titles are: *November Night; Susanna and the Elders; Triad; Niagara; The Warning;* a small cycle; declamatory, with some glissandos and half-sung passages; very chromatic; rhythmically straightforward; descriptive and atmospheric; effective.

Mourn, Mourn, Op. 53, John Dowland; incl. *NVS.*

Rec. medium and high voices (d1–f2); 4:15; Andante mesto, ritardando; closes Lento; sustained declamation; the spare accompaniment is more chordal than most Weber songs; a dramatic central section; a lament for day's passage into night; intense and powerful; recorded by McCollum on Desto (411/412).

The Ways, Op. 54, Pauline Hanson; Mobart c1964; comp. 1961; for Alice Esty

Spec. soprano (d1–g♭2), rec. any medium voice; 16:30; this seven stanza poem, in which the psyche seeks the way into death, is performed without pause; primarily lyrical over an active, independent piano score; muted dissonance; builds to a dramatic, agitated climax before the quiet, reflective ending; recorded by Herford on New World (327).

BIBLIOGRAPHY
AmerGroves, Baker, Ewen, Greene, Nathan, Thompson.
Rorem, Ned. "Thinking of Ben," from *Setting the Tone.* New York: Coward-McCann, 1983.
Salzman, Eric. "Ben Weber: Autodidact and Autographer," *New York Times,* March 19, 1961.

---

[1] Weber's real name was William Jennings Bryan.

[2] Ned Rorem suggests that the *New York Times's* misprint in the heading for its obituary "Ben Weber, 62, Tonal Composer" did not so badly miss the mark—that Weber was, in fact, lured by tonality. *Setting the Tone,* 159.

KARL WEIGL
b. Feb. 6, 1881, Vienna, Austria; d. Aug. 11, 1949, New York, NY

A student of Alexander von Zemlinsky, Karl Weigl graduated from the Vienna Music Academy. He then taught at the New Vienna Conservatory and the University of Vienna, and was an assistant to Gustav Mahler at the Imperial Opera. With his wife, Vally Weigl, who herself was a noted composer, pianist, and music therapist, he immigrated to the United States in 1938 and became a naturalized citizen in 1943. Weigl taught at several institutions including the Boston Conservatory, the Hartt School of Music, the Philadelphia Musical Academy, and Brooklyn College. His music has never received much attention in his adopted country, but since his death, primarily due to his wife's efforts, several recordings and publications have become available. Most of Weigl's large catalogue of songs are in German. In the tradition of Gustav Mahler, Hugo Wolf, and Richard Strauss, they are lyrical, intimate, and highly poetic. *Five Songs from "Phantasus"* for high voice, is commendable and representative. Along with many other songs by both Weigl and his wife, the set is available from the American Composers Alliance. Judith Raskin, Colette Boky, Betty Allen, George Shirley, and William Warfield have recorded an album exclusively devoted to Weigl's songs on Orion (ORS 81407).

BIBLIOGRAPHY
AmerGroves, Baker, Greene, Thompson.
Davis, Richard. "Karl Weigl: A Song Catalogue." *The NATS Journal* 45 (Jan/Feb 1989).

HUGO WEISGALL
b. Oct. 13, 1912, Ivancice, Czechoslovakia

Taken as a whole, Weisgall's operas, choral works, and song cycles comprise one of the most serious, sophisticated, and important achievements in the twentieth-century vocal repertoire.

Descended from generations of musicians, as a boy Weisgall sang in synagogue and played the piano, often accompanying his father, a cantor and former operatic baritone, in lieder and arias. In 1920 the family immigrated to the United States, settling in Baltimore, Maryland, and in 1926 Weisgall became an American citizen. He attended the Peabody Conservatory and later studied privately with Roger Sessions. At the Curtis Institute he studied conducting with Carl Reiner and composition with Rosario Scalero. He also received a PhD for studies in seventeenth century German poetry at Johns Hopkins University.

During World War II Weisgall served in the Army, primarily in a diplomatic capacity. Remaining in Europe after the war, he conducted and promoted his own music and that of other American composers. In 1948 he returned to Baltimore, where he founded the Hilltop Opera

Company and conducted performances of his early works including his first opera, *The Tenor.* In 1956 the New York City Opera premiered his *Six Characters in Search of an Author,* virtually securing his reputation.

Active on the American music scene, Weisgall has lectured and conducted at Johns Hopkins University, served as president of the American Music Center, and taught at the Juilliard School, Queens College, and the Jewish Theological Seminary. Married for over 50 years to Nathalie Shulman, a physiologist, with whom he raised two children, Weisgall lives in Great Neck, New York.

THE SONGS

Song has been a constant for Weisgall. Since he composed his first set in 1931, there have been published cycles from every ensuing decade with the writing steadily growing more complex. Shifting meters, intricate rhythms, fragmented and disjunct lines, dense chromaticism, and constantly varying dynamics all combine to keep the performer of his later works intensely concentrated. However, as one who "can sing anything I write,"[1] Weisgall demonstrates exceptional understanding of the voice. Though over the years his vocal lines become increasingly disjunct and declamatory, there is always that fundamental lyricism and naturalness of word setting that make his music gratifying to sing. Singers should have no trouble enunciating the serious contemporary texts that have been set over elaborate, virtuosic, but clean piano scores, which are generous in providing the vocal pitch. Unfortunately, length and musical demands discourage programming most of the large-scale cycles, but if these obstacles can be overcome, for advanced performers they offer some of the most arresting and thoughtful music in the contemporary repertoire. Carolyn Heafner has recorded *Four Songs on Poems by Adelaide Crapsey* on CRI (SD 462) and Judith Raskin has recorded *The Golden Peacock* and *Translations* on CRI (SD 417).

Four Songs on Poems by Adelaide Crapsey, Maxwell Weaner c1940.
    Rec. lyric high voices (b♭–g2); 8:00; best kept as a set; titles are: *Old Love; Song; Oh, Lady, Let the Sad Tears Fall; Dirge;* tonal with regular rhythms; much control and purity of tone needed for the delicate vocal writing; despite the generally slow tempos and quiet dynamics, there is good diversity in color and movement; stark; painfully sad, hauntingly beautiful songs on death; recorded by Heafner.

I Looked Back Suddenly, Humbert Wolfe; Presser c1977; also incl. *CAAS;* comp. 1943.

    Rec. medium and low voices; (a–e2) 1:45; Molto tranquillo; sustained, declamatory, and recitative styles intermingle over a spare chordal piano part; generally atonal; a more excited central section; reflective.

Liebeslieder (Four Songs with Interludes), Deborah Trustman;[2] Presser c1979; comp. 1979.

    Spec. high voices (c#1–bb2); 11:30; in English; titles (first lines) are: *Sound is simple; Listen: you were the victim; You were like a song; Play for me;* clearly a set, with interludes between each of the four songs; somewhat philosophical, love poems based on musical metaphors for the various moods; atonal; lyrical declamation over an intricate, virtuosic piano score; rhythms and ensemble are especially difficult; sophisticated; strong; effective.

Lyric Interval, John Hollander; Presser c1987; dedicated to the memory of Serge and Natalie Koussevitsky.

    Spec. low voice (f–f#2), several texts suggest men; 54:00; 14 songs with a piano prologue, interlude, and short postlude; excellent diversity; it would appear songs can be performed individually or in smaller groups since Weisgall gives two endings for the final song depending on whether it is performed alone or in the cycle. Nevertheless, the recurring motifs, in both poetry and music, clearly recommend that it remain an unbroken cycle. Generally atonal; rhythms, piano writing, and ensemble are extremely complex; a disjunct and primarily declamatory vocal line over an elaborate piano score; serious love songs.

Soldier Songs, various poets; Merrymount c1953; comp. 1944-46.[3]

    Spec. baritone (a–g#2), rec. high baritone or even big tenor voices as tessitura is high; 19:00; titles are: *Lord, I Have Seen Too Much* (Karl Shapiro); *Suicide in the Trenches* (Siegfried Sassoon); *The Dying Airman* (Anonymous); *My sweet old etcetera* (E. E. Cummings); *The Dying Soldier* (Isaac Rosenberg); *Fife-Tune* (John Manifold); *Futility* (Wilfred Owen); *The Leveller* (Robert Graves); *Shiloh* (Herman Melville); generally tonal, but chromatic and with considerable dissonance; rhythmically incisive, especially in some of the exciting faster songs; alternately dramatic, lyric, and declamatory over highly descriptive piano writing; vivid, powerful comments on various aspects of war; even the lightest subjects have their ironic, dark side; excellent variety; not as difficult as later Weisgall; a very moving, deadly serious cycle which should be heard more often.

Two Madrigals, Anonymous 17th century; Merion c1958; pub. separately.

A good set if the same voice can handle tessituras that are somewhat at odds.

No More I Will Thy Love Importune; comp. 1945; pub. high and low (high, c–a♭2); 1:45; Slow and sustained; desolate.

Nuptial Song (Be Nimble, Quick, Away), comp. 1955; pub. high (e#1–b♭2), rec. lyric coloraturas; 1:45; Fast and light; high tessitura; flexibility, easy articulation, and stamina all required.

Translations, various women poets; Presser c1977; comm. by and ded. to Shirley Verrett.[4]

For medium or high voices (a–a♭2[a2]); 24:30; titles are: *Knoxville, Tennessee* (Nikki Giovanni); *Song* (Adrienne Rich); *Child Song* (Deborah Trustman); *Poem: 1st Version* (Celia Dropkin); *Poem: 2nd Version* (Celia Dropkin); *The Rebel* (Mari Evans); *A City by the Sea* (Anna Margolin); three songs are translated from the Yiddish; atonal; very difficult ensemble; intricate combinations of rhythms; a highly independent and complex piano score; disjunct, in a lyrical declamation; the poems follow a woman's life from youth to old age; serious, but with good variety of tempo and mood; recorded by Raskin.

Also of interest:

The Golden Peacock (Seven Popular Songs from the Yiddish), a long set of folk songs with elaborate accompaniments, can be sung by more than one singer, recorded by Raskin.

BIBLIOGRAPHY
AmerGroves, Baker, Friedberg (III), Greene, Thompson.

Balkin, Al. "Hugo Weisgall: Controversial Man of Opera," *Music Journal* (October 1964).

Saylor, Bruce. "The Music of Hugo Weisgall," *Musical Quarterly* 59 (1973): 239–262.

———. "Pursuit of Beauty: A True Opera Composer," *Opera News* (September 1992).

---

[1] As quoted by Bruce Saylor in "The Music of Hugo Weisgall," *Musical Quarterly* (April 1973), 241.

[2] The poet Deborah Trustman is Weisgall's daughter.

[3] Although originally written for orchestra, the songs have often been performed with piano alone.

[4] Though opera star Shirley Verrett commissioned this work, contemporary music specialist Elsa Lanchester first performed it.

EMERSON WHITHORNE
b. Sept. 6, 1884, Cleveland, OH; d. March 25, 1958, Lyme, CT

After studying composition and piano with James Rogers, in 1904 Emerson Whithorne went to Vienna, where he studied piano with Leschetizky and composition with Robert Fuchs. In 1907 he married the English pianist Ethel Leginska (divorced in 1916) and moved to London. Giving up the concert piano, he composed, taught, studied Oriental music, and wrote musical criticism. Returning to America in 1915, he was executive editor for the Art Publication Society in St. Louis. In 1920 he settled in New York, where he composed and was active in the League of Composers.

During his lifetime Whithorne received considerable recognition, but since his death he has slipped into obscurity. He was considered to be something of a modernist, but his considerable catalogue of songs, primarily from the 1910s, are conventional. Most are descriptive, impressionistic, and influenced by his studies in Oriental music. Upton, who admits to having problems with the Western fascination for Oriental themes in composition, reserves judgement on Whithorne primarily for this reason. Whithorne's approximately two dozen songs are difficult to find, but of those reviewed, Op. 18 *(The King of Liang* and *The Feast)* and Op. 34 *(Tears* and *The Golden Nenuphar)* are good representatives of his Chinese settings. *Invocation* (Walt Whitman), *Sylvan Song* (Duffield Bendall), and *Dalua* (Fiona MacLeod) are also attractive.

BIBLIOGRAPHY
AmerGroves, Baker, Ewen (ACT), Thompson, Upton.

Howard, John Tasker. *Studies of Contemporary American Composers: Emerson Whithorne.* New York: Carl Fischer, Inc., 1929.

APPENDIX A

A SUPPLEMENT OF SONGS

In the process of writing this book, I occasionally came across a good song or cycle which did not, however, seem to me to have enough merit or other significance to warrant an entry for its composer in the main body of the book. At the same time, not wanting these works to be entirely overlooked, I therefore devised the following supplement. Though all of these songs have my recommendation, some are included in recognition of their former popularity, others because they have deservedly become part of the established repertoire, and still others simply because I like them.

ADAMS, LESLIE *b. 1933, Cleveland, OH*
For You There Is No Song, Edna St. Vincent Millay; incl. *ASBAC.*
    Rec. medium voices (b♭–f2); 2:30; Adagio espressivo; lyrical; flowing; melancholy; recorded by Hilda Harris on BOMC (91-6674).

AMES, WILLIAM T. *b. 1901, Cambridge, MA*
Judgement, William Rose Benét; Music Press c1947; comp. 1945.
    Rec. medium voices (b–a♭2[g2]); 3:00; Moderato; a dramatic narrative builds to central climax; declamation over a spare piano part; unusual and strong.

BALES, RICHARD *b. 1915, Alexandria, VA*
Ozymandias, Percy Bysshe Shelley; Peer c1953; also incl. *VN;* comp. 1941.
    Rec. medium voices (d1–f2); 3:00; Slowly; tempo changes; declamatory with recitative passages over a spare piano part; briefly dramatic.

BEASER, ROBERT *b. 1954, Boston, MA*
Seven Deadly Sins, Anthony Hecht; Helicon c1979; comp. 1979.
    Spec. tenors (b♭–a2) or baritones, in bass clef (A–g2); 17:15; from *Pride* to *Lust,* this interesting continuous cycle has excellent diversity; tenor and baritone lines are printed on parallel lines; moderately difficult; recorded by Paul Sperry on Albany CD (TROY058-2).

383

BONDS, MARGARET *b. 1913, Chicago, IL; d. 1972, Los Angeles, CA*
Three Dream Portraits, Langston Hughes; Ricordi c1959; incl. *AASBAC.*
Rec. lower voices (b–g♭2); 6:00; titles are: *Minstrel Man* (also recorded by Marcoulescou-Stern); *Dream Variation; I, Too;* good diversity; personal reflections on the black man's condition; recorded by Claritha Buggs on BOMC (91-6674).

DAMROSCH, WALTER *b. 1860, Breslau, Germany; d. 1950, New York, NY*
Danny Deever, Rudyard Kipling; Church c1897; to Mr. David Bispham.
Spec. baritone (A–f1); Vivo...Tempo di Marcia Funebre; becomes animated; this robust, dramatic ballad was so popular at the turn of the century that in his autobiography *(A Quaker Singer's Recollections)* Bispham, who first introduced the song, titles a chapter "Enter Danny Deever"; recorded by Bispham on New World (247) and Met CD (207), and by Hampson EMI CD (7 54051 2).

DAVIS, KATHERINE *b. 1892, St. Joseph, MO; d. 1980, Littleton, MA*
Nancy Hanks (Abraham Lincoln's Mother), Stephen Vincent Benét; Galaxy c1941.
Spec. high voice (d1–g2); 3:30; Slowly; builds dramatically over an increasingly involved accompaniment, quiet ending; melancholy; folklike.

FENNIMORE, JOSEPH *b. 1940, New York, NY*
Berlitz: Introduction to French, texts from "Berlitz: French for Travelers," a phrase book; G. Schirmer c1974; comp. 1971.
Rec. medium voices (a–a2); 10:15; in French; the seven titles, ranging from *When You Go Shopping* to *In an Emergency,* are situations in which a traveler might find himself turning to his phrase book; with their distinctly French flavor, excellent diversity, and gracious vocal writing, these clever songs make an engaging, amusing, accessible contemporary set; recorded by Joyce Castle on Albany CD (TROY023-2).

FIRESTONE, IDABELLE *b. 1874, Minnesota City, MN; d. 1954, Akron, OH*
If I Could Tell You, Madeleine Marshall; G. Schirmer c1942.
Pub. high, medium, low (high, f–a♭2); 1:45; Andante moderato con espressione.

In My Garden, Lester O'Keefe; G. Schirmer c1929.

Pub. high, medium, low (high, d1–g2); 2:00; Andante; these two theme songs, which used to open and close the famous radio and television music program, Voice of Firestone, are melodious, heartfelt, and—as demonstrated on video cassette by over two dozen first-rate artists on VAI's Voice of Firestone Classical Performances—flattering to the voice.

FOSS, LUKAS *b. 1922, Berlin, Germany*

Where the Bee Sucks, William Shakespeare; Fischer c1951.

For medium and higher voices (d1–f#2); 1:00; Allegretto; a light, elegant charmer.

GANZ, RUDOLPH *b. 1877, Zurich, Switzerland; d. 1972, Chicago, IL*

If Roses Never Bloomed Again, Franz Evers; H. W. Gray c1959.

Rec. higher voices (f#1–g2); 1:45; Andante; lyrical; sustained over a gently flowing accompaniment; chromatic; a lovely song.

A Memory, Minnie K. Breed; G. Schirmer c1919; also incl. *50AS.*

Pub. high and low (high, e1–g2); 1:00; Quietly; lyrical; chordal; delicate.

GRUENBERG, LOUIS *b. 1884, Brest, Belorussia; d. 1964, Los Angeles, CA*

Insects and Animals, Op. 22, Vachel Lindsay; Universal c1925; comp. 1924.

Spec. medium voice (a–a2); 10:00; the seven titles range from *An Explanation of the Grasshopper* to *The Spider and the Ghost of the Fly;* character sketches of animals; generally fast tempos but excellent variety; tonal; rhythmically vigorous; declamatory with fun effects and word painting; requires flexibility, picturesque piano writing; a witty, colorful set; recorded by Paul Sperry on Albany CD (TROY058-2).

GUION, DAVID *b. 1892, Ballinger, TX; d. 1981, Dallas, TX*

Mary Alone, Lucille Isbell Stall; G. Schirmer c1922; incl. *NAAS.*

Pub. high and low voices (high, d–g#2), rec. big voices; 5:45; Slowly, with deep emotion; builds several times to anguished high notes; a rich, romantic piano score; a mother compares her experience in the death of her soldier son with that of the Mother of Christ; dramatic and intense; recorded by Nancy Tatum on London (OS 26053).

HARRIS, ROY   *b. 1898, Chandler, OK; d. 1979, Santa Monica, CA*
Fog, Carl Sandburg; Fischer c1948; also incl. *CSE.*
   Rec. medium voices (medium, d1–f2); 2:15; rather slow; short, sustained vocal phrases; ominous chords depict the fog creeping in; subdued, moody, vivid.

HUHN, BRUNO   *b. 1871, London, England; d. 1950, New York, NY*
Invictus, William Ernest Henley; Schmidt c1910; to Francis Rogers.
   Pub. high, medium, low (med., c1–e♭2); Risoluto; operatic voices needed for this hearty former crowd-pleaser that builds to the stirring "I am the master of my fate, I am the captain of my soul."

KERR, HARRISON   *b. 1897, Cleveland, OH; d. 1978, Norman, OK*
Six Songs, Adelaide Crapsey; Marks c1952.
   Rec. high voices (c#1–a2); 6:00; titles are: *Triolet; Old Love; Dirge; Fate; The Old, Old Winds; A White Moth Flew;* some difficult rhythms; tonal with strongly dissonant passages; declamation with melodic passages; sombre, intense; an original and effective work.

KIM, EARL   *b. 1920, Dinuba, CA*
Letters Found Near a Suicide, Frank Horne; incl. *NVS.*
   Rec. medium voices (b♭–g2); 5:30; Lento; three poems connected; atonal; musically complex, but beautifully written for the voice in a lyrical declamation with sustained, dramatic, and melismatic passages; a clear, precise piano score; intense; profound. See Manning *(New Vocal Repertory)* for a full discussion.

LESSARD, JOHN   *b. 1920, San Francisco, CA*
Whenas in Silks My Julia Goes, Robert Herrick; General c1984.
   Rec. medium voices (e1–e2); 1:00; Lento; lyrical; liquid; sensual; evocative.

LOCKWOOD, NORMAND   *b. March 16, 1906, New York, NY*
Oh, Lady, Let the Sad Tears Fall, Adelaide Crapsey; Music Press c1947.
   Spec. medium voices (f#1–d#2); 3:15; Lamentevole; long, sustained vocal lines over slowly moving accompaniment; somber, poignant.

MANNEY, CHARLES FONTEYN   *b. 1871, Brooklyn, NY; d. 1951, New York, NY*

Orpheus with His Lute, William Shakespeare; also incl. *S30A* and *50SS*.
   Pub. high and low (high, e♭1–g2); 1:30; Andante semplice; lyrical over a simple, chordal accompaniment; tender, mellifluous, and straightforward; a lovely song that would make an excellent opener.

PORTER, QUINCY   *b. 1897, New Haven, CT; d. 1966, Bethany, CT*

Music, When Soft Voices Die, Percy Bysshe Shelley, Music Press c1947.
   Spec. medium voices (d1–c2); in a moderate tempo; lyrical over a spare accompaniment; muted dissonances; restrained; poignant.

PRICE, FLORENCE   *b. 1888, Little Rock, AK; d. 1953, Chicago, IL*

Song to the Dark Virgin, Langston Hughes; incl. *AASBAC*.
   Rec. medium and lower voices (b♭–e♭2); 1:45; Andante con moto; lyrical over flowing accompaniment; big ending; romantic and atmospheric; recorded by Marcoulescou-Stern on Gasparo CD (GSCD-287).

RASBACH, OSCAR   *b. 1888, Dayton, KY; d. 1975, Pasadena, CA*

Trees, Joyce Kilmer; G. Schirmer c1922.
   Pub. high, medium, low (c#–g#2); 1:45; Andante; lyrical and flowing; formerly very popular; recorded by Robeson on Nimbus CD (7839) and John Charles Thomas on Nimbus CD (7838).

RUGGLES, CARL   *b. 1876, Marion, MA; d. 1971, Bennington, VT*

Toys, Carl Ruggles; Presser c1920/1983.
   Rec. high lyric voices (c1–a2); 1:00; Anima; atonal; disjunct; difficult; whimsical.

SACCO, JOHN   *b. 1905, New York, NY; d. 1987, New York, NY*

Brother Will, Brother John, Elizabeth Charles Welborn; G. Schirmer c1947; also incl. *20CAS*.
   Rec. medium voices (c1–f2); 2:00; With sly jocularity; opening "You can't take it with you"; folklike; lively; recorded by Hampson on EMI CD (7 54051 2) and Marcoulescou-Stern on Gasparo CD (GSCD 287).

SARGENT, PAUL   b. 1910, Bangor, ME; d. 1987
Stopping by Woods on a Snowy Evening, Robert Frost; G. Schirmer
c1950; also incl. *CAS.*
    Rec. higher voices ([c1]d1–e2[a2]); 1:45; With quiet movement;
picturesque piano figurations; lyrical and subdued; atmospheric.

SCHONTHAL, RUTH   b. 1924, Hamburg, Germany
By the Roadside, Walt Whitman; Oxford c1979.
    Spec. soprano (c1–b♭2); 6:00; titles are: *By the Roadside;
Thought; Visor'd; To Old Age; A Farm Picture; A Child's Amaze;*
best kept as a set; good variety of mood; tonal and atonal; generally
declamatory; moderate difficulty; succinct mood pieces; some quite
intense. See Friedberg *(American Art Song and American Poetry:
Vol. III)* for a full discussion.

SCHULLER, GUNTHER   b. 1925, New York, NY
Meditation, Gertrude Stein; incl. *NVS;* comp. 1960.
    Rec. medium and higher voices (c♯1–f♯2); 3:00; Slow; atonal;
rhythmically complex; fragmented, with much detached declamatory singing; crisp, clever, and perfectly complementing Stein's singular brand of wit. See Manning *(New Vocal Repertory)* for a full
discussion.

SPROSS, CHARLES GILBERT   b. 1874, Poughkeepsie, NY; d. 1961,
    Poughkeepsie, NY
Will o' the Wisp, Torrence Benjamin; Church c1919; also incl. *AASTC.'*
    Pub. high and low (high, c1–b♭2[a2]); 1:30; Allegro; light and lyri-
cal over a busy, spirited accompaniment; very popular in its time; still
genuinely charming.

SUSA, CONRAD   b. April 26, 1935, Springfield, PA
Hymns for the Amusement of Children, Christopher Smart; E. C.
Schirmer c1980; comp. 1972.
    Spec. medium voice (b♭–b♭2); 13:15; six songs; a sophisticated,
vigorous, rhythmically incisive set with many popular elements, especially blues; recorded by Henry Herford on New World (327).

TALMA, LOUISE   *b. 1906, Arcachon, France*

Terre de France, various poets; Fischer c1978; comp. 1945.

Spec. soprano or tenor (c1–a2); 18:00; a cycle of five songs; in French; composed during World War II, these are poignant evocations of France during happier times; a lovely, lyric cycle; recorded by Sperry on Albany CD (TROY058).

WYNER, YEHUDI   *b. 1929, Calgary, Canada*

Exeunt, Richard Wilbur; incl. *Psalms and Early Songs;* Associated c1972; also incl. *AAS;* comp. 1954.

Rec. lower voices (a–f2); 2:00; Slowly - with moderate flexibility; atonal; restrained; reflective.

When You Are Old, W. B. Yeats; incl. *Psalms and Early Songs;* Associated c1972; comp. 1951.

Rec. lower voices (a–e2); 2:45; Slowly; muted dissonance; lyrical; quiet; poignant.

APPENDIX B
AMERICAN ART SONG IN ANTHOLOGY

The following multi-composer collections contain five or more American songs and are referred to in *A Singer's Guide to the American Art Song*. Each title is preceded by the abbreviation that identifies it throughout the guide. Although some of these albums include composers of other nationalities, only the songs by Americans are listed. Unless otherwise noted the collections are only available in one range. Single composer collections are only noted with that composer's entry.

A12S Album of Twelve Songs by American Composers. Boston Music and G. Schirmer (no copyright date).
   Atherton: *Oh, like a Queen* • Clough-Leighter: *My Lover he Comes on the Skee* • Colburn: *A Little Dutch Garden* • Densmore: *Mother Song* • Hadley: *Love's Matins* • Harling: *Contemplation* • Johns: *Where Blooms the Rose* • Johnson: *Song for June* • Nevin, Ethelbert: *Tell me, Bewitching Maiden* • Rogers, James: *Love has Wings* • Whelpley: *Oh, for a Breath of the Moorlands* • Whiting: *My True Love hath my Heart.*

AAS American Art Songs: A Collection of 20th Century Songs by American Composers from Charles Ives to Elliot Carter for Medium Voice and Piano. Associated c1980; compiled by Barry O'Neal.
   Ames: *A Patch of Old Snow; Fire and Ice* • Bacon: *The Commonplace* • Bowles: *In the Woods* • Carter: *Dust of Snow; The Rose Family* • Chanler: *The Lamb* • Cowell: *Spring Comes Singing* • Diamond: *Epitaph; Music When Soft Voices Die; On Death* • Dougherty: *Beauty Is Not Caused* • Graham: *After a Rain at Mokanshan* • Ives: *Sea Dirge; Evening; Peaks; Pictures; The Seer; Serenity* • Koch: *An Immorality; Calico Pie; Tame Cat* • Lockwood: *Joseph, Dearest Joseph* • Luening: *A Farm Picture* • Nordoff: *Embroidery for a Faithless Friend* • Read: *Nocturne* • Riegger: *The Dying of the Light* • Rorem: *A Song of David* • Walker: *The Bereaved Maid; I Went to Heaven; Sweet, Let Me Go* • Wyner: *Exeunt.*

AASTC *American Art Songs of the Turn of the Century.* Dover c1991; edited by Paul Sperry.

   Ayres: *Take, O Take Those Lips Away; Where the Bee Sucks; Come unto These Yellow Sands* • Barton: *It Was a Lover and His Lass* • Beach: *The Year's at the Spring; Ah, Love, But a Day; I Send My Heart up to Thee* • Bond: *Half Minute Songs* • Cadman: *From the Land of the Sky-Blue Water* • Campbell-Tipton: *After Sunset* • Carpenter: *Looking-Glass River; Les Silhouettes; When I Bring to You Colour'd Toys* • Chadwick: *The Danza; Green Grows the Willow; Adversity; The Stranger-Man* • Clough-Leighter: *It Was a Lover and His Lass* • Fisher: *Sigh No More, Ladies* • Foote: *It Was a Lover and His Lass; Song of the Forge; O Swallow, Swallow, Flying South* • Gilbert: *The Owl* • Ide: *Names* • Ives: *The Circus Band; Spring Song* • Johns: *If Love Were Not* • MacDowell: *Tyrant Love; Fair Springtide; To the Golden Rod* • Nevin: *'Twas April; Narcissus; A Song of Love* • Paine: *Early Spring Time* • Parker: *Lute-Song; The Blackbird* • Sousa: *Reveille; You'll Miss Lots of Fun When You're Married; The Stars and Stripes Forever* • Speaks: *On the Road to Mandelay; Sylvia* • Spross: *Will o' the Wisp.*

AAA *American Artsong Anthology: Volume 1: Contemporary American Songs for High Voice and Piano.*[1] Galaxy c1982; edited by John Belisle.

   Beeson: *Eldorado* • Benshoof: *The Cow; The Fox* • Berg: *Last letter* • Childs: *Virtue* • Cumming: *Other Loves* • Gideon: *Gone in Good Sooth You Are* • Green: *I Loved My Friend* • Ivey: *I Would Live in Your Love; To One Away* • Lindenfeld: *Dolor; The Cow* • Rorem: *The Youth With the Red-Gold Hair* • Ward-Steinman: *Season* • Wood: *Ants Will Not Eat Your Fingers* • Zaimont: *Soliloquy*

AASGS *Anthology of American Song: A Collection of Twenty-six Songs by Representative American Composers.* G Schirmer c1911; available high and low.

   Bartlett: *Highland Mary* • Cadman: *A Moonlight Song* • Chadwick: *In My Beloveds Eyes* • Coombs: *Her Rose* • De Koven: *Norman Cradle Song* • Hadley: *Rose-Time* • Harris: *April* • Hawley: *The Nightingale and the Rose* • Homer:

Requiem • Johns: *I Love, and the World is Mine* • La Forge: *Like the Rosebud* • MacDowell: *The Clover* • Mack: *For Ever and a Day* • Neidlinger: *Serenade* • Arthur Nevin: *Auf Wiedersehn* • Ethelbert Nevin: *Serenade* • Parker: *Milkmaid's Song* • James Rogers: *At Parting* • Winthrop Rogers: *Let Miss Lindy Pass* • Salter: *The Pine-Tree* • Shelley: *Love's Sorrow* • Smith: *Entreaty* • Thayer: *My Laddie* • Ware: *Joy of the Morning* • Whiting: *"Yet ah, that spring should vanish"* • Woodman: *Ashes of Roses.*

AASBAS *Anthology of Art Songs by Black American Composers.* Marks c1977; compiled by Willis C. Patterson.

Adams: *For You There Is No Song* • Baker: *Early in the Mornin'; A Good Assassination Should Be Quiet; Status Symbol* • Bonds: *Three Dream Portraits* • Brown: *The Barrier; Song Without Words* • Cohen: *Death of an Old Seaman* • Da Costa: *Two Songs for Julie Ju* • Fax: *Cassandra's Lullaby; Love* • Hailstork: *A Charm at Parting; I Loved You* • Hancock: *Absalom; Nunc Dimmitis* • Kerr: *Riding to Town* • Lloyd: *Compensation* • Logan: *If There Be Sorrow; Marrow of My Bone* • McCall: *Chanson Triste; Sweet Sorrow* • D. R. Moore: *Weary Blues* • U. Moore: *Love Let the Wind Cry* • Owens: *Faithful One; Genius Child* • Perkinson: *A Child's Grace; Melancholy* • Price: *Night; Song to the Dark Virgin* • Smith: *Velvet Shoes* • Still: *Grief* • Swanson: *A Death Song; I Will Lie Down in Autumn; The Negro Speaks of Rivers* • Walker: *Lament; A Red, Red Rose* • Wilson: *Wry Fragments* • Work: *Dancing in the Sun; Soliloquy.*

ASA *Art Song Argosy.* G. Schirmer c1937; compiled and edited by William Breach; available medium high and medium low.

Carpenter:*Treat Me Nice* • Salter:*The Pine Tree; Remembrance* • Guion: *All Day on the Prairie* • Rogers: *Cloud Shadows* • Homer: *Requiem.*

CAAS *Contemporary American Art Songs.* Elkan-Vogel c1965; compiled and edited by Bernard Taylor.

Bacon: *The Lamb; Stars* • Calabro: *Each a Rose; It is Forbidden* • Diamond: *Brigid's Song* • Duke:*When Slim Sophia Mounts Her Horse* • Howe: *Great Land of Mine* • Ives:

The Light That Is Felt • Kagen: *How Pleasant It Is To Have Money* • Persichetti: *Out of the Morning; Thou Child So Wise; Unquiet Heart* • Rochberg: *Ballad; I Am Baffled By This Wall; Night Piece* • Rorem: *The Lordly Hudson; Spring and Fall* • Watts: *The Poet Sings* • Weisgall: *I Looked Back Suddenly.*

CASS **Contemporary American Sacred Song.** G. Schirmer c1985.[2]
Barber: *Lord Jesus Christ* (from *Prayers of Kierkegaard*) • Chanler: *The Lamb* • Corigliano: *Christmas at the Cloisters* • Creston: *Psalm XXIII* • Effinger: *Mary's Soliloquy* • Ives: *Serenity* • Malotte: *The Lord's Prayer* • Niles: *I Wonder as I Wander* • Rorem: *A Song of David* • Thomson: *Sung by the Shepherds.*

CAS **Contemporary American Songs.** Summy-Birchard c1960; compiled and edited by Bernard Taylor; available high and low.
Beach, Bennie: *Peace* • Bialosky: *An Old Picture* • Branscombe: *Old Woman Rain* • Donato: *To My Neighbor at the Concert* • Kalmanoff: *Twentieth Century* • Kettering: *Compensation* • Kreutz: *December Lark* • Latham: *The New Love and the Old* • Lekberg: *Birds Singing at Dusk* • Murray: *The Pasture* • Pfautsh: *Lute Book Lullaby* • Raphling: *Fugue on "Money"* • Read: *A White Blossom;* Work: *Three Glimpses of Night.*

CAS28 **Contemporary Art Songs: 28 Songs by American and British Composers.** G. Schirmer c1970.
Barber: *Must the Winter Come so Soon (Vanessa)* • Beck: *Song of Devotion* • Bernstein: *Two Love Songs* • Bowles: *Heavenly Grass* • Carpenter: *When I Bring to You Colour'd Toys* • Chávez: *Segador* • Chenoweth: *Vocalise* • Corigliano: *Christmas at the Cloisters; The Unicorn* • Dougherty: *Sound the Flute* • John Duke: *Peggy Mitchell* • Hoiby: *An Immorality* • Kingsford: *Down Harley Street* • Menotti: *Lullaby (The Consul)* • Douglas Moore: *The Dove Song (Wings of the Dove)* • Sargent: *Stopping by Woods on a Snowy Evening* • Schuman: *Holiday Song* • Thomson: *English Usage; The Tiger.*

CSE Contemporary Songs in English: Songs by American and English Composers for Recital, Studio and Concert Use. Carl Fischer c1956; Edited by Bernard Taylor; available medium high and medium low.

Bergsma: *Lullee, Lullay* • Bone and Fenton: *Deborah* • Cooper: *Enough* • Dello Joio: *Mill Doors; There Is a Lady Sweet and Kind* • Duke, John: *Bells in the Rain; Luke Havergal* • Edmunds: *The Lonely* • Freed: *Chartless* • Harris: *Fog* • Helm: *Prairie Waters by Night* • Howe: *Let Us Walk in the White Snow* • Moore, Douglas: *Old Song; Under the Greenwood Tree.*

CC Cos Cob Song Volume.[3] Cos Cob c1935.

Blitzstein: *Jimmie's Got a Goil* • Bowles: *"Ainsi Parfois Nos Seuls"* • Chanler: *These, My Ophelia* • Citkowitz: *Gentle Lady* • Copland: *Song* • Heilner: *The Tide Rises* • Ives: *Where the Eagle* • Lipsky: *Lilac Time* • Sessions: *On the Beach at Fontana* • Thomson: *Susie Asado.*

50AS 50 Art Songs from the modern repertoire. G. Schirmer c1939.

Carpenter: *The Sleep that Flits on Baby's Eyes* • Deis: *Waiting* • Engel: *Sea Shell* • Ganz: *A Memory* • Griffes: *Auf geheimen Waldespfade* • Hageman: *At the Well* • Loeffler: *Adieu pour jamais; Les Paons.*

50SS Fifty Shakspere (sic) Songs; Ditson c1906; edited by Charles Vincent; available for high and low voices.

Clough-Leighter: *It was a lover and his lass.* • Fisher: *Blow, blow, thou winter wind; Sigh no more, ladies* • Loomis: *And let me the canakin clink; Crabbed age and youth* • Manney: *Orpheus with his lute.*

LF(1) Lyric Fancies: A Selection of Songs by American Composers. Schmidt c1919; in two volumes, each available in high, medium, and low, but as there are changes within the volume depending on range, ranges for each particular song are noted; therefore one must locate not only the correct volume but also the correct range.

Volume One Barbour: *Awake! It Is the Day* (medium) • Beach: *Ecstasy* (high); *Shena Van* (medium, low) • Bischoff: *The Summer Wind* (high, low) • Branscombe: *The Morning Wind* (high, medium, low) • Chadwick: *Allah* (high, low): *The*

Maiden and the Butterfly (high, low) • Clough-Leighter: *April Blossoms* (medium) • Cox: *Peggy* (medium) • Daniels: *The Lady of Dreams* (high, medium) • Foote: *The Night Has a Thousand Eyes* (high, low); *In Picardie* (medium, low) • Grant-Schaefer: *A Garden Romance* (medium) • Hadley: *My Shadow* (high) • Lang: *Arcadie* (high); *An Irish Love Song* (medium, low) • Lynes: *Hark! the Robin's Early Song* (high, low) • MacDowell: *O Lovely Rose* (high, low) • Metcalf: *The Cares of Yesterday* (high, low) • Neidlinger: *My Heart and the Rain* (high, low) • Park: *A Memory* (high, medium, low) • Risher: *Sail, White Dreams* (medium) • Salter: *My Dear* (high, low).

LF(2) **Volume Two** Beach: *Fairy Lullaby* (high); *Ah, Love, but a Day!* (medium, low) • Bischoff: *Five Little White Heads* (high, medium) • Branscombe: *I Send My Heart up to Thee* (high, medium) • *A Lovely Maiden Roaming* (low); *Only to Thee* (medium) • Chadwick: *Thou art so Like a Flower* (high, medium); *Two Folk Songs: 1. O Love and Joy , 2. The Northern Days* (low) • Clough-Leighter: *O Heart of Mine* (high, medium, low) • Foote: *On the Way to Kew* (high); *I'm Wearin Awa* (medium, low) • Friml: *At Twilight* (high, medium, low) • Lang: *Day Is Gone* (high, medium, low) • Lyncs: *Roses* (high, medium, low) • MacDowell: *Merry Maiden Spring* (high, low) • Metcalf: *The Sunshine of Thine Eyes* (high, low).

NAAS **A New Anthology of American Song: 25 Songs by Native Composers.** G. Schirmer c1942; available low and high.

Barber: *The Daises* • Beach: *Meadow-Larks* • Cadman: *A Moonlight Song* • Campbell-Tipton: *The Crying of Water* • Carpenter: *Looking-Glass River* • Charles: *And So, Goodbye* • Crist: *Knock on the Door* • Deis: *A Lover's Lament* • Farwell: *On a Faded Violet* • Griffes: *The Lament of Ian the Proud* • Guion: *Mary Alone* • Hadley: *The rose-leaves are falling like rain* • Homer: *Down Bye Street* • Horsman: *The Bird of the Wilderness* • Kingsford: *Wall-Paper* • Kramer: *I Have Seen Dawn* • La Forge: *Retreat* • Malotte: *The Homing Heart* • Manning: *Shoes* • Powell: *Heartease* • Spalding: *The Rock of Rubies* • Still: *The Breath of the Rose* • Stillman-Kelley: *Eldorado* • Watts: *Wings of Night* • Woodman: *I am thy harp.*

NVS New Vistas in Song, Marks c1964; spec. high voice.
  Babbitt: *Sounds and Words* • Cone: *Silent Noon* • Cowell: *The Pasture* • Dello Joio: *Un Sonetto di Petrarca* • Hovhaness: *O Lady Moon* • Kim: *Letters Found Near a Suicide* • Krenek: *The Flea* • Meyerowitz: *Bright Star* • Schuller: *Meditation* • Sessions: *On the Beach at Fontana* • Weber: *Mourn! Mourn!*

RAAS Romantic American Art Songs: 50 Songs by 14 Composers. G. Schirmer c1990; spec. high voice.
  Bacon: *It's all I have to bring; So bashful; Poor Little Heart; To make a prairie; And this of all my hopes* • Beach: *The Lotos Isles; Springtime; Wind o' the Westland* • Carpenter: *Slumber-Song; Serenade; Rest; Morning Fair* • Charles: *The White Swan; Beauty; Frustration; Message* • Duke, John: *February Twilight; Little Elegy; Loveliest of Trees* • Griffes: *In a Myrtle Shade; Waikiki; Symphony in Yellow* • Hageman: *Praise; Do not go, my love; Nature's Holiday; Under the Willow* • Lekberg: *The Road to Avrillé; Sweet sounds, o, beautiful music; I drank at every vine; The Spring and the Fall* • Moore, Douglas: *Thou hast made me; Batter my heart; Death be not proud* • Niles: *The Blue Madanna; Reward; Calm Is the Night; Careless Love* • Read: *Nocturne; The Unknown God; The Moon* • Rochberg: *Rise up, my love; Come, my beloved; Set me as a seal; Behold! thou art fair* • Still: *The Breath of the Rose; Grief; Winter's Approach* • Thomson: *The Tiger; Love Song; Preciosilla.*

SSSR Singable Songs for Studio and Recital: Thirty Songs. Ditson c1936; selected by Martin Mason; available high and medium.
  Cadman: *The Little Road to Kerry* • Carpenter: *May, the Maiden* • Curran: *Sonny Boy* • Edwards: *Lady Moon* • Klemm: *Sounds* • LaForge: *Song of the Open* • Rogers, James: *The time for making songs has come* • Watts: *Blue are her eyes; Isle of Beauty (Capri).*

S30A Songs by 30 Americans. Ditson c1904; edited by Rupert Hughes; available high and low.
  Baltzell: *Thou art Mine* • Bartlett: *Look Not Upon Me with Thine Eyes* • Buck: *In thy Dreams* • Bullard: *Beam from Yonder Star* • Clough-Leighter: *I Drink the Fragrance of the Rose* • De Koven: *Cradle Song* • Farwell: *Meeting* • Fisher:

When Allah Spoke • Foerster: *Tristam and Iseult* • Gilbert:
Croon of the Dew • Goldmark: *The Passionate Shepherd to his
Love* • Hadley: *How do I Love Thee* • Harris: *The Hills o' Skye*
• Huss: *My World* • Hyatt: *The Spring of Love* • Johns: *If Love
Were Not* • Loomis: *In the Foggy Dew* • Manney: *Orpheus
with his Lute* • Marshall: *O Mighty One* • Nevin: *A Bed-time
Song* • Norris: *Dearie* • Page: *The Regrets of Bokhära* •
Paine: *Matin Song* • Passmore: *A Northern Romance* • Rogers,
James: *April Weather* • Shelley: *The Ride* • Smith, David:
Rose Song • Smith, Gerrit: *Dreaming* • Smith, Wilson: *Kiss
Me, Sweetheart* • Warren: *When the Birds Go North Again.*

**S22A *Songs By 22 Americans: A Collection of Songs by Outstanding
Americans.*** Compiled by Bernard Taylor; G. Schirmer c1960; available
low and high.

Barber: *Sure On This Shining Night* • Bernstein: *Plum Pudding*
• Bowles: *Once a Lady Was Here* • Carpenter: *Serenade* •
Charles: *O Lovely World; The Sussex Sailor* • Creston: *The Bird
of Wilderness* • Dougherty: *Love in the Dictionary; Primavera*
• Duke: *A Piper; Loveliest of Trees* • Edwards: *Into the Night;
Ol' Jim* • Griffes: *By a Lonely Forest Pathway; The Lament of
Ian the Proud* • Hageman: *Do Not Go, My Love* • McArthur:
Night • Malotte: *Upstream* • Naginski: *The Pasture* • Rich:
American Lullaby • Roy: *This Little Rose* • Sacco: *That's Life*
• Sargent: *Manhattan Joy Ride* • Thomson: *Preciosilla* •
Tyson: *Sea Moods* • Warren: *Snow Toward Evening* • Wolfe:
De Glory Road.

**SE *Songs in English: 19 Contemporary Settings by American and
English Composers.*** Fischer c1970; edited by Bernard Taylor; available
high and low.

Duke, John: *Be Still As You Are Beautiful; Evening; Just-Spring;
Spring Thunder* • Dello Joio: *How Do I Love Thee; Why So
Pale and Wan, Fond Lover* • Dougherty: *Heaven-Haven; The
Taxi* • McArthur: *Spring Day* • Morgenstern: *My Apple Tree* •
Nordoff: *Song of Innocence.*

SIA **Songs of an Innocent Age.** G. Schirmer c1984; Compiled and
Edited by Paul Sperry.
  Beach: *Ariette; Take, O Take Those Lips Away; O Mistress Mine*
  • Buck: *The Capture of Bacchus* • Chadwick: *Euthanasia* •
  Gilbert: *Tell Me Where Is Fancy Bred; Pirate Song* • Griffes:
  Auf Ihrem Grab; Wohl Lag Ich Einst in Gram und Schmerz •
  Loomis: *Hark! Hark! the Lark* • MacDowell: *Long Ago; A
  Maid Sings Light* • Nevin: *Oh! That We Two Were Maying;
  One Spring Morning; Orsola's Song; Nocturne.*

20CAS **20th Century Art Songs;** G. Schirmer c1967; medium voice only.
  Barber: *Under the Willow Tree (Vanessa)* • Bernstein: *It Must
  Be Me (Candide)* • Bowles: *Cabin* • Creston: *Psalm XXIII* •
  Dougherty: *Across the Western Ocean; The K'e; A Minor Bird;
  Thy Fingers Make Early Flowers* • Duke, John: *I Watched The
  Lady Caroline; Silver* • Gold: *Music, When Soft Voices Die;
  Parting* • Guion: *At the Cry of the First Bird* • Menotti: *The
  Black Swan (The Medium); The Hero* • Sacco: *Brother Will,
  Brother John* • Schirmer: *Honey Shun* • Schuman: *Orpheus
  With His Lute* • Thomson: *My Crow Pluto* • Weaver: *Moon
  Marketing* • Weill: *The Lonesome Dove (Down in the Valley).*

VN **Vote For Names: Peer-Southern 20th Century American Song-
book;** Compiled by Paul Sperry.
  Bales: *Ozymandias* • Diamond: *For an Old Man; The
  Millennium* • Duke, John: *Acquainted With the Night;
  hist...whist* • Flanagan: *The Upside-Down Man* • Hoiby: *A
  Christmas Song; The River - Merchant's Wife: A Letter* • Ives:
  Vote for Names • Lauridsen: *As Birds Come Nearer; When
  Frost Moves Fast* • Riegger: *Ye Banks and Braes o' Bonnie
  Doon* • Rorem: *The Silver Swan* • Siegmeister: *Lonely Star* •
  Thomson: *The Bell Doth Toll; Take, O Take Those Lips Away* •
  Walker: *Nocturne* • Ward: *Sorrow of Mydath.*

WW (1–5) **Wa-Wan Press: 1901-1911.** 5 vols. Ed. by Vera Brodsky
Lawrence. New York : Arno Press and the *New York Times,* 1970. These
volumes also include instrumental music. The following titles note the
reprint volume number where each song may be found.
  Andersen: *Kinderwacht* (5) • Avery: *Eskimo Love Song* (3); *On
  a Balcony* (4) • Ayres: *Come Unto These Yellow Sands* (5);

Hesper (5); *Sea Dirge* (4); *Take, O, Take Those Lips Away* (3); *Where the Bee Sucks* (4) • John Parsons Beach: *Autumn Song* (2); *Ici-bas* (2); *In a Gondola* (3); *Is She Not Pure Gold?* (4); *'Twas in a World of living Leaves* (2); *The Kings* (2); *A Song of the Lilac* (2); *Take, O, Take Those Lips Away* (3); *A Woman's Last Word* (2) • Branscombe: *Serenade* (3); *Sleep, Then, Ah Sleep* (3); *What Are We Two ?* (3) • Campbell-Tipton: *Four Sea Lyrics* (4) • Curtis: seven *Songs from a Child's Garden of Verses* (1) • Damon: *The Valley of Lovers* (3) • Farwell: *Drake's Drum* (4) • *The Farewell* (5); *Folk Songs of the West and South: Negro, Cowboy and Spanish Californian* (3); *Love's Secret* (2); *Requiescat* (2); *A Ruined Garden*, (2) • Freer: *To a Painter* (4); *A Valentine* (5) • Gilbert: *Celtic Studies* (3); *Faery Song* (3); *Fish Wharf Rhapsody* (5); *The Lament of Deidré* (2); *Orlamonde* (4); *The Owl* (5); *Pirate Song* (1); *Salammbô's Invocation to Tänith* (1); *Tell Me Where Is Fancy Bred* (3);*Two South American Gypsy Songs* (3); *Zephyrus* (2) • Gilman: *The Heart of the Woman* (2) • Goldmark: *I Have Done, Put By the Lute* (5) • Heyman: *Lament for Adonis* (2) • Ide: *Lovers of the Wild* (4); *Names* (4) • Stillman Kelley: *Eldorado* (1); *Israfel* (1) • Kroeger: *Memory,* a song cycle (3) • Little: *I Look Into My Glass* (2); *The City of Sleep* (3); *Drink to Me Only with Thine Eyes* (1); *Helen* (1) • Loomis: *Hark! Hark! the Lark* (1); *Morning Song* (4); *O' er the Sea* (1) • McCoy: *The Only Voice* (3) • Schuyler: *In the Golden Fullness* (3) • Shepherd: *Five Songs* (5); *A Star in the Night* (3) • Troyer: *Indian Fire Song* (4); *Traditional Songs of the Zunis* (2) • Walker: *The Lonely Garden* (4); *When the Dew Is Falling* (3) • Waller: *The Spirit of Wine* (1) • Wright: *The Shadow Rose* (2).

---

1 No further volume in this series has been published.

2 Sacred song is not generally included in the main portion of *A Singer's Guide to the American Art Song.* However, this particular anthology contains several works that were clearly conceived as art song.

3 This collection, compiled by Aaron Copland of songs by a few of his friends, was lambasted in the September, 1935 issue of *Musical America:* "Let it be clearly understood that these are not songs. They are experimental compositions for voice and piano, of which only the Copland and Sessions pieces are even to be considered for a moment. The others … are more than hopeless." This album has, to the contrary, become a classic.

APPENDIX C
PUBLISHERS

The following is a directory of the publishers cited throughout this guide. Publishers, however, have a reputation for constantly merging, amalgamating, changing names, or going out of business altogether. Therefore, some of this information will be out of date before *A Singer's Guide to the American Art Song* even reaches the stores. Nevertheless, this listing both provides the abbreviation used for each publisher and starts the process for the performer who needs to locate a particular company. However, if problems arise, it is generally best to turn to your local music dealer, who is experienced in untangling the complexities of the business. Music Publishers Sales Agency List (1992) has been my principal source for this information. The term "agent" signifies either the newest distributor for the original publisher or (as in the cases where companies were disbanded decades ago) the company that now controls the copyright. Those listed without any further information or with only a city of origin went out of business a long time ago and appear to have no agents.

ACA	American Composers Alliance 170 West 74th St., New York NY 10023 (212) 362-8900
Alfred	Alfred Publishing Co., Inc. P.O. Box 10003 16380 Roscoe Blvd., Suite 200 Van Nuys, CA 91410 (818) 891-5999
Amberson	Amberson Enterprises (agent: Boosey and Hawkes)
American	American Music Press (agent: Theodore Presser)

Aquarius	Aquarius Music Company P.O. Box 71 Rock Valley Long Eddy, NY 12760
Arrow	Arrow Music Press (agent: Boosey and Hawkes)
Associated	Associated Music Press (agent: Hal Leonard)
Belwin-Mills	Belwin-Mills Publishing Corp. (agent: CPP/Belwin)
Boelke-Bomart	Boelke-Bomart Publications, Inc. (agent: Jerona Music)
Boosey	Boosey & Hawkes, Inc. 24 East 21st. St. New York, NY 10010 (212) 228-3300
Boston	Boston Music Company 9 Airport Drive Hopedale, MA 01747 (508) 478-4813
Breitkopf and Härtel	Breitkopf (agent: Hal Leonard)
Broadcast	Broadcast Music, Inc. (agent: Hal Leonard)
Broude	Alexander Broude, Inc. 575 Eighth Avenue New York, NY 10018.
Broude Bros.	Broude Brothers Limited 141 White Oaks Road Williamstown, MA 01267 (413) 458-8131
Chappell	Chappell & Co. (agent: Hal Leonard)
Church	John Church (agent: Theodore Presser)
Colombo	Franco Colombo (agent: CPP/Belwin)

Composers Library   Composers Library Edition
                           (agent: Theodore Presser)

Composers Press   Composers Press, New York, NY

Cos Cob   Cos Cob Press, Inc.
                           (agent: Boosey and Hawkes)

CPP/Belwin   CPP/Belwin Music
                           15800 N.W. 48th Ave.
                           Miami, FL 33014
                           (305) 620-1500

CVR   Classical Vocal Reprints
                           P.O. Box 20263
                           New York, NY 10023
                           (212) 517-8114

Da Capo   Da Capo Press, Inc.
                           233 Spring St.
                           New York, NY 10013
                           (212) 620-8000

Dantalian   Dantalian, Inc.
                           11 Pembroke St.
                           Newton, MA 02158
                           (617) 244-7230

Ditson   Oliver Ditson
                           (agent: Theodore Presser)

Dover   Dover Publications, Inc.
                           31 East 2nd St.
                           Mineola, NY 11501

Dragon's Teeth   Dragon's Teeth Press (Classical Vocal
                           Reprints is the agent for the songs of
                           Bacon and Edmunds)

Durand   Durand & Cie
                           21 Rue Vernet
                           F-75008
                           Paris, France

Elkan-Vogel   Elkan-Vogel, Inc.
                               (agent: Theodore Presser)

European American   European American Music Dist. Corp.
                               2480 Industrial Blvd.
                               Paoli, PA 19301
                               (215) 648-0506

Fema   Fema Music Publications
                               P.O. Box 395
                               Naperville, IL 60566
                               (312) 357-0207

Fischer   Carl Fischer, Inc.
                               62 Cooper Square
                               New York, NY 10003
                               (212) 777-0900

Foster   Mark Foster Music Co.
                               28 E. Springfield Ave.
                               Champaign, IL 61820
                               (217) 398-2760

Fredonia   Fredonia Press-Discs
                               3947 Fredonia Drive
                               Hollywood, CA 90068
                               (213) 851-3043

Galaxy   Galaxy Music Corp.,
                               (agent: E. C. Schirmer)

General   General Music Publishing Co. Inc.,
                               (agent: Boston Music)

Gray   H. W. Gray Co.,
                               (agent: CPP/Belwin-Music)

Gunmar   Gunmar Music (agent: Jerona Music)

Hargail   Hargail Music Press
                               P.O. Box 118
                               Saugerties, NY 12477

Helicon   Helicon Music Corporation
                               (agent: European American)

Henmar	Henmar Press (agent: C.F. Peters)
Highgate	Highgate Press (agent: E. C. Schirmer)
Hinshaw	Hinshaw Music, Inc. P.O. Box 470 Chapel Hill, NC 27514 (919) 933-1691
Ione	Ione Press, Inc. (agent: E. C. Schirmer)
Jerona Music	Jerona Music Corp. P.O. Box 5010 South Hackensack, NJ 07606-4210 (201) 488-0550
Leeds	Leeds Music (agent: Hal Leonard)
Leonard	Hal Leonard Publishing Corp. 7777 West Bluemound Road Milwaukee, WI 53213 (414) 774-3630
Marks	Edward B. Marks Music Corp., (agent: Hal Leonard)
Masters Music	Masters Music Publications Inc. P.O. Box 810157 Boca Raton, FL 33481-0157
Mercury	Mercury Music Corp. (agent: Theodore Presser)
Merion	Merion Music, Inc. (agent: Theodore Presser)
Merrymount	Merrymount Music, Inc., (agent: Theodore Presser)
Mills	Mills Music, Inc. (agent: CPP/Belwin)
Mobart	Mobart Music Inc., (agent: Jerona)
Morris	Edwin H. Morris & Company (agent: Hal Leonard)

Mowbray   Mowbray Music Publishers
                                 (agent: Theodore Presser)

Music Press   Music Press (agent: Theodore Presser)

Music Sales   Music Sales Corp.
                                 225 Park Ave. South
                                 New York, NY 10003
                                 (212) 254-2100

Musical Offering   Musical Offering (Classical Vocal
                                 Reprints is the agent for the songs of
                                 Bacon and Edmunds)

Musicus   Edition Musicus, Inc.
                                 P.O. Box 1341
                                 Stamford, CT 06904
                                 (203) 323-1401

New Music   New Music Press
                                 (agent: Theodore Presser)

New Valley   New Valley Music Press
                                 Sage Hall, Smith College
                                 Northampton, MA 01060

Oxford   Oxford University Press
                                 200 Madison Ave.
                                 New York, NY 10016
                                 (212) 889-0153

Peer   Peer Music
                                 810 Seventh Ave.
                                 New York, NY 10019
                                 (212) 265-3910

Peer-Southern   same as above

Peters   C. F. Peters Corp.
                                 373 Park Avenue South
                                 New York, NY 10016
                                 (212) 686-4147

Presser	Theodore Presser Company Presser Place Bryn Mawr, PA 19010 (215) 525-3636
Recital Pub. Reprint	Recital Publications P.O. Box 1697 Huntsville, TX 77342-1697
Ricordi	G. Ricordi & Co., (agent: Boosey and Hawkes)
Row	R. D. Row Music Comp., (agent: Boosey and Hawkes)
E. C. Schirmer	E. C. Schirmer Music Company 138 Ipswich St. Boston, MA 02215 (617) 236-1935
G. Schirmer	G. Schirmer, Inc., copyright; 225 Park Ave. South New York NY 10003 (212) 254-2100 (agent: Hal Leonard)
Schmidt	Arthur P. Schmidt (agent: Summy-Birchard)
Schott	Schott & Co. Ltd. London (agent: European American)
Seesaw	Seesaw Music Corp. 2067 Broadway New York, NY 10023 (212) 874-1200
Senart	Editions Maurice Senart, Paris, France
Shawnee Press	Shawnee Press, Inc. Waring Drive Delaware Water Gap, PA 18327 (717) 476-0550

Sheppard	John Sheppard Music Press P.O. Box 6784 Denver, CO (303) 320-6838
Soundings Press	Soundings Press (agent: Frog Peak Music Box A36 Hanover, NH 03755)
Southern	Southern Music Company P.O. Box 329 1100 Broadway San Antonio, TX 78215 (512) 226-8167
Summy-Birchard	Summy-Birchard Inc. 265 Secaucus Road Secaucus, NJ 07096-2037 (201) 348-0700
Valley	Valley Music Press (agent: New Valley)
Walnut Grove	Walnut Grove Press 7153 West Genesee Street Fayetteville, NY 13066
Weaner	Maxwell Weaner (agent: Shawnee Press)
Weintraub	Weintraub Music (agent: Music Sales)
White-Smith	White-Smith, Boston, MA
Williams	Ernest S. Williams
WW	Wa-Wan, Newton Center, MA

BIBLIOGRAPHY

The following is a select bibliography of collective writings and reference books, which include information about the American art song composer and his music. For works pertaining to an individual composer, the reader should see the bibliography that accompanies his or her respective entry. Abbreviations in **boldface** precede those titles most frequently consulted and, when applicable, appear at the beginning of the individual composer's bibliography. Although Noni Espina's *Repertoire for the Voice,* Sergius Kagen's *Music for the Voice,* and especially *Art-Song in the United States* (Judith Carman, et al.) are all invaluable tools which I used repeatedly, they are solely annotated song listings, and therefore I do not cite them in the individual bibliographies. The two Howard books are only cited when biographical information is scarce.

AmerGroves • *The New Grove Dictionary of American Music.* 4 vols. Hitchcock, H. Wiley and Stanley Sadie, eds. London: Macmillan Press Limited, 1986.

Ammer • Ammer, Christine. *Unsung: A History of Women in American Music.* Westport, Connecticut: Greenwood Press, 1980.

Baker • *Baker's Biographical Dictionary of Musicians.* 8th ed. Revised by Nicholas Slonimsky. New York: Schirmer Books, 1991. Probably the most comprehensive, practical, and up-to-date single volume reference.

Beatie, Rita V. "A Forgotten Legacy: The Songs of the Boston Group." *The NATS Journal* 48 (Sept/Oct 1991).

Boatwright, Helen. "A Singer's Survey of American Art Song," *Voice.* Edited by Sir Keith Falkner. A Yehudi Menuhin Music Guide. London & Sydney: Macdonald & Co, 1983.

Carman, Judith E., William K. Gaeddert and Rita M. Resch. *Art-Song in the United States, 1801–1987: An Annotated Bibliography.* 2nd ed., edited by William K. Gaeddert. The National Association of Teachers of Singing, Inc., 1987. Approximately 2,000 songs are provided with detailed annotations.

Carman, Judith Elaine. "The Song Cycle in the United States: 1900–1970." Parts 1–3. *The NATS Bulletin* 33 (October 1976, December 1976, February 1977).

Chase, Gilbert. *America's Music: From the Pilgrims to the Present.* Revised 2nd. ed. New York: McGraw-Hill Book Company, 1955.

CBY • *Current Biography Yearbook.* (1940–). New York: H. W. Wilson, 1940. Comprehensive and generally excellent profiles.

Edmunds, John and Gordon Boelzner, eds. *Some Twentieth Century American Composers: A Select Bibliography.* 2 vols. New York: The New York Public Library, 1959.

Espina, Noni. *Repertoire for the Solo Voice: Volume I.* Metuchen, N.J.: Scarecrow Press, 1977.

Ewen • Ewen, David. *American Composers: A Biographical Dictionary.* New York: G. P. Putnam's Sons, 1982. Extensive biographical material for many composers.

Ewen (ACT) • ———. *American Composers Today: A Biographical and Critical Guide.* New York: H.W. Wilson Company, 1949. Contains some information which *American Composers: A Biographical Dictionary* omits.

Ewen (1900) • ———. *Composers Since 1900: A Biographical and Critical Guide.* New York: H.W. Wilson Company, 1969.

Flanagan • Flanagan, William. "American Songs: A Thin Crop," *Musical America,* February, 1952. Emphasis is on the songs of Chanler, Copland, and Diamond.

Friedberg (I) • Friedberg, Ruth C. *American Art Song and American Poetry, Vol. I: America Comes of Age.* Metuchen, N.J.: Scarecrow Press, 1981. All three of Friedberg's volumes provides biographical sketches of the composers as well as analysis of the songs under consideration.

Friedberg (II) • ———. *American Art Song and American Poetry, Vol. II: Voices of Maturity.* Metuchen, N.J.: Scarecrow Press, 1984.

Friedberg (III) • ———. *American Art Song and American Poetry, Vol. III: The Century Advances.* Metuchen, N.J.: Scarecrow Press, 1987.

Gleason, Harold and Warren Becker. *Early American Music: Music in America from 1620 to 1920.* (Music Literature Outlines - Series III) Second Ed. Bloomington, Indiana: Frangipani Press, 1981.

———. *20th-Century American Composers* (Music Literature Outline - Series IV) 2nd ed. Bloomington, Indiana: Frangipani Press, 1980.

Goss • Goss, Madeleine. *Modern Music Makers: Contemporary American Composers.* New York: E. P. Dutton & Co., 1952. Reprint Greenwood Press, 1970.

Gratto, Christine and Scott Wheeler. "An Interview with Phyllis Curtin," *Parnassus: Poetry in Review* 10 (Fall/Winter 1982): 281–288.

Greene • Greene, David Mason. *Greene's Biographical Encyclopedia of Composers.* Garden City, New York: Doubleday & Company, Inc., 1985.

Gruen • Gruen, John. *the party's over now: reminiscences of the fifties—new york's artists, writers, musicians, and their friends.* Wainscott, New York: Pushcart Press, 1989. First paperback publication. An unusual personal account of the era. Of the composers, special attention is paid to Flanagan, Rorem, and Thomson.

———. "An Interview with Donald Gramm," *Parnassus: Poetry in Review* 10 (Fall/Winter 1982): 334–354.

Hall • Hall, James Husst. *The Art Song.* Norman, Oklahoma: University of Oklahoma Press, 1953.

Howard (OAM) • Howard, John Tasker. *Our American Music: A Comprehensive History.* 3rd ed. New York: Thomas Y. Crowell Company, 1946.

Howard (OCC) • Howard, John Tasker. *Our Contemporary Composers: American Music in the Twentieth Century.* New York: Thomas Y. Crowell Company, 1941.

Hughes • Hughes, Rupert and Arthur Elson. *American Composers.* Rev. ed. Boston: The Page Co., 1914. Though very old-fashioned, often a good source for early composers.

Ivey • Ivey, Donald. *Song: Anatomy, Imagery, and Styles.* New York: The Free Press, 1970.

Jackson, Richard. *United States Music: Sources of Bibliography and Collective Biography.* Brooklyn, NY: Institute for Studies in American Music, 1973.

Kagen, Sergius. *Music for the Voice.* Rev. ed. Bloomington, London: Indiana University Press, 1968.

Manning • Manning, Jane. *New Vocal Repertory: An Introduction.* London: Macmillan, 1986. Reprint. New York: Taplinger Publishing Co. Inc., 1987. In depth discussions for singers of many contemporary vocal works (primarily British).

Mellers • Mellers, Wilfrid. *Music in a New Found Land.* New York: Hillstone, a division of Stonehill Publishing. First Softcover Printing, 1975.

Miller, Philip L. Liner Notes, *When I Have Sung My Songs: The American Art Song, 1900–1940* (New World 247).

Nathan • Nathan, Hans. "United States of America," *A History of Song.* Edited by Denis Stevens. New York: W. W. Norton & Co., 1961. Tends to be analytical.

Reis, Claire. *Composers in America: Biographical Sketches of Living Composers with a Record of Their Works, 1912–1937.* Rev. ed. New York: Macmillan, 1947.

Rorem, Ned. "The American Art Song from 1930–1960: A Personal Survey." Liner Notes, *But Yesterday Is Not Today* (New World 243). Reprinted as "The American Art Song," *Setting the Tone.* New York: Coward McCann, 1983. Rorem evokes the era so vividly and lovingly, one longs to be there again, if only to hear the dedicated singers (many of whom were hardly known outside of the recital world) who first sang many of the songs included in this guide.

Southern • Southern, Eileen. *The Music of Black Americans.* New York: W. W. Norton & Co., 1971.

Tawa • Tawa, Nicholas E.. *The Coming of Age of American Art Music: New England's Classical Romanticists.* Westport, Connecticut: Greenwood Press, 1991.

Teat, Sue Ellen. "American Art Song and the Beginning Voice Student," *NATS Bulletin* 41 (May/June 1985).

Thompson • Thompson, Oscar. *The International Cyclopedia of Music and Musicians.* 10th ed. Edited by Bruce Bohle. New York: Dodd, Mead and Company, 1975.

Thomson, Virgil. *American Music Since 1910.* New York, Chicago and San Francisco: Holt, Rinehart & Winston, 1971.

Thorpe • Thorpe, Harry Colin. "Interpretative Studies in American Song," *Musical Quarterly* 15 (1929): 88–116.

Upton • Upton, William Treat. *Art-Song in America.* Boston: Oliver Ditson Co., 1938. (Johnson Reprint Corp., 1969, with supplement). Long considered to be the classic work on American song up to the mid 1930s.

———. "Aspects of Modern Art Song," *Musical Quarterly* 24 (Jan. 1938): 11–30.

———. "Our Musical Expatriates," *Musical Quarterly* 14 (Jan. 1928): 143–154.

———. "Recent American Song Writers," *Musical Quarterly* 11 (July 1925): 387–417.

Upton (Sup) • ————. *A Supplement to Art-Song in America, 1930–1938*. Boston: Oliver Ditson Co., 1938.

Vinton, John, ed. *Dictionary of Contemporary Music*. New York: E. P. Dutton, 1974.

Yestadt, Sister Marie. "Song Literature for the 70's: A Socio-Musical Approach," *NATS Bulletin* 29 (May/June 1973). An interesting consideration, which focuses on the numerous settings of Langston Hughes.

DISCOGRAPHY OF COLLECTIONS

Listed alphabetically by singer, each of the following recordings contains songs by at least two of the composers included in *A Singer's Guide to the American Art Song*. Individual composer recordings are noted under the appropriate composer's entry. "And others" refers to American composers not included in the guide. When earlier LP recordings have been reissued on CD, the CD version takes preference.

DeGaetani, Jan (mezzo-soprano). *Songs of America*. Elektra/Nonesuch CD (79248-2-ZK). Songs of Carter, Cadman, Crawford, Babbitt, Crumb, Fine, Bond, Cage, Schuman, Ives, Rorem, Adler, Copland, and others.

Dickinson, Meriel (mezzo-soprano). *An American Antholgy*. Unicorn (UN1-72017). Songs of Carter, Copland, Cage, Thomson, and others; also, piano solos.

Hampson, Thomas (baritone). *Lieder: Ives, Griffes, MacDowell*. Teldec CD (9031-72168-2).

———. *"An Old Song Re-sung:" American Concert Songs* EMI CD (7 54051 2). Songs of Griffes, Giannini, Speaks, Hageman, Duke, Charles, Cadman, and others.

Hanks, John (tenor). *The Art Song in America, Volume 1*. Duke University Press (DWR 6417). Songs of Bacon, Barber, Bowles, Carpenter, Chadwick, Copland, Dello Joio, Dougherty, John Duke, Finney, Griffes, Hageman, Harris, Ives, Griffes, Loeffler, MacDowell, Nordoff, and others.

———. *The Art Song in America, Volume 2*. Duke University Press (DWR 7306BX). Songs of Rorem, Persichetti, Duke, Cumming.

Haymon, Cynthia (soprano). *Where the Music Comes From: American Songs*. Argo CD (436 117-2ZH). Songs of Hoiby, Rorem, Burleigh, Barber, Nordoff, Farwell, Hundley, Dougherty, Griffes, Lekberg, and others.

Heafner, Carolyn (soprano). *Carolyn Heafner Sings Songs by Beach, Beeson, Weisgall, Hoiby, Bacon*. Composers Recordings (CRI SD 462).

Herford, Henry (baritone). *Henry Herford: Baritone.* New World (327). Songs of Corigliano, Shepherd, Susa, Weber.

Hunt, Alexandra (soprano). *Songs by Carpenter, Griffes & MacDowell.* Orion (77272).

Marcoulescou, Yolanda (soprano). *French, German, Italian, and Spanish Songs by American Composers.* Orion Cassette (OC 685). Songs of Thomson, Griffes, Bowles, MacDowell, Ives, Carpenter, and others.

Marcouleslou-Stern, Yolanda (soprano). *Art Songs by American Composers.* Gasparo CD (GSCD-287). Songs of Beach, Bonds, Bowles, Carpenter, Creston, John Duke, Griffes, Hageman, Ives, Price, Florence Price, Sacco, Thomson.

Moore, Dale (baritone). *On the Road to Mandelay & Other Favorite American Concert Songs from 1900 to 1950.* Cambridge (CRS 2715). Songs of Barber, Charles, John Duke, Griffes, Hageman, Homer, Rogers, Speaks, Stillman-Kelley.

Myers, Myron (bass). *Pomes Penyeach: Settings of Poetry by James Joyce.* Musical Heritage Society (MHS 9120167). Songs of Antheil, Sessions, Persichetti, Barber, and others (primarily British).

Parker, William (baritone). *Songs of Charles Ives, Theodore Chanler, Norman Dello Joio, Irving Fine, Robert Ward.* New World (300).

———. *Works by Arthur Farwell, Preston Ware Orem, Charles Wakefield Cadman.* New World (213).

———. *William Parker Performs Vocal Works by Ernst Bacon, Robert Evett, Charles Griffes, Lee Hoiby, John Jacob Niles, Ned Rorem.* New World (305).

Reardon, John (baritone). *John Reardon Sings Contemporary Art Songs.* Serenus (SRE 1019). Songs of Reif, Flagello, Owen, Rieti, Koch, Hundley.

Sanford, Sylvan (baritone). *Beloved That Pilgrimage.* Elektra Nonesuch CD (9 79259-2). Song cycles of Chanler, Barber, Copland.

Sharp, William (baritone). Songs of Thomson, Bowles, Hoiby, Hundley, and others. New World CD (NW 369-2).

Sperry, Paul (tenor). *Paul Sperry Sings American Cycles and Sets.* Albany CD (TROY058-2). Beaser, Gruenberg, Talma, and others.

———. *Paul Sperry Sings Romantic American Songs.* Albany CD (TROY043-2). (The CD has more songs than the original LP version). Songs of Hundley, Bowles, Thomson, Farwell, Chanler.

———. *Paul Sperry Sings Songs of an Innocent Age: Music from Turn of the Century America.* Albany CD (TROY034-2). (The CD has more songs than the original LP). Songs of Cadman, Ayres, Paine,

Sousa, Nevin, Clough-Leighter, Foote, Chadwick, Gilbert, Beach, Carpenter, MacDowell, Griffes, Ives, Bond, Buck, and others.

Suderburg, Elizabeth (soprano). *American Sampler*. Washington (OLY-104). Songs of Carpenter, Griffes, Ives, Bond, and others; also, instrumental selections.

Sylvan, Sanford (baritone). *Beloved That Pilgrimage*. Elektra Nonesuch CD (9 79259-2). Songs of Copland, Barber, Chanler.

Tatum, Nancy (soprano). *Nancy Tatum: Recital of American Songs*. London (OS26053). Songs of MacDowell, Gold, Manning, Copland, Barber, Guion, Thomson, Griffes.

Telese, Maryanne (soprano). *Let My Song Fill Your Heart: A Remembrance of the American Concert Song*. Premier (PRLP 002). Songs by Charles, Mana-Zucca, Homer, Hageman, Edwards, Strickland, and others.

Treadway, Theresa (mezzo-soprano). *Blue Moods: American Art Songs*. Orion (ORS 84476). Songs of Rorem, Beeson, Pasatieri, and others.

Various singers (Laura English-Robinson, Hilda Harris, George Shirley, Willis Patterson, and others). *Art-Songs by Black American Composers*. Book of the Month Club Records. University of Michigan (BOMC 91-6674). Songs of Bonds, Price, Hale Smith, Still, Swanson, Walker, and others.

————. (Bethany Beardslee, Donald Gramm) *But Yesterday Is Not Today*. New World (243). Songs by Barber, Bowles, Copland, Chanler, Citkowitz, Duke, Helps, Sessions.

————. (Eleanor Steber, Mildred Miller, John McCollum; Donald Gramm). *Songs by American Composers*. Desto (6411/6412). Songs by Diamond, Persichetti, Luening, Fine, Flanagan, Rorem, Ives, Douglas Moore, Beeson, Bowles, Edmunds, Carpenter, Bacon, Barber, Bergsma, Griffes, La Montaine, Thomson, MacDowell, Chanler, Copland, Ward, Pinkham, Weber, Cowell.

————. (Alma Gluck, Johanna Gadski, Emma Eames, Emilio de Gogorza, John McCormack, David Bispham, Roland Hayes, Marian Anderson, Paul Robeson, Mary Garden, Eleanor Steber, Rose Bampton, Povla Frijsh, Kirsten Flagstad, Radiana Pazmor).*When I Have Sung My Songs: The American Art Song 1900-1940*. New World (247). Songs by MacDowell, Beach, Parker, Kramer, Damrosch, Burleigh, Cadman, Griffes, Hageman, Carpenter, Thompson, Charles, Ives.

INDEX TO SONG TITLES

INDEX TO POETS

ABOUT THE AUTHOR

For over two decades soprano Victoria Villamil performed in opera, concert, and recital throughout the United States and Europe. With more than 30 major operatic roles to her credit, she portrayed such diverse heroines as Bizet's Carmen, Mozart's Countess Almaviva, and Menotti's Saint of Bleeker Street with companies that included the Philadelphia Grand Opera, the Rittenhouse Opera Society, the Wilmington Opera Society, the Des Moines Metro Opera, and the Pennsylvania Opera. Proficient in contemporary music, she won acclaim in John Cage's "Solo for Voice 1" in performances with the Pennsylvania Ballet, was a frequent soloist with the Philadelphia New Music Group, and for ten years performed regularly with New York's renowned contemporary group, Continuum, in its series at Lincoln Center, at the Library of Congress, at festivals in Europe, and in college residencies throughout the United States. As a seasoned recitalist she performed the standard classical repertoire, but especially attracted to the largely unexplored repertoire in English, she also toured college campuses and concert halls giving programs of American and British song. In 1989 she retired from professional singing to concentrate on her writing.

This book
is set in Adobe types:
Times, Frutiger, and Minion,
on Apple Macintosh equipment.
It was designed by
Michael Höhne.